The Editor

WAYNE FRANKLIN is Professor of English and head of the English Department at the University of Connecticut. He is the author of *James Fenimore Cooper: The Early Years* (the first volume of his definitive biography, from Yale University Press), *The New World of James Fenimore Cooper,* and *Discoverers, Explorers, Settlers: The Diligent Writers of Early America.* He is editor of *American Voices, American Lives: A Documentary Reader* and co-editor of *The Norton Anthology of American Literature* and of, with Michael Steiner, *Mapping American Culture.*

A NORTON CRITICAL EDITION

THE SELECTED WRITINGS OF THOMAS JEFFERSON

AUTHORITATIVE TEXTS
CONTEXTS
CRITICISM

Edited by

WAYNE FRANKLIN
UNIVERSITY OF CONNECTICUT

W • W • NORTON & COMPANY • *New York* • *London*

W. W. Norton & Company has been independent since its founding in 1923, when William Warder Norton and Mary D. Herter Norton first published lectures delivered at the People's Institute, the adult education division of New York City's Cooper Union. The firm soon expanded its program beyond the Institute, publishing books by celebrated academics from America and abroad. By mid-century, the two major pillars of Norton's publishing program—trade books and college texts—were firmly established. In the 1950s, the Norton family transferred control of the company to its employees, and today—with a staff of four hundred and a comparable number of trade, college, and professional titles published each year—W. W. Norton & Company stands as the largest and oldest publishing house owned wholly by its employees.

Manufacturing by the Courier Companies—Westford division.
Book design by Antonina Krass
Production manager: Eric Pier-Hocking

Library of Congress Cataloging-in-Publication Data

Jefferson, Thomas, 1743–1826.
   [Selections. 2010]
   The selected writings of Thomas Jefferson : authoritative texts, contexts, criticism / edited by Wayne Franklin.—1st ed.
      p. cm.—(A Norton critical edition)
   Includes bibliographical references.
   ISBN 978-0-393-97407-2 (pbk.)
   1. United States—Politics and government—1775–1783—Sources. 2. United States—Politics and government—1783–1809—Sources. 3. Virginia—Politics and government—1775–1865—Sources. I. Franklin, Wayne. II. Tittle.
   E302.J442 2010
   973.4'6092—dc22

2009030347

W. W. Norton & Company, Inc., 500 Fifth Avenue, New York, N.Y. 10110
www.wwnorton.com

W. W. Norton & Company Ltd., Castle House, 75/76 Wells Street,
London W1T 3QT

1 2 3 4 5 6 7 8 9 0

Contents

Contexts   369

Preface

In several senses, Thomas Jefferson stands at the origin point of American society and culture. He was the first intellectual (some would say the only real one) to serve as U.S. president. Before he assumed that office in 1801, he had been by turns a lawyer, an architect, a bibliophile, an extraordinary rhetorician, and a political leader. In the process of following those various vocations and avocations, he had articulated the highest ideals of his country: "We hold these truths to be self-evident: that all men are created equal; that they are endowed by their creator with certain inalienable rights; that among these are life, liberty, & the pursuit of happiness."

To have written just *that* would have been enough for most of his contemporaries. What did Washington or Adams or Hamilton, after all, ever say or write that continues to so deeply define American (and indeed human) aspirations? And Jefferson was as familiar as those other leaders with the practical affairs of everyday life. He defended his homeland from foreign detractors, gathering detailed information and live or dead specimens to prove the Western Hemisphere the equal of the Eastern. Sensing an opportunity for the United States amid the chaos of the Napoleonic era, Jefferson purchased (through his hand-picked agents, James Madison and Robert R. Livingston) the French title to a piece of real estate that overnight doubled the territory of the new nation. Then he dispatched an expedition to cross the continent, thereby asserting the government's title to it. (Because Jefferson was an eminent multitasker, Lewis and Clark also brought back from the west more specimens to drive home Jefferson's point about America's equality with Europe.) Moreover, it was not just the grand sweep of geopolitics and scientific argumentation that intrigued Jefferson. Equally interested in practical improvements, he tinkered with clocks and plows and dumbwaiters. And he was a man of affairs, as people used to say. Jefferson owned and managed several plantations in his native state of Virginia, most notably the one surrounding his beloved mountain near Charlottesville, atop which he sited the extraordinary mansion he called Monticello.

Visitors who tour that building today will notice that Jefferson laid out his private quarters in such a way that his bed defined the boundary between his dressing room and his study, which connected with his "bookroom." This spatial diagram was another result of his tinkering, but it also provides a deeper key to his personality. If he turned one way as he arose in the morning, he could tend to his bodily needs. If he turned the other, he stood amid his papers and books. And what books those were! He had assembled the finest collection in America at the time and was so generous intellectually (and so land-rich and cash-poor) that in 1814 he sold his books to the government to provide the basis for the second collection of the Library of Congress, the first having been burned during the British attack on Washington that summer.

It is an oddity of Jefferson's life, nonetheless, that the man who so loved books left us, aside from the tangible items in that great public institution, so few from his own hand. The one genuine book he wrote, modestly titled *Notes on the State of Virginia*, was not even begun as a book. He had collected data about Virginia because of a deep attachment to his native country, as he called it. When the French became the allies of the fledging nation during the Revolution, they wanted information about America's landscape and demography and institutions. For Virginia, of which Jefferson was then governor, the task fell to him. Following a British attack against the heart of the state, which sent Jefferson flying from Monticello, he managed to draw together, from the corners of his mind and the scattered documents he could lay his hands on, the longest response to the French queries that anyone from any state provided. At that point, in 1781, it was not to be a book but a document of state. Only later did Jefferson, wishing copies to send to a few friends, have it privately printed. And only when one of those private copies made its way to a translator in Paris did Jefferson reluctantly arrange for a public edition.

Earlier than *Notes on Virginia*, he had written a pamphlet on the crisis with Britain, which had been published by the colony of Virginia in 1774, and the Declaration he drafted for Congress two years later was, after being revised by that body, printed and reprinted across the country and abroad at its order—without, however, being known as primarily Jefferson's work. Jefferson would later issue other small items through the press, and of course during his service as governor and then president many of his words found their way into print. One other time, when he was vice president under Adams and therefore presided in the Senate, Jefferson was moved to intrude a book on the public—the rule book for that body, published in 1801 as *A Manual of Parliamentary Practice*, still in use today. Otherwise, the man known around the world for what he could do with language on paper (he rarely was comfortable speaking in public) left very few publications.

The best of them, including that 1774 *Summary View of the Rights of British America*, the Declaration of Independence (in the original and revised texts Jefferson provided in his draft memoirs in the 1820s), and *Notes on the State of Virginia*, are included in full in this fresh edition of his writings. So is a generous selection from the man's immense body of letters, numbering in the tens of thousands. The overall principle of selection has been a desire to represent both the historical spread of Jefferson's activities and the range and verbal acuity of his intellect. The letters in particular are chosen so as to give insight into Jefferson as father and friend, in addition to revealing his public activities in the United States and while abroad—and his masterly skill as a correspondent. Materials from other hands meant to show some of the sources of his thought and activities have been included in the "Contexts" section for each of the major items from Jefferson himself. Another section, "Early Responses to Jefferson and His Writings" is meant to show the often polarizing effect he had on his fellow Americans and his extraordinary influence as a thinker, especially on the question of political rights. This group of items is intended to round out a story that is of exceptional complexity.

Of recent years, we have been reminded of that complexity in arresting ways. Owing to the first serious investigation of charges dating from the

1790s and early 1800s, we now can conclude that Thomas Jefferson did not just own slaves when he penned the Declaration of Independence and inhabited the new presidential mansion, built by slave labor, in Washington. It is likely, many scholars have concluded, that Jefferson had a sexual liaison with one of his own slaves, Sally Hemings, that began after fifteen-year-old Sally accompanied Jefferson's younger daughter, Polly, to Paris in 1787. That liaison continued well into the new century. Furthermore, children born to Hemings between 1790 and 1808 have shown, through analysis of the DNA of some of their known descendents as well as of the DNA of descendents of some of Jefferson's kin, to have Jefferson as well as Hemings ancestry. Jefferson was in this regard, one may well conclude, the true father of his country.

When rumors of an illicit relationship between Jefferson and "Black Sal" (as the press called her) first circulated—the original story is included in the "Early Responses" section, along with several other relevant documents—they formed part of an effort by his Federalist political opponents to discredit Jefferson. But by the time of Jefferson's death in 1826, when his political reputation was secure, those rumors had been largely forgotten or silenced. As racial theories designed to shore up slavery and its associated social practices took root in the United States in the 1820s and 1830s, the white elite had a desire to keep such complicating tales out of circulation.

The story of their reemergence, and of the archival research and genetic tests they stimulated, forms part of the "Modern Analysis and Criticism" section herein. By its combination of early evidence and the latest argumentation on this subject, this book provides a rich and balanced array of material for consideration of what Jefferson did, not just what he said, in regard to race and race relations. The purpose is to redeem the truth from two centuries of obfuscation but also to reclaim Jefferson himself for truly modern consideration as an archetypal American—a man in whom we can witness both our own aspirations and the failings that have kept those aspirations from being fulfilled for so long. But the final section of the book is intended to reclaim Jefferson as a whole, not just on this one important subject. It includes an array of historical and literary perspectives that can help us see Jefferson the writer and public actor as a crucial figure—perhaps *the* crucial figure—of the founding era of the United States. It is a humbling experience to come into the acquaintance of such a mind and such a record. But it is something we all have to do.

A Note on the Texts

As there is no single reliable source of the texts reproduced here, the reader wishing detailed information on any single item is referred to the first note appended to each of them. However, some patterns can be usefully described. Jefferson himself, as a collector and reader of books, had fairly acute notions of how texts worked. When he advised others on the purchase of books, for instance, he often was careful to distinguish among editions. And when he was involved in the production of printed texts, his own or someone else's, he could be expected to pay close attention to the details. That said, he also exhibited some elements of the older, more fluid attitude toward texts that carried over from the age of manuscripts into the age of print, and that lingered long in the southern states. His own manuscript of what became *Notes on the State of Virginia*, now in the collection of the Massachusetts Historical Society, is a complex of original entries, later revisions, and a dizzying assemblage of overlays. (On this question, see Douglas Wilson's description of the manuscript in his essay on p. 533 herein). Plans for a scholarly edition of that manuscript, announced some time ago, seem now to be on hold. Although it would be good for those plans to proceed, it is hard to imagine how a printed text reproducing the actual complexities of the manuscript could be at the same time, in the usual sense, "readable." In the absence of such a publication, the first public edition, carefully scrutinized, is the best alternative.

To give modern readers as lively a sense as possible of how books in Jefferson's period actually looked and worked, the selections from his writings are derived from the best edition of his own time in every instance, usually the first printed edition, when that has been reasonable and possible. Antiquated textual features such as the long S that might be confusing have been silently modernized, but some instructive misspellings that indicate Jefferson's habits (such as *peice* for *piece*) have been left standing as they give a flavor of the past without poisoning the reader.

Jefferson's first publication, the pamphlet called *A Summary View of the Rights of British America*, is copied from the first edition, printed at the order of the Virginia legislature in Williamsburg in 1774. In the case of the Declaration of Independence, I have used Jefferson's complexly interlineated version inserted in his 1821 memoirs, which was first published by his grandson, Thomas Jefferson Randolph, in Charlottesville in 1829, and freshly edited from the manuscript by Paul Leicester Ford for the first volume of his *The Writings of Thomas Jefferson* (New York, 1892–99). For *Notes on the State of Virginia*, I have used the first public edition, that issued in London in 1787 by John Stockdale. The original map is omitted, but the three appendices and the extensive list of source materials on Virginia history (all of which are often left out of modern editions) are included. So is the so-called fourth appendix, on the Indian leader Logan, which was first issued by Jefferson as a separate pamphlet in Philadelphia in 1800, the copy text for the reprint herein.

A prodigious correspondent, Jefferson kept copies of many of his letters; others survive in collections around the world. He has been the lucky recipient of meticulous editing on the part of a chain of scholars beginning with the work of Julian P. Boyd, commenced in 1950. The result is *The Papers of Thomas Jefferson*, now running to 36 volumes, published by Princeton University Press. For the years so far covered by this edition and its supplements, including the *Retirement Series* (1760–1802 and 1809–1813, respectively), all letters and other documents in the book as a whole derive from this magnificent resource. Some additional materials come from modern editions that have special focus, most notably Donald Jackson's *Letters of the Lewis and Clark Expedition with Related Documents, 1783–1854*, 2nd ed. (Urbana, Ill., 1978). For periods or topics not yet covered by Boyd and his successors or by such topical collections, I have derived texts from H. A. Washington. ed., *The Writings of Thomas Jefferson*, 9 vols. (Washington, D.C., 1853–54); Andrew A. Lipscomb and Albert E. Bergh, ed., *The Writings of Thomas Jefferson*, 20 vols. (Washington, D.C., 1903–04); and Paul Leicester Ford, ed., *The Writings of Thomas Jefferson*, 10 vols. (New York, 1892–99). In items taken from these various sources, a few obvious errors have been silently corrected or indicated with a bracketed "[*sic*]." Finally, materials contemporary with Jefferson are reproduced from the best early sources or reliable modern reprints, as indicated in the notes. More recent materials come from the original publication cited in each instance.

Abbreviations

AJL *The Adams-Jefferson Letters*, ed. Lester J. Cappon, 2 vols. (Chapel Hill: University of North Carolina Press, 1959).

PTJ *The Papers of Thomas Jefferson*, ed. Julian P. Boyd et al., 36 vols. to date (Princeton, N.J.: Princeton University Press, 1950–2009).

PTJ: RS *The Papers of Thomas Jefferson: Retirement Series*, ed. J. Jefferson Looney et al., 6 vols. to date (Princeton, N.J.: Princeton University Press, 2004–09).

LLCE *Letters of the Lewis and Clark Expedition and Related Documents, 1783–1854*, ed. Donald Jackson, 2 vols. (Urbana: University of Illinois Press, 1978).

Peden *Notes on the State of Virginia*, ed. William Peden, (Chapel Hill: University of North Carolina Press, 1955).

THE SELECTED WRITINGS
OF THOMAS JEFFERSON

A Summary View of the Rights of British America. Set forth in Some Resolutions Intended for the Inspection of the Present Delegates of the People of Virginia Now in Convention. By a Native, and Member of the House of Burgesses.[1]

EST PROPRIUM MUNUS MAGISTRATUS INTELLIGERE, SED GERERE PERSONAM CIVITATIS, DEBEREQUE; EJUS DIGNITATEM & DECUS SISTINERE, SERVARE LEGES, JURE DISCRIBERE, EA FIDEI SUAE COMMISSA MEMINISSE.

CICERO, DE OF. L. i, C. 34.

It is the indispensable duty of the supreme magistrate to consider himself as acting for the whole community, and obliged to support its dignity, and assign to the people, with justice, their various rights, as he would be faithful to the great trust reposed in him.

THE PREFACE OF THE EDITORS

THE *following piece was intended to convey to the late meeting of* DELE-GATES *the sentiments of one of their body, whose personal attendance was prevented by an accidental illness. In it the sources of our present unhappy differences are traced with such faithful accuracy, and the opinions entertained by every free American expressed with such a manly firmness, that it must be pleasing to the present, and may be useful to future ages. It will evince to the world the moderation of our late convention, who have only touched with tenderness many of the claims insisted on in this pamphlet, though every heart acknowledged their justice. Without the knowledge of the author, we have ventured to communicate his sentiments to the public; who have certainly a right to know what the best and wisest of their members have thought on a subject in which they are so deeply interested.*

Resolved, that it be an instruction to the said deputies,[2] when assembled in general congress with the deputies from the other states of British America, to propose to the said congress that an humble and dutiful address be presented to his majesty, begging leave to lay before him, as chief magistrate of the British empire, the united complaints of his majesty's subjects in America; complaints which are excited by many unwarrantable encroachments and usurpations, attempted to be made by the legislature of one part of the empire, upon those rights which God and the laws have given equally and independently to all. To represent to his majesty that these his states have often individually made humble application to his imperial throne to obtain, through its intervention, some redress of their injured rights, to none of which was ever even an answer condescended; humbly to hope that

---

1. The text is that of the first American edition (Williamsburg. Va.: Clementina Rind, 1774). All notes are by present editor unless otherwise specified. Spellings remain unchanged, except when noted.
2. In his *Autobiography*, Jefferson explained that in 1774, having been chosen as one of Virginia's delegates (or "deputies") to the Continental Congress, he "prepared a draught of instructions to be given to the delegates" for dealing with the perceived abuses of Parliament and King George III. Prevented by illness from attending a meeting of the Virginia delegation, Jefferson forwarded two copies of his manuscript to Williamsburg, where the delegates ordered it printed as a pamphlet. *Thomas Jefferson: Writings* (New York: Library of America, 1984), 9.

this their joint address, penned in the language of truth, and divested of those expressions of servility which would persuade his majesty that we are asking favours, and not rights, shall obtain from his majesty a more respectful acceptance. And this his majesty will think we have reason to expect when he reflects that he is no more than the chief officer of the people, appointed by the laws, and circumscribed with definite powers, to assist in working the great machine of government, erected for their use, and consequently subject to their superintendance. And in order that these our rights, as well as the invasions of them, may be laid more fully before his majesty, to take a view of them from the origin and first settlement of these countries.

To remind him that our ancestors, before their emigration to America, were the free inhabitants of the British dominions in Europe, and possessed a right which nature has given to all men, of departing from the country in which chance, not choice, has placed them, of going in quest of new habitations, and of there establishing new societies, under such laws and regulations as to them shall seem most likely to promote public happiness. That their Saxon ancestors had, under this universal law, in like manner left their native wilds and woods in the north of Europe, had possessed themselves of the island of Britain, then less charged with inhabitants, and had established there that system of laws which has so long been the glory and protection of that country. Nor was ever any claim of superiority or dependence asserted over them by that mother country from which they had migrated; and were such a claim made, it is believed that his majesty's subjects in Great Britain have too firm a feeling of the rights derived to them from their ancestors, to bow down the sovereignty of their state before such visionary pretensions. And it is thought that no circumstance has occurred to distinguish materially the British from the Saxon emigration. America was conquered, and her settlements made, and firmly established, at the expence of individuals, and not of the British public. Their own blood was spilt in acquiring lands for their settlement, their own fortunes expended in making that settlement effectual; for themselves they fought, for themselves they conquered, and for themselves alone they have right to hold. Not a shilling was ever issued from the public treasures of his majesty, or his ancestors, for their assistance, till of very late times, after the colonies had become established on a firm and permanent footing. That then, indeed, having become valuable to Great Britain for her commercial purposes, his parliament was pleased to lend them assistance against an enemy, who would fain have drawn to herself the benefits of their commerce, to the great aggrandizement of herself, and danger of Great Britain. Such assistance, and in such circumstances, they had often before given to Portugal, and other allied states, with whom they carry on a commercial intercourse; yet these states never supposed, that by calling in her aid, they thereby submitted themselves to her sovereignty. Had such terms been proposed, they would have rejected them with disdain, and trusted for better to the moderation of their enemies, or to a vigorous exertion of their own force. We do not, however, mean to under-rate those aids, which to us were doubtless valuable, on whatever principles granted; but we would shew that they cannot give a title to that authority which the British parliament would arrogate over us, and that they may amply be repaid by our giving to the inhabitants of Great Britain such exclusive privileges in trade as may be advantageous to them, and at the same time not too restrictive to ourselves. That settlements having been thus effected in the wilds of America, the emigrants thought proper to adopt that system of laws under which they had hitherto lived in the mother country, and to continue their union with her by submitting themselves to the same common sovereign, who was thereby made the central link connecting the several parts of the empire thus newly multiplied.

But that not long were they permitted, however far they thought themselves removed from the hand of oppression, to hold undisturbed the rights thus acquired, at the hazard of their lives, and loss of their fortunes. A family of princes was then on the British throne, whose treasonable crimes against their people brought on them afterwards the exertion of those sacred and sovereign rights of punishment reserved in the hands of the people for cases of extreme necessity, and judged by the constitution unsafe to be delegated to any other judicature.[3] While every day brought forth some new and unjustifiable exertion of power over their subjects on that side the water, it was not to be expected that those here, much less able at that time to oppose the designs of despotism, should be exempted from injury.

Accordingly that country, which had been acquired by the lives, the labours, and the fortunes, of individual adventurers, was by these princes, at several times, parted out and distributed among the favourites and followers[4] of their fortunes, and, by an assumed right of the crown alone, were erected into distinct and independent governments; a measure which it is believed his majesty's prudence and understanding would prevent him from imitating at this day, as no exercise of such a power, of dividing and dismembering a country, has ever occurred in his majesty's realm of England, though now of very antient standing; nor could it be justified or acquiesced under there, or in any other part of his majesty's empire.

That the exercise of a free trade with all parts of the world, possessed by the American colonists, as of natural right, and which no law of their own had taken away or abridged, was next the object of unjust encroachment. Some of the colonies having thought proper to continue the administration of their government in the name and under the authority of his majesty king Charles the first, whom, notwithstanding his late deposition by the commonwealth of England, they continued in the sovereignty of their state; the parliament for the commonwealth took the same in high offence, and assumed upon themselves the power of prohibiting their trade with all other parts of the world, except the island of Great Britain. This arbitrary act, however, they soon recalled, and by solemn treaty, entered into on the 12th

---

3. The Stuart dynasty ended with the execution of Charles I in 1649. The dynasty returned to power in 1660, however, with the coronation of his son, Charles II.
4. 1632 Maryland was granted to lord Baltimore, 14. c. 2. Pennsylvania to Penn, and the province of Carolina was in the year 1663 granted by letters patent of majesty, king Charles II. in the 15th year of his reign, in propriety, unto the right honourable Edward earl of Clarendon, George duke of Albemarle, William earl of Craven, John lord Berkeley, Anthony lord Ashley, sir George Carteret, sir John Coleton, knight and baronet, and sir William Berkeley, knight; by which letters patent the laws of England were to be in force in Carolina: But the lords proprietors had power, *with the consent of the inhabitants*, to make bye-laws for the better government of the said province; so that no money could be received, or law made, without the consent of the inhabitants, or their representatives [Jefferson's note].

day of March, 1651, between the said commonwealth by their commissioners, and the colony of Virginia by their house of burgesses, it was expressly stipulated, by the 8th article of the said treaty, that they should have "free trade as the people of England do enjoy to all places and with all nations, according to the laws of that commonwealth." But that, upon the restoration of his majesty king Charles the second, their rights of free commerce fell once more a victim to arbitrary power; and by several acts[5] of his reign, as well as of some of his successors, the trade of the colonies was laid under such restrictions, as shew what hopes they might form from the justice of a British parliament, were its uncontrouled power admitted over these states. History has informed us that bodies of men, as well as individuals, are susceptible of the spirit of tyranny. A view of these acts of parliament for regulation, as it has been affectedly called, of the American trade, if all other evidence were removed out of the case, would undeniably evince the truth of this observation. Besides the duties they impose on our articles of export and import, they prohibit our going to any markets northward of Cape Finesterre, in the kingdom of Spain, for the sale of commodities which Great Britain will not take from us, and for the purchase of others, with which she cannot supply us, and that for no other than the arbitrary purposes of purchasing for themselves, by a sacrifice of our rights and interests, certain privileges in their commerce with an allied state, who in confidence that their exclusive trade with America will be continued, while the principles and power of the British parliament be the same, have indulged themselves in every exorbitance which their avarice could dictate, or our necessities extort; have raised their commodities, called for in America, to the double and treble of what they sold for before such exclusive privileges were given them, and of what better commodities of the same kind would cost us elsewhere, and at the same time give us much less for what we carry thither than might be had at more convenient ports. That these acts prohibit us from carrying in quest of other purchasers the surplus of our tobaccoes remaining after the consumption of Great Britain is supplied; so that we must leave them with the British merchant for whatever he will please to allow us, to be by him reshipped to foreign markets, where he will reap the benefits of making sale of them for full value. That to heighten still the idea of parliamentary justice, and to shew with what moderation they are like to exercise power, where themselves are to feel no part of its weight, we take leave to mention to his majesty certain other acts of British parliament, by which they would prohibit us from manufacturing for our own use the articles we raise on our own lands with our own labour. By an act[6] passed in the 5th Year of the reign of his late majesty king George the second, an American subject is forbidden to make a hat for himself of the fur which he has taken perhaps on his own soil; an instance of despotism to which no parrallel can be produced in the most arbitrary ages of British history. By one other act,[7] passed in the 23d year of the same reign, the iron which we make we are forbidden to manufacture, and heavy as that article is, and necessary in every branch of husbandry, besides commission and insurance, we are to pay freight for it to Great Britain, and freight for

5. 12. c. 2. c. 18. 15. c. 2. c. 11. 25. c. 2. c. 7. 7. 8. W. M. c. 22. 11. W. 3. 4. Anne. 6. G. 2. c. 13 [Jefferson's note].
6. 5. G. 2 [Jefferson's note].
7. 23. G. 2. c. 29 [Jefferson's note].

it back again, for the purpose of supporting not men, but machines, in the island of Great Britain. In the same spirit of equal and impartial legislation is to be viewed the act of parliament,[8] passed in the 5th year of the same reign, by which American lands are made subject to the demands of British creditors, while their own lands were still continued unanswerable for their debts; from which one of these conclusions must necessarily follow, either that justice is not the same in America as in Britain, or else that the British parliament pay less regard to it here than there. But that we do not point out to his majesty the injustice of these acts, with intent to rest on that principle the cause of their nullity; but to shew that experience confirms the propriety of those political principles which exempt us from the jurisdiction of the British parliament. The true ground on which we declare these acts void is, that the British parliament has no right to exercise authority over us.

That these exercises of usurped power have not been confined to instances alone, in which themselves were interested, but they have also intermeddled with the regulation of the internal affairs of the colonies. The act of the 9th of Anne for establishing a post office in America seems to have had little connection with British convenience, except that of accommodating his majesty's ministers and favourites with the sale of a lucrative and easy office.

That thus have we hastened through the reigns which preceded his majesty's, during which the violations of our right were less alarming, because repeated at more distant intervals than that rapid and bold succession of injuries which is likely to distinguish the present from all other periods of American story. Scarcely have our minds been able to emerge from the astonishment into which one stroke of parliamentary thunder has involved us, before another more heavy, and more alarming, is fallen on us. Single acts of tyranny may be ascribed to the accidental opinion of a day; but a series of oppressions, begun at a distinguished[9] period, and pursued unalterably through every change of ministers, too plainly prove a deliberate and systematical plan of reducing us to slavery.

That the act[1] passed in the 4th year of his majesty's reign, intitled "An act for granting certain duties in the British colonies and plantations in America, &c."

One other act,[2] passed in the 5th year of his reign, intitled "An act for granting and applying certain stamp duties and other duties in the British colonies and plantations in America, &c."

One other act,[3] passed in the 6th year of his reign, intituled "An act for the better securing the dependency of his majesty's dominions in America upon the crown and parliament of Great Britain;" and one other act,[4] passed in the 7th year of his reign, intituled "An act for granting duties on paper, tea, &c." form that connected chain of parliamentary usurpation, which has already been the subject of frequent applications to his majesty, and the houses of lords and commons of Great Britain; and no answers having yet

---

8. 5. G. 270 [Jefferson's note].
9. Distinct. Compare this passage with that in the second paragraph of the Declaration of Independence.
1. 4. G. 3. c. 15 [Jefferson's note].
2. 5. G. 3. c. 12 [Jefferson's note].
3. 6, G. 3. c. 12 [Jefferson's note].
4. 7. G. 3 [Jefferson's note].

been condescended to any of these, we shall not trouble his majesty with a repetition of the matters they contained.

But that one other act,[5] passed in the same 7th year of the reign, having been a peculiar attempt, must ever require peculiar mention; it is intituled. "An act for suspending the legislature of New York." One free and independent legislature hereby takes upon itself to suspend the powers of another, free and independent as itself; thus exhibiting a phœnomenon unknown in nature, the creator and creature of its own power. Not only the principles of common sense, but the common feelings of human nature, must be surrendered up before his majesty's subjects here can be persuaded to believe that they hold their political existence at the will of a British parliament. Shall these governments be dissolved, their property annihilated, and their people reduced to a state of nature, at the imperious breath of a body of men, whom they never saw, in whom they never confided, and over whom they have no powers of punishment or removal, let their crimes against the American public be ever so great? Can any one reason be assigned why 160,000 electors in the island of Great Britain[6] should give law to four millions in the states of America, every individual of whom is equal to every individual of them, in virtue, in understanding, and in bodily strength? Were this to be admitted, instead of being a free people, as we have hitherto supposed, and mean to continue ourselves, we should suddenly be found the slaves, not of one, but of 160,000 tyrants, distinguished too from all others by this singular circumstance, that they are removed from the reach of fear, the only restraining motive which may hold the hand of a tyrant.

That by "an act[7] to discontinue in such manner and for such time as are therein mentioned the landing and discharging, lading or shipping, of goods, wares, and merchandize, at the town and within the harbour of Boston, in the province of Massachusetts Bay, in North America," which was passed at the last session of British parliament; a large and populous town, whose trade was their sole subsistence, was deprived of that trade, and involved in utter ruin. Let us for a while suppose the question of right suspended, in order to examine this act on principles of justice: An act of parliament had been passed imposing duties on teas, to be paid in America, against which act the Americans had protested as inauthoritative. The East India company, who till that time had never sent a pound of tea to America on their own account, step forth on that occasion the assertors of parliamentary right, and send hither many ship loads of that obnoxious commodity. The masters of their several vessels, however, on their arrival in America, wisely attended to admonition, and returned with their cargoes. In the province of New England alone the remonstrances of the people were disregarded, and a compliance, after being many days waited for, was flatly refused. Whether in this the master of the vessel was governed by his obstinacy, or his instructions, let those who know, say. There are extraordinary situations which require extraordinary interposition. An exasperated people, who feel that they possess power, are not easily restrained within limits strictly regular. A number of them assembled in the town of Boston, threw the tea into the ocean, and dispersed without doing any other act of violence. If in this they

5. 7. G. 3. c. 59 [Jefferson's note].
6. Only a relatively small minority of British subjects had the right to elect members of Parliament at the time.
7. 14. G. 3 [Jefferson's note].

did wrong, they were known and were amenable to the laws of the land, against which it could not be objected that they had ever, in any instance, been obstructed or diverted from their regular course in favour of popular offenders. They should therefore not have been distrusted on this occasion. But that ill fated colony had formerly been bold in their enmities against the house of Stuart, and were now devoted to ruin by that unseen hand which governs the momentous affairs of this great empire. On the partial representations of a few worthless ministerial dependents, whose constant office it has been to keep that government embroiled, and who, by their treacheries, hope to obtain the dignity of the British knighthood, without calling for a party accused, without asking a proof, without attempting a distinction between the guilty and the innocent, the whole of that antient and wealthy town is in a moment reduced from opulence to beggary. Men who had spent their lives in extending the British commerce, who had invested in that place the wealth their honest endeavours had merited, found themselves and their families thrown at once on the world for subsistence by its charities. Not the hundredth part of the inhabitants of that town had been concerned in the act complained of; many of them were in Great Britain and in other parts beyond sea; yet all were involved in one indiscriminate ruin, by a new executive power, unheard of till then, that of a British parliament. A property, of the value of many millions of money, was sacrificed to revenge, not repay, the loss of a few thousands. This is administering justice with a heavy hand indeed! and when is this tempest to be arrested in its course? Two wharfs are to be opened again when his majesty shall think proper. The residue which lined the extensive shores of the bay of Boston are forever interdicted the exercise of commerce. This little exception seems to have been thrown in for no other purpose than that of setting a precedent for investing his majesty with legislative powers. If the pulse of his people shall beat calmly under this experiment, another and another will be tried, till the measure of despotism be filled up. It would be an insult on common sense to pretend that this exception was made in order to restore its commerce to that great town. The trade which cannot be received at two wharfs alone must of necessity be transferred to some other place; to which it will soon be followed by that of the two wharfs. Considered in this light, it would be an insolent and cruel mockery at the annihilation of the town of Boston.

By the act[8] for the suppression of riots and tumults in the town of Boston, passed also in the last session of parliament, a murder committed there is, if the governor pleases, to be tried in the court of King's Bench, in the island of Great Britain, by a jury of Middlesex. The witnesses, too, on receipt of such a sum as the governor shall think it reasonable for them to expend, are to enter into recognizance to appear at the trial. This is, in other words, taxing them to the amount of their recognizance, and that amount may be whatever a governor pleases; for who does his majesty think can be prevailed on to cross the Atlantic for the sole purpose of bearing evidence to a fact? His expences are to be borne, indeed, as they shall be estimated by a governor; but who are to feed the wife and children whom he leaves behind, and who have had no other subsistence but his daily labour? Those epidemical disorders, too, so terrible in a foreign climate, is the cure of them

8. 14. G. 3 [Jefferson's note].

to be estimated among the articles of expence, and their danger to be warded off by the almighty power of parliament? And the wretched criminal, if he happen to have offended on the American side, stripped of his privilege of trial by peers of his vicinage, removed from the place where alone full evidence could be obtained, without money, without counsel, without friends, without exculpatory proof, is tried before judges predetermined to condemn. The cowards who would suffer a countryman to be torn from the bowels of their society, in order to be thus offered a sacrifice to parliamentary tyranny, would merit that everlasting infamy now fixed on the authors of the act! A clause[9] for a similar purpose had been introduced into an act, passed in the 12th year of his majesty's reign, intitled "An act for the better securing and preserving his majesty's dockyards, magazines, ships, ammunition, and stores;" against which, as meriting the same censures, the several colonies have already protested.

That these are the acts of power, assumed by a body of men, foreign to our constitutions, and unacknowledged by our laws, against which we do, on behalf of the inhabitants of British America, enter this our solemn and determined protest; and we do earnestly entreat his majesty, as yet the only mediatory power between the several states of the British empire, to recommend to his parliament of Great Britain the total revocation of these acts, which, however nugatory they be, may yet prove the cause of further discontents and jealousies among us.

That we next proceed to consider the conduct of his majesty, as holding the executive powers of the laws of these states, and mark out his deviations from the line of duty: By the constitution of Great Britain, as well as of the several American states, his majesty possesses the power of refusing to pass into a law any bill which has already passed the other two branches of legislature. His majesty, however, and his ancestors, conscious of the impropriety of opposing their single opinion to the united wisdom of two houses of parliament, while their proceedings were unbiassed by interested principles, for several ages past have modestly declined the exercise of this power in that part of his empire called Great Britain. But by change of circumstances, other principles than those of justice simply have obtained an influence on their determinations; the addition of new states to the British empire has produced an addition of new, and sometimes opposite interests. It is now, therefore, the great office of his majesty, to resume the exercise of his negative power, and to prevent the passage of laws by any one legislature of the empire, which might bear injuriously on the rights and interests of another. Yet this will not excuse the wanton exercise of this power which we have seen his majesty practise on the laws of the American legislatures. For the most trifling reasons, and sometimes for no conceivable reason at all, his majesty has rejected laws of the most salutary tendency. The abolition of domestic slavery is the great object of desire in those colonies, where it was unhappily introduced in their infant state. But previous to the enfranchisement of the slaves we have, it is necessary to exclude all further importations from Africa; yet our repeated attempts to effect this by prohibitions, and by imposing duties which might amount to a prohibition, have been hitherto defeated by his majesty's negative: Thus preferring the immediate advantages of a few African corsairs to the lasting interests of the

9. 12. G. 3. c. 24 [Jefferson's note].

American states, and to the rights of human nature, deeply wounded by this infamous practice.[1] Nay, the single interposition of an interested individual against a law was scarcely ever known to fail of success, though in the opposite scale were placed the interests of a whole country. That this is so shameful an abuse of a power trusted with his majesty for other purposes, as if not reformed, would call for some legal restrictions.

With equal inattention to the necessities of his people here has his majesty permitted our laws to lie neglected in England for years, neither confirming them by his assent, nor annulling them by his negative; so that such of them as have no suspending clause we hold on the most precarious of all tenures, his majesty's will, and such of them as suspend themselves till his majesty's assent be obtained, we have feared, might be called into existence at some future and distant period, when time, and change of circumstances, shall have rendered them destructive to his people here. And to render this grievance still more oppressive, his majesty by his instructions has laid his governors under such restrictions that they can pass no law of any moment unless it have such suspending clause; so that, however immediate may be the call for legislative interposition, the law cannot be executed till it has twice crossed the atlantic, by which time the evil may have spent its whole force.

But in what terms, reconcileable to majesty, and at the same time to truth, shall we speak of a late instruction to his majesty's governor of the colony of Virginia, by which he is forbidden to assent to any law for the division of a county, unless the new county will consent to have no representative in assembly? That colony has as yet fixed no boundary to the westward. Their western counties, therefore, are of indefinite extent; some of them are actually seated many hundred miles from their eastern limits. Is it possible, then, that his majesty can have bestowed a single thought on the situation of those people, who, in order to obtain justice for injuries, however great or small, must, by the laws of that colony, attend their county court, at such a distance, with all their witnesses, monthly, till their litigation be determined? Or does his majesty seriously wish, and publish it to the world, that his subjects should give up the glorious right of representation, with all the benefits derived from that, and submit themselves the absolute slaves of his sovereign will? Or is it rather meant to confine the legislative body to their present numbers, that they may be the cheaper bargain whenever they shall become worth a purchase.

One of the articles of impeachment against Tresilian,[2] and the other judges of Westminister Hall, in the reign of Richard the second, for which they suffered death, as traitors to their country, was, that they had advised the king that he might dissolve his parliament at any time; and succeeding kings have adopted the opinion of these unjust judges. Since the establishment, however, of the British constitution, at the glorious revolution,[3] on its free and antient principles, neither his majesty, nor his ancestors, have exercised such a power of dissolution in the island of Great Britain; and when

1. Here, as in making similar points in his draft of the Declaration of Independence, Jefferson was technically correct about unsuccessful American petitions calling for an end to the Atlantic slave trade. But the issue was more complicated by far than such charges against the crown admitted.
2. Robert Tresilian, appointed chief justice of the king's bench in 1381, was convicted of treason by Richard II's opponents in 1388 and hanged.
3. In 1688, Parliament successfully acted, in what has become known as the "Glorious Revolution," to restrain the powers of the British crown.

his majesty was petitioned, by the united voice of his people there, to dissolve the present parliament, who had become obnoxious to them, his ministers were heard to declare, in open parliament, that his majesty possessed no such power by the constitution. But how different their language and his practice here! To declare, as their duty required, the known rights of their country, to oppose the usurpations of every foreign judicature, to disregard the imperious mandates of a minister or governor, have been the avowed causes of dissolving houses of representatives in America. But if such powers be really vested in his majesty, can he suppose they are there placed to awe the members from such purposes as these? When the representative body have lost the confidence of their constituents, when they have notoriously made sale of their most valuable rights, when they have assumed to themselves powers which the people never put into their hands, then indeed their continuing in office becomes dangerous to the state, and calls for an exercise of the power of dissolution. Such being the causes for which the representative body should, and should not, be dissolved, will it not appear strange to an unbiassed observer, that that of Great Britain was not dissolved, while those of the colonies have repeatedly incurred that sentence?

But your majesty, or your governors, have carried this power beyond every limit known, or provided for, by the laws: After dissolving one house of representatives, they have refused to call another, so that, for a great length of time, the legislature provided by the laws has been out of existence. From the nature of things, every society must at all times possess within itself the sovereign powers of legislation. The feelings of human nature revolt against the supposition of a state so situated as that it may not in any emergency provide against dangers which perhaps threaten immediate ruin. While those bodies are in existence to whom the people have delegated the powers of legislation, they alone possess and may exercise those powers; but when they are dissolved by the lopping off one or more of their branches, the power reverts to the people, who may exercise it to unlimited extent, either assembling together in person, sending deputies, or in any other way they may think proper. We forbear to trace consequences further; the dangers are conspicuous with which this practice is replete.

That we shall at this time also take notice of an error in the nature of our land holdings, which crept in at a very early period of our settlement. The introduction of the feudal tenures into the kingdom of England, though antient, is well enough understood to set this matter in a proper light. In the earlier ages of the Saxon settlement feudal holdings were certainly altogether unknown; and very few, if any, had been introduced at the time of the Norman conquest. Our Saxon ancestors held their lands, as they did their personal property, in absolute dominion, disencumbered with any superior, answering nearly to the nature of those possessions which the feudalists term allodial.[4] William, the Norman, first introduced that system generally. The lands which had belonged to those who fell in the battle of Hastings,[5] and in the subsequent insurrections of his reign, formed a considerable proportion of the lands of the whole kingdom. These he granted out, subject to feudal duties, as did he also those of a great number of his new

---

4. Under feudalism, land ownership was derivative; allodial land tenure was absolute.
5. In 1066, at Hastings in the south of England, French invaders under William of Normandy defeated the army of the English king, Harold II.

subjects, who, by persuasions or threats, were induced to surrender them for that purpose. But still much was left in the hands of his Saxon subjects; held of no superior, and not subject to feudal conditions. These, therefore, by express laws, enacted to render uniform the system of military defence, were made liable to the same military duties as if they had been feuds; and the Norman lawyers soon found means to saddle them also with all the other feudal burthens. But still they had not been surrendered to the king, they were not derived from his grant, and therefore they were not holden of him. A general principle, indeed, was introduced, that "all lands in England were held either mediately or immediately of the crown," but this was borrowed from those holdings, which were truly feudal, and only applied to others for the purposes of illustration. Feudal holdings were therefore but exceptions out of the Saxon laws of possession, under which all lands were held in absolute right. These, therefore, still form the basis, or ground-work, of the common law, to prevail wheresoever the exceptions have not taken place. America was not conquered by William the Norman, nor its lands surrendered to him, or any of his successors. Possessions there are undoubtedly of the allodial nature. Our ancestors, however, who migrated hither, were farmers, not lawyers. The fictitious principle that all lands belong originally to the king, they were early persuaded to believe real; and accordingly took grants of their own lands from the crown. And while the crown continued to grant for small sums, and on reasonable rents; there was no inducement to arrest the error, and lay it open to public view. But his majesty has lately taken on him to advance the terms of purchase, and of holding to the double of what they were; by which means the acquisition of lands being rendered difficult, the population of our country is likely to be checked. It is time, therefore, for us to lay this matter before his majesty, and to declare that he has no right to grant lands of himself. From the nature and purpose of civil institutions, all the lands within the limits which any particular society has circumscribed around itself are assumed by that society, and subject to their allotment only. This may be done by themselves, assembled collectively, or by their legislature, to whom they may have delegated sovereign authority; and if they are alloted in neither of these ways, each individual of the society may appropriate to himself such lands as he finds vacant, and occupancy will give him title.

That in order to enforce the arbitrary measures before complained of, his majesty has from time to time sent among us large bodies of armed forces, not made up of the people here, nor raised by the authority of our laws: Did his majesty possess such a right as this, it might swallow up all our other rights whenever he should think proper. But his majesty has no right to land a single armed man on our shores, and those whom he sends here are liable to our laws made for the suppression and punishment of riots, routs, and unlawful assemblies; or are hostile bodies, invading us in defiance of law. When in the course of the late war it became expedient that a body of Hanoverian troops should be brought over for the defence of Great Britain, his majesty's grandfather, our late sovereign, did not pretend to introduce them under any authority he possessed. Such a measure would have given just alarm to his subjects in Great Britain, whose liberties would not be safe if armed men of another country, and of another spirit, might be brought into the realm at any time without the consent of their legislature. He therefore applied to parliament, who passed an act for that purpose, limiting the number to be brought in and the time they were to continue. In like manner is his majesty restrained in every part of the empire. He possesses, indeed, the executive power of the laws in every state; but they are the laws of the particular state which he is to administer within that state, and not those of any one within the limits of another. Every state must judge for itself the number of armed men which they may safely trust among them, of whom they are to consist, and under what restrictions they shall be laid.

To render these proceedings still more criminal against our laws, instead of subjecting the military to the civil powers, his majesty has expressly made the civil subordinate to the military. But can his majesty thus put down all law under his feet? Can he erect a power superior to that which erected himself? He has done it indeed by force; but let him remember that force cannot give right.

That these are our grievances which we have thus laid before his majesty, with that freedom of language and sentiment which becomes a free people claiming their rights, as derived from the laws of nature, and not as the gift of their chief magistrate: Let those flatter who fear; it is not an American art. To give praise which is not due might be well from the venal, but would ill beseem those who are asserting the rights of human nature. They know, and will therefore say, that kings are the servants, not the proprietors of the people. Open your breast, sire, to liberal and expanded thought. Let not the name of George the third be a blot in the page of history. You are surrounded by British counsellors, but remember that they are parties. You have no ministers for American affairs, because you have none taken from among us, nor amenable to the laws on which they are to give you advice. It behoves you, therefore, to think and to act for yourself and your people. The great principles of right and wrong are legible to every reader; to pursue them requires not the aid of many counsellors. The whole art of government consists in the art of being honest. Only aim to do your duty, and mankind will give you credit where you fail. No longer persevere in sacrificing the rights of one part of the empire to the inordinate desires of another; but deal out to all equal and impartial right. Let no act be passed by any one legislature which may infringe on the rights and liberties of another. This is the important post in which fortune has placed you, holding the balance of a great, if a well poised empire. This, sire, is the advice of your great American council, on the observance of which may perhaps depend your felicity and future fame, and the preservation of that harmony which alone can continue both to Great Britain and America the reciprocal advantages of their connection. It is neither our wish, nor our interest, to separate from her. We are willing, on our part, to sacrifice every thing which reason can ask to the restoration of that tranquillity for which all must wish. On their part, let them be ready to establish union and a generous plan. Let them name their terms, but let them be just. Accept of every commercial preference it is in our power to give for such things as we can raise for their use, or they make for ours. But let them not think to exclude us from going to other markets to dispose of those commodities which they cannot use, or to supply those wants which they cannot supply. Still less let it be proposed that our properties within our own territories shall be taxed or regulated by any power on earth but our own. The God who gave us life gave us liberty at the same time; the hand of force may destroy, but cannot disjoin them. This, sire, is our last, our determined resolution; and that you will be pleased to interpose with that efficacy which your earnest endeavours may ensure to procure redress of these our great grievances, to quiet the minds of your subjects in British America, against any apprehensions of future encroachment, to establish fraternal love and harmony through the whole empire, and that these may continue to the latest ages of time, is the fervent prayer of all British America!

From The Autobiography of Thomas Jefferson: The Declaration of Independence[1]

In Congress, Friday June 7. 1776. The delegates from Virginia moved in obedience to instructions from their constituents that the Congress should declare that these United colonies are & of right ought to be free & independent states, that they are absolved from all allegiance to the British crown, and that all political connection between them & the state of Great Britain is & ought to be, totally dissolved; that measures should be immediately taken for procuring the assistance of foreign powers, and a Confederation be formed to bind the colonies more closely together.

The house being obliged to attend at that time to some other business, the proposition was referred to the next day, when the members were ordered to attend punctually at ten o'clock.

Saturday June 8. They proceeded to take it into consideration and referred it to a committee of the whole, into which they immediately resolved themselves, and passed that day & Monday the 10th in debating on the subject.

It was argued by Wilson, Robert R. Livingston, E. Rutledge, Dickinson[2] and others

That tho' they were friends to the measures themselves, and saw the impossibility that we should ever again be united with Gr. Britain, yet they were against adopting them at this time:

That the conduct we had formerly observed was wise & proper now, of deferring to take any capital step till the voice of the people drove us into it:

That they were our power, & without them our declarations could not be carried into effect;

That the people of the middle colonies (Maryland, Delaware, Pennsylva-[nia], the Jerseys & N. York) were not yet ripe for bidding adieu to British connection, but that they were fast ripening & in a short time would join in the general voice of America:

That the resolution entered into by this house on the 15th of May for suppressing the exercise of all powers derived from the crown, had shown, by the ferment into which it had thrown these middle colonies, that they

1. The text, first published in 1829, was written by Jefferson in 1821. When he came to write his account of the drafting and approval of the Declaration of Independence by the Continental Congress in July 1776, Jefferson inserted his original draft, with alterations showing how the text had been revised by the Congress. He also inserted a set of notes (that he said were taken down "whilst these things were going on") on the debates in Congress leading to the approval of the declaration. The present selection begins with those "notes." The text is taken from Paul L. Ford, ed., *The Writings of Thomas Jefferson*, 10 vols. (New York: G. P. Putnam's Sons, 1892–99), 1:18–38.
2. John Dickinson (1732–1808) of Pennsylvania. James Wilson (1742–1798) of Pennsylvania. Robert R. Livingston (1746–1813) of New York. Edward Rutledge (1749–1800) of South Carolina.

had not yet accommodated their minds to a separation from the mother country:

That some of them had expressly forbidden their delegates to consent to such a declaration, and others had given no instructions, & consequently no powers to give such consent:

That if the delegates of any particular colony had no power to declare such colony independant, certain they were the others could not declare it for them; the colonies being as yet perfectly independant of each other:

That the assembly of Pennsylvania was now sitting above stairs, their convention would sit within a few days, the convention of New York was now sitting, & those of the Jerseys & Delaware counties would meet on the Monday following, & it was probable these bodies would take up the question of Independance & would declare to their delegates the voice of their state:

That if such a declaration should now be agreed to, these delegates must retire & possibly their colonies might secede from the Union:

That such a secession would weaken us more than could be compensated by any foreign alliance:

That in the event of such a division, foreign powers would either refuse to join themselves to our fortunes, or, having us so much in their power as that desperate declaration would place us, they would insist on terms proportionably more hard and prejudicial:

That we had little reason to expect an alliance with those to whom alone as yet we had cast our eyes:

That France & Spain had reason to be jealous of that rising power which would one day certainly strip them of all their American possessions:

That it was more likely they should form a connection with the British court, who, if they should find themselves unable otherwise to extricate themselves from their difficulties, would agree to a partition of our territories, restoring Canada to France, & the Floridas to Spain, to accomplish for themselves a recovery of these colonies:

That it would not be long before we should receive certain information of the disposition of the French court, from the agent whom we had sent to Paris for that purpose:

That if this disposition should be favorable, by waiting the event of the present campaign, which we all hoped would be successful, we should have reason to expect an alliance on better terms:

That this would in fact work no delay of any effectual aid from such ally, as, from the advance of the season & distance of our situation, it was impossible we could receive any assistance during this campaign:

That it was prudent to fix among ourselves the terms on which we should form alliance, before we declared we would form one at all events:

And that if these were agreed on, & our Declaration of Independence ready by the time our Ambassador should be prepared to sail, it would be as well as to go into that Declaration at this day.

On the other side it was urged by J. Adams, Lee, Wythe,[3] and others

That no gentleman had argued against the policy or the right of separation from Britain, nor had supposed it possible we should ever renew our connection; that they had only opposed its being now declared:

---

3. Richard Henry Lee (1732–1794) and George Wythe (1726–1806), both of Virginia. John Adams (1735–1826) of Massachusetts.

That the question was not whether, by a declaration of independance, we should make ourselves what we are not; but whether we should declare a fact which already exists:

That as to the people or parliament of England, we had alwais been independent of them, their restraints on our trade deriving efficacy from our acquiescence only, & not from any rights they possessed of imposing them, & that so far our connection had been federal only & was now dissolved by the commencement of hostilities:

That as to the King, we had been bound to him by allegiance, but that this bond was now dissolved by his assent to the late act of parliament, by which he declares us out of his protection, and by his levying war on us, a fact which had long ago proved us out of his protection; it being a certain position in law that allegiance & protection are reciprocal, the one ceasing when the other is withdrawn:

That James the IId. never declared the people of England out of his protection yet his actions proved it & the parliament declared it:

No delegates then can be denied, or ever want, a power of declaring an existing truth:

That the delegates from the Delaware counties having declared their constituents ready to join, there are only two colonies Pennsylvania & Maryland whose delegates are absolutely tied up, and that these had by their instructions only reserved a right of confirming or rejecting the measure:

That the instructions from Pennsylvania might be accounted for from the times in which they were drawn, near a twelvemonth ago, since which the face of affairs has totally changed:

That within that time it had become apparent that Britain was determined to accept nothing less than a carte-blanche, and that the King's answer to the Lord Mayor Aldermen & common council of London, which had come to hand four days ago, must have satisfied every one of this point:

That the people wait for us to lead the way:

That *they* are in favour of the measure, tho' the instructions given by some of their *representatives* are not:

That the voice of the representatives is not always consonant with the voice of the people, and that this is remarkably the case in these middle colonies:

That the effect of the resolution of the 15th of May has proved this, which, raising the murmurs of some in the colonies of Pennsylvania & Maryland, called forth the opposing voice of the freer part of the people, & proved them to be the majority, even in these colonies:

That the backwardness of these two colonies might be ascribed partly to the influence of proprietary power & connections, & partly to their having not yet been attacked by the enemy:

That these causes were not likely to be soon removed, as there seemed no probability that the enemy would make either of these the seat of this summer's war:

That it would be vain to wait either weeks or months for perfect unanimity, since it was impossible that all men should ever become of one sentiment on any question:

That the conduct of some colonies from the beginning of this contest, had given reason to suspect it was their settled policy to keep in the rear of the confederacy, that their particular prospect might be better, even in the worst event:

That therefore it was necessary for those colonies who had thrown themselves forward & hazarded all from the beginning, to come forward now also, and put all again to their own hazard:

That the history of the Dutch revolution, of whom three states only confederated at first proved that a secession of some colonies would not be so dangerous as some apprehended:

That a declaration of Independence alone could render it consistent with European delicacy for European powers to treat with us, or even to receive an Ambassador from us:

That till this they would not receive our vessels into their ports, nor acknowledge the adjudications of our courts of admiralty to be legitimate, in cases of capture of British vessels:

That though France & Spain may be jealous of our rising power, they must think it will be much more formidable with the addition of Great Britain; and will therefore see it their interest to prevent a coalition; but should they refuse, we shall be but where we are; whereas without trying we shall never know whether they will aid us or not:

That the present campaign may be unsuccessful, & therefore we had better propose an alliance while our affairs wear a hopeful aspect:

That to await the event of this campaign will certainly work delay, because during this summer France may assist us effectually by cutting off those supplies of provisions from England & Ireland on which the enemy's armies here are to depend; or by setting in motion the great power they have collected in the West Indies, & calling our enemy to the defence of the possessions they have there:

That it would be idle to lose time in settling the terms of alliance, till we had first determined we would enter into alliance:

That it is necessary to lose no time in opening a trade for our people, who will want clothes, and will want money too for the paiment of taxes:

And that the only misfortune is that we did not enter into alliance with France six months sooner, as besides opening their ports for the vent of our last year's produce, they might have marched an army into Germany and prevented the petty princes there from selling their unhappy subjects to subdue us.

It appearing in the course of these debates that the colonies of N. York, New Jersey, Pennsylvania, Delaware, Maryland, and South Carolina were not yet matured for falling from the parent stem, but that they were fast advancing to that state, it was thought most prudent to wait a while for them, and to postpone the final decision to July 1. but that this might occasion as little delay as possible a committee was appointed to prepare a declaration of independence. The committee were J. Adams, Dr. Franklin, Roger Sherman, Robert R. Livingston & myself. Committees were also appointed at the same time to prepare a plan of confederation for the colonies, and to state the terms proper to be proposed for foreign alliance. The committee for drawing the declaration of Independence desired me to do it. It was accordingly done, and being approved by them, I reported it to the house on Friday the 28th of June when it was read and ordered to lie on the table. On Monday, the 1st of July the house resolved itself into a committee of the whole & resumed the consideration of the original motion made by the delegates of Virginia, which being again debated through the day, was carried in the affirmative by the votes of N. Hampshire, Connecticut, Massachusetts, Rhode Island, N. Jersey, Maryland, Virginia, N. Carolina, & Georgia. S. Carolina and Pennsylvania voted against it. Delaware having but two members present, they were divided. The delegates for New York declared they were for it themselves & were assured their constituents were for it, but that their instructions having been drawn near a twelvemonth before, when reconciliation was still the general object, they were enjoined by them to do nothing which should impede that object. They therefore thought themselves not justifiable in voting on either side, and asked leave to withdraw from the question, which was given them. The comm[itt]ee rose & reported their resolution to the house. Mr. Edward Rutledge of S. Carolina then requested the determination might be put off to the next day, as he believed his colleagues, tho' they disapproved of the resolution, would then join in it for the sake of unanimity. The ultimate question whether the house would agree to the resolution of the committee was accordingly postponed to the next day, when it was again moved and S. Carolina concurred in voting for it. In the meantime a third member had come post from the Delaware counties and turned the vote of that colony in favour of the resolution. Members of a different sentiment attending that morning from Pennsylvania also, their vote was changed, so that the whole 12 colonies who were authorized to vote at all, gave their voices for it; and within a few days, the convention of N. York approved of it and thus supplied the void occasioned by the withdrawing of her delegates from the vote.

Congress proceeded the same day to consider the declaration of Independance which had been reported & lain on the table the Friday preceding, and on Monday referred to a commee of the whole. The pusillanimous idea that we had friends in England worth keeping terms with, still haunted the minds of many. For this reason those passages which conveyed censures on the people of England were struck out, lest they should give them offence. The clause too, reprobating the enslaving the inhabitants of Africa, was struck out in complaisance to South Carolina and Georgia, who had never attempted to restrain the importation of slaves, and who on the contrary still wished to continue it. Our northern brethren also I believe felt a little tender under those censures; for tho' their people have very few slaves themselves yet they had been pretty considerable carriers of them to others. The debates having taken up the greater parts of the 2d 3d & 4th days of July were, in the evening of the last, closed[;] the declaration was reported by the comm[itt]ee, agreed to by the house and signed by every member present except Mr. Dickinson. As the sentiments of men are known not only by what they receive, but what they reject also, I will state the form of the declaration as originally reported. The parts struck out by Congress shall be distinguished by a black line drawn under them; & those inserted by them shall be placed in the margin or in a concurrent column.

A Declaration by the Representatives of the United States of America, in General Congress Assembled.

When in the course of human events it becomes necessary for one people to dissolve the political bands which have connected them with another, and to assume among the powers of the earth the separate & equal station to which the laws of nature and of nature's God entitle them, a decent respect to the opinions of mankind requires that they should declare the causes which impel them to the separation.

We hold these truths to be self-evident: that all men are created equal; that they are endowed by their creator with <u>inherent</u>
certain
<u>and</u> inalienable rights; that among these are life, liberty, & the pursuit of happiness: that to secure these rights, governments are instituted among men, deriving their just powers from the consent of the governed; that whenever any form of government becomes destructive of these ends, it is the right of the people to alter or abolish it, & to institute new government, laying it's foundation on such principles, & organizing it's powers in such form, as to them shall seem most likely to effect their safety & happiness. Prudence indeed will dictate that governments long established should not be changed for light & transient causes; and accordingly all experience hath shown that mankind are more disposed to suffer while evils are sufferable, than to right themselves by abolishing the forms to which they are accustomed. But when a long train of abuses & usurpations <u>begun at a distinguished period and</u> pursuing invariably the same object, evinces a design to reduce them under absolute despotism, it is their right, it is their duty to throw off such government, & to provide new guards for their future security. Such has been the patient sufferance of these colonies; & such is now the necessity which constrains them to
alter   <u>expunge</u> their former systems of government. The history of the present king of Great Britain is a history
repeated   of <u>unremitting</u> injuries & usurpations, <u>among which</u>
<u>appears no solitary fact to contradict the uniform tenor of the rest but all</u> have in direct object the establishment of an absolute
all having   tyranny over these states. To prove this let facts be submitted to a candid world <u>for the truth of which we pledge a faith yet unsullied by falsehood.</u>

He has refused his assent to laws the most wholesome & necessary for the public good.

He has forbidden his governors to pass laws of immediate & pressing importance, unless suspended in their operation till his assent should be obtained; & when so suspended, he has utterly neglected to attend to them.

He has refused to pass other laws for the accommodation of large districts of people, unless those people would relinquish the right of representation in the legislature, a right inestimable to them, & formidable to tyrants only.

He has called together legislative bodies at places unusual, uncomfortable, and distant from the depository of their public records, for the sole purpose of fatiguing them into compliance with his measures.

He has dissolved representative houses repeatedly <u>& continually</u> for opposing with manly firmness his invasions on the rights of the people.

He has refused for a long time after such dissolutions to cause others to be elected, whereby the legislative powers, incapable of annihilation, have returned to the people at large for their exercise, the state remaining in the meantime exposed to all the dangers of invasion from without & convulsions within.

He has endeavored to prevent the population of these states; for that purpose obstructing the laws for naturalization of foreigners, refusing to pass others to encourage their migrations hither, & raising the conditions of new appropriations of lands.

He has <u>suffered</u> the administration of justice <u>totally</u> obstructed <u>to cease in some of</u> these states refusing his assent to by laws for establishing judiciary powers.

He has made <u>our</u> judges dependant on his will alone, for the tenure of their offices, & the amount & paiment of their salaries.

He has erected a multitude of new offices <u>by a self assumed power</u> and sent hither swarms of new officers to harass our people and eat out their substance.

He has kept among us in times of peace standing armies <u>and ships of war</u> without the consent of our legislatures.

He has affected to render the military independant of, & superior to the civil power.

He has combined with others to subject us to a jurisdiction foreign to our constitutions & unacknowledged by our laws, giving his assent to their acts of pretended legislation for quartering large bodies of armed troops among us; for protecting them by a mock-trial from punishment for any murders which they should commit on the inhabitants of these states; for cutting off our trade with all parts of the world; for imposing taxes on us without our consent; for depriving us [ ] of the benefits of trial by in many cases jury; for transporting us beyond seas to be tried for pretended offences; for abolishing the free system of English laws in a neighboring province, establishing therein an arbitrary government, and enlarging it's boundaries, so as to render it at once an example and fit instrument for introducing the same absolute rule colonies into these <u>states</u>; for taking away our charters, abolishing our most valuable laws, and altering fundamentally the forms of our governments; for suspending our own legislatures, & declaring themselves invested with power to legislate for us in all cases whatsoever.

He has abdicated government here <u>withdrawing his</u> by declaring us out of <u>governors, and declaring us out of his allegiance &</u> his protection, and <u>protection.</u> waging war against us.

He has plundered our seas, ravaged our coasts, burnt our towns, & destroyed the lives of our people.

He is at this time transporting large armies of foreign mercenaries to compleat the works of death, desolation & tyranny already begun with circumstances of cruelty and perfidy [ ] unworthy the scarcely paralleled in head of a civilized nation. the most barbarous ages, & totally

He has constrained our fellow citizens taken captive on the high seas to bear arms against their country, to become the executioners of their friends & brethren, or to fall themselves by their hands.

He has [ ] endeavored to bring on the inhabitants of our frontiers the merciless Indian savages, whose excited domestic known rule of warfare is an undistinguished destruc- insurrection among tion of all ages, sexes, & conditions <u>of existence.</u> us, & has

<u>He has incited treasonable insurrections of our fellow-citizens, with the allurements of forfeiture & confiscation of our property.</u>

<u>He has waged cruel war against human nature itself, violating it's most sacred rights of life and liberty in the persons of a distant people who never offended him, captivating & carrying them into slavery in another</u>

hemisphere, or to incur miserable death in their transportation thither. This piratical warfare, the opprobium of INFIDEL powers, is the warfare of the CHRISTIAN king of Great Britain. Determined to keep open a market where MEN should be bought & sold, he has prostituted his negative for suppressing every legislative attempt to prohibit or to restrain this execrable commerce. And that this assemblage of horrors might want no fact of distinguished die, he is now exciting those very people to rise in arms among us, and to purchase that liberty of which he has deprived them, by murdering the people on whom he also obtruded them: thus paying off former crimes committed against the LIBERTIES of one people, with crimes which he urges them to commit against the LIVES of another.

In every stage of these oppressions we have petitioned for redress in the most humble terms: our repeated petitions have been answered only by repeated injuries.

A prince whose character is thus marked by every act which may define a tyrant is unfit to be the ruler of a [ ] people who mean to be free. *free* Future ages will scarcely believe that the hardiness of one man adventured, within the short compass of twelve years only, to lay a foundation so broad & so undisguised for tyranny over a people fostered & fixed in principles of freedom.

Nor have we been wanting in attentions to our British brethren. We have warned them from time to time of attempts by their legislature to extend a jurisdiction over these our states. *an unwarrantable* We have reminded them of the circumstances of our emigration & settle-*us* ment here, no one of which could warrant so strange a pretension: that these were effected at the expense of our own blood & treasure, unassisted by the wealth or the strength of Great Britain: that in constituting indeed our several forms of government, we had adopted one common king, thereby laying a foundation for perpetual league & amity with them: but that submission to their parliament was no part of our constitution, nor ever in idea, if history may be credited: and, we [ ] appealed to their native justice and mag-*have* *and we have conjured* nanimity as well as to the ties of our common kindred *them by* to disavow these usurpations which were likely to interrupt our connection and correspondence. They too have been deaf to the voice of justice & of consan-*would inevitably* guinity, and when occasions have been given them, by the regular course of their laws, of removing from their councils the disturbers of our harmony, they have, by their free election, re-established them in power. At this very time too they are permitting their chief magistrate to send over not only soldiers of our common blood, but Scotch & foreign mercenaries to invade & destroy us. These facts have given the last stab to agonizing affection, and manly spirit bids us to renounce forever these unfeeling brethren. We must endeavor to forget our former love for them, and hold them as we hold the rest of mankind, enemies in war, in peace friends. We might have been a free and a great people together; but a communication of grandeur & of freedom it seems is below their dignity. Be it so, since they will have it. The road to happiness & to glory is *We must therefore* open to us too. We will tread it apart from them, and *and hold them as we* acquiesce in the necessity which denounces our eter-*hold the rest of man-* *kind, enemies in war, in* nal separation [ ] ! *peace friends.*

We therefore the representatives of the United States of America in General Congress assembled do in the name & by authority of the good people of these states reject & renounce all allegiance & subjection to the kings of Great Britain & all others who may hereafter claim by, through or under them: we utterly dissolve all political connection which may heretofore have subsisted between us & the people or parliament of Great Britain: & finally we do assert & declare these colonies to be free & independent states, & that as free & independent states, they have full power to levy war, conclude peace, contract alliances, establish commerce, & to do all other acts & things which independent states may of right do.

And for the support of this declaration we mutually pledge to each other our lives, our fortunes, & our sacred honor.

We therefore the representatives of the United States of America in General Congress assembled, appealing to the supreme judge of the world for the rectitude of our intentions, do in the name, & by the authority of the good people of these colonies, solemnly publish & declare that these united colonies are & of right ought to be free & independent states; that they are absolved from all allegiance to the British crown, and that all political connection between them & the state of Great Britain is, & ought to be, totally dissolved; & that as free & independent states they have full power to levy war, conclude peace, contract alliances, establish commerce & to do all other acts & things which independant states may of right do.

And for the support of this declaration, with a firm reliance on the protection of divine providence we mutually pledge to each other our lives, our fortunes, & our sacred honor.

The Declaration thus signed on the 4th, on paper was engrossed on parchment, & signed again on the 2d. of August.

Notes on the State of Virginia[1]

Advertisement

The following Notes were written in Virginia in the year 1781, and somewhat corrected and enlarged in the winter of 1782, in answer to Queries proposed to the Author, by a Foreigner of Distinction,[2] then residing among us. The subjects are all treated imperfectly; some scarcely touched on. To apologize for this by developing the circumstances of the time and place of their composition, would be to open wounds which have already bled enough. To these circumstances some of their imperfections may with truth be ascribed; the great mass to the want of information and want of talents in the writer. He had a few copies printed, which he gave among his friends: and a translation of them has been lately published in France, but with such alterations as the laws of the press in that country rendered necessary. They are now offered to the public in their original form and language.

Feb. 27, 1787.

Contents

1. The text is that of the first public edition (London: John Stockdale, 1787). Jefferson's map, based on that prepared by his father, Peter Jefferson, and Joshua Fry in 1751, and included in Stockdale's edition, is omitted here, but the three appendices originally included in it are printed here. (The fourth appendix, added in editions published after 1800, is reprinted as a separate text, as it had first appeared in 1800; see p. 178. All notes are by the present editor unless otherwise specified. Spellings remain unchanged. Key passages in Jefferson's text that are quoted from works in languages other than English have been freely translated by the editor so as to render the sense of Jefferson's argument clear.
2. François Barbé-Marbois (1745–1837), who served as secretary of the French legation to the rebellious American colonies (1779–83), and then as chargé d'affaires to the United States (1783–85).

Query I

An exact description of the limits and   Limits
boundaries of the state of Virginia?

Virginia is bounded on the East by the Atlantic: on the North by a line of latitude, crossing the Eastern Shore through Watkins's Point, being about 37°. 57'. North latitude; from thence by a streight line to Cinquac, near the mouth of Patowmac; thence by the Patowmac, which is common to Virginia and Maryland, to the first fountain of its northern branch; thence by a meridian line, passing through that fountain till it intersects a line running East and West, in latitude 39°. 43'. 42.4" which divides Maryland from Pennsylvania, and which was marked by Messrs. Mason and Dixon; thence by that line, and a continuation of it westwardly to the completion of five degrees of longitude from the eastern boundary of Pennsylvania, in the same latitude, and thence by a meridian line to the Ohio: On the West by the Ohio and Missisipi, to latitude 36°. 30'. North: and on the South by the line of latitude last-mentioned. By admeasurements through nearly the whole of this last line, and supplying the unmeasured parts from good data, the Atlantic and Missisipi, are found in this latitude to be 758 miles distant, equal to 13°. 38'. of longitude, reckoning 55 miles and 3144 feet to the degree. This being our comprehension of longitude, that of our latitude, taken between this and Mason and Dixon's line, is 3°. 13'. 42.4". equal to 223.3 miles, supposing a degree of a great circle to be 69 m. 864 f. as computed by Cassini. These boundaries include an area somewhat triangular, of 121525 square miles, whereof 79650 lie westward of the Allegany mountains, and 57034 westward of the meridian of the mouth of the Great Kanhaway. This state is therefore one third larger than the islands of Great Britain and Ireland, which are reckoned at 88357 square miles.

These limits result from, 1. The antient charters from the crown of England. 2. The grant of Maryland to the Lord Baltimore, and the subsequent determinations of the British court as to the extent of that grant. 3. The grant of Pennsylvania to William Penn, and a compact between the general assemblies of the commonwealths of Virginia and Pennsylvania as to the extent of that grant. 4. The grant of Carolina, and actual location of its northern boundary, by consent of both parties. 5. The treaty of Paris of 1763. 6. The confirmation of the charters of the neighbouring states by the convention of Virginia at the time of constituting their commonwealth. 7. The cession made by Virginia to Congress of all the lands to which they had title on the North side of the Ohio.

Query II

A notice of its rivers, rivulets,
and how far they are navigable?

An inspection of a map of Virginia, will give a better idea of the geography of its rivers, than any description in writing. Their navigation may be imperfectly noted.

Roanoke, so far as it lies within this state, is no where navigable, but for canoes, or light batteaux; and, even for these, in such detached parcels as to have prevented the inhabitants from availing themselves of it at all.

James River, and its waters, afford navigation as follows.

The whole of *Elizabeth River*, the lowest of those which run into James River, is a harbour, and would contain upwards of 300 ships. The channel is from 150 to 200 fathom wide, and at common flood tide, affords 18 feet water to Norfolk. The Strafford, a 60 gun ship, went there, lightening herself to cross the bar at Sowell's point. The Fier Rodrigue, pierced for 64 guns, and carrying 50, went there without lightening. Craney island, at the mouth of this river, commands its channel tolerably well.

Nansemond River is navigable to Sleepy hole, for vessels of 250 tons; to Suffolk, for those of 100 tons; and to Milner's, for those of 25.

Pagan Creek affords 8 or 10 feet water to Smithfeild, which admits vessels of 20 ton.

Chickahominy has at its mouth a bar, on which is only 12 feet water at common flood tide. Vessels passing that, may go 8 miles up the river; those of 10 feet draught may go four miles further, and those of six tons burthen, 20 miles further.

Appamattox may be navigated as far as Broadways, by any vessel which has crossed Harrison's bar in James river; it keeps 8 or 9 feet water a mile or two higher up to Fisher's bar, and 4 feet on that and upwards to Petersburgh, where all navigation ceases.

James River itself affords harbour for vessels of any size in Hampton Road, but not in safety through the whole winter; and there is navigable water for them as far as Mulberry island. A 40 gun ship goes to James town, and, lightening herself, may pass to Harrison's bar, on which there is only 15 feet water. Vessels of 250 tons may go to Warwick; those of 125 go to Rocket's, a mile below Richmond; from thence is about 7 feet water to Richmond; and about the center of the town, four feet and a half, where the navigation is interrupted by falls, which in a course of six miles, descend about 80 feet perpendicular: above these it is resumed in canoes and batteaux, and is prosecuted safely and advantageously to within 10 miles of the Blue ridge; and even through the Blue ridge a ton weight has been brought; and the expence would not be great, when compared with its object, to open a tolerable navigation up Jackson's river and Carpenter's creek, to within 25 miles of Howard's creek of Green briar, both of which have then water enough to float vessels into the Great Kanhaway. In some future state of population, I think it possible, that its navigation may also be made to interlock with that of the Patowmac, and through that to communicate by a short portage with the Ohio. It is to be noted, that this river is called in the maps *James River*, only to its confluence with the Rivanna; thence to the Blue ridge it is called the Fluvanna; and thence to its source, Jackson's river. But in common speech, it is called James river to its source.

The *Rivanna*, a branch of James river, is navigable for canoes and batteaux to its intersection with the South West mountains, which is about 22 miles; and may easily be opened to navigation through those mountains to its fork above Charlottesville.

York River, at York town, affords the best harbour in the state for vessels of the largest size. The river there narrows to the width of a mile, and is contained within very high banks, close under which the vessels may ride. It holds 4 fathom water at high tide for 25 miles above York to the mouth of Poropotank, where the river is a mile and a half wide, and the channel only 75 fathom, and passing under a high bank. At the confluence of *Pamunkey* and *Mattapony*, it is reduced to 3 fathom depth, which continues up Pamunkey to Cumberland, where the width is 100 yards, and up Mattapony to within two miles of Frazer's ferry, where it becomes 2½ fathom deep, and holds that about five miles. Pamunkey is then capable of navigation for loaded flats to Brockman's bridge, 50 miles above Hanover town, and Mattapony to Downer's bridge, 70 miles above its mouth.

Piankatank, the little rivers making out of *Mobjack bay* and those of the *Eastern shore*, receive only very small vessels, and these can but enter them.

Rappahanock affords 4 fathom water to Hobb's hole, and 2 fathom from thence to Fredericksburg.

Patowmac is 7½ miles wide at the mouth; 4½ at Nomony bay; 3 at Aquia; 1 at Hallooing point; 1¼ at Alexandria. Its soundings are, 7 fathom at the mouth; 5 at St. George's island; 4½ at Lower Matchodic; 3 at Swan's point, and thence up to Alexandria; thence 10 feet water to the falls, which are 13 miles above Alexandria. These falls are 15 miles in length, and of very great descent, and the navigation above them for batteaux and canoes, is so much interrupted as to be little used. It is, however, used in a small degree up the Cohongoronta branch as far as Fort Cumberland, which was at the mouth of Wills's creek: and is capable, at no great expence, of being rendered very practicable. The Shenandoah branch interlocks with James river about the Blue ridge, and may perhaps in future be opened.

The *Missisipi* will be one of the principal channels of future commerce for the country westward of the Alleghaney. From the mouth of this river to where it receives the Ohio, is 1000 miles by water, but only 500 by land, passing through the Chickasaw country. From the mouth of the Ohio to that of the Missouri, is 230 miles by water, and 140 by land. From thence to the mouth of the Illinois river, is about 25 miles. The Missisipi, below the mouth of the Missouri, is always muddy, and abounding with sand bars, which frequently change their places. However, it carries 15 feet water to the mouth of the Ohio, to which place it is from one and a half to two miles wide, and thence to Kaskaskia from one mile to a mile and a quarter wide. Its current is so rapid, that it never can be stemmed by the force of the wind alone, acting on sails. Any vessel, however, navigated with oars, may come up at any time, and receive much aid from the wind. A batteau passes from the mouth of Ohio to the mouth of Missisipi in three weeks, and is from two to three months getting up again. During its floods, which are periodical as those of the Nile, the largest vessels may pass down it, if their steerage can be ensured. These floods begin in April, and the river returns into its banks early in August. The inundation extends further on the western than eastern side, covering the lands in some places for 50 miles from its banks. Above the mouth of the Missouri, it becomes much such a river as the Ohio, like it clear, and gentle in its current, not quite so wide, the period of its floods nearly the same, but not rising to so great a height. The streets of the village at Cohoes[3] are not more than 10 feet above the ordinary level of the water, and yet were never overflowed. Its bed deepens every year. Cohoes, in the memory of many people now living, was insulated by every flood of the river. What was the Eastern channel has now become a lake, 9 miles in length and one in width, into which the river at this day never flows. This river yields turtle of a peculiar kind, perch, trout, gar, pike, mullets, herrings, carp, spatula fish of 50 lb. weight, cat fish of an hundred pounds weight, buffalo fish, and sturgeon. Alligators or crocodiles have been seen as high up as the Acansas.[4] It also abounds in herons, cranes, ducks, brant, geese, and swans. Its passage is commanded by a fort established by this state, five miles below the mouth of Ohio, and ten miles above the Carolina boundary.

The Missouri, since the treaty of Paris, the Illinois and Northern branches of the Ohio since the cession to Congress, are no longer within our limits. Yet having been so heretofore, and still opening to us channels of extensive communication with the western and north-western country, they shall be noted in their order.

The *Missouri* is, in fact, the principal river, contributing more to the common stream than does the Missisipi, even after its junction with the Illinois. It is remarkably cold, muddy and rapid. Its overflowings are considerable. They happen during the months of June and July. Their commencement being so much later than those of the Missisipi, would induce a belief that the sources of the Missouri are northward of those of the Missisipi, unless we suppose that the cold increases again with the ascent of the land from the Missisipi westwardly. That this ascent is great, is proved by the rapidity of the river. Six miles above the mouth it is brought within the compass of a quarter of a mile's width: yet the Spanish Merchants at Pancore, or St. Louis, say they go two thousand miles up it. It heads far westward of the Rio Norte, or North River. There is, in the villages of Kaskaskia, Cohoes and St. Vincennes, no inconsiderable quantity of plate, said to have been plundered during the last war by the Indians from the churches and private houses of Santa Fé, on the North River, and brought to these villages for sale. From the mouth of Ohio to Santa Fé are forty days journey, or about 1000 miles. What is the shortest distance between the navigable waters of the Missouri, and those of the North River, or how far this is navigable above Santa Fé, I could never learn. From Santa Fé to its mouth in the Gulph of Mexico is about 1200 miles. The road from New Orleans to Mexico crosses this river at the post of Rio Norte, 800 miles below Santa Fé: and from this post to New Orleans is about 1200 miles; thus making 2000 miles between Santa Fé and New Orleans, passing down the North river, Red river and Missisipi; whereas it is 2230 through the Missouri and Missisipi. From the same post of Rio Norte, passing near the mines of La Sierra and Laiguana, which are between the North river and the river Salina to Sartilla, is 375 miles; and from thence, passing the mines of Charcas, Zaccatecas and Potosi, to the city of Mexico is 375 miles; in all, 1550 miles from Santa Fé to the city of

3. Cahokia, on the Mississippi River opposite St. Louis.
4. Arkansas.

Mexico. From New Orleans to the city of Mexico is about 1950 miles: the roads, after setting out from the Red river, near Natchitoches, keeping generally parallel with the coast, and about two hundred miles from it, till it enters the city of Mexico.

The *Illinois* is a fine river, clear, gentle, and without rapids; insomuch that it is navigable for batteaux to its source. From thence is a portage of two miles only to the Chickago, which affords a batteau navigation of 16 miles to its entrance into lake Michigan. The Illinois, about 10 miles above its mouth, is 300 yards wide.

The *Kaskaskia* is 100 yards wide at its entrance into the Missisipi, and preserves that breadth to the Buffalo plains, 70 miles above. So far also it is navigable for loaded batteaux, and perhaps much further. It is not rapid.

The *Ohio* is the most beautiful river on earth. Its current gentle, waters clear, and bosom smooth and unbroken by rocks and rapids, a single instance only excepted.

It is ¼ of a mile wide at Fort Pitt:

500 yards at the mouth of the Great Kanhaway:

1 mile and 25 poles[5] at Louisville:

¼ of a mile on the rapids, three or four miles below Louisville:

½ a mile where the low country begins, which is 20 miles above Green river:

1¼ at the receipt of the Tanissee:

And a mile wide at the mouth.

Its length, as measured according to its meanders by Capt. Hutchings,[6] is as follows:

From Fort Pitt

	Miles.		Miles.
To Log's town	18½	Little Miami	126¼
Big Beaver creek	10¾	Licking creek	8
Little Beaver cr.	13½	Great Miami	26¾
Yellow creek	11¾	Big Bones	32½
Two creeks	21¾	Kentuckey	44¼
Long reach	53¾	Rapids	77¼
End Long reach	16½	Low country	155¾
Muskingum	25½	Buffalo river	64½
Little Kanhaway	12¼	Wabash	97¼
Hockhocking	16	Big cave	42¾
Great Kanhaway	82½	Shawanee river	52½
Guiandot	43¾	Cherokee river	13
Sandy creek	14½	Massac	11
Sioto	48¾	Missisipi	46
			1188

In common winter and spring tides it affords 15 feet water to Louisville, 10 feet to La Tarte's rapids, 40 miles above the mouth of the great Kanhaway, and a sufficiency at all times for light batteaux and canoes to Fort Pitt. The rapids are in latitude 38°. 8'. The inundations of this river begin

5. A surveyor's pole or rod is sixteen and a half feet long.
6. Thomas Hutchins (1730–1789) published *A Topographical Description of Virginia, Pennsylvania, Maryland, and North Carolina* in 1778.

about the last of March, and subside in July. During these a first rate man of war may be carried from Louisville to New Orleans, if the sudden turns of the river and the strength of its current will admit a safe steerage. The rapids at Louisville descend about 30 feet in a length of a mile and a half. The bed of the river there is a solid rock, and is divided by an island into two branches, the southern of which is about 200 yards wide, and is dry four months in the year. The bed of the northern branch is worn into channels by the constant course of the water, and attrition of the pebble stones carried on with that, so as to be passable for batteaux through the greater part of the year. Yet it is thought that the southern arm may be the most easily opened for constant navigation. The rise of the waters in these rapids does not exceed 10 or 12 feet. A part of this island is so high as to have been never overflowed, and to command the settlement at Louisville, which is opposite to it. The fort, however, is situated at the head of the falls. The ground on the South side rises very gradually.

The *Tanissee*, Cherokee or Hogohege river is 600 yards wide at its mouth, ¼ of a mile at the mouth of Holston, and 200 yards at Chotee, which is 20 miles above Holston, and 300 miles above the mouth of the Tanissee. This river crosses the southern boundary of Virginia, 58 miles from the Missisipi. Its current is moderate. It is navigable for loaded boats of any burthen to the Muscleshoals, where the river passes through the Cumberland mountain. These shoals are 6 or 8 miles long, passable downwards for loaded canoes, but not upwards, unless there be a swell in the river. Above these the navigation for loaded canoes and batteaux continues to the Long island. This river has its inundations also. Above the Chickamogga towns is a whirlpool called the Sucking-pot, which takes in trunks of trees or boats, and throws them out again half a mile below. It is avoided by keeping very close to the bank, on the South side. There are but a few miles portage between a branch of this river and the navigable waters of the river Mobile, which runs into the gulph of Mexico.

Cumberland, or Shawanee river, intersects the boundary between Virginia and North Carolina 67 miles from the Missisipi, and again 198 miles from the same river, a little above the entrance of Obey's river into the Cumberland. Its clear fork crosses the same boundary about 300 miles from the Missisipi. Cumberland is a very gentle stream, navigable for loaded batteaux 800 miles, without interruption; then intervene some rapids of 15 miles in length, after which it is again navigable 70 miles upwards, which brings you within 10 miles of the Cumberland mountains. It is about 120 yards wide through its whole course, from the head of its navigation to its mouth.

The *Wabash* is a very beautiful river, 400 yards wide at the mouth, and 300 at St. Vincennes, which is a post 100 miles above the mouth, in a direct line. Within this space there are two small rapids, which give very little obstruction to the navigation. It is 400 yards wide at the mouth, and navigable 30 leagues upwards for canoes and small boats. From the mouth of Maple river to that of Eel river is about 80 miles in a direct line, the river continuing navigable, and from one to two hundred yards in width. The Eel river is 150 yards wide, and affords at all times navigation for periaguas,[7] to within 18 miles of the Miami of the lake. The Wabash, from the mouth of Eel river to Little river, a distance of 50 miles direct, is interrupted with frequent rapids

7. Dugout canoes.

and shoals, which obstruct the navigation, except in a swell. Little river affords navigation during a swell to within 3 miles of the Miami, which thence affords a similar navigation into lake Erié, 100 miles distant in a direct line. The Wabash overflows periodically in correspondence with the Ohio, and in some places two leagues from its banks.

Green River is navigable for loaded batteaux at all times 50 miles upwards; but it is then interrupted by impassable rapids, above which the navigation again commences, and continues good 30 or 40 miles to the mouth of Barren river.

Kentucky river is 90 yards wide at the mouth, and also at Boonsborough, 80 miles above. It affords a navigation for loaded batteaux 180 miles in a direct line, in the winter tides.

The Great Miami of the Ohio, is 200 yards wide at the mouth. At the Piccawee towns, 75 miles above, it is reduced to 30 yards; it is, nevertheless, navigable for loaded canoes 50 miles above these towns. The portage from its western branch into the Miami of Lake Erié, is 5 miles; that from its eastern branch into Sandusky river, is of 9 miles.

Salt river is at all times navigable for loaded batteaux 70 or 80 miles. It is 80 yards wide at its mouth, and keeps that width to its fork, 25 miles above.

The Little Miami of the Ohio, is 60 or 70 yards wide at its mouth, 60 miles to its source, and affords no navigation.

The Sioto is 250 yards wide at its mouth, which is in latitude 38°. 22'. and at the Saltlick towns, 200 miles above the mouth, it is yet 100 yards wide. To these towns it is navigable for loaded batteaux, and its eastern branch affords navigation almost to its source.

Great Sandy river is about sixty yards wide, and navigable sixty miles for loaded batteaux.

Guiandot is about the width of the river last mentioned, but is more rapid. It may be navigated by canoes sixty miles.

The Great Kanhaway is a river of considerable note for the fertility of its lands, and still more, as leading towards the headwaters of James river. Nevertheless, it is doubtful whether its great and numerous rapids will admit a navigation, but at an expence to which it will require ages to render its inhabitants equal. The great obstacles begin at what are called the great falls, 90 miles above the mouth, below which are only five or six rapids, and these passable, with some difficulty, even at low water. From the falls to the mouth of Greenbriar is 100 miles, and thence to the lead mines 120. It is 280 yards wide at its mouth.

Hock-hocking is 80 yards wide at its mouth, and yields navigation for loaded batteaux to the Press-place, 60 miles above its mouth.

The Little Kanhaway is 150 yards wide at the mouth. It yields a navigation of 10 miles only. Perhaps its northern branch, called Junius's creek, which interlocks with the western of Monongahela, may one day admit a shorter passage from the latter into the Ohio.

The Muskingum is 280 yards wide at its mouth, and 200 yards at the lower Indian towns, 150 miles upwards. It is navigable for small batteaux to within one mile of a navigable part of Cayahoga river, which runs into lake Erié.

At Fort Pitt the river Ohio loses its name, branching into the Monongahela and Alleghaney.

The Monongahela is 400 yards wide at its mouth. From thence is 12 or 15 miles to the mouth of Yohoganey, where it is 300 yards wide. Thence to

Redstone by water is 50 miles, by land 30. Then to the mouth of Cheat river by water 40 miles, by land 28, the width continuing at 300 yards, and the navigation good for boats. Thence the width is about 200 yards to the western fork, 50 miles higher, and the navigation frequently interrupted by rapids; which however with a swell of two or three feet become very passable for boats. It then admits light boats, except in dry seasons, 65 miles further to the head of Tygarts valley, presenting only some small rapids and falls of one or two feet perpendicular, and lessening in its width to 20 yards. The *Western fork* is navigable in the winter 10 or 15 miles towards the northern of the Little Kanhaway, and will admit a good waggon road to it. The *Yohoganey* is the principal branch of this river. It passes through the Laurel mountain, about 30 miles from its mouth; is so far from 300 to 150 yards wide, and the navigation much obstructed in dry weather by rapids and shoals. In its passage through the mountain it makes very great falls, admitting no navigation for ten miles to the Turkey foot. Thence to the great crossing, about 20 miles, it is again navigable, except in dry seasons, and at this place is 200 yards wide. The sources of this river are divided from those of the Patowmac by the Alleghaney mountain. From the falls, where it intersects the Laurel mountain, to Fort Cumberland, the head of the navigation on the Patowmac, is 40 miles of very mountainous road. Wills's creek, at the mouth of which was Fort Cumberland, is 30 or 40 yards wide, but affords no navigation as yet. *Cheat* river, another considerable branch of the Monongahela, is 200 yards wide at its mouth, and 100 yards at the Dunkard's settlement, 50 miles higher. It is navigable for boats, except in dry seasons. The boundary between Virginia and Pennsylvania crosses it about three or four miles above its mouth.

The *Alleghaney* river, with a slight swell, affords navigation for light batteaux to Venango, at the mouth of French creek, where it is 200 yards wide; and it is practised even to Le Bœuf, from whence there is a portage of 15 miles to Presque Isle on Lake Erié.

The country watered by the Missisipi and its eastern branches, constitutes five-eighths of the United States, two of which five-eighths are occupied by the Ohio and its waters: the residuary streams which run into the Gulph of Mexico, the Atlantic, and the St. Laurence water, the remaining three-eighths.

Before we quit the subject of the western waters, we will take a view of their principal connections with the Atlantic. These are three; the Hudson's river, the Patowmac, and the Missisipi itself.[8] Down the last will pass all heavy commodities. But the navigation through the Gulph of Mexico is so dangerous, and that up the Missisipi so difficult and tedious, that it is thought probable that European merchandize will not return through that channel. It is most likely that flour, timber, and other heavy articles will be floated on rafts, which will themselves be an article for sale as well as their loading, the navigators returning by land or in light batteaux. There will therefore be a competition between the Hudson and Patowmac rivers for the residue of the commerce of all the country westward of Lake Erié, on the waters of the lakes, of the Ohio, and upper parts of the Missisipi. To go to New-York, that part of the trade which comes from the lakes or their waters must first be brought into Lake Erié. Between Lake Superior and its waters and Huron are the rapids of St. Mary, which will permit boats to pass, but

8. See Charles Thomson's comments on this passage in Appendix No. I, section 1 (page 159).

not larger vessels. Lakes Huron and Michigan afford communication with Lake Erié by vessels of 8 feet draught. That part of the trade which comes from the waters of the Missisipi must pass from them through some portage into the waters of the lakes. The portage from the Illinois river into a water of Michigan is of one mile only. From the Wabash, Miami, Muskingum, or Alleghaney, are portages into the waters of Lake Erié, of from one to fifteen miles. When the commodities are brought into, and have passed through Lake Erié, there is between that and Ontario an interruption by the falls of Niagara, where the portage is of 8 miles; and between Ontario and the Hudson's river are portages at the falls of Onondago, a little above Oswego, of a quarter of a mile; from Wood creek to the Mohawks river two miles; at the little falls of the Mohawks river half a mile, and from Schenectady to Albany 16 miles. Besides the increase of expence occasioned by frequent change of carriage, there is an increased risk of pillage produced by committing merchandize to a greater number of hands successively. The Patowmac offers itself under the following circumstances. For the trade of the lakes and their waters westward of Lake Erié, when it shall have entered that lake, it must coast along its southern shore, on account of the number and excellence of its harbours, the northern, though shortest, having few harbours, and these unsafe. Having reached Cayahoga, to proceed on to New-York it will have 825 miles and five portages: whereas it is but 425 miles to Alexandria, its emporium on the Patowmac, if it turns into the Cayahoga, and passes through that, Bigbeaver, Ohio, Yohoganey, (or Monongalia and Cheat) and Patowmac, and there are but two portages; the first of which between Cayahoga and Beaver may be removed by uniting the sources of these waters, which are lakes in the neighbourhood of each other, and in a champaign[9] country; the other from the waters of Ohio to Patowmac will be from 15 to 40 miles, according to the trouble which shall be taken to approach the two navigations. For the trade of the Ohio, or that which shall come into it from its own waters or the Missisipi, it is nearer through the Patowmac to Alexandria than to New-York by 580 miles, and it is interrupted by one portage only. There is another circumstance of difference too. The lakes themselves never freeze, but the communications between them freeze, and the Hudson's river is itself shut up by the ice three months in the year; whereas the channel to the Chesapeak leads directly into a warmer climate. The southern parts of it very rarely freeze at all, and whenever the northern do, it is so near the sources of the rivers, that the frequent floods to which they are there liable break up the ice immediately, so that vessels may pass through the whole winter, subject only to accidental and short delays. Add to all this, that in case of a war with our neighbours the Anglo-Americans or the Indians, the route to New-York becomes a frontier through almost its whole length, and all commerce through it ceases from that moment.—But the channel to New-York is already known to practice; whereas the upper waters of the Ohio and the Patowmac, and the great falls of the latter, are yet to be cleared of their fixed obstructions.

9. Flat.

Query III

A notice of the best sea-ports of the state, and how big are the vessels they can receive?

Having no ports but our rivers and creeks, this Query has been answered under the preceding one.

Query IV

Mountains   *A notice of its* Mountains?

For the particular geography of our mountains I must refer to Fry and Jefferson's map of Virginia; and to Evans's analysis of his map of America for a more philosophical view of them than is to be found in any other work.[1] It is worthy notice, that our mountains are not solitary and scattered confusedly over the face of the country; but that they commence at about 150 miles from the sea-coast, are disposed in ridges one behind another, running nearly parallel with the sea-coast, though rather approaching it as they advance north-eastwardly. To the south-west, as the tract of country between the sea-coast and the Mississipi becomes narrower, the mountains converge into a single ridge, which, as it approaches the Gulph of Mexico, subsides into plain country, and gives rise to some of the waters of that Gulph, and particularly to a river called the Apalachicola, probably from the Apalachies, an Indian nation formerly residing on it. Hence the mountains giving rise to that river, and seen from its various parts, were called the Apalachian mountains, being in fact the end or termination only of the great ridges passing through the continent. European geographers however extended the name northwardly as far as the mountains extended; some giving it, after their separation into different ridges, to the Blue ridge, others to the North mountain, others to the Alleghaney, others to the Laurel ridge, as may be seen in their different maps. But the fact I believe is, that none of these ridges were ever known by that name to the inhabitants, either native or emigrant, but as they saw them so called in European maps. In the same direction generally are the veins of lime-stone, coal and other minerals hitherto discovered: and so range the falls of our great rivers. But the courses of the great rivers are at right angles with these. James and Patowmac penetrate through all the ridges of mountains eastward of the Alleghaney; that is broken by no watercourse. It is in fact the spine of the country between the Atlantic on one side, and the Missisipi and St. Laurence on the other. The passage of the Patowmac through the Blue ridge[2] is perhaps one of the most stupendous scenes in nature. You stand on a very high point of land. On your right comes up the Shenandoah, having ranged along the foot of the mountain an hundred miles to seek a vent. On your left approaches the Patowmac, in quest of a passage also. In the moment of their junction they rush together against the mountain, rend it asunder, and pass off to the sea. The first glance of this scene hurries our senses into the opinion, that this earth has

---

1. Lewis Evans (c. 1700–1756) included an analysis of his *General Map of the Middle British Colonies* in his collection *Essays*, both published in 1755.
2. For Charles Thomson's response to this, see Appendix No. I, section 2 (page 159).

been created in time, that the mountains were formed first, that the rivers began to flow afterwards, that in this place particularly they have been dammed up by the Blue ridge of mountains, and have formed an ocean which filled the whole valley; that continuing to rise they have at length broken over at this spot, and have torn the mountain down from its summit to its base. The piles of rock on each hand, but particularly on the Shenandoah, the evident marks of their disrupture and avulsion from their beds by the most powerful agents of nature, corroborate the impression. But the distant finishing which nature has given to the picture is of a very different character. It is a true contrast to the fore-ground. It is as placid and delightful, as that is wild and tremendous. For the mountain being cloven asunder, she presents to your eye, through the cleft, a small catch of smooth blue horizon, at an infinite distance in the plain country, inviting you, as it were, from the riot and tumult roaring around, to pass through the breach and participate of the calm below. Here the eye ultimately composes itself; and that way too the road happens actually to lead. You cross the Patowmac above the junction, pass along its side through the base of the mountain for three miles, its terrible precipices hanging in fragments over you, and within about 20 miles reach Frederic town and the fine country round that. This scene is worth a voyage across the Atlantic. Yet here, as in the neighbourhood of the natural bridge, are people who have passed their lives within half a dozen miles, and have never been to survey these monuments of a war between rivers and mountains, which must have shaken the earth itself to its center.—The height of our mountains has not yet been estimated with any degree of exactness. The Alleghaney being the great ridge which divides the waters of the Atlantic from those of the Missisipi, its summit is doubtless more elevated above the ocean than that of any other mountain. But its relative height, compared with the base on which it stands, is not so great as that of some others, the country rising behind the successive ridges like the steps of stairs. The mountains of the Blue ridge, and of these the Peaks of Otter, are thought to be of a greater height, measured from their base, than any others in our country, and perhaps in North America. From data, which may found a tolerable conjecture, we suppose the highest peak to be about 4000 feet perpendicular, which is not a fifth part of the height of the mountains of South America, nor one third of the height which would be necessary in our latitude to preserve ice in the open air unmelted through the year. The ridge of mountains next beyond the Blue ridge, called by us the North mountain, is of the greatest extent; for which reason they were named by the Indians the Endless mountains.

A substance supposed to be Pumice, found floating on the Missisipi, has induced a conjecture, that there is a volcano on some of its waters: and as these are mostly known to their sources, except the Missouri, our expectations of verifying the conjecture would of course be led to the mountains which divide the waters of the Mexican Gulph from those of the South Sea; but no volcano having ever yet been known at such a distance from the sea, we must rather suppose that this floating substance has been erroneously deemed Pumice.

Query V

Its Cascades and Caverns?

The only remarkable Cascade in this country, is that of the Falling Spring in Augusta. It is a water[3] of James river, where it is called Jackson's river, rising in the warm spring mountains about twenty miles South West of the warm spring, and flowing into that valley. About three quarters of a mile from its source, it falls over a rock 200 feet into the valley below. The sheet of water is broken in its breadth by the rock in two or three places, but not at all in its height. Between the sheet and rock, at the bottom, you may walk across dry. This Cataract will bear no comparison with that of Niagara, as to the quantity of water composing it; the sheet being only 12 or 15 feet wide above, and somewhat more spread below; but it is half as high again, the latter being only 156 feet, according to the mensuration made by order of M. Vaudreuil, Governor of Canada,[4] and 130 according to a more recent account.

In the lime-stone country, there are many caverns of very considerable extent. The most noted is called Madison's Cave, and is on the North side of the Blue ridge, near the intersection of the Rockingham and Augusta line with the South fork of the southern river of Shenandoah. It is in a hill of about 200 feet perpendicular height, the ascent of which, on one side, is so steep, that you may pitch a biscuit from its summit into the river which washes its base. The entrance of the cave is, in this side, about two thirds of the way up. It extends into the earth about 300 feet, branching into subordinate caverns, sometimes ascending a little, but more generally descending, and at length terminates, in two different places, at basons of water of unknown extent, and which I should judge to be nearly on a level with the water of the river; however, I do not think they are formed by refluent water from that, because they are never turbid; because they do not rise and fall in correspondence with that in times of flood, or of drought; and because the water is always cool. It is probably one of the many reservoirs with which the interior parts of the earth are supposed to abound, and which yield supplies to the fountains of water, distinguished from others only by its being accessible. The vault of this cave is of solid lime-stone, from 20 to 40 or 50 feet high, through which water is continually percolating. This, trickling down the sides of the cave, has incrusted them over in the form of elegant drapery; and dripping from the top of the vault generates on that, and on the base below, stalactites of a conical form, some of which have met and formed massive columns.

Another of these caves is near the North mountain, in the county of Frederick, on the lands of Mr. Zane.[5] The entrance into this is on the top of an extensive ridge. You descend 30 or 40 feet, as into a well, from whence the cave then extends, nearly horizontally, 400 feet into the earth, preserving a

---

3. Tributary.
4. Pierre François, marquis de Vaudreuil-Cavagnal (1698–1765), was governor of Canada, 1755–60. Historian William Douglass, in *A Summary, Historical and Political, of the . . . British Settlements* (1760), tells of his having the falls measured.
5. Isaac Zane (d. 1795), proprietor of an ironworks in Frederick County, Virginia, was a friend and political ally of Jefferson. After many attempts to procure the recorded temperatures for the cave, in 1784 Jefferson urged James Madison to press Zane to send them for inclusion in the book, as apparently he did. See *PTJ*, vol. 7, pp. 288–290, 362.

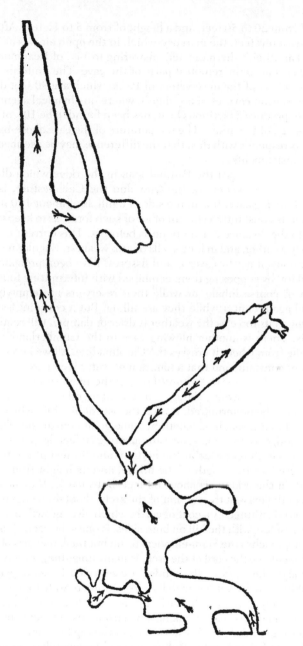

An Eye-draught of Madison's cave, on a scale of 50 feet to the inch. The arrows shew where it descends or ascends.

breadth of from 20 to 50 feet, and a height of from 5 to 12 feet. After entering this cave a few feet, the mercury, which in the open air was at 50°. rose
to 57°. of Farenheit's thermometer, answering to 11°. of Reaumur's, and it
continued at that to the remotest parts of the cave. The uniform temperature of the cellars of the observatory of Paris, which are 90 feet deep, and
of all subterranean cavities of any depth, where no chymical agents may be
supposed to produce a factitious heat, has been found to be 10°. of Reamur,
equal to 54½°. of Farenheit. The temperature of the cave above-mentioned
so nearly corresponds with this, that the difference may be ascribed to a difference of instruments.

Blowing cave   At the Panther gap, in the ridge which divides the
waters of the Cow and the Calf pasture, is what is
called the *Blowing cave*. It is in the side of a hill, is of about 100 feet diameter, and emits constantly a current of air of such force, as to keep the weeds
prostrate to the distance of twenty yards before it. This current is strongest
in dry frosty weather, and in long spells of rain weakest. Regular inspirations
and expirations of air, by caverns and fissures, have been probably enough
accounted for, by supposing them combined with intermitting fountains; as
they must of course inhale air while their reservoirs are emptying themselves, and again emit it while they are filling. But a constant issue of air,
only varying in its force as the weather is drier or damper, will require a new
hypothesis. There is another blowing cave in the Cumberland mountain,
about a mile from where it crosses the Carolina line. All we know of this is,
that it is not constant, and that a fountain of water issues from it.

Natural bridge   The *Natural bridge*,[6] the most sublime of Nature's
works, though not comprehended under the present
head, must not be pretermitted. It is on the ascent of a hill, which seems to
have been cloven through its length by some great convulsion. The fissure,
just at the bridge, is, by some admeasurements, 270 feet deep, by others only
205. It is about 45 feet wide at the bottom, and 90 feet at the top; this of
course determines the length of the bridge, and its height from the water.
Its breadth in the middle, is about 60 feet, but more at the ends, and the
thickness of the mass at the summit of the arch, about 40 feet. A part of this
thickness is constituted by a coat of earth, which gives growth to many large
trees. The residue, with the hill on both sides, is one solid rock of lime-stone.
The arch approaches the Semi-elliptical form; but the larger axis of the ellipsis, which would be the cord of the arch, is many times longer than the trans-
verse. Though the sides of this bridge are provided in some parts with a
parapet of fixed rocks, yet few men have resolution to walk to them and look
over into the abyss. You involuntarily fall on your hands and feet, creep to
the parapet and peep over it. Looking down from this height about a minute,
gave me a violent head ach. If the view from the top be painful and intolerable, that from below is delightful in an equal extreme. It is impossible for
the emotions arising from the sublime, to be felt beyond what they are here:
so beautiful an arch, so elevated, so light, and springing as it were up to
heaven, the rapture of the spectator is really indescribable! The fissure continuing narrow, deep, and streight for a considerable distance above and
below the bridge, opens a short but very pleasing view of the North mountain on one side, and Blue ridge on the other, at the distance each of them

6. Located, on land owned by Jefferson since 1774, some ten miles southwest of Lexington, Virginia.

of about five miles.[7] This bridge is in the county of Rock bridge, to which it has given name, and affords a public and commodious passage over a valley, which cannot be crossed elsewhere for a considerable distance. The stream passing under it is called Cedar creek. It is a water of James river, and sufficient in the driest seasons to turn a grist-mill, though its fountain[8] is not more than two miles above.[9]

Query VI

A notice of the mines and other subterraneous riches; its trees, plants, fruits, &c.

1. Minerals

I knew a single instance of gold found in this state.

It was interspersed in small specks through a lump of ore, of about four pounds weight, which yielded seventeen pennyweight of gold, of extraordinary ductility. This ore was found on the North side of Rappahanoc, about four miles below the falls. I never heard of any other indication of gold in its neighbourhood.

Gold

On the Great Kanhaway, opposite to the mouth of Cripple creek, and about twenty-five miles from our southern boundary, in the county of Montgomery, are mines of lead. The metal is mixed, sometimes with earth, and sometimes with rock, which requires the

Lead

7. In annotating a copy of *Notes on the State of Virginia* in 1817, Jefferson wrote: "This description was written after a lapse of several years from the time of my visit to the bridge, and under an error of recollection which requires apology. For it is from the bridge itself that the mountains are visible both ways, and not from the bottom of the fissure as my impression then was. The statement therefore in the former edition needs the corrections here given it." The revised text to which this note refers, and that replaced the 1787 passage running from "If the view . . ." to ". . . about five miles," is as follows: "This painful sensation is relieved by a short, but pleasing view of the Blue ridge along the fissure downwards, and upwards by that of the Short hills, which, with the Purgatory mountain is a divergence from the North ridge; and, descending then to the valley below, the sensation becomes delightful in the extreme. It is impossible for the emotions, arising from the sublime, to be felt beyond what they are here: so beautiful an arch, so elevated, so light, and springing, as it were, up to heaven, the rapture of the Spectator is really indiscribable! The fissure continues deep and narrow and, following the margin of the stream upwards about three eights of a mile you arrive at a limestone cavern, less remarkable, however, for height and extent than those before described. It's entrance into the hill is but a few feet above the bed of the stream."
8. Source.
9. Don Ulloa mentions a break, similar to this, in the province of Angaraez, in South America. It is from 16 to 22 feet wide, 111 feet deep, and of 1.3 miles continuance, English measures. Its breadth at top is not sensibly greater than at bottom. But the following fact is remarkable, and will furnish some light for conjecturing the probable origin of our natural bridge. "Esta caxa, ó cauce está cortada en péna viva con tanta precision, que las desigualdades del un lado entrantes, corresponden á las del otro lado salientes, como si aquella altura se hubiese abierto expresamente, con sus bueltas y tortuosidades, para darle transito á los aguas por entre los dos murallones que la forman; siendo tal su igualdad, que si llegasen á juntarse se endentarían uno con otro sin dexar hueco." Not. Amer. II. §.
10. Don Ulloa inclines to the opinion, that this channel has been affected by the wearing of the water which runs through it, rather than that the mountain should have been broken open by any convulsion of nature. But if it had been worn by the running of water, would not the rocks which form the sides, have been worn plane? or if, meeting in some parts with veins of harder stone, the water had left prominences on the one side, would not the same cause have sometimes, or perhaps generally, occasioned prominences on the other side also? Yet Don Ulloa tells us, that on the other side there are always corresponding cavities, and that these tally with the prominences so perfectly, that, were the two sides to come together, they would fit in all their indentures, without leaving any void. I think that this does not resemble the effect of running water, but looks rather as if the two sides had parted asunder. The sides of the break, over which is the Natural bridge of Virginia, consisting of a veiny rock which yields to time, the correspondence between the salient and re-entering inequalities, if it existed at all, has now disappeared. This break has the advantage of the one described by Don Ulloa in its finest circumstance; no portion in that instance having held together, during the separation of the other parts, so as to form a bridge over the Abyss [Jefferson's note].

force of gunpowder to open it; and is accompanied with a portion of silver, too small to be worth separation under any process hitherto attempted there. The proportion yielded is from 50 to 80 lb. of pure metal from 100 lb. of washed ore. The most common is that of 60 to the 100 lb. The veins are at sometimes most flattering; at others they disappear suddenly and totally. They enter the side of the hill, and proceed horizontally. Two of them are wrought at present by the public, the best of which is 100 yards under the hill. These would employ about 50 labourers to advantage. We have not, however, more than 30 generally, and these cultivate their own corn. They have produced 60 tons of lead in the year; but the general quantity is from 20 to 25 tons. The present furnace is a mile from the ore-bank, and on the opposite side of the river. The ore is first waggoned to the river, a quarter of a mile, then laden on board of canoes and carried across the river, which is there about 200 yards wide, and then again taken into waggons and carried to the furnace. This mode was originally adopted, that they might avail themselves of a good situation on a creek, for a pounding mill: but it would be easy to have the furnace and pounding mill on the same side of the river, which would yield water, without any dam, by a canal of about half a mile in length. From the furnace the lead is transported 130 miles along a good road, leading through the peaks of Otter to Lynch's ferry, or Winston's, on James river, from whence it is carried by water about the same distance to Westham. This land carriage may be greatly shortened, by delivering the lead on James river, above the blue ridge, from whence a ton weight has been brought on two canoes. The Great Kanhaway has considerable falls in the neighbourhood of the mines. About seven miles below are three falls, of three or four feet perpendicular each; and three miles above is a rapid of three miles continuance, which has been compared in its descent to the great fall of James river. Yet it is the opinion, that they may be laid open for useful navigation, so as to reduce very much the portage between the Kanhaway and James river.

A valuable lead mine is said to have been lately discovered in Cumberland, below the mouth of Red river. The greatest, however, known in the western country, are on the Missisipi, extending from the mouth of Rock river 150 miles upwards. These are not wrought, the lead used in that country being from the banks on the Spanish side of the Missisipi, opposite to Kaskaskia.

Copper   A mine of copper was once opened in the county of Amherst, on the North side of James river, and another in the opposite country, on the South side. However, either from bad management or the poverty of the veins, they were discontinued. We are told of a rich mine of native copper on the Ouabache, below the upper Wiaw.

Iron   The mines of iron worked at present are Callaway's, Ross's, and Ballendine's, on the South side of James river; Old's on the North side, in Albemarle; Miller's in Augusta, and Zane's in Frederic. These two last are in the valley between the Blue ridge and North mountain. Callaway's, Ross's, Millar's, and Zane's, make about 150 tons of bar iron each, in the year. Ross's makes also about 1600 tons of pig iron annually; Ballendine's 1000; Callaway's, Millar's, and Zane's, about 600 each. Besides these, a forge of Mr. Hunter's, at Fredericksburgh, makes about 300 tons a year of bar iron, from pigs[1] imported from Maryland; and Taylor's forge on Neapsco of Patowmac, works in the same way, but to what

1. Pig iron.

extent I am not informed. The indications of iron in other places are numerous, and dispersed through all the middle country. The toughness of the cast
iron of Ross's and Zane's furnaces is very remarkable. Pots and other uten-
sils, cast thinner than usual, of this iron, may be safely thrown into, or out
of the waggons in which they are transported. Salt-pans made of the same,
and no longer wanted for that purpose, cannot be broken up, in order to be
melted again, unless previously drilled in many parts.

In the western country, we are told of iron mines between the Muskingum and Ohio; of others on Kentucky, between the Cumberland and Barren rivers, between Cumberland and Tannissee, on Reedy creek, near the
Long island, and on Chesnut creek, a branch of the Great Kanhaway, near
where it crosses the Carolina line. What are called the iron banks, on the
Missisipi, are believed, by a good judge, to have no iron in them. In general,
from what is hitherto known of that country, it seems to want iron.

Considerable quantities of black lead[2] are taken $\quad$ Black lead
occasionally for use from Winterham, in the county of
Amelia. I am not able, however, to give a particular state of the mine. There
is no work established at it, those who want, going and procuring it for
themselves.

The country on James river, from 15 to 20 miles $\quad$ Pit coal
above Richmond, and for several miles northward and
southward, is replete with mineral coal of a very excellent quality. Being in
the hands of many proprietors, pits have been opened, and before the interruption of our commerce[3] were worked to an extent equal to the demand.

In the western country coal is known to be in so many places, as to have
induced an opinion, that the whole tract between the Laurel mountain,
Missisipi, and Ohio, yields coal. It is also known in many places on the
North side of the Ohio. The coal at Pittsburg is of very superior quality. A
bed of it at that place has been a-fire since the year 1765. Another coal-hill
on the Pike-run of Monongahela has been a-fire ten years; yet it has burnt
away about twenty yards only.

I have known one instance of an Emerald found in $\quad$ Precious stones
this country. Amethysts have been frequent, and chrys-
tals common; yet not in such numbers any of them as to be worth seeking.

There is very good marble, and in very great abun- $\quad$ Marble
dance, on James river, at the mouth of Rockfish. The
samples I have seen, were some of them of a white as pure as one might
expect to find on the surface of the earth: but most of them were variegated
with red, blue, and purple. None of it has been ever worked. It forms a very
large precipice, which hangs over a navigable part of the river. It is said there
is marble at Kentucky.

But one vein of lime-stone is known below the Blue $\quad$ Limestone
ridge. Its first appearance, in our country, is in Prince
William, two miles below the Pignut ridge of mountains; thence it passes on
nearly parallel with that, and crosses the Rivanna about five miles below it,
where it is called the South-west ridge. It then crosses Hardware, above the
mouth of Hudson's creek, James river at the mouth of Rockfish, at the
marble quarry before spoken of, probably runs up that river to where it

2. Graphite.
3. I.e., by the war with Britain.

appears again at Ross's iron-works, and so passes off south-westwardly by Flat creek of Otter river. It is never more than one hundred yards wide. From the Blue ridge westwardly the whole country seems to be founded on a rock of lime-stone, besides infinite quantities on the surface, both loose and fixed. This is cut into beds, which range, as the mountains and seacoast do, from south-west to north-east, the lamina of each bed declining from the horizon towards a parallelism with the axis of the earth. Being struck with this observation, I made, with a quadrant, a great number of trials on the angles of their declination, and found them to vary from 22°. to 60°. but averaging all my trials, the result was within one-third of a degree of the elevation of the pole or latitude of the place, and much the greatest part of them taken separately were little different from that: by which it appears, that these lamina are, in the main, parallel with the axis of the earth. In some instances, indeed, I found them perpendicular, and even reclining the other way: but these were extremely rare, and always attended with signs of convulsion, or other circumstances of singularity, which admitted a possibility of removal from their original position. These trials were made between Madison's cave and the Patowmac. We hear of lime-stone on the Missisipi and Ohio, and in all the mountainous country between the eastern and western waters, not on the mountains themselves, but occupying the vallies between them.

Near the eastern foot of the North mountain are immense bodies of *Schist*, containing impressions of shells in a variety of forms. I have received petrified shells of very different kinds from the first sources of the Kentucky, which bear no resemblance to any I have ever seen on the tide-waters. It is said that shells are found in the Andes, in South-America, fifteen thousand feet above the level of the ocean. This is considered by many, both of the learned and unlearned, as a proof of an universal deluge. To the many considerations opposing this opinion, the following may be added. The atmosphere, and all its contents, whether of water, air, or other matters, gravitate to the earth; that is to say, they have weight. Experience tells us, that the weight of all these together never exceeds that of a column of mercury of 31 inches height, which is equal to one of rain-water of 35 feet high. If the whole contents of the atmosphere then were water, instead of what they are, it would cover the globe but 35 feet deep; but as these waters, as they fell, would run into the seas, the superficial measure of which is to that of the dry parts of the globe as two to one, the seas would be raised only 52½ feet above their present level, and of course would overflow the lands to that height only. In Virginia this would be a very small proportion even of the champaign country, the banks of our tide-waters being frequently, if not generally, of a greater height. Deluges beyond this extent then, as for instance, to the North mountain or to Kentucky, seem out of the laws of nature. But within it they may have taken place to a greater or less degree, in proportion to the combination of natural causes which may be supposed to have produced them. History renders probable some instances of a partial deluge in the country lying round the Mediterranean sea. It has been often supposed,[4] and is not unlikely, that that sea was once a lake. While such, let us admit an extraordinary collection of the waters of the atmosphere from the other parts of the globe to have been discharged over that and the countries whose waters run into it. Or without supposing it a lake, admit such an extraordi-

---

4. Buffon Epoques, 96 [Jefferson's note].

nary collection of the waters of the atmosphere, and an influx of waters from the Atlantic ocean, forced by long continued Western winds. That lake, or that sea, may thus have been so raised as to overflow the low lands adjacent to it, as those of Egypt and Armenia, which, according to a tradition of the Egyptians and Hebrews, were overflowed about 2300 years before the Christian æra; those of Attica, said to have been overflowed in the time of Ogyges, about 500 years later; and those of Thessaly, in the time of Deucalion, still 300 years posterior. But such deluges as these will not account for the shells found in the higher lands. A second opinion has been entertained, which is, that, in times anterior to the records either of history or tradition, the bed of the ocean, the principal residence of the shelled tribe, has, by some great convulsion of nature, been heaved to the heights at which we now find shells and other remains of marine animals. The favourers of this opinion do well to suppose the great events on which it rests to have taken place beyond all the æras of history; for within these, certainly none such are to be found: and we may venture to say further, that no fact has taken place, either in our own days, or in the thousands of years recorded in history, which proves the existence of any natural agents, within or without the bowels of the earth, of force sufficient to heave, to the height of 15,000 feet, such masses as the Andes. The difference between the power necessary to produce such an effect, and that which shuffled together the different parts of Calabria in our days, is so immense, that, from the existence of the latter we are not authorised to infer that of the former.

M. de Voltaire[5] has suggested a third solution of this difficulty (Quest. encycl. Coquilles). He cites an instance in Touraine, where, in the space of 80 years, a particular spot of earth had been twice metamorphosed into soft stone, which had become hard when employed in building. In this stone shells of various kinds were produced, discoverable at first only with the microscope, but afterwards growing with the stone. From this fact, I suppose, he would have us infer, that, besides the usual process for generating shells by the elaboration of earth and water in animal vessels, nature may have provided an equivalent operation, by passing the same materials through the pores of calcareous earths and stones: as we see calcareous dropstones generating every day by the percolation of water through lime-stone, and new marble forming in the quarries from which the old has been taken out; and it might be asked, whether it is more difficult for nature to shoot the calcareous juice into the form of a shell, than other juices into the forms of chrystals, plants, animals, according to the construction of the vessels through which they pass? There is a wonder somewhere. Is it greatest on this branch of the dilemma; on that which supposes the existence of a power, of which we have no evidence in any other case; or on the first, which requires us to believe the creation of a body of water, and its subsequent annihilation? The establishment of the instance, cited by M. de Voltaire, of the growth of shells unattached to animal bodies, would have been that of his theory. But he has not established it. He has not even left it on ground so respectable as to have rendered it an object of enquiry to the literati of his own country. Abandoning this fact, therefore, the three hypotheses are equally unsatisfactory; and we must be contented to acknowledge, that this great phænomenon

---

5. François-Marie Arouet (1694–1778), known as Voltaire, published his *Questions on the Encyclopedia* in 1764.

is as yet unsolved. Ignorance is preferable to error; and he is less remote from the truth who believes nothing, then he who believes what is wrong.

Stone

There is great abundance (more especially when you approach the mountains) of stone, white, blue, brown, &c. fit for the chissel, good mill-stone, such also as stands the fire, and slate-stone. We are told of flint, fit for gun-flints, on the Meherrin in Brunswic, on the Missisipi between the mouth of Ohio and Kaskaskia, and on others of the western waters. Isinglass or mica is in several places; loadstone also, and an Asbestos of a ligneous texture, is sometimes to be met with.

Earths

Marle abounds generally. A clay, of which, like the Sturbridge in England, bricks are made, which will resist long the violent action of fire, has been found on Tuckahoe creek of James river, and no doubt will be found in other places. Chalk is said to be in Botetourt and Bedford. In the latter county is some earth, believed to be Gypseous. Ochres are found in various parts.

Nitre

In the lime-stone country are many caves, the earthy floors of which are impregnated with nitre. On Rich creek, a branch of the Great Kanhaway, about 60 miles below the lead mines, is a very large one, about 20 yards wide, and entering a hill a quarter or half a mile. The vault is of rock, from 9 to 15 or 20 feet above the floor. A Mr. Lynch,[6] who gives me this account, undertook to extract the nitre. Besides a coat of the salt which had formed on the vault and floor, he found the earth highly impregnated to the depth of seven feet in some places, and generally of three, every bushel yielding on an average three pounds of nitre. Mr. Lynch having made about 1000 lb. of the salt from it, consigned it to some others, who have since made 10,000 lb. They have done this by pursuing the cave into the hill, never trying a second time the earth they have once exhausted, to see how far or soon it receives another impregnation. At least fifty of these caves are worked on the Greenbriar. There are many of them known on Cumberland river.

Salt

The country westward of the Alleghaney abounds with springs of common salt. The most remarkable we have heard of are at Bullet's lick, the Big bones, the Blue licks, and on the North fork of Holston. The area of Bullet's lick is of many acres. Digging the earth to the depth of three feet, the water begins to boil up, and the deeper you go, and the drier the weather, the stronger is the brine. A thousand gallons of water yield from a bushel to a bushel and a half of salt, which is about 80 lb. of water to one lb. of salt; but of sea-water 25 lb. yield one lb. of salt. So that sea-water is more than three times as strong as that of these springs. A salt spring has been lately discovered at the Turkey foot on Yohogany, by which river it is overflowed, except at very low water. Its merit is not yet known. Duning's lick is also as yet untried, but it is supposed to be the best on this side the Ohio. The salt springs on the margin of the Onondago lake are said to give a saline taste to the waters of the lake.

Medicinal springs

There are several Medicinal springs, some of which are indubitably efficacious, while others seem to owe their reputation as much to fancy, and change of air and regimen, as to their real virtues. None of them having undergone a chemical analysis in skilful

6. Charles Lynch (1736–1796) was interested in nitre (potassium nitrate or saltpeter) because it was used for making the gunpowder needed by American forces during the Revolution. He corresponded with Jefferson on that subject.

hands, nor been so far the subject of observations as to have produced a reduction into classes of the disorders which they relieve, it is in my power to give little more than an enumeration of them.

The most efficacious of these are two springs in Augusta, near the first sources of James river, where it is called Jackson's river. They rise near the foot of the ridge of mountains, generally called the Warm spring mountain, but in the maps Jackson's mountains. The one is distinguished by the name of the Warm spring, and the other of the Hot spring. The Warm spring issues with a very bold stream, sufficient to work a grist-mill, and to keep the waters of its bason, which is 30 feet in diameter, at the vital warmth, viz. 96°. of Farenheit's thermometer. The matter with which these waters is allied is very volatile; its smell indicates it to be sulphureous, as also does the circumstance of its turning silver black. They relieve rheumatisms. Other complaints also of very different natures have been removed or lessened by them. It rains here four or five days in every week.

The *Hot spring* is about six miles from the Warm, is much smaller, and has been so hot as to have boiled an egg. Some believe its degree of heat to be lessened. It raises the mercury in Farenheit's thermometer to 112 degrees, which is fever heat. It sometimes relieves where the Warm spring fails. A fountain of common water, issuing within a few inches of its margin, gives it a singular appearance. Comparing the temperature of these with that of the Hot springs of Kamschatka, of which Krachininnikow[7] gives an account, the difference is very great, the latter raising the mercury to 200°. which is within 12°. of boiling water. These springs are very much resorted to in spite of a total want of accommodation for the sick. Their waters are strongest in the hottest months, which occasions their being visited in July and August principally.

The Sweet springs are in the county of Botetourt, at the eastern foot of the Alleghaney, about 42 miles from the Warm springs. They are still less known. Having been found to relieve cases in which the others had been ineffectually tried, it is probable their composition is different. They are different also in their temperature, being as cold as common water: which is not mentioned, however, as a proof of a distinct impregnation. This is among the first sources of James river.

On Patowmac river, in Berkeley county, above the North mountain, are Medicinal springs, much more frequented than those of Augusta. Their powers, however, are less, the waters weakly mineralized, and scarcely warm. They are more visited, because situated in a fertile, plentiful, and populous country, better provided with accommodations, always safe from the Indians, and nearest to the more populous states.

In Louisa county, on the head waters of the South Anna branch of York river, are springs of some medicinal virtue. They are not much used however. There is a weak chalybeate at Richmond; and many others in various parts of the country, which are of too little worth, or too little note, to be enumerated after those before-mentioned.

We are told of a Sulphur spring on Howard's creek of Greenbriar, and another at Boonsborough on Kentuckey.

In the low grounds of the Great Kanhaway, 7 miles above the mouth of Elk river, and 67 above that of the   Burning spring

7. Stepan Petrovich Krasheninnikov (1713–1755), Russian explorer, whose *History of Kamtschatka*, originally published as *Opisaníe zemli Kamchatki* in St. Petersburg in 1755, appeared in English translation in 1764.

Kanhaway itself, is a hole in the earth of the capacity of 30 or 40 gallons, from which issues constantly a bituminous vapour in so strong a current, as to give to the sand about its orifice the motion which it has in a boiling spring. On presenting a lighted candle or torch within 18 inches of the hole, it flames up in a column of 18 inches diameter, and four or five feet height, which sometimes burns out within 20 minutes, and at other times has been known to continue three days, and then has been left still burning. The flame is unsteady, of the density of that of burning spirits, and smells like burning pit coal. Water sometimes collects in the bason, which is remarkably cold, and is kept in ebullition by the vapour issuing through it. If the vapour be fired in that state, the water soon becomes so warm that the hand cannot bear it, and evaporates wholly in a short time. This, with the circumjacent lands, is the property of his Excellency General Washington and of General Lewis.[8]

There is a similar one on Sandy river, the flame of which is a column of about 12 inches diameter, and 3 feet high. General Clarke,[9] who informs me of it, kindled the vapour, staid about an hour, and left it burning.

Syphon fountains   The mention of uncommon springs leads me to that of Syphon fountains. There is one of these near the intersection of the Lord Fairfax's boundary with the North mountain, not far from Brock's gap, on the stream of which is a grist-mill, which grinds two bushel of grain at every flood of the spring. Another, near the Cow-pasture river, a mile and a half below its confluence with the Bull-pasture river, and 16 or 17 miles from the Hot springs, which intermits once in every twelve hours. One also near the mouth of the North Holston.

After these may be mentioned the *Natural Well*, on the lands of a Mr. Lewis in Frederick county. It is somewhat larger than a common well: the water rises in it as near the surface of the earth as in the neighbouring artificial wells, and is of a depth as yet unknown. It is said there is a current in it tending sensibly downwards. If this be true, it probably feeds some fountain, of which it is the natural reservoir, distinguished from others, like that of Madison's cave, by being accessible. It is used with a bucket and windlass as an ordinary well.

Vegetables   A complete catalogue of the trees, plants, fruits, &c. is probably not desired. I will sketch out those which would principally attract notice, as being 1. Medicinal, 2. Esculent, 3. Ornamental, or 4. Useful for fabrication; adding the Linnæan[1] to the popular names, as the latter might not convey precise information to a foreigner. I shall confine myself too to native plants.

1. Senna.   Cassia ligustrina.
Arsmart.   Polygonum Sagittatum.
Clivers, or goose-grass.   Galium spurium.
Lobelia of several species.
Palma Christi.   Ricinus.
James-town weed.   Datura Stramonium.[2]

---

8. Andrew Lewis (1720–1781), a Revolutionary officer born in Ireland, discovered Lewis Spring, near Lewisburg, West Virginia, in 1751.
9. George Rogers Clark (1752–1818), a close friend of Jefferson's.
1. Carl Linné (1707–1778), known as Linnaeus, Swedish scientist whose many publications provided the basis for the modern organization of botanical knowledge.
2. See Charles Thomson's note on this plant, also known as jimsonweed, in Appendix No. I, section 3 (p. 160).

Mallow.   Malva rotundifolia.
Syrian mallow.   Hibiscus moschentos.
                  Hibiscus virginicus.
Indian mallow.   Sida rhombifolia.
                  Sida abutilon.
Virginia Marshmallow.   Napæa hermaphrodita.
                         Napæa dioica.
Indian physic.   Spiræa trifoliata.
Euphorbia Ipecacuanhæ.
Pleurisy root.   Asclepias decumbens.
Virginia snake-root.   Aristolochia serpentaria.
Black snake-root.   Actæa racemosa.
Seneca rattlesnake-root.   Polygala Senega.
Valerian.   Valeriana locusta radiata.
Gentiana, Saponaria, Villosa & Centaurium.
Ginseng.   Panax quinquefolium.
Angelica.   Angelica sylvestris.
Cassava.   Jatropha urens.

2. Tuckahoe.   Lycoperdon tuber.
Jerusalem artichoke.   Helianthus tuberosus.
Long potatoes.   Convolvulas batatas.
Granadillas. Maycocks. Maracocks. Passiflora incarnata.
Panic.   Panicum of many species.
Indian millet.   Holcus laxus.
                  Holcus striosus.
Wild oat.   Zizania aquatica.
Wild pea.   Dolichos of Clayton.[3]
Lupine.   Lupinus perennis.
Wild hop.   Humulus lupulus.
Wild cherry.   Prunus Virginiana.
Cherokeeplumb.   Prunussylvestrisfructumajori. ⎫
Wild plumb.   Prunus sylvestris fructu minori. ⎬ Clayton.
Wild crab-apple.   Pyrus coronaria.   ⎭
Red mulberry.   Morus rubra.
Persimmon.   Diospyros Virginiana.
Sugar maple.   Acer saccharinum.
Scaly bark hiccory.   Juglans alba cortice squamoso. Clayton.
Common hiccory.   Juglans alba, fructu minore rancido. Clayton.
Paccan, or Illinois nut. Not described by Linnæus, Millar,[4] or Clayton. Were
    I to venture to describe this, speaking of the fruit from memory, and of
    the leaf from plants of two years growth, I should specify it as the Juglans
    alba, foliolis lanceolatis, acuminatis, serratis, tomentosis, fructu minore,
    ovato, compresso, vix insculpto, dulci, putamine, tenerrimo. It grows on
    the Illinois, Wabash, Ohio, and Missisipi. It is spoken of by Don Ulloa
    under the name of Pacanos, in his Noticias Americanas. Entret. 6.

3. English-born John Clayton (1694–1773) collected many plant specimens in Virginia, to which he
   emigrated early in life, but the *Flora Virginica* (1739–43; 2nd ed., 1762) to which Jefferson refers
   here and later, although based on Clayton's collections, was the work of Dutch scientist Johannes
   Gronovius.
4. Philip Miller (1691–1771), long the chief gardener of the famous Chelsea Physic Garden near
   London, author of several books on botany.

Black walnut.   Juglans nigra.
White walnut.   Juglans alba.
Chesnut.   Fagus castanea.
Chinquapin.   Fagus pumila.
Hazlenut.   Corylus avellana.
Grapes.   Vitis. Various kinds, though only three described by Clayton.
Scarlet Strawberries.   Fragaria Virginiana of Millar.
Whortleberries.   Vaccinium uliginosum?
Wild gooseberries.   Ribes grossularia.
Cranberries.   Vaccinium oxycoccos.
Black raspberries.   Rubus occidentalis.
Blackberries.   Rubus fruticosus.
Dewberries.   Rubus cæsius.
Cloud-berries.   Rubus chamæmorus.

3. Plane-tree.   Platanus occidentalis.
Poplar.   Liriodendron tulipifera.
            Populus heterophylla.
Black poplar.   Populus nigra.
Aspen.   Populus tremula.
Linden, or lime.   Tilia Americana.
Red flowering maple.   Acer rubrum.
Horse-chesnut, or Buck's-eye.   Æsculus pavia.
Catalpa.   Bignonia catalpa.
Umbrella.   Magnolia tripetala.
Swamp laurel.   Magnolia glauca.
Cucumber-tree.   Magnolia acuminata.
Portugal bay.   Laurus indica.
Red bay.   Laurus borbonia.
Dwarf-rose bay.   Rhododendron maximum.
Laurel of the western country.   Qu. species?
Wild pimento.   Laurus benzoin.
Sassafras.   Laurus sassafras.
Locust.   Robinia pseudo-acacia.
Honey-locust.   Gleditsia, 1. β.
Dogwood.   Cornus florida.
Fringe or snow-drop tree.   Chionanthus Virginica.
Barberry.   Berberis vulgaris.
Redbud, or Judas-tree.   Cercis Canadensis.
Holly.   Ilex aquifolium.
Cockspur hawthorn.   Cratægus coccinea.
Spindle-tree.   Euonymus Europæus.
Evergreen spindle-tree.   Euonymus Americanus.
Itea Virginica.
Elder.   Sambucus nigra.
Papaw.   Annona triloba.
Candleberry myrtle.   Myrica cerifera.
Dwarf-laurel.   Kalmia angustifolia. ⎫ called ivy
                Kalmia latifolia   ⎬ with us.
                                         ⎭
Ivy.   Hedera quinquefolia.
Trumpet honeysuckle.   Lonicera sempervirens.

Upright honeysuckle. Azalea nudiflora.
Yellow jasmine. Bignonia sempervirens.
Calycanthus floridus.
American aloe. Agave Virginica.
Sumach. Rhus. Qu. species?
Poke. Phytolacca decandra.
Long moss. Tillandsia Usneoides.

4. Reed. Arundo phragmitis.
Virginia hemp. Acnida cannabina.
Flax. Linum Virginianum.
Black, or pitch-pine. Pinus tæda.
White pine. Pinus strobus.
Yellow pine. Pinus Virginica.
Spruce pine. Pinus foliis singularibus. Clayton.
Hemlock spruce fir. Pinus Canadensis.
Arbor vitæ. Thuya occidentalis.
Juniper. Juniperus virginica (called cedar with us).
Cypress. Cupressus disticha.
White cedar. Cupressus Thyoides.
Black oak. Quercus nigra.
White oak. Quercus alba.
Red oak. Quercus rubra.
Willow oak. Quercus phellos.
Chesnut oak. Quercus prinus.
Black jack oak. Quercus aquatica. Clayton. Query?
Ground oak. Quercus pumila. Clayton.
Live oak. Quercus Virginiana. Millar.
Black Birch. Betula nigra.
White birch. Betula alba.
Beach Fagus sylvatica.
Ash. Fraxinus Americana.
      Fraxinus Novæ Angliæ. Millar.
Elm. Ulmus Americana.
Willow. Salix. Query species?
Sweet Gum. Liquidambar styraciflua.

The following were found in Virginia when first visited by the English; but it is not said whether of spontaneous growth, or by cultivation only. Most probably they were natives of more southern climates, and handed along the continent from one nation to another of the savages.

Tobacco. Nicotiana.
Maize. Zea mays.
Round potatoes. Solanum tuberosum.
Pumpkins. Cucurbita pepo.
Cymlings. Cucurbita verrucosa.
Squashes. Cucurbita melopepo.

There is an infinitude of other plants and flowers, for an enumeration and scientific description of which I must refer to the Flora Virginica of our great botanist Dr. Clayton, published by Gronovius at Leyden, in 1762. This accurate observer was a native and resident of this state, passed a long life in exploring and describing its plants, and is supposed to have enlarged the botanical catalogue as much as almost any man who has lived.

Besides these plants, which are native, our *Farms* produce wheat, rye, barley, oats, buck wheat, broom corn, and Indian corn. The climate suits rice well enough wherever the lands do. Tobacco, hemp, flax, and cotton, are staple commodities. Indico yields two cuttings. The silk-worm is a native, and the mulberry, proper for its food, grows kindly.

We cultivate also potatoes, both the long and the round, turnips, carrots, parsneps, pumpkins, and ground nuts (Arachis.) Our grasses are Lucerne, St. Foin, Burnet, Timothy, ray and orchard grass; red, white, and yellow clover; greenswerd, blue grass, and crab grass.

The *gardens* yield musk melons, water melons, tomatas, okra, pomegranates, figs, and the esculent plants of Europe.

The *orchards* produce apples, pears, cherries, quinces, peaches, nectarines, apricots, almonds, and plumbs.

Animals

Our quadrupeds have been mostly described by Linnæus and Mons. de Buffon.[5] Of these the Mammoth, or big buffalo, as called by the Indians, must certainly have been the largest. Their tradition is, that he was carnivorous, and still exists in the northern parts of America. A delegation of warriors from the Delaware tribe having visited the governor of Virginia,[6] during the present revolution, on matters of business, after these had been discussed and settled in council, the governor asked them some questions relative to their country, and, among others, what they knew or had heard of the animal whose bones were found at the Saltlicks, on the Ohio. Their chief speaker immediately put himself into an attitude of oratory, and with a pomp suited to what he conceived the elevation of his subject, informed him that it was a tradition handed down from their fathers, "That in antient times a herd of these tremendous animals came to the Big-bone licks, and began an universal destruction of the bear, deer, elks, buffaloes, and other animals, which had been created for the use of the Indians: that the Great Man above, looking down and seeing this, was so enraged that he seized his lightning, descended on the earth, seated himself on a neighbouring mountain, on a rock, of which his seat and the print of his feet are still to be seen, and hurled his bolts among them till the whole were slaughtered, except the big bull, who presenting his forehead to the shafts, shook them off as they fell; but missing one at length, it wounded him in the side; whereon, springing round, he bounded over the Ohio, over the Wabash, the Illinois, and finally over the great lakes, where he is living at this day." It is well known that on the Ohio, and in many parts of America further north, tusks, grinders, and skeletons of unparalleled magnitude, are found in great numbers, some lying on the surface of the earth, and some a little below it. A Mr. Stanley, taken prisoner by the Indians near the mouth of the Tanissee, relates, that, after being transferred through several tribes, from one to another, he was at length carried over the mountains west of the Missouri to a river which runs westwardly; that these bones abounded there;

5. Georges-Louis Leclerc, comte de Buffon (1707–1788), French scientist, began publishing his thirty-six-volume *Histoire Naturelle* in 1749, which proposed, among other things, the theory that life forms in the Americas were weaker and smaller than their European counterparts or originals.
6. Jefferson himself, although the exact time and circumstances of this visit remain uncertain.

and that the natives described to him the animal to which they belonged as still existing in the northern parts of their country; from which description he judged it to be an elephant. Bones of the same kind have been lately found, some feet below the surface of the earth, in salines opened on the North Holston, a branch of the Tanissee, about the latitude of 36½°. North. From the accounts published in Europe, I suppose it to be decided, that these are of the same kind with those found in Siberia. Instances are mentioned of like animal remains found in the more southern climates of both hemispheres; but they are either so loosely mentioned as to leave a doubt of the fact, so inaccurately described as not to authorize the classing them with the great northern bones, or so rare as to found a suspicion that they have been carried thither as curiosities from more northern regions. So that on the whole there seem to be no certain vestiges of the existence of this animal further south than the salines last mentioned. It is remarkable that the tusks and skeletons have been ascribed by the naturalists of Europe to the elephant, while the grinders have been given to the hippopotamus, or river-horse. Yet it is acknowledged, that the tusks and skeletons are much larger than those of the elephant, and the grinders many times greater than those of the hippopotamus, and essentially different in form. Wherever these grinders are found, there also we find the tusks and skeleton; but no skeleton of the hippopotamus nor grinders of the elephant. It will not be said that the hippopotamus and elephant came always to the same spot, the former to deposit his grinders, and the latter his tusks and skeleton. For what became of the parts not deposited there? We must agree then that these remains belong to each other, that they are of one and the same animal, that this was not a hippopotamus, because the hippopotamus had no tusks nor such a frame, and because the grinders differ in their size as well as in the number and form of their points. That it was not an elephant, I think ascertained by proofs equally decisive. I will not avail myself of the authority of the celebrated anatomist,[7] who, from an examination of the form and structure of the tusks, has declared they were essentially different from those of the elephant; because another anatomist,[8] equally celebrated, has declared, on a like examination, that they are precisely the same. Between two such authorities I will suppose this circumstance equivocal. But, 1. The skeleton of the mammoth (for so the incognitum has been called) bespeaks an animal of five or six times the cubic volume of the elephant, as Mons. de Buffon has admitted. 2. The grinders are five times as large, are square, and the grinding surface studded with four or five rows of blunt points: whereas those of the elephant are broad and thin, and their grinding surface flat. 3. I have never heard an instance, and suppose there has been none, of the grinder of an elephant being found in America. 4. From the known temperature and constitution of the elephant he could never have existed in those regions where the remains of the mammoth have been found. The elephant is a native only of the torrid zone and its vicinities: if, with the assistance of warm apartments and warm clothing, he has been preserved in life in the temperate climates of Europe, it has only been for a small portion of what would have been his

---

7. Hunter [Jefferson's note]. The reference is to John Hunter (1728–1793), who published a paper on the mammoth remains in the *Transactions* of the Royal Society in 1768.
8. D'Aubenton [Jefferson's note]. The reference is to Louis Jean Marie Daubenton (1716–1800), who provided anatomical descriptions for Buffon's *Histoire Naturelle*.

natural period, and no instance of his multiplication in them has ever been known. But no bones of the mammoth, as I have before observed, have been ever found further south than the salines of the Holston, and they have been found as far north as the Arctic circle. Those, therefore, who are of opinion that the elephant and mammoth are the same, must believe, 1. That the elephant known to us can exist and multiply in the frozen zone; or, 2. That an internal fire may once have warmed those regions, and since abandoned them, of which, however, the globe exhibits no unequivocal indications; or, 3. That the obliquity of the ecliptic,[9] when these elephants lived, was so great as to include within the tropics all those regions in which the bones are found; the tropics being, as is before observed, the natural limits of habitation for the elephant. But if it be admitted that this obliquity has really decreased, and we adopt the highest rate of decrease yet pretended, that is, of one minute in a century, to transfer the northern tropic to the Arctic circle, would carry the existence of these supposed elephants 250,000 years back; a period far beyond our conception of the duration of animal bones left exposed to the open air, as these are in many instances. Besides, though these regions would then be supposed within the tropics, yet their winters would have been too severe for the sensibility of the elephant. They would have had too but one day and one night in the year, a circumstance to which we have no reason to suppose the nature of the elephant fitted. However, it has been demonstrated, that, if a variation of obliquity in the ecliptic takes place at all, it is vibratory, and never exceeds the limits of 9 degrees, which is not sufficient to bring these bones within the tropics. One of these hypotheses, or some other equally voluntary and inadmissible to cautious philosophy, must be adopted to support the opinion that these are the bones of the elephant. For my own part, I find it easier to believe that an animal may have existed, resembling the elephant in his tusks, and general anatomy, while his nature was in other respects extremely different. From the 30th degree of South latitude to the 30th of North, are nearly the limits which nature has fixed for the existence and multiplication of the elephant known to us. Proceeding thence northwardly to 36½ degrees, we enter those assigned to the mammoth. The further we advance North, the more their vestiges multiply as far as the earth has been explored in that direction; and it is as probable as otherwise, that this progression continues to the pole itself, if land extends so far. The center of the Frozen zone then may be the Achmé of their vigour, as that of the Torrid is of the elephant. Thus nature seems to have drawn a belt of separation between these two tremendous animals, whose breadth indeed is not precisely known, though at present we may suppose it about 6½ degrees of latitude; to have assigned to the elephant the regions South of these confines, and those North to the mammoth, founding the constitution of the one in her extreme of heat, and that of the other in the extreme of cold. When the Creator has therefore separated their nature as far as the extent of the scale of animal life allowed to this planet would permit, it seems perverse to declare it the same, from a partial resemblance of their tusks and bones. But to whatever animal we ascribe these remains, it is certain such a one has existed in America, and that it has been the largest of all terrestrial beings. It should have sufficed to have rescued the earth it inhabited, and the atmosphere it breathed, from the impu-

---

9. The tilt of the earth's axis.

tation of impotence in the conception and nourishment of animal life on a large scale: to have stifled, in its birth, the opinion of a writer, the most learned too of all others in the science of animal history, that in the new world, "La nature vivante est beaucoup moins agis-sante, beaucoup moins forte:" that nature is less active, less energetic on one side of the globe than she is on Buffon. xviii. 122. ed. Paris. 1764. the other. As if both sides were not warmed by the same genial sun; as if a soil of the same chemical composition, was less capable of elaboration into animal nutriment; as if the fruits and grains from that soil and sun, yielded a less rich chyle,[1] gave less extension to the solids and fluids of the body, or produced sooner in the cartilages, membranes, and fibres, that rigidity which restrains all further extension, and terminates animal growth. The truth is, that a Pigmy and a Patagonian, a Mouse and a Mammoth, derive their dimensions from the same nutritive juices. The difference of increment depends on circumstances unsearchable to beings with our capacities. Every race of animals seems to have received from their Maker certain laws of extension at the time of their formation. Their elaborative organs were formed to produce this, while proper obstacles were opposed to its further progress. Below these limits they cannot fall, nor rise above them. What intermediate station they shall take may depend on soil, on climate, on food, on a careful choice of breeders. But all the manna of heaven would never raise the Mouse to the bulk of the Mammoth.

The opinion advanced by the Count de Buffon, is 1. That the animals common both to the old and new xviii. 100–156. world, are smaller in the latter. 2. That those peculiar to the new, are on a smaller scale. 3. That those which have been domesticated in both, have degenerated in America: and 4. That on the whole it exhibits fewer species. And the reason he thinks is, that the heats of America are less; that more waters are spread over its surface by nature, and fewer of these drained off by the hand of man. In other words, that *heat* is friendly, and *moisture* adverse to the production and developement of large quadrupeds. I will not meet this hypothesis on its first doubtful ground, whether the climate of America be comparatively more humid? Because we are not furnished with observations sufficient to decide this question. And though, till it be decided, we are as free to deny, as others are to affirm the fact, yet for a moment let it be supposed. The hypothesis, after this supposition, proceeds to another; that *moisture* is unfriendly to animal growth. The truth of this is inscrutable to us by reasonings a priori. Nature has hidden from us her modus agendi. Our only appeal on such questions is to experience; and I think that experi-ence is against the supposition. It is by the assistance of *heat* and *moisture* that vegetables are elaborated from the elements of earth, air, water, and fire. We accordingly see the more humid climates produce the greater quantity of vegetables. Vegetables are mediately or immediately the food of every ani-mal: and in proportion to the quantity of food, we see animals not only mul-tiplied in their numbers, but improved in their bulk, as far as the laws of their nature will admit. Of this opinion is the Count de Buffon himself in another part of his work: "en general il paroit que les pays un peu *froids* conviennent mieux à nos boeufs que les pays viii. 134. chauds, et qu'ils sont d'autant plus gros et plus grands que le climat est plus

---

1. Fat-laden lymphatic fluid absorbed into the bloodstream by the small intestine.

humide et plus abondans en paturages. Les boeufs de Danemarck, de la Podolie, de l'Ukraine et de la Tartarie qu'habitent les Calmouques sont les plus grands de tous."[2] Here then a race of animals, and one of the largest too, has been increased in its dimensions by *cold* and *moisture*, in direct opposition to the hypothesis, which supposes that these two circumstances diminish animal bulk, and that it is their contraries *heat* and *dryness* which enlarge it. But when we appeal to experience, we are not to rest satisfied with a single fact. Let us therefore try our question on more general ground. Let us take two portions of the earth, Europe and America for instance, sufficiently extensive to give operation to general causes; let us consider the circumstances peculiar to each, and observe their effect on animal nature. America, running through the torrid as well as temperate zone, has more *heat*, collectively taken, than Europe. But Europe, according to our hypothesis, is the *dryest*. They are equally adapted then to animal productions; each being endowed with one of those causes which befriend animal growth, and with one which opposes it. If it be thought unequal to compare Europe with America, which is so much larger, I answer, not more so than to compare America with the whole world. Besides, the purpose of the comparison is to try an hypothesis, which makes the size of animals depend on the *heat* and *moisture* of climate. If therefore we take a region, so extensive as to comprehend a sensible distinction of climate, and so extensive too as that local accidents, or the intercourse of animals on its borders, may not materially affect the size of those in its interior parts, we shall comply with those conditions which the hypothesis may reasonably demand. The objection would be the weaker in the present case, because any intercourse of animals which may take place on the confines of Europe and Asia, is to the advantage of the former, Asia producing certainly larger animals than Europe. Let us then take a comparative view of the Quadrupeds of Europe and America, presenting them to the eye in three different tables, in one of which shall be enumerated those found in both countries; in a second those found in one only; in a third those which have been domesticated in both. To facilitate the comparison, let those of each table be arranged in gradation according to their sizes, from the greatest to the smallest, so far as their sizes can be conjectured. The weights of the large animals shall be expressed in the English avoirdupoise pound and its decimals: those of the smaller in the ounce and its decimals. Those which are marked thus *, are actual weights of particular subjects, deemed among the largest of their species. Those marked thus †, are furnished by judicious persons, well acquainted with the species, and saying, from conjecture only, what the largest individual they had seen would probably have weighed. The other weights are taken from Messrs. Buffon and D'Aubenton, and are of such subjects as came casually to their hands for dissection. This circumstance must be remembered where their weights and mine stand opposed: the latter being stated, not to produce a conclusion in favour of the American species, but to justify a suspension of opinion until we are better informed, and a suspicion in the mean time that there is no uniform difference in favour of either; which is all I pretend.

---

2. In general, it appears that slightly colder lands suit our oxen better than hot ones, and they gain in weight and size in climates that are damper and richer in pasturage. The oxen of Denmark, the southwest of Russia, the Ukraine, and the part of Tartary where the Kalmucks live are the largest of all (French).

A comparative View of the Quadrupeds
of Europe and of America.

I. *Aboriginals*[3] *of both.*

	Europe.	America.
	lb.	lb.
Mammoth		
Buffalo. Bison		*1800
White bear. Ours blanc		
Caribou. Renne		
Bear. Ours	153.7	*410
Elk. Elan. Orignal, palmated		
Red deer. Cerf	288.8	*273
Fallow deer. Daim	167.8	
Wolf. Loup	69.8	
Roe. Chevreuil	56.7	
Glutton. Glouton. Carcajou		
Wild cat. Chat sauvage		†30
Lynx. Loup cervier	25.	
Beaver. Castor	18.5	*45
Badger. Blaireau	13.6	
Red Fox. Renard	13.5	
Grey Fox. Isatis		
Otter. Loutre	8.9	†12
Monax. Marmotte	6.5	
Vison. Fouine	2.8	
Hedgehog. Herisson	2.2	
Martin. Marte	1.9	†6
	oz.	
Water rat. Rat d'eau	7.5	
Wesel. Belette	2.2	oz.
Flying squirrel. Polatouche	2.2	†4
Shrew mouse. Musaraigne	1.	

II. *Aboriginals of one only.*

Europe.		America.	
	lb.		lb.
Sanglier. Wild boar	280.	Tapir	534.
Mouflon. Wild sheep	56.	Elk, round horned	†450.
Bouquetin. Wild goat		Puma	
Lievre. Hare	7.6	Jaguar	218.
Lapin. Rabbet	3.4	Cabiai	109.
Putois. Polecat	3.3	Tamanoir	109.
Genette	3.1	Tamandua	65.4
Desman. Muskrat	oz.	Cougar of N. Amer.	75.
Ecureuil. Squirrel	12.	Cougar of S. Amer.	59.4

3. Natives.

II. Table continued.

Europe.		America.	
Hermine. Ermin	8.2	Ocelot	
Rat. Rat	7.5	Pecari	46.3
Loirs	3.1	Jaguaret	43.6
Lerot. Dormouse	1.8	Alco	
Taupe. Mole	1.2	Lama	
Hamster	.9	Paco	
Zisel		Paca	32.7
Leming		Serval	
Souris. Mouse	.6	Sloth. Unau	27¼
		Saricovienne	
		Kincajou	
		Tatou Kabassou	21.8
		Urson. Urchin	
		Raccoon. Raton	16.5
		Coati	
		Coendou	16.3
		Sloth. Aï	13.
		Sapajou Ouarini	
		Sapajou Coaita	9.8
		Tatou Encubert	
		Tatou Apar	
		Tatou Cachica	7.
		Little Coendou	6.5
		Opossum. Sarigue	
		Tapeti	
		Margay	
		Crabier	
		Agouti	4.2
		Sapajou Saï	3.5
		Tatou Cirquinçon	
		Tatou Tatouate	3.3
		Mouffette Squash	
		Mouffette Chinche	
		Mouffette Conepate. Scunk	
		Mouffette. Zorilla	
		Whabus. Hare. Rabbet	
		Aperea	
		Akouchi	
		Ondatra. Muskrat	
		Pilori	
		Great grey squirrel	†2.7
		Fox squirrel of Virginia	†2.625
		Surikate	2.
		Mink	†2.
		Sapajou. Sajou	1.8
		Indian pig. Cochon d'Inde	1.6

II. TABLE continued.

Europe.	America.	
	Sapajou. Saïmiri	1.5
	Phalanger	
	Coquallin	
	Lesser grey squirrel	†1.5
	Black squirrel	†1.5
	Red squirrel	10. oz.
	Sagoin Saki	
	Sagoin Pinche	
	Sagoin Tamarin	oz.
	Sagoin Ouistiti	4.4
	Sagoin Marikine	
	Sagoin Mico	
	Cayopollin	
	Fourmillier	
	Marmose	
	Sarigue of Cayenne	
	Tucan	
	Red mole	oz.
	Ground squirrel	4.

III. *Domesticated in both.*

	Europe.	America.
	lb.	lb.
Cow	763.	*2500
Horse		*1366
Ass		
Hog		*1200
Sheep		*125
Goat		*80
Dog	67.6	
Cat	7.	

I have not inserted in the first table the Phoca[4] nor leather-winged bat, because the one living half the year in the water, and the other being a winged animal, the individuals of each species may visit both continents.

Of the animals in the 1st table Mons. de Buffon himself informs us, [XXVII. 130. XXX. 213.] that the beaver, the otter, and shrew mouse, though of the same species, are larger in America than Europe. This should therefore have corrected the generality of his expressions XVIII. 145. and elsewhere, that the animals common to the two countries, are considerably less

4. It is said, that this animal is seldom seen above 30 miles from shore, or beyond the 56th degree of latitude. The interjacent islands between Asia and America admit his passing from one continent to the other without exceeding these bounds. And, in fact, travellers tell us that these islands are places of principal resort for them, and especially in the season of bringing forth their young [Jefferson's note].

in America than in Europe, "& cela sans aucune exception."[5] He tells us too, [Quadrup. VIII. 334. edit. Paris, 1777] that on examining a bear from America, he remarked no difference, "dans *la forme* de cet ours d'Amerique comparé a celui d'Europe."[6] But adds from Bartram's[7] journal, that an American bear weighed 400 lb. English, equal to 367 lb. French: whereas we find the European bear examined by Mons. D'Aubenton, [XVII. 82.] weighed but 141 lb. French. That the palmated Elk is larger in America than Europe we are informed by Kalm,[8] a Naturalist who visited the former by public appointment for the express purpose of examining the subjects of Natural history. In this fact Pennant[9] concurs with him. [Barrington's Miscellanies.] The same Kalm tells us that the Black Moose, or Renne of America, is as high as a tall horse; and Catesby,[1] that it is about the bigness of a middle sized ox. The same account of their size has been given me by many who have seen them. But Mons. D'Aubenton says that the Renne of Europe is but about the size of a Red-deer. The wesel is larger in America than in Europe, as may be seen by comparing its dimensions as reported by Mons. D'Aubenton and Kalm. The latter tells us, that the lynx, badger, red fox, and flying squirrel, are the *same* in America as in Europe: by which expression I understand, they are the same in all material circumstances, in size as well as others: for if they were smaller, they would differ from the European. Our grey fox is, by Catesby's account, little different in size and shape from the European fox. I presume he means the red fox of Europe, as does Kalm, where he says, that in size "they do not quite come up to our foxes." For proceeding next to the red fox of America, he says "they are entirely the same with the European sort." Which shews he had in view one European sort only, which was the red. So that the result of their testimony is, that the American grey fox is somewhat less than the European red; which is equally true of the grey fox of Europe, as may be seen by comparing the measures of the Count de Buffon and Mons. D'Aubenton. The white bear of America is as large as that of Europe. The bones of the Mammoth which have been found in America, are as large as those found in the old world. It may be asked, why I insert the Mammoth, as if it still existed? I ask in return, why I should omit it, as if it did not exist? Such is the œconomy of nature, that no instance can be produced of her having permitted any one race of her animals to

I. 233. Lond. 1772.

Ib. 233.

I. xxvii.

XXIV. 162.

XV. 42.

I. 359. I. 48. 221. 251.
II. 52.

II. 78.

I. 220.

XXVII. 63. XIV. 119.
Harris, II. 387. Buffon.
Quad. IX. 1.

5. And that without a single exception (French).
6. In the form of this American bear compared to the European (French).
7. John Bartram (1699–1777), a Philadelphia botanist. The four-hundred-pound bear was mentioned in a journal he kept during a 1765–66 trip to Florida; see William Stork, *A Description of East Florida, with a Journal Kept by John Bartram* . . . (London: W. Nicoll, 1767), 138.
8. Peter Kalm (1716–1779), Finnish-Swedish botanist and student of Linnaeus's who visited North America in 1748–51; on his return to Europe, he published *En Resa til Nord Amerika* (1753–61). Jefferson's marginal note refers to the English translation published as *Travels into North America*, 2 vols. (London: T. Lowndes, 1772).
9. Thomas Pennant (1726–1798) published his *Synopsis of Quadrupeds* in 1771, the work to which Daines Barrington (1727–1800) referred in discussing the elk in his *Miscellanies* (1781).
1. Naturalist Mark Catesby (1683–1749) discussed the moose in *The Natural History of Carolina, Florida, and the Bahama Islands* . . . , 2 vols. (London: Catesby, 1731–43).

become extinct; of her having formed any link in her great work so weak as to be broken. To add to this, the traditionary testimony of the Indians, that this animal still exists in the northern and western parts of America, would be adding the light of a taper to that of the meridian sun. Those parts still remain in their aboriginal state, unexplored and undisturbed by us, or by others for us. He may as well exist there now, as he did formerly where we find his bones. If he be a carnivorous animal, as some Anatomists have conjectured, and the Indians affirm, his early retirement may be accounted for from the general destruction of the wild game by the Indians, which commences in the first instant of their connection with us, for the purpose of purchasing matchcoats, hatchets, and fire locks, with their skins. There remain then the buffalo, red deer, fallow deer, wolf, roe, glutton, wild cat, monax, vison, hedge-hog, martin, and water rat, of the comparative sizes of which we have not sufficient testimony. It does not appear that Messrs. de Buffon and D'Aubenton have measured, weighed, or seen those of America. It is said of some of them, by some travellers, that they are smaller than the European. But who were these travellers? Have they not been men of a very different description from those who have laid open to us the other three quarters of the world? Was natural history the object of their travels? Did they measure or weigh the animals they speak of? or did they not judge of them by sight, or perhaps even from report only? Were they acquainted with the animals of their own country, with which they undertake to compare them? Have they not been so ignorant as often to mistake the species? A true answer to these questions would probably lighten their authority, so as to render it insufficient for the foundation of an hypothesis. How unripe we yet are, for an accurate comparison of the animals of the two countries, will appear from the work of Mons. de Buffon. The ideas we should have formed of the sizes of some animals, from the information he had received at his first publications concerning them, are very different from what his subsequent communications give us. And indeed his candour in this can never be too much praised. One sentence of his book must do him immortal honour. "J'aime autant une personne qui me releve d'une erreur, qu'une autre qui m'apprend une verité, parce qu'en effet une erreur corrigée est une verité."[2] He seems to have thought the Cabiai he first examined wanted little of its full growth. "Il n'etoit pas encore tout-a-fait adulte."[3] Yet he weighed but 46½ lb. and he found afterwards, that these animals, when full grown, weigh 100 lb. He had supposed, from the examination of a jaguar, said to be two years old, which weighed but 16 lb. 12 oz. that, when he should have acquired his full growth, he would not be larger than a middle sized dog. But a subsequent account raises his weight to 200 lb. Further information will, doubtless, produce further corrections. The wonder is, not that there is yet something in this great work to correct, but that there is so little. The result of this view then is, that of 26 quadrupeds common to both countries, 7 are said to be larger in America, 7 of equal size, and 12 not sufficiently examined. So that the first table impeaches the first member of the assertion,

(marginal references: Quad. IX. 158. · XXV. 184. · Quad. IX. 132. · XIX. 2. · Quad. IX 41.)

2. I love a person who corrects an error of mine as much as one who teaches me a truth, for an error corrected is in effect a truth (French).
3. It was not yet fully an adult (French).

that of the animals common to both countries, the American are smallest, "et cela sans aucune exception." It shews it not just, in all the latitude in which its author has advanced it, and probably not to such a degree as to found a distinction between the two countries.

Proceeding to the second table, which arranges the animals found in one of the two countries only, Mons. de Buffon observes, that the tapir, the elephant of America, is but of the size of a small cow. To preserve our comparison, I will add that the wild boar, the elephant of Europe, is little more than half that size. I have made an elk with round or cylindrical horns, an animal of America, and peculiar to it; because I have seen many of them myself, and more of their horns; and because I can say, from the best information, that, in Virginia, this kind of elk has abounded much, and still exists in smaller numbers; and I could never learn that the palmated kind had been seen here at all. I suppose this confined to the more Northern latitudes.[4] I have made our hare or rabbet peculiar, believing it to be different from both the European animals of those denominations, and calling it therefore by its Algonquin name Whabus, to keep it distinct from these. Kalm is of the same opinion. I have enumerated the squirrels according to our own knowledge, derived from daily sight of them, because I am not able to reconcile with that the European appellations and descriptions. I have heard of other species, but they have never come within my own notice. These, I think, are the only instances in which I have departed from the authority of Mons. de Buffon in the construction of this table. I take him for my ground work, because I think him the best informed of any Naturalist who has ever written. The result is, that there are 18 quadrupeds peculiar to Europe; more than four

Kalm II. 340.I. 82.

4. The descriptions of Theodat, Denys and La Hontan, cited by Mons. de Buffon under the article Elan, authorize the supposition, that the flat-horned elk is found in the northern parts of America. It has not however extended to our latitudes. On the other hand, I could never learn that the round-horned elk has been seen further North than the Hudson's river. This agrees with the former elk in its general character, being, like that, when compared with a deer, very much larger, its ears longer, broader, and thicker in proportion, its hair much longer, neck and tail shorter, having a dewlap before the breast (caruncula gutturalis Linnæi) a white spot often, if not always; of a foot diameter, on the hinder part of the buttocks round the tail; its gait a trot, and attended with a rattling of the hoofs: but distinguished from that decisively by its horns, which are not palmated, but round and pointed. This is the animal described by Catesby as the Cervus major Americanus, the Stag of America, le Cerf de l'Amerique. But it differs from the Cervus as totally, as does the palmated elk from the dama. And in fact it seems to stand in the same relation to the palmated elk, as the red deer does to the fallow. It has abounded in Virginia, has been seen, within my knowledge, on the Eastern side of the Blue ridge since the year 1765, is now common beyond those mountains, has been often brought to us and tamed, and their horns are in the hands of many. I should designate it as the "Alces Americanus cornibus teretibus." It were to be wished, that Naturalists, who are acquainted with the renne and elk of Europe, and who may hereafter visit the northern parts of America, would examine well the animals called there by the names of grey and black moose, caribou, orignal, and elk. Mons. de Buffon has done what could be done from the materials in his hands, towards clearing up the confusion introduced by the loose application of these names among the animals they are meant to designate. He reduces the whole to the renne and flat-horned elk. From all the information I have been able to collect, I strongly suspect they will be found to cover three, if not four distinct species of animals. I have seen skins of a moose, and of the caribou: they differ more from each other, and from that of the round-horned elk, than I ever saw two skins differ which belonged to different individuals of any wild species. These differences are in the colour, length, and coarseness of the hair, and in the size, texture, and marks of the skin. Perhaps it will be found that there is, 1. the moose, black and grey, the former being said to be the male, and the latter the female. 2. The caribou or renne. 3. The flat-horned elk, or orignal. 4. The round-horned elk. Should this last, though possessing so nearly the characters of the elk, be found to be the same with the Cerf d'Ardennes or Brandhirtz of Germany, still there will remain the three species first enumerated [Jefferson's note].

times as many, to wit 74, peculiar to America; that the first[5] of these 74 weighs more than the whole column of Europeans; and consequently this second table disproves the second member of the assertion, that the animals peculiar to the new world are on a smaller scale, so far as that assertion relied on European animals for support: and it is in full opposition to the theory which makes the animal volume to depend on the circumstances of *heat* and *moisture*.

The IIId. table comprehends those quadrupeds only which are domestic in both countries. That some of these, in some parts of America, have become less than their original stock, is doubtless true; and the reason is very obvious. In a thinly peopled country, the spontaneous productions of the forests and waste fields are sufficient to support indifferently the domestic animals of the farmer, with a very little aid from him in the severest and scarcest season. He therefore finds it more convenient to receive them from the hand of nature in that indifferent state, than to keep up their size by a care and nourishment which would cost him much labour. If, on this low fare, these animals dwindle, it is no more than they do in those parts of Europe where the poverty of the soil, or poverty of the owner, reduces them to the same scanty subsistance. It is the uniform effect of one and the same cause, whether acting on this or that side of the globe. It would be erring therefore against that rule of philosophy, which teaches us to ascribe like effects to like causes, should we impute this diminution of size in America to any imbecility or want of uniformity in the operations of nature. It may be affirmed with truth that, in those countries, and with those individuals of America, where necessity or curiosity has produced equal attention as in Europe to the nourishment of animals, the horses, cattle, sheep, and hogs of the one continent are as large as those of the other. There are particular instances, well attested, where individuals of this country have imported good breeders from England, and have improved their size by care in the course of some years. To make a fair comparison between the two countries, it will not answer to bring together animals of what might be deemed the middle or ordinary size of their species; because an error in judging of that middle or ordinary size would vary the result of the comparison. Thus Monsieur D'Aubenton considers a horse of 4 feet 5 inches high and 400 lb. weight VII. 432. French, equal to 4 feet 8.6 inches and 436 lb. English, as a middle sized horse. Such a one is deemed a small horse in America. The extremes must therefore be resorted to. The same anatomist dissected a horse of 5 feet 9 inches height, French measure, equal to 6 feet 1.7 English. This is near 6 inches higher than any horse I VII. 474. have seen: and could it be supposed that I had seen the largest horses in America, the conclusion would be, that ours have diminished, or that we have bred from a smaller stock. In Connecticut and Rhode-Island, where the climate is favorable to the production of grass, bullocks have been

5. The Tapir is the largest of the animals peculiar to America. I collect his weight thus. Mons. de Buffon says, XXIII. 274. that he is of the size of a Zebu, or a small cow. He gives us the measures of a Zebu, ib. 94. as taken by himself, viz. 5 feet 7 inches from the muzzle to the root of the tail, and 5 feet 1 inch circumference behind the fore legs. A bull, measuring in the same way 6 feet 9 inches and 5 feet 2 inches, weighed 600 lb. VIII. 153. The Zebu then, and of course the Tapir, would weigh about 500 lb. But one individual of every species of European peculiars would probably weigh less than 400 lb. These are French measures and weights [Jefferson's note].

slaughtered which weighed 2500, 2200, and 2100 lb. nett; and those of 1800 lb. have been frequent. I have seen a hog[6] weigh 1050 lb. after the blood, bowels, and hair had been taken from him. Before he was killed an attempt was made to weigh him with a pair of steel-yards, graduated to 1200 lb. but he weighed more. Yet this hog was probably not within fifty generations of the European stock. I am well informed of another which weighed 1100 lb. gross. Asses have been still more neglected than any other domestic animal in America. They are neither fed nor housed in the most rigorous season of the year. Yet they are larger than those measured by Mons. D'Aubenton, of 3 feet 7¼ inches, 3 feet 4 inches, and 3 feet 2½ inches, the latter weighing only 215.8 lb. These sizes, I suppose, have been produced by the same negligence in Europe, which has produced a like diminution here. Where care has been taken of them on that side of the water, they have been raised to a size bordering on that of the horse; not by the *heat* and *dryness* of the climate, but by good food and shelter. Goats have been also much neglected in America. Yet they are very prolific here, bearing twice or three times a year, and from one to five kids at a birth. Mons. de Buffon has been sensible of a difference in this circumstance in favour of America. But what are their greatest weights I cannot say. A large sheep here weighs 100 lb. I observe Mons. D'Aubenton calls a ram of 62 lb. one of the middle size. But to say what are the extremes of growth in these and the other domestic animals of America, would require information of which no one individual is possessed. The weights actually known and stated in the third table preceding will suffice to shew, that we may conclude, on probable grounds, that, with equal food and care, the climate of America will preserve the races of domestic animals as large as the European stock from which they are derived; and consequently that the third member of Mons. de Buffon's assertion, that the domestic animals are subject to degeneration from the climate of America, is as probably wrong as the first and second were certainly so.

VIII. 48. 35. 66.

XVIII. 96.

IX. 41.

That the last part of it is erroneous, which affirms that the species of American quadrupeds are comparatively few, is evident from the tables taken all together. By these it appears that there are an hundred species aboriginal of America. Mons. de Buffon supposes about double that number existing on the whole earth. Of these Europe, Asia, and Africa, furnish suppose 126; that is, the 26 common to Europe and America, and about 100 which are not in America at all. The American species then are to those of the rest of the earth, as 100 to 126, or 4 to 5. But the residue of the earth being double the extent of America, the exact proportion would have been but as 4 to 8.

XXX. 219.

Hitherto I have considered this hypothesis as applied to brute animals only, and not in its extension to the man of America, whether aboriginal or transplanted. It is the opinion of Mons. de Buffon that the former furnishes no exception to it. "Quoique le sauvage du nouveau monde soit à-peu-près de même stature que l'homme de notre monde, cela ne suffit pas pour qu'il puisse faire une exception au

XVIII. 146.

6. In Williamsburg, April, 1769 [Jefferson's note].

fait général du rapetissement de la nature vivante dans tout ce continent:
le sauvage est foible & petit par les organes de la génération; il n'a ni poil,
ni barbe, & nulle ardeur pour sa femelle; quoique plus léger que l'Européen
parce qu'il a plus d'habitude à courir, il est cependant beaucoup moins fort
de corps; il est aussi bien moins sensible, & cependant plus craintif & plus
lâche; il n'a nulle vivacité, nulle activité dans l'ame; celle du corps est moins
un exercice, un mouvement volontaire qu'une nécessité d'action causée par
le besoin; otez lui la faim & la soif, vous détruirez en meme temps le
principe actif de tous ses mouvemens; il demeurera stupidement en repos
sur ses jambes ou couché pendant des jours entiers. Il ne faut pas aller
chercher plus loin la cause de la vie dispersée des sauvages & de leur
éloignement pour la société: la plus précieuse étincelle du feu de la nature
leur a été refusée; ils manquent d'ardeur pour leur femelle, & par consequent d'amour pour leur semblables: ne connoissant pas l'attachement le
plus vif, le plus tendre de tous, leurs autres sentimens de ce genre sont
froids & languissans; ils aiment foiblement leurs pères & leurs enfans; la
société la plus intime de toutes, celle de la même famille, n'a donc chez eux
que de foibles liens; la société d'une famille à l'autre n'en a point du tout:
dès lors nulle réunion, nulle république, nulle état social. La physique de
l'amour fait chez eux le moral des mœurs; leur cœur est glacé, leur société
froide, & leur empire dur. Ils ne regardent leurs femmes que comme des
servantes de peine ou des bêtes de somme qu'ils chargent, sans ménage-
ment, du fardeau de leur chasse, & qu'ils forcent sans pitié, sans recon-
noissance, à des ouvrages qui souvent sont audessus de leurs forces: ils
n'ont que peu d'enfans; ils en ont peu de soin; tout se ressent de leur premier défaut; ils sont indifférents parce qu'ils sont peu puissans, & cette
indifférence pour le sexe est la tâche originale qui flétrit la nature, qui l'em-
pêche de s'épanouir, & qui détruisant les germes de la vie, coupe en même
temps la racine de la société. L'homme ne fait donc point d'exception ici.
La nature en lui refusant les puissances de l'amour l'a plus maltraité & plus
rapetissé qu'aucun des animaux."[7] An afflicting picture indeed, which, for
the honor of human nature, I am glad to believe has no original. Of the
Indian of South America I know nothing; for I would not honor with the

---

7. Although the American Native is about as tall as the European, this fact does not exempt humans
   from the general rule that all life forms diminish in America. The American Native is feeble, and
   has smaller sex organs; he lacks body hair and beard, and has no passion for the female; although
   faster than the European because he is more accustomed to running, he is nevertheless weaker; he
   is less sensitive as well, and more timid and cowardly; he lacks vivacity and alertness of mind; his
   bodily activity, necessary rather than voluntary, springs from want; take away his hunger and thirst,
   and you deprive him of his motivation; he will stand around or lie down for days on end. It is pointless to seek out other explanations of the isolated life of these people, or their dislike of society: the
   most valuable spark of nature's fire has been denied them; they lack passion for the females, and
   consequently have no love for their fellow men: ignorant as they are of this strongest yet most tender affection, their other feelings are cold and languid as well; they have little love even for their
   parents and children; so that the dearest of all ties, that of family, binds them together only loosely;
   between families there is no tie at all; consequently, they lack communion, commonwealth, society. Physical love provides their only morality; their heart is chill, their society cold, their rule harsh.
   They view their wives only as workers or beasts of burden, whom they load down with their kill from
   the hunt, and whom they mercilessly force, without thanks, to perform beyond the limits of their
   strength. Of their few children they take little care. In everything, their fundamental weakness
   shows: they are indifferent because they have so little sexual capacity, and this indifference to the
   opposite sex deeply weakens their nature, preventing its full development and, by blasting the very
   seeds of life, ruins society at the same time. Man here offers no exception to the general principles.
   Nature, taking away the power of love, mistreat him, lowering him below even all the animals
   (French). For Charles Thomson's detailed response to Buffon's portrait of the Native American, see
   Appendix No. I, section 4 (p. 161).

appellation of knowledge, what I derive from the fables published of them. These I believe to be just as true as the fables of Æsop. This belief is founded on what I have seen of man, white, red, and black, and what has been written of him by authors, enlightened themselves, and writing amidst an enlightened people. The Indian of North America being more within our reach, I can speak of him somewhat from my own knowledge, but more from the information of others better acquainted with him, and on whose truth and judgment I can rely. From these sources I am able to say, in contradiction to this representation, that he is neither more defective in ardor, nor more impotent with his female, than the white reduced to the same diet and exercise: that he is brave, when an enterprize depends on bravery; education with him making the point of honor consist in the destruction of an enemy by stratagem, and in the preservation of his own person free from injury; or perhaps this is nature; while it is education which teaches us to honor[8] force more than finesse: that he will defend himself against an host of enemies, always chusing to be killed, rather than to surrender,[9] though it be to the whites, who he knows will treat him well: that in other situations also he meets death with more deliberation, and endures tortures with a firmness unknown almost to religious enthusiasm with us: that he is affectionate to his children, careful of them, and indulgent in the extreme: that his affections comprehend his other connections, weakening, as with us, from circle to circle, as they recede from the center: that his friendships are strong and faithful to the uttermost extremity:[1] that his sensibility is

8. Sol Rodomonte sprezza di venire Se non, dove la via meno è sicura. Ariosto. 14. 117 [Jefferson's note].
9. In so judicious an author as Don Ulloa, and one to whom we are indebted for the most precise information we have of South America, I did not expect to find such assertions as the following. "Los Indios vencidos son los mas cobardes y pusilanimes que se peuden vér:—se hacen inocentes, se humillan hasta el desprecio, disculpan su inconsiderado arrojo, y con las súplicas y los ruegos dán seguras pruebas de su pusilanimidad.—ó lo que resieren las historias de la Conquista, sobre sus grandes acciones, es en un sentido figurado, ó el caracter de estas gentes no es ahora segun era entonces; pero lo que no tiene duda es, que las Naciones de la parte Septentrional subsisten en la misma libertad que siempre han tenido, sin haber sido sojuzgados por algun Principe extrano, y que viven segun su régimen y costumbres de toda la vida, sin que haya habido motivo para que muden de caracter; y en estos se vé lo mismo, que succde en los del Peru, y de toda la América Meridional, reducidos, y que nunca lo han estado." Noticias Americanas. Entretenimiento XVIII. §. 1. Don Ulloa here admits, that the authors who have described the Indians of South America, before they were enslaved, had represented them as a brave people, and therefore seems to have suspected that the cowardice which he had observed in those of the present race might be the effect of subjugation. But, supposing the Indians of North America to be cowards also, he concludes the ancestors of those of South America to have been so too, and therefore that those authors have given fictions for truths. He was probably not acquainted himself with the Indians of North America, and had formed his opinion of them from hear-say. Great numbers of French, of English, and of Americans, are perfectly acquainted with these people. Had he had an opportunity of enquiring of any of these, they would have told him, that there never was an instance known of an Indian begging his life when in the power of his enemies: on the contrary, that he courts death by every possible insult and provocation. His reasoning then would have been reversed thus. "Since the present Indian of North America is brave, and authors tell us, that the ancestors of those of South America were brave also; it must follow, that the cowardice of their descendants is the effect of subjugation and ill treatment." For he observes, ib. §. 27. that "los obrages los aniquilan por la inhumanidad con que se les trata." [Jefferson's note].
1. A remarkable instance of this appeared in the case of the late Col. Byrd, who was sent to the Cherokee nation to transact some business with them. It happened that some of our disorderly people had just killed one or two of that nation. It was therefore proposed in the council of the Cherokees that Col. Byrd should be put to death, in revenge for the loss of their countrymen. Among them was a chief called Silòuee, who, on some former occasion, had contracted an acquaintance and friendship with Col. Byrd. He came to him every night in his tent, and told him not to be afraid, they should not kill him. After many days deliberation, however, the determination was, contrary to Silòuee's expectation, that Byrd should be put to death, and some warriors were dispatched as executioners. Silòuee attended them, and when they entered the tent, he threw himself between them and Byrd, and said to the warriors, "this man is my friend: before you get at him, you must kill me." On which they returned, and the council respected the principle so much as to recede from their determination [Jefferson's note].

keen, even the warriors weeping most bitterly on the loss of their children, though in general they endeavour to appear superior to human events: that his vivacity and activity of mind is equal to ours in the same situation; hence his eagerness for hunting, and for games of chance. The women are submitted to unjust drudgery. This I believe is the case with every barbarous people. With such, force is law. The stronger sex therefore imposes on the weaker. It is civilization alone which replaces women in the enjoyment of their natural equality. That first teaches us to subdue the selfish passions, and to respect those rights in others which we value in ourselves. Were we in equal barbarism, our females would be equal drudges. The man with them is less strong than with us, but their woman stronger than ours; and both for the same obvious reason; because our man and their woman is habituated to labour, and formed by it. With both races the sex which is indulged with ease is least athletic. An Indian man is small in the hand and wrist for the same reason for which a sailor is large and strong in the arms and shoulders, and a porter in the legs and thighs.—They raise fewer children than we do. The causes of this are to be found, not in a difference of nature, but of circumstance. The women very frequently attending the men in their parties of war and of hunting, child-bearing becomes extremely inconvenient to them. It is said, therefore, that they have learnt the practice of procuring abortion by the use of some vegetable; and that it even extends to prevent conception for a considerable time after. During these parties they are exposed to numerous hazards, to excessive exertions, to the greatest extremities of hunger. Even at their homes the nation depends for food, through a certain part of every year, on the gleanings of the forest: that is, they experience a famine once in every year. With all animals, if the female be badly fed, or not fed at all, her young perish: and if both male and female be reduced to like want, generation becomes less active, less productive. To the obstacles then of want and hazard, which nature has opposed to the multiplication of wild animals, for the purpose of restraining their numbers within certain bounds, those of labour and of voluntary abortion are added with the Indian. No wonder then if they multiply less than we do. Where food is regularly supplied, a single farm will shew more of cattle, than a whole country of forests can of buffaloes. The same Indian women, when married to white traders, who feed them and their children plentifully and regularly, who exempt them from excessive drudgery, who keep them stationary and unexposed to accident, produce and raise as many children as the white women. Instances are known, under these circumstances, of their rearing a dozen children. An inhuman practice once prevailed in this country of making slaves of the Indians. It is a fact well known with us, that the Indian women so enslaved produced and raised as numerous families as either the whites or blacks among whom they lived.—It has been said, that Indians have less hair than the whites, except on the head. But this is a fact of which fair proof can scarcely be had. With them it is disgraceful to be hairy on the body. They say it likens them to hogs. They therefore pluck the hair as fast as it appears. But the traders who marry their women, and prevail on them to discontinue this practice, say, that nature is the same with them as with the whites. Nor, if the fact be true, is the consequence necessary which has been drawn from it. Negroes have notoriously less hair than the whites; yet they are more ardent. But if cold and moisture be the agents of nature for diminishing the races of animals, how comes she all at once to suspend their operation as to the physical man of the new world, whom the Count acknowledges to be "à peu près de mème stature que l'homme de notre monde," and to let loose their influence on his moral faculties? How has this "combination of the elements and other physical causes, so contrary to the enlargement XVIII. 145. of animal nature in this new world, these obstacles to the developement and formation of great germs," been arrested and suspended, so as to permit the human body to acquire its just dimensions, and by what inconceivable process has their action been directed on his mind alone? To judge of the truth of this, to form a just estimate of their genius and mental powers, more facts are wanting, and great allowance to be made for those circumstances of their situation which call for a display of particular talents only. This done, we shall probably find that they are formed in mind as well as in body, on the same module with the "Homo sapiens Europæus."[2] The principles of their society forbidding all compulsion, they are to be led to duty and to enterprize by personal influence and persuasion. Hence eloquence in council, bravery and address in war, become the foundations of all consequence with them. To these acquirements all their faculties are directed. Of their bravery and address in war we have multiplied proofs, because we have been the subjects on which they were exercised. Of their eminence in oratory we have fewer examples, because it is displayed chiefly in their own councils. Some, however, we have of very superior lustre. I may challenge the whole orations of Demosthenes and Cicero, and of any more eminent orator, if Europe has furnished more eminent, to produce a single passage, superior to the speech of Logan,[3] a Mingo chief, to Lord Dunmore, when governor of this state. And, as a testimony of their talents in this line, I beg leave to introduce it, first stating the incidents necessary for understanding it. In the spring of the year 1774, a robbery and murder were committed on an inhabitant of the frontiers of Virginia, by two Indians of the Shawanee tribe. The neighbouring whites, according to their custom, undertook to punish this outrage in a summary way. Col. Cresap,[4] a man infamous for the many murders he had committed on those much-injured people, collected a party, and proceeded down the Kanhaway in quest of vengeance. Unfortunately a canoe of women and children, with one man only, was seen coming from the opposite shore, unarmed, and unsuspecting an hostile attack from the whites. Cresap and his party concealed themselves on the bank of the river, and the moment the canoe

2. Linn. Syst. Definition of a Man [Jefferson's note].
3. Logan (c. 1725–1780), son of Cayuga leader Shikellamy, was a war leader who in 1774 was living in the village of Yellow Creek, in the Ohio country. When members of his family were murdered by marauding whites that year, Logan retaliated in kind. The speech printed by Jefferson as Logan's (reportedly delivered to John Murray, fourth Earl of Dunmore [1730–1809], governor of Virginia from 1771 to 1776, who led Virginia forces against the Indians in the war that followed) had wide circulation before the publication of *Notes on the State of Virginia*, but its authenticity has often been called into question. In 1800, Jefferson, much attacked by Federalists for his original treatment of the incident, published a separate pamphlet, *An Appendix to the Notes on Virginia Relative to the Murder of Logan's Family*, which was added to later editions of *Notes on the State of Virginia* as "Appendix No. 4." In it, Jefferson provided a revised version of the description of the murders that follows after this sentence. For the appendix, see p. 178.
4. Michael Cresap (1742–1775), a Maryland native who had migrated to the Ohio country, was unfairly blamed by Logan for the murders of his family members. Cresap, understanding that war had started, did kill three Indians but in fact decided not to attack the Yellow Creek village, whose inhabitants instead were killed by a band of Virginia pioneers.

reached the shore, singled out their objects, and, at one fire, killed every person in it. This happened to be the family of Logan, who had long been distinguished as a friend of the whites. This unworthy return provoked his vengeance. He accordingly signalized himself in the war which ensued. In the autumn of the same year, a decisive battle was fought at the mouth of the Great Kanhaway, between the collected forces of the Shawanees, Mingoes, and Delawares, and a detachment of the Virginia militia. The Indians were defeated, and sued for peace. Logan however disdained to be seen among the suppliants. But, lest the sincerity of a treaty should be distrusted, from which so distinguished a chief absented himself, he sent by a messenger the following speech to be delivered to Lord Dunmore.

"I appeal to any white man to say, if ever he entered Logan's cabin hungry, and he gave him not meat; if ever he came cold and naked, and he clothed him not. During the course of the last long and bloody war, Logan remained idle in his cabin, an advocate for peace. Such was my love for the whites, that my countrymen pointed as they passed, and said, 'Logan is the friend of white men.' I had even thought to have lived with you, but for the injuries of one man. Col. Cresap, the last spring, in cold blood, and unprovoked, murdered all the relations of Logan, not sparing even my women and children. There runs not a drop of my blood in the veins of any living creature. This called on me for revenge. I have sought it: I have killed many: I have fully glutted my vengeance. For my country, I rejoice at the beams of peace. But do not harbour a thought that mine is the joy of fear. Logan never felt fear. He will not turn on his heel to save his life. Who is there to mourn for Logan?—Not one."

Before we condemn the Indians of this continent as wanting genius, we must consider that letters have not yet been introduced among them. Were we to compare them in their present state with the Europeans North of the Alps, when the Roman arms and arts first crossed those mountains, the comparison would be unequal, because, at that time, those parts of Europe were swarming with numbers; because numbers produce emulation, and multiply the chances of improvement, and one improvement begets another. Yet I may safely ask, How many good poets, how many able mathematicians, how many great inventors in arts or sciences, had Europe North of the Alps then produced? And it was sixteen centuries after this before a Newton could be formed. I do not mean to deny, that there are varieties in the race of man, distinguished by their powers both of body and mind. I believe there are, as I see to be the case in the races of other animals. I only mean to suggest a doubt, whether the bulk and faculties of animals depend on the side of the Atlantic on which their food happens to grow, or which furnishes the elements of which they are compounded? Whether nature has enlisted herself as a Cis or Trans-Atlantic partisan? I am induced to suspect, there has been more eloquence than sound reasoning displayed in support of this theory; that it is one of those cases where the judgment has been seduced by a glowing pen: and whilst I render every tribute of honor and esteem to the celebrated Zoologist, who has added, and is still adding, so many precious things to the treasures of science, I must doubt whether in this instance he has not cherished error also, by lending her for a moment his vivid imagination and bewitching language.

So far the Count de Buffon has carried this new theory of the tendency of nature to belittle her productions on this side the Atlantic. Its application to the race of whites, transplanted from Europe, remained for the Abbé Raynal.[5] "On doit etre etonné (he says) que l'Amerique n'ait pas encore produit un bon poëte, un habile mathematicien, un homme de genie dans un seul art, ou une seule science." 7. Hist. Philos. p. 92. ed. Maestricht. 1774. "America has not yet produced one good poet." When we shall have existed as a people as long as the Greeks did before they produced a Homer, the Romans a Virgil, the French a Racine and Voltaire, the English a Shakespeare and Milton, should this reproach be still true, we will enquire from what unfriendly causes it has proceeded, that the other countries of Europe and quarters of the earth shall not have inscribed any name in the roll of poets.[6] But neither has America produced 'one able mathematician, one man of genius in a single art or a single science.' In war we have produced a Washington, whose memory will be adored while liberty shall have votaries, whose name will triumph over time, and will in future ages assume its just station among the most celebrated worthies of the world, when that wretched philosophy shall be forgotten which would have arranged him among the degeneracies of nature. In physics we have produced a Franklin, than whom no one of the present age has made more important discoveries, nor has enriched philosophy with more, or more ingenious solutions of the phænomena of nature. We have supposed Mr. Rittenhouse[7] second to no astronomer living: that in genius he must be the first, because he is self-taught. As an artist he has exhibited as great a proof of mechanical genius as the world has ever produced. He has not indeed made a world; but he has by imitation approached nearer its Maker than any man who has lived from the creation to this day.[8] As in philosophy and war, so in government, in oratory, in painting, in the plastic art, we might shew that America, though but a child of yesterday, has already given hopeful proofs of genius, as well of the nobler kinds, which arouse the best feelings of man, which call him into action, which substantiate, his freedom, and conduct him to happiness, as of the subordinate, which serve to amuse him only. We therefore suppose, that this reproach is as unjust as it is unkind; and that, of the geniuses which adorn the present age, America contributes its full share. For comparing it with those countries, where genius is most cultivated, where are the most excel-

---

5. Guillaume-Thomas-François Raynal (1711–1796) published his *Histoire Philosophique et Politique des Établissements et du Commerce des Européens dans les deux Indes* in Amsterdam in 1770. Jefferson translates the quotation himself in the lines that follow.

6. Has the world as yet produced more than two poets, acknowledged to be such by all nations? An Englishman, only, reads Milton with delight, an Italian Tasso, a Frenchman the Henriade, a Portuguese Camouens: but Homer and Virgil have been the rapture of every age and nation: they are read with enthusiasm in their originals by those who can read the originals, and in translations by those who cannot [Jefferson's note].

7. David Rittenhouse (1732–1796) of Philadelphia independently produced a model of the solar system that has been known as an "orrery" following its earlier invention by the British watchmaker George Graham, whose name it for his patron, Charles Boyle, fourth Earl of Orrery. In a note (n.8), Jefferson praises another Philadelphian, Thomas Godfrey (1704–1749), who independently invented the octant, a forerunner of the sextant that is usually credited to Englishman John Hadley (1682–1744).

8. There are various ways of keeping truth out of sight. Mr. Rittenhouse's model of the planetary system has the plagiary appellation of an Orrery; and the quadrant invented by Godfrey, an American also, and with the aid of which the European nations traverse the globe, is called Hadley's quadrant [Jefferson's note].

lent models for art, and scaffoldings for the attainment of science, as France and England for instance, we calculate thus. The United States contain three millions of inhabitants; France twenty millions; and the British islands ten. We produce a Washington, a Franklin, a Rittenhouse. France then should have half a dozen in each of these lines, and Great-Britain half that number, equally eminent. It may be true, that France has: we are but just becoming acquainted with her, and our acquaintance so far gives us high ideas of the genius of her inhabitants. It would be injuring too many of them to name particularly a Voltaire, a Buffon, the constellation of Encyclopedists,[9] the Abbé Raynal himself, &c. &c. We therefore have reason to believe she can produce her full quota of genius. The present war having so long cut off all communication with Great-Britain, we are not able to make a fair estimate of the state of science in that country. The spirit in which she wages war is the only sample before our eyes, and that does not seem the legitimate offspring either of science or of civilization. The sun of her glory is fast descending to the horizon. Her philosophy has crossed the Channel, her freedom the Atlantic, and herself seems passing to that awful dissolution, whose issue is not given human foresight to scan.[1]

Having given a sketch of our minerals, vegetables, and quadrupeds, and being led by a proud theory to make a comparison of the latter with those of Europe, and to extend it to the Man of America, both aboriginal and emigrant, I will proceed to the remaining articles comprehended under the present query.

Between ninety and an hundred of our birds have been described by Catesby. His drawings are better as to form and attitude, than colouring, which is generally too high. They are the following.

9. The group of French intellectuals who, under the direction of philosopher Denis Diderot (1713–1784) and mathematician Jean le Rond d'Alembert (1717–1783), produced the great monument of enlightenment learning, *Encyclopédie ou Dictionnaire Raisonné des Sciences, des Arts et des Métiers*. (1751–72).

1. In a later edition of the Abbé Raynal's work, he has withdrawn his censure from that part of the new world inhabited by the Federo-Americans; but has left it still on the other parts. North America has always been more accessible to strangers than South. If he was mistaken then as to the former, he may be so as to the latter. The glimmerings which reach us from South America enable us only to see that its inhabitants are held under the accumulated pressure of slavery, superstition, and ignorance. Whenever they shall be able to rise under this weight, and to shew themselves to the rest of the world, they will probably shew they are like the rest of the world. We have not yet sufficient evidence that there are more *lakes* and *fogs* in South America than in other parts of the earth. As little do we know what would be their operation on the mind of man. That country has been visited by Spaniards and Portugueze chiefly, and almost exclusively. These, going from a country of the old world remarkably dry in its soil and climate, fancied there were more lakes and fogs in South America than in Europe. An inhabitant of Ireland, Sweden, or Finland, would have formed the contrary opinion. Had South America then been discovered and seated by a people from a fenny country, it would probably have been represented as much drier than the old world. A patient pursuit of facts, and cautious combination and comparison of them, is the drudgery to which man is subjected by his Maker, if he wishes to attain sure knowledge [Jefferson's note].

BIRDS OF VIRGINIA.

Linnean Designation.	Catesby's Designation.		Popular Names.	Buffon oiseaux.
Lanius tyrannus	Muscicapa coronâ rubrâ	1.55	Tyrant. Field martin	8.398
Vultur aura	Buteo specie Gallo-pavonis	1.6	Turkey buzzard	1.246
Falco leucocephalus	Aquila capite albo	1.1	Bald Eagle	1.138
Falco sparverius	Accipiter minor	1.5	Little hawk. Sparrow hawk	
Falco columbarius	Accipiter palumbarius	1.3	Pigeon hawk	1.338
Falco furcatus	Accipiter caudâ furcatâ	1.4	Forked tail hawk	1.286.312
	Accipiter piscatorius	1.2	Fishing hawk	1.199
Strix asio	Noctua aurita minor	1.7	Little owl	1.141
Psittacus Caroliniensis	Psitticus Caroliniensis	1.11	Parrot of Carolina. Perroquet	11.383
Corvus cristatus	Pica glandaria, caerulea, cristata	1.15	Blue jay	5.164
Oriolus Baltimore	Icterus ex aureo nigroque varius	1.48	Baltimore bird	5.318
Oriolus spurius	Icterus minor	1.49	Bastard Baltimore	5.321
Gracula quiscula	Monedula purpurea	1.12	Purple jackdaw. Crow blackbird	5.134
Cuculus Americanus	Cuculus Caroliniensis	1.9	Carolina cuckow	12.62
Picus principalis	Picus maximus rostro albo	1.16	White bill woodpecker	13.69
Picus pileatus	Picus niger maximus, capite rubro	1.17	Larger red-crested woodpecker	13.72
Picus erythrocephalus	Picus capite toto rubro	1.20	Red-headed woodpecker	13.83
Picus auratus	Picus major alis aureis	1.18	Gold winged woodpecker. Yucker	13.59
Picus Carolinus	Picus ventre rubro	1.19	Red bellied woodpecker	13.105
Picus pubescens	Picus varius minimus	1.21	Smallest spotted woodpecker	13.113
Picus villosus	Picus medius quasi-villosus	1.19	Hairy woodpecker. Speck. woodpec.	13.111
Picus varius	Picus varius minor ventre luteo	1.21	Yellow bellied woodpecker	13.115

Sitta Europaea {	Sitta capite nigro	1.22	Nuthatch	10.213

Latin name	Latin description	No.	English name	
Sitta Europaea {	Sitta capite nigro	1.22	Nuthatch	10.213
	Sitta capite fusco	1.22	Small Nuthatch	10.214
Alcedo alcyon	Ispida	1.69	Kingfisher	13.310
Certhia pinus	Parus Americanus lutescens	1.61	Pinecreeper	9.433
Trochilus colubris	Mellivora avis Caroliniensis	1.65	Humming bird	11.16
Anas Canadensis	Anser Canadensis	1.92	Wild goose	17.122
Anas bucephala	Anas minor purpureo capite	1.95	Buffel's head duck	17.356
Anas rustica	Anas minor ex albo & fusco vario	1.98	Little brown duck	17.413
Anas discors	Querquedula Americana variegata	1.100	White face teal	17.403
Anas discors. β.	Querquedula Americana fusca	1.99	Blue wing teal	17.405
Anas sponsa	Anas Americanus cristatus elegans	1.97	Summer duck	17.351
	Anas Americanus lato rostro	1.96	Blue wing shoveler	17.275
Mergus cucullatus	Anas cristatus	1.94	Round crested duck	15.437
Colymbus podiceps	Prodicipes minor rostro vario	1.91	Pied bill dopchick	15.383
Ardea Herodias	Ardea cristata maxima Americana	3.10	Largest crested heron	14.113
Ardea violacea	Ardea stellaris cristata Americana	1.79	Crested bittern	14.134
Ardea cærulea	Ardea cærulea	1.76	Blue heron. Crane	14.131
Ardea virescens	Ardea stellaris minima	1.80	Small bittern	14.142
Ardea æquinoctialis	Ardea alba minor Caroliniensis	1.77	Little white heron	14.136
	Ardea stellaris Americana	1.78	Brown bittern. Indian hen	14.175
Tantalus loculator	Pelicanus Americanus	1.81	Wood pelican	13.403
Tantalus alber	Numenius albus	1.82	White curlew	15.62
Tantalus fuscus	Numenius fuscus	1.83	Brown curlew	15.64
Charadrius vociferus	Pluvialis vociferus	1.71	Chattering plover. Kildee	15.151
Haematopus ostralegus	Haematopus	1.85	Oyster Catcher	15.185
Rallus Virginianus	Gallinula Americana	1.70	Soree. Ral-bird	15.256
Meleagris Gallopavo	Gallopavo Sylvestris	xliv.	Wild turkey	3.187.229

Linnean Designation.	Catesby's Designation.		Popular Names.	*Buffon oiseaux.*
Tetrao Virginianus	Perdix Sylvestris Virginiana	3.12	American partridge. American quail	4.237
	Urogallus minor, or a kind of Lagopus	3.1	Pheasant. Mountain partridge	3.409
Columba passerina	Turtur minimus guttatus	1.26	Ground dove	4.404
Columba migratoria	Palumbus migratorius	1.23	Pigeon of passage. Wild pigeon	4.351
Columba Caroliniensis	Turtur Caroliniensis	1.24	Turtle. Turtle dove	4.401
Alauda alpestris	Alauda gutture flavo	1.32	Lark. Sky lark	9.79
Alauda magna	Alauda magna	1.33	Field lark. Large lark	6.59
	Sturnus niger alis superné rubentibus	1.13	Red winged starling. Marsh blackbird	5.293
Turdus migratorius	Turdus pilaris migratorius	1.29	Fieldfare of Carolina. Robin redbreast	{ 5.426 / 9.257
Turdus rufus	Turdus ruffus	1.28	Fox coloured thrush. Thrush	5.449
Turdus polyglottos	Turdus minor cinereo albus non maculatus	1.27	Mocking bird	5.451
	Turdus minimus	1.31	Little thrush	5.400
Ampelis garrulus. β.	Garrulus Caroliniensis	1.46	Chatterer	6.162
Loxia Cardinalis	Coccothraustes rubra	1.38	Red bird. Virginia nightingale	6.185
Loxia Cærulea	Coccothraustes cærulea	1.39	Blue gross beak	8.125
Emberiza hyemalis	Passer nivalis	1.36	Snow bird	8.47
Emberiza Oryzivora	Hortulanus Caroliniensis	1.14	Rice bird	8.49
Emberiza Ciris	Fringilla tricolor	1.44	Painted finch	7.247
Tanagra cyanea	Linaria cærulea	1.45	Blue linnet	7.122
	Passerculus	1.35	Little sparrow	7.120
	Passer fuscus	1.34	Cowpen bird	7.196

Fringilla erythrophthalma	Passer niger oculis rubris	1.34	Towhe bird	7.201
Fringilla tristis	Carduelis Americanus	1.43	American goldfinch. Lettuce bird	7.297
	Fringilla purpurea	1.41	Purple finch	8.129
Muscicapa crinita	Muscicapa cristata vent-e luteo	1.52	Crested flycather	8.379
Muscicapa rubra	Muscicapa rubra	1.56	Summer red bird	8.410
Muscicapa ruticilla	Ruticilla Americana	1.67	Red start	{ 8.349 / 9.259
Muscicapa Caroliniensis	Muscicapa vertice nigro	1.66	Cat bird	8.372
	Muscicapa nigrescens	1.53	Black-cap flycatcher	8.341
	Muscicapa fusca	1.54	Little brown flycatcher	8.344
	Muscicapa oculis rubris	1.54	Red-eyed flycather	8.337
Motacilla Sialis	Rubicula Americana cærulea	1.47	Blue bird	9.308
Motacilla regulus	Regulus cristatus	3.13	Wren	10.58
Motacilla trochilus. β.	Oenanthe Americana pectore luteo	1.50	Yellow-breasted chat	6.96
Parus bicolor	Parus cristatus	1.57	Crested titmouse	10.181
Parus Americanus	Parus fringillaris	1.64	Finch creeper	9.442
Parus Virginianus	Parus uropygeo luteo	1.58	Yellow rump	10.184
	Parus cucullo nigro	1.60	Hooded titmouse	10.183
	Parus Americanus gutture luteo	1.62	Yellow-throated creeper	
	Parus Caroliniensis	1.63	Yellow titmouse	
Hirundo Pelasgia	Hirundo cauda aculeata Americana	3.8	American swallow	9.431
Hirundo purpurea	Hirundo purpurea	1.51	Purple martin. House martin	12.478
Caprimulgus Europaeus α	Caprimulgus	1.8	Goatsucker. Great bat	12.445
Caprimulgus Europaeus β	Caprimulgus minor Americanus	3.16	Whip-poor Will	12.243 / 12.246

Besides these, we have

The Royston crow. Corvus
    cornix.
Crane. Ardea Canadensis.
House swallow. Hirundo
    rustica.
Ground swallow. Hirundo
    riparia.
Greatest grey eagle.
Smaller turkey buzzard,
    with a feathered head.
Greatest owl, or night-
    hawk.
Wethawk, which feeds
    flying.
Raven.
Water pelican of the Missi-
    sipi, whose pouch holds
    a peck.
Swan.
Loon.

The Cormorant.
Duck and Mallard.
Widgeon.
Sheldrach, or Canvas back.
Black head.
Ballcoot.
Sprigtail.
Didapper, or Dopchick.
Spoon billed duck.
Water-witch.
Water-pheasant.
Mow-bird.
Blue peter.
Water wagtail.
Yellow-legged snipe.
Squatting snipe.
Small plover.
Whistling plover.
Woodcock.
Red bird, with black head,
    wings and tail.

And doubtless many others which have not yet been described and classed.

To this catalogue of our indigenous animals, I will add a short account of an anomaly of nature, taking place sometimes in the race of negroes brought from Africa, who, though black themselves, have in rare instances, white children, called Albinos. I have known four of these myself, and have faithful accounts of three others. The circumstances in which all the individuals agree are these. They are of a pallid cadaverous white, untinged with red, without any coloured spots or seams; their hair of the same kind of white, short, coarse, and curled as is that of the negro; all of them well formed, strong, healthy, perfect in their senses, except that of sight, and born of parents who had no mixture of white blood. Three of these Albinos were sisters, having two other full sisters, who were black. The youngest of the three was killed by lightning, at twelve years of age. The eldest died at about 27 years of age, in child-bed, with her second child. The middle one is now alive in health, and has issue, as the eldest had, by a black man, which issue was black. They are uncommonly shrewd, quick in their apprehensions and in reply. Their eyes are in a perpetual tremulous vibration, very weak, and much affected by the sun: but they see better in the night than we do. They are of the property of Col. Skipwith, of Cumberland. The fourth is a negro woman, whose parents came from Guinea, and had three other children, who were of their own colour. She is freckled, her eye-sight so weak that she is obliged to wear a bonnet in the summer; but it is better in the night than day. She had an Albino child by a black man. It died at the age of a few weeks. These were the property of Col. Carter, of Albemarle. A sixth instance is a woman of the property of a Mr. Butler, near Petersburgh. She is stout and robust, has issue a daughter, jet black, by a black man. I am not informed as to her eye sight. The seventh instance is of a male belonging to a Mr. Lee, of Cumberland. His eyes are tremulous and weak. He is tall of stature, and now advanced in years. He is the only male of the Albinos which have come within my information. Whatever be the cause of the disease in the skin, or in its colouring matter, which produces this change, it seems more incident to the female than male sex. To these I may add the mention of a negro man within my own knowledge, born black, and of black parents; on whose chin, when a boy, a white spot appeared. This continued to increase till he became a man, by which time it had extended over his chin, lips, one cheek, the under jaw and neck on that side. It is of the Albino white, without any mixture of red, and has for several years been stationary. He is robust and healthy, and the change of colour was not accompanied with any sensible disease, either general or topical.

Of our fish and insects there has been nothing like a full description or collection. More of them are described in Catesby than in any other work. Many also are to be found in Sir Hans Sloane's[2] Jamaica, as being common to that and this country. The honey-bee is not a native of our continent. Marcgrave[3] indeed mentions a species of honey-bee in Brasil. But this has no sting, and is therefore different from the one we have, which resembles perfectly that of Europe. The Indians concur with us in the tradition that it was brought from Europe; but when, and by whom, we know not. The bees have generally extended themselves into the country, a little in advance, of the white settlers. The Indians therefore call them the white man's fly, and consider their approach as indicating the approach of the settlements of the whites. A question here occurs, How far northwardly have these insects been found? That they are unknown in Lapland, I infer from Scheffer's[4] information, that the Laplanders eat the pine bark, prepared in a certain way, instead of those things sweetened with sugar. "Hoc comedunt pro rebus saccharo conditis." Scheff. Lapp. c. 18. Certainly, if they had honey, it would be a better substitute for sugar than any preparation of the pine bark. Kalm tells us the honey bee cannot live through the winter in Canada. They furnish then an additional proof of the remarkable fact first observed by the Count de Buffon, I. 126. and which has thrown such a blaze of light on the field of natural history, that no animals are found in both continents, but those which are able to bear the cold of those regions where they probably join.

2. Sir Hans Sloane (1660–1753), British physician and collector, published A Voyage to the Islands of Madera, Barbados, Nieves, St. Christophers and Jamaica, often referred to as his Natural History of Jamaica, in two parts, in 1707 and 1725.
3. Astronomer Georg Marcgraf (1610–1644) and physician Willem Piso (1611–1678) jointly produced Historia Naturalis Brasiliae (1648).
4. Johannes Scheffer (1621–1679) published his account of Lapland, Joannis Schefferi Argentoratensis Lapponis . . . in 1673; although it was translated into English the following year, Jefferson here quotes (and translates) the Latin original.

Query VII

A notice of all what can increase the   Climate
progress of human knowledge?

Under the latitude of this query, I will presume it not improper nor unacceptable to furnish some data for estimating the climate of Virginia. Journals of observations on the quantity of rain, and degree of heat, being lengthy, confused, and too minute to produce general and distinct ideas, I have taken five years observations, to wit, from 1772 to 1777, made in Williamsburgh and its neighbourhood, have reduced them to an average for every month in the year, and stated those averages in the following table, adding an analytical view of the winds during the same period.

The rains of every month, (as of January for instance) through the whole period of years, were added separately, and an average drawn from them. The coolest and warmest point of the same day in each year of the period were added separately, and an average of the greatest cold and greatest heat of that day, was formed. From the averages of every day in the month, a general average for the whole month was formed. The point from which the wind blew was observed two or three times in every day. These observations, in the month of January for instance, through the whole period amounted to 337. At 73 of these, the wind was from the North; at 47, from the North-east, &c. So that it will be easy to see in what proportion each wind usually prevails in each month: or, taking the whole year, the total of observations through the whole period having been 3698, it will be observed that 611 of them were from the North, 558 from the North-east, &c.

Though by this table it appears we have on an average 47 inches of rain annually, which is considerably more than usually falls in Europe, yet from the information I have collected, I suppose we have a much greater proportion of sunshine here than there. Perhaps it will be found there are twice as many cloudy days in the middle parts of Europe, as in the United States of America. I mention the middle parts of Europe, because my information does not extend to its northern or southern parts.

In an extensive country, it will of course be expected that the climate is not the same in all its parts. It is remarkable that, proceeding on the same parallel of latitude westwardly, the climate becomes colder in like manner as when you proceed northwardly. This continues to be the case till you attain the summit of the Alleghaney, which is the highest land between the ocean and the Missisipi. From thence, descending in the same latitude to the Missisipi, the change reverses; and, if we may believe travellers, it becomes warmer there than it is in the same latitude on the sea side. Their testimony is strengthened by the vegetables and animals which subsist and multiply there naturally, and do not on our sea coast. Thus Catalpas grow spontaneously on the Missisipi, as far as the latitude of 37°. and reeds as far as 38°. Perroquets even winter on the Sioto, in the 39th degree of latitude. In the summer of 1779, when the thermometer was at 90°. at Monticello, and 96 at Williamsburgh, it was 110°. at Kaskaskia. Perhaps the mountain, which overhangs this village on the North side, may, by its reflexion, have contributed somewhat to produce this heat. The difference of temperature of the air at the sea coast, or on Chesapeak bay, and at the Alleghaney, has not been ascertained; but cotemporary observations, made

	Fall of rain, &c. in inches.	Least & greatest daily heat by Farenheit's thermometer. 8.A.M.	to 4.P.M.	N.	N. E.	E.	S. E.	S.	S. W.	W.	N. W.	Total.
								W I N D S.				
Jan.	3.192	38½	44	72	47	32	10	11	78	40	46	337
Feb.	2.049	41	47½	61	52	24	11	4	63	30	31	276
Mar.	3.95	48	54½	49	44	38	28	14	83	29	33	318
April	3.68	56	62½	35	44	54	19	9	58	18	20	257
May	2.871	63	70½	27	36	62	23	7	74	32	20	281
June	3.751	71½	78¼	22	34	43	24	13	81	25	25	267
July	4.497	77	82½	41	44	75	15	7	95	32	19	328
Aug.	9.153	76¼	81	43	52	40	30	9	103	27	30	334
Sept.	4.761	69½	74¼	70	60	51	18	10	81	18	37	345
Oct.	3.633	61¼	66½	52	77	64	15	6	56	23	34	327
Nov.	2.617	47¾	53½	74	21	20	14	9	63	35	58	294
Dec.	2.877	43	48¾	64	37	18	16	10	91	42	56	334
Total.	47.038	8.A.M.	4.P.M.	611	548	521	223	109	926	351	409	3698

at Williamsburgh, or in its neighbourhood, and at Monticello, which is on the most eastern ridge of mountains, called the South West, where they are intersected by the Rivanna, have furnished a ratio by which that difference may in some degree be conjectured. These observations make the difference between Williamsburgh and the nearest mountains, at the position before mentioned, to be on an average 6⅛ degrees of Farenheit's thermometer. Some allowance however is to be made for the difference of latitude between these two places, the latter being 38°. 8'. 17". which is 52'. 22". North of the former. By cotemporary observations of between five and six weeks, the averaged and almost unvaried difference of the height of mercury in the barometer, at those two places, was .784 of an inch, the atmosphere at Monticello being so much the lightest, that is to say, about 1/37 of its whole weight. It should be observed, however, that the hill of Monticello is of 500 feet perpendicular height above the river which washes its base. This position being nearly central between our northern and southern boundaries, and between the bay and Alleghaney, may be considered as furnishing the best average of the temperature of our climate. Williamsburgh is much too near the South-eastern corner to give a fair idea of our general temperature.

But a more remarkable difference is in the winds which prevail in the different parts of the country. The following table exhibits a comparative view of the winds prevailing at Williamsburgh, and at Monticello. It is formed by reducing nine months observations at Monticello to four principal points, to wit, the North-east, South-east, South-west, and North-west; these points being perpendicular to, or parallel with our coast, mountains and rivers: and by reducing, in like manner, an equal number of observations, to wit, 421. from the preceding table of winds at Williamsburgh, taking them proportionably from every point.

	N. E.	S. E.	S. W.	N. W.	Total.
Williamsburgh	127	61	132	101	421
Monticello	32	91	126	172	421

By this it may be seen that the South-west wind prevails equally at both places; that the North-east is, next to this, the principal wind towards the sea coast, and the North-west is the predominant wind at the mountains. The difference between these two winds to sensation, and in fact, is very great. The North-east is loaded with vapour, insomuch, that the salt makers have found that their crystals would not shoot while that blows; it brings a distressing chill, is heavy and oppressive to the spirits: the North-west is dry, cooling, elastic and animating. The Eastern and South-eastern breezes come on generally in the afternoon. They have advanced into the country very sensibly within the memory of people now living. They formerly did not penetrate far above Williamsburgh. They are now frequent at Richmond, and every now and then reach the mountains. They deposit most of their moisture however before they get that far. As the lands become more cleared, it is probable they will extend still further westward.

Going out into the open air, in the temperate, and in the warm months of the year, we often meet with bodies of warm air, which, passing by us in two or three seconds, do not afford time to the most sensible thermometer to seize their temperature. Judging from my feelings only, I think they approach the ordinary heat of the human body. Some of them perhaps go a little beyond it. They are of about 20 or 30 feet diameter horizontally. Of their height we have no experience; but probably they are globular volumes wafted or rolled along with the wind. But whence taken, where found, or how generated? They are not to be ascribed to Volcanos, because we have none. They do not happen in the winter when the farmers kindle large fires in clearing up their grounds. They are not confined to the spring season, when we have fires which traverse whole counties, consuming the leaves which have fallen from the trees. And they are too frequent and general to be ascribed to accidental fires. I am persuaded their cause must be sought for in the atmosphere itself, to aid us in which I know but of these constant circumstances; a dry air; a temperature as warm at least as that of the spring or autumn; and a moderate current of wind. They are most frequent about sun-set; rare in the middle parts of the day; and I do not recollect having ever met with them in the morning.

The variation in the weight of our atmosphere, as indicated by the barometer, is not equal to two inches of mercury. During twelve months observation at Williamsburgh, the extremes were 29, and 30.86 inches, the difference being 1.86 of an inch: and in nine months, during which the height of the mercury was noted at Monticello, the extremes were 28.48 and 29.69 inches, the variation being 1.21 of an inch. A gentleman, who has observed his barometer many years, assures me it has never varied two inches. Cotemporary observations, made at Monticello and Williamsburgh, proved the variations in the weight of air to be simultaneous and corresponding in these two places.

Our changes from heat to cold, and cold to heat, are very sudden and great. The mercury in Farenheit's thermometer has been known to descend from 92°. to 47°. in thirteen hours.

It is taken for granted, that the preceding table of averaged heat will not give a false idea on this subject, as it proposes to state only the ordinary heat and cold of each month, and not those which are extraordinary. At Williamsburgh in August 1766, the mercury in Farenheit's thermometer was at 98°. corresponding with 29⅓ of Reaumur. At the same place in January 1780, it was at 6°. corresponding with 11 ½ below 0. of Reaumur. I believe these[5] may be considered to be nearly the extremes of heat and cold in that part of the country. The latter may most certainly, as, at that time, York river, at York town, was frozen over, so that people walked across it; a circumstance which proves it to have been colder than the winter of 1740, 1741, usually called the cold winter, when York river did not freeze over at that place. In the same season of 1780, Chesapeak bay was solid, from its head to the mouth of Patowmac. At Annapolis, where it is 5¼ miles over between the nearest points of land, the ice was from 5 to 7 inches thick quite across, so that loaded carriages went over on it. Those, our extremes of heat and cold, of 6°. and 98°. were indeed very distressing to us, and were thought to put the extent of the human constitution to considerable

5. At Paris, in 1753, the mercury in Reaumur's thermometer was at 30½ above 0, and in 1776, it was at 16 below 0. The extremities of heat and cold therefore at Paris, are greater than at Williamsburgh, which is in the hottest part of Virginia [Jefferson's note].

trial. Yet a Siberian would have considered them as scarcely a sensible variation. At Jenniseitz in that country, in latitude 58°. 27'. we are told, that the cold in 1735 sunk the mercury by Farenheit's scale to 126°. below nothing; and the inhabitants of the same country use stove rooms two or three times a week, in which they stay two hours at a time, the atmosphere of which raises the mercury to 135°. above nothing. Late experiments shew that the human body will exist in rooms heated to 140°. of Reaumur, equal to 347°. of Farenheit, and 135°. above boiling water. The hottest point of the 24 hours is about four o'clock, P.M. and the dawn of day the coldest.

The access of frost in autumn, and its recess in the spring, do not seem to depend merely on the degree of cold; much less on the air's being at the freezing point. White frosts are frequent when the thermometer is at 47°. have killed young plants of Indian corn at 48°. and have been known at 54°. Black frost, and even ice, have been produced at 38½°. which is 6½ degrees above the freezing point. That other circumstances must be combined with the cold to produce frost, is evident from this also, that on the higher parts of mountains, where it is absolutely colder than in the plains on which they stand, frosts do not appear so early by a considerable space of time in autumn, and go off sooner in the spring, than in the plains. I have known frosts so severe as to kill the hiccory trees round about Monticello, and yet not injure the tender fruit blossoms then in bloom on the top and higher parts of the mountain; and in the course of 40 years, during which it has been settled, there have been but two instances of a general loss of fruit on it: while, in the circumjacent country, the fruit has escaped but twice in the last seven years. The plants of tobacco, which grow from the roots of those which have been cut off in the summer, are frequently green here at Christmas. This privilege against the frost is undoubtedly combined with the want of dew on the mountains. That the dew is very rare on their higher parts, I may say with certainty, from 12 years observations, having scarcely ever, during that time, seen an unequivocal proof of its existence on them at all during summer. Severe frosts in the depth of winter prove that the region of dews extends higher in that season than the tops of the mountains: but certainly, in the summer season, the vapours, by the time they attain that height, are become so attenuated as not to subside and form a dew when the sun retires.

The weavil has not yet ascended the high mountains.

A more satisfactory estimate of our climate to some, may perhaps be formed, by noting the plants which grow here, subject however to be killed by our severest colds. These are the fig, pomegranate, artichoke, and European walnut. In mild winters, lettuce and endive require no shelter; but generally they need a slight covering. I do not know that the want of long moss, reed, myrtle, swamp laurel, holly and cypress, in the upper country, proceeds from a greater degree of cold, nor that they were ever killed with any degree of cold in the lower country. The aloe lived in Williamsburgh in the open air through the severe winter of 1779, 1780.

A change in our climate however is taking place very sensibly. Both heats and colds are become much more moderate within the memory even of the middle-aged. Snows are less frequent and less deep. They do not often lie, below the mountains, more than one, two, or three days, and very rarely a week. They are remembered to have been formerly frequent, deep, and of long continuance. The elderly inform me the earth used to be covered with snow about three months in every year. The rivers, which then seldom failed to freeze over in the course of the winter, scarcely ever do so now. This change has produced an unfortunate fluctuation between heat and cold, in the spring of the year, which is very fatal to fruits. From the year 1741 to 1769, an interval of twenty-eight years, there was no instance of fruit killed by the frost in the neighbourhood of Monticello. An intense cold, produced by constant snows, kept the buds locked up till the sun could obtain, in the spring of the year, so fixed an ascendency as to dissolve those snows, and protect the buds, during their developement, from every danger of returning cold. The accumulated snows of the winter remaining to be dissolved all together in the spring, produced those overflowings of our rivers, so frequent then, and so rare now.

Having had occasion to mention the particular situation of Monticello for other purposes, I will just take notice that its elevation affords an opportunity of seeing a phænomenon which is rare at land, though frequent at sea. The seamen call it *looming*. Philosophy is as yet in the rear of the seamen, for so far from having accounted for it, she has not given it a name. Its principal effect is to make distant objects appear larger, in opposition to the general law of vision, by which they are diminished. I knew an instance, at York town, from whence the water prospect eastwardly is without termination, wherein a canoe with three men, at a great distance, was taken for a ship with its three masts. I am little acquainted with the phænomenon as it shews itself at sea; but at Monticello it is familiar. There is a solitary mountain about 40 miles off, in the South, whose natural shape, as presented to view there, is a regular cone; but, by the effect of looming, it sometimes subsides almost totally into the horizon; sometimes it rises more acute and more elevated; sometimes it is hemispherical; and sometimes its sides are perpendicular, its top flat, and as broad as its base. In short it assumes at times the most whimsical shapes, and all these perhaps successively in the same morning. The Blue ridge of mountains comes into view, in the North East, at about 100 miles distance, and, approaching in a direct line, passes by within 20 miles, and goes off to the South-west. This phænomenon begins to shew itself on these mountains, at about 50 miles distance, and continues beyond that as far as they are seen. I remark no particular state, either in the weight, moisture, or heat of the atmosphere, necessary to produce this. The only constant circumstances are, its appearance in the morning only, and on objects at least 40 or 50 miles distant. In this latter circumstance, if not in both, it differs from the looming on the water. Refraction will not account for this metamorphosis. That only changes the proportions of length and breadth, base and altitude, preserving the general outlines. Thus it may make a circle appear elliptical, raise or depress a cone, but by none of its laws, as yet developed, will it make a circle appear a square, or a cone a sphere.

Query VIII

The number of its inhabitants?   Population

The following table shews the number of persons imported for the establishment of our colony in its infant state, and the census of inhabitants at different periods, extracted from our historians and public records, as particularly as I have had opportunities and leisure to examine them. Successive lines in the same year shew successive periods of time in that year. I have stated the census in two different columns, the whole inhabitants having been sometimes numbered, and sometimes the *tythes* only. This term, with us, includes the free males above 16 years of age, and slaves above that age of both sexes. A further examination of our records would render this history of our population much more satisfactory and perfect, by furnishing a greater number of intermediate terms. Those however which are here stated will enable us to calculate, with a considerable degree of precision, the rate at which we have increased. During the infancy of the colony, while numbers were small, wars, importations, and other accidental circumstances render the progression fluctuating and irregular. By the year 1654, however, it becomes tolerably uniform, importations having in a great measure ceased from the dissolution of the company, and the inhabitants become too numerous to be sensibly affected by Indian wars. Beginning at that period, therefore, we find that from thence to the year 1772, our tythes had increased from 7209 to 153,000. The whole term being of 118 years, yields a duplication once in every 27¼ years. The intermediate enumerations taken in 1700, 1748, and 1759, furnish proofs of the uniformity of this progression. Should this rate of increase continue, we shall have between six and seven millions of inhabitants within 95 years. If we suppose our country to be bounded, at some future day, by the meridian of the mouth of the Great Kanhaway, (within which it has been before conjectured, are 64,491 square miles) there will then be 100 inhabitants for every square mile, which is nearly the state of population in the British islands.

Here I will beg leave to propose a doubt. The present desire of America is to produce rapid population by as great importations of foreigners as possible. But is this founded in good policy? The advantage proposed is the multiplication of numbers. Now let us suppose (for example only) that, in this state, we could double our numbers in one year by the importation of foreigners; and this is a greater accession than the most sanguine advocate for emigration has a right to expect. Then I say, beginning with a double stock, we shall attain any given degree of population only 27 years and 3 months sooner than if we proceed on our single stock. If we propose four millions and a half as a competent population for this state, we should be 54½ years attaining it, could we at once double our numbers; and 81¾ years, if we rely on natural propagation, as may be seen by the following table.

In the first column are stated periods of 27¼ years; in the second are our numbers, at each period, as they will be if we proceed on our actual stock; and in the third are what they would be, at the same periods, were we to set out from the double of our present stock. I have taken the term of four millions and a half of inhabitants for example's sake only. Yet I am persuaded it is a greater number than the country spoken of, considering how much inarrable land it contains, can clothe and feed, without a material change in the quality of their diet. But are there no inconveniences to be thrown into the scale against the advantage expected from a multiplication of numbers by the importation of foreigners? It is for the happiness of those united in society to harmonize as much as possible in matters which they must of

Years	Settlers imported.	Census of Inhabitants.	Census of Tythes.
1607	100		
		40	
	120		
1608		130	
	70		
1609		490	
	16		
		60	
1610	150		
		200	
1611	3 ship loads		
	300		
1612	80		
1617		400	
1618	200		
	40		
		600	
1619	1216		
1621	1300		
1622		3800	
		2500	
1628		3000	
1632			2000
1644			4822
1645			5000
1652			7000
1654			7209
1700			22,000
1748			82,100
1759			105,000
1772			153,000
1782		567,614	

necessity transact together. Civil government being the sole object of forming societies, its administration must be conducted by common consent. Every species of government has its specific principles. Ours perhaps are more peculiar than those of any other in the universe. It is a composition of the freest principles of the English constitution, with others derived from natural right and natural reason. To these nothing can be more opposed than the maxims of absolute monarchies. Yet, from such, we are to expect the greatest number of emigrants. They will bring with them the principles of the governments they leave, imbibed in their early youth; or, if able to throw them off, it will be in exchange for an unbounded licentiousness, passing, as is usual, from one extreme to another. It would be a miracle were they to stop precisely at the point of temperate liberty. These principles, with their language, they will transmit to their children. In proportion to their numbers, they will share with us the legislation. They will infuse into it their spirit, warp and bias its direction, and render it a heterogeneous, incoherent, distracted mass. I may appeal to experience, during the present contest, for a verification of these conjectures. But, if they be not certain in event, are they not possible, are they not probable? Is it not safer to wait with patience 27 years and three months longer, for the attainment of any degree of

	Proceeding on our present stock.	Proceeding on a double stock.
1781	567,614	1,135,228
1808 ¼	1,135,228	2,270,456
1835 ½	2,270,456	4,540,912
1862 ¾	4,540,912	

population desired, or expected? May not our government be more homogeneous, more peaceable, more durable? Suppose 20 millions of republican Americans thrown all of a sudden into France, what would be the condition of that kingdom? If it would be more turbulent, less happy, less strong, we may believe that the addition of half a million of foreigners to our present numbers would produce a similar effect here. If they come of themselves, they are entitled to all the rights of citizenship: but I doubt the expediency of inviting them by extraordinary encouragements. I mean not that these doubts should be extended to the importation of useful artificers. The policy of that measure depends on very different considerations. Spare no expence in obtaining them. They will after a while go to the plough and the hoe; but, in the mean time, they will teach us something we do not know. It is not so in agriculture. The indifferent state of that among us does not proceed from a want of knowledge merely; it is from our having such quantities of land to waste as we please. In Europe the object is to make the most of their land, labour being abundant: here it is to make the most of our labour, land being abundant.

It will be proper to explain how the numbers for the year 1782 have been obtained; as it was not from a perfect census of the inhabitants. It will at the same time develope the proportion between the free inhabitants and slaves. The following return of taxable articles for that year was given in.

  53,289 free males above 21 years of age.
 211,698 slaves of all ages and sexes.
  23,766 not distinguished in the returns, but said to be titheable
       slaves.
 195,439 horses.
 609,734 cattle.
   5,126 wheels of riding-carriages.
    191 taverns.

There were no returns from the 8 counties of Lincoln, Jefferson, Fayette, Monongalia, Yohogania, Ohio, Northampton, and York. To find the number of slaves which should have been returned instead of the 23,766 titheables, we must mention that some observations on a former census had given reason to believe that the numbers above and below 16 years of age were equal. The double of this number, therefore, to wit, 47,532 must be added to 211,698, which will give us 259,230 slaves of all ages and sexes. To find the number of free inhabitants, we must repeat the observation, that those above and below 16 are nearly equal. But as the number 53,289 omits the males between 16 and 21, we must supply them from conjecture. On a former experiment it had appeared that about one-third of our militia, that is, of the males between 16 and 50, were unmarried. Knowing how early marriage takes place here, we shall not be far wrong in supposing that the unmarried part of our militia are those between 16 and 21. If there be young men who do not marry till after 21, there are as many who marry before that age. But as the men above 50 were not included in the militia, we will suppose the unmarried, or those between 16 and 21, to be one-fourth of the whole number above 16, then we have the following calculation:

53,289	free males above 21 years of age.
17,763	free males between 16 and 21.
71,052	free males under 16.
142,104	free females of all ages.
284,208	free inhabitants of all ages.
259,230	slaves of all ages.

543,438 inhabitants, exclusive of the 8 counties from which were no returns. In these 8 counties in the years 1779 and 1780 were 3,161 militia. Say then,

3,161	free males above the age of 16.
3,161	ditto under 16.
6,322	free females.

12,644 free inhabitants in these 8 counties. To find the number of slaves, say, as 284,208 to 259,230, so is 12,644 to 11,532. Adding the third of these numbers to the first, and the fourth to the second, we have,

296,852	free inhabitants,
270,762	slaves.

567,614 inhabitants of every age, sex, and condition. But 296,852, the number of free inhabitants, are to 270,762, the number of slaves, nearly as 11 to 10. Under the mild treatment our slaves experience, and their wholesome, though coarse, food, this blot in our country increases as fast, or faster, than the whites. During the regal government, we had at one time obtained a law, which imposed such a duty on the importation of slaves, as amounted nearly to a prohibition, when one inconsiderate assembly, placed under a peculiarity of circumstance, repealed the law. This repeal met a joyful sanction from the then sovereign, and no devices, no expedients, which could ever after be attempted by subsequent assemblies, and they seldom met without attempting them, could succeed in getting the royal assent to a renewal of the duty. In the very first session held under the republican government, the assembly passed a law for the perpetual prohibition of the importation of slaves. This will in some measure stop the increase of this great political and moral evil, while the minds of our citizens may be ripening for a complete emancipation of human nature.

Query IX

The number and condition of the militia and   Military
regular troops, and their pay?

The following is a state of the militia, taken from returns of 1780 and 1781, except in those counties marked with an asterisk, the returns from which are somewhat older.

Situation.	Counties.	Militia.	Situation.	Counties.	Militia.
Westward of the Allegany. 4458.	Lincoln	600	Between James river and Carolina. 6959.	Greenesville	500
	Jefferson	300		Dinwiddie	*750
	Fayette	156		Chesterfield	655
	Ohio			Prince George	382
	Monongalia	*1000		Surry	380
	Washington	*829		Sussex	*700
	Montgomery	1071		Southampton	874
	Green-briar	502		Isle of Wight	*600
				Nansemond	*644
Between the Allegany and Blue ridge. 7673.	Hampshire	930		Norfolk	*880
	Berkeley	*1100		Princess Anne	*594
	Frederick	1143	Between James and York rivers. 3009.	Henrico	619
	Shenando	*925		Hanover	796
	Rockingham	875		New Kent	*418
	Augusta	1375		Charles City	286
	Rockbridge	*625		James city	235
	Botetourt	*700		Williamsburg	129
Between the Blue ridge and Tide waters. 18,828	Loudoun	1746		York	*244
	Fauquier	1078		Warwick	*100
	Culpeper	1513		Elizabeth City	182
	Spotsylvania	480	Between York and Rappahanock. 3269.	Caroline	805
	Orange	*600		King William	436
	Louisa	603		King & Queen	500
	Goochland	*550		Essex	468
	Fluvanna	*296		Middlesex	*210
	Albemarle	873		Gloucester	850
	Amherst	896	Between Rappahanoc & Patowmac. 4137.	Fairfax	652
	Buckingham	*625		Prince William	614
	Bedford	1300		Stafford	*500
	Henry	1004		King George	483
	Pittsylvania	*725		Richmond	412
	Halifax	*1139		Westmoreland	544
	Charlotte	612		Northumberl.	630
	Prince Edward	589		Lancaster	302
	Cumberland	408	East. Shore. 1638.	Accomac	*1208
	Powhatan	330		Northampton	*430
	Amelia	*1125	Whole Militia of the State		49,971
	Lunenburg	677			
	Mecklenburg	1100			
	Brunswic	559			

ON THE TIDE WATERS AND IN THAT PARALLEL. 19,012.

Every able-bodied freeman, between the ages of 16 and 50, is enrolled in the militia. Those of every county are formed into companies, and these again into one or more battalions, according to the numbers in the county. They are commanded by colonels, and other subordinate officers, as in the regular service. In every county is a county-lieutenant, who commands the whole militia of his county, but ranks only as a colonel in the field. We have no general officers always existing. These are appointed occasionally, when an invasion or insurrection happens, and their commission determines with the occasion. The governor is head of the military, as well as civil power. The law requires every militia-man to provide himself with the arms usual in the regular service. But this injunction was always indifferently complied with, and the arms they had have been so frequently called for to arm the regulars, that in the lower parts of the country they are entirely disarmed. In the middle country a fourth or fifth part of them may have such firelocks as they had provided to destroy the noxious animals which infest their farms; and on the western side of the Blue ridge they are generally armed with rifles. The pay of our militia, as well as of our regulars, is that of the Continental regulars. The condition of our regulars, of whom we have none but Continentals, and part of a battalion of state troops, is so constantly on the change, that a state of it at this day would not be its state a month hence. It is much the same with the condition of the other Continental troops, which is well enough known.

Query X

The marine? Marine

Before the present invasion of this state by the British under the command of General Phillips,[6] we had three vessels of 16 guns, one of 14, five small gallies, and two or three armed boats. They were generally so badly manned as seldom to be in condition for service. Since the perfect possession of our rivers assumed by the enemy, I believe we are left with a single armed boat only.

Query XI

A description of the Indians established Aborigines
in that state?

When the first effectual settlement of our colony was made, which was in 1607, the country from the sea-coast to the mountains, and from Patowmac to the most southern waters of James river, was occupied by upwards of forty different tribes of Indians. Of these the *Powhatans*, the *Mannahoacs*, and *Monacans*, were the most powerful. Those between the sea-coast and falls of the rivers, were in amity with one another, and attached to the *Powhatans* as their link of union. Those between the falls of the rivers and

---

6. William Phillips (1731–1781), British general who led the invasion of Virginia in 1781, had been Jefferson's guest at Monticello earlier in the war, following his capture at Saratoga.

	TRIBES.	COUNTRY.	CHIEF TOWN.	1607	1669	TRIBES.
	M A N N A H O A C S.			WARRIORS.		
Between PATOWMAC and RAPPAHANOC.	Whonkenties	Fauquier				Tauxenents
	Tegninaties	Culpeper				Patówomekes
						Cuttatawomans
	Ontponies	Orange				Pissasecs
						Onaumanients
	Tàuxitanians	Fauquier				Rappahànocs
						Moràughtacunds
						Secacaonies
	Hassinungaes	Culpeper				Wighcocòmicoes
						Cuttatawomans
Between RAPPAHANOC and YORK.	Stegarakies	Orange				Nantaughtacunds
	Shackakonies	Spotsylvania				Màttapomènts
	Mannahoacs	Stafford				Pamùnkies
		Spotsylvania				Wèrowocòmicos
						Payànkatanks
	M O N A C A N S.					Youghtanunds
						Chickahòminies
Between YORK and JAMES.	Monacans	James R. above the falls	Fork of James R.		30	Powhatàns
						Arrowhàtocs
						Wèanocs
						Paspahèghes
	Monasicca panoes	Louisa. Fluvanna				Chìskiacs
						Kecoughtáns
Between JAMES and CAROLINA.	Monahassanoes	Bedford. Buckingham				Appamàttocs
						Quiocohànocs
	Massinacacs	Cumberland				Wàrrasqeaks
	Mohemenchoes	Powhatan				Nansamònds
						Chèsapeaks
EASTERN SHORE.						Accohanocs
						Accomàcks

the mountains, were divided into two confederacies; the tribes inhabiting the head waters of Patowmac and Rappahanoc being attached to the *Mannahoacs*; and those on the upper parts of James river to the *Monacans*. But the *Monacans* and their friends were in amity with the *Mannahoacs* and their friends, and waged joint and perpetual war against the *Powhatans*. We are told that the *Powhatans*, *Mannahoacs*, and *Monacans*, spoke languages so radically different, that interpreters were necessary when they transacted business. Hence we may conjecture, that this was not the case between all the tribes, and probably that each spoke the language of the nation to which it was attached; which we know to have been the case in many particular instances. Very possibly there may have been antiently three different stocks, each of which multiplying in a long course of time, had separated into so many little societies. This practice results from the circumstance of their having never submitted themselves to any laws, any coercive power, any shadow of government. Their only controuls are their manners, and that moral sense of right and wrong, which, like the sense of tasting and feeling, in every man makes a part of his nature. An offence against these is punished by contempt, by exclusion from society, or, where the case is serious, as that of murder, by the individuals whom it concerns.

N O R T H.

| P | O | W | H | A | T | A | N | S. |

Country.	Chief Town.	Warriors.		
		1607	1669	
Fairfax	About General Washington's	40		
Stafford. King George	Patowmac creek	200		By the name of
King George	About Lamb creek	20		Matchotics. U.
King Geo. Richmond	Above Leeds town	–	60	Matchodic. Nanza-
Westmoreland	Nomony river	100		ticos. Nanzatico.
Richmond county	Rappahanoc creek	100	30	Appamatox Matox.
Lancaster. Richmond	Moratico river	80	40	
Northumberland	Coan river	30		by the name of
Northumberland	Wicocomico river	130	70	Totuskeys.
Lancaster	Corotoman	30		
Essex. Caroline	Port tobacco creek	150	60	
Mattapony river	– – – –	30	20	
King William	Romuncock	300	50	
Gloucester	About Rosewell	40		
Piankatank river	Turk's Ferry. Grimesby	55		
Pamunkey river	– – – –	60		
Chickahominy river	Orapaks	250	60	
Henrico	Powhatan. Mayo's	40	10	
Henrico	Arrohatocs	30		
Charles city	Weynoke	100	15	
Charles city. James city	Sandy point	40		
York	Chiskiac	45	15	
Elizabeth city	Roscows	20		
Chesterfield	Bermuda hundred	60	50	
Surry	About Upper Chipoak	25	3 Pohics	Nottoways 1669
Isle of Wight	Warrasqueac			Meherrics 90
Nansamond	About the mouth of West. branch	200	45	Tuteloes 50
Princess Anne	About Lynhaven river	100		
Accom. Northampton	Accohanoc river	40		
Northampton	About Cheriton's	80		

S O U T H.

Imperfect as this species of coercion may seem, crimes are very rare among them: insomuch that were it made a question, whether no law, as among the savage Americans, or too much law, as among the civilized Europeans, submits man to the greatest evil, one who has seen both conditions of existence would pronounce it to be the last: and that the sheep are happier of themselves, than under care of the wolves. It will be said, that great societies cannot exist without government. The Savages therefore break them into small ones.

The territories of the *Powhatan* confederacy, south of the Patowmac, comprehended about 8000 square miles, 30 tribes, and 2400 warriors. Capt. Smith[7] tells us, that within 60 miles of James town were 5000 people, of whom 1500 were warriors. From this we find the proportion of their warriors to their whole inhabitants, was as 3 to 10. The *Powhatan* confederacy then would consist of about 8000 inhabitants, which was one for every square mile; being about the twentieth part of our present population in the same territory, and the hundredth of that of the British islands.

7. Captain John Smith (1580–1631), soldier and adventurer, had been one of the early leaders of the Jamestown settlement and later compiled *The Generall Historie of New-England, Virginia and the Summer Isles* (1624).

Besides these, were the *Nottoways*, living on Nottoway river, the *Meherrins* and *Tuteloes* on Meherrin river, who were connected with the Indians of Carolina, probably with the Chowanocs.

The preceding table contains a state of these several tribes, according to their confederacies and geographical situation, with their numbers when we first became acquainted with them, where these numbers are known. The numbers of some of them are again stated as they were in the year 1669, when an attempt was made by the assembly to enumerate them. Probably the enumeration is imperfect, and in some measure conjectural, and that a further search into the records would furnish many more particulars. What would be the melancholy sequel of their history, may however be augured from the census of 1669; by which we discover that the tribes therein enumerated were, in the space of 62 years, reduced to about one-third of their former numbers. Spirituous liquors, the small-pox, war, and an abridgment of territory, to a people who lived principally on the spontaneous productions of nature, had committed terrible havock among them, which generation,[8] under the obstacles opposed to it among them, was not likely to make good. That the lands of this country were taken from them by conquest, is not so general a truth as is supposed. I find in our historians and records, repeated proofs of purchase, which cover a considerable part of the lower country; and many more would doubtless be found on further search.[9] The upper country we know has been acquired altogether by purchases made in the most unexceptionable form.

Westward of all these tribes, beyond the mountains, and extending to the great lakes, were the *Massawomecs*, a most powerful confederacy, who harrassed unremittingly the *Powhatans* and *Manahoacs*. These were probably the ancestors of the tribes known at present by the name of the *Six Nations*.

Very little can now be discovered of the subsequent history of these tribes severally. The *Chickahominies* removed, about the year 1661, to Mattapony river. Their chief, with one from each of the tribes of the Pamunkies and Mattaponies, attended the treaty of Albany in 1685. This seems to have been the last chapter in their history. They retained however their separate name so late as 1705, and were at length blended with the Pamunkies and Mattaponies, and exist at present only under their names. There remain of the *Mattaponies* three or four men only, and they have more negro than Indian blood in them. They have lost their language, have reduced themselves, by voluntary sales, to about fifty acres of land, which lie on the river of their own name, and have, from time to time, been joining the Pamunkies, from whom they are distant but 10 miles. The *Pamunkies* are reduced to about 10 or 12 men, tolerably pure from mixture with other colours. The older ones among them preserve their language in a small degree, which are the last vestiges on earth, as far as we know, of the Powhatan language. They have about 300 acres of very fertile land, on Pamunkey river, so encompassed by water that a gate shuts in the whole. Of the *Nottoways*, not a male is left. A few women constitute the remains of that tribe. They are seated on Nottoway river, in Southampton county, on very fertile lands. At a very early period, certain lands were marked out and appropriated to these tribes, and

---

8. Reproduction.
9. Here Jefferson's manuscript contains the deleted observation, "it is true that these purchases were sometimes made with the price in one hand and the sword in the other" (Peden, 281).

were kept from encroachment by the authority of the laws. They have usually had trustees appointed, whose duty was to watch over their interests, and guard them from insult and injury.

The *Monacans* and their friends, better known latterly by the name of *Tuscaroras*, were probably connected with the Massawomecs, or Five Nations. For though we are told[1] their languages were so different that the intervention of interpreters was necessary between them, yet do we also learn[2] that the Erigas, a nation formerly inhabiting on the Ohio, were of the same original stock with the Five Nations, and that they partook also of the Tuscarora language. Their dialects might, by long separation, have become so unlike as to be unintelligible to one another. We know that in 1712, the Five Nations received the Tuscaroras into their confederacy, and made them the Sixth Nation. They received the Meherrins and Tuteloes also into their protection: and it is most probable, that the remains of many other of the tribes, of whom we find no particular account, retired westwardly in like manner, and were incorporated with one or other of the western tribes.[3]

I know of no such thing existing as an Indian monument: for I would not honour with that name arrow, points, stone hatchets, stone pipes, and half-shapen images. Of labour on the large scale, I think there is no remain as respectable as would be a common ditch for the draining of lands: unless indeed it be the Barrows, of which many are to be found all over this country. These are of different sizes, some of them constructed of earth, and some of loose stones. That they were repositories of the dead, has been obvious to all: but on what particular occasion constructed, was matter of doubt. Some have thought they covered the bones of those who have fallen in battles fought on the spot of interment. Some ascribed them to the custom, said to prevail among the Indians, of collecting, at certain periods, the bones of all their dead, wheresoever deposited at the time of death. Others again supposed them the general sepulchres for towns, conjectured to have been on or near these grounds; and this opinion was supported by the quality of the lands in which they are found, (those constructed of earth being generally in the softest and most fertile meadow-grounds on river sides) and by a tradition, said to be handed down from the Aboriginal Indians, that, when they settled in a town, the first person who died was placed erect, and earth put about him, so as to cover and support him; that, when another died, a narrow passage was dug to the first, the second reclined against him, and the cover of earth replaced, and so on. There being one of these in my neighbourhood, I wished to satisfy myself whether any, and which of these opinions were just. For this purpose I determined to open and examine it thoroughly. It was situated on the low grounds of the Rivanna, about two miles above its principal fork, and opposite to some hills, on which had been an Indian town. It was of a spheroidical form, of about 40 feet diameter at the base, and had been of about twelve feet altitude, though now reduced by the plough to seven and a half, having been under cultivation about a dozen years. Before this it was covered with trees of twelve inches diameter, and round the base was an excavation of five feet depth and width, from whence the earth had been taken of which

1. Smith [Jefferson's note].
2. Evans [Jefferson's note].
3. For Charles Thomson's discussion of the tribes of the middle colonies, see Appendix No. I, section 5 (p. 162).

the hillock was formed. I first dug superficially in several parts of it, and came to collections of human bones, at different depths, from six inches to three feet below the surface. These were lying in the utmost confusion, some vertical, some oblique, some horizontal, and directed to every point of the compass, entangled, and held together in clusters by the earth. Bones of the most distant parts were found together, as, for instance, the small bones of the foot in the hollow of a scull, many sculls would sometimes be in contact, lying on the face, on the side, on the back, top or bottom, so as, on the whole, to give the idea of bones emptied promiscuously from a bag or basket, and covered over with earth, without any attention to their order. The bones of which the greatest numbers remained, were sculls, jaw-bones, teeth, the bones of the arms, thighs, legs, feet, and hands. A few ribs remained, some vertebræ of the neck and spine, without their processes, and one instance only of the bone[4] which serves as a base to the vertebral column. The sculls were so tender, that they generally fell to pieces on being touched. The other bones were stronger. There were some teeth which were judged to be smaller than those of an adult; a scull, which, on a slight view, appeared to be that of an infant, but it fell to pieces on being taken out, so as to prevent satisfactory examination; a rib, and a fragment of the under-jaw of a person about half grown; another rib of an infant; and part of the jaw of a child, which had not yet cut its teeth. This last furnishing the most decisive proof of the burial of children here, I was particular in my attention to it. It was part of the right-half of the under-jaw. The processes, by which it was articulated to the temporal bones, were entire; and the bone itself firm to where it had been broken off, which, as nearly as I could judge, was about the place of the eye-tooth. Its upper edge, wherein would have been the sockets of the teeth, was perfectly smooth. Measuring it with that of an adult, by placing their hinder processes together, its broken end extended to the penultimate grinder of the adult. This bone was white, all the others of a sand colour. The bones of infants being soft, they probably decay sooner, which might be the cause so few were found here. I proceeded then to make a perpendicular cut through the body of the barrow, that I might examine its internal structure. This passed about three feet from its center, was opened to the former surface of the earth, and was wide enough for a man to walk through and examine its sides. At the bottom, that is, on the level of the circumjacent plain, I found bones; above these a few stones, brought from a cliff a quarter of a mile off, and from the river one-eighth of a mile off; then a large interval of earth, then a stratum of bones, and so on. At one end of the section were four strata of bones plainly distinguishable; at the other, three; the strata in one part not ranging with those in another. The bones nearest the surface were least decayed. No holes were discovered in any of them, as if made with bullets, arrows, or other weapons. I conjectured that in this barrow might have been a thousand skeletons. Every one will readily seize the circumstances above related, which militate against the opinion, that it covered the bones only of persons fallen in battle; and against the tradition also, which would make it the common sepulchre of a town, in which the bodies were placed upright, and touching each other. Appearances certainly indicate that it has derived both origin and growth from the accustomary collection of bones, and deposition of them together; that the first collection had been deposited on the common surface

4. The os sacrum [Jefferson's note].

of the earth, a few stones put over it, and then a covering of earth, that the second had been laid on this, had covered more or less of it in proportion to the number of bones, and was then also covered with earth; and so on. The following are the particular circumstances which give it this aspect, 1. The number of bones. 2. Their confused position. 3. Their being in different strata. 4. The strata in one part having no correspondence with those in another. 5. The different states of decay in these strata, which seem to indicate a difference in the time of inhumation. 6. The existence of infant bones among them.

But on whatever occasion they may have been made, they are of considerable notoriety among the Indians: for a party passing, about thirty years ago, through the part of the country where this barrow is, went through the woods directly to it, without any instructions or enquiry, and having staid about it some time, with expressions which were construed to be those of sorrow, they returned to the high road, which they had left about half a dozen miles to pay this visit, and pursued their journey. There is another barrow, much resembling this in the low grounds of the South branch of Shenandoah, where it is crossed by the road leading from the Rock-fish gap to Staunton. Both of these have, within these dozen years, been cleared of their trees and put under cultivation, are much reduced in their height, and spread in width, by the plough, and will probably disappear in time. There is another on a hill in the Blue ridge of mountains, a few miles North of Wood's gap, which is made up of small stones thrown together. This has been opened and found to contain human bones, as the others do. There are also many others in other parts of the country.[5]

Great question has arisen from whence came those aboriginal inhabitants of America? Discoveries, long ago made, were sufficient to shew that a passage from Europe to America was always practicable, even to the imperfect navigation of ancient times. In going from Norway to Iceland, from Iceland to Groenland, from Groenland to Labrador, the first traject is the widest: and this having been practised from the earliest times of which we have any account of that part of the earth, it is not difficult to suppose that the subsequent trajects may have been sometimes passed. Again, the late discoveries of Captain Cook,[6] coasting from Kamschatka to California, have proved that, if the two continents of Asia and America be separated at all, it is only by a narrow streight. So that from this side also, inhabitants may have passed into America: and the resemblance between the Indians of America and the Eastern inhabitants of Asia, would induce us to conjecture, that the former are the descendants of the latter, or the latter of the former: excepting indeed the Eskimaux, who, from the same circumstance of resemblance, and from identity of language, must be derived from the Groenlanders, and these probably from some of the northern parts of the old continent. A knowledge of their several languages would be the most certain evidence of their derivation which could be produced. In fact, it is the best proof of the affinity of nations which ever can be referred to. How many ages have elapsed since the English, the Dutch, the Germans, the Swiss, the Norwegians, Danes and Swedes have separated from their common stock? Yet how many more must elapse before the proofs of their common origin, which exist in their several languages, will disappear? It is to be lamented then, very much to be lamented, that we have suffered so many of the Indian tribes already

5. Thomson's comment on Native American burial customs is found in Appendix No. I, section 6 (p. 166).
6. Captain James Cook (1728–1779), explorer of North America and the Pacific Ocean.

to extinguish, without our having previously collected and deposited in the records of literature, the general rudiments at least of the languages they spoke. Were vocabularies formed of all the languages spoken in North and South America, preserving their appellations of the most common objects in nature, of those which must be present to every nation barbarous or civilised, with the inflections of their nouns and verbs, their principles of regimen and concord, and these deposited in all the public libraries, it would furnish opportunities to those skilled in the languages of the old world to compare them with these, now, or at any future time, and hence to construct the best evidence of the derivation of this part of the human race.

But imperfect as is our knowledge of the tongues spoken in America, it suffices to discover the following remarkable fact. Arranging them under the radical ones to which they may be palpably traced, and doing the same by those of the red men of Asia, there will be found probably twenty in America, for one in Asia, of those radical languages, so called because, if they were ever the same, they have lost all resemblance to one another. A separation into dialects may be the work of a few ages only, but for two dialects to recede from one another till they have lost all vestiges of their common origin, must require an immense course of time; perhaps not less than many people give to the age of the earth. A greater number of those radical changes of language having taken place among the red men of America, proves them of greater antiquity than those of Asia.

I will now proceed to state the nations and numbers of the Aborigines which still exist in a respectable and independant form. And as their undefined boundaries would render it difficult to specify those only which may be within any certain limits, and it may not be unacceptable to present a more general view of them, I will reduce within the form of a Catalogue all those within, and circumjacent to, the United States, whose, names and numbers have come to, my notice.[7] These are taken from four different lists, the first of which was given in the year 1759 to General Stanwix by George Croghan, Deputy agent for Indian affairs under Sir William Johnson; the second was drawn up by a French trader of considerable note, resident among the Indians many years, and annexed to Colonel Bouquet's printed account of his expedition in 1764. The third was made out by Captain Hutchins, who visited most of the tribes, by order, for the purpose of learning their numbers in 1768. And the fourth by John Dodge,[8] an Indian trader, in 1779, except the numbers marked*, which are from other information.

But, apprehending these might be different appellations for some of the tribes already enumerated, I have not inserted them in the table, but state them separately as worthy of further inquiry. The variations observable in numbering the same tribe may sometimes be ascribed to imperfect

7. For Thomson's comments and corrections on tribes listed in Jefferson's table, see Appendix No. I, section 7 (p. 166).
8. Jefferson's sources all shared deep familiarity with the emergent frontier of the late colonial era. John Dodge (1751–1800), Indian trader in the Great Lakes basin. John Stanwix (c. 1690–1765), British army officer who saw service on the Pennsylvania and New York frontiers in the 1750s. Irish-born George Croghan (c. 1720–1782), Indian agent and land developer in Pennsylvania and New York. Sir William Johnson (1715–1774), also a native of Ireland, soldier, New York land developer, and superintendent for Indian affairs in the northern colonies before the Revolution. Henry Bouquet (1719–1766), Swiss-born British officer who served in western Pennsylvania and then, during Pontiac's War (1764–65), in the Ohio country.

TRIBES.	Croghan. 1759.	Bouquet. 1764.	Hutchins. 1768.	Where they reside.
Oswegatchies	— —	— —	100	At Swagatchy, on the river St. Laurence
Connasedagoes	— —	— —		
Cohunnewagoes	— —	200	300	Near Montreal
Orondocs	— —	— —	100	Near Trois Rivieres
Abenakies	— —	350	150	Near Trois Rivieres
Little Algonkins	— —	— —	100	Near Trois Rivieres
Michmacs	— —	700	— —	River St. Laurence
Amelistes	— —	550	— —	River St. Laurence
Chalas	— —	130	— —	River St. Laurence
Nipissins	— —	400	— —	Towards the heads of the Ottawas river
Algonquins	— —	300	— —	Towards the heads of the Ottawas river
Round heads	— —	2500	— —	Riviere aux Tetes boules on the East side of Lake Superior
Messasagues	— —	2000	— —	Lakes Huron and Superior
Christinaux. Kris	— —	3000	— —	Lake Christinaux
Assinaboes	— —	1500	— —	Lake Assinaboes
Blancs, or Barbus	— —	1500	— —	
Sioux of the Meadows		2500		
Sioux of the Woods	10,000	1800	10,000	On the heads of the Missisipi and Westward
Sioux		—		of that river
Ajoues	— —	1100	— —	North of the Padoucas
Panis. White	— —	2000	— —	South of the Missouri
Panis. Freckled	— —	1700	— —	South of the Missouri
Padoucas	— —	500	— —	South of the Missouri
Grandes eaux	— —	1000	— —	
Canses	— —	1600	— —	South of the Missouri
Osages	— —	600	— —	South of the Missouri
Missouris	400	3000	— —	On the river Missouri
Arkanzas	— —	2000	— —	On the river Arkanzas
Caouitas	— —	700	— —	East of the Alibamous

Northward and Westward of the United States.

<table>
<tr><td></td><td>Croghan. 1759.</td><td>Bouquet. 1764.</td><td>Hutchins. 1768.</td><td>Dodge. 1779.</td><td>Where they reside.</td></tr>
</table>

TRIBES.	Croghan. 1759.	Bouquet. 1764.	Hutchins. 1768.	Dodge. 1779.	Where they reside.
Mohocks	—	——	160	100	Mohocks river. [of Susquehanna.
Onèidas	—	——	300	400	E. side of Oneida L. and head branches
Tuscaròras	—	——	200		Between the Oneidas and Onondagoes.
Onondàgoes	—	1550	260	230	Near Onondago L. [of Susquehanna.
Cayùgas	—	——	200	220	On the Cayuga L. near the N. branch
Sènecas	—	——	1000	650	On the waters of Susquehanna, of Ontario, and the heads of the Ohio.
Aughquàgahs	—	——	150	—	East branch of Susquehanna, and on Aughquagah.
Nánticocs	—	——	100	—	Utsanango, Chaghtnet, and Owegy, on the East branch of Susquehanna.
Mohìccons	—	——	100	—	In the same parts.
Conòies	—	——	30	—	In the same parts.
Sapòonies	—	——	30	—	At Diahago and other villages up the N. branch of Susquehanna.
Mùnsies	—	——	150	*150	At Diahago and other villages up the N. branch of Susquehanna.
Delawares, or Linnelinopies	—	—	150	*500	At Diahago and other villages up the N. branch of Susquehanna.
Delawares, or Linnelinopies	600	600	600		Between Ohio and L. Erie and the branches of Beaver creek, Cayahoga and Muskingham.
Shàwanees	400	500	300	300	Sioto and the branches of Muskingham.
Mìngoes	—	—	——	60	On a branch of Sioto.
Mohìccons	—	—	——	*60	
Cohunnewagos	—	—	300	—	Near Sandusky.
Wyandots	300	300	250	180	Near Fort St. Joseph's and Detroit.
Wyandots					
Twightwees	300	—	250	—	Miami river near Fort Miami.
Miamis	—	350	——	300	Miami river, about Fort St. Joseph.

Within the Limits of the United States.

TRIBES.	Croghan. 1759.	Bouquet. 1764.	Hutchins. 1768.	Dodge. 1779.	Where they reside.
Ouiàtonons	200	400	300	*300	On the banks of the Wabash, near Fort Ouiatonon.
Piànkishas	300	250	300	*400	On the banks of the Wabash, near Fort Ouiatonon.
Shàkies	—	—	200	—	On the banks of the Wabash, near Fort Ouiatonon.
Kaskaskias	— }	600	300	—	Near Kaskaskia.
Illinois	400 {		300	—	Near Cahokia. Qu. If not the same with the Mitchigamis?
Piorias	—	800	— —	—	On the Illinois R. called Pianrias, but supposed to mean Piorias.
Pouteòtamies	—	350	300	450	Near St. Joseph's and Fort Detroit.
Ottàwas	—	—	550	*300	Near St. Joseph's and Fort Detroit.
Chìppawas	—	—		—	On Saguinam bay of Lake Huron.
Ottawas	—	—	200	—	On Saguinam bay of Lake Huron.
Chippawas	—	—	400	—	Near Michillimakinac.
Ottawas	—	—	250	5450	Near Michillimakinac.
Chippawas	2000	5900	400		Near Fort St. Mary's on Lake Superior.
Chippawas	—	—	— —	—	Several other villages along the banks of Lake Superior. Numbers unknown.
Chippawas	—	—	— —	—	Near Puans bay, on Lake Michigan.
Shakies	200	400	550	—	Near Puans bay, on Lake Michigan.
Mynonàmies	—	—	— —	—	Near Puans bay, on Lake Michigan.
Ouisconsings	—	550	— —	—	Ouisconsing River.
Kìckapous	600	300	— —	250	
Otogamies. Foxes	—	—	— —	—	
Màscoutens	—	500		—	On Lake Michigan, and between that and the Missisipi.
Miscòthins	—	—	4000	—	
Outimacs	—	—	— —	—	
Musquakies	200	250	— —	250	

	TRIBES.	Croghan. 1759.	Bouquet. 1764.	Hutchins. 1768.	Dodge. 1779.	Where they reside.
Within the Limits of the United States.	Sioux. Eastern	—	—	——	500	On the Eastern heads of Missisipi, and the islands of Lake Superior.
				Galphin. 1768.		
	Cherokees	1500	2500	3000	—	Western parts of North Carolina.
	Chickasaws	—	750	500	—	Western parts of Georgia.
	Catawbas	—	150	——	—	On the Catawba R. in S. Carolina.
	Chacktaws	2000	4500	6000	—	Western parts of Georgia.
	Upper Creeks	—	—⎫	3000	—	Western parts of Georgia.
	Lower Creeks	—	1180⎰	3000		
	Natchez	—	150	——	—	
	Alibamous	—	600	——	—	Alibama R. in the Western parts of Georgia.

The following tribes are also mentioned:

Croghan's catal.
Lezar	400	From the mouth of Ohio to the mouth of Wabash.
Webings	200	On the Missisipi below the Shakies.
Ousasoys. Grand Tuc.	4000	On White creek, a branch of the Missisipi.
Linways	1000	On the Missisipi.

Bouquet's.
Les Puans	700	Near Puans bay.
Folle avoine	350	Near Puans bay.
Ouanakina	300	
Chiakanessou	350	
Machecous	800	Conjectured to be tribes of the creeks.
Souikilas	200	

Dodge's.
| Mineamis | 2000 | North-west of L. Michigan, to the heads of Missisipi, and up to L. Superior. |
| Piankishas Mascoutins Vermillions | 800 | On and near the Wabash, towards the Illinois. |

information, and sometimes to a greater or less comprehension of settlements under the same name.

Query XII

A *notice of the counties, cities,*   Counties, Towns
townships, and villages?

The counties have been enumerated under Query IX. They are 74 in
number, of very unequal size and population. Of these 35 are on the tide
waters, or in that parallel; 23 are in the Midlands, between the tide waters
and Blue ridge of mountains; 8 between the Blue ridge and Alleghaney; and
8 westward of the Alleghaney.

The state, by another division, is formed into parishes, many of which are
commensurate with the counties: but sometimes a county comprehends
more than one parish, and sometimes a parish more than one county. This
division had relation to the religion of the state, a Parson of the Anglican
church, with a fixed salary, having been heretofore established in each
parish. The care of the poor was another object of the parochial division.

We have no townships. Our country being much intersected with navigable waters, and trade brought generally to our doors, instead of our being
obliged to go in quest of it, has probably been one of the causes why we have
no towns of any consequence. Williamsburgh, which, till the year 1780, was
the seat of our government, never contained above 1800 inhabitants; and
Norfolk, the most populous town we ever had, contained but 6000. Our
towns, but more properly our villages or hamlets, are as follows.

On *James river* and its waters, Norfolk, Portsmouth, Hampton, Suffolk,
Smithfield, Williamsburgh, Petersburg, Richmond the seat of our government, Manchester, Charlottesville, New London.

On *York river* and its waters, York, Newcastle, Hanover.

On *Rappahannoc*, Urbanna, Portroyal, Fredericksburg, Falmouth.

On *Patowmac* and its waters, Dumfries, Colchester, Alexandria, Winchester, Staunton.

On *Ohio*, Louisville.

There are other places at which, like some of the foregoing, the *laws* have
said there shall be towns; but *Nature* has said there shall not, and they
remain unworthy of enumeration. *Norfolk* will probably be the emporium for
all the trade of the Chesapeak bay and its waters; and a canal of 8 or 10 miles
will bring to it all that of Albemarle sound and its waters. Secondary to this
place, are the towns at the head of the tidewaters, to wit, Petersburgh on
Appamattox, Richmond on James river, Newcastle on York river, Alexandria
on Patowmac, and Baltimore on the Patapsco. From these the distribution
will be to subordinate situations in the country. Accidental circumstances
however may controul the indications of nature, and in no instances do they
do it more frequently than in the rise and fall of towns.

Query XIII

Constitution   *The constitution of the state, and*
its several charters?

Queen Elizabeth by her letters-patent, bearing date March 25, 1584,
licensed Sir Walter Raleigh to search for remote heathen lands, not inhabited by Christian people, and granted to him, in fee simple, all the soil within
200 leagues of the places where his people should, within 6 years, make their
dwellings or abidings; reserving only, to herself and her successors, their allegiance and one fifth part of all the gold and silver ore they should obtain. Sir
Walter immediately sent out two ships which visited Wococon island in
North Carolina, and the next year dispatched seven with 107 men, who settled in Roanoke island, about latitude 35°. 50'. Here Okisko, king of the
Weopomeiocs, in a full council of his people, is said to have acknowledged
himself the homager of the Queen of England, and, after her, of Sir Walter
Raleigh. A supply of 50 men were sent in 1586, and 150 in 1587. With these
last, Sir Walter sent a Governor, appointed him twelve assistants, gave them
a charter of incorporation, and instructed them to settle on Chesapeak bay.
They landed however at Hatorask. In 1588, when a fleet was ready to sail
with a new supply of colonists and necessaries, they were detained by the
Queen to assist against the Spanish Armada. Sir Walter having now
expended 40,000 l. in these enterprizes, obstructed occasionally by the
crown, without a shilling of aid from it, was under a necessity of engaging
others to adventure their money. He therefore, by deed bearing date the 7th
of March 1589, by the name of Sir Walter Raleigh, Chief Governor of
Assamàcomòc, (probably Acomàc), alias Wingadacoia, alias Virginia, granted
to Thomas Smith and others, in consideration of their adventuring certain
sums of money, liberty of trade to his new country, free from all customs and
taxes for seven years, excepting the fifth part of the gold and silver ore to be
obtained; and stipulated with them, and the other assistants, then in Virginia, that he would confirm the deed of incorporation which he had given
in 1587, with all the prerogatives, jurisdictions, royalties and privileges
granted to him by the Queen. Sir Walter, at different times, sent five other
adventures hither, the last of which was in 1602: for in 1603 he was
attainted, and put into close imprisonment, which put an end to his cares
over his infant colony. What was the particular fate of the colonists he had
before sent and seated, has never been known: whether they were murdered,
or incorporated with the savages.

Some gentlemen and merchants, supposing that by the attainder of Sir
Walter Raleigh the grant to him was forfeited, not enquiring over carefully
whether the sentence of an English court could affect lands not within the
jurisdiction of that court, petitioned king James for a new grant of Virginia to
them. He accordingly executed a grant to Sir Thomas Gates and others, bearing date the 9th of March 1607, under which, in the same year a settlement
was effected at Jamestown and ever after maintained. Of this grant however
no particular notice need be taken, as it was superseded by letters-patent of
the same king, of May 23, 1609, to the Earl of Salisbury and others, incorporating them by the name of 'the Treasurer and Company of adventurers and
planters of the City of London for the first colony in Virginia,' granting to them
and their successors all the lands in Virginia from Point Comfort along the sea

coast to the northward 200 miles, and from the same point along the sea coast to the southward 200 miles, and all the space from this precinct on the sea coast up into the land, West and North-west, from sea to sea, and the islands within one hundred miles of it, with all the commodities, jurisdictions, royalties, privileges, franchises and preeminences within the same, and thereto and thereabouts, by sea and land, appertaining, in as ample manner as had before been granted to any adventurer: to be held of the king and his successors, in common soccage, yielding one fifth part of the gold and silver ore to be therein found, for all manner of services; establishing a council in England for the direction of the enterprise, the members of which were to be chosen and displaced by the voice of the majority of the company and adventurers, and were to have the nomination and revocation of governors, officers, and ministers, which by them should be thought needful for the colony, the power of establishing laws and forms of government and magistracy, obligatory not only within the colony, but also on the seas in going and coming to and from it; authorising them to carry thither any persons who should consent to go, freeing them for ever from all taxes and impositions on any goods or merchandize on importation into the colony, or exportation out of it, except the five per cent. due for custom on all goods imported into the British dominions, according to the ancient trade of merchants; which five per cent. only being paid, they might, within 13 months, re-export the same goods into foreign parts, without any custom, tax, or other duty, to the king or any his officers or deputies: with powers of waging war against those who should annoy them: giving to the inhabitants of the colony all the rights of natural subjects, as if born and abiding in England; and declaring that these letters should be construed, in all doubtful parts, in such manner as should be most for the benefit of the grantees.

Afterwards, on the 12th of March 1612, by other letters-patent, the king added to his former grants, all islands in any part of the ocean between the 30th and 41st degrees of latitude, and within 300 leagues of any of the parts before granted to the Treasurer and company, not being possessed or inhabited by any other christian prince or state, nor within the limits of the northern colony.

In pursuance of the authorities given to the company by these charters, and more especially of that part in the charter of 1609, which authorised them to establish a form of government, they on the 24th of July 1621, by charter under their common seal, declared that from thenceforward there should be two supreme councils in Virginia, the one to be called the council of state, to be placed and displaced by the treasurer, council in England, and company, from time to time, whose office was to be that of assisting and advising the governor; the other to be called the general assembly, to be convened by the governor once yearly or oftener, which was to consist of the council of state, and two burgesses out of every town, hundred, or plantation, to be respectively chosen by the inhabitants. In this all matters were to be decided by the greater part of the votes present; reserving to the governor a negative voice; and they were to have power to treat, consult, and conclude all emergent occasions concerning the public weal, and to make laws for the behoof and government of the colony, imitating and following the laws and policy of England as nearly as might be: providing that these laws should have no force till ratified in a general quarter court of the company in England, and returned under their common seal, and declaring that, after the government of the colony should be well framed and settled, no orders of the council in England should bind the colony unless ratified in the said general assembly. The king and company quarrelled, and, by a mixture of law and force, the latter were ousted of all their rights, without retribution, after having expended 100,000 l. in establishing the colony, without the smallest aid from government. King James suspended their powers by proclamation of July 15, 1624, and Charles I. took the government into his own hands. Both sides had their partisans in the colony: but in truth the people of the colony in general thought themselves little concerned in the dispute. There being three parties interested in these several charters, what passed between the first and second it was thought could not affect the third. If the king seized on the powers of the company, they only passed into other hands, without increase or diminution, while the rights of the people remained as they were. But they did not remain so long. The northern parts of their country were granted away to the Lords Baltimore and Fairfax, the first of these obtaining also the rights of separate jurisdiction and government. And in 1650 the parliament, considering itself as standing in the place of their deposed king, and as having succeeded to all his powers, without as well as within the realm, began to assume a right over the colonies, passing an act for inhibiting their trade with foreign nations. This succession to the exercise of the kingly authority gave the first colour for parliamentary interference with the colonies, and produced that fatal precedent which they continued to follow after they had retired, in other respects, within their proper functions. When this colony, therefore, which still maintained its opposition to Cromwell and the parliament, was induced in 1651 to lay down their arms, they previously secured their most essential rights, by a solemn convention, which having never seen in print, I will here insert literally from the records.

"ARTICLES[9] agreed on & concluded at James Cittie in Virginia for the surrendering and settling of that plantation under the obedience & goverment of the common wealth of England by the Commissioners of the Councill of state by authoritie of the parliamt. of England & by the Grand assembly of the Governour, Councill & Burgesses of that countrey.

"First it is agreed and consted that the plantation of Virginia, and all the inhabitants thereof shall be and remaine in due obedience and subjection to the Comon wealth of England, according to the lawes there established, and that this submission and subscription bee acknowledged a voluntary act not forced nor constrained by a conquest upon the countrey, and that they shall have & enjoy such freedomes and priviledges as belong to the free borne people of England, and that the former government by the Comissions and Instructions be void and null.

"2ly, Secondly that the Grand assembly as formerly shall convene & transact the affairs of Virginia wherein nothing is to be acted or done contrarie to the government of the Comon wealth of England & the lawes there established.

"3ly, That there shall be a full & totall remission and indempnitie of all acts, words, or writeings done or spoken against the parliament of England in relation to the same.

9. In this document and the one that follows it, Jefferson's source employed *ye*, the antique form of "the." This usage has been modernized here.

"4ly, That Virginia shall have & enjoy the antient bounds and Lymitts granted by the charters of the former kings, and that we shall seek a new charter from the parliament to that purpose against any that have intrencht upon the rights thereof.

"5ly, That all the patterns of land granted under the collony seale by any of the precedent governours shall be & remaine in their full force & strength.

"6ly, That the priviledge of haveing ffiftie acres of land for every person transported in that collonie shall continue as formerly granted.

"7ly, That the people of Virginia have free trade as the people of England do enjoy to all places and with all nations according to the lawes of that common wealth, and that Virginia shall enjoy all priviledges equall with any English plantations in America.

"8ly, That Virginia shall be free from all taxes, customs & impositions whatsoever, & none to be imposed on them without consent of the Grand assembly, And soe that neither ffortes nor castles bee erected or garrisons maintained without their consent.

"9ly, That noe charge shall be required from this country in respect of this present ffleet.

"10ly, That for the future settlement of the countrey in their due obedience, the Engagement shall be tendred to all the inhabitants according to act of parliament made to that purpose, that all persons who shall refuse to subscribe the said engagement, shall have a yeare's time if they please to remove themselves & their estates out of Virginia, and in the mean time during the said yeare to have equall justice as formerly.

"11ly, That the use of the booke of common prayer shall be permitted for one yeare ensueinge with referrence to the consent of the major part of the parishes, provided that those things which relate to kingshipp or that government be not used publiquely, and the continuance of ministers in their places, they not misdemeaning themselves, and the payment of their accustomed dues and agreements made with them respectively shall be left as they now stand dureing this ensueing yeare.

"12ly, That no man's cattell shall be questioned as the companies unles such as have been entrusted with them or have disposed of them without order.

"13ly, That all ammunition, powder & armes, other then for private use, shall be delivered up, securitie being given to make satisfaction for it.

"14ly, That all goods allreadie brought hither by the Dutch or others which are now on shoar shall be free from surprizall.

"15ly, That the quittrents granted unto us by the late kinge for seaven yeares bee confirmed.

"16ly, That the commissioners for the parliament subscribeing these articles engage themselves & the honour of the parliament for the full performance thereof: and that the present governour & the councill & the burgesses do likewise subscribe & engage the whole collony on their parts.

RICH. BENNETT.————Seale.
W^m. CLAIBORNE.————Seale.
EDMOND CURTIS.————Seale.

"Theise articles were signed & sealed by the Commissioners of the Councill of state for the Commonwealth of England the twelveth day of March 1651."

Then follow the articles stipulated by the governor and council, which relate merely to their own persons and property, and then the ensuing instrument:

"An act of indempnitie made att the surrender of the countrey."

"Whereas by the authoritie of the parliament of England wee the commissioners appointed by the councill of state authorized thereto having brought a fleete & force before James cittie in Virginia to reduce that collonie under the obedience of the commonwealth of England, & findeing force raised by the Governour & countrey to make opposition against the said ffleet whereby assured danger appearinge of the ruine & destruction of the plantation, for prevention whereof the Burgesses of all the severall plantations being called to advise & assist therein, uppon long & serious debate, and in sad contemplation of the greate miseries & certaine destruction which were soe neerely hovering over the whole countrey; Wee the said Comissioners have thought fitt & condescended and granted to signe & confirme under our hands, seales, & by our oath, Articles bearinge date with theise presents, and do further declare that by the authoritie of the parliament & commonwealth of England derived unto us theire Comissioners, that according to the articles in generall wee have granted an act of indempnitie and oblivion to all the inhabitants of this colloney from all words, actions, or writings that have been spoken acted or writt against the parliament or commonwealth of England or any other person from the beginning of the world to this daye. And this wee have done that all the inhabitants of the collonie may live quietly & securely under the comonwealth of England. And wee do promise that the parliament and commonwealth of England shall confirme & make good all those transactions of ours. Wittnes our hands & seales this 12th of March 1651. Richard Bennett—Seale. W^m. Claiborne—Seale. Edm. Curtis—Seale.'

The colony supposed, that, by this solemn convention, entered into with arms in their hands, they had secured the antient[1] limits of their country, its[2] free trade, its exemption from taxation[3] but by their own assembly, and exclusion of military[4] force from among them. Yet in every of these points was this convention violated by subsequent kings and parliaments, and other infractions of their constitution, equally dangerous, committed. Their General Assembly, which was composed of the council of state and burgesses, sitting together and deciding by plurality of voices, was split into two houses, by which the council obtained a separate negative on their laws. Appeals from their supreme court, which had been fixed by law in their General Assembly, were arbitrarily revoked to England, to be there heard before the king and council. Instead of four hundred miles on the sea coast, they were reduced, in the space of thirty years, to about one hundred miles. Their trade with foreigners was totally suppressed, and, when carried to Great-Britain, was there loaded with imposts. It is unnecessary, however, to glean up the several instances of injury, as scattered through American and British history, and the more especially as, by passing on to the accession of the present king, we shall find specimens of them all, aggravated, multiplied and

1. Art. 4 [Jefferson's note].
2. Art. 7 [Jefferson's note].
3. Art. 8 [Jefferson's note].
4. Art. 8 [Jefferson's note].

crouded within a small compass of time, so as to evince a fixed design of considering our rights natural, conventional and chartered as mere nullities. The following is an epitome of the first fifteen years of his reign. The colonies were taxed internally and externally; their essential interests sacrificed to individuals in Great-Britain; their legislatures suspended; charters annulled; trials by juries taken away; their persons subjected to transportation across the Atlantic, and to trial before foreign judicatories; their supplications for redress thought beneath answer; themselves published as cowards in the councils of their mother country and courts of Europe; armed troops sent among them to enforce submission to these violences; and actual hostilities commenced against them. No alternative was presented but resistance, or unconditional submission. Between these could be no hesitation. They closed in the appeal to arms. They declared themselves independent States. They confederated together into one great republic; thus securing to every state the benefit of an union of their whole force. In each state separately a new form of government was established. Of ours particularly the following are the outlines. The executive powers are lodged in the hands of a governor, chosen annually, and incapable of acting more than three years in seven. He is assisted by a council of eight members. The judiciary powers are divided among several courts, as will be hereafter explained. Legislation is exercised by two houses of assembly, the one called the house of Delegates, composed of two members from each county, chosen annually by the citizens possessing an estate for life in 100 acres of uninhabited land, or 25 acres with a house on it, or in a house or lot in some town: the other called the Senate, consisting of 24 members, chosen quadrennially by the same electors, who for this purpose are distributed into 24 districts. The concurrence of both houses is necessary to the passage of a law. They have the appointment of the governor and council, the judges of the superior courts, auditors, attorney-general, treasurer, register of the land office, and delegates to congress. As the dismemberment of the state had never had its confirmation, but, on the contrary, had always been the subject of protestation and complaint, that it might never be in our own power to raise scruples on that subject, or to disturb the harmony of our new confederacy, the grants to Maryland, Pennsylvania, and the two Carolinas, were ratified.

This constitution[5] was formed when we were new and unexperienced in the science of government. It was the first too which was formed in the whole United States. No wonder then that time and trial have discovered very capital defects in it.

1. The majority of the men in the state, who pay and fight for its support, are unrepresented in the legislature, the roll of freeholders intitled to vote, not including generally the half of those on the roll of the militia, or of the tax-gatherers.

2. Among those who share the representation, the shares are very unequal. Thus the county of Warwick, with only one hundred fighting men, has an equal representation with the county of Loudon, which has 1746. So that every man in Warwick has as much influence in the government as 17 men in Loudon. But lest it should be thought that an equal interspersion of small among large counties, through the whole state, may prevent any danger of

5. Jefferson printed the Virginia Constitution as Appendix No. II (p. 167).

	Square miles.	Fighting men.	Dele-gates	Sena-tors.
Between the sea-coast and falls of the rivers	11,205[6]	19,012	71	12
Between the falls of the rivers and the Blue ridge of mountains	18,759	18,828	46	8
Between the Blue ridge and the Alleghaney	11,911	7,673	16	2
Between the Alleghaney and the Ohio	79,650[7]	4,458	16	2
Total	121,525	49,971	149	24

injury to particular parts of it, we will divide it into districts, and shew the proportions of land, of fighting men, and of representation in each.

An inspection of this table will supply the place of commentaries on it. It will appear at once that nineteen thousand men, living below the falls of the rivers, possess half the senate, and want four members only of possessing a majority of the house of delegates; a want more than supplied by the vicinity of their situation to the seat of government, and of course the greater degree of convenience and punctuality with which their members may and will attend in the legislature. These nineteen thousand, therefore, living in one part of the country, give law to upwards of thirty thousand, living in another, and appoint all their chief officers executive and judiciary. From the difference of their situation and circumstances, their interests will often be very different.

3. The senate is, by its constitution, too homogeneous with the house of delegates. Being chosen by the same electors, at the same time, and out of the same subjects, the choice falls of course on men of the same description. The purpose of establishing different houses of legislation is to introduce the influence of different interests or different principles. Thus in Great-Britain it is said their constitution relies on the house of commons for honesty, and the lords for wisdom; which would be a rational reliance if honesty were to be bought with money, and if wisdom were hereditary. In some of the American states the delegates and senators are so chosen, as that the first represent the persons, and the second the property of the state. But with us, wealth and wisdom have equal chance for admission into both houses. We do not therefore derive from the separation of our legislature into two houses, those benefits which a proper complication of principles is capable of producing, and those which alone can compensate the evils which may be produced by their dissensions.

4. All the powers of government, legislative, executive, and judiciary, result to the legislative body. The concentrating these in the same hands is precisely the definition of despotic government. It will be no alleviation that these powers will be exercised by a plurality of hands, and not by a single one. 173 despots would surely be as oppressive as one. Let those who doubt it turn their eyes on the republic of Venice. As little will it avail us that they are chosen by ourselves. An *elective despotism* was not the government we fought for; but one which should not only be founded on free principles, but in which the powers of government should be so divided and balanced among several bodies of magistracy, as that no one could transcend their legal limits, without being effectually checked and restrained by the others. For this reason

6. Of these, 542 are on the Eastern shore [Jefferson's note].
7. Of these, 22,616 are Eastward of the meridian of the mouth of the Great Kanhaway [Jefferson's note].

that convention, which passed the ordinance of government, laid its foundation on this basis, that the legislative, executive and judiciary departments
should be separate and distinct, so that no person should exercise the powers
of more than one of them at the same time. But no barrier was provided
between these several powers. The judiciary and executive members were left
dependant on the legislative, for their subsistence in office, and some of them
for their continuance in it. If therefore the legislature assumes executive and
judiciary powers, no opposition is likely to be made; nor, if made, can it be
effectual; because in that case they may put their proceedings into the form
of an act of assembly, which will render them obligatory on the other
branches. They have accordingly, in many instances, decided rights which
should have been left to judiciary controversy: and the direction of the executive, during the whole time of their session, is becoming habitual and familiar. And this is done with no ill intention. The views of the present members
are perfectly upright. When they are led out of their regular province, it is by
art in others, and inadvertence in themselves. And this will probably be the
case for some time to come. But it will not be a very long time. Mankind soon
learn to make interested uses of every right and power which they possess,
or may assume. The public money and public liberty, intended to have been
deposited with three branches of magistracy, but found inadvertently to be in
the hands of one only, will soon be discovered to be sources of wealth and
dominion to those who hold them; distinguished too by this tempting circumstance, that they are the instrument, as well as the object of acquisition.
With money we will get men, said Cæsar, and with men we will get money.
Nor should our assembly be deluded by the integrity of their own purposes,
and conclude that these unlimited powers will never be abused, because
themselves are not disposed to abuse them. They should look forward to a
time, and that not a distant one, when corruption in this, as in the country
from which we derive our origin, will have seized the heads of government,
and be spread by them through the body of the people; when they will purchase the voices of the people, and make them pay the price. Human nature
is the same on every side of the Atlantic, and will be alike influenced by the
same causes. The time to guard against corruption and tyranny, is before they
shall have gotten hold on us. It is better to keep the wolf out of the fold, than
to trust to drawing his teeth and talons after he shall have entered. To render
these considerations the more cogent, we must observe in addition,

    5. That the ordinary legislature may alter the constitution itself. On the
discontinuance of assemblies, it became necessary to substitute in their place
some other body, competent to the ordinary business of government, and to
the calling forth the powers of the state for the maintenance of our opposition to Great-Britain. Conventions were therefore introduced, consisting of
two delegates from each county, meeting together and forming one house, on
the plan of the former house of Burgesses, to whose places they succeeded.
These were at first chosen anew for every particular session. But in March
1775, they recommended to the people to chuse a convention, which should
continue in office a year. This was done accordingly in April 1775, and in the
July following that convention passed an ordinance for the election of delegates in the month of April annually. It is well known, that in July 1775, a separation from Great-Britain and establishment of Republican government
had never yet entered into any person's mind. A convention therefore, chosen under that ordinance, cannot be said to have been chosen for purposes

which certainly did not exist in the minds of those who passed it. Under this ordinance, at the annual election in April 1776, a convention for the year was chosen. Independance, and the establishment of a new form of government, were not even yet the objects of the people at large. One extract from the pamphlet called Common Sense[8] had appeared in the Virginia papers in February, and copies of the pamphlet itself had got into a few hands. But the idea had not been opened to the mass of the people in April, much less can it be said that they had made up their minds in its favor. So that the electors of April 1776, no more than the legislators of July 1775, not thinking of independance and a permanent republic, could not mean to vest in these delegates powers of establishing them, or any authorities other than those of the ordinary legislature. So far as a temporary organization of government was necessary to render our opposition energetic, so far their organization was valid. But they received in their creation no powers but what were given to every legislature before and since. They could not therefore pass an act transcendant to the powers of other legislatures. If the present assembly pass any act, and declare it shall be irrevocable by subsequent assemblies, the declaration is merely void, and the act repealable, as other acts are. So far, and no farther authorized, they organized the government by the ordinance entitled a Constitution or Form of government. It pretends to no higher authority than the other ordinances of the same session; it does not say, that it shall be perpetual; that it shall be unalterable by other legislatures; that it shall be transcendant above the powers of those, who they knew would have equal power with themselves. Not only the silence of the instrument is a proof they thought it would be alterable, but their own practice also: for this very convention, meeting as a House of Delegates in General Assembly with the new Senate in the autumn of that year, passed acts of assembly in contradiction to their ordinance of government; and every assembly from that time to this has done the same. I am safe therefore in the position, that the constitution itself is alterable by the ordinary legislature. Though this opinion seems founded on the first elements of common sense, yet is the contrary maintained by some persons. 1. Because, say they, the conventions were vested with every power necessary to make effectual opposition to Great-Britain. But to complete this argument, they must go on, and say further, that effectual opposition could not be made to Great-Britain, without establishing a form of government perpetual and unalterable by the legislature; which is not true. An opposition which at some time or other was to come to an end, could not need a perpetual institution to carry it on: and a government, amendable as its defects should be discovered, was as likely to make effectual resistance, as one which should be unalterably wrong. Besides, the assemblies were as much vested with all powers requisite for resistance as the conventions were. If therefore these powers included that of modelling the form of government in the one case, they did so in the other. The assemblies then as well as the conventions may model the government; that is, they may alter the ordinance of government. 2. They urge, that if the convention had meant that this instrument should be alterable, as their other ordinances were, they would have called it an ordinance: but they have called it a *constitution*, which ex vi termini[9] means "an act above the power of the ordinary legislature." I answer

8. *Common Sense*, by British immigrant Thomas Paine (1737–1809), first appeared in Philadelphia in January 1776.
9. From the force of the term (Latin).

that *constitutio, constitutum, statutum, lex,* are convertible terms. "*Constitutio* dicitur jus quod a principe conditur." "*Constitutum,* quod ab imperatoribus rescriptum statutumve est." "*Statutum,* idem quod lex." Calvini Lexicon juridicum.[1] *Constitution* and *statute* were originally terms of the civil law,[2] and from thence introduced by Ecclesiastics into the English law. Thus in the statute 25 Hen. 8. c. 19. §. 1.[3] "*Constitutions* and *ordinances*" are used as synonimous. The term *constitution* has many other significations in physics and in politics; but in Jurisprudence, whenever it is applied to any act of the legislature, it invariably means a statute, law, or ordinance, which is the present case. No inference then of a different meaning can be drawn from the adoption of this title: on the contrary, we might conclude, that, by their affixing to it a term synonimous with ordinance, or statute, they meant it to be an ordinance or statute. But of what consequence is their meaning, where their power is denied? If they meant to do more than they had power to do, did this give them power? It is not the name, but the authority which renders an act obligatory. Lord Coke[4] says, "an article of the statute II R. 2. c. 5. that no person should attempt to revoke any ordinance then made, is repealed, for that such restraint is against the jurisdiction and power of the parliament." 4. inst. 42. and again, "though divers parliaments have attempted to restrain subsequent parliaments, yet could they never effect it; for the latter parliament hath ever power to abrogate, suspend, qualify, explain, or make void the former in the whole or in any part thereof, notwithstanding any words of restraint, prohibition, or penalty, in the former: for it is a maxim in the laws of the parliament, quod leges posteriores priores contrarias abrogant."[5] 4. inst. 43.—To get rid of the magic supposed to be in the word *constitution*, let us translate it into its definition as given by those who think it above the power of the law; and let us suppose the convention instead of saying, "We, the ordinary legislature, establish a *constitution,*" had said, "We, the ordinary legislature, establish an act *above the power of the ordinary legislature.*" Does not this expose the absurdity of the attempt? 3. But, say they, the people have acquiesced, and this has given it an authority superior to the laws. It is true, that the people did not rebel against it: and was that a time for the people to rise in rebellion? Should a prudent acquiescence, at a critical time, be construed into a confirmation of every illegal thing done during that period? Besides, why should they rebel? At an annual election, they had chosen delegates for the year, to exercise the ordinary powers of legislation, and to manage the great contest in which they were engaged. These delegates thought the contest would be best managed by an organized government. They therefore, among others, passed an ordinance of government. They did not presume to call it perpetual and unalterable. They well knew they had no power

1. Jefferson quotes from the *Magnum Lexicon Juridicum* (1600) by the German jurist Johannis Kahl (c. 1550–1610), known as Johannes Calvinus. The English versions of the various Latin quotations, as given by Peden (123), run as follows: "A *constitution* is called that which is made by the ruler. An *ordinance,* that which is rewritten by emperors or ordained. A *statute* is called the same as a law."
2. To *bid,* to *set,* was the antient legislative word of the English. Ll. Hlotharii & Eadrici. Ll Inae. Ll. Eadwerdi. Ll. Aathelstani. [Jefferson's note]. Civil law is the system of law on the Continent that evolved from Roman practice. In his footnote, Jefferson refers to the "laws" (Ll.) dating from the reigns of various early local rulers in Britain.
3. Standard legal shorthand for referring to laws dating from the reigns of various English sovereigns— in this instance, to one derived from the twenty-fifth year of the reign of Henry VIII, chapter 9, section 1.
4. Edward Coke (1552–1634), lord chief justice of England and author of *Institutes of the Lawes of England* (1628-1644).
5. Because later laws cancel earlier ones (Latin).

to make it so; that our choice of them had been for no such purpose, and at a time when we could have no such purpose in contemplation. Had an unalterable form of government been meditated, perhaps we should have chosen a different set of people. There was no cause then for the people to rise in rebellion. But to what dangerous lengths will this argument lead? Did the acquiescence of the colonies under the various acts of power exercised by Great-Britain in our infant state, confirm these acts, and so far invest them with the authority of the people as to render them unalterable, and our present resistance wrong? On every unauthoritative exercise of power by the legislature, must the people rise in rebellion, or their silence be construed into a surrender of that power to them? If so, how many rebellions should we have had already? One certainly for every session of assembly. The other states in the Union have been of opinion, that to render a form of government unalterable by ordinary acts of assembly, the people must delegate persons with special powers. They have accordingly chosen special conventions to form and fix their governments. The individuals then who maintain the contrary opinion in this country, should have the modesty to suppose it possible that they may be wrong and the rest of America right. But if there be only a possibility of their being wrong, if only a plausible doubt remains of the validity of the ordinance of government, is it not better to remove that doubt, by placing it on a bottom which none will dispute? If they be right, we shall only have the unnecessary trouble of meeting once in convention. If they be wrong, they expose us to the hazard of having no fundamental rights at all. True it is, this is no time for deliberating on forms of government. While an enemy is within our bowels, the first object is to expel him. But when this shall be done, when peace shall be established, and leisure given us for intrenching within good forms, the rights for which we have bled, let no man be found indolent enough to decline a little more trouble for placing them beyond the reach of question. If any thing more be requisite to produce a conviction of the expediency of calling a convention, at a proper season, to fix our form of government, let it be the reflection,

6. That the assembly exercises a power of determining the Quorum of their own body which may legislate for us. After the establishment of the new form they adhered to the *Lex majoris partis*,[6] founded in common[7] law as well as common right. It is the natural[8] law of every assembly of men, whose numbers are not fixed by any other law. They continued for some time to require the presence of a majority of their whole number, to pass an act. But the British parliament fixes its own quorum: our former assemblies fixed their own quorum: and one precedent in favour of power is stronger than an hundred against it. The house of delegates therefore have lately[9] voted that, during the present dangerous invasion,[1] forty members shall be a house to proceed to business. They have been moved to this by the fear of not being able to collect a house. But this danger could not authorize them to call that a house which was none: and if they may fix it at one number, they may at another, till it loses its fundamental character of being a representative body.

6. The principle of majority rule.
7. Bro. abr. Corporations. 31. 34. Hakewell, 93 [Jefferson's note].
8. Puff. Off, hom. l. 2. c. 6. §. 12 [Jefferson's note].
9. June 4, 1781 [Jefferson's note].
1. Jefferson's contemporary reference to the British invasion of Virginia in 1781, which, early in June, forced the legislature to flee Charlottesville and Jefferson himself to run from Monticello.

As this vote expires with the present invasion, it is probable the former rule will be permitted to revive: because at present no ill is meant. The power however of fixing their own quorum has been avowed, and a precedent set. From forty it may be reduced to four, and from four to one: from a house to a committee, from a committee to a chairman or speaker, and thus an oligarchy or monarchy be substituted under forms supposed to be regular. "Omnia mala exempla ex bonis orta sunt: sed ubi imperium ad ignaros aut minus bonos pervenit, novum illud exemplum ab dignis et idoneis ad indignos et non idoneos fertur."[2] When therefore it is considered, that there is no legal obstacle to the assumption by the assembly of all the powers legislative, executive, and judiciary, and that these may come to the hands of the smallest rag of delegation, surely the people will say, and their representatives, while yet they have honest representatives, will advise them to say, that they will not acknowledge as laws any acts not considered and assented to by the major part of their delegates.

In enumerating the defects of the constitution, it would be wrong to count among them what is only the error of particular persons. In December 1776, our circumstances being much distressed, it was proposed in the house of delegates to create a *dictator*, invested with every power legislative, executive and judiciary, civil and military, of life and of death, over our persons and over our properties: and in June 1781, again under calamity, the same proposition was repeated, and wanted a few votes only of being passed.—One who entered into this contest from a pure love of liberty, and a sense of injured rights, who determined to make every sacrifice, and to meet every danger, for the re-establishment of those rights on a firm basis, who did not mean to expend his blood and substance for the wretched purpose of changing this master for that, but to place the powers of governing him in a plurality of hands of his own choice, so that the corrupt will of no one man might in future oppress him, must stand confounded and dismayed when he is told, that a considerable portion of that plurality had meditated the surrender of them into a single hand, and, in lieu of a limited monarch, to deliver him over to a despotic one! How must we find his efforts and sacrifices abused and baffled, if he may still by a single vote be laid prostrate at the feet of one man! In God's name, from whence have they derived this power? Is it from our ancient laws? None such can be produced. Is it from any principle in our new constitution, expressed or implied? Every lineament of that expressed or implied, is in full opposition to it. Its fundamental principle is, that the state shall be governed as a commonwealth. It provides a republican organization, proscribes under the name of *prerogative* the exercise of all powers undefined by the laws; places on this basis the whole system of our laws; and, by consolidating them together, chuses that they shall be left to stand or fall together, never providing for any circumstances, nor admitting that such could arise, wherein either should be suspended, no, not for a moment. Our antient laws expressly declare, that those who are but delegates themselves shall not delegate to others powers which require judgment and integrity in their exercise.—Or was this proposition moved on a supposed right in the movers of abandoning their posts in a moment of distress? The

---

2. All bad examples derive from good ones: but where power comes into the hands of the ignorant or those who lack virtue, the new example passes from the worthy and proper to the unworthy and unfit (Latin).

same laws forbid the abandonment of that post, even on ordinary occasions; and much more a transfer of their powers into other hands and other forms, without consulting the people. They never admit the idea that these, like sheep or cattle, may be given from hand to hand without an appeal to their own will.—Was it from the necessity of the case? Necessities which dissolve a government, do not convey its authority to an oligarchy or a monarchy. They throw back, into the hands of the people, the powers they had delegated, and leave them as individuals to shift for themselves. A leader may offer, but not impose himself, nor be imposed on them. Much less can their necks be submitted to his sword, their breath be held at his will or caprice. The necessity which should operate these tremendous effects should at least be palpable and irresistible. Yet in both instances, where it was feared, or pretended with us, it was belied by the event. It was belied too by the preceding experience of our sister states, several of whom had grappled through greater difficulties without abandoning their forms of government. When the proposition was first made, Massachusets had found even the government of committees sufficient to carry them through an invasion. But we at the time of that proposition were under no invasion. When the second was made, there had been added to this example those of Rhode-Island, New-York, New-Jersey, and Pennsylvania, in all of which the republican form had been found equal to the task of carrying them through the severest trials. In this state alone did there exist so little virtue, that fear was to be fixed in the hearts of the people, and to become the motive of their exertions and the principle of their government? The very thought alone was treason against the people; was treason against mankind in general; as rivetting for ever the chains which bow down their necks, by giving to their oppressors a proof, which they would have trumpeted through the universe, of the imbecility of republican government, in times of pressing danger, to shield them from harm. Those who assume the right of giving away the reins of government in any case, must be sure that the herd, whom they hand on to the rods and hatchet of the dictator, will lay their necks on the block when he shall nod to them. But if our assemblies supposed such a resignation in the people, I hope they mistook their character. I am of opinion, that the government, instead of being braced and invigorated for greater exertions under their difficulties, would have been thrown back upon the bungling machinery of county committees for administration, till a convention could have been called, and its wheels again set into regular motion. What a cruel moment was this for creating such an embarrassment, for putting to the proof the attachment of our countrymen to republican government! Those who meant well, of the advocates for this measure, (and most of them meant well, for I know them personally, had been their fellow-labourer in the common cause, and had often proved the purity of their principles), had been seduced in their judgment by the example of an ancient republic, whose constitution and circumstances were fundamentally different. They had sought this precedent in the history of Rome, where alone it was to be found, and where at length too it had proved fatal. They had taken it from a republic, rent by the most bitter factions and tumults, where the government was of a heavy-handed unfeeling aristocracy, over a people ferocious, and rendered desperate by poverty and wretchedness; tumults which could not be allayed under the most trying circumstances, but by the omnipotent hand of a single despot. Their constitution therefore allowed a temporary tyrant to be erected, under the name of a Dictator; and that temporary tyrant, after a few examples, became perpetual. They misapplied this precedent to a people, mild in their dispositions, patient under their trial, united for the public liberty, and affectionate to their leaders. But if from the constitution of the Roman government there resulted to their Senate a power of submitting all their rights to the will of one man, does it follow, that the assembly of Virginia have the same authority? What clause in our constitution has substituted that of Rome, by way of residuary provision, for all cases not otherwise provided for? Or if they may step ad libitum into any other form of government for precedents to rule us by, for what oppression may not a precedent be found in this world of the bellum omnium in omnia?[3]—Searching for the foundations of this proposition, I can find none which may pretend a colour of right or reason, but the defect before developed, that there being no barrier between the legislative, executive, and judiciary departments, the legislature may seize the whole: that having seized it, and possessing a right to fix their own quorum, they may reduce that quorum to one, whom they may call a chairman, speaker, dictator, or by any other name they please.—Our situation is indeed perilous, and I hope my countrymen will be sensible of it, and will apply, at a proper season, the proper remedy; which is a convention to fix the constitution, to amend its defects, to bind up the several branches of government by certain laws, which when they transgress their acts shall become nullities; to render unnecessary an appeal to the people, or in other words a rebellion, on every infraction of their rights, on the peril that their acquiescence shall be construed into an intention to surrender those rights.

Query XIV

The administration of justice   Laws
and description of the laws?

The state is divided into counties. In every county are appointed magistrates, called justices of the peace, usually from eight to thirty or forty in number, in proportion to the size of the county, of the most discreet and honest inhabitants. They are nominated by their fellows, but commissioned by the governor, and act without reward. These magistrates have jurisdiction both criminal and civil. If the question before them be a question of law only, they decide on it themselves: but if it be of fact, or of fact and law combined, it must be referred to a jury. In the latter case, of a combination of law and fact, it is usual for the jurors to decide the fact, and to refer the law arising on it to the decision of the judges. But this division of the subject lies with their discretion only. And if the question relate to any point of public liberty, or if it be one of those in which the judges may be suspected of bias, the jury undertake to decide both law and fact. If they be mistaken, a decision against right, which is casual only, is less dangerous to the state, and less afflicting to the loser, than one which makes part of a regular and uniform system. In truth, it is better to toss up cross and pile[4] in a cause, than to refer it to a judge whose mind is warped by any motive whatever, in that particular case. But the common sense of twelve honest men gives still a better

3. A war of all against all (Latin).
4. A British term for heads or tails.

chance of just decision, than the hazard of cross and pile. These judges exe-cute their process by the sheriff or coroner of the county, or by constables of their own appointment. If any free person commit an offence against the commonwealth, if it be below the degree of felony, he is bound by a justice to appear before their court, to answer it on indictment or information. If it amount to felony, he is committed to jail, a court of these justices is called; if they on examination think him guilty, they send him to the jail of the gen-eral court, before which court he is to be tried first by a grand jury of 24, of whom 13 must concur in opinion: if they find him guilty, he is then tried by a jury of 12 men of the county where the offence was committed, and by their verdict, which must be unanimous, he is acquitted or condemned with-out appeal. If the criminal be a slave the trial by the county court is final. In every case however, except that of high treason, there resides in the gover-nor a power of pardon. In high treason, the pardon can only flow from the general assembly. In civil matters these justices have jurisdiction in all cases of whatever value, not appertaining to the department of the admiralty. This jurisdiction is twofold. If the matter in dispute be of less value than 4⅙ dol-lars, a single member may try it at any time and place within his county, and may award execution on the goods of the party cast. If it be of that or greater value, it is determinable before the county court, which consists of four at the least of those justices, and assembles at the court-house of the county on a certain day in every month. From their determination, if the matter be of the value of ten pounds sterling, or concern the title or bounds of lands, an appeal lies to one of the superior courts.

There are three superior courts, to wit, the high-court of chancery, the general court, and court of admiralty. The first and second of these receive appeals from the county courts, and also have original jurisdiction where the subject of controversy is of the value of ten pounds sterling, or where it con-cerns the title or bounds of land. The jurisdiction of the admiralty is origi-nal altogether. The high-court of chancery is composed of three judges, the general court of five, and the court of admiralty of three. The two first hold their sessions at Richmond at stated times, the chancery twice in the year, and the general court twice for business civil and criminal, and twice more for criminal only. The court of admiralty sits at Williamsburgh whenever a controversy arises.

There is one supreme court, called the court of appeals, composed of the judges of the three superior courts, assembling twice a year at stated times at Richmond. This court receives appeals in all civil cases from each of the superior courts, and determines them finally. But it has no original juris-diction.

If a controversy arise between two foreigners of a nation in alliance with the United States, it is decided by the Consul for their State, or, if both par-ties chuse it, by the ordinary courts of justice. If one of the parties only be such a foreigner, it is triable before the courts of justice of the country. But if it shall have been instituted in a county court, the foreigner may remove it into the general court, or court of chancery, who are to determine it at their first sessions, as they must also do if it be originally commenced before them. In cases of life and death, such foreigners have a right to be tried by a jury, the one half foreigners, the other natives.

All public accounts are settled with a board of auditors, consisting of three members, appointed by the general assembly, any two of whom may act. But an individual, dissatisfied with the determination of that board, may carry his case into the proper superior court.

A description of the laws.

The general assembly was constituted, as has been already shewn, by letters-patent of March the 9th, 1607, in the 4th year of the reign of James the First. The laws of England seem to have been adopted by consent of the settlers, which might easily enough be done whilst they were few and living all together. Of such adoption however we have no other proof than their practice, till the year 1661, when they were expressly adopted by an act of the assembly, except so far as 'a difference of condition' rendered them inapplicable. Under this adoption, the rule, in our courts of judicature was, that the common law of England, and the general statutes previous to the 4th of James,[5] were in force here; but that no subsequent statutes were, *unless we were named in them*, said the judges and other partisans of the crown, but *named or not named*, said those who reflected freely. It will be unnecessary to attempt a description of the laws of England, as that may be found in English publications. To those which were established here, by the adoption of the legislature, have been since added a number of acts of assembly passed during the monarchy, and ordinances of convention and acts of assembly enacted since the establishment of the republic. The following variations from the British model are perhaps worthy of being specified.

Debtors unable to pay their debts, and making faithful delivery of their whole effects, are released from confinement, and their persons for ever discharged from restraint for such previous debts: but any property they may afterwards acquire will be subject to their creditors.

The poor, unable to support themselves, are maintained by an assessment on the titheable persons in their parish. This assessment is levied and administered by twelve persons in each parish, called vestrymen, originally chosen by the housekeepers of the parish, but afterwards filling vacancies in their own body by their own choice. These are usually the most discreet farmers, so distributed through their parish, that every part of it may be under the immediate eye of some one of them. They are well acquainted with the details and œconomy of private life, and they find sufficient inducements to execute their charge well, in their philanthropy, in the approbation of their neighbours, and the distinction which that gives them. The poor who have neither property, friends, nor strength to labour, are boarded in the houses of good farmers, to whom a stipulated sum is annually paid. To those who are able to help themselves a little, or have friends from whom they derive some succours, inadequate however to their full maintenance, supplementory aids are given, which enable them to live comfortably in their own houses, or in the houses of their friends. Vagabonds, without visible property or vocation, are placed in workhouses, where they are well cloathed, fed, lodged, and made to labour. Nearly the same method of providing for the poor prevails through all our states; and from Savannah to Portsmouth you will seldom meet a beggar. In the larger towns indeed they sometimes present themselves. These are usually foreigners, who have never obtained a settlement in any parish. I never yet saw a native American begging in the streets or highways. A subsistence is easily gained here: and if, by misfortunes, they are thrown on the charities of the world, those provided by their own country are so comfortable and so

---

5. I.e., 1607, the year of Jamestown's founding; King James I assumed the throne of England in 1603.

certain, that they never think of relinquishing them to become strolling beggars. Their situation too, when sick, in the family of a good farmer, where every member is emulous to do them kind offices, where they are visited by all the neighbours, who bring them the little rarities which their sickly appetites may crave, and who take by rotation the nightly watch over them, when their condition requires it, is without comparison better than in a general hospital, where the sick, the dying, and the dead are crammed together, in the same rooms, and often in the same beds. The disadvantages, inseparable from general hospitals, are such as can never be counterpoised by all the regularities of medicine and regimen. Nature and kind nursing save a much greater proportion in our plain way, at a smaller expence, and with less abuse. One branch only of hospital institution is wanting with us; that is, a general establishment for those labouring under difficult cases of chirurgery. The aids of this art are not equivocal. But an able chirurgeon cannot be had in every parish. Such a receptacle should therefore be provided for those patients: but no others should be admitted.

Marriages must be solemnized either on special licence, granted by the first magistrate of the county, on proof of the consent of the parent or guardian of either party under age, or after solemn publication, on three several Sundays, at some place of religious worship, in the parishes where the parties reside. The act of solemnization may be by the minister of any society of Christians, who shall have been previously licensed for this purpose by the court of the county. Quakers and Menonists however are exempted from all these conditions, and marriage among them is to be solemnized by the society itself.

A foreigner of any nation, not in open war with us, becomes naturalized by removing to the state to reside, and taking an oath of fidelity: and thereupon acquires every right of a native citizen: and citizens may divest themselves of that character, by declaring, by solemn deed, or in open court, that they mean to expatriate themselves, and no longer to be citizens of this state.

Conveyances of land must be registered in the court of the county wherein they lie, or in the general court, or they are void, as to creditors, and subsequent purchasers.

Slaves pass by descent and dower as lands do. Where the descent is from a parent, the heir is bound to pay an equal share of their value in money to each of his brothers and sisters.

Slaves, as well as lands, were entailable during the monarchy: but, by an act of the first republican assembly, all donees in tail, present and future, were vested with the absolute dominion of the entailed subject.

Bills of exchange, being protested, carry 10 per cent. interest from their date.

No person is allowed, in any other case, to take more than five per cent. per annum simple interest, for the loan of monies.

Gaming debts are made void, and monies actually paid to discharge such debts (if they exceeded 40 shillings) may be recovered by the payer within three months, or by any other person afterwards.

Tobacco, flour, beef, pork, tar, pitch, and turpentine, must be inspected by persons publicly appointed, before they can be exported.

The erecting iron-works and mills is encouraged by many privileges; with necessary cautions however to prevent their dams from obstructing the navigation of the water-courses. The general assembly have on several occasions shewn a great desire to encourage the opening the great falls of James and Patowmac rivers. As yet, however, neither of these have been effected.

The laws have also descended to the preservation and improvement of the races of useful animals, such as horses, cattle, deer; to the extirpation of those which are noxious, as wolves, squirrels, crows, blackbirds; and to the guarding our citizens against infectious disorders, by obliging suspected vessels coming into the state, to perform quarantine, and by regulating the conduct of persons having such disorders within the state.

The mode of acquiring lands, in the earliest times of our settlement, was by petition to the general assembly. If the lands prayed for were already cleared of the Indian title, and the assembly thought the prayer reasonable, they passed the property by their vote to the petitioner. But if they had not yet been ceded by the Indians, it was necessary that the petitioner should previously purchase their right. This purchase the assembly verified, by enquiries of the Indian proprietors; and being satisfied of its reality and fairness, proceeded further to examine the reasonableness of the petition, and its consistence with policy; and, according to the result, either granted or rejected the petition. The company also sometimes, though very rarely, granted lands, independantly of the general assembly. As the colony increased, and individual applications for land multiplied, it was found to give too much occupation to the general assembly to enquire into and execute the grant in every special case. They therefore thought it better to establish general rules, according to which all grants should be made, and to leave to the governor the execution of them, under these rules. This they did by what have been usually called the land laws, amending them from time to time, as their defects were developed. According to these laws, when an individual wished a portion of unappropriated land, he was to locate and survey it by a public officer, appointed for that purpose: its breadth was to bear a certain proportion to its length: the grant was to be executed by the governor: and the lands were to be improved in a certain manner, within a given time. From these regulations there resulted to the state a sole and exclusive power of taking conveyances of the Indian right of soil: since, according to them, an Indian conveyance alone could give no right to an individual, which the laws would acknowledge. The state, or the crown, thereafter, made general purchases of the Indians from time to time, and the governor parcelled them out by special grants, conformed to the rules before described, which it was not in his power, or in that of the crown, to dispense with. Grants, unaccompanied by their proper legal circumstances, were set aside regularly by *scire facias*,[6] or by bill in Chancery. Since the establishment of our new government, this order of things is but little changed. An individual, wishing to appropriate to himself lands still unappropriated by any other, pays to the public treasurer a sum of money proportioned to the quantity he wants. He carries the treasurer's receipt to the auditors of public accompts, who thereupon debit the treasurer with the sum, and order the register of the land-office to give the party a warrant for his land. With this warrant from the register, he goes to the surveyor of the county where the land lies on which he has cast his eye. The surveyor lays it off for him, gives him its exact description, in the form of a certificate, which certificate he returns to the land-office, where a grant is

---

6. A writ requiring someone to show cause (in this case, why title to the grant in question should not be "set aside" or vacated).

made out, and is signed by the governor. This vests in him a perfect dominion in his lands, transmissible to whom he pleases by deed or will, or by
descent to his heirs if he die intestate.

Many of the laws which were in force during the monarchy being relative
merely to that form of government, or inculcating principles inconsistent
with republicanism, the first assembly which met after the establishment of
the commonwealth appointed a committee to revise the whole code, to
reduce it into proper form and volume, and report it to the assembly. This
work has been executed by three gentlemen,[7] and reported; but probably will
not be taken up till a restoration of peace shall leave to the legislature leisure
to go through such a work.

The plan of the revisal was this. The common law of England, by which
is meant, that part of the English law which was anterior to the date of the
oldest statutes extant, is made the basis of the work. It was thought dangerous to attempt to reduce it to a text: it was therefore left to be collected
from the usual monuments of it. Necessary alterations in that, and so much
of the whole body of the British statutes, and of acts of assembly, as were
thought proper to be retained, were digested into 126 new acts, in which
simplicity of stile was aimed at, as far as was safe. The following are the
most remarkable alterations proposed:

To change the rules of descent, so as that the lands of any person dying
intestate shall be divisible equally among all his children, or other representatives, in equal degree.

To make slaves distributable among the next of kin, as other moveables.

To have all public expences, whether of the general treasury, or of a parish
or county, (as for the maintenance of the poor, building bridges, court-houses,
&c.) supplied by assessments on the citizens, in proportion to their property.

To hire undertakers for keeping the public roads in repair, and indemnify
individuals through whose lands new roads shall be opened.

To define with precision the rules whereby aliens should become citizens,
and citizens make themselves aliens.

To establish religious freedom on the broadest bottom.

To emancipate all slaves born after passing the act. The bill reported by the
revisors does not itself contain this proposition; but an amendment containing it was prepared, to be offered to the legislature whenever the bill should
be taken up, and further directing, that they should continue with their parents to a certain age, then be brought up, at the public expence, to tillage, arts
or sciences, according to their geniusses, till the females should be eighteen,
and the males twenty-one years of age, when they should be colonized to such
place as the circumstances of the time should render most proper, sending
them out with arms, implements of houshold and of the handicraft arts,
seeds, pairs of the useful domestic animals, &c. to declare them a free and
independant people, and extend to them our alliance and protection, till they
shall have acquired strength; and to send vessels at the same time to other
parts of the world for an equal number of white inhabitants; to induce whom
to migrate hither, proper encouragements were to be proposed. It will probably be asked, Why not retain and incorporate the blacks into the state, and
thus save the expence of supplying, by importation of white settlers, the
vacancies they will leave? Deep rooted prejudices entertained by the whites;

---

7. Jefferson was one of them.

ten thousand recollections, by the blacks, of the injuries they have sustained; new provocations; the real distinctions which nature has made; and many other circumstances, will divide us into parties, and produce convulsions which will probably never end but in the extermination of the one or the other race.—To these objections, which are political, may be added others, which are physical and moral. The first difference which strikes us is that of colour. Whether the black of the negro resides in the reticular membrane between the skin and scarf-skin, or in the scarf-skin itself; whether it proceeds from the colour of the blood, the colour of the bile, or from that of some other secretion, the difference is fixed in nature, and is as real as if its seat and cause were better known to us. And is this difference of no importance? Is it not the foundation of a greater or less share of beauty in the two races? Are not the fine mixtures of red and white, the expressions of every passion by greater or less suffusions of colour in the one, preferable to that eternal monotony, which reigns in the countenances, that immoveable veil of black which covers all the emotions of the other race? Add to these, flowing hair, a more elegant symmetry of form, their own judgment in favour of the whites, declared by their preference of them, as uniformly as is the preference of the Oranootan for the black women over those of his own species. The circumstance of superior beauty, is thought worthy attention in the propagation of our horses, dogs, and other domestic animals; why not in that of man? Besides those of colour, figure, and hair, there are other physical distinctions proving a difference of race. They have less hair on the face and body. They secrete less by the kidnies, and more by the glands of the skill, which gives them a very strong and disagreeable odour. This greater degree of transpiration renders them more tolerant of heat, and less so of cold, than the whites. Perhaps too a difference of structure in the pulmonary apparatus, which a late ingenious experimentalist[8] has discovered to be the principal regulator of animal heat, may have disabled them from extricating, in the act of inspiration, so much of that fluid from the outer air, or obliged them in expiration, to part with more of it. They seem to require less sleep. A black, after hard labour through the day, will be induced by the slightest amusements to sit up till midnight, or later, though knowing he must be out with the first dawn of the morning. They are at least as brave, and more adventuresome. But this may perhaps proceed from a want of forethought, which prevents their seeing a danger till it be present. When present, they do not go through it with more coolness or steadiness than the whites. They are more ardent after their female: but love seems with them to be more an eager desire, than a tender delicate mixture of sentiment and sensation. Their griefs are transient. Those numberless afflictions, which render it doubtful whether heaven has given life to us in mercy or in wrath, are less felt, and sooner forgotten with them. In general, their existence appears to participate more of sensation than reflection. To this must be ascribed their disposition to sleep when abstracted from their diversions, and unemployed in labour. An animal whose body is at rest, and who does not reflect, must be disposed to sleep of course. Comparing them by their faculties of memory, reason, and imagination, it appears to me, that in memory they are equal to the whites; in reason much inferior, as I think one could scarcely be found capable of tracing and comprehending

8. Crawford [Jefferson's note]. Jefferson's note refers to British scientist Adair Crawford (1748–1795), who published his *Experiments and Observations on Animal Heat* in 1779.

the investigations of Euclid; and that in imagination they are dull, tasteless, and anomalous. It would be unfair to follow them to Africa for this investigation. We will consider them here, on the same stage with the whites, and where the facts are not apocryphal on which a judgment is to be formed. It will be right to make great allowances for the difference of condition, of education, of conversation, of the sphere in which they move. Many millions of them have been brought to, and born in America. Most of them indeed have been confined to tillage, to their own homes, and their own society: yet many have been so situated, that they might have availed themselves of the conversation of their masters; many have been brought up to the handicraft arts, and from that circumstance have always been associated with the whites. Some have been liberally educated, and all have lived in countries where the arts and sciences are cultivated to a considerable degree, and have had before their eyes samples of the best works from abroad. The Indians, with no advantages of this kind, will often carve figures on their pipes not destitute of design and merit. They will crayon out an animal, a plant, or a country, so as to prove the existence of a germ in their minds which only wants cultivation. They astonish you with strokes of the most sublime oratory; such as prove their reason and sentiment strong, their imagination glowing and elevated. But never yet could I find that a black had uttered a thought above the level of plain narration; never see even an elementary trait of painting or sculpture. In music they are more generally gifted than the whites with accurate ears for tune and time, and they have been found capable of imagining a small catch.[9] Whether they will be equal to the composition of a more extensive run of melody, or of complicated harmony, is yet to be proved. Misery is often the parent of the most affecting touches in poetry.—Among the blacks is misery enough, God knows, but no poetry. Love is the peculiar œstrum of the poet. Their love is ardent, but it kindles the senses only, not the imagination. Religion indeed has produced a Phyllis Whately;[1] but it could not produce a poet. The compositions published under her name are below the dignity of criticism. The heroes of the Dunciad are to her, as Hercules to the author of that poem.[2] Ignatius Sancho[3] has approached nearer to merit in composition; yet his letters do more honour to the heart than the head. They breathe the purest effusions of friendship and general philanthropy, and shew how great a degree of the latter may be compounded with strong religious zeal. He is often happy in the turn of his compliments, and his stile is easy and familiar, except when he affects a Shandean fabrication of words. But his imagination is wild and extravagant, escapes incessantly from every restraint of reason and taste, and, in the course of its vagaries, leaves a tract of thought as incoherent and eccentric, as is the course of a meteor through the sky. His subjects should often have led him to a process of sober reasoning: yet we find him always substituting sentiment for demonstration. Upon the whole, though we admit him to the first place among those

9. The instrument proper to them is the Banjar, which they brought hither from Africa, and which is the original of the guitar, its chords being precisely the four lower chords of the guitar [Jefferson's note].
1. Phillis Wheatley (c. 1753–1784), born in Africa and brought as a slave to America, published her Poems on Various Subjects, Religious and Moral in 1773.
2. Alexander Pope published the first version of the Dunciad, a satire on dull literature, in 1728.
3. Charles Ignatius Sancho (c. 1729–1780), born on a slave ship and brought to England in his infancy, later became the friend of Laurence Sterne, the author of Tristram Shandy (1760–67), and other literary figures. His Letters appeared in London in 1782.

of his own colour who have presented themselves to the public judgment, yet when we compare him with the writers of the race among whom he lived, and particularly with the epistolary class, in which he has taken his own stand, we are compelled to enroll him at the bottom of the column. This criticism supposes the letters published under his name to be genuine, and to have received amendment from no other hand; points which would not be of easy investigation. The improvement of the blacks in body and mind, in the first instance of their mixture with the whites, has been observed by every one, and proves that their inferiority is not the effect merely of their condition of life. We know that among the Romans, about the Augustan age especially, the condition of their slaves was much more deplorable than that of the blacks on the continent of America. The two sexes were confined in separate apartments, because to raise a child cost the master more than to buy one. Cato, for a very restricted indulgence to his slaves in this particular, took[4] from them a certain price. But in this country the slaves multiply as fast as the free inhabitants. Their situation and manners place the commerce between the two sexes almost without restraint.—The same Cato, on a principle of œconomy, always sold his sick and superannuated slaves. He gives it as a standing precept to a master visiting his farm, to sell his old oxen, old waggons, old tools, old and diseased servants, and every thing else become useless. "Vendat boves vetulos, plaustrum vetus, ferramenta vetera, servum senem, servum morbosum, & si quid aliud supersit vendat." Cato[5] de re rusticâ. c. 2. The American slaves cannot enumerate   Suet. Cloud. 25. this among the injuries and insults they receive. It was the common practice to expose in the island of Æsculapius, in the Tyber, diseased slaves, whose cure was like to become tedious. The Emperor Claudius, by an edict, gave freedom to such of them as should recover, and first declared, that if any person chose to kill rather than to expose them, it should be deemed homicide.[6] The exposing them is a crime of which no instance has existed with us; and were it to be followed by death, it would be punished capitally. We are told of a certain Vedius Pollio, who, in the presence of Augustus, would have given a slave as food to his fish, for having broken a glass. With the Romans, the regular method of taking the evidence of their slaves was under torture. Here it has been thought better never to resort to their evidence. When a master was murdered, all his slaves, in the same house, or within hearing, were condemned to death. Here punishment falls on the guilty only, and as precise proof is required against him as against a freeman. Yet notwithstanding these and other discouraging circumstances among the Romans, their slaves were often their rarest artists. They excelled too in science, insomuch as to be usually employed as tutors to their master's children. Epictetus, Terence, and Phædrus, were slaves. But they were of the race of whites. It is not their condition then, but nature, which has produced the distinction.—Whether

4. Τὸς δόλὃς εταξεν ὡρισμενὃ νομισματος ὁμιλειν ταις ϑεραπαινισιν. —Plutarch. Cato [Jefferson's note].
5. Marcus Porcius Cato (234–149 B.C.E.), a farmer's son who became a Roman political figure and moral leader, wrote De Re Rustica as a tough-nosed guide to the profitable running of a farm. Jefferson himself translates his quotation from Cato in the sentence preceding it. The quotation in Jefferson's footnote (no. 4) from the life of Cato by the Greek historian Mestrius Plutarchus (c. 46–120 C.E.) may be translated as follows: "He provided that his male slaves should consort with the females for a set price."
6. Jefferson's marginal note refers to the life of Emperor Claudius in the Lives of the Caesars by Roman historian Suetonius Tranquillus (c. 70–c. 140 C.E).

further observation will or will not verify the conjecture, that nature has been less bountiful to them in the endowments of the head, I believe that in those of the heart she will be found to have done them justice. That disposition to theft with which they have been branded, must be ascribed to their situation, and not to any depravity of the moral sense. The man, in whose favour no laws of property exist, probably feels himself less bound to respect those made in favour of others. When arguing for ourselves, we lay it down as a fundamental, that laws, to be just, must give a reciprocation of right: that, without this, they are mere arbitrary rules of conduct, founded in force, and not in conscience: and it is a problem which I give to the master to solve, whether the religious precepts against the violation of property were not framed for him as well as his slave? And whether the slave may not as justifiably take a little from one, who has taken all from him, as he may slay one who would slay him? That a change in the relations in which a man is placed should change his ideas of moral right and wrong, is neither new, nor peculiar to the colour of the blacks. Homer tells us it was so 2600 years ago.

'Ημισυ, γαζ τ' ἀρετῆς ἀποαίνυ|αι εὐρύθπα Ζεὺς.
'Ανερος, ευτ' ἄν μιν κατὰ δȣ́λιον ἦμαζ ἕλησιν.

Od. 17. 323.

Jove fix'd it certain, that whatever day
Makes man a slave, takes half his worth away.

But the slaves of which Homer speaks were whites. Notwithstanding these considerations which must weaken their respect for the laws of property, we find among them numerous instances of the most rigid integrity, and as many as among their better instructed masters, of benevolence, gratitude, and unshaken fidelity.—The opinion, that they are inferior in the faculties of reason and imagination, must be hazarded with great diffidence. To justify a general conclusion, requires many observations, even where the subject may be submitted to the Anatomical knife, to Optical glasses, to analysis by fire, or by solvents. How much more then where it is a faculty, not a substance, we are examining; where it eludes the research of all the senses; where the conditions of its existence are various and variously combined; where the effects of those which are present or absent bid defiance to calculation; let me add too, as a circumstance of great tenderness, where our conclusion would degrade a whole race of men from the rank in the scale of beings which their Creator may perhaps have given them. To our reproach it must be said, that though for a century and a half we have had under our eyes the races of black and of red men, they have never yet been viewed by us as subjects of natural history. I advance it therefore as a suspicion only, that the blacks, whether originally a distinct race, or made distinct by time and circumstances, are inferior to the whites in the endowments both of body and mind. It is not against experience to suppose, that different species of the same genus, or varieties of the same species, may possess different qualifications. Will not a lover of natural history then, one who views the gradations in all the races of animals with the eye of philosophy, excuse an effort to keep those in the department of man as distinct as nature has formed them? This unfortunate difference of colour, and perhaps of faculty, is a powerful obstacle to the emancipation of these people. Many of their advocates, while they wish to vindicate the liberty of human nature, are anxious also to preserve its dignity and beauty. Some of these, embarrassed by the question "What further is to be done with them?" join themselves in opposition with those who are actuated by sordid avarice only. Among the Romans emancipation required but one effort. The slave, when made free, might mix with, without staining the blood of his master. But with us a second is necessary, unknown to history. When freed, he is to be removed beyond the reach of mixture.

The revised code further proposes to proportion crimes and punishments. This is attempted on the following scale.

I. Crimes whose punishment extends to *Life*.
    1. High treason. Death by hanging.
                    Forfeiture of lands and goods to the common-wealth.
    2. Petty treason. Death by hanging. Dissection.
                    Forfeiture of half the lands and goods to the representatives of the party slain.
    3. Murder. 1. by poison. Death by poison.
                                  Forfeiture of one-half as before.
                2. in Duel. Death by hanging. Gibbeting, if the challenger.
                                  Forfeiture of one-half as before, unless it be the party challenged, then the forfeiture is to the commonwealth.
                3. in any other way. Death by hanging.
                                  Forfeiture of one-half as before.
    4. Manslaughter. The second offence is murder.
II. Crimes whose punishment goes to *Limb*.
    1. Rape,
    2. Sodomy, } Dismemberment.
    3. Maiming, } Retaliation, and the forfeiture of half the lands
    4 Disfiguring, and goods to the sufferer.
III. Crimes punishable by *Labour*.
    1. Manslaughter, 1st offence. Labour VII. years   Forfeiture of half as for the public. in murder.
    2. Counterfeiting money. Labour VI. years. Forfeiture of lands and goods to the commonwealth.
    3. Arson.
    4. Asportation of vessels. } Labour V. years. Reparation three-fold.
    5. Robbery.
    6. Burglary. } Labour IV. years. Reparation double.
    7. Housebreaking.
    8. Horse-stealing. } Labour III. years. Reparation.
    9. Grand Larcency. Labour II. years. Reparation. Pillory.
    10. Petty Larcency. Labour I. year. Reparation. Pillory.
    11. Pretensions to witch-craft, &c. Ducking. Stripes.
    12. Excusable homicide.
    13. Suicide. } to be pitied, not punished.
    14. Apostacy. Heresy.

Pardon and privilege of clergy are proposed to be abolished; but if the verdict be against the defendant, the court in their discretion, may allow a new trial. No attainder to cause a corruption of blood, or forfeiture of dower. Slaves guilty of offences punishable in others by labour, to be transported to Africa, or elsewhere, as the circumstances of the time admit, there to be continued in slavery. A rigorous regimen proposed for those condemned to labour.

Another object of the revisal is, to diffuse knowledge more generally through the mass of the people. This bill proposes to lay off every county into small districts of five or six miles square, called hundreds, and in each of them to establish a school for teaching reading, writing, and arithmetic. The tutor to be supported by the hundred, and every person in it entitled to send their children three years gratis, and as much longer as they please, paying for it. These schools to be under a visitor, who is annually to chuse the boy, of best genius in the school, of those whose parents are too poor to give them further education, and to send him forward to one of the grammar schools, of which twenty are proposed to be erected in different parts of the country, for teaching Greek, Latin, geography, and the higher branches of numerical arithmetic. Of the boys thus sent in any one year, trial is to be made at the grammar schools one or two years, and the best genius of the whole selected, and continued six years, and the residue dismissed. By this means twenty of the best geniusses will be raked from the rubbish annually, and be instructed, at the public expence, so far as the grammer schools go. At the end of six years instruction, one half are to be discontinued (from among whom the grammar schools will probably be supplied with future masters); and the other half, who are to be chosen for the superiority of their parts and disposition, are to be sent and continued three years in the study of such sciences as they shall chuse, at William and Mary college, the plan of which is proposed to be enlarged, as will be hereafter explained, and extended to all the useful sciences. The ultimate result of the whole scheme of education would be the teaching all the children of the state reading, writing, and common arithmetic: turning out ten annually of superior genius, well taught in Greek, Latin, geography, and the higher branches of arithmetic: turning out ten others annually, of still superior parts, who, to those branches of learning, shall have added such of the sciences as their genius shall have led them to: the furnishing to the wealthier part of the people convenient schools, at which their children may be educated, at their own expence.—The general objects of this law are to provide an education adapted to the years, to the capacity, and the condition of every one, and directed to their freedom and happiness. Specific details were not proper for the law. These must be the business of the visitors entrusted with its execution. The first stage of this education being the schools of the hundreds, wherein the great mass of the people will receive their instruction, the principal foundations of future order will be laid here. Instead therefore of putting the Bible and Testament into the hands of the children, at an age when their judgments are not sufficiently matured for religious enquiries, their memories may here be stored with the most useful facts from Grecian, Roman, European and American history. The first elements of morality too may be instilled into their minds; such as, when further developed as their judgments advance in strength, may teach them how to work out their own greatest happiness, by shewing them that it does not depend on the condition of life in which chance has placed them, but is always the result of a good conscience, good health, occupation, and freedom in all just pursuits.—Those whom either the wealth of their parents or the adoption of the state shall destine to higher degrees of learning, will go on to the grammar schools, which constitute the next stage, there to be instructed in the languages. The learning Greek and Latin, I am told, is going into disuse in Europe. I know not what their manners and occupations may call for: but it would be very ill-judged in us to follow their example in this instance. There is a certain period of life, say from eight to fifteen or sixteen years of age, when the mind, like the body, is not yet firm enough for laborious and close operations. If applied to such, it falls an early victim to premature exertion; exhibiting indeed at first, in these young and tender subjects, the flattering appearance of their being men while they are yet children, but ending in reducing them to be children when they should be men. The memory is then most susceptible and tenacious of impressions; and the learning of languages being chiefly a work of memory, it seems precisely fitted to the powers of this period, which is long enough too for acquiring the most useful languages antient and modern. I do not pretend that language is science. It is only an instrument for the attainment of science. But that time is not lost which is employed in providing tools for future operation: more especially as in this case the books put into the hands of the youth for this purpose may be such as will at the same time impress their minds with useful facts and good principles. If this period be suffered to pass in idleness, the mind becomes lethargic and impotent, as would the body it inhabits if unexercised during the same time. The sympathy between body and mind during their rise, progress and decline, is too strict and obvious to endanger our being misled while we reason from the one to the other.—As soon as they are of sufficient age, it is supposed they will be sent on from the grammar schools to the university, which constitutes our third and last stage, there to study those sciences which may be adapted to their views.—By that part of our plan which prescribes the selection of the youths of genius from among the classes of the poor, we hope to avail the state of those talents which nature has sown as liberally among the poor as the rich, but which perish without use, if not sought for and cultivated.—But of all the views of this law none is more important, none more legitimate, than that of rendering the people the safe, as they are the ultimate, guardians of their own liberty. For this purpose the reading in the first stage, where *they* will receive their whole education, is proposed, as has been said, to be chiefly historical. History by apprising them of the past will enable them to judge of the future; it will avail them of the experience of other times and other nations; it will qualify them as judges of the actions and designs of men; it will enable them to know ambition under every disguise it may assume; and knowing it, to defeat its views. In every government on earth is some trace of human weakness, some germ of corruption and degeneracy, which cunning will discover, and wickedness insensibly open, cultivate, and improve. Every government degenerates when trusted to the rulers of the people alone. The people themselves therefore are its only safe depositories. And to render even them safe their minds must be improved to a certain degree. This indeed is not all that is necessary, though it be essentially necessary. An amendment of our constitution must here come in aid of the public education. The influence over government must be shared among all the people. If every individual which composes their mass participates of the ultimate authority, the government will be safe; because the corrupting the whole mass will exceed any private resources of wealth: and public ones cannot be provided but by levies on the people. In this case every man would have to pay his own price. The government of Great-Britain has been corrupted, because but one man in ten has a right to vote for members of parliament. The sellers of the government therefore get nine-tenths of their price clear. It has been thought that corruption is restrained by confining the right of suffrage to a few of the wealthier of the people: but it would be more effectually restrained by an extension of that right to such numbers as would bid defiance to the means of corruption.

Lastly, it is proposed, by a bill in this revisal, to begin a public library and gallery, by laying out a certain sum annually in books, paintings, and statues.

Query XV

Colleges,
Buildings,
Roads, &c.

The colleges and public establishments,
the roads, buildings, &c.?

The college of William and Mary is the only public seminary of learning in this state. It was founded in the time of king William and queen Mary, who granted to it 20,000 acres of land, and a penny a pound duty on certain tobaccoes exported from Virginia and Maryland, which had been levied by the statute of 25 Car. 2. The assembly also gave it, by temporary laws, a duty on liquors imported, and skins and firs exported. From these resources it received upwards of 3000 l. communibus annis.[7] The buildings are of brick, sufficient for an indifferent accommodation of perhaps an hundred students. By its charter it was to be under the government of twenty visitors, who were to be its legislators, and to have a president and six professors, who were incorporated. It was allowed a representative in the general assembly. Under this charter, a professorship of the Greek and Latin languages, a professorship of mathematics, one of moral philosophy, and two of divinity, were established. To these were annexed, for a sixth professorship, a considerable donation by Mr. Boyle[8] of England, for the instruction of the Indians, and their conversion to Christianity. This was called the professorship of Brafferton, from an estate of that name in England, purchased with the monies given. The admission of the learners of Latin and Greek filled the college with children. This rendering it disagreeable and degrading to young gentlemen already prepared for entering on the sciences, they were discouraged from resorting to it, and thus the schools for mathematics and moral philosophy, which might have been of some service, became of very little. The revenues too were exhausted in accommodating those who came only to acquire the rudiments of science. After the present revolution, the visitors, having no power to change those circumstances in the constitution of the college which were fixed by the charter, and being therefore confined in the number of professorships, undertook to change the objects of the professorships. They excluded the two schools for divinity, and that for the Greek and Latin languages, and substituted others; so that at present they stand thus:

---

7. I.e., three thousand pounds in an average year.
8. Robert Boyle (1627–1691), born in Ireland, was a celebrated scientist who promoted missionary work among Native Americans.

A Professorship for Law and Police:
  Anatomy and Medicine:
  Natural Philosophy and Mathematics:
  Moral Philosophy, the Law of Nature
    and Nations, the Fine Arts:
  Modern Languages:
  For the Brafferton.

And it is proposed, so soon as the legislature shall have leisure to take up this subject, to desire authority from them to increase the number of professorships, as well for the purpose of subdividing those already instituted, as of adding others for other branches of science. To the professorships usually established in the universities of Europe, it would seem proper to add one for the antient languages and literature of the North, on account of their connection with our own language, laws, customs, and history. The purposes of the Brafferton institution would be better answered by maintaining a perpetual mission among the Indian tribes, the object of which, besides instructing them in the principles of Christianity, as the founder requires, should be to collect their traditions, laws, customs, languages, and other circumstances which might lead to a discovery of their relation with one another, or descent from other nations. When these objects are accomplished with one tribe, the missionary might pass on to another.

The roads are under the government of the county courts, subject to be controuled by the general court. They order new roads to be opened wherever they think them necessary. The inhabitants of the county are by them laid off into precincts, to each of which they allot a convenient portion of the public roads to be kept in repair. Such bridges as may be built without the assistance of artificers, they are to build. If the stream be such as to require a bridge of regular workmanship, the court employs workmen to build it, at the expence of the whole county. If it be too great for the county, application is made to the general assembly, who authorize individuals to build it, and to take a fixed toll from all passengers, or give sanction to such other proposition as to them appears reasonable.

Ferries are admitted only at such places as are particularly pointed out by law, and the rates of ferriage are fixed.

Taverns are licensed by the courts, who fix their rates from time to time.

The private buildings are very rarely constructed of stone or brick; much the greatest proportion being of scantling[9] and boards, plaistered with lime. It is impossible to devise things more ugly, uncomfortable, and happily more perishable. There are two or three plans, on one of which, according to its size, most of the houses in the state are built. The poorest people build huts of logs, laid horizontally in pens, stopping the interstices with mud. These are warmer in winter, and cooler in summer, than the more expensive constructions of scantling and plank. The wealthy are attentive to the raising of vegetables, but very little so to fruits. The poorer people attend to neither, living principally on milk and animal diet. This is the more inexcusable, as the climate requires indispensably a free use of vegetable food, for health as well as comfort, and is very friendly to the raising of fruits.—The only public buildings worthy mention are the Capitol, the Palace, the College, and the Hospital for Lunatics, all of them in Williamsburg, heretofore the seat

9. Timber framing.

of our government. The Capitol is a light and airy structure, with a portico in front of two orders, the lower of which, being Doric, is tolerably just in its proportions and ornaments, save only that the intercolonnations are too large. The upper is Ionic, much too small for that on which it is mounted, its ornaments not proper to the order, nor proportioned within themselves. It is crowned with a pediment, which is too high for its span. Yet, on the whole, it is the most pleasing piece of architecture we have. The Palace is not handsome without: but it is spacious and commodious within, is prettily situated, and, with the grounds annexed to it, is capable of being made an elegant seat. The College and Hospital are rude, mis-shapen piles, which, but that they have roofs, would be taken for brick-kilns. There are no other public buildings but churches and court-houses, in which no attempts are made at elegance. Indeed it would not be easy to execute such an attempt, as a workman could scarcely be found here capable of drawing an order. The genius of architecture seems to have shed its maledictions over this land. Buildings are often erected, by individuals, of considerable expence. To give these symmetry and taste would not increase their cost. It would only change the arrangement of the materials, the form and combination of the members. This would often cost less than the burthen of barbarous ornaments with which these buildings are sometimes charged. But the first principles of the art are unknown, and there exists scarcely a model among us sufficiently chaste to give an idea of them. Architecture being one of the fine arts, and as such within the department of a professor of the college, according to the new arrangement, perhaps a spark may fall on some young subjects of natural taste, kindle up their genius, and produce a reformation in this elegant and useful art. But all we shall do in this way will produce no permanent improvement to our country, while the unhappy prejudice prevails that houses of brick or stone are less wholesome than those of wood. A dew is often observed on the walls of the former in rainy weather, and the most obvious solution is, that the rain has penetrated through these walls. The following facts however are sufficient to prove the error of this solution. 1. This dew on the walls appears when there is no rain, if the state of the atmosphere be moist. 2. It appears on the partition as well as the exterior walls. 3. So also on pavements of brick or stone. 4. It is more copious in proportion as the walls are thicker; the reverse of which ought to be the case, if this hypothesis were just. If cold water be poured into a vessel of stone, or glass, a dew forms instantly on the outside: but if it be poured into a vessel of wood, there is no such appearance. It is not supposed, in the first case, that the water has exuded through the glass, but that it is precipitated from the circumambient air; as the humid particles of vapour, passing from the boiler of an alembic through its refrigerant, are precipitated from the air, in which they were suspended, on the internal surface of the refrigerant. Walls of brick or stone act as the refrigerant in this instance. They are sufficiently cold to condense and precipitate the moisture suspended in the air of the room, when it is heavily charged therewith. But walls of wood are not so. The question then is, whether air in which this moisture is left floating, or that which is deprived of it, be most wholesome? In both cases the remedy is easy. A little fire kindled in the room, whenever the air is damp, prevents the precipitation on the walls: and this practice, found healthy in the warmest as well as coldest seasons, is as necessary in a wooden as in a stone or a brick house. I do not mean to say, that the rain never penetrates through walls of brick. On the contrary I have seen instances of it. But with us it is only through the northern and eastern walls of the house, after a north-easterly storm, these being the only ones which continue long enough to force through the walls. This however happens too rarely to give a just character of unwholesomeness to such houses. In a house, the walls of which are of well-burnt brick and good mortar, I have seen the rain penetrate through but twice in a dozen or fifteen years. The inhabitants of Europe, who dwell chiefly in houses of stone or brick, are surely as healthy as those of Virginia. These houses have the advantage too of being warmer in winter and cooler in summer than those of wood, of being cheaper in their first construction, where lime is convenient, and infinitely more durable. The latter consideration renders it of great importance to eradicate this prejudice from the minds of our countrymen. A country whose buildings are of wood, can never increase in its improvements to any considerable degree. Their duration is highly estimated at 50 years. Every half century then our country becomes a tabula rasa, whereon we have to set out anew, as in the first moment of seating it. Whereas when buildings are of durable materials, every new edifice is an actual and permanent acquisition to the state, adding to its value as well as to its ornament.

Query XVI

The measures taken with regard of the   Tories
estates and possessions of the rebels, commonly
called Tories?

A Tory has been properly defined to be a traitor in thought, but not in deed. The only description, by which the laws have endeavoured to come at them, was that of non-jurors, or persons refusing to take the oath of fidelity to the state. Persons of this description were at one time subjected to double taxation, at another to treble, and lastly were allowed retribution, and placed on a level with good citizens. It may be mentioned as a proof both of the lenity of our government, and unanimity of its inhabitants, that though this war has now raged near seven years, not a single execution for treason has taken place.

Under this query I will state the measures which have been adopted as to British property, the owners of which stand on a much fairer footing than the Tories. By our laws, the same as the English in this respect, no alien can hold lands, nor alien enemy maintain an action for money, or other moveable thing. Lands acquired or held by aliens become forfeited to the state; and, on an action by an alien enemy to recover money, or other moveable property, the defendant may plead that he is an alien enemy. This extinguishes his right in the hands of the debtor or holder of his moveable property. By our separation from Great-Britain, British subjects became aliens, and being at war, they were alien enemies. Their lands were of course forfeited, and their debts irrecoverable. The assembly however passed laws, at various times, for saving their property. They first sequestered their lands, slaves, and other property on their farms, in the hands of commissioners, who were mostly the confidential friends or agents of the owners, and directed their clear profits to be paid into the treasury: and they gave leave to all persons owing debts to British subjects to pay them also into the treasury. The monies so to be brought in were declared to remain the property of the British subject, and, if used by the state, were to be repaid, unless an improper conduct in Great-Britain should render a detention of it reasonable. Depreciation had at that time, though unacknowledged and unperceived by the Whigs, begun in some small degree. Great sums of money were paid in by debtors. At a later period, the assembly, adhering to the political principles which forbid an alien to hold lands in the state, ordered all British property to be sold: and, become sensible of the real progress of depreciation, and of the losses which would thence occur, if not guarded against, they ordered that the proceeds of the sales should be converted into their then worth in tobacco, subject to the future direction of the legislature. This act has left the question of retribution more problematical. In May 1780 another act took away the permission to pay into the public treasury debts due to British subjects.

Query XVII

Religion   *The different religions received*
into that state?

The first settlers in this country were emigrants from England, of the English church, just at a point of time when it was flushed with complete victory over the religious of all other persuasions. Possessed, as they became, of the powers of making, administering, and executing the laws, they shewed equal intolerance in this country with their Presbyterian brethren, who had emigrated to the northern government.[1] The poor Quakers were flying from persecution in England. They cast their eyes on these new countries as asylums of civil and religious freedom; but they found them free only for the reigning sect. Several acts of the Virginia assembly of 1659, 1662, and 1693, had made it penal in parents to refuse to have their children baptized; had prohibited the unlawful assembling of Quakers; had made it penal for any master of a vessel to bring a Quaker into the state; had ordered those already here, and such as should come thereafter, to be imprisoned till they should abjure the country; provided a milder punishment for their first and second return, but death for their third; had inhibited all persons from suffering their meetings in or near their houses, entertaining them individually, or disposing of books which supported their tenets. If no capital execution took place here, as did in New-England, it was not owing to the moderation of the church, or spirit of the legislature, as may be inferred from the law itself; but to historical circumstances which have not been handed down to us. The Anglicans retained full possession of the country about a century. Other opinions began then to creep in, and the great care of the government to support their own church, having begotten an equal degree of indolence in its clergy, two-thirds of the people had become dissenters at the commencement of the present revolution. The laws indeed were still oppressive on them, but the spirit of the one party had subsided into moderation, and of the other had risen to a degree of determination which commanded respect.

1. I.e., the Puritans of New England.

The present state of our laws on the subject of religion is this. The convention of May 1776, in their declaration of rights, declared it to be a truth, and a natural right, that the exercise of religion should be free; but when they proceeded to form on that declaration the ordinance of government, instead of taking up every principle declared in the bill of rights, and guarding it by legislative sanction, they passed over that which asserted our religious rights, leaving them as they found them. The same convention, however, when they met as a member of the general assembly in October 1776, repealed all *acts of parliament* which had rendered criminal the maintaining any opinions in matters of religion, the forbearing to repair to church, and the exercising any mode of worship; and suspended the laws giving salaries to the clergy, which suspension was made perpetual in October 1779. Statutory oppressions in religion being thus wiped away, we remain at present under those only imposed by the common law, or by our own acts of assembly. At the common law, *heresy* was a capital offence, punishable by burning. Its definition was left to the ecclesiastical judges, before whom the conviction was, till the statute of the 1 El. c. 1. circumscribed it, by declaring, that nothing should be deemed heresy, but what had been so determined by authority of the canonical scriptures, or by one of the four first general councils, or by some other council having for the grounds of their declaration the express and plain words of the scriptures. Heresy, thus circumscribed, being an offence at the common law, our act of assembly of October 1777, c. 17. gives cognizance of it to the general court, by declaring, that the jurisdiction of that court shall be general in all matters at the common law. The execution is by the writ *De hæretico comburendo.* By our own act of assembly of 1705, c. 30, if a person brought up in the Christian religion denies the being of a God, or the Trinity, or asserts there are more Gods than one, or denies the Christian religion to be true, or the scriptures to be of divine authority, he is punishable on the first offence by incapacity to hold any office or employment ecclesiastical, civil, or military; on the second by disability to sue, to take any gift or legacy, to be guardian, executor, or administrator, and by three years imprisonment, without bail. A father's right to the custody of his own children being founded in law on his right of guardianship, this being taken away, they may of course be severed from him, and put, by the authority of a court, into more orthodox hands. This is a summary view of that religious slavery, under which a people have been willing to remain, who have lavished their lives and fortunes for the establishment of their civil freedom. The[2] error seems not sufficiently eradicated, that the operations of the mind, as well as the acts of the body, are subject to the coercion of the laws. But our rulers can have authority over such natural rights only as we have submitted to them. The rights of conscience we never submitted, we could not submit. We are answerable for them to our God. The legitimate powers of government extend to such acts only as are injurious to others. But it does me no injury for my neighbour to say there are twenty gods, or no god. It neither picks my pocket nor breaks my leg. If it be said, his testimony in a court of justice cannot be

2. Furneaux passim [Jefferson's note]. Jefferson here refers to Philip Furneaux (1726–1783), an English dissenting minister, who published *Letters to the Honourable Mr. Justice Blackstone*, concerned with religious toleration, in 1770.

relied on, reject it then, and be the stigma on him. Constraint may make him worse by making him a hypocrite, but it will never make him a truer man. It may fix him obstinately in his errors, but will not cure them. Reason and free enquiry are the only effectual agents against error. Give a loose to them, they will support the true religion, by bringing every false one to their tribunal, to the test of their investigation. They are the natural enemies of error, and of error only. Had not the Roman government permitted free enquiry, Christianity could never have been introduced. Had not free enquiry been indulged, at the æra of the reformation, the corruptions of Christianity could not have been purged away. If it be restrained now, the present corruptions will be protected, and new ones encouraged. Was the government to prescribe to us our medicine and diet, our bodies would be in such keeping as our souls are now. Thus in France the emetic was once forbidden as a medicine, and the potatoe as an article of food. Government is just as infallible too when it fixes systems in physics. Galileo was sent to the inquisition for affirming that the earth was a sphere: the government had declared it to be as flat as a trencher, and Galileo was obliged to abjure his error. This error however at length prevailed, the earth became a globe, and Descartes declared it was whirled round its axis by a vortex. The government in which he lived was wise enough to see that this was no question of civil jurisdiction, or we should all have been involved by authority in vortices. In fact, the vortices have been exploded, and the Newtonian principle of gravitation is now more firmly established, on the basis of reason, than it would be were the government to step in, and to make it an article of necessary faith. Reason and experiment have been indulged, and error has fled before them. It is error alone which needs the support of government. Truth can stand by itself. Subject opinion to coercion: whom will you make your inquisitors? Fallible men; men governed by bad passions, by private as well as public reasons. And why subject it to coercion? To produce uniformity. But is uniformity of opinion desireable? No more than of face and stature. Introduce the bed of Procrustes then, and as there is danger that the large men may beat the small, make us all of a size, by lopping the former and stretching the latter. Difference of opinion is advantageous in religion. The several sects perform the office of a Censor morum over each other. Is uniformity attainable? Millions of innocent men, women, and children, since the introduction of Christianity, have been burnt, tortured, fined, imprisoned; yet we have not advanced one inch towards uniformity. What has been the effect of coercion? To make one half the world fools, and the other half hypocrites. To support roguery and error all over the earth. Let us reflect that it is inhabited by a thousand millions of people. That these profess probably a thousand different systems of religion. That ours is but one of that thousand. That if there be but one right, and ours that one, we should wish to see the 999 wandering sects gathered into the fold of truth. But against such a majority we cannot effect this by force. Reason and persuasion are the only practicable instruments. To make way for these, free enquiry must be indulged; and how can we wish others to indulge it while we refuse it ourselves. But every state, says an inquisitor, has established some religion. No two, say I, have established the same. Is this a proof of the infallibility of establishments? Our sister states of Pennsylvania and New York, however, have long subsisted without any establishment at all. The experiment was new and doubtful when they made it. It has

answered beyond conception. They flourish infinitely. Religion is well supported; of various kinds, indeed, but all good enough; all sufficient to preserve peace and order: or if a sect arises, whose tenets would subvert morals,
good sense has fair play, and reasons and laughs it out of doors, without suffering the state to be troubled with it. They do not hang more malefactors
than we do. They are not more disturbed with religious dissensions. On the
contrary, their harmony is unparalleled, and can be ascribed to nothing but
their unbounded tolerance, because there is no other circumstance in
which they differ from every nation on earth. They have made the happy
discovery, that the way to silence religious disputes, is to take no notice of
them. Let us too give this experiment fair play, and get rid, while we may,
of those tyrannical laws. It is true, we are as yet secured against them by
the spirit of the times. I doubt whether the people of this country would
suffer an execution for heresy, or a three years imprisonment for not comprehending the mysteries of the Trinity. But is the spirit of the people an
infallible, a permanent reliance? Is it government? Is this the kind of protection we receive in return for the rights we give up? Besides, the spirit of
the times may alter, will alter. Our rulers will become corrupt, our people
careless. A single zealot may commence persecutor, and better men be his
victims. It can never be too often repeated, that the time for fixing every
essential right on a legal basis is while our rulers are honest, and ourselves
united. From the conclusion of this war we shall be going down hill. It will
not then be necessary to resort every moment to the people for support.
They will be forgotten, therefore, and their rights disregarded. They will forget themselves, but in the sole faculty of making money, and will never
think of uniting to effect a due respect for their rights. The shackles, therefore, which shall not be knocked off at the conclusion of this war, will
remain on us long, will be made heavier and heavier, till our rights shall
revive or expire in a convulsion.[3]

Query XVIII

The particular *customs and manners*   Manners
that *may happen to be received*
in that state?

It is difficult to determine on the standard by which the manners of a
nation may be tried, whether *catholic*, or *particular*. It is more difficult for
a native to bring to that standard the manners of his own nation, famil-
iarized to him by habit. There must doubtless be an unhappy influence on
the manners of our people produced by the existence of slavery among us.
The whole commerce between master and slave is a perpetual exercise of
the most boisterous passions, the most unremitting despotism on the one
part, and degrading submissions on the other. Our children see this, and
learn to imitate it; for man is an imitative animal. This quality is the germ
of all education in him. From his cradle to his grave he is learning to do

---

3. Jefferson had the Virginia "Act for establishing Religious Freedom" printed as a pamphlet in Paris
in 1786 and included it as Appendix No. III in the Stockdale edition of *Notes on the State of Virginia* the next year. It is printed as Appendix No. III herein (p. 176).

what he sees others do. If a parent could find no motive either in his philanthropy or his self-love, for restraining the intemperance of passion towards his slave, it should always be a sufficient one that his child is present. But generally it is not sufficient. The parent storms, the child looks on, catches the lineaments of wrath, puts on the same airs in the circle of smaller slaves, gives a loose to his worst of passions, and thus nursed, educated, and daily exercised in tyranny, cannot but be stamped by it with odious peculiarities. The man must be a prodigy who can retain his manners and morals undepraved by such circumstances. And with what execration should the statesman be loaded, who permitting one half the citizens thus to trample on the rights of the other, transforms those into despots, and these into enemies, destroys the morals of the one part, and the amor patriæ of the other. For if a slave can have a country in this world, it must be any other in preference to that in which he is born to live and labour for another: in which he must lock up the faculties of his nature, contribute as far as depends on his individual endeavours to the evanishment of the human race, or entail his own miserable condition on the endless generations proceeding from him. With the morals of the people, their industry also is destroyed. For in a warm climate, no man will labour for himself who can make another labour for him. This is so true, that of the proprietors of slaves a very small proportion indeed are ever seen to labour. And can the liberties of a nation be thought secure when we have removed their only firm basis, a conviction in the minds of the people that these liberties are of the gift of God? That they are not to be violated but with his wrath? Indeed I tremble for my country when I reflect that God is just: that his justice cannot sleep for ever: that considering numbers, nature and natural means only, a revolution of the wheel of fortune, an exchange of situation, is among possible events: that it may become probable by supernatural interference! The Almighty has no attribute which can take side with us in such a contest.—But it is impossible to be temperate and to pursue this subject through the various considerations of policy, of morals, of history natural and civil. We must be contented to hope they will force their way into every one's mind. I think a change already perceptible, since the origin of the present revolution. The spirit of the master is abating, that of the slave rising from the dust, his condition mollifying, the way I hope preparing, under the auspices of heaven, for a total emancipation, and that this is disposed, in the order of events, to be with the consent of the masters, rather than by their extirpation.

Query XIX

Manufactures   *The present state of manufactures,*
commerce, interior and exterior trade?

We never had an interior trade of any importance. Our exterior commerce has suffered very much from the beginning of the present contest. During this time we have manufactured within our families the most necessary articles of cloathing. Those of cotton will bear some comparison with the same kinds of manufacture in Europe; but those of wool, flax and hemp are very coarse, unsightly, and unpleasant: and such is our attachment to agriculture, and such our preference for foreign manufactures, that be it wise or unwise, our people will certainly return as soon as they can, to the raising raw materials, and exchanging them for finer manufactures than they are able to execute themselves.

The political œconomists of Europe have established it as a principle that every state should endeavour to manufacture for itself: and this principle, like many others, we transfer to America, without calculating the difference of circumstance which should often produce a difference of result. In Europe the lands are either cultivated, or locked up against the cultivator. Manufacture must therefore be resorted to of necessity not of choice, to support the surplus of their people. But we have an immensity of land courting the industry of the husbandman. Is it best then that all our citizens should be employed in its improvement, or that one half should be called off from that to exercise manufactures and handicraft arts for the other? Those who labour in the earth are the chosen people of God, if ever he had a chosen people, whose breasts he has made his peculiar deposit for substantial and genuine virtue. It is the focus in which he keeps alive that sacred fire, which otherwise might escape from the face of the earth. Corruption of morals in the mass of cultivators is a phænomenon of which no age nor nation has furnished an example. It is the mark set on those, who not looking up to heaven, to their own soil and industry, as does the husbandman, for their subsistance, depend for it on the casualties and caprice of customers. Dependance begets subservience and venality, suffocates the germ of virtue, and prepares fit tools for the designs of ambition. This, the natural progress and consequence of the arts, has sometimes perhaps been retarded by accidental circumstances: but, generally speaking, the proportion which the aggregate of the other classes of citizens bears in any state to that of its husbandmen, is the proportion of its unsound to its healthy parts, and is a good-enough barometer whereby to measure its degree of corruption. While we have land to labour then, let us never wish to see our citizens occupied at a workbench, or twirling a distaff. Carpenters, masons, smiths, are wanting in husbandry: but, for the general operations of manufacture, let our workshops remain in Europe. It is better to carry provisions and materials to workmen there, than bring them to the provisions and materials, and with them their manners and principles. The loss by the transportation of commodities across the Atlantic will be made up in happiness and permanence of government. The mobs of great cities add just so much to the support of pure government, as sores do to the strength of the human body. It is the manners and spirit of a people which preserve a republic in vigour. A degeneracy in these is a canker which soon eats to the heart of its laws and constitution.

Query XX

*A notice of the commercial productions
particular to the state, and of those objects
which the inhabitants are obliged to get from
Europe and from other parts of the world?*

Before the present war we exported, communibus annis, according to the best information I can get, nearly as follows:

A R T I C L E S.	Quantity.	Price in dollars.	Am. in dollars.
Tobacco	55,000 hhds. of 1000 lb.	at 30 d. per hhd.	1,650,000
Wheat	800,000 bushels	at ⅚ d. per bush.	666,666⅔
Indian corn	600,000 bushels	at ⅓ d. per bush.	200,000
Shipping	— — —	— —	100,000
Masts, planks, skantling, shingles, staves	— — —	— —	66,666⅔
Tar, pitch, turpentine	30,000 barrels	at 1⅓ d. per bar.	40,000
Peltry, viz. skins of deer, beavers, otters, muskrats, racoons, foxes	180 hhds. of 600 lb.	at ⁵⁄₁₂ d. per lb.	42,000
Pork	4,000 barrels	at 10 d. per bar.	40,000
Flax-seed, hemp, cotton	— — —	— —	8,000
Pit-coal, pig-iron	— — —	— —	6,666⅔
Peas	5,000 bushels	at ⅔ d. per bush.	3,333⅓
Beef	1,000 barrels	at 3⅓ d. per bar.	3,333⅓
Sturgeon, white shad, herring	— — —	— —	3,333⅓
Brandy from peaches and apples, and whiskey	— — —	— —	1,666⅔
Horses	— — —	— —	1,666⅔
This sum is equal to 850,000 l. Virginia money, 607,142 guineas.			2,833,333⅓ D.

In the year 1758 we exported seventy thousand hogsheads of tobacco, which was the greatest quantity ever produced in this country in one year. But its culture was fast declining at the commencement of this war and that of wheat taking its place: and it must continue to decline on the return of peace. I suspect that the change in the temperature of our climate has become sensible to that plant, which, to be good, requires an extraordinary degree of heat. But it requires still more indispensably an uncommon fertility of soil: and the price which it commands at market will not enable the planter to produce this by manure. Was the supply still to depend on Virginia and Maryland alone, as its culture becomes more difficult, the price would rise, so as to enable the planter to surmount those difficulties and to live. But the western country on the Missisipi, and the midlands of Georgia, having fresh and fertile lands in abundance, and a hotter sun, will be able to undersell these two states, and will oblige them to abandon the raising tobacco altogether. And a happy obligation for them it will be. It is a culture productive of infinite wretchedness. Those employed in it are in a continued state of exertion beyond the powers of nature to support. Little food of any kind is raised by them; so that the men and animals on these farms are badly fed, and the earth is rapidly impoverished. The cultivation of wheat is the reverse in every circumstance. Besides cloathing the earth with herbage, and preserving its fertility, it feeds the labourers plentifully, requires from them only a moderate toil, except in the season of harvest, raises great numbers of animals for food and service, and diffuses plenty and happiness among the whole. We find it easier to make an hundred bushels of wheat than a thousand weight of tobacco, and they are worth more when made. The weavil indeed is a formidable obstacle to the cultivation of this grain with us. But principles are already known which must lead to a remedy. Thus a certain degree of heat, to wit, that of the common air in summer, is necessary to hatch the egg. If subterranean granaries, or others, therefore, can be contrived below that temperature, the evil will be cured by cold. A degree of heat beyond that which hatches the egg, we know will kill it. But in aiming at this we easily run into that which produces putrefaction. To produce putrefaction, however, three agents are requisite, heat, moisture, and the external air. If the absence of any one of these be secured, the other two may safely be admitted. Heat is the one we want. Moisture then, or external air, must be excluded. The former has been done by exposing the grain in kilns to the action of fire, which produces heat, and extracts moisture at the same time: the latter, by putting the grain into hogsheads, covering it with a coat of lime, and heading it up. In this situation its bulk produces a heat sufficient to kill the egg; the moisture is suffered to remain indeed, but the external air is excluded. A nicer operation yet has been attempted; that is, to produce an intermediate temperature of heat between that which kills the egg, and that which produces putrefaction. The threshing the grain as soon as it is cut, and laying it in its chaff in large heaps, has been found very nearly to hit this temperature, though not perfectly, nor always. The heap generates heat sufficient to kill most of the eggs, whilst the chaff commonly restrains it from rising into putrefaction. But all these methods abridge too much the quantity which the farmer can manage, and enable other countries to undersell him which are not infested with this insect. There is still a desideratum then to give with us decisive triumph to this branch of agriculture over that of tobacco.—The culture of wheat, by enlarging our pasture, will render the Arabian horse an article of very considerable profit. Experience has shewn that ours is the particular climate of America where he may be raised without degeneracy. Southwardly the heat of the sun occasions a deficiency of pasture, and northwardly the winters are too cold for the short and fine hair, the particular sensibility and constitution of that race. Animals transplanted into unfriendly climates, either change their nature and acquire new fences against the new difficulties in which they are placed, or they multiply poorly and become extinct. A good foundation is laid for their propagation here by our possessing already great numbers of horses of that blood, and by a decided taste and preference for them established among the people. Their patience of heat without injury, their superior wind, fit them better in this and the more southern climates even for the drudgeries of the plough and waggon. Northwardly they will become an object only to persons of taste and fortune, for the saddle and light carriages. To these, and for these uses, their fleetness and beauty will recommend them.—Besides these there will be other valuable substitutes when the cultivation of tobacco shall be discontinued, such as cotton in the eastern parts of the state, and hemp and flax in the western.

It is not easy to say what are the articles either of necessity, comfort, or luxury, which we cannot raise, and which we therefore shall be under a necessity of importing from abroad, as every thing hardier than the olive, and as hardy as the fig, may be raised here in the open air. Sugar, coffee and tea, indeed, are not between these limits; and habit having placed them among the necessaries of life with the wealthy part of our citizens, as long as these habits remain, we must go for them to those countries which are able to furnish them.

Query XXI

Weights,
Measures,
Money

The weights, measures, and the currency
of the hard money? Some details relating
to the exchange with Europe?

Our weights and measures are the same which are fixed by acts of parliament in England.—How it has happened that in this as well as the other American states the nominal value of coin was made to differ from what it was in the country we had left, and to differ among ourselves too, I am not able to say with certainty. I find that in 1631 our house of burgesses desired of the privy council in England, a coin debased to twenty-five per cent: that in 1645 they forbid dealing by barter for tobacco, and established the Spanish piece of eight at six shillings, as the standard of their currency: that in 1655 they changed it to five shillings sterling. In 1680 they sent an address to the king, in consequence of which, by proclamation in 1683, he fixed the value of French crowns, rixdollars[4] and pieces of eight at six shillings, and the coin of New-England at one shilling. That in 1710, 1714, 1727, and 1762, other regulations were made, which will be better presented to the eye stated in the form of a table as follows:

The first symptom of the depreciation of our present paper-money, was that of silver dollars selling at six shillings, which had before been worth but five shillings and ninepence. The assembly thereupon raised them by law to six shillings. As the dollar is now likely to become the money-unit of America, as it passes at this rate in some of our sister-states, and as it facilitates their computation in pounds and shillings, & e converso,[5] this seems to be more convenient than it's former denomination. But as this particular coin

4. A silver coin of several European countries.
5. Vice versa.

	1710.	1714.	1727.	1762.
Guineas	— —	26s		
British gold coin not milled, coined gold of Spain and France, chequins, Arabian gold, moidores of Portugal	— —	5s the dwt.		
Coined gold of the empire	— —	5s the dwt.	— —	4s3 the dwt.
English milled silver money, in proportion to the crown, at	— —	5s10	6s3	
Pieces of eight of Mexico, Seville, and Pillar, ducatoons of Flanders, French ecus, or silver Louis, crusados of Portugal	3¾ d. the dwt.	— —	4 d. the dwt.	
Peru pieces, cross dollars, and old rixdollars of the empire	3½ d. the dwt.	— —	3¾ d. the dwt.	
Old British silver coin not milled	— —	3¾ d. the dwt.		

now stands higher than any other in the proportion of 133⅓ to 125, or 16 to 15, it will be necessary to raise the others in the same proportion.

Query XXII

The public income and expences?   Revenue

The nominal amount of these varying constantly and rapidly, with the constant and rapid depreciation of our paper-money, it becomes impracticable to say what they are. We find ourselves cheated in every essay by the depreciation intervening between the declaration of the tax and its actual receipt. It will therefore be more satisfactory to consider what our income may be when we shall find means of collecting what the people may spare. I should estimate the whole taxable property of this state at an hundred millions of dollars, or thirty millions of pounds our money. One per cent on this, compared with any thing we ever yet paid, would be deemed a very heavy tax. Yet I think that those who manage well, and use reasonable œconomy, could pay one and a half per cent, and maintain their houshould comfortably in the mean time, without aliening[6] any part of their principal, and that the people would submit to this willingly for the purpose of supporting their present contest. We may say then, that we could raise, and ought to raise, from one million to one million and a half of dollars annually, that is from three hundred to four hundred and fifty thousand pounds, Virginia money.

Of our expences it is equally difficult to give an exact state, and for the same reason. They are mostly stated in paper money, which varying continually, the legislature endeavours at every session, by new corrections, to adapt the

6. Selling.

nominal sums to the value it is wished they should bear. I will state them therefore in real coin, at the point at which they endeavour to keep them.

	Dollars.
The annual expences of the general assembly are about	20,000
The governor	3,333⅓
The council of state	10,666⅔
Their clerks	1,166⅔
Eleven judges	11000
The clerk of the chancery	666⅔
The attorney general	1,000
Three auditors and a solicitor	5,333⅓
Their clerks	2,000
The treasurer	2,000
His clerks	2,000
The keeper of the public jail	1,000
The public printer	1,666⅔
Clerks of the inferior courts	43,333⅓
Public levy: this is chiefly for the expences of criminal justice	40,000
County levy, for bridges, court houses, prisons,&c.	40,000
Members of congress	7000
Quota of the Federal civil list, supposed ⅙ of about 78,000 dollars	13,000
Expences of collection, 6 per cent. on the above	12,310
The clergy receive only voluntary contributions: suppose them on an average ⅛ of a dollar a tythe on 200,000 tythes	25,000
Contingencies, to make round numbers not far from truth	7,523⅓
	250,000

Dollars, or 53,571 guineas. This estimate is exclusive of the military expence. That varies with the force actually employed, and in time of peace will probably be little or nothing. It is exclusive also of the public debts, which are growing while I am writing, and cannot therefore be now fixed. So it is of the maintenance of the poor, which being merely a matter of charity, cannot be deemed expended in the administration of government. And if we strike out the 25,000 dollars for the services of the clergy, which neither makes part of that administration, more than what is paid to physicians or lawyers, and being voluntary, is either much or nothing as every one pleases, it leaves 225,000 dollars, equal to 48,208 guineas, the real cost of the apparatus of government with us. This, divided among the actual inhabitants of our country, comes to about two-fifths of a dollar, 21d sterling, or 42 sols, the price which each pays annually for the protection of the residue of his property, that of his person, and the other advantages of a free government. The public revenues of Great Britain divided in like manner on its inhabitants would be sixteen times greater. Deducting even the double of the expences of government, as before estimated, from the million and a half of dollars which we before supposed might be annually paid without distress, we may conclude that this state can contribute one million of dollars annually towards supporting the federal army, paying the federal debt, building a federal navy, or opening roads, clearing rivers, forming safe ports, and other useful works.

To this estimate of our abilities, let me add a words as to the application of them, if, when cleared of the present contest, and of the debts with which that will charge us, we come to measure force hereafter with any European power. Such events are devoutly to be deprecated. Young as we are, and with such a country before us to fill with people and with happiness, we should point in that direction the whole generative force of nature, wasting none of it in efforts of mutual destruction. It should be our endeavour to cultivate the peace and friendship of every nation, even of that which has injured us most, when we shall have carried our point against her. Our interest will be to throw open the doors of commerce, and to knock off all its shackles, giving perfect freedom to all persons for the vent[7] of whatever they may chuse to bring into our ports, and asking the same in theirs. Never was so much false arithmetic employed on any subject, as that which has been employed to persuade nations that it is their interest to go to war. Were the money which it has cost to gain, at the close of a long war, a little town, or a little territory, the right to cut wood here, or to catch fish there, expended in improving what they already possess, in making roads, opening rivers, building ports, improving the arts, and finding employment for their idle poor, it would render them much stronger, much wealthier and happier. This I hope will be our wisdom. And, perhaps, to remove as much as possible the occasions of making war, it might be better for us to abandon the ocean altogether, that being the element whereon we shall be principally exposed to jostle with other nations: to leave to others to bring what we shall want, and to carry what we can spare. This would make us invulnerable to Europe, by offering none of our property to their prize, and would turn all our citizens to the cultivation of the earth; and, I repeat it again, cultivators of the earth are the most virtuous and independant citizens. It might be time enough to seek employment for them at sea, when the land no longer offers it. But the actual habits, of our countrymen attach them to commerce. They will exercise it for themselves. Wars then must sometimes be our lot; and all the wise can do, will be to avoid that half of them which would be produced by our own follies, and our own acts of injustice; and to make for the other half the best preparations we can. Of what nature should these be? A land army would be useless for offence, and not the best nor safest instrument of defence. For either of these purposes, the sea is the field on which we should meet an European enemy. On that element it is necessary we should possess some power. To aim at such a navy as the greater nations of Europe possess, would be a foolish and wicked waste of the energies of our countrymen. It would be to pull on our own heads that load of military expence, which makes the European labourer go supperless to bed, and moistens his bread with the sweat of his brows. It will be enough if we enable ourselves to prevent insults from those nations of Europe which are weak on the sea, because circumstances exist, which render even the stronger ones weak as to us. Providence has placed their richest and most defenceless possessions at our door; has obliged their most precious commerce to pass as it were in review before us. To protect this, or to assail us, a small part only of their naval force will ever be risqued across the Atlantic.

7. Sale.

The dangers to which the elements expose them here are too well known, and the greater dangers to which they would be exposed at home, were any general calamity to involve their whole fleet. They can attack us by detachment only; and it will suffice to make ourselves equal to what they may detach. Even a smaller force than they may detach will be rendered equal or superior by the quickness with which any check may be repaired with us, while losses with them will be irreparable till too late. A small naval force then is sufficient for us, and a small one is necessary. What this should be, I will not undertake to say. I will only say, it should by no means be so great as we are able to make it. Suppose the million of dollars, or 300,000 pounds, which Virginia could annually spare without distress, to be applied to the creating a navy. A single year's contribution would build, equip, man, and send to sea a force which should carry 300 guns. The rest of the confederacy, exerting themselves in the same proportion, would equip in the same time 1500 guns more. So that one year's contributions would set up a navy of 1800 guns. The British ships of the line average 76 guns; their frigates 38. 1800 guns then would form a fleet of 30 ships, 18 of which might be of the line, and 12 frigates. Allowing 8 men, the British average, for every gun, their annual expence, including subsistence, cloathing, pay, and ordinary repairs, would be about 1280 dollars for every gun, or 2,304,000 dollars for the whole. I state this only as one year's possible exertion, without deciding whether more or less than a year's exertion should be thus applied.

The value of our lands and slaves, taken conjunctly, doubles in about twenty years. This arises from the multiplication of our slaves, from the extension of culture, and increased demand for lands. The amount of what may be raised will of course rise in the same proportion.

Query XXIII

Histories, &c.   *The histories of the state, the memorials*
published in its name in the time of its being
a colony, and the pamphlets relating to its interior
or exterior affairs present or antient?

Captain Smith, who next to Sir Walter Raleigh may be considered as the founder of our colony, has written its history, from the first adventures to it till the year 1624. He was a member of the council, and afterwards president of the colony; and to his efforts principally may be ascribed its support against the opposition of the natives. He was honest, sensible, and well informed; but his style is barbarous and uncouth. His history, however, is almost the only source from which we derive any knowledge of the infancy of our state.

The reverend William Stith,[8] a native of Virginia, and president of its college, has also written the history of the same period, in a large octavo volume of small print. He was a man of classical learning, and very exact, but of no taste in style. He is inelegant, therefore, and his details often too minute to be tolerable, even to a native of the country, whose history he writes.

---

8. Stith (1707–1755), president of the College of William and Mary from 1752 to his death, published *The History of the First Discovery and Settlement of Virginia* in 1747.

Beverley,[9] a native also, has run into the other extreme; he has comprised our history, from the first propositions of Sir Walter Raleigh to the year 1700, in the hundredth part of the space which Stith employs for the fourth part of the period.

Sir William Keith[1] has taken it up at its earliest period, and continued it to the year 1725. He is agreeable enough in style, and passes over events of little importance. Of course he is short, and would be preferred by a foreigner.

During the regal government, some contest arose on the exaction of an illegal fee by governor Dinwiddie,[2] and doubtless there were others on other occasions not at present recollected. It is supposed, that these are not sufficiently interesting to a foreigner to merit a detail.

The petition of the council and burgesses of Virginia to the king, their memorial to the lords, and remonstrance to the commons in the year 1764, began the present contest: and these having proved ineffectual to prevent the passage of the stamp-act, the resolutions of the house of burgesses of 1765 were passed, declaring the independance of the people of Virginia on the parliament of Great-Britain, in matters of taxation. From that time till the declaration of independance by congress in 1776, their journals are filled with assertions of the public rights.

The pamphlets published in this state on the controverted question were,

1766, An Enquiry into the Rights of the British Colonies, by Richard Bland.
1769, The Monitor's Letters, by Dr. Arthur Lee.
1774, A summary[3] View of the Rights of British America.
—— Considerations, &c. by Robert Carter Nicholas.

Since the declaration of independence this state has had no controversy with any other, except with that of Pennsylvania, on their common boundary. Some papers on this subject passed between the executive and legislative bodies of the two states, the result of which was a happy accommodation of their rights.

To this account of our historians, memorials, and pamphlets, it may not be unuseful to add a chronological catalogue of American state-papers, as far as I have been able to collect their titles. It is far from being either complete or correct. Where the title alone, and not the paper itself, has come under my observation, I cannot answer for the exactness of the date. Sometimes I have not been able to find any date at all, and sometimes have not been satisfied that such a paper exists. An extensive collection of papers of this description has been for some time in a course of preparation by a gentleman[4] fully equal to the task, and from whom, therefore, we may hope ere long to receive it. In the mean time accept this as the result of my labours,

9. Robert Beverley (c. 1673–1722), a planter and minor public official, published *The History and Present State of Virginia* in 1705 (rev. ed. 1722).
1. The Scotsman Keith (1680–1749), governor of Pennsylvania from 1717 to 1726, projected an ambitious *History of the British Plantations in America*, of which he completed and published in 1738 only that part covering Virginia.
2. Robert Dinwiddie (1693–1770), a native of Scotland, was Virginia's lieutenant governor from 1751 to 1758. He precipitated a lively debate over colonial rights, presaging those leading up to the Revolution, by seeking to impose a quitrent on lands in 1753.
3. By the author of these Notes [Jefferson's note].
4. Mr. Hazard [Jefferson's note]. Ebenezer Hazard (1744–1817), to whom Jefferson's note refers, eventually published his pioneering *Historical Collections; Consisting of State Papers, and Other Authentic Documents; Intended as Materials, for an History of the United States of America* in 1792–94.

and as closing the tedious detail which you have so undesignedly drawn upon yourself.[5]

1496, Mar. 5.	11. H. 7.	Pro Johanne Caboto et filiis suis super terra incognita investiganda. 12. Ry. 595. 3. Hakl. 4. 2. Mem. Am. 409.
1498, Feb. 3.	13. H. 7.	Billa signata anno 13. Henrici septimi. 3. Hakluyt's voiages 5.
1502, Dec. 19.	18. H. 7.	De potestatibus ad terras incognitas investigandum. 13. Rymer. 37.
1540, Oct. 17.		Commission de François I. à Jacques Cartier pour l'establissement du Canada. L'Escarbot. 397. 2. Mem. Am. 416.
1548,	2. E. 6.	An act against the exaction of money, or any other thing, by any officer for license to traffique into Iseland and Newfoundland, made in An. 2. Edwardi sexti. 3. Hakl. 131.
1578, June 11,	20. El.	The letters-patent granted by her Majestie to Sir Humphrey Gilbert, knight, for the inhabiting and planting of our people in America. 3. Hakl. 135.
1583, Feb. 6.		Letters-patents of Queen Elizabeth to Adrian Gilbert and others, to discover the Northwest passage to China. 3. Hakl. 96.
1584, Mar. 25,	26 El.	The letters-patents granted by the Queen's majestie to M. Walter Raleigh, now knight, for the discovering and planting of new lands and countries, to continue the space of 6 years and no more. 3. Hakl. 243.
Mar. 7.	31. El.	An assignment by Sir Walter Raleigh for continuing the action of inhabiting and planting his people in Virginia. Hakl. 1st. ed. publ. in 1589, p. 815.
1603, Nov. 8.		Lettres de Lieutenant General de l'Acadie & pays circonvoisins pour le Sieur de Monts. L'Escarbot. 417.
1606, Apr. 10,	4. Jac. 1.	Letters-patent to Sir Thomas Gates, Sir George Somers and others, for two several colonies to be made in Virginia and other parts of America. Stith. Append. No. 1.
1607, Mar. 9,	4. Jac. 1.	An ordinance and constitution enlarging the council of the two colonies in Virginia and America, and augmenting their authority, M. S.

---

5. Jefferson's long list of relevant documents, like the one he sent Hazard in 1774, represents the early efforts of American intellectuals to organize the documentary record of the new nation. In citing public documents, Jefferson again employs the usual legal format (as in "1498, Feb. 3. 13. H. 7.," referring to an act of King Henry VII in 1498, the thirteenth year of his reign). Among his most important printed sources are the enlarged three-volume edition of clergyman Richard Hakluyt (1552?–1616), *Principall Navigations of the English Nations* (1598–1600), and the twenty-volume compilation of historic records by the playwright and critic Thomas Rymer (1641–1713), *Foedera, Conventiones, et cujuscunque generis Acta Publica* (1704–35).

The second charter to the treasurer and company for Virginia, erecting them into a body politick. Stith. Ap. 2.	1609, May 23.	7. Jac. 1.
Letters-patents to the E. of Northampton, granting part of the island of Newfoundland. 1. Harris. 861.	1610, Apr. 10.	Jac. 1.
A third charter to the treasurer and company for Virginia.—Stith. App. 3.	1611, Mar. 12.	9. Jac. 1.
A commission to Sir Walter Raleigh. Qu.?	1617,	Jac. 1.
Commissio specialis concernens le garbling herbæ Nicotianæ. 17. Rym. 190.	1620, Apr. 7.	18. Jac. 1.
A proclamation for restraint of the disordered trading of tobacco. 17. Rym. 233.	1620, June 29.	18. Jac. 1.
A grant of New England to the council of Plymouth.	1620, Nov. 3.	Jac. 1.
An ordinance and constitution of the treasurer, council and company in England, for a council of state and general assembly in Virginia. Stith. App. 4.	1621, July 24.	Jac. 1.
A grant of Nova Scotia to Sir William Alexander. 2. Mem. de l'Amerique. 193.	1621, Sep. 10–20.	Jac. 1.
A proclamation prohibiting interloping and disorderly trading to New England in America. 17. Rym. 416.	1622, Nov. 6.	20. Jac. 1.
De Commissione speciali Willielmo Jones militi directa. 17. Rym. 490.	1623, May 9.	21. Jac. 1.
A grant to Sir Edmund Ployden, of New Albion. Mentioned in Smith's examination. 82.	1623.	
De Commissione Henrico vice-comiti Mandevill & aliis. 17. Rym. 609.	1624, July 15.	22. Jac. 1.
De Commissione speciali concernenti gubernationem in Virginia. 17. Rym. 618.	1624, Aug. 26.	22. Jac. 1.
A proclamation concerning tobacco. 17. Rym. 621.	1624, Sep. 29.	22. Jac. 1.
De concessione demiss. Edwardo Dichfield et aliis. 17. Rym. 633.	1624, Nov. 9.	22. Jac. 1.
A proclamation for the utter prohibiting the importation and use of all tobacco which is not of the proper growth of the colony of Virginia and the Somer islands, or one of them. 17. Rym. 668.	1625, Mar. 2.	22. Jac. 1.
De commissione directa Georgio Yardeley militi et aliis. 18. Rym. 311.	1625, Mar. 4.	1. Car. 1.
Proclamatio de herba Nicotianâ. 18. Rym. 19.	1625, Apr. 9.	1. Car. 1.
A proclamation for settlinge the plantation of Virginia. 18. Rym. 72.	1625, May 13.	1. Car. 1.
A grant of the soil, barony, and domains of Nova Scotia to Sir Wm. Alexander of Minstrie. 2. Mem. Am. 226.	1625, July 12.	
Commissio directa Johanni Wolstenholme militi et aliis. 18. Ry. 831.	1626, Jan. 31.	2. Car. 1.

1626, Feb. 17.	2. Car. 1.	A proclamation touching tobacco. Ry. 848.
1627, Mar. 19. qu.?	2. Car. 1.	A grant of Massachuset's bay by the council of Plymouth to Sir Henry Roswell and others.
1627, Mar. 26.	3. Car. 1.	De concessione commissionis specialis pro concilio in Virginia. 18. Ry. 980.
1627, Mar. 30.	3. Car. 1.	De proclamatione de signatione de tobacco. 18. Ry. 886.
1627, Aug. 9.	3. Car. 1.	De proclamatione pro ordinatione de tobacco. 18. Ry. 920.
1628, Mar. 4.	3. Car. 1.	A confirmation of the grant of Massachuset's bay by the crown.
1629, Aug. 19.		The capitulation of Quebec. Champlain part. 2. 216. 2. Mem. Am. 489.
1630, Jan. 6.	5. Car. 1.	A proclamation concerning tobacco. 19. Ry. 235.
1630, April 30.		Conveyance of Nova Scotia (Port-royal excepted) by Sir William Alexander to Sir Claude St. Etienne Lord of la Tour and of Uarre and to his son Sir Charles de St. Etienne Lord of St. Denniscourt, on condition that they continue subjects to the king of Scotland under the great seal of Scotland.
1630–31, Nov. 24.	6. Car. 1.	A proclamation forbidding the disorderly trading with the salvages in New England in America, especially the furnishing the natives in those and other parts of America by the English with weapons and habiliments of warre. 19. Ry. 210. 3. Rushw. 82.
1630, Dec. 5.	6. Car. 1.	A proclamation prohibiting the selling arms, &c. to the savages in America. Mentioned 3. Rushw. 75.
1630,	Car. 1.	A grant of Connecticut by the council of Plymouth to the E. of Warwick.
1630,	Car. 1.	A confirmation by the crown of the grant of Connecticut [said to be in the petty bag office in England].
1631, Mar. 19.	6. Car. 1.	A conveiance of Connecticut by the E. of Warwick to Lord Say and Seal and others. Smith's examination, App. No. 1.
1631, June 27.	7. Car. 1.	A special commission to Edward Earle of Dorsett and others for the better plantation of the colony of Virginia. 19. Ry. 301.
1631, June 29.	7. Car. 1.	Litere continentes promissionem regis ad tradendum castrum et habitationem de Kebec in Canada ad regem Francorum. 19. Ry. 303.
1632, Mar. 29.	8. Car. 1.	Traité entre le roy Louis XIII. et Charles roi d'Angleterre pour la restitution de la nouvelle France, la Cadie et Canada et des navires et merchandises pris de part et d'autre. Fait a St. Germain. 19. Ry. 361. 2. Mem. Am. 5.

A grant of Maryland to Cæcilius Calvert, Baron of Baltimore in Ireland.	1632, June 20.	8. Car. 1.
A petition of the planters of Virginia against the grant to Lord Baltimore.	1633, July 3.	9. Car. 1.
Order of council upon the dispute between the Virginia planters and lord Baltimore. Votes of repres. of Pennsylvania. V.	1633, July 3.	
A proclamation to prevent abuses growing by the unordered retailing of tobacco. Mentioned 3. Rushw. 191.	1633, Aug. 13.	9. Car. 1.
A special commission to Thomas Young to search, discover and find out what parts are not yet inhabited in Virginia and America and other parts thereunto adjoining. 19. Ry. 472.	1633, Sept. 23.	9. Car. 1.
A proclamation for preventing of the abuses growing by the unordered retailing of tobacco. 19. Ry. 474.	1633, Oct. 13.	9. Car. 1.
A proclamation restraining the abusive venting of tobacco. 19. Rym. 522.	1634, Mar. 13.	Car. 1.
A proclamation concerning the landing of tobacco, and also forbidding the planting thereof in the king's dominions. 19. Ry. 553.	1634, May 19. 10.	Car. 1.
A commission to the Archbishop of Canterbury and 11 others, for governing the American colonies.	1634,	Car. 1.
A commission concerning tobacco. M. S.	1634, June 19.	10. Car. 1.
A commission from Lord Say and Seal, and others, to John Winthrop to be governor of Connecticut. Smith's App.	1635, July 18.	11. Car. 1.
A grant to Duke Hamilton.	1635,	Car. 1.
De commissione speciali Johanni Harvey militi pro meliori regimine coloniae in Virginia. 20. Ry. 3.	1636, Apr. 2.	12. Car. 1.
A proclamation concerning tobacco. Title in 3. Rush. 617.	1637, Mar. 14.	Car. 1.
De commissione speciali Georgio domino Goring et aliis concessâ concernente venditionem de tobacco absque licentiâ regiâ. 20. Ry. 116.	1636–7, Mar. 16.	12. Car. 1.
A proclamation against the disorderly transporting his Majesty's subjects to the plantations within the parts of America. 20. Ry. 143. 3. Rush. 409.	1637, Apr. 30.	13. Car. 1.
An order of the privy council to stay 8 ships now in the Thames from going to New-England. 3. Rush. 409.	1637, May 1.	13. Car. 1.
A warrant of the Lord Admiral to stop unconformable ministers from going beyond sea. 3. Rush. 410.	1637,	Car. 1.
Order of council upon Claiborne's petition against Lord Baltimore. Votes of representatives of Pennsylvania. vi.	1638, Apr. 4.	Car. 1.

1638, Apr. 6.	14. Car. 1.	An order of the king and council that the attorney-general draw up a proclamation to prohibit transportation of passengers to New-England without license. 3. Rush. 718.
1638, May 1.	14. Car. 1.	A proclamation to restrain the transporting of passengers and provisions to New-England without licence. 20. Ry. 223.
1639, Mar. 25.	Car. 1.	A proclamation concerning tobacco. Title 4. Rush. 1060.
1639, Aug. 19.	15. Car. 1.	A proclamation declaring his majesty's pleasure to continue his commission and letters patents for licensing retailers of tobacco. 20. Ry. 348.
1639, Dec. 16.	15. Car. 1.	De commissione speciali Henrico Ashton armigero et aliis ad amovendum Henricum Hawley gubernatorem de Barbadoes. 20. Ry. 357.
1639,	Car. 1.	A proclamation concerning retailers of tobacco. 4. Rush. 966.
1641, Aug. 9.	17. Car. 1.	De constitutione gubernatoris et concilii pro Virginia. 20. Ry. 484.
1643,	Car. 1.	Articles of union and confederacy entered into by Massachusets, Plymouth, Connecticut and New-haven. 1. Neale. 223.
1644,	Car. 1.	Deed from George Fenwick to the old Connecticut jurisdiction. An ordinance of the lords and commons assembled in parliament, for exempting from custom and imposition all commodities exported for, or imported from New-England, which has been very prosperous and without any public charge to this state, and is likely to prove very happy for the propagation of the gospel in those parts. Tit. in Amer. library 90. 5. No date. But seems by the neighbouring articles to have been in 1644.
1644, June 20.	Car. 2.	An act for charging of tobacco brought from New-England with custom and excise. Title in American library. 99. 8.
1644, Aug. 1.	Car. 2.	An act for the advancing and regulating the trade of this commonwealth. Tit. Amer. libr. 99. 9.
Sept. 18. 1. Car. 2.		Grant of the Northern neck of Virginia to Lord Hopton, Lord Jermyn, Lord Culpeper, Sir John Berkely, Sir William Moreton, Sir Dudly Wyatt, and Thomas Culpeper.
1650, Oct. 3.	2. Car. 2.	An act prohibiting trade with the Barbadoes, Virginia, Bermudas and Antego. Scoble's Acts. 1027.
1650,	Car. 2.	A declaration of Lord Willoughby, governor of Barbadoes, and of his council, against an act of

parliament of 3d of October 1650. 4. Polit. register. 2. cited from 4. Neale. hist. of the Puritans. App. No. 12. but not there.

A final settlement of boundaries between the Dutch New Netherlands and Connecticut.	1650,	Car. 2.
Instructions for Captain Robert Dennis, Mr. Richard Bennet, Mr. Thomas Stagge, and Capt. William Clabourne, appointed commissioners for the reducing of Virginia and the inhabitants thereof to their due obedience to the commonwealth of England. 1. Thurloe's state papers. 197.	1651, Sept. 26.	3. Car. 2.
An act for increase of shipping and encouragement of the navigation of this nation. Scobell's acts. 1449.	1651, Oct. 9.	3. Car. 2.
Articles agreed on and concluded at James cittie in Virginia for the surrendering and settling of that plantation under the obedience and government of the commonwealth of England, by the commissioners of the council of state, by authoritie of the parliament of England, and by the grand assembly of the governor, council, and burgesse of that state. M. S. [Ante. pa. 201.]	1651–2, Mar. 12.	4. Car. 2.
An act of indempnitie made at the surrender of the countrey [of Virginia.] [Ante. p. 206.]	1651–2, Mar. 12.	4. Car. 2.
Capitulation de Port-Royal. mem. Am. 507.	1654, Aug. 16.	
A proclamation of the protector relating to Jamaica. 3. Thurl. 75.	1655,	Car. 2.
The protector to the commissioners of Maryland. A letter. 4. Thurl. 55.	1655, Sept. 26.	7. Car. 2.
An instrument made at the council of Jamaica, Oct. 8, 1655, for the better carrying on of affairs there. 4. Thurl. 71.	1655, Oct. 8.	7. Car. 2.
Treaty of Westminster between France and England. 6. corps diplom. part 2. p. 121. 2. Mem. Am. 10.	1655, Nov. 3.	
The assembly at Barbadoes to the Protector. 4. Thurl. 651.	1656, Mar. 27.	8. Car. 2.
A grant by Cromwell to Sir Charles de Saint Etienne, a baron of Scotland, Crowne and Temple. A French translation of it. 2. Mem. Am. 511.	1656, Aug. 9.	
A paper concerning the advancement of trade. 5. Thurl. 80.	1656,	Car. 2.
A brief narration of the English rights to the Northern parts of America. 5. Thurl. 81.	1656,	Car. 2.
Mr. R. Bennet and Mr. S. Matthew to Secretary Thurloe. 5. Thurl. 482.	1656, Oct. 10.	8. Car. 2.
Objections against the Lord Baltimore's patent, and reasons why the government of Maryland	1656, Oct. 10.	8. Car. 2.

should not be put into his hands. 5. Thurl. 482.

1656, Oct. 10.	8. Car. 2.	A paper relating to Maryland. 5. Thurl. 483.
1656, Oct. 10.	8. Car. 2.	A breviet of the proceedings of the lord Baltimore and his officers and compliers in Maryland against the authority of the parliament of the commonwealth of England and against his highness the lord protector's authority laws and government. 5. Thurl. 486.
1656, Oct. 15.	8. Car. 2.	The assembly of Virginia to secretary Thurlow. 5. Thurl. 497.
1657, Apr. 4.	9. Car. 2.	The governor of Barbadoes to the protector. 6. Thurl. 169.
1661,	Car. 2.	Petition of the general court at Hartford upon Connecticut for a charter. Smith's exam. App. 4.
1662, Ap. 23.	14. Car. 2.	Charter of the colony of Connecticut. Smith's examn. App. 6.
1662–3, Mar. 24.	Apr. 4. 15. Car. 2.	The first charter granted by Charles II. to the proprietaries of Carolina, to wit, to the Earl of Clarendon, Duke of Albemarle, Lord Craven, Lord Berkeley, Lord Ashley, Sir George Carteret, Sir William Berkeley, and Sir John Colleton. 4. mem. Am. 554.
1664, Feb. 10.		The concessions and agreement of the lords proprietors of the province of New Cæsarea, or New-Jersey, to and with all and every of the adventurers and all such as shall settle or plant there. Smith's New-Jersey. App. 1.
1664, Mar. 12.	20. Car. 2.	A grant of the colony of New-York to the Duke of York.
1664, Apr. 26.	16. Car. 2.	A commission to Colonel Nichols and others to settle disputes in New-England. Hutch. Hist. Mass. Bay. App. 537.
1664, Apr. 26.		The commission to Sir Robert Carre and others to put the Duke of York in possession of New-York, New-Jersey, and all other lands thereunto appertaining.
		Sir Robert Carre and others proclamation to the inhabitants of New-York, New-Jersey, &c. Smith's N. J. 36.
1664, June 23, 24.	16. C. 2.	Deeds of lease and release of New-Jersey by the Duke of York to Lord Berkeley and Sir George Carteret.
		A conveiance of the Delaware counties to William Penn.
1664, Aug. 19–29, 20–30, 24. Aug. 25. Sept. 4.	}	Letters between Stuyvesant and Colonel Nichols on the English right. Smith's N. J. 37–42.

Treaty between the English and Dutch for the surrender of the New-Netherlands. Sm. N. Jers. 42.	1664, Aug. 27.	
Nicoll's commission to Sir Robert Carre to reduce the Dutch on Delaware bay. Sm. N. J. 47.	Sept. 3.	
Instructions to Sir Robert Carre for reducing of Delaware bay and settling the people there under his majesty's obedience. Sm. N. J. 47.		
Articles of capitulation between Sir Robert Carre and the Dutch and Swedes on Delaware bay and Delaware river. Sm. N. J. 49.	1664, Oct. 1.	
The determination of the commissioners of the boundary between the Duke of York and Connecticut. Sm. Ex. Ap. 9.	1664, Dec. 1.	16. Car. 2.
The New Haven case. Smith's Ex. Ap. 20.	1664.	
The second charter granted by Charles II. to the same proprietors of Carolina. 4. Mem. Am. 586.	1665, June 13–24.	17. C. 2.
Declaration de guerre par la France contre l'Angleterre. 3. Mem. Am. 123.	1666, Jan. 26.	
Declaration of war by the king of England against the king of France.	1666, Feb. 9.	17. Car. 2.
The treaty of peace between France and England made at Breda. 7. Corps Dipl. part 1. p. 41. 2. Mem. Am. 32.	1667, July 31.	
The treaty of peace and alliance between England and the United Provinces made at Breda. 7. Cor. Dip. p. 1. p. 44. 2. Mem. Am. 40.	1667, July 31.	
Acte de la cession de l'Acadie au roi de France. 2. Mem. Am. 292.	1667–8, Feb. 17.	
Directions from the governor and council of New York for a better settlement of the government on Delaware. Sm. N. J. 51.	1668, April 21.	
Lovelace's order for customs at the Hoarkills. Sm. N. J. 55.	1668.	
A confirmation of the grant of the northern neck of Virginia to the Earl of St. Alban's, Lord Berkeley, Sir William Moreton and John Tretheway.	16— May 8.	21. Car. 2.
Incorporation of the town of Newcastle or Amstell.	1672.	
A demise of the colony of Virginia to the Earl of Arlington and Lord Culpeper for 31 years. M. S.	1673, Feb. 25.	25. Car. 2.
Treaty at London between king Charles II. and the Dutch. Article VI.	1673–4.	

Remonstrances against the two grants of Charles II. of Northern and Southern Virginia. Ment[d]. Beverley. 65.

1674, July 13.   Sir George Carteret's instructions to Governor Carteret.

1674, Nov. 9.   Governor Andros's proclamation on taking possession of Newcastle for the Duke of York. Sm. N. J. 78.

1675, Oct. 1.   27. Car. 2.   A proclamation for prohibiting the importation of commodities of Europe into any of his majesty's plantations in Africa, Asia, or America, which were not laden in England: and for putting all other laws relating to the trade of the plantations in effectual execution.

1676, Mar. 3.   The concessions and agreements of the proprietors, freeholders and inhabitants of the province of West-New-Jersey in America. Sm. N. J. App. 2.

1676, July 1.   A deed quintipartite for the division of New-Jersey.

1676, Aug. 18.   Letter from the proprietors of New-Jersey to Richard Hartshorne. Sm. N. J. 80.

Proprietors instructions to James Wasse and Richard Hartshorne. Sm. N. J. 83.

1676, Oct. 10.   28. Car. 2.   The charter of king Charles II. to his subjects of Virginia. M. S.

1676.   Cautionary epistle from the trustees of Byllinge's part of New-Jersey. Sm. N. J. 84.

1677, Sept. 10.   Indian deed for the lands between Rankokas creek and Timber creek, in New-Jersey.

1677, Sept. 27.   Indian deed for the lands from Oldman's creek to Timber creek, in New-Jersey.

1677, Oct. 10.   Indian deed for the lands from Rankokas creek to Assunpink creek, in New-Jersey.

1678, Dec. 5.   The will of Sir George Carteret, sole proprietor of East-Jersey, ordering the same to be sold.

1680, Feb. 16.   An order of the king in council for the better encouragement of all his majesty's subjects in their trade to his majesty's plantations, and for the better information of all his majesty's loving subjects in these matters. Lond. Gaz No. 1596. Title in Amer. library. 134. 6.

1680.   Arguments against the customs demanded in New-West-Jersey by the governor of New-York, addressed to the Duke's commissioners. Sm. N. J. 117.

1680,   June 14. 23. 25.   Oct. 16.   Nov. 4. 8. 11.   }   Extracts of proceedings of the committee of trade and plantations; copies of letters, reports, &c. between the board of trade, Mr.

Penn, Lord Baltimore and Sir John Werden, in the behalf of the Duke of York and the settlement of the Pennsylvania boundaries by the L. C. J. North. Votes of Repr. Pennsyl. vii:–xiii.

> 18. 20. 23.
> Dec. 16.
> 1680–1 Jan. 15. 22.
> Feb. 24.

A grant of Pennsylvania to William Penn. Votes of Represen. Pennsylv. xviii.

1681, Mar. 4.   Car. 2.

The king's declaration to the inhabitants and planters of the province of Pennsylvania. Vo. Rep. Penn. xxiv.

1681, Apr. 2.

Certain conditions or concessions agreed upon by William Penn, proprietary and governor of Pennsylvania, and those who are the adventurers and purchasers in the same province. Votes of Rep. Pennsylv. xxiv.

1681, July 11.

Fundamental laws of the province of West-New-Jersey. Sm. N. J. 126.

1681, Nov. 9.

The methods of the commissioners for settling and regulation of lands in New-Jersey. Sm. N. J. 130.

1681–2, Jan. 14.

Indentures of lease and release by the executors of Sir George Carteret to William Penn and 11 others, conveying East-Jersey.

1681–2, Feb. 1. 2.

The Duke of York's fresh grant of East-New-Jersey to the 24 proprietors.

1682, Mar. 14.

The Frame of the government of the province of Pennsylvania, in America. Votes of Repr. Penn. xxvii.

1682, Apr. 25.

The Duke of York's deed for Pennsylvania. Vo. Repr. Penn. xxxv.

1682, Aug. 21.

The Duke of York's deed of feoffment of Newcastle and twelve miles circle to William Penn. Vo. Repr. Penn.

1682, Aug. 24.

The Duke of York's deed of feoffment of a tract of land 12 miles south from Newcastle to the Whorekills, to William Penn. Vo. Repr. Penn. xxxvii.

1682, Aug. 24.

A commission to Thomas Lord Culpeper to be lieutenant and governor-general of Virginia. M. S.

1682, Nov. 27.   34. Car. 2.

An act of union for annexing and uniting of the counties of Newcastle, Jones's and Whorekill's alias Deal, to the province of Pennsylvania, and of naturalization of all foreigners in the province and counties aforesaid.

1682, 10th month, 6th day.

An act of settlement.

1682, Dec. 6.

The frame of the government of the province of Pennsylvania and territories thereunto annexed in America.

1683, Apr. 2.

1683, Apr. 17, 27.	1684, Feb. 12.	1685, Mar. 17.	⎫ Proceedings of
May 30.	July 2, 16, 23.	Aug. 18. 26.	⎬ the committee
June 12.	Sept. 30.	Sept. 2.	
	Dec. 9.	Oct. 8. 17, 31.	of trade and
		Nov. 7.	⎭ plantations in

the dispute between Lord Baltimore and Mr. Penn. Vo. R. P. xiii–xviii.

1683, July 17.   A commission by the proprietors of East-New-Jersey to Robert Barclay to be governor. Sm. N. J. 166.

1683, July 26.   35. Car. 2.   An order of council for issuing a quo warranto against the charter of the colony of the Massachuset's bay in New-England, with his majesty's declaration that in case the said corporation of Masschuset's bay shall before prosecution had upon the same quo warranto make a full submission and entire resignation to his royal pleasure, he will then regulate their charter in such a manner, as shall be for his service and the good of that colony. Title in Amer. library. 139. 6.

1683, Sept. 28.   35. Car. 2.   A commission to Lord Howard of Effingham to be lieutenant and governor-general of Virginia. M. S.

1684, May 3.   The humble address of the chief governor, council and representatives of the island of Nevis, in the West-Indies, presented to his majesty by Colonel Netheway and Captain Jefferson, at Windsor, May 3, 1684. Title in Amer. libr. 142. 3. cites Lond. Gaz. No. 1927.

1684, Aug. 2.   A treaty with the Indians at Albany.

1686, Nov. 16.   A treaty of neutrality for America between France and England. 7. Corps. Dipl. part 2. p. 44. 2. Mem. Am. 40.

1687, Jan. 20.   By the king, a proclamation for the more effectual reducing and suppressing of pirates and privateers in America, as well on the sea as on the land in great numbers, committing frequent robberies and piracies, which hath occasioned a great prejudice and obstruction to trade and commerce, and given a great scandal and disturbance to our government in those parts. Title Amer. libr. 147. 2. cites Lond. Gaz. No. 2315.

1687, Feb. 12.   Constitution of the council of proprietors of West-Jersey. Smith's N. Jersey. 199.

1687, qu. Sept. 27.   4. Jac. 2.   A confirmation of the grant of the northern neck of Virginia to Lord Culpeper.

1687, Sept. 5.   Governor Coxe's declaration to the council of proprietors of West-Jersey. Sm. N. J. 190.

Provisional treaty of Whitehall concerning 1687, Dec. 16.
America between France and England. 2.
Mem. de l'Am. 89.

Governor Coxe's narrative relating to the division line, directed to the council of proprietors of West-Jersey. Sm. App. N. 4.

The representation of the council of proprietors
of West-Jersey to Governor Burnet. Smith.
App. No. 5.

The remonstrance and petition of the inhabitants
of East-New-Jersey to the king. Sm. App. No. 8.

The memorial of the proprietors of East-New-
Jersey to the Lords of trade. Sm. App. No. 9.

Agreement of the line of partition between East 1688, Sept. 5.
and West-New-Jersey. Sm. N. J. 196.

Conveiance of the government of West-Jersey 1691.
and territories by Dr. Coxe, to the West-Jersey
society.

A charter granted by King William and Queen 1691, Oct. 7.
Mary to the inhabitants of the province of
Massachuset's bay in New-England. 2. Mem.
de l'Am. 593.

The frame of government of the province of 1696, Nov. 7.
Pennsylvania and the territories thereunto
belonging, passed by Governor Markham.
Nov. 7, 1696.

The treaty of peace between France and En- 1697, Sept. 20.
gland, made at Ryswick. 7. Corps Dipl. part.
2. p. 399. 2. Mem. Am. 89.

The opinion and answer of the lords of trade to 1699, July 5.
the memorial of the proprietors of East-New-
Jersey. Sm. App. No. 10.

The memorial of the proprietors of East-New- 1700, Jan. 15.
Jersey to the Lords of trade. Sm. App. No. 11.

The petition of the proprietors of East and
West-New-Jersey to the Lords justices of England. Sm. App. No. 12.

A confirmation of the boundary between the 1700, W. 3.
colonies of New-York and Connecticut, by
the crown.

The memorial of the proprietors of East and 1701, Aug. 12.
West-Jersey to the king. Sm. App. No. 14.

Representation of the lords of trade to the lords 1701, Oct. 2.
justices. Sm. App. No. 13.

A treaty with the Indians. 1701.

Report of lords of trade to king William of 1701–2, Jan. 6.
draughts of a commission and instructions for
a governor of New-Jersey. Sm. N. J. 262.

Surrender from the proprietors of E. and W. N. 1702, Apr. 15.
Jersey of their pretended right of government
to her majesty Q. Anne. Sm. N. J. 211.

1702, Apr. 17.	The Queen's acceptance of the surrender of government of East and West-Jersey. Sm. N. J. 219.
1702, Nov. 16.	Instructions to lord Cornbury. Sm. N. J. 230.
1702, Dec. 5.	A commission from Queen Anne to Lord Cornbury, to be captain-general and governor in chief of New-Jersey. Sm. N. J. 220.
1703, June 27.	Recognition by the council of proprietors of the true boundary of the deeds of Sept. 10 and Oct. 10, 1677. (New Jersey). Sm. N. J. 96.
1703.	Indian deed for the lands above the falls of the Delaware in West-Jersey.
	Indian deed for the lands at the head of Rankokus river in West-Jersey.
1704, June 18.	A proclamation by Queen Anne for settling and ascertaining the current rates of foreign coins in America. Sm. N. J. 281.
1705, May 3.	Additional instructions to Lord Cornbury. Sm. N. J. 235.
1707, May 3.	Additional instructions to Lord Cornbury. Sm. N. J. 258.
1707, Nov. 20.	Additional instructions to Lord Cornbury. Sm. N. J. 259.
1707.	An answer by the council of proprietors for the western division of New-Jersey, to questions, proposed to them by Lord Cornbury. Sm. N. J. 285.
1708–9, Feb. 28.	Instructions to Colonel Vetch in his negociations with the governors of America. Sm. N. J. 364.
1708–9, Feb. 28.	Instructions to the governor of New Jersey and New-York. Sm. N. J. 361.
1710, Aug.	Earl of Dartmouth's letter to governor Hunter.
1711, Apr. 22.	Premieres propositions de la France. 6. Lamberty, 669. 2. Mem. Am. 341.
1711, Oct. 8.	Réponses de la France aux demandes préliminaires de la Grande-Bretagne. 6. Lamb. 681. 2. Mem. Amer. 344.
1711, $\frac{\text{Sept. 27.}}{\text{Oct. 8.}}$	Demandes préliminaires plus particulieres de la Grande-Bretagne, avec les réponses. 2. Mem. de l'Am. 346.
1711, $\frac{\text{Sept. 27.}}{\text{Oct. 8.}}$	L'acceptation de la part de la Grande-Bretagne. 2. Mem. Am. 356.
1711, Dec. 23.	The queen's instructions to the Bishop of Bristol and Earl of Strafford, her plenipotentiaries, to treat of a general peace. 6. Lamberty, 744. 2. Mem. Am. 358.
1712, $\frac{\text{May 24.}}{\text{June 10.}}$	A memorial of Mr. St. John to the Marquis de Torci, with regard to North America, to commerce, and to the suspension of arms. 7.

Recueil de Lamberty, 161. 2. Mem. de l'Amer. 376.

Réponse du roi de France au memoire de Londres. 7. Lamberty, p. 163. 2. Mem. Am. 380.   1712, June 10.

Traité pour une suspension d'armes entre Louis XIV. roi de France, & Anne, reigne de la Grande-Bretagne, fait à Paris. 8. Corps Diplom. part. 1. p. 308. 2. Mem. d'Am. 104.   1712, Aug. 19.

Offers of France to England, demands of England, and the answers of France. 7. Rec. de Lamb. 491. 2. Mem. Am. 390.   1712, Sept. 10.

Traité de paix & d'amitié entre Louis XIV. roi de France, & Anne, reine de la Grande-Bretagne, fait à Utrecht. 15. Corps Diplomatique de Dumont, 339. id. Latin. 2. Actes & memoires de la pais d'Utrecht, 457. id. Lat. Fr. 2. Mem. Am. 113. $1713, \frac{\text{Mar. 31.}}{\text{Apr. 11.}}$

Traité de navigation & de commerce entre Louis XIV. roi de France, & Anne, reine de la Grande-Bretagne. Fait à Utrecht. 8. Corps. Dipl. part. 1. p. 345. 2. Mem. de l'Am. 137.   1713, Mar. 31. Apr. 11.

A treaty with the Indians.   1726.

The petition of the representatives of the province of New-Jersey, to have a distinct governor. Sm. N. J. 421   1728, Jan.

Deed of release by the government of Connecticut to that of New-York.   1732,   G. 2.

The charter granted by George II. for Georgia. 4. Mem. de l'Am. 617.   1732, June 9–20.   5. G. 2.

Petition of Lord Fairfax, that a commission might issue for running and marking the dividing line between his district and the province of Virginia.   1733.

Order of the king in council for Commissioners to survey and settle the said dividing line between the proprietary and royal territory.   1733, Nov. 29.

Report of the lords of trade relating to the separating the government of the province of New-Jersey from New-York. Sm. N. J. 423.   1736, Aug. 5.

Survey and report of the commissioners appointed on the part of the crown to settle the line between the crown and Lord Fairfax.   1737, Aug. 10.

Survey and report of the commissioners appointed on the part of Lord Fairfax to settle the line between the crown and him.   1737, Aug. 11.

Order of reference of the surveys between the crown and Lord Fairfax to the council for plantation affairs.   1738, Dec. 21.

Treaty with the Indians of the 6 nations at Lancaster.   1744, June

1745, Apr. 6.		Report of the council for plantation affairs, fixing the head springs of Rappahanoc and Patowmac, and a commission to extend the line.
1745, Apr. 11.		Order of the king in council confirming the said report of the council for plantation affairs.
1748, Apr. 30.		Articles préliminaires pour parvenir à la paix, signés à Aix-la-Chapelle entre les ministres de France, de la Grande-Bretagne, & des Provinces-Unies des Pays-Bas. 2. Mem. de l'Am. 159.
1748, May 21.		Declaration des ministres de France, de la Grande-Bretagne, & des Provinces-Unies des Pays-Bas, pour rectifier les articles I. & II. des préliminaires. 2. Mem. Am. 165.
1748, Oct. 7–18.	22. G. 2.	The general and definitive treaty of peace concluded at Aix-la-Chapelle. Lond. Mag. 1748. 503 French. 2. Mem. Am. 169.
1754.		A treaty with the Indians.
1758, Aug. 7.		A conference between Governor Bernard and Indian nations at Burlington. Sm. N. J. 449.
1758, Oct. 8.		A conference between Governor Denny, Governor Bernard and others, and Indian nations at Easton. Sm. N. J. 455.
1759, July 25.	33. G. 2.	The capitulation of Niagara.
175—		The king's proclamation promising lands to souldiers.
1763, Feb. 10.	3. G. 3.	The definitive treaty concluded at Paris. Lond. Mag. 1763. 149.
1763, Oct. 7.	G. 3.	A proclamation for regulating the cessions made by the last treaty of peace. Guth. Geogr. Gram. 623.
1763.		The king's proclamation against settling on any lands on the waters, westward of the Alleghaney.
1768, Nov. 3.		Deed from the six nations of Indians to William Trent and others for lands betwixt the Ohio and Monongahela: View of the title to Indiana. Phil. Styner and Cist. 1776.
1768, Nov. 5.		Deed from the six nations of Indians to the crown for certain lands and settling a boundary. M. S.

Appendix No. I.

The preceding sheets having been submitted to my friend Mr. Charles Thomson, Secretary of Congress, he has furnished me with the following observations, which have too much merit not to be communicated.[6]

1. (PAGE [32])

Besides the three channels of communication mentioned between the western waters and the Atlantic, there are two others, to which the Pennsylvanians are turning their attention; one from Presque-isle, on Lake Erie, to Le Bœuf, down the Alleghaney to Kiskiminitas, then up the Kiskiminitas, and from thence, by a small portage, to Juniata, which falls into the Susquehanna: the other from Lake Ontario to the East Branch of the Delaware, and down that to Philadelphia. Both these are said to be very practicable: and, considering the enterprising temper of the Pennsylvanians, and particularly of the merchants of Philadelphia, whose object is concentered in promoting the commerce and trade of one city, it is not improbable but one or both of these communications will be opened and improved.

2. (PAGE [34])

The reflections I was led into on viewing this passage of the Patowmac through the Blue ridge were, that this country must have suffered some violent convulsion, and that the face of it must have been changed from what it probably was some centuries ago: that the broken and ragged faces of the mountain on each side the river; the tremendous rocks, which are left with one end fixed in the precipice, and the other jutting out, and seemingly ready to fall for want of support; the bed of the river for several miles below obstructed, and filled with the loose stones carried from this mound; in short, every thing on which you cast your eye evidently demonstrates a disrupture and breach in the mountain, and that, before this happened, what is now a fruitful vale, was formerly a great lake or collection of water, which possibly might have here formed a mighty cascade, or had its vent to the ocean by the Susquehanna, where the Blue ridge seems to terminate. Besides this, there are other parts of this country which bear evident traces of a like convulsion. From the best accounts I have been able to obtain, the place where the Delaware now flows through the Kittatinny mountain, which is a continuation of what is called the North ridge, or mountain, was not its original course, but that it passed through what is now called "the Wind-gap," a place several miles to the westward, and above an hundred

6. For the circumstances surrounding these "Observations," see Letter to Charles Thomson, December 20, 1781, on p. 217. A ten-year-old Scots-Irish orphan when he arrived in America with his brothers in 1739, Charles Thomson (1729–1824) became a Latin tutor in the Philadelphia academy that was the forerunner of the University of Pennsylvania and was one of the founders of the American Philosophical Society. Active in political affairs in the years leading up to the Revolution, he served as secretary of the First and Second Continental Congresses from the first meeting in 1774 until 1789. Thomson, who published *An Enquiry into the Causes of the Alienation of the Delaware and Shawanese Indians from the British Interest* in 1759, had particular interest in issues relative to Native Americans.

feet higher than the present bed of the river. This Wind-gap is about a mile broad, and the stones in it such as seem to have been washed for ages by water running over them. Should this have been the case, there must have been a large lake behind that mountain, and by some uncommon swell in the waters, or by some convulsion of nature, the river must have opened its way through a different part of the mountain, and meeting there with less obstruction, carried away with it the opposing mounds of earth, and deluged the country below with the immense collection of waters to which this new passage gave vent. There are still remaining, and daily discovered, innumerable instances of such a deluge on both sides of the river, after it passed the hills above the falls of Trenton, and reached the champaign. On the New-Jersey side, which is flatter than the Pennsylvania side, all the country below Croswick hills seems to have been overflowed to the distance of from ten to fifteen miles back from the river, and to have acquired a new soil by the earth and clay brought down and mixed with the native sand. The spot on which Philadelphia stands evidently appears to be made ground. The different strata through which they pass in digging to water, the acorns, leaves, and sometimes branches, which are found above twenty feet below the surface, all seem to demonstrate this. I am informed that at York town in Virginia, in the bank of York river, there are different strata of shells and earth, one above another, which seem to point out that the country there has undergone several changes; that the sea has, for a succession of ages, occupied the place where dry land now appears; and that the ground has been suddenly raised at various periods. What a change would it make in the country below, should the mountains at Niagara, by any accident, be cleft asunder, and a passage suddenly opened to drain off the waters of Erie and the Upper lakes! While ruminating on these subjects, I have often been hurried away by fancy, and led to imagine, that what is now the bay of Mexico, was once a champaign country; and that from the point or cape of Florida, there was a continued range of mountains through Cuba, Hispaniola, Porto rico, Martinique, Guadaloupe, Barbadoes, and Trinidad, till it reached the coast of America, and formed the shores which bounded the ocean, and guarded the country behind: that, by some convulsion or shock of nature, the sea had broken through these mounds, and deluged that vast plain, till it reached the foot of the Andes; that being there heaped up by the trade-winds, always blowing from one quarter, it had found its way back, as it continues to do, through the gulph between Florida and Cuba, carrying with it the loom and sand it may have scooped from the country it had occupied, part of which it may have deposited on the shores of North America, and with part formed the banks of Newfoundland.—But these are only the visions of fancy.

3. (page [46])

There is a plant, or weed, called the James town weed, of a very singular quality.[7] The late Dr. Bond[8] informed me, that he had under his care a patient, a young girl, who had put the seeds of this plant into her eye, which dilated the pupil to such a degree, that she could see in the dark, but in the

---

7. Datura pericarpiis erectis ovatis. Linn [Jefferson's note].
8. Probably Phineas Bond (1717–1773), who was on the staff of the Philadelphia Hospital.

light was almost blind. The effect that the leaves had when eaten by a ship's crew that arrived at James town, are well known.[9]

4. (PAGE [63])

Mons. Buffon has indeed given an afflicting picture of human nature in his description of the man of America. But sure I am there never was a picture more unlike the original. He grants indeed that his stature is the same as that of the man of Europe. He might have admitted, that the Iroquois were larger, and the Lenopi, or Delawares, taller than people in Europe generally are. But he says their organs of generation are smaller and weaker than those of Europeans. Is this a fact? I believe not; at least it is an observation I never heard before.—"They have no beard." Had he known the pains and trouble it costs the men to pluck out by the roots the hair that grows on their faces, he would have seen that nature had not been deficient in that respect. Every nation has its customs. I have seen an Indian beau, with a looking glass in his hand, examining his face for hours together, and plucking out by the roots every hair he could discover, with a kind of tweezer made of a piece of fine brass wire, that had been twisted around a stick, and which he used with great dexterity.—"They have no ardour for their female." It is true, they do not indulge those excesses, nor discover that fondness which is customary in Europe; but this is not owing to a defect in nature, but to manners. Their soul is wholly bent upon war. This is what procures them glory among the men, and makes them the admiration of the women. To this they are educated from their earliest youth. When they pursue game with ardour, when they bear the fatigues of the chase, when they sustain and suffer patiently hunger and cold; it is not so much for the sake of the game they pursue, as to convince their parents and the council of the nation that they are fit to be enrolled in the number of the warriors. The songs of the women, the dance of the warriors, the sage counsel of the chiefs, the tales of the old, the triumphal entry of the warriors returning with success from battle, and the respect paid to those who distinguish themselves in war and in subduing their enemies; in short, every thing they see or hear tends to inspire them with an ardent desire for military fame. If a young man were to discover a fondness for women before he has been to war, he would become the contempt of the men, and the scorn and ridicule of the women. Or were he to indulge himself with a captive taken in war, and much more were he to offer violence in order to gratify his lust, he would incur indelible disgrace. The seeming frigidity of the men, therefore, is the effect of manners, and not a defect of nature. Besides, a celebrated warrior is oftener courted by the females, than he has occasion to court: and this is a point of honour which the men aim at. Instances similar to that of Ruth and Boaz[1] are not uncommon among them. For though the women are modest and diffident, and so bashful that they seldom lift up their eyes, and scarce ever look a man full in the face, yet, being brought up in great subjection, custom and manners reconcile them to modes of acting, which,

9. An instance of temporary imbelicity produced by them is mentioned, Beverl. H. of Virg., B. 2. c. 4 [Jefferson's note].
1. When Boas had eaten and drank, and his heart was merry, he went to lie down at the end of the heap of corn; and Ruth came softly, and uncovered his feet, and laid her down. Ruth iii. 7 [Jefferson's note].

judged of by Europeans, would be deemed inconsistent with the rules of female decorum and propriety. I once saw a young widow, whose husband, a warrior, had died about eight days before, hastening to finish her grief, and who by tearing her hair, beating her breast, and drinking spirits, made the tears flow in great abundance, in order that she might grieve much in a short space of time, and be married that evening to another young warrior. The manner in which this was viewed by the men and women of the tribe, who stood round, silent and solemn spectators of the scene, and the indifference with which they answered my question respecting it, convinced me that it was no unusual custom. I have known men advanced in years, whose wives were old and past childbearing, take young wives, and have children, though the practice of polygamy is not common. Does this savour of frigidity, or want of ardour for the female? Neither do they seem to be deficient in natural affection. I have seen both fathers and mothers in the deepest affliction, when their children have been dangerously ill; though I believe the affection is stronger in the descending than the ascending scale, and though custom forbids a father to grieve immoderately for a son slain in battle.—"That they are timorous and cowardly," is a character with which there is little reason to charge them, when we recollect the manner in which the Iroquois met Mons. ———, who marched into their country; in which the old men, who scorned to fly, or to survive the capture of their town, braved death, like the old Romans in the time of the Gauls, and in which they soon after revenged themselves by sacking and destroying Montreal. But above all, the unshaken fortitude with which they bear the most excruciating tortures and death when taken prisoners, ought to exempt them from that character. Much less are they to be characterised as a people of no vivacity, and who are excited to action or motion only by the calls of hunger and thirst. Their dances in which they so much delight, and which to a European would be the most severe exercise, fully contradict this, not to mention their fatiguing marches, and the toil they voluntarily and cheerfully undergo in their military expeditions. It is true, that when at home, they do not employ themselves in labour or the culture of the soil: but this again is the effect of customs and manners, which have assigned that to the province of the women. But it is said, they are averse to society and a social life. Can any thing be more inapplicable than this to a people who always live in towns or clans? Or can they be said to have no "republique," who conduct all their affairs in national councils, who pride themselves in their national character, who consider an insult or injury done to an individual by a stranger as done to the whole, and resent it accordingly? In short, this picture is not applicable to any nation of Indians I have ever known or heard of in North America.

5. (PAGE [91])

As far as I have been able to learn, the country from the sea coast to the Alleghaney, and from the most southern waters of James river up to Patuxent river, now in the state of Maryland, was occupied by three different nations of Indians, each of which spoke a different language, and were under separate and distinct governments. What the original or real names of those nations were, I have not been able to learn with certainty: but by us they are distinguished by the names of Powhatàns, Mannahòacs, and

Mònacans, now commonly called Tuscaròras. The Powhatàns, who occupied the country from the sea shore up to the falls of the rivers, were a powerful nation, and seem to have consisted of seven tribes five on the western
and two on the eastern shore. Each of these tribes was subdivided into
towns, families, or clans, who lived together. All the nations of Indians in
North America lived in the hunter state, and depended for subsistence on
hunting, fishing, and the spontaneous fruits of the earth, and a kind of
grain which was planted and gathered by the women, and is now known by
the name of Indian corn. Long potatoes, pumpkins of various kinds, and
squashes, were also found in use among them. They had no flocks, herds,
or tamed animals of any kind. Their government is a kind of patriarchal confederacy. Every town or family has a chief, who is distinguished by a particular title, and whom we commonly call "Sachem." The several towns or
families that compose a tribe, have a chief who presides over it, and the several tribes composing a nation have a chief who presides over the whole
nation. These chiefs are generally men advanced in years, and distinguished
by their prudence and abilities in council. The matters which merely regard
a town or family are settled by the chief and principal men of the town:
those which regard a tribe, such as the appointment of head warriors or
captains, and settling differences between different towns and families, are
regulated at a meeting or council of the chiefs from the several towns; and
those which regard the whole nation, such as the making war, concluding
peace, or forming alliances with the neighbouring nations, are deliberated
on and determined in a national council composed of the chiefs of the tribe,
attended by the head warriors and a number of the chiefs from the towns,
who are his counsellors. In every town there is a council house, where the
chief and old men of the town assemble, when occasion requires, and consult what is proper to be done. Every tribe has a fixed place for the chiefs
of the towns to meet and consult on the business of the tribe: and in every
nation there is what they call the central council house, or central council
fire, where the chiefs of the several tribes, with the principal warriors, convene to consult and determine on their national affairs. When any matter
is proposed in the national council, it is common for the chiefs of the several tribes to consult thereon apart with their counsellors, and, when they
have agreed, to deliver the opinion of the tribe at the national council: and,
as their government seems to rest wholly on persuasion, they endeavour, by
mutual concessions, to obtain unanimity. Such is the government that still
subsists among the Indian nations bordering upon the United States. Some
historians seem to think, that the dignity of office of Sachem was hereditary. But that opinion does not appear to be well founded. The Sachem or
chief of the tribe seems to be by election. And sometimes persons who are
strangers, and adopted into the tribe, are promoted to this dignity, on
account of their abilities. Thus on the arrival of Capt. Smith, the first
founder of the colony of Virginia, Opechàncanough, who was Sachem or
chief of the Chickahòminies, one of the tribes of the Powhàtans, is said to
have been of another tribe, and even of another nation, so that no certain
account could be obtained of his origin or descent. The chiefs of the nation
seem to have been by a rotation among the tribes. Thus when Capt. Smith,
in the year 1609, questioned Powhatàn (who was the chief of the nation,
and whose proper name is said to have been Wahunsonacock) respecting
the succession, the old chief informed him, "that he was very old and had

seen the death of all his people thrice;[2] that not one of these generations were then living except himself, that he must soon die and the succession descend in order to his brothers Opichapàn, Opechàncanough, and Catatàugh, and then to his two sisters, and their two daughters." But these were appellations designating the tribes in the confederacy. For the persons named are not his real brothers, but the chiefs of different tribes. Accordingly in 1618, when Powhatan died, he was succeeded by Opichapàn, and after his decease Opechàncanough became chief of the nation. I need only mention another instance to shew that the chiefs of the tribes claimed this kindred with the head of the nation. In 1622, when Raleigh Crashaw was with Japazàw, the Sachem or chief of the Patowmacs, Opechàncanough, who had great power and influence, being the second man in the nation, and next in succession to Opichapan, and who was a bitter but secret enemy to the English, and wanted to engage his nation in a war with them, sent two baskets of beads to the Patowmac chief, and desired him to kill the Englishman that was with him. Japazaw replied, that the English were his friends, and Opichapàn his *brother,* and that therefore there should be no blood shed between them by his means. It is also to be observed, that when the English first came over, in all their conferences with any of the chiefs, they constantly heard him make mention of his *brother,* with whom he must consult, or to whom he referred them, meaning thereby either the chief of the nation, or the tribes in confederacy. The Manahòacks are said to have been a confederacy of four tribes, and in alliance with the Monacans, in the war which they were carrying on against the Powhatans.

To the northward of these there was another powerful nation, which occupied the country from the head of the Chesapeak-bay up to the Kittatinney mountains, and as far eastward as Connecticut river, comprehending that part of New-York which lies between the highlands and the ocean, all the state of New-Jersey, that part of Pennsylvania which is watered, below the range of the Kittatinney mountains, by the rivers or streams falling into the Delaware, and the county of Newcastle in the state of Delaware, as far as Duck creek. It is to be observed, that the nations of Indians distinguished their countries one from another by natural boundaries, such as ranges of mountains, or streams of water. But as the heads of rivers frequently interlock, or approach near to each other, as those who live upon a stream claim the country watered by it, they often encroached on each other, and this is a constant source of war between the different nations. The nation occupying the tract of country last described, called themselves Lenopi. The French writers call them Loups; and among the English they are now commonly called Delawares. This nation or confederacy consisted of five tribes, who all spoke one language. 1. The Chihohocki, who dwelt on the West side of the river now called Delaware, a name which it took from Lord De la War, who put into it on his passage from Vir-

---

2. This is one generation more than the poet ascribes to the life of Nestor [Jefferson's note]. Jefferson here inserted the Greek original, as well as Pope's translation of Homer:

> Two generations now had past away,
> Wise by his rules, and happy by his sway;
> Two ages o'er his native realm he reign'd,
> And now th' example of the third remain'd.
> [Alexander] Pope

ginia in the year [1611],[3] but which by the Indians was called Chihohocki. 2. The Wanami, who inhabited the country, called New-Jersey, from the Rariton to the sea. 3. The Munsey, who dwelt on the upper streams of the Delaware, from the Kittatinney mountains down to the Leheigh or western branch of the Delaware. 4. The Wabinga, who are sometimes called River Indians, sometimes Mohickanders, and who had their dwelling between the west branch of Delaware and Hudson's river, from the Kittatinney ridge down to the Rariton: and 5. The Mahiccon, or Mahattan, who occupied Staten island, York island, (which from its being the principal seat of their residence was formerly called Mahatton), Long island, and that part of New-York and Connecticut which lies between Hudson and Connecticut rivers, from the highland, which is a continuation of the Kittatinney ridge down to the sound. This nation had a close alliance with the Shawanese, who lived on the Susquehannah and to the westward of that river, as far as the Alleghaney mountains, and carried on a long war with another powerful nation or confederacy of Indians, which lived to the north of them between the Kittatinney mountains, or highlands, and the lake Ontario, and who call themselves Mingos, and are called by the French writers Iroquois, by the English the Five Nations, and by the Indians to the southward, with whom they were at war, Massawomacs. This war was carrying on, in its greatest fury, when Captain Smith first arrived in Virginia. The Mingo warriors had penetrated down the Susquehanna to the mouth of it. In one of his excursions up the bay, at the mouth of the Susequehanna, in 1608, Captain Smith met with six or seven of their canoes full of warriors, who were coming to attack their enemies in the rear. In an excursion which he had made a few weeks before, up the Rappahanock, and in which he had a skirmish with a party of the Manahoacs, and taken a brother of one of their chiefs prisoner, he first heard of this nation. For when he asked the prisoner, why his nation attacked the English? the prisoner said, because his nation had heard that the English came from under the world to take their world from them. Being asked, how many worlds he knew? he said, he knew but one, which was under the sky that covered him, and which consisted of the Powhatàns, the Mànakins, and the Massawòmacs. Being questioned concerning the latter, he said, they dwelt on a great water to the North, that they had many boats, and so many men that they waged war with all the rest of the world. The Mingo confederacy then consisted of five tribes; three who are called the elder, to wit, the Senecas, who live to the West, the Mohawks to the East, and the Onondagas between them; and two who are called the younger tribes, namely, the Cayugas, and Oneidas. All these tribes speak one language, and were then united in a close confederacy, and occupied the tract of country from the East end of lake Erie to lake Champlain, and from the Kittatinney and Highlands to the lake Ontario and the river Cadaraqui, or St. Laurence. They had, some time before that, carried on a war with a nation, who lived beyond the lakes, and were called Adirondacs. In this war they were worsted: but having made a peace with them, through the intercession of the French, who were then settling Canada, they turned their arms against the Lenopi; and as this war was long and doubtful, they, in the course of it, not only exerted their whole force, but put

3. Date supplied by the editor.

in practice every measure which prudence or policy could devise to bring it to a successful issue. For this purpose they bent their course down the Susquehanna, warring with the Indians in their way, and having penetrated as far as the mouth of it, they, by the terror of their arms, engaged a nation, now known by the name of Nanticocks, Conoys, and Tùteloes, and who lived between Chesapeak and Delaware bays, and bordering on the tribe of Chihohocki, to enter into an alliance with them. They also formed an alliance with the Monakans, and stimulated them to a war with the Lenopi and their confederates. At the same time the Mohawks carried on a furious war down the Hudson against the Mohiccons and River indians, and compelled them to purchase a temporary and precarious peace, by acknowledging them to be their superiors, and paying an annual tribute: The Lenopi being surrounded with enemies, and hard pressed, and having lost many of their warriors, were at last compelled to sue for peace, which was granted to them on the condition that they should put themselves under the protection of the Mingoes, confine themselves to raising corn, hunting for the subsistence of their families, and no longer have the power of making war. This is what the Indians call making them women. And in this condition the Lenopis were when William Penn first arrived and began the settlement of Pennsylvania in 1682.

6. (page [93])

From the figurative language of the Indians, as well as from the practice of those we are still acquainted with, it is evident that it was, and still continues to be, a constant custom among the Indians to gather up the bones of the dead, and deposit them in a particular place. Thus, when they make peace with any nation, with whom they have been at war, after burying the hatchet, they take up the belt of wampum, and say, "We now gather up all the bones of those who have been slain, and bury them, &c." See all the treaties of peace. Besides, it is customary when any of them die at a distance from home, to bury them, and afterwards to come and take up the bones, and carry them home. At a treaty which was held at Lancaster with the six nations, one of them died, and was buried in the woods a little distance from the town. Some time after a party came and took up the body, separated the flesh from the bones by boiling and scraping them clean, and carried them to be deposited in the sepulchres of their ancestors. The operation was so offensive and disagreeable, that nobody could come near them while they were performing it.

7. (page [94])

The Oswegàtchies, Connosedàgos and Cohunnegàgoes, or, as they are commonly called, Caghnewàgos, are of the Mingo or Six-nation Indians, who, by the influence of the French missionaries, have been separated from their nation, and induced to settle there.

I do not know of what nation the Augquàgahs are; but suspect they are a family of the Senecas.

The Nànticocks and Conòies were formerly of a nation that lived at the head of Chesapeak bay, and who, of late years, have been adopted into the Mingo or Iroquois confederacy, and make a seventh nation. The Monacans or Tuscaroras, who were taken into the confederacy in 1712, making the sixth.

The Saponies are families of the Wanamies, who removed from New-Jersey, and, with the Mohiccons, Munsies, and Delawares, belong to the Lenopi nation. The Mingos are a war colony from the six nations; so are the Cohunnewagos.

Of the rest of the northern tribes I never have been able to learn any thing certain. But all accounts seem to agree in this, that there is a very powerful nation, distinguished by a variety of names taken from the several towns or families, but commonly called Tàwas or Outawas, who speak one language, and live round and on the waters that fall into the western lakes, and extend from the waters of the Ohio quite to the waters falling into Hudson's bay.

Appendix No. II.

In the Summer of the Year 1783, it was expected, that the
ASSEMBLY OF VIRGINIA would call a CONVENTION for the
Establishment of a CONSTITUTION. The following DRAUGHT
of a FUNDAMENTAL CONSTITUTION for the COMMONWEALTH
OF VIRGINIA was then prepared, with a Design of being
proposed in such Convention, had it taken place.[4]

To the Citizens of the Commonwealth of Virginia, and all others whom it may concern, the Delegates for the said Commonwealth in Convention assembled, send greeting.

It is known to you, and to the world, that the government of Great Britain, with which the American States were not long since connected, assumed over them an authority unwarrantable and oppressive; that they endeavoured to enforce this authority by arms, and that the States of New Hampshire, Massachusets, Rhode island, Connecticut, New York, New Jersey, Pennsylvania, Delaware, Maryland, Virginia, North Carolina, South Carolina, and Georgia, considering resistance, with all its train of horrors, as a lesser evil than abject submission, closed in the appeal to arms. It hath pleased the Sovereign Disposer of all human events to give to this appeal an issue favourable to the rights of the States; to enable them to reject for ever all dependance on a government which had shewn itself so capable of abusing the trusts reposed in it; and to obtain from that government a solemn and explicit acknowledgment that they are free, sovereign, and independant States. During the progress of that war, through which we had to labour for the establishment of our rights, the legislature of the commonwealth of Virginia found it necessary to make a temporary organization of government for preventing anarchy, and pointing our efforts to the two important objects of war against our invaders, and peace and happiness among ourselves. But this, like all other their acts of legislation, being subject to change by subsequent legislatures, possessing equal powers with themselves, it has been thought expedient, that it should receive those amendments which time and trial have suggested, and be rendered permanent by a power superior to that of the ordinary legislature. The general

4. Jefferson himself prepared this proposed revision of Virginia's constitution in 1783 and printed it in both the private 1785 edition of *Notes on the State of Virginia* and the Stockdale edition of 1787.

assembly therefore of this state recommend it to the good people thereof, to chuse delegates to meet in general convention, with powers to form a constitution of government for them, and to declare those fundamentals to which all our laws present and future shall be subordinate: and, in compliance with this recommendation, they have thought proper to make choice of us, and to vest us with powers for this purpose.

We therefore, the delegates, chosen by the said good people of this state for the purpose aforesaid, and now assembled in general convention, do, in execution of the authority with which we are invested, establish the following constitution and fundamentals of government for the said state of Virginia.

The said state shall for ever hereafter be governed as a commonwealth.

The powers of government shall be divided into three distinct departments, each of them to be confided to a separate body of magistracy; to wit, those which are legislative to one, those which are judiciary to another, and those which are executive to another. No person, or collection of persons, being of one of these departments, shall exercise any power properly belonging to either of the others, except in the instances hereinafter expressly permitted.

I. LEGISLATURE.

The legislature shall consist of two branches, the one to be called the House of Delegates, the other the Senate, and both together the General Assembly. The concurrence of both of these, expressed on three several readings, shall be necessary to the passage of a law.

ELECTION.

Delegates for the general assembly shall be chosen on the last Monday of November in every year. But if an election cannot be concluded on that day, it may be adjourned from day to day till it can be concluded.

DELEGATES.

The number of delegates which each county may send shall be in proportion to the number of its qualified electors; and the whole number of delegates for the state shall be so proportioned to the whole number of qualified electors in it, that they shall never exceed 300, nor be fewer than 100. Whenever such excess or deficiency shall take place, the House of Delegates so deficient or excessive shall, notwithstanding this, continue in being during its legal term; but they shall, during that term, re-adjust the proportion, so as to bring their number within the limits beforementioned at the ensuing election. If any county be reduced in its qualified electors below the number authorized to send one delegate, let it be annexed to some adjoining county.

SENATE.

For the election of senators, let the several counties be allotted by the senate, from time to time, into such and so many districts as they shall find best; and let each county at the time of electing its delegates, chuse senatorial electors, qualified as themselves are, and four in number for each delegate their county is entitled to send, who shall convene, and conduct themselves, in such manner as the legislature shall direct, with the senatorial electors from the other counties of their district, and then chuse, by ballot, one senator for every six delegates which their district is entitled to chuse. Let the senatorial districts be divided into two classes, and let the members elected for one of them be dissolved at the first ensuing general election of delegates, the other at the next, and so on alternately for ever.

ELECTORS.

All free male citizens, of full age, and sane mind, who for one year before shall have been resident in the county, or shall through the whole of that time have possessed therein real property of the value of   or shall for the same time have been enrolled in the milita, and no others, shall have a right to vote for delegates for the said county, and for senatorial electors for the district. They shall give their votes personally, and *vivâ voce.*

GENERAL ASSEMBLY.

The general assembly shall meet at the place to which the last adjournment was, on the 42d day after the day of the election of delegates, and thenceforward at any other time or place on their own adjournment, till their office expires, which shall be on the day preceding that appointed for the meeting of the next general assembly. But if they shall at any time adjourn for more than one year, it shall be as if they had adjourned for one year precisely. Neither house, without the concurrence of the other, shall adjourn for more than one week, nor to any other place than the one at which they are sitting. The governor shall also have power, with the advice of the council of state, to call them at any other time to the same place, or to a different one, if that shall have become, since the last adjournment, dangerous from an enemy, or from infection.

QUORUM.

A majority of either house shall be a quorum, and shall be requisite for doing business: but any smaller proportion which from time to time shall be thought expedient by the respective houses, shall be sufficient to call for, and to punish, their non-attending members, and to adjourn themselves for any time not exceeding one week.

PRIVILEGES.

The members, during their attendance on the general assembly, and for so long a time before and after as shall be necessary for travelling to and from the same, shall be privileged from all personal restraint and assault, and shall have no other privilege whatsoever. They shall receive during the same time, daily wages in gold or silver, equal to the value of two bushels of wheat. This value shall be deemed one dollar by the bushel till the year 1790, in which, and in every tenth year thereafter, the general court, at their first sessions in the year, shall cause a special jury, of the most respectable merchants and farmers, to be summoned, to declare what shall have been the averaged value of wheat during the last ten years; which averaged value shall be the measure of wages for the ten subsequent years.

EXCLUSIONS.

Of this general assembly, the treasurer, attorney general, register, ministers of the gospel, officers of the regular armies of this state, or of the United States, persons receiving salaries or emoluments from any power foreign to our confederacy, those who are not resident in the county for which they are chosen delegates, or districts for which they are chosen senators, those who are not qualified as electors, persons who shall have committed treason, felony, or such other crime as would subject them to infamous punishment, or who shall have been convicted by due course of law of bribery or corruption, in endeavouring to procure an election to the said assembly, shall be incapable of being members. All others, not herein elsewhere excluded, who may elect, shall be capable of being elected thereto.

Any member of the said assembly accepting any office of profit under this state, or the United States, or any of them, shall thereby vacate his seat, but shall be capable of being re-elected.

VACANCIES.

Vacancies occasioned by such disqualifications, by death, or otherwise, shall be supplied by the electors, on a writ from the speaker of the respective house.

LIMITS OF POWER.

The general assembly shall not have power to infringe this constitution; to abridge the civil rights of any person on account of his religious belief; to restrain him from professing and supporting that belief, or to compel him to contributions, other than those he shall have personally stipulated, for the support of that or any other; to ordain death for any crime but treason or murder, or military offences; to pardon, or give a power of pardoning persons duly convicted of treason or felony, but instead thereof they may substitute one or two new trials, and no more; to pass laws for punishing actions done before the existence of such laws; to pass any bill of attainder of treason or felony; to prescribe torture in any case whatever; nor to permit the introduction of any more slaves to reside in this state, or the continuance of slavery beyond the generation which shall be living on the thirty-first day of December, one thousand eight hundred: all persons born after that day being hereby declared free.

The general assembly shall have power to sever from this state all or any part of its territory westward of the Ohio, or of the meridian of the mouth of the great Kanhaway, and to cede to Congress one hundred square miles of territory in any other part of this state, exempted from the jurisdiction and government of this state so long as Congress shall hold their sessions therein, or in any territory adjacent thereto, which may be ceded to them by any other state.

They shall have power to appoint the speakers of their respective houses, treasurer, auditors, attorney-general, register, all general officers of the military, their own clerks and serjeants, and no other officers, except where, in other parts of this constitution, such appointment is expressly given them.

II. EXECUTIVE. GOVERNOR.

The executive powers shall be exercised by a *governor*, who shall be chosen by joint ballot of both houses of assembly, and when chosen shall remain in office five years, and be ineligible a second time. During his term he shall hold no other office or emolument under this state, or any other state or power whatsoever. By executive powers, we mean no reference to those powers exercised under our former government by the crown as of its prerogative, nor that these shall be the standard of what may or may not be deemed the rightful powers of the governor. We give him those powers only, which are necessary to execute the laws (and administer the government) and which are not in their nature either legislative or judiciary. The application of this idea must be left to reason. We do however expressly deny him the prerogative powers of erecting courts, offices, boroughs, corporations, fairs, markets, ports, beacons, light-houses, and sea-marks; of laying embargoes, of establishing precedence, of retaining within the state or recalling to it any citizen thereof, and of making denizens, except so far as he may be authorised from time to time by the legislature to exercise any of those powers. The powers of declaring war and concluding peace, of contracting alliances, of issuing letters of marque and reprisal, of raising or introducing armed forces, of building armed vessels, forts, or strong holds, of coining money or regulating its value, of regulating weights and measures, we leave to be exercised under the authority of the confederation: but in all cases respecting them which are out of the said confederation, they shall be exercised by the governor, under the regulation of such laws as the legislature may think it expedient to pass.

The whole military of the state, whether regular, or of militia, shall be subject to his directions; but he shall leave the execution of those directions to the general officers appointed by the legislature.

His salary shall be fixed by the legislature at the session of assembly in which he shall be appointed, and before such appointment be made; or if it be not then fixed, it shall be the same which his next predecessor in office was entitled to. In either case he may demand it quarterly out of any money which shall be in the public treasury; and it shall not be in the power of the legislature to give him less or more, either during his continuance in office, or after he shall have gone out of it. The lands, houses, and other things appropriated to the use of the governor, shall remain to his use during his continuance in office.

COUNCIL OF STATE.

A *council of state* shall be chosen by joint ballot of both houses of assembly, who shall hold their offices seven years, and be ineligible a second time, and who, while they shall be of the said council, shall hold no other office or emolument, under this state, or any other state or power whatsoever. Their duty shall be to attend and advise the governor when called on by him, and their advice in any case shall be a sanction to him. They shall also have power, and it shall be their duty, to meet at their own will, and to give their advice, though not required by the governor, in cases where they shall think the public good calls for it. Their advice and proceedings shall be entered in books to be kept for that purpose, and shall be signed as approved of disapproved by the members present. These books shall be laid before either house of assembly when called for by them. The said council shall consist of eight members for the present: but their numbers may be increased or reduced by the legislature, whenever they shall think it necessary: provided such reduction be made only as the appointments become vacant by death, resignation, disqualification, or regular deprivation. A majority of their actual number, and not fewer, shall be a quorum. They shall be allowed for the present each by the year, payable quarterly out of any money which shall be in the public treasury. Their salary however may be increased or abated from time to time, at the discretion of the legislature; provided such increase or abatement shall not, by any ways or means, be made to affect either then, or at any future time, any one of those then actually in office. At the end of each quarter their salary shall be divided into equal portions by the number of days on which, during that quarter, a council has been held, or required by the governor, or by their own adjournment, and one of those portions shall be withheld from each member for every of the said days which, without cause allowed good by the board, he failed to attend, or departed before adjournment without their leave. If no board should have been held during that quarter, there shall be no deduction.

PRESIDENT.

They shall annually chuse a *president*, who shall preside in council in the absence of the governor, and who, in case of his office becoming vacant by death or otherwise, shall have authority to exercise all his functions, till a new appointment be made, as he shall also in any interval during which the governor shall declare himself unable to attend to the duties of his office.

III. JUDICIARY.

The *Judiciary* powers shall be exercised by county courts and such other inferior courts as the legislature shall think proper to continue or to erect, by three superior courts, to wit, a Court of Admiralty, a General Court of Common Law, and a High Court of Chancery; and by one supreme court to be called the Court of Appeals.

The judges of the High Court of Chancery, General Court, and Court of Admiralty, shall be four in number each, to be appointed by joint ballot of both houses of assembly, and to hold their offices during good behaviour. While they continue judges, they shall hold no other office or emolument, under this state, or any other state or power whatsoever, except that they may be delegated to Congress, receiving no additional allowance.

These judges, assembled together, shall constitute the Court of Appeals, whose business shall be to receive and determine appeals from the three superior courts, but to receive no original causes, except in the cases expressly permitted herein.

A majority of the members of either of these courts, and not fewer, shall be a quorum. But in the Court of Appeals nine members shall be necessary to do business. Any smaller numbers however may be authorized by the legislature to adjourn their respective courts.

They shall be allowed for the present   each by the year, payable quarterly out of any money which shall be in the public treasury. Their salaries however may be increased or abated, from time to time, at the discretion of the legislature, provided such increase or abatement shall not, by any ways or means, be made to affect, either then, or at any future time, any one of those then actually in office. At the end of each quarter their salary shall be divided into equal portions by the number of days on which, during that quarter, their respective courts sat, or should have sat, and one of these portions shall be withheld from each member for every of the said days, which, without cause allowed good by his court, he failed to attend, or departed before adjournment without their leave. If no court should have been held during the quarter, there shall be no deduction.

There shall moreover be a court of *Impeachments* to consist of three members of the council of state, one of each of the superior Courts of Chancery, Common Law, and Admiralty, two members of the House of Delegates and one of the Senate, to be chosen by the body respectively of which they are. Before this court any member of the three branches of government, that is to say, the governor, any member of the council, of the two houses of legislature, or of the superior courts, may be impeached by the governor, the council, or either of the said houses or courts, and by no other, for such misbehaviour in office as would be sufficient to remove him therefrom: and the only sentence they shall have authority to pass shall be that of deprivation and future incapacity of office. Seven members shall be requisite to make a court, and two-thirds of those present must concur in the sentence. The offences cognisable by this court shall be cognisable by no other, and they shall be triers of the fact as well as judges of the law.

The justices or judges of the inferior courts already erected, or hereafter to be erected, shall be appointed by the governor, on advice of the council of state, and shall hold their offices during good behaviour, or the existence of their court. For breach of the good behaviour, they shall be tried according to the laws of the land, before the Court of Appeals, who shall be judges of the fact as well as of the law. The only sentence they shall have authority to pass, shall be that of deprivation and future incapacity of office, and two thirds of the members present must concur in this sentence.

All courts shall appoint their own clerks, who shall hold their offices during good behaviour, or the existence of their court: they shall also appoint all other their attending officers to continue during their pleasure. Clerks appointed by the supreme or the superior courts shall be removeable by their respective courts. Those to be appointed by other courts shall have been previously examined, and certified to be duly qualified, by some two members of the general court, and shall be removeable for breach of the good behaviour by the Court of Appeals only, who shall be judges of the fact as well as of the law. Two-thirds of the members present must concur in the sentence.

The justices or judges of the inferior courts may be members of the legislature.

The judgment of no inferior court shall be final, in any civil case, of greater value than 50 bushels of wheat, as last rated in the general court for settling the allowance to the members of the general assembly, nor in any case of treason, felony, or other crime which would subject the party to infamous punishment.

In all causes depending before any court, other than those of impeachments, of appeals, and military courts, facts put in issue shall be tried by jury, and in all courts whatever witnesses shall give their testimony vivâ voce in open court, wherever their attendance can be procured: and all parties shall be allowed counsel and compulsory process for their witnesses.

Fines, amercements, and terms of imprisonment left indefinite by the law, other than for contempts, shall be fixed by the jury, triers of the offence.

IV. COUNCIL OF REVISION.

The governor, two councellors of state, and a judge from each of the superior Courts of chancery, Common Law, and Admiralty, shall be a council to revise all bills which shall have passed both houses of assembly, in which council the governor, when present, shall preside. Every bill, before it becomes a law, shall be presented to this council, who shall have a right to advise its rejection, returning the bill, with their advice and reasons in writing, to the house in which it originated, who shall proceed to reconsider the said bill. But if after such reconsideration, two thirds of the house shall be of opinion the bill should pass finally, they shall pass and send it, with the advice and written reasons of the said council of revision to the other house, wherein, if two thirds also shall be of opinion it should pass finally, it shall thereupon become law: otherwise it shall not.

If any bill, presented to the said council, be not, within one week (exclusive of the day of presenting it) returned by them, with their advice of rejection and reasons, to the house wherein it originated, or to the clerk of the said house, in case of its adjournment over the expiration of the week, it shall be law from the expiration of the week, and shall then be demandable by the clerk of the House of Delegates, to be filed of record in his office.

The bills which they approve shall become law from the time of such approbation, and shall then be returned to, or demandable by, the clerk of the House of Delegates, to be filed of record in his office.

A bill rejected on advice of the Council of Revision may again be proposed, during the same session of assembly, with such alterations as will render it conformable to their advice.

The members of the said Council of Revision shall be appointed from time to time by the board or court of which they respectively are. Two of the executive and two of the judiciary members shall be requisite to do business: and to prevent the evils of non-attendance, the board and courts may, at any time, name all, or so many as they will, of their members, in the particular order in which they would chuse the duty of attendance to devolve from preceding to subsequent members, the preceding failing to attend. They shall have additionally for their services in this council the same allowance as members of assembly have.

CONFEDERACY.

The Confederation is made a part of this constitution, subject to such future alterations as shall be agreed to by the legislature of this state, and by all the other confederating states.

DELEGATES TO CONGRESS.

The delegates to Congress shall be five in number; any three of whom, and no fewer, may be a representation. They shall be appointed by joint ballot of both houses of assembly for any term not exceeding one year, subject to be recalled, within the term, by joint vote of both the said houses. They may at the same time be members of the legislative or judiciary departments, but not of the executive.

HAB. CORP.

The benefits of the writ of Habeas Corpus shall be extended, by the legislature, to every person within this state, and without fee, and shall be so facilitated that no person may be detained in prison more than ten days after he shall have demanded and been refused such writ by the judge appointed by law, or if none be appointed, then by any judge of a superior court, nor more than ten days after such writ shall have been served on the person detaining him, and no order given, on due examination, for his remandment or discharge.

MILITARY.

The military shall be subordinate to the civil power.

PRINTING.

Printing-presses shall be subject to no other restraint than liableness to legal prosecution for false facts printed and published.

CONVENTION.

Any two of the three branches of government concurring in opinion, each by the voices of two thirds of their whole existing number, that a convention is necessary for altering this constitution, or correcting breaches of it, they shall be authorized to issue writs to every county for the election of so many delegates as they are authorized to send to the General Assembly, which elections shall be held, and writs returned, as the laws shall have provided in the case of elections of Delegates to assembly, mutatis mutandis, and the said Delegates shall meet at the usual place of holding assemblies, three months after the date of such writs, and shall be acknowledged to have equal powers with this present convention. The said writs shall be signed by all the members approving the same.

To introduce this government, the following special and temporary provision is made.

This convention being authorized only to amend those laws which constituted the form of government, no general dissolution of the whole system of laws can be supposed to have taken place: but all laws in force at the meeting of this convention, and not inconsistent with this constitution, remain in full force, subject to alterations by the ordinary legislature.

The present General Assembly shall continue till the 42d day after the last Monday of November in this present year. On the said last Monday of

November in this present year, the several counties shall, by their electors, qualified as provided by this constitution, elect delegates, which for the present shall be, in number, one for every   militia of the said county, according to the latest returns in possession of the governor, and shall also chuse senatorial electors in proportion thereto, which senatorial electors shall meet on the 14th day after the day of their election, at the Court-house of that county of their present district which would stand first in an alphabetical arrangement of their counties, and shall chuse senators in the proportion fixed by this constitution. The elections and returns shall be conducted, in all circumstances not hereby particularly prescribed, by the same persons and under the same forms, as prescribed by the present laws in elections of Senators and Delegates of Assembly. The said Senators and Delegates shall constitute the first General Assembly of the new government, and shall specially apply themselves to the procuring an exact return from every county of the number of its qualified electors, and to the settlement of the number of Delegates to be elected for the ensuing General Assembly.

The present Governor shall continue in office to the end of the term for which he was elected.

All other officers of every kind shall continue in office as they would have done had their appointment been under this constitution, and new ones, where new are hereby called for, shall be appointed by the authority to which such appointment is referred. One of the present judges of the general court, he consenting thereto, shall by joint ballot of both houses of assembly, at their first meeting, be transferred to the High Court of Chancery.

Appendix No. III.

An ACT for establishing RELIGIOUS FREEDOM, passed in the Assembly of Virginia in the beginning of the year 1786.[5]

Well aware that Almighty God hath created the mind free; that all attempts to influence it by temporal punishments or burthens, or by civil incapacitations, tend only to beget habits of hypocrisy and meanness, and are a departure from the plan of the Holy Author of our religion, who, being Lord both of body and mind, yet chose not to propagate it by coercions on either, as was in his Almighty power to do; that the impious presumption of legislators and rulers, civil as well as ecclesiastical, who, being themselves but fallible and uninspired men have assumed dominion over the faith of others, setting up their own opinions and modes of thinking as the only true and infallible, and as such endeavouring to impose them on others, hath established and maintained false religions over the greatest part of the world, and through all time; That to compel a man to furnish contributions of money for the propagation of opinions which he disbelieves, is sinful and tyrannical; that even the forcing him to support this or that teacher of his own religious persuasion, is depriving him of the comfortable liberty of giving his contributions to the particular pastor whose morals he would make his pattern, and whose powers he feels most persuasive to righteousness, and is withdrawing from the ministry

5. Separately printed as a pamphlet in Paris in spring 1786, this document was included by Jefferson as the third and last appendix in Stockdale's 1787 edition of *Notes on the State of Virginia*. The act in question had been passed by the Virginia general assembly in January 1786.

those temporal rewards which, proceeding from an approbation of their personal conduct, are an additional incitement to earnest and unremitting labours for the instruction of mankind; that our civil rights have no dependence on our religious opinions, more than on our opinions in physics or geometry; that therefore the proscribing any citizen as unworthy the public confidence by laying upon him an incapacity of being called to offices of trust and emolument, unless he profess or renounce this or that religious opinion, is depriving him injuriously of those privileges and advantages to which in common with his fellow citizens he has a natural right; that it tends also to corrupt the principles of that very religion it is meant to encourage, by bribing, with a monopoly of worldly honors and emoluments, those who will externally profess and conform to it; that though indeed these are criminal who do not withstand such temptation, yet neither are those innocent who lay the bait in their way; that to suffer the civil magistrate to intrude his powers into the field of opinion, and to restrain the profession or propagation of principles, on supposition of their ill tendency, is a dangerous fallacy, which at once destroys all religious liberty, because he being of course judge of that tendency, will make his opinions the rule of judgment, and approve or condemn the sentiments of others only as they shall square with or differ from his own; that it is time enough for the rightful purposes of civil government for its officers to interfere when principles break out into overt acts against peace and good order; and finally, that truth is great and will prevail if left to herself, that she is the proper and sufficient antagonist to error, and has nothing to fear from the conflict, unless by human interposition disarmed of her natural weapons, free argument and debate, errors ceasing to be dangerous when it is permitted freely to contradict them.

Be it therefore enacted by the General Assembly, That no man shall be compelled to frequent or support any religious worship, place or ministry whatsoever, nor shall be enforced, restrained, molested, or burthened in his body or goods, nor shall otherwise suffer on account of his religious opinions or belief; but that all men shall be free to profess, and by argument to maintain, their opinions in matters of religion, and that the same shall in no wise diminish, enlarge, or affect their civil capacities.

And though we well know that this Assembly, elected by the people for the ordinary purposes of legislation only, have no power to restrain the acts of succeeding Assemblies, constituted with powers equal to our own, and that therefore to declare this act irrevocable, would be of no effect in law, yet we are free to declare, and do declare, that the if any act shall be hereafter passed to repeal the present, or to narrow rights hereby asserted are of the natural rights of mankind, and that its operation, such act will be an infringement of natural right.

178

An Appendix to the Notes on Virginia Relative
to the Murder of Logan's Family[1]

A Letter to Governor Henry,[2] of Maryland

Philadelphia, December 31st 1797.

Dear Sir,

Mr. Tazewell has communicated to me the enquiries you have been so kind as to make, relative to a passage in the Notes on Virginia, which has lately excited some newspaper publications. I feel, with great sensibility, the interest you take in this business, and with pleasure, go into explanations with one whose objects I know to be truth and justice alone. Had Mr. Martin[3] thought proper to suggest to me, that doubts might be entertained of the transaction respecting Logan, as stated in the Notes on Virginia, and to enquire on what grounds that statement was founded, I should have felt myself obliged by the enquiry, have informed him candidly of the grounds, and cordially have cooperated in every means of investigating the fact, and correcting whatsoever in it should be found to have been erroneous. But he chose to step at once into the newspapers, and in his publications there and the letters he wrote to me, adopted a style which forbade the respect of an answer. Sensible, however, that no act of his could absolve me from the justice due to others, as soon as I found that the story of Logan could be doubted, I determined to enquire into it as accurately as the testimony remaining, after a lapse of twenty odd years, would permit, and that the result should be made known, either in the first new edition which should be printed of the Notes on Virginia, or by publishing an appendix. I thought that so far as that work had contributed to impeach the memory of Cresap, by handing on an erroneous charge, it was proper it should be made the vehicle of retribution. Not that I was at all the author of the injury. I had only concurred, with thousands and thousands of others, in believing a transaction on authority which merited respect. For the story of Logan is only repeated in the Notes on Virginia, precisely as it had been current for more than a dozen years before they were published. When Lord Dunmore returned from the expedition against the Indians, in 1774, he and his officers brought the speech of Logan, and related the circumstances connected with it. These were so affecting, and the speech itself so fine a morsel of eloquence, that it became the theme of every conversation, in Williamsburgh particularly, and generally, indeed, wheresoever any of the officers resided or resorted. I learned it in Williamsburgh; I believe at lord Dunmore's; and I find in my pocket-book of that year (1774) an entry of the narrative, as taken from the mouth of some person, whose name, however, is not noted, nor rec-

---

1. The text is derived from the first edition, published in Philadelphia in 1800.
2. John Henry (1750–1798), a Federalist politician, graduated from the College of New Jersey (Princeton) in 1769, then studied law in the Middle Temple, London, before returning home in 1775. A member of the Continental Congress and then the U.S. Senate, he became governor of Maryland in 1797. As mentioned in the opening sentence of the pamphlet, Henry had communicated his "enquiries" to Jefferson through Henry Tazewell (1753–1799), U.S. Senator from Virginia and Jefferson's friend.
3. Luther Martin (1748–1826), a Maryland Federalist, began a newspaper campaign against Jefferson following the latter's election as vice president in 1797 (for one of his published letters, see p. 402 herein). The son-in-law of Michael Cresap, Martin also had personal motives for attacking the credibility of the account of Logan and Cresap in *Notes on the States of Virginia*.

ollected, precisely in the words stated in the notes on Virginia. The speech was published in the Virginia Gazette of that time (I have it myself in the volume of gazettes of that year) and though in a style by no means elegant, yet it was so admired, that it flew through all the public papers of the continent, and through the magazines and other periodical publications of Great Britain; and those who were boys at that day will now attest, that the speech of Logan used to be given them as a school exercise for repetition. It was not till about thirteen or fourteen years after the newspaper publications, that the Notes on Virginia were published in America. Combating, in these, the contumelious theory of certain European writers, whose celebrity gave currency and weight to their opinions, that our country, from the combined effects of soil and climate, degenerated animal nature, in the general, and particularly the moral faculties of man, I considered the speech of Logan as an apt proof of the contrary, and used it as such; and I copied, verbatim, the narrative I had taken down in 1774, and the speech as it had been given us in a better translation by lord Dunmore. I knew nothing of the Cresaps, and could not possibly have a motive to do them an injury with design. I repeated what thousands had done before, on as good authority as we have for most of the facts we learn through life, and such as, to this moment, I have seen no reason to doubt. That any body questioned it, was never suspected by me, till I saw the letter of Mr. Martin in the Baltimore paper. I endeavoured then to recollect who among my cotemporaries, of the same circle of society, and consequently of the same recollections, might still be alive. Three and twenty years of death and dispersion had left very few. I remembered, however, that general Gibson[4] was still living, and knew that he had been the translator of the speech. I wrote to him immediately. He, in answer, declares to me, that he was the very person sent by lord Dunmore to the Indian town; that, after he had delivered his message there, Logan took him out to a neighbouring wood; sat down with him, and rehearsing, with tears, the catastrophe of his family, gave him that speech for lord Dunmore; that he carried it to lord Dunmore; translated it for him; has turned to it in the Encyclopedia, as taken from the Notes on Virginia, and finds that it was his translation I had used, with only two or three verbal variations of no importance These, I suppose, had arisen in the course of successive copies. I cite general Gibson's letter by memory, not having it with me; but I am sure I cite it substantially right. It establishes unquestionably, that the speech of Logan is genuine; and that being established, it is Logan himself who is author of all the important facts. "Colonel Cresap," says he, "in cold blood and unprovoked, murdered all the relations of Logan, not sparing even my women and children. There runs not a drop of my blood in the veins of any living creature." The person and the fact, in all its material circumstances, are here given by Logan himself. General Gibson, indeed, says, that the title was mistaken; that Cresap was a captain, and not a colonel. This was Logan's mistake. He also observes, that it was on the Ohio, and not on the Kanhaway itself, that his family was killed. This is an error which has crept into the traditionary account; but surely of little moment in the moral view of the

---

4. Pennsylvania native John Gibson (1740–1822), an Indian captive in the Ohio country during Pontiac's War, and husband of one of Logan's female relatives, translated Logan's speech for Lord Dunmore. After military service on the western frontier during the Revolution, he was appointed secretary of Indiana Territory in 1800 and served in the territorial government throughout Jefferson's administration.

subject. The material question is; was Logan's family murdered, and by whom? That it was murdered has not, I believe, been denied; that it was by one of the Cresaps, Logan affirms. This is a question which concerns the memories of Logan and Cresap; to the issue of which I am as indifferent as if I had never heard the name of either. I have begun and shall continue to enquire into the evidence additional to Logan's, on which the fact was founded. Little, indeed, can now be heard of, and that little dispersed and distant. If it shall appear on enquiry, that Logan has been wrong in charging Cresap with the murder of his family, I will do justice to the memory of Cresap, as far as I have contributed to the injury, by believing and repeating what others had believed and repeated before me. If, on the other hand, I find that Logan was right in his charge, I will vindicate, as far as my suffrage may go, the truth of a Chief, whose talents and misfortunes have attached to him the respect and commiseration of the world.

I have gone, my dear Sir, into this lengthy detail to satisfy a mind, in the candour and rectitude of which I have the highest confidence. So far as you may incline to use the communication for rectifying the judgments of those who are willing to see things truly as they are, you are free to use it. But I pray that no confidence which you may repose in any one, may induce you to let it go out of your hands, so as to get into a newspaper. Against a contest in that field I am entirely decided. I feel extraordinary gratification, indeed, in addressing this letter to you, with whom shades of difference in political sentiment have not prevented the interchange of good opinion, nor cut off the friendly offices of society and good correspondence. This political tolerance is the more valued by me, who consider social harmony as the first of human felicities, and the happiest moments, those which are given to the effusions of the heart. Accept them sincerely, I pray you, from one who has the honor to be, with sentiments of high respect and attachment,

> *Dear Sir,*
> *Your most obedient*
> *And most humble servant,*
> THOMAS JEFFERSON

The Notes on Virginia were written, in Virginia, in the years 1781 and 1782, in answer to certain queries proposed to me by Mons. de Marbois, then secretary of the French legation in the United States; and a manuscript copy was delivered to him. A few copies, with some additions, were afterwards, in 1784,[5] printed in Paris, and given to particular friends. In speaking of the animals of America, the theory of M. de Buffon, the Abbe Raynal, and others, presented itself to consideration. They have supposed that there is something in the soil, climate and other circumstances of America, which occasions animal nature to degenerate, not excepting even the man, native or adoptive, physical or moral. This theory, so unfounded and degrading to one third of the globe, was called to the bar of fact and reason. Among other proofs adduced in contradiction of this hypothesis,

---

5. Jefferson mistakes the date of the private edition, which came off the press on May 10, 1785 (see letter to James Madison, May 11, 1785, on p. 223). To add to the confusion, the date on the title page read "MDCCLXXXII," 1782 being the year during which Jefferson had finished much of his early work on the project.

the speech of Logan, an Indian chief, delivered to lord Dunmore in 1774, was produced, as a specimen of the talents of the aboriginals of this country, and particularly of their eloquence; and it was believed that Europe had never produced any thing superior to this morsel of eloquence. In order to make it intelligible to the reader, the transaction, on which it was founded, was stated, as it had been generally related in America at the time, and as I had heard it myself, in the circle of lord Dunmore, and the officers who accompanied him: and the speech itself was given as it had, ten years before the printing of that book, circulated in the newspapers through all the then colonies, through the magazines of Great-Britain, and periodical publications of Europe. For three and twenty years it passed uncontradicted; nor was it ever suspected that it even admitted contradiction. In 1797 however, for the first time, not only the whole transaction respecting Logan was affirmed in the public papers to be false, but the speech itself suggested to be a forgery, and even a forgery of mine, to aid me in proving that the man of America was equal in body and in mind, to the man of Europe. But wherefore the forgery? Whether Logan's or mine, it would still have been American. I should indeed consult my own fame if the suggestion, that this speech is mine, were suffered to be believed. He would have a just right to be proud who could with truth claim that composition. But it is none of mine; and I yield it to whom it is due.

On seeing then that this transaction was brought into question, I thought it my duty to make particular enquiry into its foundation. It was the more my duty, as it was alledged that, by ascribing to an individual therein named, a participation in the murder of Logan's family, I had done an injury to his character, which it had not deserved. I had no knowledge personally of that individual. I had no reason to aim an injury at him. I only repeated what I had heard from others, and what thousands had heard and believed as well as myself; and which no one indeed, till then, had been known to question. Twenty three years had now elapsed, since the transaction took place. Many of those acquainted with it were dead, and the living dispersed to very distant parts of the earth. Few of them were even known to me. To those however of whom I knew, I made application by letter; and some others, moved by a regard for truth and justice, were kind enough to come forward, of themselves, with their testimony. These fragments of evidence, the small remains of a mighty mass which time has consumed, are here presented to the public, in the form of letters, certificates, or affidavits, as they came to me. I have rejected none of these forms, nor required other solemnities from those whose motives and characters were pledges of their truth. Historical transactions are deemed to be well vouched by the simple declarations of those who have borne a part in them; and especially of persons having no interest to falsify or disfigure them. The world will now see whether they, or I, have injured Cresap, by believing Logan's charge against him: and they will decide between Logan and Cresap, whether Cresap was innocent, and Logan a calumniator?

In order that the reader may have a clear conception of the transactions, to which the different parts of the following declarations refer, he must take notice that they establish four different murders. 1. Of two Indians, a little above Wheeling. 2. Of others at Grave Creek, among whom were some of Logan's relations. 3. The massacre at Baker's bottom, on the Ohio, opposite the mouth of Yellow Creek, where were other relations of Logan. 4. Of those killed at the same place, coming in canoes to the relief of their friends. I place the numbers 1, 2, 3, 4, against certain paragraphs of the evidence, to indicate the particular murder to which the paragraph relates, and present also a small sketch or map of the principal scenes of these butcheries, for their more ready comprehension.

Extract of a letter from the honourable Judge INNES[6] *of Frankfort in Kentucky to* THOMAS JEFFERSON; *dated Kentucky, near Frankfort March 2d, 1799.*

I recollect to have seen Logan's speech in 1775, in one of the public prints. That Logan conceived Cresap to be the author of the murder at Yellow Creek, it is in my power to give, perhaps, a more particular information, than any other person you can apply to.

In 1774 I lived in Fincastle county, now divided into Washington, Montgomery and part of Wythe. Being intimate in Col. Preston's family, I happened in July to be at his house, when an Express was sent to him as the County Lieut. requesting a guard of the militia to be ordered out for the protection of the inhabitants residing low down on the north fork of Holston river. The Express brought with him a War Club, and a note which was left tied to it at the house of one Robertson, whose family were cut off by the Indians, and gave rise for the application to Col. Preston, of which the following is a copy, then taken by me in my memorandum book.

"Captain Cresap,
  What did you kill my people on Yellow Creek for? The white people killed my kin, at Conestoga, a great while ago; and I thought nothing of that. But you killed my kin again, on Yellow Creek, and took my Cousin Prisoner. Then I thought I must kill too; and I have been three times to war since; but the Indians are not angry: only myself."

Captain JOHN LOGAN.

July 21st, 1774.

With great respect, I am, Dear Sir,
your most obedient servant,

HARRY INNES.

Allegeney County, ss. }
State of Pennsylvania.

Before me the Subscriber, a justice of the peace in and for said county, personally appeared John Gibson, Esquire, an associate Judge of same county, who being duly sworn deposeth and saith that he traded with the Shawnese and other tribes of Indians then settled on the Siota in the year 1773, and in the beginning of the year 1774, and that in the month of April of the same year, he left the same Indian towns, and came to this place, in order to procure some goods and provisions, that he remained here only a few days, and then set out in company with a certain Alexander Blaine and M. Elliot by water to return to the towns on Siota, and that one evening as

---

6. Virginian Harry Innes (1752–1816), educated at William and Mary, studied law under George Wythe. Moving to the Kentucky district of Virginia in 1783, he favored Kentucky statehood and held a variety of offices there, including first judge of the federal district court, to which he was appointed by George Washington. He and Jefferson were frequent correspondents.

they were drifting in their Canoes near the Long Reach on the Ohio, they were hailed by a number of white men on the South West Shore, who requested them to put ashore, as they had disagreeable news to inform them of; that we then landed on shore; and found amongst the party, a Major Angus M'Donald from West Chester, a Doctor Woods from same place, and a party as they said of 150 men. We then asked the news. They informed us that some of the party who had been taken up, and improving lands near the Big Kanhawa river, had seen another party of white men, who informed them that they and some others had fell in with a party of Shawnese, who had been hunting on the South West side of the Ohio, that they had killed the whole of the Indian party, and that the others had gone across the country to Cheat river with the horses and plunder, the consequence of which they apprehended would be an Indian War, and that they were flying away. On making enquiry of them when this murder should have happened, we found that it must have been some considerable time before we left the Indian towns, and that there was not the smallest foundation for the report, as there was not a single man of the Shawnese, but what returned from hunting long before this should have happened.

We then informed them that if they would agree to remain at the place we then were, one of us would go to Hock Hocking river with some of their party, where we should find some of our people making Canoes, and that if we did not find them there, we might conclude that everything was not right. Doctor Wood and another person then proposed going with me; the rest of the party seemed to agree, but said they would send and consult captain Cresap who was about two miles from that place. They sent off for him, and during the greatest part of the night they behaved in the most disorderly manner, threatening to kill us, and saying the damned traders were worse than the Indians and ought to be killed. In the morning captain Michael Cresap come to the camp. I then gave him the information as above related. They then met in Council, and after an hour or more captain Cresap returned to me and informed that he could not prevail on them to adopt the proposal I had made to them, that as he had a great regard for captain R. Callender, a brother In law of mine with whom I was connected in trade, he advised me by no means to think of proceeding any further, as he was convinced the present party would fall on and kill every Indian they met on the river, that for his part he should not continue with them, but go right across the country to Red Stone to avoid the consequences. That we then proceeded to Hocking and went up the same to the canoe place, where we found our people at work, and after some days we proceeded to the towns on Siota by land. On our arrival there, we heard of the different murders committed by the party on their way up the Ohio.

This Deponent further saith that in the year 1774, he accompanied Lord Dunmore on the Expedition against the Shawnese and other Indians on the Siota, that on their arrival within 15 Miles of the towns, they were met by a flag, and a white man of the name of Elliot, who informed Lord Dunmore that the Chiefs of the Shawnese had sent to request his Lordship to halt his army and send in some person, who understood their language; that this Deponent, at the request of Lord Dunmore and the whole of the officers with him, went in; that on his arrival at the towns, Logan, the Indian, came to where this deponent was sitting with the Corn-Stalk, and the other chiefs of the Shawnese, and asked him to walk out with him; that they went into a copse of wood, where they sat down, when Logan, after shedding abundance of tears, delivered to him the speech, nearly as related by Mr. Jefferson in his notes on the State of Virginia; that he the Deponent told him then that it was not Col. Cressap who had murdered his relations, and that although his son captain Michael Cressap was with the party who killed a Shawnese chief and other Indians, yet he was not present when his relations were killed at Baker's, near the mouth of Yellow Creek on the Ohio; that this Deponent on his return to camp delivered the speech to Lord Dunmore; and that the murders perpetrated as above were considered as ultimately the cause of the War of 1774, commonly called Cressap's war.

Sworn and subscribed the 4th April, ⎱
1800, at Pittsburgh, before me, ⎰   JOHN GIBSON.

JER. BARKER.

Extract of a letter from Col. EBENEZER ZANE,
to the honourable JOHN BROWN,[7] *one of the Senators*
in Congress from Kentucky; dated Wheeling, Feb. 4th, 1800.

I was myself, with many others, in the practice of making improvements on lands upon the Ohio, for the purpose of acquiring rights to the same. Being on the Ohio at the mouth of Sandy Creek, in company with many others, news circulated that the Indians had robbed some of the Land jobbers. This news induced the people generally to ascend the Ohio. I was among the number. On our arrival at the Wheeling, being informed that there were two Indians with some traders near and above Wheeling, a proposition was made by the then captain Michael Cresap to way lay and kill the Indians upon the river. This measure I opposed with much violence, alledging that the killing of those Indians might involve the country in a war. But the opposite party prevailed, and proceeded up the Ohio with captain Cresap at their head.

In a short time the party returned, and also the traders, in a canoe; but there were no Indians in the company. I enquired what had become of the Indians, and was informed by the traders and Cresap's party that they had fallen overboard. I examined the canoe, and saw much fresh blood and some bullet holes in the canoe. This fully convinced me that the party had killed the two Indians, and thrown them into the river.

On the afternoon of the day this action happened, a report prevailed that there was a camp, or party of Indians on the Ohio below and near the Wheeling. In consequence of this information, captain Cresap with his party, joined by a number of recruits, proceeded immediately down the Ohio for the purpose, as was then generally understood, of destroying the Indians above mentioned. On the succeeding day, captain Cresap and his party returned to Wheeling, and it was generally reported by the party that they had killed a number of Indians. Of the truth of this report I had no doubt, as one of Cresap's party was badly wounded, and the party had a

---

7. Virginia native Ebenezer Zane (1747–1811) was an early settler and soldier in the Ohio country, serving under Lord Dunmore before fighting on the American side in the Revolution. John Brown (1757–1837), also born in Virginia, likewise fought in the Revolution. He represented Virginia in the Congress before serving as U.S. senator from Kentucky (1792–1805).

fresh scalp, and a quantity of property, which they called Indian plunder. At the time of the last mentioned transaction, it was generally reported that the party of Indians down the Ohio were Logan and his family; but I have reason to believe that this report was unfounded.

Within a few days after the transaction above mentioned, a party of Indi- 3 ans were killed at Yellow Creek. But I must do the memory of captain Cresap the justice to say that I do not believe that he was present at the killing of the Indians at Yellow Creek. But there is not the least doubt in my mind, that the massacre at Yellow Creek was brought on by the two transactions first stated.

All the transactions, which I have related happened in the latter end of April 1774: and there can scarcely be a doubt that they were the cause of the war which immediately followed, commonly called Dunmore's War.

I am with much Esteem,
Yours, &c.
EBENEZER ZANE

The Certificate of WILLIAM HUSTON[8] of Washington
county, in the state of Pennsylvania, communicated by
DAVID RIDDICK, Esquire, Prothonotary of Washington county,
Pennsylvania; who in the letter inclosing it says "Mr. WILLIAM
HUSTON is a man of established reputation in point of Integrity."

I WILLIAM HUSTON of Washington county, in the State of Pennsylvania, do hereby certify to whom it may concern, that in the year 1774 I resided at Catfishes camp, on the main path from Wheeling to Red-stone: that Michael Cresap, who resided on or near the Potowmac river, on his way up from the river Ohio, at the head of a party of armed men, lay some time at my cabbin.

I had previously heard the report of Mr. Cresap having killed some Indi- 2 ans, said to be the relations of "Logan" an Indian Chief. In a variety of conversations with several of Cresap's party, they boasted of the deed; and that in the presence of their chief. They acknowledged they had fired first on the Indians. They had with them one man on a litter, who was in the skirmish.

I do further certify that, from what I learned from the party themselves, I then formed the opinion, and have not had any reason to change the opinion since, that the killing, on the part of the whites, was what I deem the grossest murder. I further certify that some of the party, who afterwards 3 killed some women and other Indians at Baker's Bottom, also lay at my cabbin, on their march to the interior part of the country; they had with them a little girl, whose life had been spared by the interference of some more humane than the rest. If necessary I will make affidavit to the above to be true. Certified at Washington, this 18th day of April, Anno Domini, 1798.
WILLIAM HUSTON.

---

8. William Huston was the first settler in Catfish Camp (Washington), in western Pennsylvania.

The Certificate of JACOB NEWLAND,[9] *of Shelby
County, Kentucky, communicated by the Honorable
Judge Innes, of Kentucky.*

In the year 1774, I lived on the waters of Short Creek, a branch of the
Ohio, 12 miles above Wheeling. Sometime in June or July of that year, capt.
Michael Cresap raised a party of men, and came out under col. M'Daniel,
of Hampshire County, Virginia, who commanded a detachment against the
Wappotommaka towns on the Muskinghum. I met with capt. Cresap, at
Redstone fort, and entered his company. Being very well acquainted with
him, we conversed freely; and he, among other conversations, informed me
2 several times of falling in with some Indians on the Ohio some distance
below the mouth of Yellow Creek, and killed two or three of them; and that
3 this murder was before that of the Indians by Great-house and others, at
Yellow Creek. I do not recollect the reason which capt. Cresap assigned for
committing the act, but never understood that the Indians gave any offence.
Certified under my hand this 15th day of November, 1799, being an inhabitant of Shelby county, and State of Kentucky.

JACOB NEWLAND.

The Certificate of JOHN ANDERSON, *a merchant in
Fredericksburg, Virginia; communicated by Mann Page,
Esq. of Mansfield, near Fredericksburg, who, in the letter
accompanying it, says, "Mr. John Anderson has for many years
past been settled in Fredericksburg, in the mercantile line. I have
known him in prosperous and adverse situations. He has always
shewn the greatest degree of Equanimity, his honesty and veracity
are unimpeachable. These things can be attested by all the
respectable part of the town and neighborhood of Fredericksburg."*

Mr. John Anderson, a merchant in Fredericksburg, says, that in the year
1774, being a trader in the Indian country, he was at Pittsburg, to which place
he had a cargo brought up the river in a boat navigated by a Delaware Indian
and a white man. That on their return down the river, with a cargo, belong-
1 ing to Messrs. Butler, Michael Cresap fired on the boat, and killed the
Indian, after which two men of the name of Gatewood and others of the name
of Tumblestone,[1] who lived on the opposite side of the river from the Indians,
3 with whom they were on the most friendly terms, invited a party of them to
come over and drink with them; and that, when the Indians were drunk, they
4 murdered them to the number of six, among whom was Logan's mother. That
five other Indians uneasy at the absence of their friends, came over the river
to enquire after them; when they were fired upon, and two were killed, and
the others wounded. This was the origin of the war.

I certify the above to be true to the best of my recollection.

JOHN ANDERSON.

Attest.
DAVID BLAIR, 30th June 1798.

---

9. Jacob Newland is listed among the soldiers serving under Michael Cresap during Lord Dunmore's
War.
1. The popular pronunciation of Tomlinson, which was the real name [Jefferson's note].

The Deposition of JAMES CHAMBERS, communicated
by David Riddick, Esq. Prothonotary of Washington County,
Pennsylvania, who in the letter enclosing it shews that he entertains
the most perfect confidence in the truth of MR. CHAMBERS.

Washington County, sc.

Personally came before me Samuel Shannon, Esq. one of the Commonwealth justices for the County of Washington in the state of Pennsylvania,
James Chambers, who being sworn according to law, deposeth and saith
that in the spring of the year 1774, he resided on the frontiers near Baker's
bottom on the Ohio: that he had an intimate companion, with whom he
sometimes lived, named "Edward King:" That a report reached him that 2
Michael Cresap had killed some Indians near Grave Creek, friends to an
Indian, known by the name of "Logan:" That other of his friends, following 3
down the river, having received intelligence, and fearing to proceed, lest
Cresap might fall in with them, encamped near the mouths of Yellow Creek,
opposite Baker's bottom; that Daniel Great-house had determined to kill
them; had made the secret known to the deponent's companion, King; that
the deponent was earnestly solicited to be of the party, and, as an inducement, was told that they would get a great deal of plunder; and further, that
the Indians would be made drunk by Baker, and that little danger would follow the expedition. The deponent refused to have any hand in killing unoffending people. His companion, King, went with Great-house, with divers
others, some of whom had been collected at a considerable distance under
an idea that Joshua Baker's family was in danger from the Indians, as war
had been commenced between Cresap and them already; that Edward
King, as well as others of the party, did not conceal from the deponent the
most minute circumstances of this affair; they informed him that Great-
house, concealing his people, went over to the Indian encampments and
counted their number, and found that they were too large a party to attack
with his strength; that he then requested Joshua Baker, when any of them
came to his house, (which they had been in the habit of) to give them what
rum they could drink, and to let him know when they were in a proper train,
and that he would then fall on them; that accordingly they found several
men and women at Baker's house; that one of these women had cautioned
Great-house, when over in the Indian camp, that he had better return home,
as the Indian men were drinking, and that having heard of Cresap's attack
on their relations down the river, they were angry, and, in a friendly manner, told him to go home. Great-house, with his party, fell on them, and
killed all except a little girl, which the deponent saw with the party after the
slaughter: that the Indians in the camp hearing the firing, manned two
canoes, supposing their friends at Baker's to be attacked, as was supposed:
the party under Great-house prevented their landing by a well directed fire, 4
which did execution in the canoes: that Edward King shewed the deponent
one of the scalps.—The deponent further saith, that the settlements near
the river broke up, and he the deponent immediately repaired to Catfish's
camp, and lived some time with mr. William Huston: that not long after his
arrival, Cresap, with his party, returning from the Ohio, came to Mr. Huston's and tarried some time: that in various conversations with the party,
and in particular with a Mr. Smith, who had one arm only, he was told that 2
the Indians were acknowledged and known to be Logan's friends which

they had killed, and that he heard the party say, that Logan would probably
avenge their deaths.

They acknowledged that the Indians passed Cresap's encampment on the
bank of the river in a peaceable manner, and encamped below him; that they
2 went down and fired on the Indians, and killed several; that the survivors flew
to their arms and fired on Cresap, and wounded one man, whom the depon-
3 ent saw carried on a litter by the party; that the Indians killed by Cresap were
not only Logan's relations, but of the women killed at Baker's, one was said
and generally believed to be Logan's sister. The deponent further saith, that
on the relation of the attack by Cresap on the unoffending Indians, he
exclaimed in their hearing, that it was an atrocious murder: on which Mr.
Smith threatened the deponent with the tomahawk: so that he was obliged to
be cautious, fearing an injury, as the party appeared to have lost, in a great
degree, sentiments of humanity as well as the effects of civilization. Sworn
and subscribed at Washington, the 20th day of April, anno Domini 1798.

JAMES CHAMBERS.

Before Samuel Shannon.

Washington county, sc.

I, David Reddick, prothonotary of the court of common pleas, for
the county of Washington, in the state of Pennsylvania, do cer-
SEAL.   tify, that Samuel Shannon, esq. before whom the within affidavit
was made, was, at the time thereof, and still is, a justice of the peace in and
for the county of Washington aforesaid; and that full credit is due to all his
judicial acts as such as well in courts of justice as thereout.

In testimony whereof I have hereunto set my hand and affixed the seal
of my office at Washington, the 26th day of April, anno Dom. 1798.

DAVID REDDICK.

*The Certificate of CHARLES POLKE, of Shelby county,
in Kentucky, communicated by the hon. Judge Innes, of Kentucky,
who in the letter inclosing it, together with Newland's certificate,
and his own declaration of the information given him by Baker,
says, "I am well acquainted with Jacob Newland, he is a man
of integrity. Charles Polke and Joshua Baker both support
respectable characters."*

About the latter end of April or beginning of May 1774, I lived on the
waters of Cross creek, about 16 miles from Joshua Baker, who lived on the
3 Ohio, opposite the mouth of Yellow creek. A number of persons collected
at my house, and proceeded to the said Baker's and murdered several Indians, among whom was a woman said to be the sister of the Indian chief,
Logan. The principal leader of the party was Daniel Great-house.[2] To the
best of my recollection the cause which gave rise to the murder was, a general idea that the Indians were meditating an attack on the frontiers. Capt.

2. Daniel Greathouse (c. 1750–1775), born in Maryland, moved to the Ohio country of Virginia
around 1770. It was Greathouse, rather than Cresap, who led the band of armed men that murdered members of Logan's family at Joshua Baker's tavern, located near the mouth of the Yellow
Creek, in late April 1774.

Michael Cresap was not of the party; but I recollect that some time before the perpetration of the above fact it was currently reported that capt. Cresap 2 had murdered some Indians on the Ohio, one or two, some distance below Wheeling.

Certified by me, an inhabitant of Shelby county and state of Kentucky, this 15th day of November, 1799.

CHARLES POLKE.

The declaration of the hon. JUDGE INNES,
of Frankfort, in Kentucky.

On the 14th of November, 1799, I accidentally met upon the road Joshua Baker, the person referred to in the certificate signed by Polke, who informed me that the murder of the Indians in 1774, opposite the mouth 3 of Yellow creek, was perpetrated at his house by 32 men, led on by Daniel Great-house; that 12 were killed and 6 or 8 wounded; among the slain was a sister and other relations of the Indian chief Logan. Baker says captain Michael Cresap was not of the party; that some days preceding the murder at his house two Indians left him and were on their way home; that they fell 1 in with capt. Cresap and a party of land improvers on the Ohio, and were murdered, if not by Cresap himself, with his approbation; he being the leader of the party, and that he had this information from Cresap.

HARRY INNES.

The declaration of WILLIAM ROBINSON.

William Robinson, of Clarksburg, in the county of Harrison, and state of Virginia, subscriber to these presents, declares that he was, in the year 1774, a resident on the west fork of Monongahela river, in the county then called West Augusta, and being in his field on the 12th of July, with two other men, they were surprised by a party of eight Indians, who shot down one of the others and made himself and the remaining one prisoners; this subscriber's wife and four children having been previously conveyed by him for safety to a fort about 24 miles off; that the principal Indian of the party which took them was captain Logan; that Logan spoke English well, and very soon manifested a friendly disposition to this subscriber, and told him to be of good heart, that he would not be killed, but must go with him to his town, where he would probably be adopted in some of their families; but above all things that he must not attempt to run away; that in the course of the journey to the Indian town he generally endeavoured to keep close to Logan, who had a great deal of conversation with him, always encouraging him to be chearful and without fear; for that he would not be killed, but should become one of them; and constantly impressing on him not to attempt to run away; that in these conversations he always charged capt. Michael Cresap with the murder of his family: that on his arrival in the town, which was on the 18th of July, he was tied to a stake, and a great debate arose whether he should not be burnt; Logan insisting on having him adopted, while others contended to burn him: that at length Logan prevailed, tied a belt of wampum round him as the mark of adoption, loosed him from the post and carried him to the cabin of an old squaw, where Logan pointed out a person who he said was this subscriber's cousin; and he afterwards understood that the old woman was his aunt, and two others his brothers, and that he now stood in the place of a warrior of the family who had been killed at Yellow creek: that about three days after this Logan brought him a piece of paper, and told him he must write a letter for him, which he meant to carry and leave in some house where he should kill somebody: that he made ink with gunpowder, and the subscriber proceeded to write the letter by his direction, addressing captain Michael Cresap in it, and that the purport of it was, to ask "why he had killed his people? That some time before they had killed his people at some place (the name of which the subscriber forgets) which he had forgiven; but since that he had killed his people again at Yellow creek, and taken his cousin, a little girl, prisoner; that therefore he must war against the whites; but that he would exchange the subscriber for his cousin." And signed it with Logan's name, which letter Logan took and set out again to war; and the contents of this letter, as recited by the subscriber, calling to mind, that stated by Judge Innes to have been left, tied to a war club, in a house, where a family was murdered, and that being read to the subscriber, he recognises it, and declares he verily believes it to have been the identical letter which he wrote, and supposes he was mistaken in stating as he has done before from memory, that the offer of the exchange was proposed in the letter; that it is probable it was only promised him by Logan, but not put in the letter; that while he was with the old woman, she repeatedly endeavored to make him sensible that she had been of the party at Yellow Creek, and, by signs, shewed him how they decoyed her friends over the river to drink, and when they were reeling and tumbling about, tomahawked them all, and that whenever she entered on this subject she was thrown into the most violent agitations, and that he afterwards understood that, amongst the Indians killed at Yellow Creek, was a sister of Logan, very big with child, whom they ripped open, and stuck on a pole: that he continued with the Indians till the month of November, when he was released in consequence of the peace made by them with Lord Dunmore: that, while he remained with them, the Indians in general were very kind to him; and especially those who were his adopted relations; but above all, the old woman and family in which he lived, who served him with every thing in their power, and never asked, or even suffered him to do any labour, seeming in truth to consider and respect him, as the friend they had lost. All which several matters and things, so far as they are stated to be of his own knowledge, this subscriber solemnly declares to be true, and so far as they are stated on information from others, he believes them to be true. Given and declared under his hand at Philadelphia, this 28th day of February, 1800.

WILLIAM ROBINSON.

The deposition of Col. William M'Kee, of Lincoln County, Kentucky, communicated by the hon. John Brown, one of the Senators in Congress from Kentucky.

Colonel William M'Kee of Lincoln County, declareth, that in autumn 1774, he commanded as a captain in the Bottetourt Regiment under col. Andrew Lewis, afterwards Gen. Lewis; and fought in the battle at the mouth of Kanhawa, on the 10th of October in that year. That after the battle, col. Lewis marched the militia across the Ohio, and proceeded towards the

Shawnee Towns on Sciota; but before they reached the Towns, Lord Dunmore, who was commander in chief of the army, and had, with a large part thereof, been up the Ohio about Hockhockin, when the battle was fought, overtook the militia, and informed them of his having since the battle concluded a Treaty with the Indians; upon which the whole army returned.

And the said William declareth that, on the evening of that day on which the junction of the troops took place, he was in company with Lord Dunmore and several of his officers, and also conversed with several who had been with Lord Dunmore at the Treaty; said William, on that evening, heard repeated conversations concerning an extraordinary speech made at the Treaty, or sent there by a chieftain of the Indians named Logan, and heard several attemps at a rehearsal of it. The speech as rehearsed excited the particular attention of said William, and the most striking members of it were impressed on his memory.

And he declares that when Thomas Jefferson's notes on Virginia were published, and he came to peruse the same, he was struck with the speech of Logan as there set forth, as being substantially the same, and accordant with the Speech he heard rehearsed in the camp as aforesaid.

Signed,

WILLIAM M'KEE.

Danville, December 18th, 1799.

We certify that Col. William M'Kee this day signed the original certificate, of which the foregoing is a true copy, in our presence.

JAMES SPEED, Jun.

J.H. DEWEES.

The Certificate of the Honorable STEVENS THOMPSON MASON, one of the Senators in Congress from the State of Virginia. "LOGAN'S speech, delivered at the Treaty, after the Battle in which Col. LEWIS was killed in 1774."

[Here follows a copy of the speech agreeing verbatim with that printed in Dixon and Hunter's Virginia Gazette of February 4, 1775, under the Williamsburg head. At the foot is this certificate.

"The foregoing is a copy taken by me, when a boy, at school, in the year 1775, or at farthest in 1776, and lately found in on old pocketbook, containing papers and maunscripts of that period.]

STEVENS THOMPSON MASON.

January 20th, 1798.

A copy of LOGAN'S speech given by the late General MERCER, who fell in the battle of Trenton, January 1776, to LEWIS WILLIS, Esquire, of Fredericksburg, in Virginia, upwards of 20 years ago, (from the date of February 1798,) communicated through MANN PAGE Esquire.

"The SPEECH of LOGAN, a Shawanese chief, to Lord Dunmore."

[Here follows a copy of the speech, agreeing verbatim with that in the Notes on Virginia.]

A Copy of LOGAN'S SPEECH from the Notes on Virginia having been sent to captain ANDREW RODGERS of Kentucky, he subjoined the following certificate.

In the year 1774 I was out with the Virginia Volunteers, and was in the battle at the mouth of Canhawee, and afterwards proceeded over the Ohio to the Indian Towns. I did not hear Logan make the above speech; but, from the unanimous accounts of those in camp, I have reason to think that said speech was delivered to Dunmore. I remember to have heard the very things contained in the above speech, related by some of our people in camp at that time.

ANDREW RODGERS.

The declaration of MR. JOHN HECKEWELDER,[3] for
several years a missionary from the Society of Moravians,
among the western Indians.

In the spring of the year 1774, at a time when the interior part of the Indian country all seemed peace and tranquil, the Villagers on the Muskingum were suddenly alarmed by two Runners (Indians,) who reported "that the Big Knife, (Virginians) had attacked the Mingoe settlement, on the Ohio, and butchered even the women with their children in their arms, and that Logan's family were among the slain." A day or two after this, several Mingoes made their appearance; among whom were one or two wounded, who had in this manner effected their escape. Exasperated to a high degree, after relating the particulars of this transaction, (which for humanity's sake I forbear to mention,) after resting some time on the treachery of the Big Knives, of their barbarity to those who are their friends, they gave a figurative description of the perpetrators; named Cresap as having been at the head of this murderous act. They made mention of nine being killed, and two wounded; and were prone to take revenge on any person of a white colour; for which reason the missionaries had to shut themselves up during their stay. From this time terror daily increased. The exasperated friends and relations of these murdered women and children, with the nations to whom they belonged, passed and repassed through the villages of the quiet Delaware towns, in search of white people, making use of the most abusive language to these (the Delawares,) since they would not join in taking revenge. Traders had either to hide themselves, or try to get out of the country the best way they could. And even, at this time, they yet found such true friends among the Indians, who, at the risk of their own lives, conducted them, with the best part of their property, to Pittsburg; although, (shameful to relate!) these benefactors were, on their return from this mission, *waylaid,* and fired upon by whites, while crossing Big Beaver in a canoe, and had one man, a Shawanese, named Silverheels, (a man of note in his nation) wounded in the body. This exasperated the Shawanese so much, that they, or at least a great part of them, immediately took an active part in the cause; and the Mingoes, (nearest connected with the former,) became unbounded in their rage. A Mr. Jones, son to a respectable family of this neighbourhood (Bethlehem,) who was then on his passage up Muskinghum, with two other men, was fortu-

3. Johann Gottlieb Ernestus Heckewelder (1743–1823), born in England to German parents who immigrated to Pennsylvania in 1754, became the most famous missionary of the Moravian church (or United Brethren) among the Indian tribes of the Ohio country. He would publish two important historical narratives in the final decade of his life.

nately espied by a friendly Indian woman, at the falls of Muskinghum; who through motives of humanity alone, informed Jones of the nature of the times, and that he was running right in the hands of the enraged; and put him on the way, where he might perhaps escape the vengeance of the strolling parties. One of Jones's men, fatigued by travelling in the woods, declared he would rather die than remain longer in this situation; and hitting accidentally on a path, he determined to follow the same. A few hundred yards decided *his* fate. He was met by a party of about fifteen Mingoes, (and as it happened, almost within sight of White Eyes Town,) murdered, and cut to pieces; and his limbs and flesh stuck up on the bushes. White Eyes, on hearing the Scalp Halloo, ran immediately out with his men, to see what the matter was; and finding the mangled body in this condition, gathered the whole and buried it. But next day, when some of the above party found on their return the body interred, they instantly tore up the ground, and endeavored to destroy, or scatter about, the parts at a greater distance. White Eyes, with the Delawares, watching their motions, gathered and interred the same a second time. The war party finding this out, ran furiously into the Delaware Village, exclaiming against the conduct of these people, setting forth the cruelty of Cresap towards women and children, and declaring at the same time, that they would, in consequence of this cruelty, serve every white man they should meet with in the same manner. Times grew worse and worse, war parties went out and took scalps and prisoners, and the latter, in hopes it might be of service in saving their lives, exclaimed against the barbarous act which gave rise to these troubles and against the perpetrators. The name of Greathouse was mentioned as having been accomplice to Cresap. So detestable became the latter name among the Indians, that I have frequently heard them apply it to the worst of things; also in quieting or stilling their children, I have heard them say, Hush! Cresap will fetch you; whereas otherwise, they name the Owl. The warriors having afterwards bent their course more toward the Ohio, and down the same, peace seemed with us already on the return; and this became the case soon after the decided battle fought on the Kanhaway. Traders, returning now into the Indian country, again related the story of the above mentioned massacre, *after the same manner, and with the same words*, we have heard it related hitherto. So the report remained, and was believed, by all who resided in the Indian country. So it was represented numbers of times, in the peaceable Delaware Towns, by the Enemy. So the Christian Indians were continually told they would one day be served. With *this* impression, a petty Chief hurried all the way from Wabash in 1779 to take his relations (who were living with the peaceable Delawares near Coshachking), out of the reach of the Big Knives, in whose friendship he never more would place any confidence. And when this man found that his numerous relations, would not break friendship with the Americans, nor be removed, he took two of his relations (women) off by force, saying "The whole crop should not be destroyed; I will have seed out of it for a new crop": alluding to, and repeatingly reminding these of the family of Logan, who, he said, had been real friends to the whites, and yet were cruelly murdered by them.

In Detroit, where I arrived the same spring, the report respecting the murder of the Indians on Ohio (amongst whom was Logan's family) was the same as related above; and on my return to the United States in the fall of 1786, and from that time, whenever and wherever in my presence, this subject was the topic of conversation, I found the report still the same; *viz.* that a person, bearing the name of Cresap, was the author, or perpetrator of this deed.

LOGAN was the second son of SHIKELLEMUS, a celebrated chief of the Cayuga nation. This chief, on account of his attachment to the English government, was of great service to the country, having the confidence of all the Six Nations, as well as that of the English, he was very useful in settling disputes, &c. &c. He was highly esteemed by Conrad Weisser, Esq. (an officer for government in the Indian department,) with whom he acted conjunctly, and was faithful unto his death. His residence was at Shamokin, where he took great delight in acts of hospitality to such of the white people whose business led them that way.[4] His name and fame were so high on record, that count Zinzendorf, when in this country in 1742, became desirous of seeing him, and actually visited him at his house in Shamokin.[5] About the year 1772, Logan was introduced to me, by an Indian friend; as son to the late reputable chief Shikellemus, and as a friend to the white people. In the course of conversation, I thought him a man of superior talents, than Indians generally were. The subject turning on vice and immorality, he confessed his too great share of this, especially his fondness for liquor. He exclaimed against the white people, for imposing liquors upon the Indians; he otherwise admired their ingenuity; spoke of gentlemen, but observed the Indians unfortunately had but few of these as their neighbours, &c. He spoke of his friendship to the white people, wished always to be a neighbour to them, intended to settle on the Ohio, below Big Beaver; was (to the best of my recollection) then encamped at the mouth of this river, (Beaver) urged me to pay him a visit, &c. *Note.* I was then living at the Moravian Town on this River, in the neighbourhood of Cuskuskee. In April 1773, while on my passage down the Ohio for Muskinghum, I called at Logan's settlement; where I received every civility I could expect from such of the family as were at home.

Indian reports concerning Logan, after the death of his family, ran to this; that he exerted himself during the Shawnee war, (then so called) to take all the revenge he could, declaring he had lost all confidence in the white people. At the time of negotiation, he declared his reluctance in laying down the hatchet, not having (in his opinion) yet taken ample satisfaction; yet, for the sake of the nation, he would do it. His expressions, from time to time, denoted a deep melancholy. Life (said he) had become a torment to him: He knew no more what pleasure was: He thought it had been better if he had never existed, &c. &c. Report further states, that he became in some measure delirious, declared he would kill himself, went to Detroit, drank very freely, and did not seem to care what he did, and what became of himself. In this condition he left Detroit, and, on his way between that place and Miami, was murdered. In October 1781, (while as prisoner on my way to Detroit) I was shown the spot where this shall have happened. Having had an opportunity since last June of seeing the Rev. David Zeisberger, senior, missionary to the Delaware nation of Indians, who had resided among the same on Muskingum, at the time when the murder was com-

4. The preceding account of Shikellemus (Logan's father) is copied from the manuscripts of the Rev. C. Pyrlœus written between the years 1741 and 1748 [Jefferson's note]. Jefferson refers to Johann Christopher Pyrlœus (1713–1779).
5. See. G. H. Hoskiel's history of the Mission of the United Brethren, &c. Part II, Chap. 11, page 31 [Jefferson's note] Jefferson refers to George Henry Loskiel, whose *Geschichte der Mission der Evangelischen Brüder unter den Indianern in Nordamerika* (1789) was translated into English as *History of the Mission of the United Brethren among the Indians of North America* (1794).

mitted on the family of Logan, I put the following questions to him. 1. Who he had understood it was that had committed the murder on Logan's family? And secondly, whether he had any knowledge of a speech sent to lord Dunmore by Logan, in consequence of this affair, &c. To which Mr. Zeisberger's answer was: That he had, from that time when this murder was committed to the present day, firmly believed the common report (which he had never heard contradicted) *viz.* that one Cresap was the author of the massacre; or that it was committed by his orders: and that he had known Logan as a boy, had frequently seen him from that time, and doubted not in the least, that Logan had sent such a speech to Lord Dunmore on this occasion, as he understood from me had been published; that expressions of that kind from Indians were familiar to him; that Logan in particular, was a man of quick comprehension, good judgment and talents. Mr. Zeisberger has been a missionary upwards of fifty years; his age is about eighty; speaks both the language of the Onondagoes and the Delawares; resides at present on the Muskingum, with his Indian congregation; and is beloved and respected by all who are acquainted with him.

JOHN HECKEWELDER.

• •

From this testimony the following historical statement results:

In April or May 1774, a number of people being engaged in looking out for settlements on the Ohio, information was spread among them, that the Indians had robbed some of the *land-jobbers*, as those adventurers were called. Alarmed for their safety, they collected together at Wheeling creek. Hearing there that there were two Indians and some traders a little above Wheeling, Captain Michael Cresap, one of the party, proposed to waylay and kill them. The proposition, though opposed, was adopted. A party went up the river, with Cresap at their head, and killed the two Indians.

1st murder of the two Indians by Cresap.

The same afternoon it was reported that there was a party of Indians on the Ohio, a little below Wheeling. Cresap and his party immediately proceeded down the river, and encamped on the bank. The Indians passed him peaceably, and encamped at the mouth of Grave creek, a little below. Cresap and his party attacked them, and killed several. The Indians returned the fire, and wounded one of Cresap's party. Among the slain of the Indians were some of Logan's family. Colonel Zane indeed expresses a doubt of it; but it is affirmed by Huston and Chambers. Smith, one of the murderers, said they were known and acknowledged to be Logan's friends, and the party themselves generally said so; boasted of it in presence of Cresap; pretended no provocation; and expressed their expectations that Logan would probably avenge their deaths.

2d murder on Grave creek.

Pursuing these examples, Daniel Great-house and one Tomlinson, who lived on the opposite side of the river from the Indians, and were in habits of friendship with them, collected at the house of Polke on Cross creek, about 16 miles from Baker's Bottom a party of 32 men. Their object was to attack a hunting encampment of Indians, consisting of men, women and children, at the mouth of Yellow creek, some distance above Wheeling.—They proceeded, and when arrived near Baker's Bottom, they concealed themselves,

3d Massacre at Baker's Bottom opposite Yellow Creek, by Greathouse.

and Great-house crossed the river to the Indian camp. Being among them as a friend he counted them, and found them too strong for an open attack with his force. While here, he was cautioned by one of the women not to stay, for that the Indian men were drinking, and having heard of Cresap's murder of *their relations* at Grave creek, were angry, and she pressed him, in a friendly manner, to go home; whereupon, after inviting them to come over and drink, he returned to Baker's, which was a tavern, and desired that when any of them should come to his house he would give them as much rum as they would drink. When his plot was ripe and a sufficient number of them were collected at Baker's, and intoxicated, he and his party fell on them and massacred the whole, except a little girl, whom they preserved as a prisoner. Among these was the very woman who had saved his life, by pressing him to retire from the drunken wrath of her friends, when he was spying their camp at Yellow creek. Either she herself, or some other of the murdered women, was the sister of Logan, very big with child, and inhumanly and indecently butchered; and there were others of his relations who fell here.

4th *murders by* *Greathouse.*   The party on the other side of the river, alarmed for their friends at Baker's, on hearing the report of the guns manned two canoes and sent them over. They were received, as they approached the shore, by a well directed fire from Great-house's party, which killed some, wounded others, and obliged the rest to put back. Baker tells us there were twelve killed, and six or eight wounded.

This commenced the war, of which Logan's war-club and note left in the house of a murdered family, was the notification. In the course of it, during the ensuing summer, great numbers of innocent men, women and children, fell victims to the tomahawk and scalping knife of the Indians, till it was arrested in the autumn following by the battle at Point-Pleasant and the pacification with Lord Dunmore, at which the speech of Logan was delivered.

Of the genuineness of that speech nothing need be said. It was known to the camp where it was delivered; it was given out by Lord Dunmore and his officers; it ran through the public papers of these states; was rehearsed as an exercise at schools; published in the papers and periodical works of Europe; and all this, a dozen years before it was copied into the notes on Virginia. In fine, gen. Gibson concludes the question for ever, by declaring that he received it from Logan's hand, delivered it to Lord Dunmore, translated it for him, and that the copy in the notes on Virginia is a faithful copy.

The popular account of these transactions, as stated in the notes on Virginia, appears, on collecting exact information, imperfect and erroneous in its details. It was the belief of the day; but how far its errors were to the prejudice of Cresap, the reader will now judge. That he, and those under him, murdered two Indians above Wheeling; that they murdered a larger number at Grave creek, among whom were a part of the family and relations of Logan, cannot be questioned; and as little that this led to the massacre of the rest of the family at Yellow creek. Logan imputed the whole to Cresap in his war-note and peace-speech: the Indians generally imputed it to Cresap: Lord Dunmore and his officers imputed it to Cresap: the country, with one accord, imputed it to him; and whether he was innocent, let the universal verdict now declare.

I propose that in any future edition of the Notes on Virginia, the passage relating to this subject shall stand in the following form:

"In the spring of the year 1774, a robbery was committed by some Indians on certain land adventurers on the river Ohio. The whites in that quarter, according to their custom, undertook to punish this outrage in a summary way. Captain Michael Cresap, and a certain Daniel Great-house, leading on these parties, surprized, at different times, travelling and hunting parties of the Indians, having their women and children with them, and murdered many. Among these were unfortunately the family of Logan, a chief celebrated in peace and war, and long distinguished as the friend of the whites. This unworthy return provoked his vengeance. He accordingly signalized himself in the war which ensued. In the autumn of the same year a decisive battle was fought at the mouth of the Great Kanhaway, between the collected forces of the Shawanese, Mingoes and Delawares, and a detachment of the Virginia militia. The Indians were defeated and sued for peace. Logan, however, disdained to be seen among the suppliants. But lest the sincerity of a treaty should be distrusted, from which so distinguished a chief absented himself, he sent, by a messenger, the following speech, to be delivered to Lord Dunmore.

"I appeal to any white man to say, if ever he entered Logan's cabin hungry, and he gave him not meat: if ever he came cold and naked, and he cloathed him not. During the course of the last long and bloody war Logan remained idle in his cabin, an advocate for peace. Such was my love for the whites, that my countrymen pointed as they passed, and said, 'Logan is the friend of white men.' I had even thought to have lived with you, but for the injuries of one man. Colonel Cresap, the last spring, in cold blood, and unprovoked, murdered all the relations of Logan, not even sparing my women and children. There runs not a drop of my blood in the veins of any living creature. This called on me for revenge. I have sought it: I have killed many: I have fully glutted my vengeance: for my country I rejoice at the beams of peace. But do not harbour a thought that mine is the joy of fear. Logan never felt fear. He will not turn on his heel to save his life. Who is there to mourn for Logan?—Not one."

FINIS.

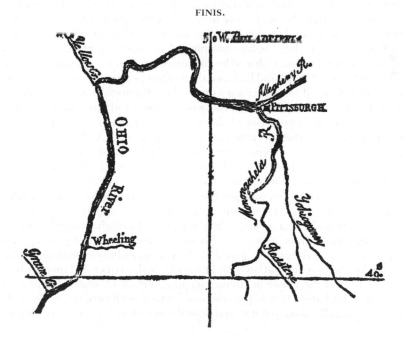

The declaration of JOHN SAPPINGTON, received after the publication of the preceding Appendix.

• •

I, JOHN SAPPINGTON, declare myself to be intimately acquainted with all the circumstances respecting the destruction of Logan's family, and do give in the following narrative, a true statement of that affair.

Logan's family (if it was his family) was not killed by Cresap, nor with his knowledge, nor by his consent, but by the Great-houses and their associates. They were killed 30 miles above Wheeling, near the mouth of Yellow Creek. Logan's camp was on one side of the river Ohio, and the house, where the murder was committed, opposite to it on the other side. They had encamped there only four or five days, and during that time had lived peaceably and neighbourly with the whites on the opposite side, until the very day the affair happened. A little before the period alluded to, letters had been received by the inhabitants from a man of great influence in that country, and who was then I believe at Capteener [Captiva Island], informing them that war was at hand, and desiring them to be on their guard. In consequence of those letters and other rumours of the same import, almost all the inhabitants fled for safety into the settlements. It was at the house of one Baker the murder was committed. Baker was a man who sold rum, and the Indians had made frequent visits at his house, induced, probably, by their fondness for that liquor. He had been particularly desired by Cresap to remove and take away his rum, and he was actually preparing to move at the time of the murder. The evening before a squaw came over to Baker's house, and by her crying seemed to be in great distress. The cause of her uneasiness being asked, she refused to tell; but getting Baker's wife alone, she told her, that the Indians were going to kill her and all her family the next day, that she loved her, did not wish her to be killed, and therefore told her what was intended, that she might save herself. In consequence of this information, Baker got a number of men to the amount of 21, to come to his house, and they were all there before morning. A council was held, and it was determined that the men should lie concealed in the back appartment; that if the Indians did come and behaved themselves peaceably, they should not be molested; but if not, the men were to shew themselves and act accordingly. Early in the morning seven Indians, four men and three squaws, came over. Logan's brother was one of them. They immediately got rum, and all, except Logan's brother, became very much intoxicated. At this time all the men were concealed, except the man of the house, Baker, and two others who staid out with him. Those Indians came unarmed. After some time Logan's brother took down a coat and hat belonging to Baker's brother-in-law, who lived with him, and put them on, and setting his arms a kimbo began to strut about, till at length coming up to one of the men, he attempted to strike him, saying "white man, son of a bitch." The white man, whom he treated thus, kept out of his way for some time; but growing irritated he jumped to his gun, and shot the Indian as he was making to the door with the coat and hat on him. The men who lay concealed then rushed out, and killed the whole of them, excepting one child, which I believe is alive yet. But before this happened, one [canoe] with two, the other with five Indians, all naked, painted and armed completely for war, were discovered to start from the shore on which Logan's camp was. Had it not been for this circumstance, the white men would not have acted as they did; but this confirmed what the squaw had told before. The white men, having killed as aforesaid the Indians in the house, ranged themselves along the bank of the river, to receive the canoes. The canoe with the two Indians came near, being the foremost. Our men fired upon them and killed them both. The other canoe then went back. After this two other canoes started, the one containing 11, the other 7 Indians, painted and armed as the first. They attempted to land below our men; but were fired upon, had one killed, and retreated, at the same time firing back. To the best of my recollection there were three of the Greathouses engaged in this business. This is a true representation of the affair from beginning to end. I was intimately acquainted with Cresap, and know he had no hand in that transaction. He told me himself afterwards at Redstone old fort, that the day before Logan's people were killed, he, with a small party, had an engagement with a party of Indians on Capteneer, about 44 miles lower down. Logan's people were killed at the mouth of Yellow Creek on the 24th of May 1774, and on the 23d, the day before, Cresap was engaged as already stated. I know likewise that he was generally blamed for it, and believed by all who were not acquainted with the circumstances, to have been the perpetrator of it. I know that he despised and hated the Great-houses ever afterwards on account of it. I was intimately acquainted with general Gibson, and served under him during the late war, and I have a discharge from him now lying in the land office at Richmond, to which I refer any person for my charac- ter, who might be disposed to scruple my veracity. I was likewise at the treaty held by lord Dunmore with the Indians, at Chelicothe. As for the speech said to have been delivered by Logan on that occasion, it might have been, or might not, for any thing I know, as I never heard of it till long after- wards. I do not believe that Logan had any relations killed, except his brother. Neither of the squaws who were killed was his wife. Two of them were old women, and the third, with her child which was saved, I have the best reason in the world to believe was the wife and child of general Gib- son. I know he educated the child, and took care of it, as if it had been his own. Whether Logan had a wife or not, I cant say; but it is probable that as he was a chief, he considered them all as his people. All this I am ready to be qualified to at any time.

JOHN SAPPINGTON.

Attest, SAMUEL M'KEE, JUNR.

MADISON COUNTY, Feb. 13th, 1800.

I do certify further that the above-named John Sappington told me, at the same time and place at which he gave me the above narrative, that he him- self was the man who shot the brother of Logan in the house as above related, and that he likewise killed one of the Indians in one of the canoes, which came over from the opposite shore.

He likewise told me, that Cresap never said an angry word to him about the matter, although he was frequently in company with Cresap, and indeed had been, and continued to be, in habits of intimacy with that gen- tleman, and was always befriended by him on every occasion. He further told me, that after they had perpetrated the murder, and were flying into the settlements, he met with Cresap (if I recollect right, at Redstone old fort),

and gave him a scalp, a very large fine one, as he expressed it, and adorned with silver. This scalp, I think he told me, was the scalp of Logan's brother; though as to this I am not absolutely certain.
Certified by
SAMUEL M'KEE, JUNR.

Message to Congress on the Lewis and Clark Expedition

Confidential.[1]   18 January 1803
Gentlemen of the Senate and of the House of Representatives.

As the continuance of the Act for establishing trading houses with the Indian tribes will be under the consideration of the legislature at it's present session, I think it my duty to communicate the views which have guided me in the execution of that act; in order that you may decide on the policy of continuing it, in the present or any other form, or to discontinue it altogether if that shall, on the whole, seem most for the public good.

The Indian tribes residing within the limits of the U.S. have for a considerable time been growing more & more uneasy at the constant diminution of the territory they occupy, altho' effected by their own voluntary sales: and the policy has long been gaining strength with them of refusing absolutely all further sale on any conditions, insomuch that, at this time, it hazards their friendship, and excites dangerous jealousies & perturbations in their minds to make any overture for the purchase of the smallest portions of their land. A very few tribes only are not yet obstinately in these dispositions. In order peaceably to counteract this policy of theirs, and to provide an extension of territory which the rapid increase of our numbers will call for, two measures are deemed expedient. First, to encourage them to abandon hunting, to apply to the raising [of] stock, to agriculture and domestic manufacture, and thereby prove to themselves that less land & labour will maintain them in this, better than in their former mode of living. The extensive forests necessary in the hunting life, will then become useless, & they will see advantage in exchanging them for the means of improving their farms, & of increasing their domestic comforts. Secondly to multiply trading houses among them, & place within their reach those things which will contribute more to their domestic comfort than the possession of extensive, but uncultivated wilds. Experience & reflection will develope to them the wisdom of exchanging what they can spare & we want, for what we can spare and they want. In leading them thus to agriculture, to manufactures & civilization, in bringing together their & our settlements, & in preparing them ultimately to participate in the benefits of our government, I trust and believe we are acting for their greatest good. At these trading houses we have pursued the principles of the act of Congress, which directs that the commerce shall be carried on liberally, & requires only that the capital stock shall not be diminished. We consequently undersell private traders, foreign & domestic, drive them from the competition, & thus, with the good will of

1. Jefferson had first intended to submit his tentative plan for the Lewis and Clark expedition to Congress in his annual message the previous December, but concerns about keeping it secret led him to delay it for a month. Congress approved the plan in February.

the Indians, rid ourselves of a description of men who are constantly endeavoring to excite in the Indian mind suspicions, fears & irritations towards us. A letter now inclosed shows the effect of our competition on the operations of the traders, while the Indians, percieving the advantage of purchasing from us, are solliciting generally our establishment of trading houses among them. In one quarter this is particularly interesting. The legislature, reflecting on the late occurrences on the Missisipi, must be sensible how desireable it is to possess a respectable breadth of country on that river, from our Southern limit to the Illinois at least; so that we may present as firm a front on that as on our Eastern border. We possess what is below the Yazoo, & can probably acquire a certain breadth from the Illinois & Wabash to the Ohio. But between the Ohio and Yazoo, the country all belongs to the Chickasaws, the most friendly tribe within our limits, but the most decided against the alienation of lands. The portion of their country most important for us is exactly that which they do not inhabit. Their settlements are not on the Missisipi, but in the interior country. They have lately shown a desire to become agricultural, and this leads to the desire of buying implements & comforts. In the strengthening and gratifying of these wants, I see the only prospect of planting on the Missisipi itself the means of it's own safety. Duty has required me to submit these views to the judgment of the legislature. But as their disclosure might embarrass & defeat their effect, they are committed to the special confidence of the two houses.

While the extension of the public commerce among the Indian tribes may deprive of that source of profit such of our citizens as are engaged in it, it might be worthy the attention of Congress, in their care of individual as well as of the general interest to point in another direction the enterprize of these citizens, as profitably for themselves, and more usefully for the public. The river Missouri, & the Indians inhabiting it, are not as well known as is rendered desireable by their connection with the Missisipi, & consequently with us. It is however understood that the country on that river is inhabited by numerous tribes, who furnish great supplies of furs & peltry to the trade of another nation[2] carried on in a high latitude, through an Infinite number of portages and lakes, shut up by ice through a long season. The commerce on that line could bear no competition with that of the Missouri, traversing a moderate climate, offering according to the best accounts a continued navigation from it's source, and, possibly with a single portage, from the Western ocean, and finding to the Atlantic a choice of channels through the Illinois or Wabash, the Lakes and Hudson, through the Ohio and Susquehanna or Potomac or James rivers, and through the Tennessee and Savannah rivers. An intelligent officer with ten or twelve chosen men, fit for the enterprize and willing to undertake it, taken from our posts, where they may be spared without inconvenience, might explore the whole line, even to the Western ocean, have conferences with the natives on the subject of commercial intercourse, get admission among them for our traders as others are admitted, agree on convenient deposits for an interchange of articles, and return with the information acquired in the course of two summers. Their arms & accoutrements, some instruments of observation, & light & cheap presents for the Indians would be all the apparatus they could carry, and with an expectation of a soldier's portion of land on

2. Great Britain.

their return would constitute the whole expense. Their pay would be going on, whether here or there. While other civilized nations have encountered great expense to enlarge the boundaries of knowledge, by undertaking voyages of discovery, & for other literary purposes, in various parts and directions, our nation seems to owe to the same object, as well as to its own interest, to explore this, the only line of easy communication across the continent, and so directly traversing our own part of it. The interests of commerce place the principal object within the constitutional powers and care of Congress, and that it should incidentally advance the geographical knowledge of our own continent can not but be an additional gratification. The nation claiming the territory, regarding this as a literary pursuit which it is in the habit of permitting within it's dominions, would not be disposed to view it with jealousy, even if the expiring state of it's interest there did not render it a matter of indifference. The appropriation of two thousand five hundred dollars "for the purpose of extending the external commerce of the U.S.," while understood and considered by the Executive as giving the legislative sanction, would cover the undertaking from notice, and prevent the obstructions which interested individuals might otherwise previously prepare in it's way.

TH: JEFFERSON

Selected Letters†

To John Harvie[1]

SIR Shadwell, Jan. 14, 1760.

I was at Colo. Peter Randolph's about a Fortnight ago, and my Schooling falling into Discourse, he said he thought it would be to my Advantage to go to the College, and was desirous I should go, as indeed I am myself for several Reasons. In the first place as long as I stay at the Mountains the Loss of one fourth of my Time is inevitable, by Company's coming here and detaining me from School. And likewise my Absence will in a great Measure put a Stop to so much Company, and by that Means lessen the Expences of the Estate in House-Keeping. And on the other Hand by going to the College I shall get a more universal Acquaintance, which may hereafter be serviceable to me; and I suppose I can pursue my Studies in the Greek and Latin as well there as here, and likewise learn something of the Mathematics. I shall be glad of your opinion.

To John Page[2]

DEAR PAGE Fairfeilds Dec: 25. 1762.

This very day, to others the day of greatest mirth and jollity, sees me overwhelmed with more and greater misfortunes than have befallen a descendant of Adam for these thousand years past I am sure; and perhaps, after excepting Job, since the creation of the world. I think his misfortunes were somewhat greater than mine: for although we may be pretty nearly on a level in other respects, yet I thank my God I have the advantage of brother Job in this, that Satan has not as yet put forth his hand to load me with bodily afflictions. You must know, dear Page, that I am now in a house surrounded with enemies, who take counsel together against my soul and when I lay me down to rest they say among themselves Come let us destroy him. I am sure if there is such a thing as a devil in this world, he must have been here last night and have had some hand in contriving what happened to me. Do you think the cursed rats (at his instigation I suppose) did not eat up my pocket-book which was in my pocket within a foot of my head? And not contented with plenty for the present they carried away my Jemmy worked silk garters and half a dozen new minuets I had just got, to serve I suppose as provision for the winter. But of this I should not have accused

† The letters on pages 203–85 and 315–32 are from *PTJ*. Copyright © 1950–2009 Princeton University Press. Reprinted by permission of Princeton University Press.

1. This first surviving letter from Jefferson, then aged sixteen, was addressed to one of his guardians, to whom the young student reported a conversation about his education with another guardian, his mother's cousin Colonel. Peter Randolph (1708–1767) of Chatsworth.
2. John Page (1744–1808), Jefferson's closest friend at school, became a soldier and politician, serving several terms as a congressman from Virginia and as governor of the state.

the devil (because you know rats will be rats, and hunger without the addition of his instigations might have urged them to do this) if something worse and from a different quarter had not happened. You know it rained last night, or if you do not know it I am sure I do. When I went to bed I laid my watch in the usual place, and going to take her up after I arose this morning I found her, in the same place it's true but! Quantum mutatus ab illo![3] all afloat in water let in at a leak in the roof of the house, and as silent and still as the rats that had eat my pocket-book. Now you know if Chance had had any thing to do in this matter, there were a thousand other spots where it might have chanced to leak as well as at this one which was perpendicularly over my watch. But I'll tell you: It's my opinion that the Devil came and bored the hole over it on purpose. Well as I was saying, my poor watch had lost her speech: I should not have cared much for this, but something worse attended it: the subtle particles of the water with which the case was filled had by their penetration so overcome the cohesion of the particles of the paper of which my dear picture and watch paper were composed that in attempting to take them out to dry them Good God! mens horret referre![4] my cursed fingers gave them such a rent as I fear I never shall get over. This, cried I, was the last stroke Satan had in reserve for me: he knew I cared not for any thing else he could do to me, and was determined to try this last most fatal expedient. * * * However whatever misfortunes may attend the picture or lover, my hearty prayers shall be that all the health and happiness which heaven can send may be the portion of the original, and that so much goodness may ever meet with what may be most agreeable in this world, as I am sure it must in the next. And now although the picture be defaced there is so lively an image of her imprinted in my mind that I shall think of her too often I fear for my peace of mind, and too often I am sure to get through Old Cooke [Coke][5] this winter: for God knows I have not seen him since I packed him up in my trunk in Williamsburgh.

Well, Page, I do wish the Devil had old Cooke, for I am sure I never was so tired of an old dull scoundrel in my life. What! are there so few inquietudes tacked to this momentary life of ours that we must need be loading ourselves with a thousand more? Or as brother Job sais (who by the bye I think began to whine a little under his afflictions) "Are not my days few? Cease then that I may take comfort a little before I go whence I shall not return, even to the land of darkness and the shadow of death." But the old-fellows say we must read to gain knowledge; and gain knowledge to make us happy and be admired. Mere jargon! Is there any such thing as happiness in this world? No: And as for admiration I am sure the man who powders most, parfumes most, embroiders most, and talks most nonsense, is most admired. Though to be candid, there are some who have too much good sense to esteem such monkey-like animals as these, in whose formation, as the saying is, the taylors and barbers go halves with God almighty: and since these are the only persons whose esteem is worth a wish, I do not know but that upon the whole the advice of these old fellows may be worth following.

You cannot conceive the satisfaction it would give me to have a letter from you: Write me very circumstantially everything which happened at the wed-

---

3. How greatly changed from itself! (Latin).
4. The mind bristles at the recollection (Latin).
5. Edward Coke (1552–1634), lord chief justice of England under King James I. His treatises on English law were standard fare for students in Jefferson's youth, especially those aiming at a career in the law.
6. Rebecca Burwell, sister of another student at William and Mary.

ding. Was SHE[6] there? Because if she was I ought to have been at the devil for not being there too. If there is any news stirring in town or country, such as deaths, courtships and marriages in the circle of my acquaintance let me know it. Remember me affectionately to all the young ladies of my acquaintance, particularly the Miss Burwells and Miss Potters, and tell them that though that heavy earthly part of me, my body, be absent, the better half of me, my soul, is ever with them, and that my best wishes shall ever attend them. Tell Miss Alice Corbin that I verily believe the rats knew I was to win a pair of garters from her, or they never would have been so cruel as to carry mine away. This very consideration makes me so sure of the bet that I shall ask every body I see from that part of the world what pretty gentleman is making his addresses to her. I would fain ask the favor of Miss Becca Burwell to give me another watch paper, of her own cutting which I should esteem much more though it were a plain round one, than the nicest in the world cut by other hands: however I am afraid she would think this presumption after my suffering the other to get spoiled. If you think you can excuse me to her for this I should be glad if you would ask her. Tell Miss Suckey Potter that I heard just before I came out of town that she was offended with me about something: what it is I know not: but this I know, that I never was guilty of the least disrespect to her in my life either in word or deed: as far from it as it has been possible for me to be: I suppose when we meet next she will be endeavoring to repay an imaginary affront with a real one: but she may save herself the trouble, for nothing that she can say or do to me shall ever lessen her in my esteem. And I am determined allways to look upon her as the same honest-hearted good-humored agreeable lady I ever did. Tell—tell—In short tell them all ten thousand things more than either you or I can now or ever shall think of as long as we live.

My mind has been so taken up with thinking of my acquaintances that till this moment I almost imagined myself in Williamsburgh talking to you in our old unreserved way, and never observed till I turned over this leaf to what an immoderate size I had swelled my letter: however that I may not tire your patience by further additions I will make but this one more that I am sincerely and affectionately Dr Page your friend and servant,

T: JEFFERSON

P. S. I am now within an easy day's ride of Shadwell whither I shall proceed in two or three days.

To Robert Skipwith,[7]

with a List of Books for a Private Library

TH: JEFFERSON TO R. SHIPWITH   Monticello. Aug. 3. 1771.

I sat down with a design of executing your request to form a catalogue of books amounting to about 30. lib. sterl. but could by no means satisfy myself with any partial choice I could make. Thinking therefore it might be as agreeable to you, I have framed such a general collection as I think you would wish, and might in time find convenient, to procure. Out of this you will chuse for yourself to the amount you mentioned for the present year, and may hereafter as shall be convenient proceed in completing the whole.

7. Robert Skipwith (or Shipwith), of an estate called Rowantee in Dinwiddie County, Virginia, was the husband of a half-sister of Martha Wayles Skelton, who was to marry Jefferson at the start of 1772.

A view of the second column in this catalogue would I suppose extort a smile from the face of gravity. Peace to it's wisdom! Let me not awaken it. A little attention however to the nature of the human mind evinces that the entertainments of fiction are useful as well as pleasant. That they are pleasant when well written, every person feels who reads. But wherein is it's utility, asks the reverend sage, big with the notion that nothing can be useful but the learned lumber of Greek and Roman reading with which his head is stored? I answer, every thing is useful which contributes to fix us in the principles and practice of virtue. When any signal act of charity or of gratitude, for instance, is presented either to our sight or imagination, we are deeply impressed with it's beauty and feel a strong desire in ourselves of doing charitable and grateful acts also. On the contrary when we see or read of any atrocious deed, we are disgusted with it's deformity and conceive an abhorrence of vice. Now every emotion of this kind is an exercise of our virtuous dispositions; and dispositions of the mind, like limbs of the body, acquire strength by exercise. But exercise produces habit; and in the instance of which we speak, the exercise being of the moral feelings, produces a habit of thinking and acting virtuously. We never reflect whether the story we read be truth or fiction. If the painting be lively, and a tolerable picture of nature, we are thrown into a reverie, from which if we awaken it is the fault of the writer. I appeal to every reader of feeling and sentiment whether the fictitious murther of Duncan by Macbeth in Shakespeare does not excite in him as great horror of villainy, as the real one of Henry IV by Ravaillac as related by Davila? And whether the fidelity of Nelson, and generosity of Blandford in Marmontel do not dilate his breast, and elevate his sentiments as much as any similar incident which real history can furnish? Does he not in fact feel himself a better man while reading them, and privately covenant to copy the fair example? We neither know nor care whether Lawrence Sterne really went to France, whether he was there accosted by the poor Franciscan, at first rebuked him unkindly, and then gave him a peace offering; or whether the whole be not a fiction. In either case we are equally sorrowful at the rebuke, and secretly resolve *we* will never do so: we are pleased with the subsequent atonement, and view with emulation a soul candidly acknowleging it's fault, and making a just reparation. Considering history as a moral exercise, her lessons would be too unfrequent if confined to real life. Of those recorded by historians few incidents have been attended with such circumstances as to excite in any high degree this sympathetic emotion of virtue. We are therefore wisely framed to be as warmly interested for fictitious as for a real personage. The spacious field of imagination is thus laid open to our use, and lessons may be formed to illustrate and carry home to the mind every moral rule of life. Thus a lively and lasting sense of filial duty is more effectually impressed on the mind of a son or daughter by reading King Lear, than by all the dry volumes of ethics and divinity that ever were written. This is my idea of well-written Romance, of Tragedy, Comedy, and Epic Poetry.—If you are fond of speculation, the books under the head of Criticism, will afford you much pleasure. Of Politicks and Trade I have given you a few only of the best books, as you would probably chuse to be not unacquainted with those commercial principles which bring wealth into our country, and the constitutional security we have for the enjoiment of that wealth. In Law I mention a few systematical books, as a knowlege of the minutiae of that science is not necessary for a private gentleman. In Religion, History, Natural philosophy, I have followed the same plan in general.—But whence the necessity of this collection? Come to the new Rowanty,[8] from which you may reach your hand to a library formed on a more extensive plan. Separated from each other but a few paces, the possessions of each would be open to the other. A spring, centrically situated, might be the scene of every evening's joy. There we should talk over the lessons of the day, or lose them in Musick, Chess, or the merriments of our family companions. The heart thus lightened, our pillows would be soft, and health and long life would attend the happy scene. Come then and bring our dear Tibby with you; the first in your affections, and second in mine. Offer prayers for me too at that shrine to which, tho' absent, I pay continual devotion. In every scheme of happiness she is placed in the fore-ground of the picture, as the principal figure. Take that away, and it is no picture for me. Bear my affections to Wintipock,[9] cloathed in the warmest expressions of sincerity; and to yourself be every human felicity. Adieu.

ENCLOSURE[1]

FINE ARTS

Observations on gardening. Payne. 5/

Webb's essay on painting. 12mo 3/

Pope's Iliad. 18/

_____Odyssey. 15/

Dryden's Virgil. 12mo. 12/

Milton's works. 2 v. 8vo. Donaldson. Edinburgh 1762. 10/

Hoole's Tasso. 12mo. 5/

Ossian with Blair's criticisms. 2 v. 8vo. 10/

Telemachus by Dodsley. 6/

Capell's Shakespear. 12mo. 30/

Dryden's plays. 6 v. 12mo. 18/

Addison's plays. 12mo. 3/

Otway's plays. 3 v. 12mo. 9/

Rowe's works. 2 v. 12mo. 6/

Thompson's works. 4 v. 12mo. 12/

Young's works. 4 v. 12mo. 12/

Home's plays. 12mo. 3/

Mallet's works. 3 v. 12mo. 9/

Mason's poetical works. 5/

Terence. Eng. 3/

Moliere. Eng. 15/

Farquhar's plays. 2 v. 12mo. 6/

Vanbrugh's plays. 2 v. 12mo. 6/

Steele's plays. 3/

Congreve's works. 3 v. 12mo. 9/

Garric's dramatic works. 2 v. 8vo. 10/

Foote's dramatic works. 2 v. 8vo. 10/

Rousseau's Eloisa. Eng. 4 v. 12mo. 12/

_____ Emilius and Sophia. Eng. 4 v. 12mo. 12/

Marmontel's moral tales. Eng. 2 v. 12mo. 9/

Gil Bias, by Smollett. 6/

Don Quixot. by Smollett 4 v. 12mo. 12/

David Simple. 2 v. 12mo. 6/

Roderic Random. 2 v. 12mo. 6/
Peregrine Pickle. 4 v. 12mo. 12/
Launcelot Graves. 6/
Adventures of a guinea. 2 v. 12mo. 6/ } *these are written by Smollett.*

8. Monticello.

9. A Virginia estate of the Eppes family, into which a sister of Martha Wayles Skelton had married.

1. As Andrew Burstein has emphasized, Skipwith had asked Jefferson for a list of books "suited to the capacity of a common reader who understands little of the classicks and who has not leisure for any intricate or tedious study." Jefferson's reply hardly met those criteria, instead revealing far more about his own ambitious appetite for books. See Andrew Burstein, *The Inner Jefferson: Portrait of a Grieving Optimist* (Charlottesville: University of Virginia Press, 1995), 28.

Pamela. 4 v. 12mo. ⎤
  12/ |
Clarissa. 8 v. 12mo. |
  24/   } *these are by*
Grandison. 7 v. | *Richardson.*
  12mo. 21/ |
Fool of quality. 3 v. |
  12mo. 9/   ⎦
Feilding's works. 12 v. 12mo. £1.16
Constantia. 2 v. ⎤
  12mo. 6/ |
Solyman and   } *by Langhorne.*
Almena 12 mo. |
  3/   ⎦
Belle assemblee. 4 v. 12mo. 12/
Vicar of Wakefeild. 2 v. 12mo. 6/.
  by Dr. Goldsmith
Sidney Bidulph. 5 v. 12mo. 15/
Lady Julia Mandeville. 2 v. 12mo.
  6/
Almoran and Hamet. 2 v. 12mo. 6/
Tristam Shandy. 9 v. 12mo. £1.7
Sentimental journey. 2 v. 12mo. 6/
Fragments of antient poetry. Edin-
  burgh. 2/
Percy's Runic poems. 3/
Percy's reliques of antient English
  poetry. 3 v. 12mo. 9/
Percy's Han Kiou Chouan. 4 v.
  12mo. 12/
Percy's Miscellaneous Chinese
  peices. 2 v. 12mo. 6/
Chaucer. 10/
Spencer. 6 v. 12mo. 15/
Waller's poems. 12mo. 3/
Dodsley's collection of poems. 6 v.
  12mo. 18/
Pearch's collection of poems. 4 v.
  12mo. 12/
Gray's works. 5/
Ogilvie's poems. 5/
Prior's poems. 2 v. 12mo. Foulis. 6/
Gay's works. 12mo. Foulis. 3/
Shenstone's works. 2 v. 12mo. 6/
Dryden's works. 4 v. 12mo. Foulis.
  12/
Pope's works. by Warburton. 12mo.
  £1.4
Churchill's poems. 4 v. 12mo. 12/
Hudibrass. 3/

Swift's works. 21 v. small 8vo.
  £3.3
Swift's literary correspondence. 3 v.
  9/
Spectator. 9 v. 12mo. £1.7
Tatler. 5 v. 12mo. 15/
Guardian. 2 v. 12mo. 6/
Freeholder. 12mo. 3/
Ld. Lyttleton's Persian letters.
  12mo. 3/

C R I T I C I S M   O N   T H E
F I N E   A R T S
Ld. Kaim's elements of criticism. 2
  v. 8vo. 10/
Burke on the sublime and beautiful.
  8 vo. 5/
Hogarth's analysis of beauty. 4to.
  £1.1
Reid on the human mind. 8vo. 5/
Smith's theory of moral sentiments.
  8vo. 5/
Johnson's dictionary. 2 v. fol. £3
Capell's prolusions. 12mo. 3/

P O L I T I C K S   T R A D E
Montesquieu's spirit of laws. 2 v.
  12mo. 6/
Locke on government. 8vo. 5/
Sidney on government. 4to. 15/
Marmontel's Belisarius. 12mo. Eng.
  3/
Ld. Bolingbroke's political works. 5
  v. 8vo. £1.5
Montesquieu's rise & fall of the
  Roman governmt. 12mo. 3/
Steuart's Political oeconomy. 2 v.
  4to. £1.10
Petty's Political arithmetic. 8vo. 5/

R E L I G I O N
Locke's conduct of the mind in
  search of truth. 12mo. 3/
Xenophon's memoirs of Socrates. by
  Feilding. 8vo. 5/
Epictetus. by Mrs. Carter. 2 v.
  12mo. 6/
Antoninus by Collins. 3/
Seneca. by L'Estrange. 8vo. 5/
Cicero's Offices. by Guthrie. 8vo.
  5/

Cicero's Tusculan questions. Eng. 3/
Ld. Bolingbroke's Philosophical
works. 5 v. 8vo. £1.5
Hume's essays. 4 v. 12mo. 12/
Ld. Kaim's Natural religion. 8vo.
6/
Philosophical survey of Nature. 3/
Oeconomy of human life. 2/
Sterne's sermons. 7 v. 12mo. £1.1
Sherlock on death. 8vo. 5/
Sherlock on a future state. 5/

LAW
Ld. Kaim's Principles of equity. fol.
£1.1
Blackstone's Commentaries. 4 v.
4to. £4.4
Cuningham's Law dictionary. 2 v.
fol. £3

HISTORY. ANTIENT
Bible. 6/
Rollin's Antient history. Eng. 13 v.
12mo. £1.19
Stanyan's Graecian history. 2 v. 8vo.
10/
Livy. (the late translation). 12/
Sallust by Gordon. 12mo. 12/
Tacitus by Gordon. 12mo. 15/
Caesar by Bladen. 8vo. 5/
Josephus. Eng. 1.0
Vertot's Revolutions of Rome. Eng. 9/
Plutarch's lives. by Langhorne. 6 v.
8vo. £1.10
Bayle's Dictionary. 5 v. fol. £7.10.
Jeffery's Historical & Chronological
chart. 15/
HISTORY. MODERN.
Robertson's History of Charles the
Vth. 3 v. 4to. £3.3
Bossuet's history of France. 4 v.
12mo. 12/

Davila. by Farneworth. 2 v. 4to.
£1.10.
Hume's history of England. 8 v. 8vo.
£2.8.
Clarendon's history of the rebellion.
6 v. 8vo. £1.10.
Robertson's history of Scotland. 2 v.
8vo. 12/
Keith's history of Virginia. 4to. 12/
Stith's history of Virginia. 6/

NATURAL PHILOSOPHY.
NATURAL HISTORY &c.
Nature displayed. Eng. 7 v. 12mo.
Franklin on Electricity. 4to. 10/
Macqueer's elements of Chemistry.
2 v. 8vo. 10/
Home's principles of agriculture.
8vo. 4/
Tull's horse-hoeing husbandry. 8vo.
5/
Duhamel's husbandry. 4to. 15/
Millar's Gardener's dict. fol. £2.10.
Buffon's natural history. Eng.
£2.10.
A compendium of Physic & Surgery.
Nourse. 12mo. 1765. 3/
Addison's travels. 12mo. 3/
Anson's voiage. 8vo. 6/
Thompson's travels. 2 v. 12mo. 6/
Lady M. W. Montague's letters. 3 v.
12mo. 9/

MISCELLANEOUS
Ld. Lyttleton's dialogues of the
dead. 8vo. 5/
Fenelon's dialogues of the dead.
Eng. 12mo. 3/
Voltaire's works. Eng. £4.
Locke on Education. 12mo. 3/
Owen's Dict. of arts & sciences. 4 v.
8vo. £2.

These books if bound quite plain will cost the prices affixed in this catalogue. If bound elegantly, gilt, lettered, and marbled on the leaves, they will cost 20. p. cent more. If bound by Bumgarden in fine Marbled bindings, they will cost 50. p. cent more.

Apply to Thomas Waller, bookseller, Fleet-street London.

This whole catalogue as rated here comes to £107.10.

To Charles McPherson[2]

DEAR SIR   Albemarle in Virga. Feb. 25. 1773.
    Encouraged by the small acquaintance which I had the pleasure of having contracted with you during your residence in this country, I take the liberty of making the present application to you. I understood you were related to the gentleman of your name Mr. James Macpherson to whom the world is so much indebted for the collection, arrangement and elegant translation, of Ossian's poems. These peices have been, and will I think during my life continue to be to me, the source of daily and exalted pleasure. The tender, and the sublime emotions of the mind were never before so finely wrought up by human hand. I am not ashamed to own that I think this rude bard of the North the greatest Poet that has ever existed. Merely for the pleasure of reading his works I am become desirous of learning the language in which he sung and of possessing his songs in their original form. Mr. Macpherson I think informs us he is possessed of the originals. Indeed a gentleman has lately told me he had seen them in print; but I am afraid he has mistaken the specimen from Temora annexed to some of the editions of the translation, for the whole works. If they are printed, it will abridge my request and your trouble to the sending me a printed copy. But if there be none such, my petition is that you would be so good as to use your interest with Mr. Mcpherson to obtain leave to take a manuscript copy of them; and procure it to be done. I would chuse it in a fair, round, hand, on fine paper, with a good margin, bound in parchment as elegantly as possible, lettered on the back and marbled or gilt on the edges of the leaves. I should not regard expence in doing this. I would further beg the favor of you to give me a catalogue of books written in that language, and to send me such of them as may be necessary for learning it. These will of course include a grammar and dictionary. The cost of these as well as of the copy of Ossian will be answered for me on demand by Mr. Alexr. McCaul sometime of Virga. merchant but now of Glasgow, or by your friend Mr. Ninian Minzies of Richmond in Virga. to whose care the books may be sent. You can perhaps tell me whether we may ever hope to see any more of those Celtic peices published. Manuscript copies of any which are not in print it would at any time give me the greatest happiness to receive. The glow of one warm thought is to me worth more than money. I hear with pleasure from your friends that your path through life is likely to be smoothed by success. I wish the business and the pleasures of your situation could admit leisure now and then to scribble a line to one who wishes you every felicity and would willingly merit the appellation of Dr. Sir Your friend and humble servt.

---

2. Merchant Charles McPherson of Edinburgh had earlier been in business in Virginia. His cousin James Macpherson (1736–1796) claimed that *Fingal* (1762) and *Temora* (1763) were translations from the Gaelic epics of a legendary poet named Ossian. Although he did have traditional sources, the works were largely his own creation. Calls for him to produce the manuscripts from which he claimed to have worked were frequent in the period.

To John Adams[3]

DEAR SIR   Williamsburgh May 16. 1777.
   Matters in our part of the continent are too much in quiet to send you
news from hence. Our battalions for the Continental service were some
time ago so far filled as rendered the recommendation of a draught from the
militia hardly requisite, and the more so as in this country it ever was the
most unpopular and impracticable thing that could be attempted. Our
people even under the monarchical government had learnt to consider it as
the last of all oppressions. I learn from our delegates that the Confederation is again on the carpet. A great and a necessary work, but I fear almost
desperate. The point of representation is what most alarms me, as I fear the
great and small colonies are bitterly determined not to cede. Will you be so
good as to recollect the proposition I formerly made you in private and try
if you can work it into some good to save our union? It was that any proposition might be negatived by the representatives of a majority of the people
of America, or of a majority of the colonies of America. The former secures
the larger the latter the smaller colonies. I have mentioned it to many here.
The good whigs I think will so far cede their opinions for the sake of the
Union, and others we care little for. The journals of congress not being
printed earlier gives more uneasiness than I would ever wish to see produced by any act of that body, from whom alone I know our salvation can
proceed. In our assembly even the best affected think it an indignity to
freemen to be voted away life and fortune in the dark. Our house have lately
written for a M.S. copy of your journals, not meaning to desire a communication of any thing ordered to be kept secret. I wish the regulation of the
post office adopted by Congress last September could be put in practice. It
was for the riders to travel night and day, and to go their several stages three
times a week. The speedy and frequent communication of intelligence is
really of great consequence. So many falshoods have been propagated that
nothing now is beleived unless coming from Congress or camp. Our people
merely for want of intelligence which they may rely on are become lethargick and insensible of the state they are in. Had you ever a leisure moment
I should ask a letter from you sometimes directed to the care of Mr. Dick,
Fredericksburgh: but having nothing to give in return it would be a tax on
your charity as well as your time. The esteem I have for you privately, as well
as for your public importance will always render assurances of your health
and happiness agreeable. I am Dear Sir Your friend & servt:

                                                        TH: JEFFERSON

To Giovanni Fabbroni[4]

SIR   Williamsburgh in Virginia June. 8. 1778
   Your letter of Sep. 15. 1776 from Paris came safe to hand. We have not
however had the pleasure of seeing Mr. De Crenis,[5] the bearer of it in this

---

3. This is the earliest surviving letter between Jefferson and John Adams (1735–1826). The two leaders would suffer alienation owing to political differences in the 1790s but resumed their correspondence and friendship in 1813.
4. Giovanni Fabbroni (1752–1822) of Florence was a young scholar then working in Paris.
5. The chevalier de Crenis joined the Pulaski cavalry legion as a lieutenant in 1778. In his letter to
   Jefferson in September 1776, Fabbroni described him as "an officer of Some distinction in the
   Servise of the croun of France," adding that he was "a person of merit whose good qualities receive
   a new Luster from the particular estim he has for the Country he is going to" (*PTJ* 1:519).

country, as he joined the army in Pennsylvania as soon as he arrived. I should have taken particular pleasure in serving him on your recommendation. From the kind anxiety expressed in your letters as well as from other sources of information we discover that our enemies have filled Europe with Thrasonic[6] accounts of victories they had never won and conquests they were fated never to make. While these accounts alarmed our friends in Europe they afforded us diversion. We have long been out of all fear for the event of the war. I inclose you a list of the killed, wounded, and captives of the enemy from the Commencement of hostilities at Lexington in April 1775. till November 1777. since which there has been no event of any consequence. This is the best history of the war which can be brought within the compass of a letter. I believe the account to be near the truth, tho' it is difficult to get at the numbers lost by an enemy with absolute precision. Many of the articles have been communicated to us from England as taken from the official returns made by their General. I wish it were in my power to send you as just an account of our [losses] but this cannot be done without an application to the war office which being in another country is at this time out of my reach. I think that upon the whole it has been about one half the number lost by them. In some instances more, but in others less. This difference is ascribed to our superiority in taking aim when we fire; every soldier in our army having been intimate with his gun from his infancy. If there could have been a doubt before as to the event of the war, it is now totally removed by the interposition of France; and the generous alliance she has entered into with us.

Tho' much of my time is employed in the councils of America I have yet a little leisure to indulge my fondness for philosophical studies. I could wish to correspond with you on subjects of that kind. It might not be unacceptable to you to be informed for instance of the true power of our climate as discoverable from the Thermometer, from the force and direction of the winds, the quantity of rain, the plants which grow without shelter in the winter &c. On the other hand we should be much pleased with cotemporary observations on the same particulars in your country, which will give us a comparative view of the two climates. Farenheit's thermometer is the only one in use with us. I make my daily observations as early as possible in the morning and again about 4. o'clock in the afternoon, these generally showing the maxima of cold and heat in the course of 24 hours. I wish I could gratify your Botanical taste; but I am acquainted with nothing more than the first principles of that science, yet myself and my friends may furnish you with any Botanical subjects which this country affords, and are not to be had with you: and I shall take pleasure in procuring them when pointed out by you. The greatest difficulty will be the means of conveyance during the continuance of the war.

If there is a gratification which I envy any people in this world it is to your country its music. This is the favorite passion of my soul, and fortune has cast my lot in a country where it is in a state of deplorable barbarism. From the [line] of life in which we conjecture you to be, I have for some time lost the hope of seeing you here. Should the event prove so, I shall ask your assistance in procuring a substitute who may be a proficient in singing and on the harpsichord. I should be contented to receive such an one two or three years hence, when it is hoped he may come more safely, and find here a greater plenty of those useful things which commerce alone can furnish.

6. Boastful, from a braggart soldier named Thraso in a play by Roman writer Terence.

The bounds of an American fortune will not admit the indulgence of a domestic band of musicians. Yet I have thought that a passion for music might be reconciled with that oeconomy which we are obliged to observe. I retain for instance among my domestic servants a gardener (Ortolano), weaver (Tessitore di lino e lan[o],] a cabinet maker (Stipettaio) and a stone-cutter (scalpellino lavorante in piano) to which I would add a Vigneron. In a country where, like yours, music is cultivated and practised by every class of men I suppose there might be found persons of those trades who could perform on the French horn, clarinet or hautboy and bassoon, so that one might have a band of two French horns, two clarinets and hautboys and a bassoon, without enlarging their domest[ic] expences. A certainty of employment for a half dozen years, and at [the] end of that time to find them if they chose it a conveyance to their own country might induce [them] to come here on reasonable wages. Without meaning to give you trouble, perhaps it mig[ht] be practicable for you in your ordinary intercourse with your pe[ople] to find out such men disposed to come to America. Sobriety and good nature would be desireable parts of their characters. If you think such a plan practicable, and will be so kind as to inform me what will be necessary to be done on my part, I will take care that it shall be done. The necessary expences, when informed of them, I can remit before they are wanting, to any port in France with which country alone we have safe correspondence.

I am Sir with much esteem your humble servt.,

T. J.

ENCLOSURE[7]

Number of the Killed, Wounded, and Captives of the British Army in the Course of the American War.

1775	killed	Wounded	Prisoners
At Lexington & Concord	43	70	
Bunker's hill	746	1,150	
Ticonderoga, St. John, & Quebeck	81	110	340
1776			
on the Lakes by general Arnold	53	64	
at Fort Sulivan in South Carolina	197	260	
at the Cedars in Canada	40	70	
at Norfolk, & the great bridge in Virginia	129	175	40
in Long Island	840	1600	65
at Harlem & Hellgate near New York	136	157	49
at New York on Landing	57	100	
at Fort Washington near New York	900	1,500	
at Fort Lee	20	35	
at Trenton the 26 of Decber.	35	60	948
at Princeton in New Jersey	74	100	
1777			
in Boston road by Commodore Harding	52	90	750
in Sundry transports			390
at Danbury	260	350	

---

7. In writing Jefferson, Fabbroni had asked for "particulars of the present War" (*PTJ* 1:519). Hence this statistical report, which survives in a copy made by the British, who intercepted the original as it made its way to Fabbroni "by way of Spain" (*PTJ* 2:198).

at Iron hill in Delaware State	59	80	20
at Brandwine in Pensylvania the 11th. Sepber.	800	1,176	
on Reading road by Genal. Maxwell	40	60	
at german Town near Philadelphia the 4th. Octber.	180	975	20
on Staten Island by Genal. Sulivan	94	150	278
at Bennington near the Lakes the 4th. Octber.	900	1,300	30
at Forts Montgomery & Clinton Hudsons River	580	700	
at Forts Mifflin & Red-Bank near Philada.	328	70	84
Genal. Burgoin's Army at Saratoga	2,100	1,126	5,752
Prisoners, & deserters before the Surrender			1,100
Total	8,844	11,528	9,866.

In all Wounded, Killed, and Prisoners,   30,238
Men already Lost to England   18,710

To the Chevalier d'Anmours[8]

DEAR SIR   Richmond Nov. 30. 1780.

I received your favor from Baltimore and shall carefully attend to the notifying you of the arrival of any fleet here from your nation or other circumstance which I may think interesting to you. The enemy have left us as you will before have heard. Tho' I do not wish for new occasions of calling together my countrymen to try their valour, yet I really wish, as they were called together that the enemy had staid to give them a little exercise and some lessons in real war. Were it not that an invasion of our state at Portsmouth shuts the only door of our commerce, I had rather fight our share of them here than send 300 miles to seek them in a climate more fatal than their sword. I am at present busily employed for Monsr. Marbois without his knowing it, and have to acknolege to him the mysterious obligation for making me much better acquainted with my own country than I ever was before. His queries as to this country put into my hands by Mr. Jones[9] I take every occasion which presents itself of procuring answers to. Some of them however can never be answered till I shall [have] leisure to go to Monticello where alone the materials exist which can enable any one to answer them. I am exceedingly anxious to get a copy of Le grande Encyclopedie,[1] but am really frightened from attempting it thro' the mercantile channel, dear as it is originally and loaded as it would come with the enormous advance which they lay on under pretext of insurance out and in. You

8. The chevalier d'Anmours had begun serving as French consul for Virginia and Maryland at the start of 1780. He had written Jefferson from Baltimore in October to inform him of the rumored approach of a French fleet.
9. Joseph Jones (1727–1780), Virginia delegate in the Continental Congress, had forwarded the queries of Marbois to Jefferson.
1. The *Encyclopédie ou dictionnaire raisonné des sciences, des arts et des matiers* (1751–72, with later additions and revisions), the joint project of Diderot and Alembert, to which Jefferson would refer in *Notes on the State of Virginia*.

once thought that some means might be fallen on of effecting this importation by some vessel of war and perhaps of making the remittance in tobacco in the same way. Should any such occur I shall be greatly obliged by your availing me of it, and will surely answer every engagement you can make for me.

I am with great sincerity Your friend & servt.

To J. P. G. Muhlenberg[2]

SIR   Richmond Jan. 31. 1781.

Acquainted as you are with the treasons of Arnold, I need say nothing for your information, or to give you a proper sentiment of them. You will readily suppose that it is above all things desireable to drag him from those under whose wing he is now sheltered. On his march to and from this place I am certain it might have been done with facility by men of enterprize and firmness. I think it may still be done though perhaps not quite so easily. Having peculiar confidence in the men from the Western side of the mountains, I meant as soon as they should come down to get the enterprize proposed to a chosen number of them, such whose courage and whose fidelity would be above all doubt. Your perfect knowlege of those men personally, and my confidence in your discretion, induce me to ask you to pick from among them proper characters, in such number as you think best, to reveal to them our desire, and engage them [to] undertake to seize and bring off this greatest of all traitors. Whether this may be best effected by their going in as friends and awaiting their opportunity, or otherwise is left to themselves. The smaller the number the better; so that they be sufficient to manage him. Every necessary caution must be used on their part to prevent a discovery of their design by the enemy, as should they be taken, the laws of war will justify against them the most rigorous sentence. I will undertake if they are succesful in bringing him off alive, that they shall receive five thousand guineas reward among them, and to men formed for such an enterprize it must be a great incitement to know that their names will be recorded with glory in history with those of Vanwert, Paulding and Williams.[3] *I shall be sorry to suppose that any circumstances may put it out of their power to bring him off alive after they shall have taken him and of course oblige them to put him to death. Should this happen, however, and America be deprived of the satisfaction of seeing him exhibited as a public spectacle of infamy, and of vengeance, I must give my approbation to their putting him to death. I do this considering him as a deserter from the American army, who has incurred the pain of death by his desertion, which we have a right to inflict on him and against which he cannot be protected by any act of our enemies. I distinguish him from an honourable enemy, who, in his station, would never be considered by me as a justifiable object of such an enterprize. In event of his death, however, I must reduce the reward proposed to 2000*

---

2. John Peter Gabriel Muhlenberg (1746–1807), Lutheran clergyman in Woodstock, Virginia, before he became an American general.

3. Isaac Van Wart (1760–1828), John Paulding (1758–1818), and David Williams (1754–1831) were the three New York militiamen who captured British spy John André on his return from a secret meeting with American general Benedict Arnold in September 1780. The captors thus ensured the failure of the British plan to seize West Point, although Arnold's escape allowed him, now as a British officer, to harass various areas, including Virginia early in 1781. The italicized passage that follows was deleted in the draft manuscript by Jefferson.

guineas, in proportion as our satisfaction would be reduced. The inclosed order from Baron Steuben[4] will authorize you to call for and to dispose of any force you may think necessary to place in readiness for covering the enterprize and securing the retreat of the party. Mr. Newton the bearer of this, and to whom it's contents are communicated in confidence, will provide men of trust to go as guides. These may be associated in the enterprize or not as you please; but let that point be previously settled that no difficulties may arise as to the parties entitled to participate of the reward. You know how necessary profound secrecy is in this business, even if it be not undertaken.

To François Barbé-Marbois[5]

SIR   Richmond Mar. 4. 1781.
    I have been honoured with your letter of Feb. 5. Mr. Jones did put into my hands a paper containing sundry enquiries into the present state of Virginia, which he informed me was from yourself, some of which I meant to do myself the honour of answering. Hitherto it has been in my power to collect a few materials only, which my present occupations disable me from compleating. I mean however, shortly, to be in a condition which will leave me quite at leisure to take them up, when it shall certainly be one of my first undertakings to give you as full information as I shall be able to do on such of the subjects as are within the sphere of my acquaintance. On some of them however I trust Mr. Jones will engage abler hands, those in particular which relate to the commerce of the state, a subject with which I am totally unacquainted, and which is probably the most important in your plan.
    I have the honour to be with sentiments of the highest esteem & respect Sir your most obedient & most humble sert.,
                                                      TH: JEFFERSON

To François Barbé-Marbois

SIR   Richmond Dec. 20. 1781.
    I now do myself the honour of inclosing you answers to the quaeries which Mr. Jones put into my hands. I fear your patience has been exhausted in attending them, but I beg you to be assured there has been no avoidable delay on my part. I retired from the public service in June only, and after that the general confusion of our state put it out of my power to procure the informations necessary till lately. Even now you will find them very imperfect and not worth offering but as a proof of my respect for your wishes. I have taken the liberty of referring to you my friend Mr. Charles Thompson for a perusal of them when convenient to you. Particular reasons subsisting between him and myself induced me to give you this trouble.
    If his Excellency the Chevalier de la Luzerne[6] will accept the respects of a stranger I beg you to present mine to him, and to consider me as being

4. Friedrich Wilhelm Augustus von Steuben (1730–1794), Prussian general who was recruited for the United States by Benjamin Franklin and who was especially effective in instituting a training regimen for American forces. In 1781 he was operating in Virginia.
5. François Barbe-Marbois (1745–1837), then the secretary of the French legation in the United States, had queried the various states, through their representatives in the Continental Congress, on conditions prevailing in them.
6. Anne-César, chevalier de la Luzerne (1741–1791), French minister to the United States. Marbois was his secretary.

with the greatest regard & esteem Sir Your most obedient and most humble
servt.,

TH: JEFFERSON

To Charles Thomson[7]

DEAR SIR   Richmond Dec. 20. 1781.
   I received notice from the secretary of the American Philosophical society some time ago that they had done me the honour of appointing me a
counsellor of that body. The particular duties of that office I am quite a
stranger to, and indeed know too little of the nature of their institution to
judge what objects it comprehends. In framing answers to some queries
which Monsr. de Marbois sent me, it occurred to me that some of the subjects which I had then occasion to take up, might, if more fully handled, be
a proper tribute to the Philosophical society, and the aversion I have to
being counted as a drone in any society induced me to determine to recur
to you as my antient friend, to ask the favor of you to peruse those answers,
and to take the trouble of communicating to me your opinion whether any
and which of the subjects there treated would come within the scope of that
learned institution, and to what degree of minuteness one should descend
in treating it; perhaps also you would be so friendly as to give me some idea
of the subjects which would at any time be admissible into their transactions. Had I known nothing but the load of business under which you
labour I should not have ventured on this application, but knowing your
friendly disposition also I thought you would take some spare half hour to
satisfy a friend who can assure you that he is with great sincerity & esteem
Your most obedt. humble servt.,

TH: JEFFERSON

To François Barbé-Marbois

SIR   Monticello Mar. 24. 1782.
   I am very sorry that the papers I had taken the liberty to trouble you with
have been so unfortunately delayed. I retired from office in the month of
June last, and was obliged by the movements of the enemy to retire from my
house at the same time, to which I did not return till the month of Aug. I
immediately engaged in the work of digesting the materials I had collected
in answer to your quæries, and supplying their defects. This I completed in
a short time except as to some few articles which requiring information
from very distant parts of the country, I referred forwarding the whole to
you till our assembly should meet in October when I hoped to get the information I wanted. That meeting was unexpectedly protracted so that I did not
go to Richmond till December. On leaving that place without having had a
good opportunity of sending my letter to you, I put that and some others into
the hands of the honbl. Mr. Ambler[8] a member of the council desiring he
would forward them by some of those safe conveyances which I supposed

---

7. Charles Thomson (1729–1824), the Irish native and Pennsylvania radical who served as secretary of
   the Continental Congress throughout the war. Jefferson included his comments on various topics, and
   particularly on Native American questions, as Appendix No. I to *Notes on the State of Virginia*.
8. Jacquelin Ambler (1742–1798) explained (*PTJ* 6:165) that he delayed conveying the materials to Marbois because he thought Jefferson was more concerned with their safety than with speedy delivery.

government would have. On receipt of your favor of January—[29] I became uneasy lest they should have miscarried, and wrote to Mr. Ambler to be informed of the channel of conveyance. I take the liberty of subjoining his answer as it will explain to you the cause of the one letter being delayed while it's companion went on safely. The trifle which has exposed you to this detail was not worth a thought on your part and I trouble you with it merely to satisfy you of the attention I payd to your wishes. I hope before this you will have received it safely and that it will have effected the sole purpose I could expect which was that of shewing you with how much respect I have the honour of considering whatever comes from you and of the very profound regard with which I am Sir Your mo. ob. & mo hble servt.

To François-Jean de Beauvoir, Chevalier de Chastellux[9]

DEAR SIR   Ampthiil Nov. 26. 1782.
    I received your friendly letters of   and June 30 but the latter not till the 17th. of Oct. It found me a little emerging from that stupor of mind which had rendered me as dead to the world as she[1] was whose loss occasioned it. Your letter recalled to my memory, that there were persons still living of much value to me. If you should have thought me remiss in not testifying to you sooner how deeply I had been impressed with your worth in the little time I had the happiness of being with you you will I am sure ascribe it to it's true cause the state of dreadful suspence in which I had been kept all the summer and the catastrophe which closed it. Before that event my scheme of life had been determined. I had folded myself in the arms of retirement, and rested all prospects of future happiness on domestic and literary objects. A single event wiped away all my plans and left me a blank which I had not the spirits to fill up. In this state of mind an appointment from Congress found me requiring me to cross the Atlantic, and that temptation might be added to duty I was informed at the same time from his Excy. the Chevalier de la Luzerne that a vessel of force would be sailing about the middle of Dec. in which you would be passing to France. I accepted the appointment and my only object now is so to hasten over those obstacles which would retard my departure as to be ready to join you in your voiage, fondly measuring your affections by my own and presuming your consent. It is not certain that by any exertions I can be in Philadelphia by the middle of December. The contrary is most probable. But hoping it will not be much later and counting on those procrastinations which usually attend the departure of vessels of size I have hopes of being with you in time. This will give me full Leisure to learn the result of your observations on the Natural bridge, to communicate to you my answers to the queries of Monsr. de Marbois, to receive edification from you on these and on other subjects of science, considering chess too as a matter of science. Should I be able to set out in tolerable time and any extraordinary delays attend the

9. François-Jean de Beauvoir, chevalier de Chastellux (1734–1788), one of the French generals in Rochambeau's expeditionary force. He had visited Monticello in the summer of 1782 and would leave a warm portrait of it and its owner in his *Voyages de M. le Marquis de Chastellux dans l'Amérique Septentrionale* (1786).
1. Martha Wayles Skelton Jefferson (1748–1782), Jefferson's wife and the widow of a young man he had known in college, had died on September 6, 1782. During her final illness, Jefferson attended her as a nurse every day. Following her death, he kept to his room for three weeks, then spent long hours riding through his woods, wracked by "many a violent burst of grief," as his daughter Patsy (who accompanied him) recalled.

sailing of the vessel I shall certainly do myself the honour of waiting on his
Excy. Count Rochambeau[2] at his Headquarters and of assuring him in person of my high respect and esteem for him—an object of which I have never
lost sight. To yourself I am unable to express the warmth of those sentiments of friendship and attachment with which I have the honour to be Dr
Sir Your most obedt. & mo. hble. servt.

To George Rogers Clark[3]

DEAR SIR   Nov. 26. 1782.
    I received in August your favour wherein you give me hopes of your being
able to procure for me some of the big bones.[4] I should be unfaithful to my
own feelings were I not to express to you how much I am obliged by your
attention to the request I made you on that subject. A specimen of each of
the several species of bones now to be found is to me the most desireable
object in Natural history, and there is no expence of package or of safe
transportation which I will not gladly reimburse to procure them safely.
Elkhorns of very extraordinary size, petrifactions, or any thing else uncommon would be very acceptable. New London in Bedford, Staunton in Augusta,
or Fredericksburg are places from whence I can surely get them. Mr. Step-
toe in the first place, Colo. Matthews in the second, Mr. Dick in the third
will take care of them for me. You will perhaps hear of my being gone to Europe, but my trip there will be short. I mention this lest you should hesitate
in forwarding any curiosities for me. Any observations of your own on the
subject of the big bones or their history, or on any thing else in the Western
country, will come acceptably to me, because I know you see the works of
nature in the great, and not merely in detail. Descriptions of animals, vegetables, minerals, or other curious things, notes as to the Indians, information of the country between the Missisipi and waters of the South sea &c.
&c. will strike your mind as worthy being communicated. I wish you had
more time to pay attention to them.
    I perceive by your letter you are not unapprised that your services to your
country have not made due impression on every mind. That you have enemies you must not doubt, when you reflect that you have made yourself eminent. If you meant to escape malice you should have confined yourself
within the sleepy line of regular duty. When you transgressed this and
enterprized deeds which will hand down your name with honour to future
times, you made yourself a mark for malice and envy to shoot at. Of these
there is enough both in and out of office. I was not a little surprized however to find one person hostile to you as far as he has personal courage to
shew hostility to any man. Who he is you will probably have heard, or may

2. Jean Baptiste Donatien de Vimeur, Comte de Rochambeau (1725–1807), commander of the French
   army in America, 1780–83.
3. George Rogers Clark (1752–1818), Virginia-born soldier who had distinguished himself in the Western theater of the Revolution by winning several key victories over the British. His brother was
   William Clark, whom Jefferson would appoint to share command of the Lewis and Clark expedition in 1803.
4. Jefferson had written Clark in December 1781 asking him to procure "some of the teeth of the great
   animal whose remains are found on the Ohio" (*PTJ* 6:139). Replying the following February, Clark
   informed Jefferson, "I am unhappy that it hath been out of my power to procure you those Curiosities you want except a large thigh Bone that dont please me being broke." He was eager to comply
   with Jefferson's request: "Nothing of this nature escape[s] me am anxious of being possessd of your
   Sentiments Respecting the big bones, what those Animals ware and how they Came into this part
   of the Globe" (*PTJ* 6:159).

know him by this description as being all tongue without either head or heart.[5] In the variety of his crooked schemes however, his interests may probably veer about so as to put it in your power to be useful to him; in which case he certainly will be your friend again if you want him. That you may long continue a fit object for his enemity and for that of every person of his complexion in the state, which I know can only be by your continuing to do good to your country and honour to yourself is the earnest prayer of one who subscribes himself with great truth & sincerity Dr. Sir Your friend & servt.,

TH: JEFFERSON

To Thomas Walker[6]

DEAR SIR   Monticello Sep. 25. 1783.
    The inclosed are part of some papers I wrote in answer to certain queries sent me by Monsr. de Marbois in 1781. Another foreigner of my acquaintance,[7] now beyond the water, having asked a copy of them, I undertook to revise and correct them in some degree. There are still a great number of facts defective and some probably not to be depended on. Knowing nobody so able as yourself to set me right in them I take the liberty of sending you that part of the answers which I am most anxious to have as accurate as possible, and of asking the favour of you to peruse them with a pen in your hand, noting on a peice of paper as you proceed what facts and observations you think may be corrected, or added to, or should be withdrawn altogether. That part particularly which relates to the positions of Monsr. de Buffon I would wish to have very correct in matters of fact. You will observe in the table of animals that the American columns are almost entirely blank. I think you can better furnish me than any body else with the heaviest weights of our animals which I would ask the favour of you to do from the mouse to the mammoth as far as you have known them actually weighed, and where not weighed, you can probably conjecture pretty nearly. It is of no consequence how loose and rough your notes are, as I shall be able to incorporate them into the work and would wish to give you as little trouble as possible. If you could be as pointed as possible as to those circumstances relating to the Indians I should be much obliged to you: as I think it may happen that this may be the subject of further discussions. I fear you will think me too free in giving you trouble and more especially when I further ask the favour of you to get through them by the 4th. of the next month when I shall be returned from a journey I am now setting out on, and shall be preparing for my departure to Philadelphia. I know not what apology to make you unless my necessity be one, and my knowing no body else who can give me equal information on all the points. I am with very great esteem Dr. Sir Your most obedt. humble servt.,

TH: JEFFERSON

---

5. Jefferson is referring to Patrick Henry, who in this period also targeted Jefferson himself (see *PTJ* 6:205).
6. Thomas Walker (1715–1794), Virginia planter, soldier, and politician, had visited the Kentucky lands then belonging to Virginia some years before Daniel Boone. He had been a good friend of Jefferson's father.
7. Chastellux.

To George Rogers Clark

DEAR SIR   Annapolis Dec. 4. 1783.
I received here about a week ago your obliging letter of Oct. 12. 1783.
with the shells and seeds for which I return you many thanks. You are also
so kind as to keep alive the hope of getting for me as many of the different
species of bones, teeth and tusks of the *Mammoth* as can now be found.
This will be most acceptable. Pittsburg and Philadelphia or Winchester will
be the surest channel of conveyance. I find they have subscribed a very large
sum of money in England for exploring the country from the Missisipi to
California. They pretend it is only to promote knolege. I am afraid they have
thoughts of colonising into that quarter. Some of us have been talking here
in a feeble way of making the attempt to search that country. But I doubt
whether we have enough of that kind of spirit to raise the money. How
would you like to lead such a party? Tho I am afraid our prospect is not
worth asking the question. The definitive treaty of peace is at length
arrived. It is not altered from the preliminaries. The cession of the territory
West of Ohio to the United states has been at length accepted by Congress
with some small alterations of the conditions. We are in daily expectation
of receiving it with the final approbation of Virginia. Congress have been
lately agitated by questions where they should fix their residence. They first
resolved on Trentown. The Southern states however contrived to get a vote
that they would give half their time to Georgetown at the Falls of Patowmac. Still we consider the matter as undecided between the Delaware and
Patowmac. We urge the latter as the only point of union which can cement
us to our Western friends when they shall be formed into separate states. I
shall always be happy to hear from you and am with very particular esteem
Dr. Sir Your friend & humble servt.,

TH: JEFFERSON

To François-Jean de Beauvoir, Chevalier de Chastellux

DEAR SIR   Annapolis Jan. 16. 1784.
Lt. Colo. Franks[8] being appointed to carry to Paris one of the copies of
our ratification of the Definitive treaty, and being to depart in the instant
of his appointment furnishes me a hasty opportunity of obtruding myself on
your recollection. Should this prove troublesome you must take the blame
as having exposed yourself to my esteem by letting me become acquainted
with your merit. Our transactions on this side the water must now have
become uninteresting to the rest of the world. We are busy however among
ourselves endeavouring to get our new governments into regular and con-
certed motion. For this purpose I beleive we shall find some additions requisite to our Confederation. As yet every thing has gone smoothly since the
war. We are diverted with the European accounts of the anarchy and opposition to government in America. Nothing can be more untrue than these
relations. There was indeed some disatisfaction in the army at not being
paid off before they were disbanded, and a very trifling mutiny of 200

8. David Solebury Franks (c. 1742–1793), a Montreal native who, breaking with his Loyalist father
during the American occupation of that city, joined the staff of Benedict Arnold. In 1784, after
delivering the ratified treaty mentioned by Jefferson, he served for a time as U.S. consul at Marseilles.

souldiers in Philadelphia. On the latter occasion, Congress left that place disgusted with the pusillanimity of the government and not from any want of security to their own persons. The indignation which the other states felt at this insult to their delegates has enlisted them more warmly in support of Congress; and the people, the legislature and the Executive themselves of Pennsva. have made the most satisfactory atonements. Some people also of warm blood undertook to resolve as committees for proscribing the refugees. But they were few, scattered here and there through the several states, were absolutely unnoticed by those both in and out of power, and never expressed an idea of not acquiescing ultimately under the decisions of their governments. The greatest difficulty we find is to get money from them. The reason is not founded in their unwillingness, but in their real inability. You were a witness to the total destruction of our commerce, devastation of our country, and absence of the precious metals. It cannot be expected that these should flow in but through the channels of commerce, or that these channels can be opened in the first instant of peace. Time is requisite to avail ourselves of the productions of the earth, and the first of these will be applied to renew our stock of those necessaries of which we had been totally exhausted. But enough of America it's politics and poverty.—Science I suppose is going on with you rapidly as usual. I am in daily hopes of seeing something from your pen which may portray us to ourselves. Aware of the bias of self love and prejudice in myself and that your pictures will be faithful I am determined to annihilate my own opinions and give full credit to yours. I must caution you to distrust information from my answers to Monsr. de Marbois' queries. I have lately had a little leisure to revise them. I found some things should be omitted, many corrected, and more supplied and enlarged. They are swelled nearly to treble bulk. Being now too much for M.S. copies, I think the ensuing spring to print a dozen or 20 copies to be given to my friends, not suffering another to go out. As I have presumed to place you in that number I shall take the liberty of sending you a copy as a testimony of the sincere esteem and affection with which I have the honour to be Dr Sir Your mo. ob. & mo. hbl servt.

To Charles Thomson

DEAR SIR   Philadelphia May. 21. 1784.
    I received your favor of the 16th. last night. I was out when it was delivered, so know not how it came; a circumstance no otherwise important than as I am at a loss how or where to enquire for the packet which should have accompanied it containing the commissions, instructions &c.[9] I shall immediately however make the enquiry. I am obliged to you for the order for the journals. I shall make use of it to procure those of 1779, 1783, and part of 1784, which my set wants.[1] My matter in the printing way is dropped. Aitken had formerly told me he would print it for £4. a sheet. He now asked £5–10 which raised the price from £48 to £66. but what was a

9. Jefferson was preparing to leave for Paris, where he would join John Adams and Benjamin Franklin in negotiating "Treaties of Amity and Commerce" for the new nation. The "commissions, instructions, etc." about which Jefferson expressed concern dealt with that mission. These were sent separately; they are printed in *PTJ* 7:262–271.
1. Thomson had sent an order on the printer, D. C. Claypoole of Philadelphia, for copies of the journals of the Continental Congress that he had issued for 1779, 1781, 1782, and part of 1783 (*PTJ* 7:261).

more effectual and insuperable bar was that he could not complete it under three weeks, a time I could not wait for it. Dunlap happened to be out of town; so I relinquished the plan. Perhaps I may have a few copies struck off in Paris if there be an English printer there. If I do you shall assuredly have one. I shall take the liberty of adding some of your notes. Those which were amendatory merely will have their effect on the body of the work. I left all the papers belonging to the Grand committee in the hands of Mr. Blanchard. Among these were the papers relating to Vermont. My reason for not delivering them to you, as I did the others, was that the committee was to sit that morning. There are vessels arrived here which left London as late as the 14th. of April. Nothing important however has yet been communicated from them. The principal interesting occurrence here is a very daring insult committed on Mr. Marbois by a Frenchman who calls himself the Chevalr. de Longchamps,[2] but is in fact the nephew of the Minister's steward's wife. He obliged him in his own defence to box in the streets like a porter. He is demanded by the Minister to be delivered up by the Executive here to be sent to France for punishment. They are plodding over the case. Whether he be a citizen of America or not is not yet decided. I shall endeavor to make myself acquainted with the facts because it will possibly be the cause of something disagreeable here, and perhaps on the other side the water. I think there is a desire in the Executive here to give every satisfaction they can. But whether it is in the syllables and letters of the law that a Frenchman committing an outrage may be delivered up to his master for punishment is matter of dubiety. You will hear enough of it, as it comes to Congress of course, so I will add no more than my respectful compliments to Mrs. Thomson & assurances to yourself that I am with much esteem Dr. Sir Your friend & servt,

TH: JEFFERSON

P.S. I find your letter came by post but no packet with it. The arrival of so late a vessel is now contradicted.

To James Madison[3]

DEAR SIR   Paris May 11. 1785.
    Your favor of Jan. 9. came to my hands on the 13th. of April. The very full and satisfactory detail of the proceedings of assembly which it contained, gave me the highest pleasure. The value of these communications cannot be calculated at a shorter distance than the breadth of the Atlantic. Having lately made a cypher on a more convenient plan than the one we have used, I now transmit it to you by a Monsr. Doradour who goes to settle in Virginia. His family will follow him next year. Should he have occasion of your patronage I beg leave to solicit it for him. They yesterday finished printing my notes.[4] I had 200 copies printed, but do not put them out of my own

---

2. Charles Jullien de Longchamps was quickly apprehended and convicted in Pennsylvania, but an impasse developed when France demanded his extradition. Jefferson was interested in the episode not only because of his ties to Marbois but also because he was about to go to Paris as minister plenipotentiary (and soon, with Franklin's resignation, U.S. minister) to France and hence would have to deal with the repercussions.
3. Jefferson had first become allied with James Madison (1751–1836) during his efforts at revising the laws of Virginia in 1779. The two became especially close while rooming together during the session of Congress in Philadelphia over the winter of 1782–83. Madison's letter of April 13, 1785, some four thousand words long, contained extensive summaries of key congressional enactments.
4. I.e., *Notes on the State of Virginia.*

hands, except two or three copies here, and two which I shall send to America, to yourself and Colo. Monroe, if they can be ready this evening as promised. In this case you will receive one by Monsr. Doradour. I beg you to peruse it carefully because I ask your advice on it and ask nobody's else. I wish to put it into the hands of the young men at the college, as well on account of the political as physical parts. But there are sentiments on some subjects which I apprehend might be displeasing to the country perhaps to the assembly or to some who lead it. I do not wish to be exposed to their censure, nor do I know how far their influence, if exerted, might effect a misapplication of law to such a publication were it made. Communicate it then in confidence to those whose judgments and information you would pay respect to: and if you think it will give no offence I will send a copy to each of the students of W.M.C.[5] and some others to my friends and to your disposal. Otherwise I shall only send over a very few copies to particular friends in confidence and burn the rest. Answer me soon and without reserve. Do not view me as an author, and attached to what he has written. I am neither. They were at first intended only for Marbois. When I had enlarged them, I thought first of giving copies to three or four friends. I have since supposed they might set our young students into a useful train of thought and in no event do I propose to admit them to go to the public at large. A variety of accidents have postponed my writing to you till I have no further time to continue my letter. The next packet will sail from Havre. I will then send your books and write more fully. But answer me immediately on the preceding subject. I am with much affection Dr. Sir Your friend and servt.,

TH: JEFFERSON

To François-Jean de Beauvoir, Chevalier de Chastellux

DEAR SIR   Paris June 7, 1785
   I have been honoured with the receipt of your letter of the 2d. instant, and am to thank you, as I do sincerely for the partiality with which you receive the copy of the Notes on my country. As I can answer for the facts therein reported on my own observation, and have admitted none on the report of others which were not supported by evidence sufficient to command my own assent, I am not afraid that you should make any extracts you please for the Journal de physique which come within their plan of publication. The strictures on slavery and on the constitution of Virginia are not of that kind, and they are the parts which I do not wish to have made public, at least till I know whether their publication would do most harm or good. It is possible that in my own country these strictures might produce an irritation which would indispose the people towards the two great objects I have in view, that is the emancipation of their slaves, and the settlement of their constitution on a firmer and more permanent basis. If I learn from thence, that they will not produce that effect, I have printed and reserved just copies enough to be able to give one to every young man at the College. It is to them I look, to the rising generation, and not to the one now in power for these great reformations. The other copy delivered at your hotel was for Monsr. de Buffon. I meant to ask the favour of you to have it sent to him, as I was ignorant how to do it. I have one also for Monsr.

---

5. William and Mary College.

Daubenton: but being utterly unknown to him I cannot take the liberty of presenting it till I can do it through some common acquaintance.

I will beg leave to say here a few words on the general question of the degeneracy of animals in America. 1. As to the degeneracy of the man of Europe transplanted to America, it is no part of Monsr. de Buffon's system. He goes indeed within one step of it, but he stops there. The Abbé Raynal alone has taken that step. Your knowlege of America enables you to judge this question, to say whether the lower class of people in America, are less informed and less susceptible of information than the lower class in Europe: and whether those in America who have received such an education as that country can give, are less improved by it than Europeans of the same degree of education. 2. As to the Aboriginal man of America, I know of no respectable evidence on which the opinion of his inferiority of genius has been founded but that of Don Ulloa.[6] As to Robertson,[7] he never was in America, he relates nothing on his own knowlege, he is a compiler only of the relations of others, and a mere translator of the opinions of Monsr. de Buffon. I should as soon therefore add the translators of Robertson to the witnesses of this fact, as himself. Paw,[8] the beginner of this charge, was a compiler from the works of others; and of the most unlucky description; for he seems to have read the writings of travellers only to collect and republish their lies. It is really remarkable that in three volumes 12mo. of small print it is scarcely possible to find one truth, and yet that the author should be able to produce authority for every fact he states, as he says he can. Don Ulloa's testimony is of the most respectable. He wrote of what he saw. But he saw the Indian of South America only, and that after he had passed through ten generations of slavery. It is very unfair, from this sample, to judge of the natural genius of this race of men: and after supposing that Don Ulloa had not sufficiently calculated the allowance which should be made for this circumstance, we do him no injury in considering the picture he draws of the present Indians of S. America as no picture of what their ancestors were 300 years ago. It is in N. America we are to seek their original character: and I am safe in affirming that the proofs of genius given by the Indians of N. America, place them on a level with Whites in the same uncultivated state. The North of Europe furnishes subjects enough for comparison with them, and for a proof of their equality. I have seen some thousands myself, and conversed much with them, and have found in them a male, sound understanding. I have had much information from men who had lived among them, and whose veracity and good sense were so far known to me as to establish a reliance on their information. They have all agreed in bearing witness in favour of the genius of this people. As to their bodily strength, their manners rendering it disgraceful to labour, those muscles employed in labour will be weaker with them than with the European labourer: but those which are exerted in the chase and those faculties which are employed in the tracing an enemy or a wild beast, in contriving ambuscades for him, and in carrying them through their execution, are much stronger than with us, because they are more exercised. I beleive the Indian then to be in body and mind equal to the whiteman. I have supposed the

---

6. Don Antonio de Ulloa (1716–1795), first Spanish governor of Louisiana, published several works on the Americas, beginning with *Relación historica del viaje a la America Meridional y observaciones sobre Astronomica e Fisica* (1748).
7. The first part of the *History of America* by Scottish historian William Robertson (1721–1793), covering the Spanish colonies, appeared in 1777.
8. Cornelius De Pauw (1737–1799), a native of the Netherlands, published *Recherches Philosophiques sur les Américains* in 1768–69.

blackman, in his present state, might not be so. But it would be hazardous to affirm that, equally cultivated for a few generations, he would not become so. 3. As to the inferiority of the other animals of America, without more facts I can add nothing to what I have said in my Notes. As to the theory of Monsr. de Buffon that heat is friendly and moisture adverse to the production of large animals, I am lately furnished with a fact by Doctr. Franklin which proves the air of London and of Paris to be more humid than that of Philadelphia, and so creates a suspicion that the opinion of the superior humidity of America may perhaps have been too hastily adopted. And supposing that fact admitted, I think the physical reasonings urged to shew that in a moist country animals must be small, and that in a hot one they must be large, are not built on the basis of experiment. These questions however cannot be decided ultimately at this day. More facts must be collected, and more time flow off, before the world will be ripe for decision. In the mean time doubt is wisdom.

I have been fully sensible of the anxieties of your situation, and that your attentions were wholly consecrated, where alone they were wholly due, to the succour of friendship and worth. However much I prize your society I wait with patience the moment when I can have it without taking what is due to another. In the mean time I am solaced with the hope of possessing your friendship, and that it is not ungrateful to you to receive assurances of that with which I have the honour to be Dear Sir Your most obedient and most humble servt.,

TH: JEFFERSON

To the Reverend Richard Price[9]

SIR   Paris Aug. 7. 1785.
    Your favor of July 2. came duly to hand. The concern you therein express as to the effect of your pamphlet in America, induces me to trouble you with some observations on that subject. From my acquaintance with that country I think I am able to judge with some degree of certainty of the manner in which it will have been received. Southward of the Chesapeak it will find but few readers concurring with it in sentiment on the subject of slavery. From the mouth to the head of the Chesapeak, the bulk of the people will approve it in theory, and it will find a respectable minority ready to adopt it in practice, a minority which for weight and worth of character preponderates against the greater number, who have not the courage to divest their families of a property which however keeps their consciences inquiet. Northward of the Chesapeak you may find here and there an opponent to your doctrine as you may find here and there a robber and a murderer, but in no greater number. In that part of America, there being but few slaves, they can easily disencumber themselves of them, and emancipation is put

9. Richard Price (1723–1791), Welsh non-conformist minister and pro-American political writer, whose *Observations on the Importance of the American Revolution* (1784) included a call for the extension of liberty by the elimination of slavery. On hearing that the pamphlet had been condemned in South Carolina, he wrote Jefferson in his July 2 letter: "Should such a disposition prevail in the other United States, I shall have reason to fear that I have made myself ridiculous by Speaking of the American Revolution in the manner I have done; it will appear that the people who have been Struggling so earnestly to save *themselves* from Slavery are very ready to enslave *others*; the friends of liberty and humanity in Europe will be mortify'd, and an event which had raised their hopes will prove only an introduction to a new Scene of aristocratic tyranny and human debasement" (*PTJ* 8:258–259).

into such a train that in a few years there will be no slaves Northward of Maryland. In Maryland I do not find such a disposition to begin the redress of this enormity as in Virginia. This is the next state to which we may turn our eyes for the interesting spectacle of justice in conflict with avarice and oppression: a conflict wherein the sacred side is gaining daily recruits from the influx into office of young men grown and growing up. These have sucked in the principles of liberty as it were with their mother's milk, and it is to them I look with anxiety to turn the fate of this question. Be not therefore discouraged. What you have written will do a great deal of good: and could you still trouble yourself with our welfare, no man is more able to give aid to the labouring side. The college of William and Mary in Williamsburg, since the remodelling of it's plan, is the place where are collected together all the young men of Virginia under preparation for public life. They are there under the direction (most of them) of a Mr. Wythe one of the most virtuous of characters, and whose sentiments on the subject of slavery are unequivocal. I am satisfied if you could resolve to address an exhortation to those young men, with all that eloquence of which you are master, that it's influence on the future decision of this important question would be great, perhaps decisive. Thus you see that, so far from thinking you have cause to repent of what you have done, I wish you to do more, and wish it on an assurance of it's effect. The information I have received from America of the reception of your pamphlet in the different states agrees with the expectations I had formed.—Our country is getting into a ferment against yours, or rather have caught it from yours. God knows how this will end: but assuredly in one extreme or the other. There can be no medium between those who have loved so much. I think the decision is in your power as yet, but will not be so long. I pray you to be assured of the sincerity of the esteem & respect with which I have the honour to be Sir Your most obedt. humble servt.,

TH: JEFFERSON

P.S. I thank you for making me acquainted with Monsr. D'Ivernois.[1]

To Peter Carr[2]

DEAR PETER   Paris Aug. 19. 1785.

I received by Mr. Mazzei[3] your letter of April 20. I am much mortified to hear that you have lost so much time, and that when you arrived in Williamsburgh you were not at all advanced from what you were when you left Monticello. Time now begins to be precious to you. Every day you lose, will retard a day your entrance on that public stage whereon you may begin to be useful to yourself. However the way to repair the loss is to improve the future time. I trust that with your dispositions even the acquisition of science is a pleasing employment. I can assure you that the possession of it is

---

1. François D'Ivernois (1757–1842), who bore Price's letter to Jefferson, would later propose transplanting the College of Geneva to the United States.
2. Jefferson remained at this time the guardian of Peter Carr (1770–1815), his nephew. Jefferson knew from other sources (including a letter from James Madison) that Carr had delayed his preparation for entrance into college. Carr blamed his "great loss of time" on "want of horses" and "want of money" (*PTJ* 8:96).
3. Filippo (or Philip) Mazzei (1730–1816), Italian physician and then merchant in London, had been Jefferson's neighbor in Virginia from 1773 to 1779. The two men collaborated on the introduction of commercial wine production there, but their deeper ties sprang from their shared love of liberty. Returning to Italy in 1779 as a covert agent for Virginia, Mazzei had shipped arms to America.

what (next to an honest heart) will above all things render you dear to your friends, and give you fame and promotion in your own country. When your mind shall be well improved with science, nothing will be necessary to place you in the highest points of view but to pursue the interests of your country, the interests of your friends, and your own interests also with the purest integrity, the most chaste honour. The defect of these virtues can never be made up by all the other acquirements of body and mind. Make these then your first object. Give up money, give up fame, give up science, give the earth itself and all it contains rather than do an immoral act. And never suppose that in any possible situation or under any circumstances that it is best for you to do a dishonourable thing however slightly so it may appear to you. Whenever you are to do a thing tho' it can never be known but to yourself, ask yourself how you would act were all the world looking at you, and act accordingly. Encourage all your virtuous dispositions, and exercise them whenever an opportunity arises, being assured that they will gain strength by exercise as a limb of the body does, and that exercise will make them habitual. From the practice of the purest virtue you may be assured you will derive the most sublime comforts in every moment of life and in the moment of death. If ever you find yourself environed with difficulties and perplexing circumstances, out of which you are at a loss how to extricate yourself, do what is right, and be assured that that will extricate you the best out of the worst situations. Tho' you cannot see when you fetch one step, what will be the next, yet follow truth, justice, and plain-dealing, and never fear their leading you out of the labyrinth in the easiest manner possible. The knot which you thought a Gordian one will untie itself before you. Nothing is so mistaken as the supposition that a person is to extricate himself from a difficulty, by intrigue, by chicanery, by dissimulation, by trimming, by an untruth, by an injustice. This increases the difficulties tenfold, and those who pursue these methods, get themselves so involved at length that they can turn no way but their infamy becomes more exposed. It is of great importance to set a resolution, not to be shaken, never to tell an untruth. There is no vice so mean, so pitiful, so contemptible and he who permits himself to tell a lie once, finds it much easier to do it a second and third time, till at length it becomes habitual, he tells lies without attending to it, and truths without the world's beleiving him. This falshood of the tongue leads to that of the heart, and in time depraves all it's good dispositions.

An honest heart being the first blessing, a knowing head is the second. It is time for you now to begin to be choice in your reading, to begin to pursue a regular course in it and not to suffer yourself to be turned to the right or left by reading any thing out of that course. I have long ago digested a plan for you, suited to the circumstances in which you will be placed. This I will detail to you from time to time as you advance. For the present I advise you to begin a course of antient history, reading every thing in the original and not in translations. First read Goldsmith's history of Greece. This will give you a digested view of that feild. Then take up antient history in the detail, reading the following books in the following order. Herodotus. Thucydides. Xenophontis hellenica. Xenophontis Anabasis. Quintus Curtius. Justin. This shall form the first stage of your historical reading, and is all I need mention to you now. The next will be of Roman history. From that we will come down to Modern history. In Greek and Latin poetry, you have read or will read at school Virgil, Terence, Horace, Anacreon, Theocritus, Homer. Read also Milton's paradise lost, Ossian, Pope's works, Swift's works in order to form your style in your own language. In morality read Epictetus, Xenophontis memorabilia, Plato's Socratic dialogues, Cicero's philosophies. In order to assure a certain progress in this reading, consider what hours you have free from the school and the exercises of the school. Give about two of them every day to exercise; for health must not be sacrificed to learning. A strong body makes the mind strong. As to the species of exercise, I advise the gun. While this gives a moderate exercise to the body, it gives boldness, enterprize, and independance to the mind. Games played with the ball and others of that nature, are too violent for the body and stamp no character on the mind. Let your gun therefore be the constant companion of your walks. Never think of taking a book with you. The object of walking is to relax the mind. You should therefore not permit yourself even to think while you walk. But divert your attention by the objects surrounding you. Walking is the best possible exercise. Habituate yourself to walk very far. The Europeans value themselves on having subdued the horse to the uses of man. But I doubt whether we have not lost more than we have gained by the use of this animal. No one has occasioned so much the degeneracy of the human body. An Indian goes on foot nearly as far in a day, for a long journey, as an enfeebled white does on his horse, and he will tire the best horses. There is no habit you will value so much as that of walking far without fatigue. I would advise you to take your exercise in the afternoon. Not because it is the best time for exercise for certainly it is not: but because it is the best time to spare from your studies; and habit will soon reconcile it to health, and render it nearly as useful as if you gave to that the more precious hours of the day. A little walk of half an hour in the morning when you first rise is adviseable also. It shakes off sleep, and produces other good effects in the animal œconomy. Rise at a fixed and an early hour, and go to bed at a fixed and early hour also. Sitting up late at night is injurious to the health, and not useful to the mind.—Having ascribed proper hours to exercise, divide what remain (I mean of your vacant hours) into three portions. Give the principal to history, the other two, which should be shorter, to Philosophy and Poetry. Write me once every month or two and let me know the progress you make. Tell me in what manner you employ every hour in the day. The plan I have proposed for you is adapted to your present situation only. When that is changed, I shall propose a corresponding change of plan. I have ordered the following books to be sent to you from London to the care of Mr. Madison. Herodotus. Thucydides. Xenophon's Hellenics, Anabasis, and Memorabilia. Cicero's works. Baretti's Spanish and English dictionary. Martin's philosophical grammar and Martin's philosophia Britannica. I will send you the following from hence. Bezout's mathematics. De la Lande's astronomy. Muschenbroek's physics. Quintus Curtius. Justin, a Spanish grammar, and some Spanish books. You will observe that Martin, Bezout, De la Lande and Muschenbroek are not in the preceding plan. They are not to be opened till you go to the University. You are now I expect learning French. You must push this: because the books which will be put into your hands when you advance into Mathematics, Natural philosophy, Natural history, &c. will be mostly French, these sciences being better treated by the French than the English writers. Our future connection with Spain renders that the most necessary of the modern languages, after the French. When you become a public man you may have occasion for it, and the circumstance of your possessing that language may give you a preference over other candidates. I have nothing further to add for the present, than to husband well your time, cherish your instructors, strive to make every body your friend, & be assured that nothing will be so pleasing, as your success, to Dear Peter yours affectionately,

TH: JEFFERSON

To John Banister Jr.[4]

DEAR SIR   Paris Oct. 15. 1785.
I should sooner have answered the paragraph in your favor of Sep. 19. respecting the best seminary for the education of youth in Europe, but that it was necessary for me to make enquiries on the subject. The result of these has been to consider the competition as resting between Geneva and Rome. They are equally cheap, and probably are equal in the course of education pursued. The advantage of Geneva is that students acquire there the habits of speaking French. The advantages of Rome are the acquiring a local knowlege of a spot so classical and so celebrated; the acquiring the true pronuntiation of the Latin language; the acquiring a just taste in the fine arts, more particularly those of painting, sculpture, Architecture, and Music; a familiarity with those objects and processes of agriculture which experience has shewn best adapted to a climate like ours; and lastly the advantage of a fine climate for health. It is probable too that by being boarded in a French family the habit of speaking that language may be obtained. I do not count on any advantage to be derived in Geneva from a familiar acquaintance with the principles of it's government. The late revolution has rendered it a tyrannical aristocracy more likely to give ill than good ideas to an American. I think the balance in favor of Rome. Pisa is sometimes spoken of as a place of education. But it does not offer the 1st. and 3d. of the advantages of Rome. But why send an American youth to Europe for education? What are the objects of an useful American education? Classical knowlege, modern languages and chiefly French, Spanish, and Italian; Mathematics; Natural philosophy; Natural History; Civil History; Ethics. In Natural philosophy I mean to include Chemistry and Agriculture, and in Natural history to include Botany as well as the other branches of those departments. It is true that the habit of speaking the modern languages cannot be so well acquired in America, but every other article can be as well acquired at William and Mary College as at any place in Europe. When College education is done with and a young man is to prepare himself for public life, he must cast his eyes (for America) either on Law or Physic. For the former where can he apply so advantageously as to Mr. Wythe? For the latter he must come to Europe; the medical class of students therefore is the only one which need come to Europe. Let us view the disadvantages of sending a youth to Europe. To enumerate them all would require a volume. I will select a few. If he goes to England he learns drinking, horse-racing and boxing. These are the peculiarities of English education. The following circumstances are common to education in that and the other countries of Europe. He acquires a fondness for European luxury and dissipation and a contempt for the simplicity of his own country; he is fascinated with the privileges of the European aristocrats, and sees with abhorrence the lovely equality which the poor enjoys with the rich in his

4. John Banister Jr. (d. 1788), a young man from Petersburg, Virginia, with whose father, Colonel John Banister, Jefferson was well acquainted, had written asking advice on where his brother might study in Europe.

own country: he contracts a partiality for aristocracy or monarchy; he forms foreign friendships which will never be useful to him, and loses the season of life for forming in his own country those friendships which of all others are the most faithful and permanent: he is led by the strongest of all the human passions into a spirit for female intrigue destructive of his own and others happiness, or a passion for whores destructive of his health, and in both cases learns to consider fidelity to the marriage bed as an ungentlemanly practice and inconsistent with happiness: he recollects the voluptuary dress and arts of the European women and pities and despises the chaste affections and simplicity of those of his own country; he retains thro' life a fond recollection and a hankering after those places which were the scenes of his first pleasures and of his first connections; he returns to his own country, a foreigner, unacquainted with the practices of domestic œconomy necessary to preserve him from ruin; speaking and writing his native tongue as a foreigner, and therefore unqualified to obtain those distinctions which eloquence of the pen and tongue ensures in a free country; for I would observe to you that what is called style in writing or speaking is formed very early in life while the imagination is warm, and impressions are permanent. I am of opinion that there never was an instance of a man's writing or speaking his native tongue with elegance who passed from 15. to 20. years of age out of the country where it was spoken. Thus no instance exists of a person writing two languages perfectly. That will always appear to be his native language which was most familiar to him in his youth. It appears to me then that an American coming to Europe for education loses in his knowlege, in his morals, in his health, in his habits, and in his happiness. I had entertained only doubts on this head before I came to Europe: what I see and hear since I come here proves more than I had even suspected. Cast your eye over America: who are the men of most learning, of most eloquence, most beloved by their country and most trusted and promoted by them? They are those who have been educated among them, and whose manners, morals and habits are perfectly homogeneous with those of the country.—Did you expect by so short a question to draw such a sermon on yourself? I dare say you did not. But the consequences of foreign education are alarming to me as an American. I sin therefore through zeal whenever I enter on the subject. You are sufficiently American to pardon me for it. Let me hear of your health and be assured of the esteem with which I am Dear Sir Your friend & servant,

TH: JEFFERSON

To James Madison

DEAR SIR   Fontainebleau Oct. 28. 1785.
Seven o'clock, and retired to my fireside, I have determined to enter into conversation with you; this is a village of about 5,000 inhabitants when the court is not here and 20,000 when they are, occupying a valley thro' which runs a brook, and on each side of it a ridge of small mountains most of which are naked rock. The king comes here in the fall always, to hunt. His court attend him, as do also the foreign diplomatic corps. But as this is not indispensably required, and my finances do not admit the expence of a continued residence here, I propose to come occasionally to attend the king's levees, returning again to Paris, distant 40 miles. This being the first trip, I set out yesterday morning to take a view of the place. For this purpose I shaped

my course towards the highest of the mountains in sight, to the top of which was about a league. As soon as I had got clear of the town I fell in with a poor woman walking at the same rate with myself and going the same course. Wishing to know the condition of the labouring poor I entered into conversation with her, which I began by enquiries for the path which would lead me into the mountain: and thence proceeded to enquiries into her vocation, condition and circumstance. She told me she was a day labourer, at 8. sous or 4 d. sterling the day; that she had two children to maintain, and to pay a rent of 30 livres for her house (which would consume the hire of 75 days), that often she could get no emploiment, and of course was without bread. As we had walked together near a mile and she had so far served me as a guide, I gave her, on parting 24 sous. She burst into tears of a gratitude which I could perceive was unfeigned, because she was unable to utter a word. She had probably never before received so great an aid. This little attendrissement,[5] with the solitude of my walk led me into a train of reflections on that unequal division of property which occasions the numberless instances of wretchedness which I had observed in this country and is to be observed all over Europe. The property of this country is absolutely concentered in a very few hands, having revenues of from half a million of guineas a year downwards. These employ the flower of the country as servants, some of them having as many as 200 domestics, not labouring. They employ also a great number of manufacturers, and tradesmen, and lastly the class of labouring husbandmen. But after all these comes the most numerous of all the classes, that is, the poor who cannot find work. I asked myself what could be the reason that so many should be permitted to beg who are willing to work, in a country where there is a very considerable proportion of uncultivated lands? These lands are kept idle mostly for the sake of game. It should seem then that it must be because of the enormous wealth of the proprietors which places them above attention to the increase of their revenues by permitting these lands to be laboured. I am conscious that an equal division of property is impracticable. But the consequences of this enormous inequality producing so much misery to the bulk of mankind, legislators cannot invent too many devices for subdividing property, only taking care to let their subdivisions go hand in hand with the natural affections of the human mind. The descent of property of every kind therefore to all the children, or to all the brothers and sisters, or other relations in equal degree is a politic measure, and a practicable one. Another means of silently lessening the inequality of property is to exempt all from taxation below a certain point, and to tax the higher portions of property in geometrical progression as they rise. Whenever there is in any country, uncultivated lands and unemployed poor, it is clear that the laws of property have been so far extended as to violate natural right. The earth is given as a common stock for man to labour and live on. If, for the encouragement of industry we allow it to be appropriated, we must take care that other employment be furnished to those excluded from the appropriation. If we do not the fundamental right to labour the earth returns to the unemployed. It is too soon yet in our country to say that every man who cannot find employment but who can find uncultivated land, shall be at liberty to cultivate it, paying a moderate rent. But it is not too soon to provide by every possible means that as few as possible shall be without a little portion of land. The small landholders are the most precious part of a state.—The next object which struck

5. Tenderness (French).

my attention in my walk was the deer with which the wood abounded. They were of the kind called "Cerfs" and are certainly of the same species with ours. They are blackish indeed under the belly, and not white as ours, and they are more of the chesnut red: but these are such small differences as would be sure to happen in two races from the same stock, breeding separately a number of ages.—Their hares are totally different from the animal we call by that name: but their rabbet is almost exactly like him. The only difference is in their manners; the land on which I walked for some time being absolutely reduced to a honeycomb by their burrowing. I think there is no instance of ours burrowing.—After descending the hill again I saw a man cutting fern. I went to him under the pretence of asking the shortest road to the town, and afterwards asked for what use he was cutting fern. He told me that this part of the country furnished a great deal of fruit to Paris. That when packed in straw it acquired an ill taste, but that dry fern preserved it perfectly without communicating any taste at all. I treasured this observation for the preservation of my apples on my return to my own country. They have no apple here to compare with our Newtown pipping. They have nothing which deserves the name of a peach; there being not sun enough to ripen the plumbpeach and the best of their soft peaches being like our autumn peaches. Their cherries and strawberries are fair, but I think less flavoured. Their plumbs I think are better; so also the gooseberries, and the pears infinitely beyond any thing we possess. They have no grape better than our sweet-water. But they have a succession of as good from very early in the summer till frost. I am tomorrow to go to Mr. Malsherbes (an uncle of the Chevalr. Luzerne's) about 7. leagues from hence, who is the most curious man in France as to his trees. He is making for me a collection of the vines from which the Burgundy, Champagne, Bourdeaux, Frontignac, and other the most valuable wines of this country are made. Another gentleman is collecting for me the best eating grapes, including what we call the raisin. I propose also to endeavor to colonize their hare, rabbet, red and grey partridge, pheasants of different kinds, and some other birds. But I find that I am wandering beyond the limits of my walk and will therefore bid you Adieu. Yours affectionately,

TH: JEFFERSON

To James Madison

DEAR SIR   Paris Feb. 8. 1786.
   My last letters have been of the 1st. and 20th. of Sep. and the 28th. of Oct. Yours unacknoleged are of Aug. 20. Oct. 3. and Nov. 15. I take this the first safe opportunity of inclosing you the bills of lading for your books, and two others for your name sake of Williamsburgh and for the attorney which I will pray you to forward. I thank you for the communication of the remonstrance against the assessment. Mazzei who is now in Holland promised me to have it published in the Leyden gazette. It will do us great honour. I wish it may be as much approved by our assembly as by the wisest part of Europe. I have heard with great pleasure that our assembly have come to the resolution of giving the regulation of their commerce to the federal head. I will venture to assert that there is not one of it's opposers who, placed on this ground, would not see the wisdom of this measure. The politics of Europe render it indispensably necessary that with respect to every thing external we be one nation only, firmly hooped together. Interior government is what

each state should keep to itself. If it could be seen in Europe that all our states could be brought to concur in what the Virginia assembly has done, it would produce a total revolution in their opinion of us, and respect for us. And it should ever be held in mind that insult and war are the consequences of a want of respectability in the national character. As long as the states exercise separately those acts of power which respect foreign nations, so long will there continue to be irregularities committing by some one or other of them which will constantly keep us on an ill footing with foreign nations.

I thank you for your information as to my Notes.[6] The copies I have remaining shall be sent over to be given to some of my friends and to select subjects in the college. I have been unfortunate here with this trifle. I gave out a few copies only, and to confidential persons, writing in every copy a restraint against it's publication. Among others I gave a copy to a Mr. Williamos.[7] He died. I immediately took every precaution I could to recover this copy. But by some means or other a book seller had got hold of it. He had employed a hireling translator and was about publishing it in the most injurious form possible. An Abbé Morellet, a man of letters here to whom I had given a copy, got notice of this. He had translated some passages for a particular purpose: and he compounded with the bookseller to translate and give him the whole, on his declining the first publication. I found it necessary to confirm this, and it will be published in French, still mutilated however in it's freest parts. I am now at a loss what to do as to England. Every thing, good or bad, is thought worth publishing there; and I apprehend a translation back from the French and publication there. I rather believe it will be most eligible to let the original come out in that country: but am not yet decided.

I have purchased little for you in the book way since I sent the catalogue of my former purchases. I wish first to have your answer to that, and your information what parts of those purchases went out of your plan. You can easily say buy more of this kind, less of that &c. My wish is to conform myself to yours. I can get for you the original Paris edition in folio of the Encyclopedic for 620 livres, 35. vols: a good edition in 39. vols 4to, for 380 [livres] and a good one in 39. vols. 8vo. for 280 [livres]. The new one will be superior in far the greater number of articles: but not in all. And the pos-

6. In his November 15, 1785, letter, Madison, responding to Jefferson's concerns about how Notes on the State of Virginia might be received and whether it might be useful to distribute copies of the "private" edition to William and Mary students, wrote that he (with the concurrence of George Wythe) thought "the facts and remarks" Jefferson had collected "too [valuable] not to be made known," adding, however, that Wythe "suggested it might be better" if Jefferson deposit the copies he intended for the college in "the library, rather than to distribute them among the Students." That alternative would ensure the continued availability of the privately printed book; besides, Madison went on, "Perhaps too an indiscriminate gift might offend some [narrow-minded parents]" (PTJ 9:38; bracketed words were written in code by Madison and translated by Jefferson on the manuscript, indicating how sensitive the correspondents thought these issues).
7. Charles Williamos or Willyamoz (d. 1785), a Swiss native, had long served the British interest in America, being commissioned as a lieutenant in the 80th Regiment of Light Armed Foot in 1757 and later becoming a deputy of Sir William Johnson, Superintendent of Indian Affairs in the Northern Department. It is possible that Jefferson met him as early as 1766 in Virginia; certainly by the time of Jefferson's residence in Paris in the 1780s, he and the former soldier (who had sat out the Revolution) were very close friends, so close that Williamos was among those to whom Jefferson gave a copy of the private edition of his Notes. They subsequently had a falling-out so severe that it called forth from Jefferson a letter notable for its bitterness, and following the death of Williamos, as Jefferson informed Madison, that man's copy of the book unfortunately fell into the hands of the French bookseller Louis François Barrois, who proceeded to commission a translation in the hopes of publishing it. Availing himself of the Abbé André Morellet (1727–1819), a philosophe who had translated the Italian criminologist Beccaria and to whom he had in fact given another copy of the book, Jefferson managed to have an somewhat better (though still inadequate) version prepared, which was finally issued by Barrois in 1787 (PTJ 8:269–273).

session of the ancient one has more over the advantage of supplying present use. I have bought one for myself, but wait your orders as to you. I remember your purchase of a watch in Philadelphia. If she should not have proved good, you can probably sell her. In that case I can get for you here, one made as perfect as human art can make it for about 24. louis. I have had such a one made by the best and most faithful hand in Paris. She has a second hand, but no repeating, no day of the month, nor other useless thing to impede and injure the movements which are necessary. For 12. louis more you can have in the same cover, but on the backside, and absolutely unconnected with the movements of the watch, a pedometer which shall render you an exact account of the distances you walk. Your pleasure hereon shall be awaited.

Houdon[8] is returned. He called on me the other day to remonstrate against the inscription proposed for Genl. W's statue. He says it is too long to be put on the pedestal. I told him I was not at liberty to permit any alteration, but I would represent his objection to a friend who could judge of it's validity, and whether a change could be authorized. This has been the subject of conversations here, and various devices and inscriptions have been suggested. The one which has appeared best to me may be translated as follows: "Behold, Reader, the form of George Washington. For his worth, ask History: that will tell it, when this stone shall have yeilded to the decays of time. His country erects this monument: Houdon makes it." This for one side. On the 2d. represent the evacuation of Boston with the motto "hostibus primum fugatis." On the 3d. the capture of the Hessians with "hostibus iterum devictis." On the 4th. the surrender of York, with "hostibus ultimum debellatis."[9] This is seising the three most brilliant actions of his military life. By giving out here a wish of receiving mottos for this statue, we might have thousands offered, of which still better might be chosen. The artist made the same objection of *length* to the inscription for the bust of the M. de la fayette. An alteration of that might come in time still, if an alteration was wished. However I am not certain that it is desireable in either case. The state of Georgia has given 20,000 acres of land to the Count d'Estaing. This gift is considered here as very honourable to him, and it has gratified him much. I am persuaded that a gift of lands by the state of Virginia to the Marquis de la fayette would give a good opinion here of our character, and would reflect honour on the Marquis. Nor am I sure that the day will not come when it might be an useful asylum to him. The time of life at which he visited America was too well adapted to receive good and lasting impressions to permit him ever to accommodate himself to the principles of monarchical government; and it will need all his own prudence and that of his friends to make this country a safe residence for him. How glorious, how comfortable in reflection will it be to have prepared a refuge for him in case of a reverse. In the mean time he could settle it with tenants from the freest part of this country, Bretagny. I have never suggested the smallest idea of this kind to him: because the execution of it should convey the first notice. If the state has not a right to give him lands with their own officers, they could buy up at cheap prices the shares of others.—I am not certain however whether in the public or private opinion, a similar gift to

8. Jean-Antoine Houdon (1741–1828), whose life-size statue of George Washington was commissioned by the Virginia legislature and stands today in the rotunda of the capitol building in Richmond.
9. The enemy for the first time put to flight; The enemy again overcome; The enemy finally subdued (Latin). The inscription objected to by Houdon as too long for the statue had been written by Madison.

Count Rochambeau could be dispensed with. If the state could give to both, it would be better: but in any event I think they should to the Marquis. C. Rochambeau too has really deserved more attention than he has received. Why not set up his bust, that of Gates, Greene, Franklin in your new Capitol? à propos of the Capitol, do my dear friend exert yourself to get the plan begun or set aside, and that adopted which was drawn here.[1] It was taken from a model which has been the admiration of 16. centuries, which has been the object of as many pilgrimages as the tomb of Mahomet; which will give unrivalled honour to our state, and furnish a model whereon to form the taste of our young men. It will cost much less too than the one begun, because it does not cover one half the Area. Ask if you please, a sight of my letter of Jan. 26. to Messrs. Buchanan and Hay, which will spare me the repeating it's substance here.

Every thing is quiet in Europe. I recollect but one new invention in the arts which is worth mentioning. It is a mixture of the arts of engraving and printing, rendering both cheaper. Write or draw any thing on a plate of brass with the ink of the inventor, and in half an hour he gives you copies of it so perfectly like the original that they could not be suspected to be copies. His types for printing a whole page are all in one solid peice. An author therefore only prints a few copies of his work from time to time as they are called for. This saves the loss of printing more copies than may possibly be sold, and prevents an edition from being ever exhausted.

I am with a lively esteem Dear Sir your sincere friend & servant,

TH: JEFFERSON

P.S. Could you procure and send me an hundred or two nuts of the Paccan? They would enable me to oblige some characters here whom I should be much gratified to oblige. They should come packed in sand. The seeds of the sugar maple too would be a great present.

To Maria Cosway[2]

[MY DEAR] MADAM   Paris Octob. 12. 1786
    Having performed the last sad office of handing you into your carriage at the Pavilion de St. Denis, and seen the wheels get actually into motion, I turned on my heel and walked, more dead than alive, to the opposite door, where my own was awaiting me. Mr. Danquerville was missing. He was sought for, found, and dragged down stairs. [We] were crammed into the carriage, like recruits for the Bastille, and not having [sou]l enough to give orders to the coachman, he presumed Paris our destination, [and] drove off. After a considerable interval, silence was broke with a "je suis vraiment affligé du depart de ces bons gens."[3] This was the signal for a mutual confession [of dist]ress. We began immediately to talk of Mr. and Mrs. Cosway, of their goodness, their [talents], their amability, and tho we spoke of noth-

---

1. Jefferson himself completed, with the assistance of the architect Charles-Louis Clérisseau, a design for the Virginia capitol based on the Maison Carrée (sometimes written "Maison quarrée" by Jefferson), a famous Roman temple in Nîmes, France (see PTJ 9:220–223). That design was adopted and the building erected.
2. Jefferson was introduced to the Anglo-Italian artist Maria Hadfield Cosway (1760–1838) by the American painter John Trumbull in Paris in August 1786 and quickly became infatuated with her. This letter, composed after her departure for London with her husband, miniaturist Richard Cosway, on October 5, was written with Jefferson's left hand—for he had dislocated his right wrist when vaulting over a fence during one of his walks with her about Paris.
3. I am truly afflicted to part with those good people (French).

ing else, we seemed hardly to have entered into matter when the coachman announced the rue St. Denis, and that we were opposite Mr. Danquerville's. He insisted on descending there and traversing a short passage to his lodgings. I was carried home. Seated by my fire side, solitary and sad, the following dialogue took place between my Head and my Heart.

Head. Well, friend, you seem to be in a pretty trim.

Heart. I am indeed the most wretched of all earthly beings. Overwhelmed with grief, every fibre of my frame distended beyond it's natural powers to bear, I would willingly meet whatever catastrophe should leave me no more to feel or to fear.

Head. These are the eternal consequences of your warmth and precipitation. This is one of the scrapes into which you are ever leading us. You confess your follies indeed: but still you hug and cherish them, and no reformation can be hoped, where there is no repentance.

Heart. Oh my friend! This is no moment to upbraid my foibles. I am rent into fragments by the force of my grief! If you have any balm, pour it into my wounds: if none, do not harrow them by new torments. Spare me in this awful moment! At any other I will attend with patience to your admonitions.

Head. On the contrary I never found that the moment of triumph with you was the moment of attention to my admonitions. While suffering under your follies you may perhaps be made sensible of them, but, the paroxysm over, you fancy it can never return. Harsh therefore as the medecine may be, it is my office to administer it. You will be pleased to remember that when our friend Trumbull used to be telling us of the merits and talents of these good people, I never ceased whispering to you that we had no occasion for new acquaintance; that the greater their merit and talents, the more dangerous their friendship to our tranquillity, because the regret at parting would be greater.

Heart. Accordingly, Sir, this acquaintance was not the consequence of my doings. It was one of your projects which threw us in the way of it. It was you, remember, and not I, who desired the meeting, at Legrand & Molinos. I never trouble myself with domes nor arches. The Halle aux bleds[4] might have rotted down before I should have gone to see it. But you, forsooth, who are eternally getting us to sleep with your diagrams and crotchets, must go and examine this wonderful piece of architecture. And when you had seen it, oh! it was the most superb thing on earth! What you had seen there was worth all you had yet seen in Paris! I thought so too. But I meant it of the lady and gentleman to whom we had been presented, and not of a parcel of sticks and chips put together in pens. You then, Sir, and not I, have been the cause of the present distress.

Head. It would have been happy for you if my diagrams and crotchets had gotten you to sleep on that day, as you are pleased to say they eternally do. My visit to Legrand & Molinos had publick utility for it's object. A market is to be built in Richmond. What a commodious plan is that of Legrand & Molinos: especially if we put on it the noble dome of the Halle aux bleds. If such a bridge as they shewed us can be thrown across the Schuylkill at Philadelphia, the floating bridges taken up, and the navigation of that river opened, what a copious resource will be added, of wood and provisions, to warm and feed the poor of that city. While I was occupied with these objects, you were dilating with your new acquaintances, and contriving how

---

4. The magnificently domed Paris grain market, which had been designed by Jacques Molinos and Jacques-Guillaume Legrand, where Jefferson had first met the Cosways.

to prevent a separation from them. Every soul of you had an engagement for the day. Yet all these were to be sacrificed, that you might dine together. Lying messengers were to be dispatched into every quarter of the city with apologies for your breach of engagement. You particularly had the effrontery [to] send word to the Dutchess Danville that, in the moment we were setting out to d[ine] with her, dispatches came to hand which required immediate attention. You [wanted] me to invent a more ingenious excuse; but I knew you were getting into a scrape, and I would have nothing to do with it. Well, after dinner to St. Cloud, from St. Cloud to Ruggieri's, from Ruggieri to Krumfoltz, and if the day had been as long as a Lapland summer day, you would still have contrived means, among you, to have filled it.[5]

   Heart. Oh! my dear friend, how you have revived me by recalling to my mind the transactions of that day! How well I remember them all, and that when I came home at night and looked back to the morning, it seemed to have been a month agone. Go on then, like a kind comforter, and paint to me the day we went to St. Germains. How beautiful was every object! the Port de Neuilly, the hills along the Seine, the rainbows of the machine of Marly, the terras of St. Germains, the chateaux, the gardens, the [statues] of Marly, the pavillon of Lucienne. Recollect too Madrid, Bagatelle, the King's garden, the Dessert. How grand the idea excited by the remains of such a column! The spiral staircase too was beautiful. Every moment was filled with something agreeable. The wheels of time moved on with a rapidity of which those of our carriage gave but a faint idea, and yet in the evening, when one took a retrospect of the day, what a mass of happiness had we travelled over! Retrace all those scenes to me, my good companion, and I will forgive the unkindness with which you were chiding me. The day we went to St. Germains was a little too warm, I think, was not it?

   Head. Thou art the most incorrigible of all the beings that ever sinned! I reminded you of the follies of the first day, intending to deduce from thence some useful lessons for you, but instead of listening to these, you kindle at the recollection, you retrace the whole series with a fondness which shews you want nothing but the opportunity to act it over again. I often told you during it's course that you were imprudently engaging your affections under circumstances that must cost you a great deal of pain: that the persons indeed were of the greatest merit, possessing good sense, good humour, honest hearts, honest manners, and eminence in a lovely art: that the lady had moreover qualities and accomplishments, belonging to her sex, which might form a chapter apart for her: such as music, modesty, beauty, and that softness of disposition which is the ornament of her sex and charm of ours. But that all these considerations would increase the pang of separation: that their stay here was to be short: that you rack our whole system when you are parted from those you love, complaining that such a separation is worse than death, inasmuch as this ends our sufferings, whereas that only begins them: and that the separation would in this instance be the more severe as you would probably never see them again.

   Heart. But they told me they would come back again the next year.

   Head. But in the mean time see what you suffer: and their return too depends on so many circumstances that if you had a grain of prudence you would not count upon it. Upon the whole it is improbable and therefore you should abandon the idea of ever seeing them again.

---

5. The Cosways, Jefferson, and Trumbull all had engagements for the evening, but had enjoyed each other's company so much that each sent word to their respective hosts expressing their regrets.

Heart. May heaven abandon me if I do!

Head. Very well. Suppose then they come back. They are to stay here two months, and when these are expired, what is to follow? Perhaps you flatter yourself they may come to America?

Heart. God only knows what is to happen. I see nothing impossible in that supposition, and I see things wonderfully contrived sometimes to make us happy. Where could they find such objects as in America for the exercise of their enchanting art? especially the lady, who paints landscape so inimitably. She wants only subjects worthy of immortality to render her pencil immortal. The Falling spring, the Cascade of Niagara, the Passage of the Potowmac thro the Blue mountains, the Natural bridge. It is worth a voiage across the Atlantic to see these objects;[6] much more to paint, and make them, and thereby ourselves, known to all ages. And our own dear Monticello, where has nature spread so rich a mantle under the eye? mountains, forests, rocks, rivers. With what majesty do we there ride above the storms! How sublime to look down into the workhouse of nature, to see her clouds, hail, snow, rain, thunder, all fabricated at our feet! And the glorious Sun, when rising as if out of a distant water, just gilding the tops of the mountains, and giving life to all nature!——I hope in god no circumstance may ever make either seek an asylum from grief! With what sincere sympathy I would open every cell of my composition to receive the effusion of their woes! I would pour my tears into their wounds: and if a drop of balm could be found at the top of the Cordilleras, or at the remotest sources of the Missouri, I would go thither myself to seek and to bring it. Deeply practised in the school of affliction, the human heart knows no joy which I have not lost, no sorrow of which I have not drank! Fortune can present no grief of unknown form to me! Who then can so softly bind up the wound of another as he who has felt the same wound himself? But Heaven forbid they should ever know a sorrow!—Let us turn over another leaf, for this has distracted me.

Head. Well. Let us put this possibility to trial then on another point. When you consider the character which is given of our country by the lying newspapers of London, and their credulous copyers in other countries; when you reflect that all Europe is made to believe we are a lawless banditti, in a state of absolute anarchy, cutting one another's throats, and plundering without distinction, how can you expect that any reasonable creature would venture among us?

Heart. But you and I know that all this is false: that there is not a country on earth where there is greater tranquillity, where the laws are milder, or better obeyed: where every one is more attentive to his own business, or meddles less with that of others: where strangers are better received, more hospitably treated, and with a more sacred respect.

Head. True, you and I know this, but your friends do not know it.

Heart. But they are sensible people who think for themselves. They will ask of impartial foreigners who have been among us, whether they saw or heard on the spot any instances of anarchy. They will judge too that a people occupied as we are in opening rivers, digging navigable canals, making roads, building public schools, establishing academies, erecting busts and statues to our great men, protecting religious freedom, abolishing sanguinary punishments, reforming and improving our laws in general, they will judge I say for themselves whether these are not the occupations of a people at

---

6. Here, Jefferson playfully mimics his own description of the last two of these "subjects" in *Notes on the State of Virginia*.

their ease, whether this is not better evidence of our true state than a London newspaper, hired to lie, and from which no truth can ever be extracted but by reversing everything it says.

Head. I did not begin this lecture my friend with a view to learn from you what America is doing. Let us return then to our point. I wished to make you sensible how imprudent it is to place your affections, without reserve, on objects you must so soon lose, and whose loss when it comes must cost you such severe pangs. Remember the last night. You knew your friends were to leave Paris to-day. This was enough to throw you into agonies. All night you tossed us from one side of the bed to the other. No sleep, no rest. The poor crippled wrist too, never left one moment in the same position, now up, now down, now here, now there; was it to be wondered at if all it's pains returned? The Surgeon then was to be called, and to be rated as an ignoramus because he could not devine the cause of this extraordinary change.— In fine, my friend, you must mend your manners. This is not a world to live at random in as you do. To avoid these eternal distresses, to which you are for ever exposing us, you must learn to look forward before you take a step which may interest our peace. Everything in this world is matter of calculation. Advance then with caution, the balance in your hand. Put into one scale the pleasures which any object may offer; but put fairly into the other the pains which are to follow, and see which preponderates. The making an acquaintance is not a matter of indifference. When a new one is proposed to you, view it all round. Consider what advantages it presents, and to what inconveniencies it may expose you. Do not bite at the bait of pleasure till you know there is no hook beneath it. The art of life is the art of avoiding pain: and he is the best pilot who steers clearest of the rocks and shoals with which it is beset. Pleasure is always before us; but misfortune is at our side: while running after that, this arrests us. The most effectual means of being secure against pain is to retire within ourselves, and to suffice for our own happiness. Those, which depend on ourselves, are the only pleasures a wise man will count on: for nothing is ours which another may deprive us of. Hence the inestimable value of intellectual pleasures. Ever in our power, always leading us to something new, never cloying, we ride, serene and sublime, above the concerns of this mortal world, contemplating truth and nature, matter and motion, the laws which bind up their existence, and that eternal being who made and bound them up by these laws. Let this be our employ. Leave the bustle and tumult of society to those who have not talents to occupy themselves without them. Friendship is but another name for an alliance with the follies and the misfortunes of others. Our own share of miseries is sufficient: why enter then as volunteers into those of another? Is there so little gall poured into our own cup that we must needs help to drink that of our neighbor? A friend dies or leaves us: we feel as if a limb was cut off. He is sick: we must watch over him, and participate of his pains. His fortune is shipwrecked: ours must be laid under contribution. He loses a child, a parent or a partner: we must mourn the loss as if it was our own.

Heart. And what more sublime delight than to mingle tears with one whom the hand of heaven hath smitten! To watch over the bed of sickness, and to beguile it's tedious and it's painful moments! To share our bread with one to whom misfortune has left none! This world abounds indeed with misery: to lighten it's burthen we must divide it with one another. But let us now try the virtues of your mathematical balance, and as you have put into one scale the burthens of friendship, let me put it's comforts into the other. When languishing then under disease, how grateful is the solace of our friends! How are we penetrated with their assiduities and attentions! How much are we supported by their encouragements and kind offices! When Heaven has taken from us some object of our love, how sweet is it to have a bosom whereon to recline our heads, and into which we may pour the torrent of our tears! Grief, with such a comfort, is almost a luxury! In a life where we are perpetually exposed to want and accident, yours is a wonderful proposition, to insulate ourselves, to retire from all aid, and to wrap ourselves in the mantle of self-sufficiency! For assuredly nobody will care for him who cares for nobody. But friendship is precious not only in the shade but in the sunshine of life: and thanks to a benevolent arrangement of things, the greater part of life is sunshine. I will recur for proof to the days we have lately passed. On these indeed the sun shone brightly! How gay did the face of nature appear! Hills, vallies, chateaux, gardens, rivers, every object wore it's liveliest hue! Whence did they borrow it? From the presence of our charming companion. They were pleasing, because she seemed pleased. Alone, the scene would have been dull and insipid: the participation of it with her gave it relish. Let the gloomy Monk, sequestered from the world, seek unsocial pleasures in the bottom of his cell! Let the sublimated philosopher grasp visionary happiness while pursuing phantoms dressed in the garb of truth! Their supreme wisdom is supreme folly: and they mistake for happiness the mere absence of pain. Had they ever felt the solid pleasure of one generous spasm of the heart, they would exchange for it all the frigid speculations of their lives, which you have been vaunting in such elevated terms. Believe me then, my friend, that that is a miserable arithmetic which would estimate friendship at nothing, or at less than nothing. Respect for you has induced me to enter into this discussion, and to hear principles uttered which I detest and abjure. Respect for myself now obliges me to recall you into the proper limits of your office. When nature assigned us the same habitation, she gave us over it a divided empire. To you she allotted the field of science, to me that of morals. When the circle is to be squared, or the orbit of a comet to be traced; when the arch of greatest strength, or the solid of least resistance is to be investigated, take you the problem: it is yours: nature has given me no cognisance of it. In like manner in denying to you the feelings of sympathy, of benevolence, of gratitude, of justice, of love, of friendship, she has excluded you from their controul. To these she has adapted the mechanism of the heart. Morals were too essential to the happiness of man to be risked on the incertain combinations of the head. She laid their foundation therefore in sentiment, not in science. That she gave to all, as necessary to all: this to a few only, as sufficing with a few. I know indeed that you pretend authority to the sovereign controul of our conduct in all it's parts: and a respect for your grave saws and maxims, a desire to do what is right, has sometimes induced me to conform to your counsels. A few facts however which I can readily recall to your memory, will suffice to prove to you that nature has not organised you for our moral direction. When the poor wearied souldier, whom we overtook at Chickahominy with his pack on his back, begged us to let him get up behind our chariot, you began to calculate that the road was full of souldiers, and that if all should be taken up our horses would fail in their journey. We drove on therefore. But soon becoming sensible you had made me do wrong, that tho we cannot relieve all the distressed we should relieve as many as we can, I turned about to take up the souldier; but he had entered a bye path, and was no more to be found: and from that moment to this I could never find him out to ask his forgiveness. Again, when the poor woman came to ask a charity in Philadelphia, you whispered that she looked like a drunkard, and that half a dollar was enough to give her for the ale-house. Those who want the dispositions to give, easily find reasons why they ought not to give. When I sought her out afterwards, and did what I should have done at first, you know that she employed the money immediately towards placing her child at school. If our country, when pressed with wrongs at the point of the bayonet, had been governed by it's heads instead of it's hearts, where should we have been now? hanging on a gallows as high as Haman's.[7] You began to calculate and to compare wealth and numbers: we threw up a few pulsations of our warmest blood: we supplied enthusiasm against wealth and numbers: we put our existence to the hazard, when the hazard seemed against us, and we saved our country: justifying at the same time the ways of Providence, whose precept is to do always what is right, and leave the issue to him. In short, my friend, as far as my recollection serves me, I do not know that I ever did a good thing on your suggestion, or a dirty one without it. I do for ever then disclaim your interference in my province. Fill paper as you please with triangles and squares: try how many ways you can hang and combine them together. I shall never envy nor controul your sublime delights. But leave me to decide when and where friendships are to be contracted. You say I contract them at random, so you said the woman at Philadelphia was a drunkard. I receive no one into my esteem till I know they are worthy of it. Wealth, title, office, are no recommendations to my friendship. On the contrary great good qualities are requisite to make amends for their having wealth, title and office. You confess that in the present case I could not have made a worthier choice. You only object that I was so soon to lose them. We are not immortal ourselves, my friend; how can we expect our enjoiments to be so? We have no rose without it's thorn; no pleasure without alloy. It is the law of our existence; and we must acquiesce. It is the condition annexed to all our pleasures, not by us who receive, but by him who gives them. True, this condition is pressing cruelly on me at this moment. I feel more fit for death than life. But when I look back on the pleasures of which it is the consequence, I am conscious they were worth the price I am paying. Notwithstanding your endeavors too to damp my hopes, I comfort myself with expectations of their promised return. Hope is sweeter than despair, and they were too good to mean to deceive me. In the summer, said the gentleman; but in the spring, said the lady: and I should love her forever, were it only for that! Know then, my friend, that I have taken these good people into my bosom: that I have lodged them in the warmest cell I could find: that I love them, and will continue to love them thro life: that if fortune should dispose them on one side the globe, and me on the other, my affections shall pervade it's whole mass to reach them. Knowing then my determination, attempt not to disturb it. If you can at any time furnish matter for their amusement, it will be the office of a good neighbor to do it. I will in like manner seize any occasion which may offer to do the like good turn for you with Condorcet, Rittenhouse, Madison, La Cretelle, or any other of those worthy sons of science whom you so justly prize.

I thought this a favorable proposition whereon to rest the issue of the dialogue. So I put an end to it by calling for my nightcap. Methinks I hear you wish to heaven I had called a little sooner, and so spared you the ennui of such a tedious sermon. I did not interrupt them sooner because I was in a

---

7. See the story of the villainous Haman in Esther 7:10: "So Haman was put to death by hanging him on the pillar he had made for Mordecai."

mood for hearing sermons. You too were the subject; and on such a thesis I never think the theme long; not even if I am to write it, and that slowly and awkwardly, as now, with the left hand. But that you may not be discoraged from a correspondence which begins so formidably, I will promise you on my honour that my future letters shall be of a reasonable length. I will even agree to express but half my esteem for you, for fear of cloying you with too full a dose. But, on your part, no curtailing. If your letters are as long as the bible, they will appear short to me. Only let them be brim full of affection. I shall read them with the dispositions with which Arlequin in les deux billets spelt the words "je t'aime" and wished that the whole alphabet had entered into their composition.[8]

We have had incessant rains since your departure. These make me fear for your health, as well as that you have had an uncomfortable journey. The same cause has prevented me from being able to give you any account of your friends here. This voiage to Fontainbleau will probably send the Count de Moutier and the Marquise de Brehan to America. Danquerville promised to visit me, but has not done it as yet. De latude comes sometimes to take family soupe with me, and entertains me with anecdotes of his five and thirty years imprisonment. How fertile is the mind of man which can make the Bastille and Dungeon of Vincennes yeild interesting anecdotes. You know this was for making four verses on Mme. de Pompadour. But I think you told me you did not know the verses. They were these. "Sans esprit, sans sentiment, Sans etre belle, ni neuve, En France on peut avoir le premier amant: Pompadour en est l'epreuve."[9] I have read the memoir of his three escapes. As to myself my health is good, except my wrist which mends slowly, and my mind which mends not at all, but broods constantly over your departure. The lateness of the season obliges me to decline my journey into the South of France. Present me in the most friendly terms to Mr. Cosway, and receive me into your own recollection with a partiality and a warmth, proportioned, not to my own poor merit, but to the sentiments of sincere affection and esteem with which I have the honour to be, my dear Madam, your most obedient humble servant,

TH: JEFFERSON

To J. Hector St. John de Crèvecoeur[1]

DEAR SIR   Paris Jan. 15. 1787.
I see by the Journal of this morning that they are robbing us of another of our inventions to give it to the English. The writer indeed only admits

---

8. Les Deux Billets of Jean-Pierre Claris de Florian was first performed in 1779. In it, the comic character Arlequin woos Argentine.
9. Without spirit, without feeling, without being beautiful, or young—in France one can still have the foremost lover: Pompadour is the proof (French). Madame Pompadour (1721–1764), the mistress of Louis XV, had Jean Henri Latude (1725–1805) imprisoned for meddling with her, and through a series of mishaps he escaped and was recaptured several times before his final release in 1784. His Memoirs, though full of exaggeration, were widely published in the last two decades of the 18th century.
1. Michel-Guillaume Jean de Crèvecoeur (1735–1813), born near Caen, Normandy, had served in Canada under Montcalm before settling in New York. His Letters from an American Farmer (1782), written in English and published in London while he was on his way back to his homeland, had given him considerable celebrity (under the assumed name "J. Hector St. John") as an interpreter of American life for pre-Revolutionary France. He and Jefferson had corresponded and met after Crèvecoeur returned to America as French consul for the middle states in 1784.

them to have revived what he thinks was known to the Greeks, that is the making the circumference of a wheel of one single peice. The farmers in New Jersey were the first who practised it, and they practised it commonly. Dr. Franklin, in one of his trips to London, mentioned this practice to the man, now in London, who has the patent for making those wheels (I forget his name.) The idea struck him. The Doctor promised to go to his shop and assist him in trying to make the wheel of one peice. The Jersey farmers did it by cutting a young sapling, and bending it, while green and juicy, into a circle; and leaving it so till it became perfectly seasoned. But in London there are no saplings. The difficulty was then to give to old wood the pliancy of young. The Doctor and the workman laboured together some weeks, and succeeded, and the man obtained a patent for it which has made his fortune. I was in his shop in London, he told me the whole story himself, and acknowleged, not only the origin of the idea, but how much the assistance of Dr. Franklin had contributed to perform the operation on dry wood. He spoke of him with love and gratitude. I think I have had a similar account from Dr. Franklin, but cannot be certain quite. I know that being in Philadelphia when the first set of patent wheels arrived from London, and were spoken of by the gentleman (an Englishman) who brought them as a wonderful discovery. The idea of it's being a new discovery was laughed at by the Philadelphians, who in their Sunday parties across the Delaware had seen every farmer's cart mounted on such wheels. The writer in the paper supposes the English workman got his idea from Homer. But it is more likely that the Jersey farmer got the idea from thence, because ours are the only farmers who can read Homer: because too the Jersey practice is precisely that stated by Homer; the English practice very different. Homer's words are (comparing a young hero killed by Ajax to a poplar felled by a workman)————

> ὅ δ' εν κονιηςι, χαμαι πεςεν, αιγειρος ὡς
> Ἡ ῥα τ'εν ειαμενη ελεος μεγαλοιο πεφυκε
> Λειη αταρ τε ὁι οζοι επ' ακροτατη πεφυαςι
> Την μεν θάρματοπηγος ανηρ αιθωνι ςιδηρῷ
> Εξεταμ' οφρα ιτυν καμψη περικαλλεϊ διφρῳ,
> Ἡ μεν τ'αζομενη κειται ποταμοιο παρ οχθας   4. Il. 482.

literally thus "he fell on the ground, like a poplar, which has grown, smooth, in the wet part of a great meadow; with it's branches shooting from it's summit. But the Chariot-maker with his sharp axe, has felled it, that he may bend a wheel for a beautiful chariot. It lies drying on the banks of the river." Observe the circumstances which coincide with the Jersey practice. 1. It is a tree growing in a moist place, full of juices, and easily bent. 2. It is cut while green. 3. It is bent into the circumference of a wheel. 4. It is left to dry in that form. You, who write French well and readily, should write a line for the Journal to reclaim the honour of our farmers.[2] Adieu. Your's affectionately,

TH: JEFFERSON

---

2. Jefferson had found the offending story in the *Journal de Paris* on January 15, 1787; Crèvecoeur obliged his friend by sending an embellished translation of Jefferson's answer to the *Journal*, where it appeared on January 31. See *PTJ* 11: 44–45.

To John Stockdale³

SIR   Paris Feb. 27. 1787.

By the Diligence of tomorrow I will send you a corrected copy of my Notes, which I will pray you to print precisely as they are, without additions, alterations, preface, or any thing else but what is there. They will require a very accurate corrector of the press, because they are filled with tables, which will become absolutely useless if they are not printed with a perfect accuracy. I beg you therefore to have the most particular attention paid to the correcting of the press. With respect to the plate of the map, it is impossible to send it at the same time. It was engraved in London, and on examination I found a prodigious number of orthographical errors. Being determined that it shall not go out with a single error, an engraver is now closely employed in correcting them. He promises to have it finished the next week, say by the 10th. of March: but I suppose you must expect he will not be punctual to a day. The map will be worth more than the book, because it is very particular, made on the best materials which exist, and is of a very convenient size, bringing the states of Virginia, Maryland, Delaware and Pennsylvania into a single sheet. It will make the book sell. I think it would be worth your while to print 400 copies of the book for America, sending 200. to Richmond in Virginia, and 200 to Philadelphia. If you have no correspondents there, you might send those for Richmond to Mr. James Buchanan merchant there, and those for Philadelphia to Aitken bookseller there. These are men on whose punctuality you may depend. But they should be restrained from selling but for ready money: so that you may always find in their hands either the money or the books. I set out on my journey tomorrow: but Mr. Short, my secretary, remains here, and will hasten, and forward the plate to you by the Diligence.

Be so good as to send by the next Diligence a copy of Mr. Adams's book on the American constitutions printed by Dilly, in boards,⁴ it being for a bookseller here. I am Sir your very humble servt.,

TH: JEFFERSON

To Madame la Comtesse de Tessé⁵

Nismes. Mar. 20. 1787.

Here I am, Madam, gazing whole hours at the Maison quarrée, like a lover at his mistress. The stocking-weavers and silk spinners around it consider me as an hypochondriac Englishman, about to write with a pistol the last chapter of his history. This is the second time I have been in love since I left Paris. The first was with a Diana at the Chateau de Laye Epinaye in the Beaujolois, a delicious morsel of sculpture, by Michael Angelo Slodtz. This, you will say, was in rule, to fall in love with a fine woman: but, with a house! It is out of all precedent! No, madam, it is not without a precedent in my own history. While at Paris, I was violently smitten with the hotel de

---

3. John Stockdale (c. 1749–1814) was the London bookseller who issued the first "public" edition of *Notes on the State of Virginia* in 1787.
4. John Adams wrote his *Defence of the Constitutions of Government in the United States of America* while in Britain. It was first published by Charles Dilly in London in 1787.
5. Adrienne Catherine de Noailles, Madame de Tessé, a devotee of botany, was the aunt of Lafayette's wife.

Salm, and used to go to the Thuileries almost daily to look at it. The loueuse
des chaises, inattentive to my passion, never had the complaisance to place
a chair there; so that, sitting on the parapet, and twisting my neck round to
see the object of my admiration, I generally left it with a torticollis.[6] From
Lyons to Nismes I have been nourished with the remains of Roman
grandeur. They have always brought you to my mind, because I know your
affection for whatever is Roman and noble. At Vienne I thought of you. But
I am glad you were not there; for you would have seen me more angry than
I hope you will ever see me. The Pretorian palace, as it is called, comparable for it's fine proportions to the Maison quarrée, totally defaced by the
Barbarians who have converted it to it's present purpose; it's beautiful,
fluted, Corinthian columns cut out in part to make space for Gothic windows, and hewed down in the residue to the plane of the building. At Orange
too I thought of you. I was sure you had seen with rapture the sublime triumphal arch at the entrance into the city. I went then to the Arenas. Would
you believe Madam, that in this 18th. Century, in France, under the reign
of Louis XVI, they are at this moment pulling down the circular wall of this
superb remain to pave a road? And that too from a hill which is itself an
entire mass of stone just as fit, and more accessible. A former Intendant, a
Monsr. de Baville has rendered his memory dear to travellers and amateurs
by the pains he took to preserve and to restore these monuments of antiquity. The present one (I do not know who he is) is demolishing the object
to make a good road to it. I thought of you again, and I was then in great
good humour, at the Pont du Gard, a sublime antiquity, and well preserved.
But most of all here, where Roman taste, genius, and magnificence excite
ideas analogous to yours at every step, I could no longer oppose the inclination to avail myself of your permission to write to you, a permission given
with too much complaisance by you, taken advantage of with too much
indiscretion by me. Madame de Tott[7] too did me the same honour. But she
being only the descendant of some of those puny heroes who boiled their
own kettles before the walls of Troy, I shall write to her from a Graecian,
rather than a Roman canton; when I shall find myself for example among
her Phocean relations at Marseilles. Loving, as you do Madam, the precious
remains of antiquity, loving architecture, gardening, a warm sun, and a
clear sky, I wonder you have never thought of moving Chaville to Nismes.
This is not so impracticable as you may think. The next time a Surintendant
des batiments du roi,[8] after the example of M. Colbert, sends persons to
Nismes to move the Maison Carrée to Paris, that they may not come empty-
handed, desire them to bring Chaville with them to replace it. À propos of
Paris. I have now been three weeks from there without knowing any thing
of what has past. I suppose I shall meet it all at Aix, where I have directed
my letters to be lodged poste restante.[9] My journey has given me leisure to
reflect on this Assemblée des Notables.[1] Under a good and young king as
the present, I think good may be made of it. I would have the deputies then
by all means so conduct themselves as to encorage him to repeat the calls of
this assembly. Their first step should be to get themselves divided into two
chambers, instead of seven, the Noblesse and the commons separately. The

6. Wrenched neck.
7. A mutual friend of Jefferson' and Madame de Tessé's.
8. Superintendent of the king's buildings (French).
9. I.e., general delivery (French).
1. Facing large shortfalls in income and wishing to increase taxes, the French government had called
   an assembly of notables that opened in February 1787 at Versailles.

2d. to persuade the king, instead of chusing the deputies of the commons himself, to summon those chosen by the people for the Provincial adminis- trations. The 3d. as the Noblesse is too numerous to be all admitted into the assemblée to obtain permission for that body to chuse it's own deputies. The rest would follow. Two houses so elected would contain a mass of wisdom which would make the people happy, and the king great; would place him in history where no other act can possibly place him. This is my plan Madam; but I wish to know yours, which I am sure is better.

From a correspondent at Nismes you will not expect news. Were I to attempt to give you news, I should tell you stories a thousand years old. I should detail to you the intrigues of the courts of the Caesars, how they affect us here, the oppressions of their Praetors, Praefects &c. I am immersed in antiquities from morning to night. For me the city of Rome is actually existing in all the splendor of it's empire. I am filled with alarms for the event of the irruptions dayly making on us by the Goths, Ostrogoths, Visigoths and Vandals, lest they should reconquer us to our original bar- barism. If I am sometimes induced to look forward to the eighteenth century, it is only when recalled to it by the recollection of your goodness and friend- ship, and by those sentiments of sincere esteem and respect with which I have the honor to be, Madam, your most obedient & most humble servant,

TH: JEFFERSON

To Martha Jefferson[2]

Aix en Provence March. 28. 1787.

I was happy, my dear Patsy, to receive, on my arrival here, your letter informing me of your health and occupations. I have not written to you sooner because I have been almost constantly on the road.[3] My journey hitherto has been a very pleasing one. It was undertaken with the hope that the mineral waters of this place might restore strength to my wrist. Other considerations also concurred. Instruction, amusement, and abstraction from business, of which I had too much at Paris I am glad to learn that you are employed in things new and good in your music and drawing. You know what have been my fears for some time past; that you do not employ your- self so closely as I could wish. You have promised me a more assiduous attention, and I have great confidence in what you promise. It is your future happiness which interests me, and nothing can contribute more to it (moral rectitude always excepted) than the contracting a habit of industry and activity. Of all the cankers of human happiness, none corrodes it with so silent, yet so baneful a tooth, as indolence. Body and mind both unem- ployed, our being becomes a burthen, and every object about us loathsome, even the dearest. Idleness begets ennui, ennui the hypochrondria, and that a diseased body. No laborious person was ever yet hysterical. Exercise and application produce order in our affairs, health of body, chearfulness of mind, and these make us precious to our friends. It is while we are young

---

2. Martha or "Patsy" (1772–1836), Jefferson's oldest child, accompanied her father to France in 1784 and at the time of this letter was living at the convent school at the Abbey Royale de Pentemont in Paris. In 1790, shortly after the family's return to America, she was to marry her cousin, Thomas Mann Randolph (1768–1828).

3. Patsy had upbraided her father in her own letter of March 25: ". . . you promised to write to me every week. Until now you have not kept your word the least in the world, but I hope you will make up for your silence by writing me a fine, long letter by the first opportunity" (*PTJ* 11:238).

that the habit of industry is formed. If not then, it never is afterwards. The fortune of our lives therefore depends on employing well the short period of youth. If at any moment, my dear, you catch yourself in idleness, start from it as you would from the precipice of a gulph. You are not however to consider yourself as unemployed while taking exercise. That is necessary for your health, and health is the first of all objects. For this reason if you leave your dancing master for the summer, you must increase your other exercise. I do not like your saying that you are unable to read the antient print of your Livy, but with the aid of your master.[4] We are always equal to what we undertake with resolution. A little degree of this will enable you to decypher your Livy. If you always lean on your master, you will never be able to proceed without him. It is a part of the American character to consider nothing as desperate; to surmount every difficulty by resolution and contrivance. In Europe there are shops for every want. It's inhabitants therefore have no idea that their wants can be furnished otherwise. Remote from all other aid, we are obliged to invent and to execute; to find means within ourselves, and not to lean on others. Consider therefore the conquering your Livy as an exercise in the habit of surmounting difficulties, a habit which will be necessary to you in the country where you are to live, and without which you will be thought a very helpless animal, and less esteemed. Music, drawing, books, invention and exercise will be so many resources to you against ennui. But there are others which to this object add that of utility. These are the needle, and domestic oeconomy. The latter you cannot learn here, but the former you may. In the country life of America there are many moments when a woman can have recourse to nothing but her needle for employment. In a dull company and in dull weather for instance. It is ill manners to read; it is ill manners to leave them; no card-playing there among genteel people; that is abandoned to blackguards. The needle is then a valuable resource. Besides without knowing to use it herself, how can the mistress of a family direct the works of her servants? You ask me to write you long letters. I will do it my dear, on condition you will read them from time to time, and practice what they will inculcate. Their precepts will be dictated by experience, by a perfect knowlege of the situation in which you will be placed, and by the fondest love for you. This it is which makes me wish to see you more qualified than common. My expectations from you are high: yet not higher than you may attain. Industry and resolution are all that are wanting. No body in this world can make me so happy, or so miserable as you. Retirement from public life will ere long become necessary for me. To your sister and yourself I look to render the evening of my life serene and contented. It's morning has been clouded by loss after loss till I have nothing left but you. I do not doubt either your affection or dispositions. But great exertions are necessary, and you have little time left to make them. Be industrious then, my dear child. Think nothing unsurmountable by resolution and application, and you will be all that I wish you to be. You ask me if it is my desire you should dine at the abbess's table? It is. Propose it as such to Madame de Taubenheim[5] with my respectful compliments and thanks for her care of you. Continue to love me with all the warmth with which you are beloved by, my dear Patsy, yours affectionately,

TH: JEFFERSON

4. Patsy had written, apropos of the Roman historian Livy, "*Titus Livius* puts me out of my wits. I cannot read a word of it myself, and I read of it very seldom with my master; however, I hope I shall soon be able to take it up again" (*PTJ* 11:238).
5. Madame de Taubenheim looked after Patsy at Pentemont.

To The Marquis de Lafayette[6]

Nice, April 11, 1787.

Your head, my dear friend, is full of Notable things; and being better employed, therefore, I do not expect letters from you. I am constantly roving about, to see what I have never seen before and shall never see again. In the great cities, I go to see what travellers think alone worthy of being seen; but I make a job of it, and generally gulp it all down in a day. On the other hand, I am never satiated with rambling through the fields and farms, examining the culture and cultivators, with a degree of curiosity which makes some take me to be a fool, and others to be much wiser than I am. I have been pleased to find among the people a less degree of physical misery than I had expected. They are generally well clothed, and have a plenty of food, not animal indeed, but vegetable, which is as wholesome. Perhaps they are over worked, the excess of the rent required by the landlord, obliging them to too many hours of labor, in order to produce that, and wherewith to feed and clothe themselves. The soil of Champagne and Burgundy I have found more universally good than I had expected, and as I could not help making a comparison with England, I found that comparison more unfavorable to the latter than is generally admitted. The soil, the climate, and the productions are superior to those of England, and the husbandry as good, except in one point; that of manure. In England, long leases for twenty-one years, or three lives, to wit, that of the farmer, his wife, and son, renewed by the son as soon as he comes to the possession, for his own life, his wife's and eldest child's, and so on, render the farms there almost hereditary, make it worth the farmer's while to manure the lands highly, and give the landlord an opportunity of occasionally making his rent keep pace with the improved state of the lands. Here the leases are either during pleasure, or for three, six, or nine years, which does not give the farmer time to repay himself for the expensive operation of well manuring, and therefore, he manures ill, or not at all. I suppose, that could the practice of leasing for three lives be introduced in the whole kingdom, it would, within the term of your life, increase agricultural productions fifty per cent; or were any one proprietor to do it with his own lands, it would increase his rents fifty per cent, in the course of twenty-five years. But I am told the laws do not permit it. The laws then, in this particular, are unwise and unjust, and ought to give that permission. In the southern provinces, where the soil is poor, the climate hot and dry, and there are few animals, they would learn the art, found so precious in England, of making vegetable manure, and thus improving these provinces in the article in which nature has been least kind to them. Indeed, these provinces afford a singular spectacle. Calculating on the poverty of their soil, and their climate by its latitude only, they should have been the poorest in France. On the contrary, they are the richest, from one fortuitous circumstance. Spurs or ramifications of high mountains, making down from the Alps, and as it were, reticulating these provinces, give to the vallies the protection of a particular inclosure to each, and the

6. The marquis de Lafayette (1757–1834), a young nobleman who had volunteered to assist the revolutionaries in America and then, following his success there, had helped persuade the French government to formally support the American cause, was back in France during Jefferson's service there as American minister. Having first met Jefferson during the Virginia campaign late in the war, Lafayette thought him an ideal appointment to that diplomatic post and became his essential go-between with the government.

benefit of a general stagnation of the northern winds produced by the whole of them, and thus countervail the advantage of several degrees of latitude. From the first olive fields of Pierrelate, to the orangeries of Hieres, has been continued rapture to me. I have often wished for you. I think you have not made this journey. It is a pleasure you have to come, and an improvement to be added to the many you have already made. It will be a great comfort to you to know, from your own inspection, the condition of all the provinces of your own country, and it will be interesting to them at some future day to be known to you. This is perhaps the only moment of your life in which you can acquire that knolege. And to do it most effectually you must be absolutely incognito, you must ferret the people out of their hovels as I have done, look into their kettles, eat their bread, loll on their beds under pretence of resting yourself, but in fact to find if they are soft. You will feel a sublime pleasure in the course of this investigation, and a sublimer one hereafter when you shall be able to apply your knolege to the softening of their beds, or the throwing a morsel of meat into the kettle of vegetables. You will not wonder at the subjects of my letter: they are the only ones which have been present to my mind for some time past, and the waters must always be what are the fountain from which they flow. According to this indeed I should have intermixed from beginning to end warm expressions of friendship to you: but according to the ideas of our country we do not permit ourselves to speak even truths when they may have the air of flattery. I content myself therefore with saying once for all that I love you, your wife and children. Tell them so and Adieu. Your's affectionately,

TH: JEFFERSON

To Maria Cosway

Paris Apr. 24. 1788.

I arrived here, my dear friend, the last night, and in a bushel of letters presented me by way of reception, I saw that one was of your handwriting. It is the only one I have yet opened, and I answer it before I open another. I do not think I was in arrears in our epistolary account when I left Paris. In affection I am sure you were greatly my debtor. I often determined during my journey to write to you: but sometimes the fatigue of exercise, and sometimes a fatigued attention hindered me. At Dusseldorp I wished for you much. I surely never saw so precious a collection of paintings. Above all things those of Van der Werff affected me the most. His picture of Sarah delivering Agar to Abraham is delicious. I would have agreed to have been Abraham though the consequence would have been that I should have been dead five or six thousand years.[7] Carlo Dolce became also a violent favorite. I am so little of a connoisseur that I preferred the works of these two authors to the old faded red things of Rubens. I am but a son of nature, loving what I see and feel, without being able to give a reason, nor caring much whether there be one. At Heidelberg I wished for you too. In fact I led you by the hand thro' the whole garden. I was struck with the resemblance of this scene to that of Vaucluse as seen from what is called the chateau of Petrarch. Nature has formed both on the same sketch, but she has filled up

---

7. Adriaen van der Werff (1659–1722), Dutch Baroque painter. The 1699 painting to which Jefferson refers portrays the famous biblical scene in which Sarah, the infertile wife of Abraham, offers him her young servant Hagar as a sexual partner (see Genesis 16).

that of Heidelberg with a bolder hand. The river is larger, the mountains more majestic and better clothed. Art too has seconded her views. The chateau of Petrarch is the ruin of a modest country house, that of Heidelbourg would stand well along side the pyramids of Egypt. It is certainly the most magnificent ruin after those left us by the antients. At Strasbourg I sat down to write to you. But for my soul I could think of nothing at Strasbourg but the promontory of noses, of Diego, of Slawkenburgius his historian, and the procession of the Strasburgers to meet the man with the nose. Had I written to you from thence it would have been a continuation of Sterne upon noses, and I knew that nature had not formed me for a Continuator of Sterne: so I let it alone till I came here and received your angry letter.[8] It is a proof of your esteem, but I love better to have soft testimonials of it. You must therefore now write me a letter teeming with affection; such as I feel for you.[9] So much I have no right to ask.—Being but just arrived I am not au fait of the small news respecting your acquaintance here. I know only that the princess Lubomirski is still here, and that she has taken the house that was M. de Simoulin's. When you come again therefore you will be somewhat nearer to me, but not near enough: and still surrounded by a numerous cortege, so that I shall see you only by scraps as I did when you were here last. The time before we were half days, and whole days together, and I found this too little. Adieu! God bless you! Your's affectionately,

TH: JEFFERSON

To J. Hector St. John de Crèvecoeur

DEAR SIR   Paris Aug. 9. 1788.
   While our second revolution is just brought to a happy end with you, yours here is but cleverly under way. For some days I was really melancholy with the apprehensions that arms would be appealed to, and the opposition crushed in it's first efforts. But things seem now to wear a better aspect. While the opposition keeps at it's highest wholsome point, government, unwilling to draw the sword, is not forced to do it. The contest here is exactly what it was in Holland: a contest between the monarchical and aristocratical part of the government for a monopoly of despotism over the people. The aristocracy in Holland, seeing that their common prey was likely to escape out of their clutches, chose rather to retain it's former portion and therefore coalesced with the single head. The people remained victims. Here I think it will take a happier turn. The parliamentary part of the aristocracy is alone firmly united. The Noblesse and clergy, but especially the

---

8. Jefferson's most recent surviving letter to Cosway dates from January 1788, a month after her departure from another visit to Paris. The two friends did not see each other much at that time, apparently, and by March 6, Cosway, having heard little from Jefferson since then, was upset: "I have waited some time to trie if I could recover my usual peace with you, but I find it is impossible yet, therefore Must address Myself to you still *angry*. Your long silence is impardonable. . . . But I begin to runn on and my intention was only to say, *nothing*, send a blank paper; as a Lady in a Passion is not fit for Any thing" (*PTJ* 12:645).
9. On April 29, Cosway answered from London: "At last I receive a letter from you, am I to be angry or not? . . . The fatigue of your journey the different occupations the & & & & prevented your writing, I agree, but how could you le[a]d me by the hand all the way, think of me, have Many things to say, and not find One word to write, *but on Noses?*" The reference to "noses" here and in Jefferson's letter derives from Laurence Sterne, who in *Tristram Shandy* (1760–67) introduces Hafen Slawkenbergius, supposed author of a treatise on noses. Slawkenbergius tells the story of huge-nosed Diego, who, on his way through Strasbourg on a visit to the "Promontory of Noses," causes much excitement among the townspeople, particularly the nuns. The sexual meanings of the story, and of Jefferson's use of it here, are obvious.

former are divided partly between the parliamentary and the despotic party, and partly united with the real patriots who are endeavoring to gain for the nation what they can both from the parliamentary and the single despotism. I think I am not mistaken in believing that the king and some of his ministers are well affected to this band: and surely that they will make great cessions to the people rather than small ones to the parliament. They are accordingly yielding daily to the national reclamations, and will probably end in according a well tempered constitution. They promise the states general for the next year and we have reason to believe they will take place in May. How they will be composed, and what they will do, cannot be foreseen. Their convocation however will tranquillize the public mind in a great degree, till their meeting. There are however two intervening difficulties. 1. Justice cannot till then continue completely suspended as it now is. The parliament will not resume their functions but in their entire body. The baillages are afraid to accept of them. What will be done? 2. There are well-founded fears of a bankruptcy before the month of May. In the mean time the war is spreading from nation to nation. Sweden has commenced hostilities against Russia; Denmark is shewing it's teeth against Sweden; Prussia against Denmark, and England too deeply engaged in playing the back-game to avoid coming forward and dragging this country and Spain in with her. But even war will not prevent the assembly of the States general, because it cannot be carried on without them. War however is not the most favorable moment for divesting the monarchy of power. On the contrary it is the moment when the energy of a single hand shews itself in the most seducing form.

Your friend the Countess D'Houdetot[1] has had a long illness at Sanois. She was well enough the other day to come to Paris and was so good as to call on me, as I did also on her, without finding each other. The Dutchess Danville is in the country altogether. Your sons are well. Their master speaks very highly of the genius and application of Aly, and more favorably of the genius than application of the younger. They are both fine lads, and will make you very happy. I am not certain whether more exercise than the rules of the school admit would not be good for Aly. I confered the other day on this subject with M. le Moine, who seems to be of that opinion, and disposed to give him every possible indulgence.

A very considerable portion of this country has been desolated by a hail. I considered the newspaper accounts of hailstones of 10. pounds weight as exaggerations. But in a conversation with the Duke de la Rochefoucaut the other day, he assured me that tho' he could not say he had seen such himself, yet he considered the fact as perfectly established. Great contributions public and private are making for the sufferers. But they will be like the drop of water from the finger of Lazarus. There is no remedy for the present evil, nor way to prevent future ones but to bring the people to such a state of ease as not to be ruined by the loss of a single crop. This hail may be considered as the coup de grace to an expiring victim. In the arts there is nothing new discovered since you left us which is worth communicating. Mr. Payne's iron bridge was exhibited here with great approbation. An idea has been encouraged of executing it in three arches at the King's garden,

1. The witty and charming Élisabeth-Sophie, comtesse de Houdetot (1730–1813) had befriended Crèvecoeur on his arrival in France at the start of the decade, thus providing him access to the highest literary circles in Paris. Jefferson met her through Benjamin Franklin and spent much time at her salon. Both Jefferson and Houdetot took great interest in the education of the widowed Crèvecoeur's sons, Guillaume-Alexandre (Aly) and Philippe-Louis.

but it will probably not be done. I am with sentiments of perfect esteem & attachment Dear Sir Your most obedient & most humble servt.,

TH: JEFFERSON

To the Reverend Richard Price

DEAR SIR   Paris Jan. 8. 1789.
I was favoured with your letter of Oct. 26. and far from finding any of it's subjects uninteresting as you apprehend, they were to me, as every thing which comes from you, pleasing and instructive. I concur with you strictly in your opinion of the comparative merits of atheism and demonism, and really see nothing but the latter in the being worshipped by many who think themselves Christians. Your opinions and writings will have effect in bringing others to reason on this subject.[2]—Our new constitution, of which you speak also, has succeded beyond what I apprehended it would have done. I did not at first believe that 11. states out of 13. would have consented to a plan consolidating them so much into one. A change in their dispositions, which had taken place since I left them, had rendered this consolidation necessary, that is to say, had called for a federal government which could walk upon it's own legs, without leaning for support on the state legislatures. A sense of this necessity, and a submission to it, is to me a new and consolatory proof that wherever the people are well informed they can be trusted with their own government; that whenever things get so far wrong as to attract their notice, they may be relied on to set them to rights.—You say you are not sufficiently informed about the nature and circumstances of the present struggle here. Having been on the spot from it's first origin and watched it's movements as an uninterested spectator, with no other bias than a love of mankind I will give you my ideas of it. Tho' celebrated writers of this and other countries had already sketched good principles on the subject of government, yet the American war seems first to have awakened the thinking part of this nation in general from the sleep of despotism in which they were sunk. The officers too, who had been to America, were mostly young men, less shackled by habit and prejudice, and more ready to assent to the dictates of common sense and common right. They came back impressed with these. The press, notwithstanding it's shackles, began to disseminate them: conversation too assumed new freedoms; politics became the theme of all societies, male and female, and a very extensive and zealous party was formed, which may be called the Patriotic party, who sensible of the abusive government under which they lived, longed for occasions of reforming it. This party comprehended all the honesty of the kingdom, sufficiently at it's leisure to think: the men of letters, the easy bourgeois, the young nobility, partly from reflection partly, from mode; for those sentiments became a matter of mode, and as such united most of the young women to the party. Happily for the nation, it happened

2. In his letter of October 26, 1788, the radical theorist Price had informed Jefferson that he had been reading the recently published treatise, De l'importance des opinions religieuses (1788), by the Swiss native Jacques Necker (1732–1804), a banker who had served as director general of finances for France from 1776 to 1781 and was again appointed to that post as the 1788 financial crisis deepened. Price had thought Necker's book "an extraordinary work for a minister of state," but thought it failed to distinguish "rational and liberal religion" from "the Superstitions that go under the name of religion." Commenting on the current troubles in France, Price added that he had "been made very happy by the adoption of the new federal Constitution in America," which, he added, fulfilled his "ideas in most of its parts" (PTJ 14:39).

that at the same moment, the dissipations of the court had exhausted the money and credit of the state, and M. de Calonnes[3] found himself obliged to appeal to the nation and to develope to it the ruin of their finances. He had no ideas of supplying the deficit by economies; he saw no means but new taxes. To tempt the nation to consent to these some douceurs[4] were necessary. The Notables were called in 1787. The leading vices of the constitution and administration were ably sketched out, good remedies proposed, and under the splendor of these propositions a demand of more money was couched. The Notables concurred with the minister in the necessity of reformation, adroitly avoided the demand of money, got him displaced, and one of their leading men placed in his room. The Archbishop of Thoulouse by the aid of the hopes formed of him, was able to borrow some money, and he reformed considerably the expences of the court. Notwithstanding the prejudices since formed against him, he appeared to me to pursue the reformation of the laws and constitution as steadily as a man could do who had to drag the court after him, and even to conceal from them the consequences of the measures he was leading them into. In his time the Criminal laws were reformed, provincial assemblies and states established in most of the provinces, the States general promised, and a solemn acknolegement made by the king that he could not impose a new tax without the consent of the nation. It is true he was continually goaded forward by the public clamours excited by the writings and workings of the Patriots, who were able to keep up the public fermentation at the exact point which borders on resistance without entering on it. They had taken into their alliance the parliaments also, who were led by very singular circumstances to espouse, for the first time, the rights of the nation. They had from old causes had personal hostility against M. de Calonne. They refused to register his loans or his taxes, and went so far as to acknolege they had no power to do it. They persisted in this with his successor, who therefore exiled them. Seeing that the nation did not interest themselves much for their recall, they began to fear that the new judicatures proposed in their place would be established and that their own suppression would be perpetual. In short they found their own strength insufficient to oppose that of the king. They therefore insisted the states general should be called. Here they became united with and supported by the Patriots, and their joint influence was sufficient to produce the promise of that assembly. I always suspected that the Archbishop had no objections to this force under which they laid him. But the patriots and parliament insist it was their efforts which extorted the promise against his will. The reestablishment of the parliament was the effect of the same coalition between the patriots and parliament: but, once reestablished, the latter began to see danger in that very power, the States general, which they had called for in a moment of despair, but which they now foresaw might very possibly abridge their powers. They began to prepare grounds for questioning their legality, as a rod over the head of the states, and as a refuge if they should really extend their reformations to them. Mr. Neckar came in at this period, and very dexterously disembarrassed the administration of these disputes by calling the Notables to advise the form of calling and constituting the states. The court was well disposed towards the people; not from principles of justice or love

---

3. Charles Alexandre de Calonne (1734–1802), a lawyer who had assumed the post of comptroller general of France in 1783, discovered the deep deficits in the treasury and, on calling together the Assembly of Notables early in 1787, was dismissed by Louis XVI that April and sent into exile.
4. Sweeteners; i.e., inducements (French).

to them. But they want money. No more can be had from the people. They are squeezed to the last drop. The clergy and nobles, by their privileges and influence, have kept their property in a great measure untaxed hitherto. They then remain to be squeezed, and no agent is powerful enough for this but the people. The court therefore must ally itself with the people. But the Notables, consisting mostly of privileged characters, had proposed a method of composing the states, which would have rendered the voice of the people, or tiers etat,[5] in the states general, inefficient for the purposes of the court. It concurred then with the patriots in intriguing with the parliament to get them to pass a vote in favor of the rights of the people. This vote balancing that of the Notables has placed the court at liberty to follow it's own views, and they have determined that the tiers etat shall have in the States general as many votes as the clergy and nobles put together. Still a great question remains to be decided: that is, shall the states general vote by orders or by persons? Precedents are both ways. The clergy will move heaven and earth to obtain the suffrage by orders, because that parries the effect of all hitherto done for the people. The people will probably send their deputies expressly instructed to consent to no tax, to no adoption of the public debts, unless the unprivileged part of the nation has a voice equal to that of the privileged; that is to say unless the voice of the tiers etat be equalled to that of the clergy and nobles. They will have the young noblesse in general on their side, and the king and court. Against them will be the antient nobles and the clergy. So that I hope upon the whole, that by the time they meet there will be a majority of the nobles themselves in favor of the tiers etat. So far history. We are now to come to prophecy; for you will ask, to what will all this lead? I answer, if the States general do not stumble at the threshold on the question before stated, and which must be decided before they can proceed to business, then they will in their first session easily obtain 1. the future periodical convocation of the States: 2. their exclusive right to raise and appropriate money, which includes that of establishing a civil list. 3. a participation in legislation; probably, at first, it will only be a transfer to them of the portion of it now exercised by parliament, that is to say a right to propose amendments and a negative: but it must infallibly end in a right of origination. 4. perhaps they may make a declaration of rights. It will be attempted at least. Two other objects will be attempted, viz. a habeas corpus law, and free press. But probably they may not obtain these in the first session, or with modifications only, and the nation must be left to ripen itself more for their unlimited adoption.

Upon the whole it has appeared to me that the basis of the present struggle is an illumination of the public mind as to the rights of the nation, aided by fortunate incidents; that they can never retrograde, but from the natural progress of things must press forward to the establishment of a constitution which shall assure to them a good degree of liberty. They flatter themselves they shall form a better constitution than the English. I think it will be better in some points, worse in others. It will be better in the article of representation which will be more equal. It will be worse, as their situation obliges them to keep up the dangerous machine of a standing army. I doubt too whether they will obtain the trial by jury, because they are not sensible of it's value.

5. Third estate (French), i.e., the commoners, who together with the clergy and the nobles constituted the "states (or estates) general" (*états généraux*).

I am sure I have by this time heartily tired you with this long epistle, and that you will be glad to see it brought to an end with assurances of the sentiments of esteem and respect with which I have the honor to be Dear Sir Your most obedient & most humble servt,

TH: JEFFERSON

To John Trumbull[6]

DEAR SIR   Paris Feb. 15. 1789.
I have duly received your favor of the 5th. inst. with respect to the busts and pictures. I will put off till my return from America all of them except Bacon, Locke and Newton, whose pictures I will trouble you to have copied for me: and as I consider them as the three greatest men that have ever lived, without any exception, and as having laid the foundation of those superstructures which have been raised in the Physical and Moral sciences, I would wish to form them into a knot on the same canvas, that they may not be confounded at all with the herd of other great men. To do this I suppose we need only desire the copyist to draw the three busts in three ovals all contained in a larger oval in some such forms as this each bust to be the 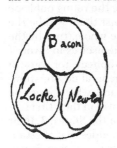 size of the life. The large oval would I suppose be about between four and five feet. Perhaps you can suggest a better way of accomplishing my idea. In your hands be it, as well as the subaltern expences you mention. I trouble you with a letter to Mrs. Church. We have no important news here but of the revolution of Geneva which is not yet sufficiently explained. But they have certainly reformed their government. I am with great esteem Dr. Sir Your affectionate friend & humble servt.,

TH: JEFFERSON

To Francis Hopkinson[7]

DEAR SIR   Paris Mar. 13. 1789.
Since my last, which was of Dec. 21. yours of Dec. 9. and 21. are received. Accept my thanks for the papers and pamphlets which accompanied them, and mine and my daughter's for the book of songs. I will not tell you how much they have pleased us nor how well the last of them merits praise for it's pathos, but relate a fact only, which is that while my elder daughter was playing it on the harpsichord, I happened to look towards the fire and saw the younger one all in tears. I asked her if she was sick? She said "no; but the tune was so mournful."—The Editor of the Encyclopedie has published something as to an advanced price on his future volumes,

---

6. In January, Jefferson had asked the painter John Trumbull (1756–1843), who had introduced him to the Cosways in 1786, whether "the pictures" (or "the busts") "of Newton, Locke, Bacon, Sydney, Hampden, Shakespeare exist," and if so whether Trumbull could arrange for "some good young hand" to copy them for him (*PTJ* 14:467–468). Trumbull replied on February 5 with the details of the arrangements he had been able to make (*PTJ* 14:524–525).
7. Pennsylvanian Francis Hopkinson (1737–1791), a lawyer, composer, and writer, had become Jefferson's friend during sessions of the Continental Congress in Philadelphia. Accompanying his December 1, 1788, letter to Jefferson, Hopkinson had sent not only the "papers and pamphlets" to which Jefferson refers but also, as Hopkinson wrote, "a Book of Songs, which I composed"—*Seven Songs for the Harpsichord or Forte Piano*, published in 1788.

which I understand alarms the subscribers. It was in a paper which I do not take and therefore I have not yet seen it, nor can say what it is.—I hope that by this time you have ceased to make wry faces about your vinegar,[8] and that you have received it safe and good. You say that I have been dished up to you as an antifederalist, and ask me if it be just. My opinion was never worthy enough of notice to merit citing: but since you ask it I will tell it you. I am not a Federalist, because I never submitted the whole system of my opinions to the creed of any party of men whatever in religion, in philosophy, in politics, or in any thing else where I was capable of thinking for myself. Such an addiction is the last degradation of a free and moral agent. If I could not go to heaven but with a party, I would not go there at all. Therefore I protest to you I am not of the party of federalists. But I am much farther from that of the Antifederalists. I approved from the first moment, of the great mass of what is in the new constitution, the consolidation of the government, the organisation into Executive, legislative and judiciary, the subdivision of the legislative, the happy compromise of interests between the great and little states by the different manner of voting in the different houses, the voting by persons instead of states, the qualified negative on laws given to the Executive which however I should have liked better if associated with the judiciary also as in New York, and the power of taxation. I thought at first that the latter might have been limited. A little reflection soon convinced me it ought not to be. What I disapproved from the first moment also was the want of a bill of rights to guard liberty against the legislative as well as executive branches of the government, that is to say to secure freedom in religion, freedom of the press, freedom from monopolies, freedom from unlawful imprisonment, freedom from a permanent military, and a trial by jury in all cases determinable by the laws of the land. I disapproved also the perpetual reeligibility of the President. To these points of disapprobation I adhere. My first wish was that the 9. first conventions[9] might accept the constitution, as the means of securing to us the great mass of good it contained, and that the 4. last might reject it, as the means of obtaining amendments. But I was corrected in this wish the moment I saw the much better plan of Massachusets and which had never occurred to me. With respect to the declaration of rights I suppose the majority of the United states are of my opinion: for I apprehend all the antifederalists, and a very respectable proportion of the federalists think that such a declaration should now be annexed. The enlightened part of Europe have given us the greatest credit for inventing this instrument of security for the rights of the people, and have been not a little surprised to see us so soon give it up. With respect to the re-eligibility of the president, I find myself differing from the majority of my countrymen, for I think there are but three states of the 11. which have desired an alteration of this. And indeed, since the thing is established, I would wish it not to be altered during the life of our great leader, whose executive talents are superior to those I beleive of any man in the world, and who alone by the authority of his name and the confidence reposed in his perfect integrity, is fully qualified to put the new government so under way as to secure it against the efforts of opposition. But having derived from our error all the good there was in it I hope we shall correct it the moment we can no longer have the same person at the helm. These, my dear friend, are my sentiments, by which you will see I was right

8. The vinegar shipment had been promised to the composer but apparently was delayed if not lost. "I am much *sower'd* by the Disappointment," Hopkinson added (*PTJ* 14:324).
9. I.e., state-by-state meetings to vote on the constitution.

in saying I am neither federalist nor antifederalist; that I am of neither party, nor yet a trimmer between parties. These my opinions I wrote within a few hours after I had read the constitution, to one or two friends in America. I had not then read one single word printed on the subject. I never had an opinion in politics or religion which I was afraid to own. A costive reserve on these subjects might have procured me more esteem from some people, but less from myself. My great wish is to go on in a strict but silent performance of my duty: to avoid attracting notice and to keep my name out of newspapers, because I find the pain of a little censure, even when it is unfounded, is more acute than the pleasure of much praise. The attaching circumstance of my present office is that I can do it's duties unseen by those for whom they are done.—You did not think, by so short a phrase in your letter,[1] to have drawn on yourself such an egoistical dissertation. I beg your pardon for it, and will endeavor to merit that pardon by the constant sentiments of esteem & attachment with which I am Dear Sir, Your sincere friend & servant,

TH: JEFFERSON

P.S. Affectionate respects to Dr. Franklin Mr. Rittenhouse, their and your good families.

To John Jay[2]

DEAR SIR   Paris July 19. 1789.
I am become very uneasy lest you should have adopted some channel for the conveiance of your letters to me which is unfaithful. I have none from you of later date than Nov. 25. 1788. and of consequence no acknolegement of the receipt of any of mine since that of Aug. 11. 1788. Since that period I have written to you of the following dates. 1788. Aug. 20. Sep. 3. 5. 24. Nov. 14. 19. 29. 1789. Jan. 11. 14. 21. Feb. 4. Mar. 1. 12. 14. 15. May. 9. 11. 12. Jun. 17. 24. 29. I know through another person that you have received mine of Nov. 29. and that you have written an answer; but I have never received the answer, and it is this which suggests to me the fear of some general source of miscarriage.

The capture of three French merchant ships by the Algerines under different pretexts, has produced great sensation in the seaports of this country, and some in it's government. They have ordered some frigates to be armed at Toulon to punish them. There is a possibility that this circumstance, if not too soon set to rights by the Algerines, may furnish occasion to the States general, when they shall have leisure to attend to matters of this kind, to disavow any future tributary treaty with them. These pyrates respect still less their treaty with Spain, and treat the Spaniards with an insolence greater than was usual before the treaty.

The scarcity of bread begins to lessen in the Southern parts of France where the harvest is commenced. Here it is still threatening because we have

1. "By the bye, you have been often dish'd up to me as a strong Antifederalist, which is almost equivalent to what *a Tory* was in the Days of the War, for what Reason I know not, but I don't believe it and have utterly denied the Insinuation" (*PTJ* 14:324).
2. John Jay (1745–1829), member of the Continental Congress, espionage officer, and diplomat during the Revolution, had written strongly on behalf of the Constitution in the *Federalist Papers* with Hamilton and Madison. As American secretary of foreign affairs from 1784 to the establishment of the new government in 1789, Jay corresponded frequently with Jefferson both as a friend and as a diplomat serving in France. Jefferson's letter to Jay represents the first extensive discussion in his correspondence of the July 14 storming of the Bastille prison and events over the week following.

yet two or three weeks to the beginning of harvest, and I think there has not been three days provision beforehand in Paris for two or three weeks past. Monsieur de Mirabeau,[3] who is very hostile to Mr. Necker, wished to find a ground for censuring him in a proposition to have a great quantity of flour furnished from the United states, which he supposed me to have made to Mr. Necker, and to have been refused by him; and he asked time of the states general to furnish proofs. The Marquis de la Fayette immediately gave me notice of this matter, and I wrote him a letter to disavow having ever made any such proposition to Mr. Necker, which I desired him to communicate to the states. I waited immediately on Mr. Necker and Monsieur de Montmorin, satisfied them that what had been suggested was absolutely without foundation from me, and indeed they had not needed this testimony. I gave them copies of my letter to the Marquis de la Fayette, which was afterwards printed. The Marquis on the receipt of my letter, shewed it to Mirabeau, who turned then to a paper from which he had drawn his information, and found he had totally mistaken it. He promised immediately that he would himself declare his error to the States general, and read to them my letter, which he did. I state this matter to you, tho' of little consequence in itself, because it might go to you mistated in the English papers.—Our supplies to the Atlantic ports of France during the months of March, April, and May, were only 12,220 quintals 33 [lb] of flour, and 44,115 quintals 40 [lb] of wheat, in 21. vessels.

My letter of the 29th. of June brought down the proceedings of the States and Government to the reunion of the orders, which took place on the 27th. Within the Assembly matters went on well. But it was soon observed that troops, and particularly the foreign troops, were on their march towards Paris from various quarters and that this was against the opinion of Mr. Necker. The king was probably advised to this under pretext of preserving peace in Paris and Versailles, and saw nothing else in the measure. But his advisers are supposed to have had in view, when he should be secured and inspirited by the presence of the troops, to take advantage of some favorable moment and surprize him into an act of authority for establishing the Declaration of the 23d of June, and perhaps dispersing the States general. The Marshal de Broglio was appointed to command all the troops within the Isle of France, a high flying Aristocrat, cool and capable of every thing. Some of the French guards were soon arrested under other pretexts, but in reality on account of their dispositions in favor of the national cause. The people of Paris forced the prison, released them, and sent a deputation to the States general to sollicit a pardon. The States by a most moderate and prudent Arreté recommended these prisoners to the king, and peace to the people of Paris. Addresses came in to them from several of the great cities expressing 8th. sincere allegiance to the king, but a determined resolution to support the States general. On the 8th. of July they vote an address to the king to remove the troops. This[4] peice of masculine eloquence, written by Monsieur de Mirabeau, is worth attention, on account of the bold matter it expresses or covers, thro the whole. The king refuses to remove the troops and says they

3. Honoré Gabriel Riqueti, comte de Mirabeau (1749–1791), a colorful and controversial figure, had passed much of his time in exile from France, but returned in 1787 and in 1789 succeeded in being elected to the Estates General, due to meet in May, as a representative of the third estate from Aix. A political moderate who had written a good deal against monarchy and who, therefore, had a popular following, he also was a longtime associate of the French foreign secretary (Jefferson's "Monsieur de Montmarin"; i.e., Armand Marc, comte de Montmarin), to whom he provided information from the Estates General as well as astute policy proposals. Mirabeau thus came to occupy strategic ground during the early months of the French Revolution.
4. See it in the paper called Point du jour. No. 23 [Jefferson's note].

may remove themselves if they please to Noyons or Soissons. They proceed
9th. to fix the order in which they will take up the several branches of their future
constitution, from which it appears they mean to build it from the bottom,
confining themselves to nothing in their antient form, but a king. A Declaration of rights, which forms the first chapter of their work was then pro-
11th. posed by the Marquis de la Fayette. This was on the 11th.—In the mean
time troops to the number of about 25. or 30,000 had arrived and were
posted in and between Paris and Versailles. The bridges and passes were
guarded. At 3. oclock in the afternoon the Count de la Luzerne was sent to
notify Mr. Necker of his dismission, and to enjoin him to retire instantly
without saying a word of it to any body. He went home, dined, proposed to
his wife a visit to a friend, but went in fact to his country house at St. Ouen,
12th. and at midnight set out from thence for Brussels. This was not known till the
next day, when the whole ministry was changed except Villedeuil of the
Domestic department and Barentin Garde des sceaux.[5] These changes were
as follows. The Baron de Breteuil President of the council of finance, and
de la Galaisiere Comptroller General in the room of Mr. Necker; the Mare-
shal de Broglio minister of war, and Foulon under him, in the room of Puy-
segur; Monsieur de la Vauguyon minister of foreign affairs instead of
Monsieur de Montmorin; de la Porte, minister of marine, in place of the
Count de la Luzerne; St. Priest was also removed from the council. It is to
be observed that Luzerne and Puy-segur had been strongly of the aristocratical party in council; but they were not considered as equal to bear their
shares in the work now to be done. For this change, however sudden it may
have been in the mind of the king, was, in that of his advisers, only the second chapter of a great plan, of which the bringing together the foreign
troops had been the first. He was now completely in the hands of men, the
principal among whom had been noted thro' their lives for the Turkish
despotism of their characters, and who were associated about the king as
proper instruments for what was to be executed.—The news of this change
began to be known in Paris about 1. or 2. oclock. In the afternoon a body of
about 100. German cavalry were advanced and drawn up in the Place Louis
XV. and about 300 Swiss posted at a little distance in their rear. This drew
people to that spot, who naturally formed themselves in front of the troops,
at first merely to look at them. But as their numbers increased their indignation arose: they retired a few steps, posted themselves on and behind large
piles of loose stone collected in that Place for a bridge adjacent to it, and
attacked the horse with stones. The horse charged, but the advantageous
position of the people, and the showers of stones obliged them to retire, and
even to quit the field altogether, leaving one of their number on the ground.
The Swiss in their rear were observed never to stir. This was the signal for
universal insurrection, and this body of cavalry, to avoid being massacred,
retired towards Versailles. The people now armed themselves with such
weapons as they could find in Armourer's shops and private houses, and with
bludgeons, and were roaming all night through all parts of the city without
any decided and practicable object. The next day the States press on the king
to send away the troops, to permit the Bourgeoisie of Paris to arm for the
13th. preservation of order in the city, and offer to send a deputation from their
body to tranquillize them. He refuses all their propositions. A Committee of
magistrates and electors of the city are appointed, by their bodies, to take
upon them it's government. The mob, now openly joined by the French

5. Guardian of the (royal) seal (French).

guards, force the prisons of St. Lazare, release all the prisoners, and take a great store of corn, which they carry to the corn market. Here they get some arms, and the French guards begin to form and train them. The City committee determine to raise 48,000 Bourgeois, or rather to restrain their numbers to 48,000. On the 14th. they send one of their members (Monsieur de 14th. Corny, whom we knew in America) to the Hotel des Invalides to ask arms for their Garde Bourgeoise.[6] He was followed by, or he found there, a great mob. The Governor of the Invalids came out and represented the impossibility of his delivering arms without the orders of those from whom he received them. De Corney advised the people then to retire, retired himself, and the people took possession of the arms. It was remarkable that not only the Invalids themselves made no opposition, but that a body of 5000 foreign troops, encamped within 400. yards, never stirred. Monsieur de Corny and five others were then sent to ask arms of Monsieur de Launai, Governor of the Bastille. They found a great collection of people already before the place, and they immediately planted a flag of truce, which was answered by a like flag hoisted on the parapet. The deputation prevailed on the people to fall back a little, advanced themselves to make their demand of the Governor, and in that instant a discharge from the Bastille killed 4. people of those nearest to the deputies. The deputies retired, the people rushed against the place, and almost in an instant were in possession of a fortification, defended by 100 men, of infinite strength, which in other times had stood several regular sieges and had never been taken. How they got in, has as yet been impossible to discover. Those, who pretend to have been of the party tell so many different stories as to destroy the credit of them all. They took all the arms, discharged the prisoners and such of the garrison as were not killed in the first moment of fury, carried the Governor and Lieutenant governor to the Greve (the place of public execution) cut off their heads, and set them through the city in triumph to the Palais royal. About the same instant, a treacherous correspondence having been discovered in Monsieur de Flesselles prevot des marchands,[7] they seize him in the hotel de ville, where he was in the exercise of his office, and cut off his head. These events carried imperfectly to Versailles were the subject of two successive deputations from the States to the King, to both of which he gave dry and hard answers, for it has transpired that it had been proposed and agitated in Council to seize on the principal members of the States general, to march the whole army down upon Paris and to suppress it's tumults by the sword. But at night the Duke de Liancourt forced his way into the king's bedchamber, and obliged him to hear a full and animated detail of the disasters of the day in Paris. He went to bed deeply impressed. The decapitation of de Launai[8] worked powerfully thro' the night on the whole Aristocratical party, insomuch that in the morning those of the greatest influence on the Count d'Artois[9] represented to him the absolute necessity that the king should give up every thing to the states. This according well enough with the dispositions of the king, he went about 11. oclock, accompanied only by his brothers, to

6. Dominique-Louis Ethis de Corny (1736–1790), who had come to America with Lafayette on the latter's return in 1780, served briefly as advance commissary for the expeditionary force under Rochambeau. The impressive "Hôtel des Invalides," on the left bank of the Seine, housed French military veterans.
7. Jacques de Flesselles (1721–1789) served as "provost of merchants," a position roughly equivalent to that of mayor, and had his office in the *hôtel de ville,* or city hall.
8. Bernard, marquis de Launay (1740–1789), governor of the Bastille.
9. Charles, comte d'Artois (1757–1836) the brother of the king and himself destined to rule France as Charles X (1824–30).

the States general, and there read to them a speech, in which he asked their interposition to re-establish order. Tho this be couched in terms of some caution, yet the manner in which it was delivered made it evident that it was meant as a surrender at discretion. He returned to the chateau afoot, accompanied by the States. They sent off a deputation, the Marquis de la Fayette at their head, to quiet Paris. He had the same morning been named Commandant en chef of the milice Bourgeoise,[1] and Monsieur Bailly, former President of the States general, was called for as Prevost des marchands. The demolition of the Bastille was now ordered, and begun. A body of the Swiss guards, of the regiment of Ventimille, and the city horse guards join the people. The alarm at Versailles increases instead of abating. They believed that the Aristocrats of Paris were under pillage and carnage, that 150,000 men were in arms coming to Versailles to massacre the Royal family, the court, the ministers and all connected with them, their practices and principles. The Aristocrats of the Nobles and Clergy in the States general vied with each other in declaring how sincerely they were converted to the justice of voting by persons, and how determined to go with the nation all it's lengths. The foreign troops were ordered off instantly. Every minister resigned. The king confirmed Bailly as Prevost des marchands, wrote to Mr. Necker to recall him, sent his letter open to the States general to be forwarded by them, and invited them to go with him to Paris the next day to satisfy the city of his dispositions: and that night and the next morning the

16th. Count d'Artois and a Monsieur de Montesson (a deputy) connected with him, Madame de Polignac, Madame de Guiche and the Count de Vaudreuil favorites of the queen, the Abbé de Vermont her confessor, the Prince of Condé and Duke de Bourbon, all fled, we know not whither. The king came to Paris, leaving the queen in consternation for his return. Omitting the less important figures of the procession, I will only observe that the king's carriage was in the center, on each side of it the States general, in two ranks, afoot, at their head the Marquis de la Fayette as commander in chief, on horseback, and Bourgeois guards before and behind. About 60,000 citizens of all forms and colours, armed with the muskets of the Bastille and Invalids as far as they would go, the rest with pistols, swords, pikes, pruning hooks, scythes &c. lined all the streets thro' which the procession passed, and, with the crowds of people in the streets, doors and windows, saluted them every where with cries of "vive la nation." But not a single "vive le roy" was heard. The king landed at the Hotel de ville. There Monsieur Bailly presented and put into his hat the popular cockade, and addressed him. The king being unprepared and unable to answer, Bailly went to him, gathered from him some scraps of sentences, and made out an answer, which he delivered to the Audience as from the king. On their return the popular cries were "vive le roy et la nation." He was conducted by a garde Bourgeoise to his palace at Versailles, and thus concluded such an Amende honorable as no sovereign ever made, and no people ever received. Letters written with his own hand to the Marquis de la Fayette remove the scruples of his position. Tranquillity is now restored to the Capital: the shops are again opened; the people resuming their labours, and, if the want of bread does not disturb our peace, we may hope a continuance of it. The demolition of the Bastille is going on, and the milice Bourgeoise organising and training. The antient police of the city is abolished by the authority of the people, the introduction of king's troops will probably be proscribed, and a watch or city guards substituted,

---

1. The national guard in Paris.

which shall depend on the city alone. But we cannot suppose this paroxysm confined to Paris alone. The whole country must pass successively thro' it, and happy if they get thro' it as soon and as well as Paris has done. I went yesterday to Versailles to satisfy myself what had passed there; for nothing can be believed but what one sees, or has from an eye witness. They believe there still that 3000 people have fallen victims to the tumults of Paris. Mr. Short[2] and myself have been every day among them in order to be sure of what was passing. We cannot find with certainty that any body has been killed but the three beforementioned, and those who fell in the assault or defence of the Bastille. How many of the garrison were killed no body pretends to have ever heard. Of the assailants accounts vary from 6. to 600. The most general belief is that there fell about 30. There have been many reports of instantaneous executions by the mob, on such of their body as they caught in acts of theft or robbery. Some of these may perhaps be true. There was a severity of honesty observed of which no example has been known. Bags of money offered on various occasions, thro fear or guilt, have been uniformly refused by the mobs. The churches are now occupied in singing "De profundis" and "Requiems for the repose of the souls of the brave and valiant citizens who have sealed with their blood the liberty of the nation."— Monsieur de Montmorin is this day replaced in the department of foreign affairs, and Monsieur de St. Priest is named to the Home department. The gazettes of France and Leyden accompany this. I send also a paper (called the Point du jour) which will give you some idea of the proceedings of the National assembly. It is but an indifferent thing; however it is the best.—I have the honor to be with great esteem and respect, Sir, your most obedient and most humble servt.,

TH: JEFFERSON

P.S. July 21. Mr. Necker had left Brussels for Francfort before the Courier got there. We expect however to hear of him in a day or two. Monsieur le Comte de la Luzerne has resumed the department of the marine this day. Either this is an office of friendship effected by Monsr. de Montmorin (for tho they had taken different sides, their friendship continued) or he comes in as a stop-gap till somebody else can be found. Tho' very unequal to his office, all agree that he is an honest man. The Count d'Artois was at Valenciennes. The Prince of Condé and Duke de Bourbon[3] had passed that place.

To James Madison

DEAR SIR   Paris September 6. 1789.
    I sit down to write to you without knowing by what occasion I shall send my letter. I do it because a subject comes into my head which I would wish to develope a little more than is practicable in the hurry of the moment of making up general dispatches.
    The question Whether one generation of men has a right to bind another, seems never to have been started either on this or our side of the water. Yet it is a question of such consequences as not only to merit decision, but place also, among the fundamental principles of every government. The course of

2. William Short (1759–1849) was Jefferson's secretary.
3. Louis Joseph de Bourbon, prince of Condé (1736–1818), and his son, Louis-Henri de Bourbon-Condé (1756?–1830), close kinsmen of Louis XVI, both managed to escape execution by fleeing to England.

reflection in which we are immersed here on the elementary principles of society has presented this question to my mind; and that no such obligation can be so transmitted I think very capable of proof.—I set out on this ground, which I suppose to be self evident, *"that the earth belongs in usufruct to the living"*: that the dead have neither powers nor rights over it. The portion occupied by any individual ceases to be his when himself ceases to be, and reverts to the society. If the society has formed no rules for the appropriation of it's lands in severality, it will be taken by the first occupants. These will generally be the wife and children of the decedent. If they have formed rules of appropriation, those rules may give it to the wife and children, or to some one of them, or to the legatee of the deceased. So they may give it to his creditor. But the child, the legatee, or creditor takes it, not by any natural right, but by a law of the society of which they are members, and to which they are subject. Then no man can, by *natural right*, oblige the lands he occupied, or the persons who succeed him in that occupation, to the paiment of debts contracted by him. For if he could, he might, during his own life, eat up the usufruct of the lands for several generations to come, and then the lands would belong to the dead, and not to the living, which would be the reverse of our principle.

What is true of every member of the society individually, is true of them all collectively, since the rights of the whole can be no more than the sum of the rights of the individuals.—To keep our ideas clear when applying them to a multitude, let us suppose a whole generation of men to be born on the same day, to attain mature age on the same day, and to die on the same day, leaving a succeeding generation in the moment of attaining their mature age all together. Let the ripe age be supposed of 21. years, and their period of life 34. years more, that being the average term given by the bills of mortality to persons who have already attained 21. years of age. Each successive generation would, in this way, come on, and go off the stage at a fixed moment, as individuals do now. Then I say the earth belongs to each of these generations, during it's course, fully, and in their own right. The 2d. generation receives it clear of the debts and incumberances of the 1st. the 3d of the 2d. and so on. For if the 1st. could charge it with a debt, then the earth would belong to the dead and not the living generation. Then no generation can contract debts greater than may be paid during the course of it's own existence. At 21. years of age they may bind themselves and their lands for 34. years to come: at 22. for 33: at 23. for 32. and at 54. for one year only; because these are the terms of life which remain to them at those respective epochs.—But a material difference must be noted between the succession of an individual, and that of a whole generation. Individuals are parts only of a society, subject to the laws of the whole. These laws may appropriate the portion of land occupied by a decedent to his creditor rather than to any other, or to his child on condition he satisfies the creditor. But when a whole generation, that is, the whole society dies, as in the case we have supposed, and another generation or society succeeds, this forms a whole, and there is no superior who can give their territory to a third society, who may have lent money to their predecessors beyond their faculties of paying.

What is true of a generation all arriving to self-government on the same day, and dying all on the same day, is true of those in a constant course of decay and renewal, with this only difference. A generation coming in and going out entire, as in the first case, would have a right in the 1st. year of their self-dominion to contract a debt for 33. years, in the 10th. for 24. in the 20th. for 14. in the 30th for 4. whereas generations, changing daily by daily deaths and births, have one constant term, beginning at the date of their contract, and ending when a majority of those of full age at that date shall be dead. The length of that term may be estimated from the tables of mortality, corrected by the circumstances of climate, occupation &c. peculiar to the country of the contractors. Take, for instance, the table of M. de Buffon wherein he states 23,994 deaths, and the ages at which they happened.[4] Suppose a society in which 23,994 persons are born every year, and live to the ages stated in this table. The conditions of that society will be as follows. 1st. It will consist constantly of 617,703. persons of all ages. 2ly. Of those living at any one instant of time, one half will be dead in 24. years 8. months. 3dly. 10,675 will arrive every year at the age of 21. years complete. 4ly. It will constantly have 348,417 persons of all ages above 21. years. 5ly. And the half of those of 21. years and upwards living at any one instant of time will be dead in 18. years 8. months, or say 19. years as the nearest integral number. Then 19. years is the term beyond which neither the representatives of a nation, nor even the whole nation itself assembled, can validly extend a debt.

To render this conclusion palpable by example, suppose that Louis XIV. and XV. had contracted debts in the name of the French nation to the amount of 10,000 milliards[5] of livres, and that the whole had been contracted in Genoa. The interest of this sum would be 500. milliards, which is said to be the whole rent roll or nett proceeds of the territory of France. Must the present generation of men have retired from the territory in which nature produced them, and ceded it to the Genoese creditors? No. They have the same rights over the soil on which they were produced, as the preceding generations had. They derive these rights not from their predecessors, but from nature. They then and their soil are by nature clear of the debts of their predecessors.

Again suppose Louis XV. and his cotemporary generation had said to the money-lenders of Genoa, give us money that we may eat, drink, and be merry in our day; and on condition you will demand no interest till the end of 19. years you shall then for ever after receive an annual interest of 12⅝ per cent.[6] The money is lent on these conditions, is divided among the living, eaten, drank, and squandered. Would the present generation be obliged to apply the produce of the earth and of their labour to replace their dissipations? Not at all.

I suppose that the recieved opinion, that the public debts of one generation devolve on the next, has been suggested by our seeing habitually in private life that he who succeeds to lands is required to pay the debts of his ancestor or testator: without considering that this requisition is municipal only, not moral; flowing from the will of the society, which has found it convenient to appropriate lands, become vacant by the death of their occupant, on the condition of a paiment of his debts: but that between society and society, or generation and generation, there is no municipal obligation, no umpire but the law of nature. We seem not to have percieved that, by the law of nature, one generation is to another as one independant nation to another.

The interest of the national debt of France being in fact but a two thousandth part of it's rent roll, the paiment of it is practicable enough: and so

---

4. Buffon had published an essay on what we now call life expectancy as an appendix to his *Histoire Naturelle* in the 1749 edition.
5. A billion.
6. 100£, at a compound interest of 5. per cent, makes, at the end of 19. years, an aggregate of principal and interest of £252-14, the interest of which is 12£-12s-7d which is nearly 12⅝ per cent on the first capital of 100.£ [Jefferson's note].

becomes a question merely of honor, or of expediency. But with respect to future debts, would it not be wise and just for that nation to declare, in the constitution they are forming, that neither the legislature, nor the nation itself, can validly contract more debt than they may pay within their own age, or within the term of 19. years? And that all future contracts will be deemed void as to what shall remain unpaid at the end of 19. years from their date? This would put the lenders, and the borrowers also, on their guard. By reducing too the faculty of borrowing within it's natural limits, it would bridle the spirit of war, to which too free a course has been procured by the inattention of money-lenders to this law of nature, that succeeding generations are not responsible for the preceding.

On similar ground it may be proved that no society can make a perpetual constitution, or even a perpetual law. The earth belongs always to the living generation. They may manage it then, and what proceeds from it, as they please, during their usufruct. They are masters too of their own persons, and consequently may govern them as they please. But persons and property make the sum of the objects of government. The constitution and the laws of their predecessors extinguished then in their natural course with those who[21] gave them being. This could preserve that being till it ceased to be itself, and no longer. Every constitution then, and every law, naturally expires at the end of 19 years. If it be enforced longer, it is an act of force, and not of right.—It may be said that the succeeding generation exercising in fact the power of repeal, this leaves them as free as if the constitution or law had been expressly limited to 19 years only. In the first place, this objection admits the right, in proposing an equivalent. But the power of repeal is not an equivalent. It might be indeed if every form of government were so perfectly contrived that the will of the majority could always be obtained fairly and without impediment. But this is true of no form. The people cannot assemble themselves. Their representation is unequal and vicious. Various checks are opposed to every legislative proposition. Factions get possession of the public councils. Bribery corrupts them. Personal interests lead them astray from the general interests of their constituents: and other impediments arise so as to prove to every practical man that a law of limited duration is much more manageable than one which needs a repeal.

This principle that the earth belongs to the living, and not to the dead, is of very extensive application and consequences, in every country, and most especially in France. It enters into the resolution of the questions Whether the nation may change the descent of lands holden in tail?[7] Whether they may change the appropriation of lands given antiently to the church, to hospitals, colleges, orders of chivalry, and otherwise in perpetuity? Whether they may abolish the charges and privileges attached on lands, including the whole catalogue ecclesiastical and feudal? It goes to hereditary offices, authorities and jurisdictions; to hereditary orders, distinctions and appellations; to perpetual monopolies in commerce, the arts and sciences; with a long train of et ceteras: and it renders the question of reimbursement a question of generosity and not of right. In all these cases, the legislature of the day could authorize such appropriations and establishments for their own time, but no longer; and the present holders, even where they, or their ancestors, have purchased, are in the case of bonâ fide purchasers of what the seller had no right to convey.

7. Lands passing to the children of the owner.

Turn this subject in your mind, my dear Sir, and particularly as to the power of contracting debts; and develope it with that perspicuity and cogent logic so peculiarly yours. Your station in the councils of our country gives you an opportunity of producing it to public consideration, of forcing it into discussion. At first blush it may be rallied, as a theoretical speculation: but examination will prove it to be solid and salutary. It would furnish matter for a fine preamble to our first law for appropriating the public revenue; and it will exclude at the threshold of our new government the contagious and ruinous errors of this quarter of the globe, which have armed despots with means, not sanctioned by nature, for binding in chains their fellow men. We have already given in example one effectual check to the Dog of war by transferring the power of letting him loose from the Executive to the Legislative body, from those who are to spend to those who are to pay.[8] I should be pleased to see this second obstacle held out by us also in the first instance. No nation can make a declaration against the validity of long-contracted debts so disinterestedly as we, since we do not owe a shilling which may not be paid with ease, principal and interest, within the time of our own lives.—Establish the principle also in the new law to be passed for protecting copyrights and new inventions, by securing the exclusive right for 19. instead of 14. years. Besides familiarising us to this term, it will be an instance the more of our taking reason for our guide, instead of English precedent,[9] the habit of which fetters us with all the political heresies of a nation equally remarkeable for it's early excitement from some errors, and long slumbering under others.

I write you no news, because, when an occasion occurs, I shall write a separate letter for that. I am always with great & sincere esteem, dear Sir Your affectionate friend & servt,

TH: JEFFERSON

To Mary Jefferson[1]

New York Apr. 11. 1790.

Where are you, my dear Maria? How do you do? How are you occupied? Write me a letter by the first post and answer me all these questions. Tell me whether you see the sun rise every day? How many pages a-day you read in Don Quixot? How far you are advanced in him? Whether you repeat a Grammar lesson every day? What else you read? How many hours a day you sew? Whether you have an opportunity of continuing your music? Whether you know how to make a pudding yet, to cut out a beef stake, to sow spinach? Or to set a hen? Be good, my dear, as I have always found you, never be angry with any body, nor speak harm of them, try to let every body's faults be forgotten, as you would wish yours to be; take more pleasure in giving what is best to another than in having it yourself, and then all the world will love you, and I more than all the world. If your sister is with you kiss her and tell her how much I love her also, and present my affections to Mr. Randolph. Love your Aunt and Uncle, and be dutiful and obliging to them

8. Jefferson refers to Article 1, section 8 of the U.S. Constitution: "Congress shall have power . . . to declare war."
9. The English law known as the "Statute of Anne," dating from 1710, set the term of copyright at fourteen years. Congress in 1790 followed that precedent rather than Jefferson's suggestion to Madison.
1. Mary or "Polly" or later "Maria" (1778–1804), Jefferson's younger daughter, at this time eleven years old. She had come to France (with the fifteen-year-old family slave Sally Hemings) in 1787 and entered the same convent school as her sister Martha.

for all their kindness to you. What would you do without them, and with such a vagrant for a father? Say to both of them a thousand affectionate things for me: and Adieu my dear Maria,

TH: JEFFERSON

To Mary Jefferson

MY DEAR MARIA   New York June 13. 1790.
   I have recieved your letter of May 23. which was in answer to mine of May 2. but I wrote you also on the 23d. of May, so that you still owe me an answer to that, which I hope is now on the road. In matters of correspondence as well as of money you must never be in debt. I am much pleased with the account you give me of your occupations, and the making the pudding is as good an article of them as any. When I come to Virginia I shall insist on eating a pudding of your own making, as well as on trying other specimens of your skill. You must make the most of your time while you are with so good an aunt[2] who can learn you every thing. We had not peas nor strawberries here till the 8th. day of this month. On the same day I heard the first Whip-poor-will whistle. Swallows and martins appeared here on the 21st. of April. When did they appear with you? And when had you peas, strawberries, and whip-poor-wills in Virginia? Take notice hereafter whether the whip-poor-wills always come with the strawberries and peas. Send me a copy of the maxims I gave you, also a list of the books I promised you. I have had a long touch of my periodical head-ach, but a very moderate one.[3] It has not quite left me yet. Adieu, my dear, love your uncle, aunt and cousins, and me more than all. Your's affectionately,

TH: JEFFERSON

To Martha Jefferson Randolph

MY DEAR DAUGHTER   Philadelphia Dec. 23. 1790.
   This is a scolding letter for you all. I have not recieved a scrip of a pen from home since I left it which is now eleven weeks. I think it so easy for you to write me one letter every week, which will be but once in three weeks for each of you, when I write one every week who have not one moment's repose from business from the first to the last moment of the week. Perhaps you think you have nothing to say to me. It is a great deal to say you are all well, or that one has a cold, another a fever &c., besides that there is not a sprig of grass that shoots uninteresting to me, nor any thing that moves, from yourself down to Bergere or Grizzle.[4] Write then my dear daughter punctually on

---

2. As she had before her trip to France, Mary Jefferson at this time was residing with her mother's sister, Elizabeth Wayles Eppes, and Elizabeth's husband, Francis Eppes, at their James River plantation, Eppington. In 1797 she would marry their son, her first cousin, John Wayles Eppes. By the end of the present year, as Jefferson's December 23, 1790, letter to her sister Martha indicates, Mary was living with Martha and her husband Thomas M. Randolph.
3. Merrill D. Peterson points out that Jefferson's "inveterate headache" typically afflicted him at "times of emotional stress." The first recorded attack occurred shortly after he learned that an early love, Rebecca Burwell, was to marry someone else. Merrill D. Peterson, *Thomas Jefferson and the New Nation: A Biography* (New York: Oxford University Press, 1970), 84.
4. Bergere and Grizzle were puppies born to a pregnant dog Jefferson acquired just before departing from France in October 1789. Jefferson had been in New York and then Philadelphia since March attending to his duties as President George Washington's secretary of state.

your day, and Mr. Randolph and Polly on theirs. I suspect you may have news to tell me of yourself of the most tender interest to me. Why silent then?

I am still without a house, and consequently without a place to open my furniture. This has prevented my sending you what I was to send for Monticello. In the mean time the river is frozen up so as that no vessel can get out, nor probably will these two months: so that you will be much longer without them than I had hoped. I know how inconvenient this will be and am distressed at it; but there is no help. I send a pamphlet for Mr. Randolph. My best affections to him, Polly, & yourself. Adieu my dear,

TH: JEFFERSON

To the Reverend William Smith[5]

DEAR SIR   Philadelphia Feb. 19. 1791.

I feel both the wish and the duty to communicate, in compliance with your request, whatever, within my knowledge, might render justice to the memory of our great countryman Dr. Franklin, in whom Philosophy has to deplore one of it's principal luminaries extinguished. But my opportunities of knowing the interesting facts of his life have not been equal to my desire of making them known. I could indeed relate a number of those bons mots, with which he was used to charm every society, as having heard many of them. But these are not your object. Particulars of greater dignity happened not to occur during his stay of nine months after my arrival in France.[6]

A little before that, Argand had invented his celebrated lamp, in which the flame is spread into a hollow cylinder, and thus brought into contact with the air within as well as without. Doctr. Franklin had been on the point of the same discovery. The idea had occurred to him; but he had tried a bullrush as a wick, which did not succeed. His occupations did not permit him to repeat and extend his trials to the introduction of a larger column of air than could pass through the stem of a bull-rush.

The Animal magnetism too of the Maniac, Mesmer, had just recieved it's death's wound from his hand in conjunction with his brethren of the learned committee appointed to unveil that compound of fraud and folly.[7] But after this, nothing very interesting was before the public, either in philosophy or politicks, during his stay: and he was principally occupied in winding up his affairs there.

I can only therefore testify in general that there appeared to me more respect and veneration attached to the character of Doctor Franklin in France than to that of any other person in the same country, foreign or native. I had opportunities of knowing particularly how far these sentiments were felt by the foreign Ambassadors and ministers at the court of Versailles. The fable

5. The Reverend William Smith (1727–1803), a native of Scotland whom Benjamin Franklin had encouraged to come to Philadelphia, served as the first provost of what became the University of Pennsylvania and at the time of Jefferson's letter was one of the two vice presidents of the American Philosophical Society, David Rittenhouse being the other. After Franklin's death in April 1790, Smith and Rittenhouse were chosen to prepare the official eulogy in his memory, but not until early the following year did Smith finally begin to work on it. He wrote fellow society member Jefferson asking him to contribute information and anecdotes.
6. Franklin in fact had stayed on in Paris for almost a year after Jefferson's arrival there in the summer of 1784. Jefferson was appointed to succeed him as American minister to France in March 1785, but word of the change did not arrive until May, and not until July did Franklin leave for home.
7. In 1784, Franklin had been appointed to a French royal commission charged with reviewing the claims of Franz Anton Mesmer (1734–1815) about what he called "animal magnetism," a precursor of hypnotism.

of his capture by the Algerines, propagated by the English news-papers, excited no uneasiness;[8] as it was seen at once to be a dish cooked up to the palate of their readers. But nothing could exceed the anxiety of his diplomatic brethren, on a subsequent report of his death, which, tho' premature, bore some marks of authenticity.

I found the ministers of France equally impressed with the talents and integrity of Doctr. Franklin. The Ct. de Vergennes[9] particularly gave me repeated and unequivocal demonstrations of his entire confidence in him.

When he left Passy, it seemed as if the village had lost it's Patriarch. On taking leave of the court, which he did by letter, the king ordered him to be handsomely complimented, and furnished him with a litter and mules of his own, the only kind of conveyance the state of his health could bear.

No greater proof of his estimation in France can be given than the late letters of condoleance on his death from the National assembly of that country, and the community of Paris, to the President of the U.S. and to Congress, and their public mourning on that event. It is I believe the first instance of that homage having been paid by a public body of one nation to a private citizen of another.

His death was an affliction which was to happen to us at some time or other. We had reason to be thankful he was so long spared: that the most useful life should be the longest also: that it was protracted so far beyond the ordinary span allotted to man, as to avail us of his wisdom in the establishment of our own freedom, and to bless him with a view of it's dawn in the east, where they seemed till now to have learned every thing, but how to be free.

The succession to Dr. Franklin at the court of France, was an excellent school of humility. On being presented to any one as the Minister of America, the common-place question, used in such cases, was "c'est vous, Monsieur, qui remplace le Docteur Franklin?" "It is you, Sir, who replace Doctor Franklin?" I generally answered "no one can replace him, Sir; I am only his successor."

These small offerings to the memory of our great and dear friend, whom time will be making greater while it is spunging us from it's records, must be accepted by you, Sir, in that spirit of love and veneration for him in which they are made: and not according to their insignificance in the eyes of a world, who did not want this mite to fill up the measure of his worth.—I pray you to accept in addition assurances of the sincere esteem and respect with which I have the honor to be, Sir, your most obedient & most humble servant,

Tʜ: Jᴇғғᴇʀsᴏɴ

To Benjamin Banneker[1]

Sɪʀ   Philadelphia Aug. 30. 1791.

I thank you sincerely for your letter of the 19th. instant and for the Almanac it contained. No body wishes more than I do to see such proofs as

---

8. After Franklin's departure for the United States in 1785, rumors of his capture by Barbary pirates spread through Europe.
9. Charles Gravier, comte de Vergennes (1717–1787), had been Louis XVI's foreign minister during Franklin's stay in France.
1. In the summer of 1791, the free African American farmer Benjamin Banneker (1731–1806), a self-trained mathematician and astronomer from Maryland who had been employed in conducting the survey of the new federal capital of the District of Columbia, a process supervised by Jefferson, sent Secretary of State Jefferson a manuscript copy of an almanac that he had created and that he would soon publish. In his cover letter, Banneker directly but politely challenged Jefferson to see that the

you exhibit, that nature has given to our black brethren, talents equal to those of the other colours of men, and that the appearance of a want of them is owing merely to the degraded condition of their existence both in Africa and America. I can add with truth that no body wishes more ardently to see a good system commenced for raising the condition both of their body and mind to what it ought to be, as fast as the imbecillity[2] of their present existence, and other circumstances which cannot be neglected, will admit.—I have taken the liberty of sending your almanac to Monsieur de Condorcet, Secretary of the Academy of sciences at Paris, and member of the Philanthropic society because I considered it as a document to which your whole colour had a right for their justification against the doubts which have been entertained of them.[3] I am with great esteem, Sir Your most obedt. humble servt.,

TH: JEFFERSON

To Martha Jefferson Randolph

MY DEAR MARTHA   Philadelphia Jan. 15. 1792.
    Having no particular subject for a letter, I find none more soothing to my mind than to indulge itself in expressions of the love I bear you, and the delight with which I recall the various scenes thro which we have passed together, in our wanderings over the world. These reveries alleviate the toils and inquietudes of my present situation, and leave me always impressed with the desire of being at home once more, and of exchanging labour, envy, and malice, for ease, domestic occupation, and domestic love and society, where I may once more be happy with you, with Mr. Randolph, and dear little Anne, with whom even Socrates might ride on a stick without being ridiculous. Indeed it is with difficulty that my resolution will bear me through what yet lies between the present day and that which, on mature consideration of all circumstances respecting myself and others, my mind has determined to be the proper one for relinquishing my office. Tho' not very distant, it is not near enough for my wishes.[4] The ardor of these however would be abated if I thought that on coming home I should be left alone. On the contrary I hope that Mr. Randolph will find a convenience in making only leisurely preparations for a settlement, and that I shall be able to make you both happier than you have been at Monticello, and relieve you from *desagremens*[5] to which I

---

principles of liberty articulated in the Declaration of Independence, and secured by the sacrifices of the Revolution, were no less precious to his own "race of beings, who have long labored under the abuse and censure of the world." When Jefferson sent the mathematician this reply, Banneker proceeded to publish both letters in a small pamphlet in Philadelphia. Banneker would continue to issue his popular *Almanac* through the next decade.

2. In Jefferson's time, this word had a broader meaning of weakness, especially physical weakness.
3. Jefferson's August 30, 1791, letter to Condorcet read in part: "I am happy to be able to inform you that we have now in the United States a negro, the son of a black man born in Africa, and of a black woman born in the United States, who is a very respectable Mathematician. I procured him to be employed under one of our chief directors in laying out the new federal city on the Patowmac, and in the intervals of his leisure, while on that work, he made an Almanac for the next year, which he sent me in his own handwriting, and which I enclose to you. I have seen very elegant solutions of Geometrical problems by him. Add to this that he is a very worthy and respectable member of society. He is a free man, I shall be delighted to see these instances of moral eminence so multiplied as to prove that the want of talent observed in them is merely the effect of their degraded condition, and not proceeding from any difference in the structure of the parts on which intellect depends" (*PTJ* 22:98–99).
4. Jefferson did not resign as secretary of state until the end of the following year.
5. Unpleasantness, difficulties (French). The Randolphs were contemplating the purchase of a property near Monticello, where they had been residing for some time.

have been sensible you were exposed, without the power in myself to prevent it, but by my own presence. Remember me affectionately to Mr. Randolph and be assured of the tender love of Yours,

TH: JEFFERSON

To Thomas Paine[6]

DEAR SIR   Philadelphia June 19. 1792
I received with great pleasure the present of your pamphlets, as well for the thing itself as that it was a testimony of your recollection. Would you believe it possible that in this country there should be high and important characters who need your lessons in republicanism, and who do not heed them? It is but too true that we have a sect preaching up and panting after an English constitution of king, lords, and commons, and whose heads are itching for crowns, coronets and mitres. But our people, my good friend, are firm and unanimous in their principles of republicanism, and there is no better proof of it than that they love what you write and read it with delight. The printers season every newspaper with extracts from your last, as they did before from your first part of the Rights of man. They have both served here to separate the wheat from the chaff, and to prove that tho the latter appears on the surface, it is on the surface only. The bulk below is sound and pure. Go on then in doing with your pen what in other times was done with the sword; shew that reformation is more practicable by operating on the mind than on the body of man, and be assured that it has not a more sincere votary, nor you a more ardent well-wisher than, Dear Sir, Your friend & servt,

TH: JEFFERSON

To André Michaux

ca. 30 Apr. 1793
Sundry persons having subscribed certain sums of money for your encouragement to explore the country along the Missouri, and thence Westwardly to the Pacific ocean, having submitted the plan of the enterprize to the direction of the American Philosophical society, and the Society having accepted of the trust, they proceed to give you the following instructions.
They observe to you that the chief objects of your journey are to find the shortest and most convenient route of communication between the US. and the Pacific ocean, within the temperate latitudes, and to learn such particulars as can be obtained of the country through which it passes, it's productions, inhabitants and other interesting circumstances.
As a channel of communication between these states and the Pacific ocean, the Missouri, so far as it extends, presents itself under circumstances of unquestioned preference. It has therefore been declared as a fundamental object of the subscription, (not to be dispensed with) that this river

6. By the time the famous political pamphleteer Thomas Paine (1737–1809), author of *Common Sense* (1776), wrote a letter to Jefferson from England in February 1792, political parties had already begun to emerge in the United States, especially because of the widening split between Jefferson and Alexander Hamilton, George Washington's treasury secretary. Hence Jefferson's comments on the fortunes of Republicanism in America. Paine had included with his own letter six copies of the second part of *The Rights of Man*, published in London on February 16. Despite the evident warmth in Jefferson's tone in this letter, over the next decade he neglected to answer all of the increasingly radical Paine's letters to him.

shall be considered and explored as a part of the communication sought for. To the neighborhood of this river therefore, that is to say to the town of Kaskaskia, the society will procure you a conveyance in company with the Indians of that town now in Philadelphia.

From thence you will cross the Missisipi and pass by land to the nearest part of the Missouri above the Spanish settlements, that you may avoid the risk of being stopped.

You will then pursue such of the largest streams of that river, as shall lead by the shortest way, and the lowest latitudes to the Pacific ocean.

When, pursuing these streams, you shall find yourself at the point from whence you may get by the shortest and most convenient route to some principal river of the Pacific ocean, you are to proceed to such river, and pursue it's course to the ocean. It would seem by the latest maps as if a river called Oregon interlocked with the Missouri for a considerable distance, and entered the Pacific ocean, not far Southward of Nootka sound. But the Society are aware that these maps are not to be trusted so far as to be the ground of any positive instruction to you. They therefore only mention the fact, leaving to yourself to verify it, or to follow such other as you shall find to be the real truth.

You will, in the course of your journey, take notice of the country you pass through, it's general face, soil, rivers, mountains, it's productions animal, vegetable, and mineral so far as they may be new to us and may also be useful or very curious; the latitude of places or materials for calculating it by such simple methods as your situation may admit you to practice, the names, numbers, and dwellings of the inhabitants, and such particularities as you can learn of their history, connection with each other, languages, manners, state of society and of the arts and commerce among them.

Under the head of Animal history, that of the Mammoth is particularly recommended to your enquiries. As it is also to learn whether the Lama, or Paca of Peru is found in those parts of this continent, or how far North they come.

The method of preserving your observations is left to yourself, according to the means which shall be in your power. It is only suggested that the noting them on the skin might be best for such as are most important, and that further details may be committed to the bark of the paper birch, a substance which may not excite suspicions among the Indians, and little liable to injury from wet, or other common accidents. By the means of the same substance you may perhaps find opportunities, from time to time, of communicating to the society information of your progress, and of the particulars you shall have noted.

When you shall have reached the Pacific ocean, if you find yourself within convenient distance of any settlement of Europeans, go to them, commit to writing a narrative of your journey and observations and take the best measures you can for conveying it by duplicates or triplicates thence to the society by sea.

Return by the same, or such other route, as you shall think likely to fulfill with most satisfaction and certainty the objects of your mission; furnishing yourself with the best proofs the nature of the case will admit of the reality and extent of your progress. Whether this shall be by certificates from Europeans settled on the Western coast of America, or by what other means, must depend on circumstances.

Ignorance of the country thro' which you are to pass and confidence in your judgment, zeal, and discretion, prevent the society from attempting more minute instructions, and even from exacting rigorous observance of those already given, except indeed what is the first of all objects, that you seek for and pursue that route which shall form the shortest and most convenient communication between the higher parts of the Missouri and the Pacific ocean.

It is strongly recommended to you to expose yourself in no case to unnecessary dangers, whether such as might affect your health or your personal safety: and to consider this not merely as your personal concern, but as the injunction of Science in general which expects it's enlargement from your enquiries, and of the inhabitants of the US. in particular, to whom your Report will open new feilds and subjects of Commerce, Intercourse, and Observation.

If you reach the Pacific ocean and return, the Society assign to you all the benefits of the subscription beforementioned. If you reach the waters only which run into that ocean, the society reserve to themselves the apportionment of the reward according to the conditions expressed in the subscription.

They will expect you to return to the city of Philadelphia to give in to them a full narrative of your journey and observations, and to answer the enquiries they shall make of you, still reserving to yourself the benefits arising from the publication[7] of them.

To James Madison

June 9. 1793.

I have to acknolege the receipt of your two favors of May 27. and 29. since the date of my last which was of the 2d. inst.—In that of the 27th. you say "you must not make your final exit from public life till it will be marked with justifying circumstances which all good citizens will respect, and to which your friends can appeal." To my fellow-citizens the debt of service has been fully and faithfully paid. I acknolege that such a debt exists: that a tour of duty, in whatever line he can be most useful to his country, is due from every individual. It is not easy perhaps to say of what length exactly this tour should be. But we may safely say of what length it should not be. Not of our whole life, for instance, for that would be to be born a slave. Not even of a very large portion of it. I have now been in the public service four and twenty years; one half of which has been spent in total occupation with their affairs, and absence from my own. I have served my tour then.—No positive engagement, by word or deed, binds me to their further service.—No commitment of their interests in any enterprize by me requires that I should see them through it.— I am pledged by no act which gives any tribunal a call upon me before I withdraw. Even my enemies do not pretend this. I stand clear then of public right in all points.—My friends I have not committed. No circumstances have attended my passage from office to office, which could lead them, and others through them, into deception as to the time I might remain; and particularly they and all have known with what reluctance I engaged and have continued in the present one, and of my uniform determination to retire from

7. French botanist Andre Michaux (1746–1802), resident in the United States from 1785 to 1796, proposed to Jefferson in 1792 undertaking an expedition, to be funded by the American Philosophical Society, across the continent to the Pacific. Jefferson, a member of a five-person committee of the society, drew up these instructions in April 1793, but political tensions associated with the intrigues of Edmund-Charles Genêt (1763–1834), French envoy to the United States, forced the cancellation of the planned expedition. Michaux did manage to travel to the Mississippi at his own expense and, once back in France, published two books about American plants.

it at an early day. If the public then has no claim on me, and my friends nothing to justify, the decision will rest on my own feelings alone. There has been a time when these were very different from what they are now: when perhaps the esteem of the world was of higher value in my eye than every thing in it. But age, experience, and reflection, preserving to that only it's due value, have set a higher on tranquility. The motion of my blood no longer keeps time with the tumult of the world. It leads me to seek for happiness in the lap and love of my family, in the society of my neighbors and my books, in the wholesome occupations of my farm and my affairs, in an interest or affection in every bud that opens, in every breath that blows around me, in an entire freedom of rest or motion, of thought or incogitancy,[8] owing account to myself alone of my hours and actions. What must be the principle of that calculation which should balance against these the circumstances of my present existence! Worn down with labours from morning till night, and day to day; knowing them as fruitless to others as they are vexatious to myself, committed singly in desperate and eternal contest against a host who are systematically undermining the public liberty and prosperity, even the rare hours of relaxation sacrificed to the society of persons in the same intentions, of whose hatred I am conscious even in those moments of conviviality when the heart wishes most to open itself to the effusions of friendship and confidence, cut off from my family and friends, my affairs abandoned to chaos and derangement, in short giving every thing I love, in exchange for every thing I hate, and all this without a single gratification in possession or prospect, in present enjoyment or future wish.—Indeed my dear friend, duty being out of the question, inclination cuts off all argument, and so never let there be more between you and me, on this subject.

I inclose you some papers which have passed on the subject of a new loan. You will see by them that the paper-Coryphaeus[9] is either undaunted, or desperate. I believe that the statement inclosed has secured a decision against his proposition.—I dined yesterday in a company where Morris and Bingham were, and happened to set between them. In the course of a conversation after a dinner Morris made one of his warm declarations that, after the expiration of his present Senatorial term, nothing on earth should ever engage him to serve again in any public capacity. He did this with such solemnity as renders it impossible he should not be in earnest.—The President is not well. Little lingering fevers have been hanging about him for a week or ten days, and have affected his looks most remarkably. He is also extremely affected by the attacks made and kept up on him in the public papers. I think he feels those things more than any person I ever yet met with. I am sincerely sorry to see them. I remember an observation of yours, made when I first went to New York, that the satellites and sycophants which surrounded him had wound up the ceremonials of the government to a pitch of stateliness which nothing but his personal character could have supported, and which no character after him could ever maintain. It appears now that even his will be insufficient to justify them in the appeal of the times to common sense as the arbiter of every thing. Naked he would have been sanctimoniously reverenced. But inveloped in the rags of royalty, they can hardly be torn off without laceration. It is the more unfortunate that this attack is planted on popular ground, on the love of the people to France and it's cause, which is universal.—Genet mentions freely enough in conversation

8. Thoughtlessness.
9. Coryphaeus was the leader of the chorus in Greek drama.

that France does not wish to involve us in the war by our guarantee. The information from St. Domingo and Martinique is that those two islands are disposed and able to resist any attack which Great Britain can make on them by land. A blockade would be dangerous, could it be maintained in that climate for any length of time. I delivered to Genet your letter to Roland. As the latter is out of office, he will direct it to the Minister of the Interior. I found every syllable of it strictly proper. Your ploughs shall be duly attended to. Have you ever taken notice of Tull's[1] horse-houghing plough? I am persuaded that that, where you wish your work to be very exact, and our great plough where a less degree will suffice, leave us nothing to wish for from other countries as to ploughs, under our circumstances.—I have not yet received my threshing machine. I fear the late long and heavy rains must have extended to us, and affected our wheat. Adieu. Your's affectionately.

To Angelica Schuyler Church[2]

Germantown Nov. 27. 1793.

I have received, my very good friend, your, kind letter of Aug. 19. with the extract from that of La Fayette, for whom my heart has been constantly bleeding.[3] The influence of the United States has been put into action, as far as it could be either with decency or effect. But I fear that distance and difference of principle give little hold to Genl. Washington on the jailors of La Fayette. However his friends may be assured that our zeal has not been inactive. Your letter gives me the first information that our dear friend Madame de Corny has been, as to her fortune, among the victims of the times. Sad times indeed! and much lamented victim! I know no country where the remains of a fortune could place her so much at her ease as this, and where public esteem is so attached to worth, regardless of wealth. But our manners, and the state of society here are so different from those to which her habits have been formed, that she would lose more perhaps in that scale.—And Madame Cosway in a convent! I knew that, to much goodness of heart, she joined enthusiasm and religion: but I thought that very enthusiasm would have prevented her from shutting up her adoration of the god of the Universe within the walls of a cloyster; that she would rather have sought the *mountain-top*. How happy should I be that it were *mine* that you, she and Mde. de Corny would seek. You say indeed that you are coming to America. But I know that means New York. In the mean time I am going to Virginia. I have at length been able to fix that to the beginning of the new year. I am then to be liberated from the hated occupations of politics, and to sink into the bosom of my family, my farm and my books. I have my house to build, my feilds to form, and to watch for the happiness of those who labor for mine. I have one daughter married to a man of science, sense, virtue, and competence; in whom indeed I have nothing more

1. Jethro Tull (1674–1741), English agricultural innovator and author of *The New Horse-Hoeing Husbandry; or, an Essay on the Principles of Tillage and Vegetation* (1731).
2. Angelica Schuyler Church (1756–1815), daughter of Revolutionary hero General Philip Schuyler and New York heiress Catharine van Rensselaer and wife of Anglo-American merchant John Barker Church, was introduced to Jefferson by Maria Cosway and became his close friend. For a time her daughter Kitty was in the same convent school as Jefferson's daughters in Paris, and Jefferson looked after her. Church and her husband moved in the highest social circles in London; at the time of this letter she was thinking of returning to New York, and in 1797 finally did so.
3. Lafayette, opposed to the execution of Louis XVI and Marie Antoinette, fled France in 1793 intending to take refuge in the United States but was captured by Austrian authorities and imprisoned.

to wish. They live with me. If the other shall be as fortunate in due process of time, I shall imagine myself as blessed as the most blessed of the patriarchs. Nothing could then withdraw my thoughts a moment from home, but the recollection of my friends abroad. I often put the question Whether yourself and Kitty will ever come to see your friends at Monticello? But it is my affection, and not my experience of things, which has leave to answer. And I am determined to believe the answer; because, in that belief, I find I sleep sounder and wake more chearful. En attendant, god bless you; accept the homage of my sincere & constant affection.

TH: JEFFERSON

To John Adams

DEAR SIR   Monticello Dec. 28. 1796.
  The public and the public papers have been much occupied lately in placing us in a point of opposition to each other. I trust with confidence that less of it has been felt by ourselves personally. In the retired canton where I am, I learn little of what is passing: pamphlets I see never; papers but a few; and the fewer the happier. Our latest intelligence from Philadelphia at present is of the 16th inst. but tho' at that date your election to the first magistracy[4] seems not to have been known as a fact, yet with me it has never been doubted. I knew it impossible you should lose a vote North of the Delaware, and even if that of Pennsylvania should be against you in the mass, yet that you would get enough South of that to place your succession out of danger. I have never one single moment expected a different issue; and tho' I know I shall not be believed, yet it is not the less true that I have never wished it. My neighbors, as my compurgators,[5] could aver that fact, because they see my occupations and my attachment to them. Indeed it is possible that you may be cheated of your succession by a trick worthy the subtlety of your arch-friend of New York,[6] who has been able to make of your real friends tools to defeat their and your just wishes. Most probably he will be disappointed as to you; and my inclinations place me out of his reach. I leave to others the sublime delights of riding in the storm, better pleased with sound sleep and a warm birth below, with the society of neighbors, friends and fellow laborers of the earth, than of spies and sycophants. No one then will congratulate you with purer disinterestedness than myself. The share indeed which I may have had in the late vote, I shall still value highly, as an evidence of the share I have in the esteem of my fellow citizens. But while, in this point of view, a few votes less would be little sensible, the difference in the effect of a few more would be very sensible and oppressive to me. I have no ambition to govern men.[7] It is a painful and thankless office. Since the day too on which you signed the treaty of Paris our horizon was never so overcast. I devoutly wish you may be able to shun for us this war by which our agriculture, commerce and credit will be destroyed. If you are, the glory will be all your own; and that your administration may be filled with glory and happiness to yourself and advantage to us is the sincere wish of one who tho', in the course of our voyage thro' life,

---

4. The presidency.
5. Witnesses testifying to a defendant's innocence.
6. Alexander Hamilton.
7. Jefferson nonetheless, as the presidential candidate with the second-highest number of votes, was elected vice president in 1796.

various little incidents have happened or been contrived to separate us, retains still for you the solid esteem of the moments when we were working for our independance, and sentiments of respect and affectionate attachment.

TH: JEFFERSON

To James Madison

Jan. 1. [17]97.

Yours of Dec. 19. has come safely. The event of the election has never been a matter of doubt in my mind. I knew that the Eastern states were disciplined in the schools of their town meetings to sacrifice differences of opinion to the great object of operating in phalanx, and that the more free and moral agency practised in the other states would always make up the supplement of their weight. Indeed the vote comes much nearer an equality than I had expected. I know the difficulty of obtaining belief to one's declarations of a disinclination to honors, and that it is greatest with those who still remain in the world. But no arguments were wanting to reconcile me to a relinquishment of the first office or acquiescence under the second. As to the first it was impossible that a more solid unwillingness settled on full calculation, could have existed in any man's mind, short of the degree of absolute refusal. The only view on which I would have gone into it for a while was to put our vessel on her republican tack before she should be thrown too much to leeward of her true principles. As to the second, it is the only office in the world about which I am unable to decide in my own mind whether I had rather have it or not have it. Pride does not enter into the estimate; for I think with the Romans that the General of to-day should be a soldier tomorrow if necessary. I can particularly have no feelings which would revolt at a secondary position to Mr. Adams. I am his junior in life, was his junior in Congress, his junior in the diplomatic line, his junior lately in our civil government. Before the receipt of your letter I had written the inclosed one to him. I had intended it some time, but had deferred it from time to time under the discoragement of a despair of making him believe I could be sincere in it. The papers by the last post not rendering it necessary to change any thing in the letter I inclose it open for your perusal, not only that you may possess the actual state of dispositions between us, but that if any thing should render the delivery of it ineligible in your opinion, you may return it to me. If Mr. Adams can be induced to administer the government on it's true principles, and to relinquish his bias to an English constitution, it is to be considered whether it would not be on the whole for the public good to come to a good understanding with him as to his future elections. He is perhaps the only sure barrier against Hamilton's getting in.

Since my last I have recieved a packet of books and pamphlets, the choiceness of which testifies that they come from you. The Incidents of Hamilton's insurrection is a curious work indeed.[8] The hero of it exhibits himself in all the attitudes of a dexterous balance master.

---

8. Jefferson refers to *Incidents of the Insurrection in the Western Parts of Pennsylvania, in the Year 1794* (1795) by Hugh Henry Brackenridge. The Whiskey Rebellion among frontier farmers came in response to Treasury Secretary Hamilton's successful proposal of an excise tax covering whiskey.

The Political progress[9] is a work of value and of a singular complexion. The eye of the author seems to be a natural achromatic, which divests every object of the glare of colour. The preceding work under the same title had the same merit. One is disgusted indeed with the ulcerated state which it presents of the human mind: but to cure an ulcer we must go to it's bottom: and no writer has ever done this more radically than this one. The reflections into which he leads one are not flattering to our species. In truth I do not recollect in all the Animal kingdom a single species but man which is eternally and systematically engaged in the destruction of it's own species. What is called civilization seems to have no other effect on him than to teach him to pursue the principle of bellum omnium in omnia[1] on a larger scale, and in place of the little contests of tribe against tribe, to engage all the quarters of the earth in the same work of destruction. When we add to this that as to the other species of animals, the lions and tygers are mere lambs compared with man as a destroyer, we must conclude that it is in man alone that Nature has been able to find a sufficient barrier against the too great multiplication of other animals and of man himself, an equilibriating power against the fecundity of generation. My situation points my views chiefly to his wars in the physical world: yours perhaps exhibit him as equally warring in the Moral one. We both, I believe, join in wishing to see him softened. Adieu.

To Mary Jefferson Eppes

Philadelphia Jan. 7. [17]98.

I acknowleged, my dear Maria, the reciept of yours in a letter I wrote to mr Eppes. It gave me the welcome news that your sprain was well, but you are not to suppose it entirely so. The joint will remain weak for a considerable time, & give you occasional pains much longer. The state of things at Chesnut grove is truly distressing. Mr B.'s[2] habitual intoxication will destroy himself, his fortune & family. of all calamities this is the greatest. I wish my sister could bear his misconduct with more patience. It might lessen his attachment to the bottle, & at any rate would make her own time more tolerable. When we see ourselves in a situation which must be endured & gone through, it is best to make up our minds to it, meet it with firmness, & accomodate every thing to it in the best way practicable. This lessens the evil. while fretting & fuming only serves to increase our own torment. The errors and misfortunes of others should be a school for our own instruction. Harmony in the marriage state is the very first object to be aimed at. Nothing can preserve affections uninterrupted but a firm resolution never to differ in will, and a determination in each to consider the love of the other as of more value than any object whatever on which a wish has been fixed. How light in fact is the sacrifice of any other wish, when weighed against the affections of one with whom we are to pass our whole life. And though opposition in a single instance will hardly of itself produce alienation; yet every

---

9. Jefferson refers to the second part of *The Political Progress of Britain* (1795), by James T. Callender, at the time a republican and supporter of Jefferson. By 1802, disappointed in his pursuit of political appointment, Callender published his charge that Jefferson had fathered children with his slave Sally Hemings.
1. War of all against all (Latin).
2. Jefferson refers to John Boiling, husband of his sister, Mary.

one has their pouch into which all these little oppositions are put: while that is filling, the alienation is insensibly going on, & when filled, it is complete. it would puzzle either to say why; because no one difference of opinion has been marked enough to produce a serious effect by itself. But he finds his affections wearied out by a constant stream of little checks & obstacles. Other sources of discontent, very common indeed, are the little cross purposes of husband & wife in common conversation, a disposition in either to criticise & question whatever the other says, a desire always to demonstrate & make him feel himself in the wrong, & especially in company. Nothing is so goading. much better therefore, if our companion views a thing in a light different from what we do, to leave him in quiet possession of his view. What is the use of rectifying him if the thing be unimportant; & if important let it pass for the present, & wait a softer moment, and more conciliatory occasion of revising the subject together. It is wonderful how many persons are rendered unhappy by inattention to these little rules of prudence. I have been insensibly led, by the particular case you mention, to sermonize to you on the subject generally. However if it be the means of saving you from a single heart-ache, it will have contributed a great deal to my happiness. But before I finish the sermon, I must add a word on economy. The unprofitable condition of Virginia estates in general, leaves it now next to impossible for the holder of one to avoid ruin. And this condition will continue until some change takes place in the mode of working them. In the mean time nothing can save us & our children from beggary but a determination to get a year before hand, & restrain ourselves rigorously this year to the clear profits of the last. If a debt is once contracted by a farmer, it is never paid but by a sale. The article of dress is perhaps that in which economy is the least to be recommended. It is so important to each to continue to please the other, that the happiness of both requires the most pointed attention to whatever may contribute to it. And the more as time makes greater inroads on our person. Yet generally we become slovenly in proportion as personal decay requires the contrary. I have great comfort in believing that your understanding & dispositions will engage your attention to these considerations: and that you are connected with a person & family who, of all within the circle of my acquaintance, are most in the dispositions which will make you happy. Cultivate their affections my dear, with assiduity. think every sacrifice a gain which shall tend to attach them to you. my only object in life is to see yourself & your sister, & those deservedly dear to you, not only happy, but in no danger of becoming unhappy.

I have lately recieved a letter from your friend Kitty Church. I inclose it to you, & think the affectionate expressions relative to yourself, & the advance she has made, will require a letter from you to her. It will be impossible to get a chrystal here to fit your watch without the watch itself. If you should know of any one coming to Philadelphia, send it to me, & I will get you a stock of chrystals. The river being frozen up, I shall not be able to send your things till it opens, which will probably be some time in February.—I inclose to mr Eppes some pamphlets. Present me affectionately to all the family, & be assured of my tenderest love to yourself. Adieu

                                                        TH: JEFFERSON

To Joseph Priestley[3]

DEAR SIR   Philadelphia Jan. 18. 1800.

I have to thank you for the pamphlets you were so kind as to send me. you will know what I thought of them by my having before sent a dozen sets to Virginia to distribute among my friends. yet I thank you not the less for these which I value the more as they came from yourself. the stock of them which Campbell had was I believe exhausted the first or second day of advertising them. the papers of Political arithmetic both in your's & Mr. Cooper's pamphlets[4] are the most precious gifts that can be made to us; for we are running navigation-mad, & commerce-mad, and navy-mad, which is worst of all. how desireable is it that you could pursue that subject for us. from the Porcupines[5] of our country you will receive no thanks; but the great mass of our nation will edify & thank you. how deeply have I been chagrined & mortified at the persecutions which fanaticism & monarchy have excited against you even here! at first I believed it was merely a continuance of the English persecution. but I observe that on the demise of Porcupine & division of his inheritance between Fenno & Brown,[6] the latter (tho' succeeding only to the *federal* portion of Porcupinism, not the *Anglican* which is Fenno's part) serves up for the palate of his sect dishes of abuse against you as high-season as Porcupine's were. you have sinned against church & king & can therefore never be forgiven. how sincerely have I regretted that your friend,[7] before he fixed his choice of a position, did not visit the vallies on each side of the blue ridge in Virginia, as mr. Madison & myself so much wished. you would have found there equal soil, the finest climate & most healthy one on the earth, the homage of universal reverence & love, & the power of the country spread over you as a shield. but since you would not make it your country by adoption, you must now do it by your good offices. I have one to propose to you which will produce their good & gratitude to your [ages?], and in the way to which you have devoted a long life, that of spread[ing?] light among men.

We have in that state a college (Wm. & Mary) just well enough endowed to draw out the miserable existence to which a miserable constitution has doomed it. it is moreover eccentric in it's position, exposed to bilious diseases as all the lower country is, & therefore abandoned by the public care, as that part of the country itself is in a considerable degree by it's inhabitants. We wish to establish in the upper & healthier country, & more centrally for the state an University[8] on a plan so broad & liberal & *modern*, as to be worth patronising with the public support, and be a temptation to the youth of other states to come, and drink of the cup of knolege & fraternize with us. the first step is to obtain a good plan; that is a judicious selection of the sciences, & a

---

3. Joseph Priestley (1734–1804), radical English theologian and scientist who supported the French Revolution, had fled political persecution in England in 1794 and settled in Pennsylvania.
4. Priestley apparently had sent Jefferson copies of his own *Letters to the Inhabitants of Northumberland and its Neighborhood* (1799), which incorporated his "Maxims of Political Arithmetic, Applied to the Case of the United States of America," and of the *Political Essays* (1799) of his fellow immigrant Thomas Cooper (1759–1840).
5. William Cobbett (1763–1835), an English immigrant who during his first residence in the United States (1792–1800) became famous under the pseudonym "Peter Porcupine" for his journalistic writings, which supported Britain against France (and the United States).
6. John Ward Fenno (1778–1802) succeeded his father, John Fenno (1751–1798) as editor of the *Gazette of the United States*, a partisan paper backed by Hamilton, who often wrote for it. Andrew Brown Jr. (1774–1847) similarly took over from his father, the Irish-born Andrew Brown Sr. (c. 1744–1797), the pro-Federalist *Philadelphia Gazette*.
7. Thomas Cooper.
8. The University of Virginia opened in Charlottesville, near Monticello, in March 1825.

practicable grouping of some of them together, & ramifying of others, so as to adapt the professorships to our uses, & our means. in an institution meant chiefly for use, some branches of science, formerly esteemed, may be now omitted, so may others now valued in Europe, but useless to us for ages to come. take, as an example of the former, the Oriental learning, and of the latter almost the whole of the institution proposed to Congress by the Secretary of war's report of the 5th. inst.[9] now there is no one to whom this subject is so familiar as yourself. there is no one in the world who equally with yourself unites this full possession of the subject with such a knolege of the state of our existence, as enables you to fit the garment to him who is to *pay* for it & to *wear* it. to you therefore we address our sollicitations. and to lessen to you as much as possible the ambiguities of our object, I will venture even to sketch the sciences which seem useful & practicable for us, as they occur to me while holding my pen. Botany. Chemistry. Zoology. Anatomy. Surgery. Medecine. Natl. Philosophy. Agriculture. Mathematics. Astronomy. Geology. Geography. Politics. Commerce. History. Ethics. Law. Arts. Fine arts. this list is imperfect because I make it hastily, and because I am unequal to the subject. it is evident that some of these articles are too much for one professor & must therefore be ramified; others may be ascribed in groupes to a single professor. this is the difficult part of the work, & requires a hand perfectly knowing the extent of each branch, & the limits within which it may be circumscribed; so as to bring the whole within the powers of the fewest professors possible, & consequently within the degree of expence practicable for us. we should propose that the professors follow no other calling, so that their whole time may be given to their academical functions: and we should propose to draw from Europe the first characters in science, by considerable temptations, which would not need to be repeated after the first set should have prepared fit successors & given reputation to the institution. from some splendid characters I have received offers most perfectly reasonable & practicable.

I do not propose to give you all this trouble merely of my own head. that would be arrogance. it has been the subject of consultation among the ablest and highest characters of our state, who only wait for a plan to make a joint & I hope succesful effort to get the thing carried into effect. they will recieve your ideas with the greatest deference & thankfulness. we shall be here certainly for two months to come; but should you not have leisure to think of it before Congress adjourns, it will come safely to me afterwards by post, the nearest post office being Milton.

Will not the arrival of Dupont tempt you to make a visit to this quarter?[1] I have no doubt the Alarmists are already whetting their shafts for him also, but their glass is nearly run out; and the day I believe is approaching when we shall be as free to pursue what is true wisdom as the effects of their follies will permit: for some of them we shall be forced to wade through because we are immerged in them.

Wishing you that pure happiness which your pursuits and circumstances offer, and which I am sure you are too wise to suffer a diminution of by the pigmy assaults made on you, and with every sentiment of affectionate esteem & respect I am Dear Sir

Your most obedt. & most humble servt

TH: JEFFERSON

9. Secretary of War James McHenry proposed the founding of a national military academy shortly before Jefferson wrote to Priestley in 1800.
1. Members of the Du Pont family arrived in America from France on January 1, 1800, with plans to set up various business ventures, and were soon headed to Philadelphia, where Jefferson (a close friend of the family's patriarch, Pierre S. du Pont) then was living in his capacity as vice president.

To Dr. Joseph Priestley

DEAR SIR   Philadelphia Jan. 27. 1800.

In my letter of the 18th. I omitted to say any thing of the languages as part of our proposed university. it was not that I think, as some do, that they are useless. I am of a very different opinion. I do not think them essential to the obtaining eminent degrees of science, but I think them very useful towards it. I suppose there is a portion of life during which our faculties are ripe enough for this & for nothing more useful. I think the Greeks & Romans have left us the purest models which exist of fine composition, whether we examine them as works of reason, or of style & fancy; and to them we probably owe these characteristics of modern composition: I know of no composition of any other antient people which merits the least regard as a model for it's matter or style. to all this I add that to read the Latin & Greek authors in their original is a sublime luxury; and I deem luxury in science to be at least as justifiable as in architecture, painting, gardening or the other arts. I enjoy Homer in his own language infinitely beyond Pope's translation of him, & both beyond the dull narrative of the same events by Dares Phrygius,[2] & it is an innocent enjoyment. I thank on my knees him who directed my early education for having put into my possession this rich source of delight: and I would not exchange it for any thing which I could then have acquired & have not since acquired. with this regard for those languages you will acquit me of meaning to omit them. about 20. years ago I drew a bill for our legislature which proposed to lay off every county into hundreds or townships of 5 or 6. miles square, in the center of each of which was to be a free English school; the whole state was further laid off into 10. districts in each of which was to be a college for teaching the languages, geography, surveying and other useful things of that grade; and then a single University for the sciences. it was recieved with enthusiasm; but as I had proposed that Wm. & Mary, under an improved form should be the University, & that was at that time pretty highly Episcopal, the dissenters after a while began to apprehend some secret design of a preference to that sect, and nothing could then be done. about 3. years ago they enacted that part of my bill which related to English schools, except that instead of obliging, they left it optional in the court of every county, to carry it into execution or not. I think it probable the part of the plan for the middle grade of education, may also be brought forward in due time. in the mean while we are not without a sufficient number of good country schools where the languages, geography & the first elements of Mathematics are taught. having omitted this information in my former letter, I thought it necessary now to supply it, that you might know on what base your superstructure was to be reared.—I have a letter from M. Dupont since his arrival at N. York, dated the 20th. in which he says he will be in Philadelphia within about a fortnight from that time; but only on a visit. how much would it delight me if a visit from you at the same time were to shew us two such illustrious foreigners embracing each other in my country as the asylum for whatever is great & good. pardon, I pray you, the temporary delirium which has been excited here, but which is fast passing away. the Gothic idea that we are to look backwards instead of

---

2. Dares Phrygius, mentioned in the *Iliad*, was thought by some ancient Greeks to be the author of a prose account of the destruction of Troy.

forwards for the improvement of the human mind, and to recur to the annals of our ancestors for what is most perfect in government, in religion & in learning, is worthy of those bigots in religion & government, by whom it has been recommended, & whose purposes it would answer, but it is not an idea which this country will endure; and the moment of their shewing it is fast ripening. and the signs of it will be their respect for you & growing detestation of those who have dishonored our country by endeavors to disturb your tranquility in it. no one has felt this with more sensibility, than, my dear Sir, Your respectful & affectionate friend & servt

TH: JEFFERSON

To Dr. Joseph Priestley

DEAR SIR   Washington Mar. 21. 1801.

I learnt some time ago that you were in Philadelphia, but that it was only for a fortnight, & supposed you were gone. it was not till yesterday I recieved information that you were still there, had been very ill but were on the recovery. I sincerely rejoice that you are so. yours is one of the few lives precious to mankind, & for the continuance of which every thinking man is solicitous. bigots may be an exception. what an effort, my dear Sir, of bigotry in Politics & Religion have we gone through. the barbarians really flattered themselves they should even be able to bring back the times of Vandalism, when ignorance put every thing into the hands of power & priestcraft. all advances in science were proscribed as innovations. they pretended to praise & encourage education, but it was to be vain the education of our ancestors. we were to look backwards not forwards for improvement, the President himself declaring in one of his answers to addresses that we were never to expect to go beyond them in real science. this was the real ground of all the attacks on you: those who live by mystery & charlatanerie, fearing you would render them useless by simplifying the Christian philosophy, the most sublime & benevolent, but most perverted system that ever shone on man, endeavored to crush your well earnt, & well deserved fame. but it was the Lilliputians upon Gulliver. our countrymen have recovered from the alarm into which art & industry had thrown them, science & honesty are replaced on their high ground, and you, my dear Sir, as their great apostle, are on it's pinnacle. it is with heartfelt satisfaction that, in the first moment of my public action, I can hail you with welcome to our land, tender to you the homage of it's respect & esteem, cover you under the protection of those laws which were made for the wise & the good like you, and disclaim the legitimacy of that libel on legislation which under the form of a law was for sometime placed among them.[3] as the storm is now subsiding & the horison becoming serene, it is pleasant to consider the phaenomenon with attention. we can no longer say there is nothing new under the sun. for this whole chapter in the history of man is new. the great extent of our republic is new. it's sparse habitation is new. the mighty wave of public opinion which has rolled over it is new. but the most pleasing novelty is it's so quickly subsiding, over such an extent of surface, to it's true level again. the order & good sense displayed in this recovery from delusion, and in the momentous crisis which lately arose, really bespeak a

3. Jefferson explained this with a marginal reference to the "Alien law," one of a group of five acts supported by the Federalists in 1798. As president, Jefferson freed and pardoned those convicted under these acts.

strength of character in our nation which augurs well for the duration of our republic, & I am much better satisfied now of it's stability, than I was before it was tried. I have been above all things solaced by the prospect which opened on us in the event of a non election of a president;[4] in which case the federal government would have been in the situation of a clock or watch run down. there was no idea of force, nor of any occasion for it. a Convention, invited by the republican members of Congress with the virtual President & Vice President, would have been on the ground in 8. weeks, would have repaired the constitution where it was defective & wound it up again. this peaceable & legitimate resource, to which we are in the habit of implicit obedience, superseding all appeal to force, and being always within our reach, shews a precious principle of self-preservation in our composition, till a change of circumstances shall take place, which is not within prospect at any definite period.—but I have got into a long disquisition on politics when I only meant to express my sympathy in the state of your health, and to tender you all the affections of public & private hospitality. I should be very happy indeed to see you here. I leave this about the 30th. inst. to return about the 25th. of April. if you do not leave Philadelphia before that, a little excursion hither would help your health. I should be much gratified with the possession of a guest I so much esteem, and should claim a right to lodge you should you make such an excursion. accept the homage of my high consideration & respect, & assurances of affectionate attachment.

TH: JEFFERSON

To Samuel Adams[5]

Washington Mar. 29. 1801

I addressed a letter to you, my very dear & antient friend, on the 4th. of March: not indeed to you by name, but through the medium of some of my fellow citizens, whom occasion called on me to address. in meditating the matter of that address, I often asked myself, is this exactly in the spirit of the patriarch of liberty, Samuel Adams? is it as he would express it? will he approve of it? I have felt a great deal for our country in the times we have seen: but individually for no one so much as yourself. when I have been told that you were avoided, insulated, frowned on, I could but ejaculate "Father, forgive them, for they know not what they do." I confess I felt an indignation for you, which for myself I have been able under every trial to keep entirely passive. however, the storm is over, and we are in port. the ship was not rigged for the service she was put on. we will shew the smoothness of her motions on her republican tack. I hope we shall once more see harmony restored among our citizens, & an entire oblivion of past feuds. some of the leaders who have most committed themselves cannot come into this. but I hope the great body of our fellow citizens will do it. I will sacrifice every thing but principle to procure it. a few examples of justice on officers who have perverted their functions to the oppression of their fellow citizens, must, in justice to those citizens, be made. but opinion, & the just maintenance of it

4. Jefferson had defeated John Adams in the popular vote for president in 1800, but a tie between Jefferson and Aaron Burr in the electoral vote in December threw the election into the house of Representatives. Jefferson's opponents tried to deny him the victory, but on the thirty-sixth ballot he was at last victorious and took office on March 4, 1801.
5. Samuel Adams (1722–1803), political writer and radical opponent of British policy during the Revolutionary era, had served in the Continental Congress and, in the 1790s, had been first lieutenant governor and then governor of Massachusetts.

shall never be a crime in my view; nor bring injury on the individual. those whose misconduct in office ought to have produced their removal even by my predecessor, must not be protected by the delicacy due only to honest men.—how much I lament that time has deprived us of your aid: it would have been a day of glory which should have called you to the first office of the administration. but give us your counsel my friend, and give us your blessing: and be assured that there exists not in the heart of man a more faithful esteem than mine to you, & that I shall ever bear you the most affectionate veneration & respect.

TH: JEFFERSON

To James Monroe[6]

DEAR SIR,—   WASHINGTON, November 24, 1801.

I had not been unmindful of your letter of June 15th, covering a resolution of the House of Representatives of Virginia, and referred to in yours of the 17th inst. The importance of the subject, and the belief that it gave us time for consideration till the next meeting of the Legislature, have induced me to defer the answer to this date. You will perceive that some circumstances connected with the subject, and necessarily presenting themselves to view, would be improper but for yours and the legislative ear. Their publication might have an ill effect in more than one quarter. In confidence of attention to this, I shall indulge greater freedom in writing.

Common malefactors, I presume, make no part of the object of that resolution. Neither their numbers, nor the nature of their offences, seem to require any provisions beyond those practised heretofore, and found adequate to the repression of ordinary crimes. Conspiracy, insurgency, treason, rebellion, (among that description of persons who brought on us the alarm, and on themselves the tragedy, of 1800,) were doubtless within the view of every one; but many perhaps contemplated, and one expression of the resolution might comprehend, a much larger scope. Respect to both opinions makes it my duty to understand the resolution in all the extent of which it is susceptible.

The idea seems to be to provide for these people by a purchase of lands; and it is asked whether such a purchase can be made of the United States in their western territory? A very great extent of country, north of the Ohio, has been laid off into townships, and is now at market, according to the provisions of the acts of Congress, with which you are acquainted. There is nothing which would restrain the State of Virginia either in the purchase or the application of these lands; but a purchase, by the acre, might perhaps be a more expensive provision than the House of Representatives contemplated. Questions would also arise whether the establishment of such a colony within our limits, and to become a part of our union, would be desirable to the State of Virginia itself, or to the other States—especially those who would be in its vicinity?

---

6. James Monroe (1758–1831), Revolutionary leader and then the governor of Virginia, had studied law under Jefferson from 1780 to 1783, becoming his close friend. In the present instance, he wrote Jefferson, then president, asking his advice on a subject of considerable urgency to white politicians in his state. The resolution to which Jefferson refers, designed to allow the removal westward of troublesome slaves from Virginia, had been triggered by the ill-fated conspiracy led by an enslaved blacksmith named Gabriel, who had been hanged along with two of his brothers and many other conspirators in Richmond in October 1800.

Could we procure lands beyond the limits of the United States to form a receptacle for these people? On our northern boundary, the country not occupied by British subjects, is the property of Indian nations, whose title would be to be extinguished, with the consent of Great Britain; and the new settlers would be British subjects. It is hardly to be believed that either Great Britain or the Indian proprietors have so disinterested a regard for us, as to be willing to relieve us, by receiving such a colony themselves; and as much to be doubted whether that race of men could long exist in so rigorous a climate. On our western and southern frontiers, Spain holds an immense country, the occupancy of which, however, is in the Indian natives, except a few insulated spots possessed by Spanish subjects. It is very questionable, indeed, whether the Indians would sell? whether Spain would be willing to receive these people? and nearly certain that she would not alienate the sovereignty. The same question to ourselves would recur here also, as did in the first case: should we be willing to have such a colony in contact with us? However our present interests may restrain us within our own limits, it is impossible not to look forward to distant times, when our rapid multiplication will expand itself beyond those limits, and cover the whole northern, if not the southern continent, with a people speaking the same language, governed in similar forms, and by similar laws; nor can we contemplate with satisfaction either blot or mixture on that surface. Spain, France, and Portugal hold possessions on the southern continent, as to which I am not well enough informed to say how far they might meet our views. But either there or in the northern continent, should the constituted authorities of Virginia fix their attention, of preference, I will have the dispositions of those powers sounded in the first instance.

The West Indies offer a more probable and practicable retreat for them. Inhabited already by a people of their own race and color; climates congenial with their natural constitution; insulated from the other descriptions of men; nature seems to have formed these islands to become the receptacle of the blacks transplanted into this hemisphere. Whether we could obtain from the European sovereigns of those islands leave to send thither the persons under consideration, I cannot say; but I think it more probable than the former propositions, because of their being already inhabited more or less by the same race. The most promising portion of them is the island of St. Domingo, where the blacks are established into a sovereignty *de facto*, and have organized themselves under regular laws and government. I should conjecture that their present ruler might be willing, on many considerations, to receive over that description which would be exiled for acts deemed criminal by us, but meritorious, perhaps, by him. The possibility that these exiles might stimulate and conduct vindicative or predatory descents on our coasts, and facilitate concert with their brethren remaining here, looks to a state of things between that island and us not probable on a contemplation of our relative strength, and of the disproportion daily growing; and it is overweighed by the humanity of the measures proposed, and the advantages of disembarrassing ourselves of such dangerous characters. Africa would offer a last and undoubted resort, if all others more desirable should fail us. Whenever the Legislature of Virginia shall have brought its mind to a point, so that I may know exactly what to propose to foreign authorities, I will execute their wishes with fidelity and zeal. I hope, however, they will pardon me for suggesting a single question for their own consideration. When we contemplate the variety of countries and of sovereigns towards which we may direct our views, the vast resolutions and changes of circumstances which are now in a course of progression, the possibilities that arrangements now to be made, with a view to any particular plea, may, at no great distance of time, be totally deranged by a change of sovereignty, of government, or of other circumstances, it will be for the Legislature to consider whether, after they shall have made all those general provisions which may be fixed by legislative authority, it would be reposing too much confidence in their Executive to leave the place of relegation to be decided on by *them*. They could accommodate their arrangements to the actual state of things, in which countries or powers may be found to exist at the day; and may prevent the effect of the law from being defeated by intervening changes. This, however, is for them to decide. Our duty will be to respect their decision.

Accept assurances of my constant affection, and high consideration and respect.

To Brother Handsome Lake[7]—

WASHINGTON, November 3, 1802.

I have received the message in writing which you sent me through Captain Irvine, our confidential agent, placed near you for the purpose of communicating and transacting between us, whatever may be useful for both nations. I am happy to learn yon have been so far favored by the Divine spirit as to be made sensible of those things which are for your good and that of your people, and of those which are hurtful to you; and particularly that you and they see the ruinous effects which the abuse of spirituous liquors have produced upon them. It has weakened their bodies, enervated their minds, exposed them to hunger, cold, nakedness, and poverty, kept them in perpetual broils, and reduced their population. I do not wonder then, brother, at your censures, not only on your own people, who have voluntarily gone into these fatal habits, but on all the nations of white people who have supplied their calls for this article. But these nations have done to you only what they do among themselves. They have sold what individuals wish to buy, leaving to every one to be the guardian of his own health and happiness. Spirituous liquors are not in themselves bad, they are often found to be an excellent medicine for the sick; it is the improper and intemperate use of them, by those in health, which makes them injurious. But as you find that your people cannot refrain from an ill use of them, I greatly applaud your resolution not to use them at all. We have too affectionate a concern for your happiness to place the paltry gain on the sale of these articles in competition with the injury they do you. And as it is the desire of your nation, that no spirits should be sent among them, I am authorized by the great council of the United States to prohibit them. I will sincerely cöoperate with your wise men in any proper measures for this purpose, which shall be agreeable to them.

You remind me, brother, of what I said to you, when you visited me the last winter, that the lands you then held would remain yours, and shall never go from you but when you should be disposed to sell. This I now repeat, and will ever abide by. We, indeed, are always ready to buy land; but we will never ask but when you wish to sell; and our laws, in order to protect you against imposition, have forbidden individuals to purchase lands from you; and have ren-

7. Handsome Lake or Ganioda'yo (1735–1815), Seneca religious leader, had renounced alcohol in 1799 and begun efforts to help the Seneca, who had fought on the British side in the Revolution, adapt to their new cultural and political circumstances. He had visited Jefferson in Washington with other Iroquois leaders earlier in 1802.

dered it necessary, when you desire to sell, even to a State, that an agent from the United States should attend the sale, see that your consent is freely given, a satisfactory price paid, and report to us what has been done, for our approbation. This was done in the late case of which you complain. The deputies of your nation came forward, in all the forms which we have been used to consider as evidence of the will of your nation. They proposed to sell to the State of New York certain parcels of land, of small extent, and detached from the body of your other lands; the State of New York was desirous to buy. I sent an agent, in whom we could trust, to see that your consent was free, and the sale fair. All was reported to be free and fair. The lands were your property. The right to sell is one of the rights of property. To forbid you the exercise of that right would be a wrong to your nation. Nor do I think, brother, that the sale of lands is, under all circumstances, injurious to your people. While they depended on hunting, the more extensive the forest around them, the more game they would yield. But going into a state of agriculture, it may be as advantageous to a society, as it is to an individual, who has more land than he can improve, to sell a part, and lay out the money in stocks and implements of agriculture, for the better improvement of the residue. A little land well stocked and improved, will yield more than a great deal without stock or improvement. I hope, therefore, that on further reflection, you will see this transaction in a more favorable light, both as it concerns the interest of your nation, and the exercise of that superintending care which I am sincerely anxious to employ for their subsistence and happiness. Go on then, brother, in the great reformation you have undertaken. Persuade our red brethren then to be sober, and to cultivate their lands; and their women to spin and weave for their families. You will soon see your women and children well fed and clothed, your men living happily in peace and plenty, and your numbers increasing from year to year. It will be a great glory to you to have been the instrument of so happy a change, and your children's children, from generation to generation, will repeat your name with love and gratitude forever. In all your enterprises for the good of your people, you may count with confidence on the aid and protection of the United States, and on the sincerity and zeal with which I am myself animated in the furthering of this humane work. You are our brethren of the same land; we wish your prosperity as brethren should do. Farewell.

To Benjamin Hawkins[8]

DEAR SIR,—   WASHINGTON, Feb. 18, 1803.

Mr. Hill's return to you offers so safe a conveyance for a letter, that I feel irresistibly disposed to write one, tho' there is but little to write about. You have been so long absent from this part of the world, and the state of society so changed in that time, that details respecting those who compose it are no longer interesting or intelligible to you. One source of great change in social intercourse arose while you were with us, tho' it's effects were as yet scarcely sensible on society or government. I mean the British treaty, which produced a schism that went on widening and rankling till the years '98, '99, when a

---

8. Benjamin Hawkins (1754–1816), a political and military figure from North Carolina during the Revolution, became U.S. superintendent of Indian affairs south of the Ohio River in 1796. In 1803, allied to Jefferson politically, he was living among the Creek in Georgia and encouraging them in their adoption of Euro-American farming methods.

final dissolution of all bonds, civil & social, appeared imminent.[9] In that awful crisis, the people awaked from the phrenzy into which they had been thrown, began to return to their sober and ancient principles, & have now become five-sixths of one sentiment, to wit, for peace, economy, and a government bottomed on popular election in its legislative & executive branches. In the public counsels the federal party hold still one-third. This, however, will lessen, but not exactly to the standard of the people; because it will be forever seen that of bodies of men even elected by the people, there will always be a greater proportion aristocratic than among their constituents. The present administration had a task imposed on it which was unavoidable, and could not fail to exert the bitterest hostility in those opposed to it. The preceding administration left 99. out of every hundred in public offices of the federal sect. Republicanism had been the mark on Cain which had rendered those who bore it exiles from all portion in the trusts & authorities of their country. This description of citizens called imperiously & justly for a restoration of right. It was intended, however, to have yielded to this in so moderate a degree as might conciliate those who had obtained exclusive possession; but as soon as they were touched, they endeavored to set fire to the four corners of the public fabric, and obliged us to deprive of the influence of office several who were using it with activity and vigilance to destroy the confidence of the people in their government, and thus to proceed in the drudgery of removal farther than would have been, had not their own hostile enterprises rendered it necessary in self-defence. But I think it will not be long before the whole nation will be consolidated in their ancient principles, excepting a few who have committed themselves beyond recall, and who will retire to obscurity & settled disaffection.

Altho' you will receive, thro' the official channel of the War Office, every communication necessary to develop to you our views respecting the Indians, and to direct your conduct, yet, supposing it will be satisfactory to you, and to those with whom you are placed, to understand my personal dispositions and opinions in this particular, I shall avail myself of this private letter to state them generally. I consider the business of hunting as already become insufficient to furnish clothing and subsistence to the Indians. The promotion of agriculture, therefore, and household manufacture, are essential in their preservation, and I am disposed to aid and encourage it liberally. This will enable them to live on much smaller portions of land, and indeed will render their vast forests useless but for the range of cattle; for which purpose, also, as they become better farmers, they will be found useless, and even disadvantageous. While they are learning to do better on less land, our increasing numbers will be calling for more land, and thus a coincidence of interests will be produced between those who have lands to spare, and want other necessaries, and those who have such necessaries to spare, and want lands. This commerce, then, will be for the good of both, and those who are friends to both ought to encourage it. You are in the station peculiarly charged with this interchange, and who have it peculiarly in your power to promote among the Indians a sense of the superior value of a little land, well cultivated, over a great deal, unimproved, and to encourage them to make this estimate truly. The wisdom of the animal which amputates & abandons to the hunter the parts for which he is pursued should be theirs, with this

9. In 1795, Federalist John Jay negotiated an unpopular treaty with Great Britain that aimed to settle disputes lingering from the Revolutionary era. Jefferson refers as well to the rise of fierce partisanship in the United States in the 1790s and the passage of the Alien and Sedition Acts during the Adams administration.

difference, that the former sacrifices what is useful, the latter what is not. In truth, the ultimate point of rest & happiness for them is to let our settlements and theirs meet and blend together, to intermix, and become one people. Incorporating themselves with us as citizens of the U. S., this is what the natural progress of things will of course bring on, and it will be better to promote than to retard it. Surely it will be better for them to be identified with us, and preserved in the occupation of their lands, than be exposed to the many casualties which may endanger them while a separate people. I have little doubt but that your reflections must have led you to view the various ways in which their history may terminate, and to see that this is the one most for their happiness. And we have already had an application from a settlement of Indians to become citizens of the U. S. It is possible, perhaps probable, that this idea may be so novel as that it might shock the Indians, were it even hinted to them. Of course, you will keep it for your own reflection; but, convinced of its soundness, I feel it consistent with pure morality to lead them towards it, to familiarize them to the idea that it is for their interest to cede lands at times to the U S, and for us thus to procure gratifications to our citizens, from time to time, by new acquisitions of land. From no quarter is there at present so strong a pressure on this subject as from Georgia for the residue of the fork of Oconee & Ockmulgee; and indeed I believe it will be difficult to resist it. As it has been mentioned that the Creeks had at one time made up their minds to sell this, and were only checked in it by some indiscretions of an individual, I am in hopes you will be able to bring them to it again. I beseech you to use your most earnest endeavors; for it will relieve us here from a great pressure, and yourself from the unreasonable suspicions of the Georgians which you notice, that you are more attached to the interests of the Indians than of the U S, and throw cold water on their willingness to part with lands. It is so easy to excite suspicion, that none are to be wondered at; but I am in hopes it will be in your power to quash them by effecting the object.

Mr. Madison enjoys better health since his removal to this place than he had done in Orange. Mr. Giles is in a state of health feared to be irrecoverable, although he may hold on for some time, and perhaps be re-established. Browze Trist is now in the Mississippi territory, forming an establishment for his family, which is still in Albemarle, and will remove to the Mississippi in the spring. Mrs. Trist, his mother, begins to yield a little to time. I retain myself very perfect health, having not had 20. hours of fever in 42 years past. I have sometimes had a troublesome headache, and some slight rheumatic pains; but now sixty years old nearly, I have had as little to complain of in point of health as most people. I learn you have the gout. I did not expect that Indian cookery or Indian fare would produce that; but it is considered as a security for good health otherwise. That it may be so with you, I sincerely pray, and tender you my friendly and respectful salutations.

To William H. Harrison[1]

DEAR SIR,—   WASHINGTON, February 27, 1803.

While at Monticello in August last I received your favor of August 8th, and meant to have acknowledged it on my return to the seat of government at the close of the ensuing month, but on my return I found that you were

1. Future president William H. Harrison (1773–1841) at this time was governor of Indiana Territory.

expected to be on here in person, and this expectation continued till winter. I have since received your favor of December 30th.

In the former you mentioned the plan of the town which you had done me the honor to name after me, and to lay out according to an idea I had formerly expressed to you. I am thoroughly persuaded that it will be found handsome and pleasant, and I do believe it to be the best means of preserving the cities of America from the scourge of the yellow fever, which being peculiar to our country, must be derived from some peculiarity in it. That peculiarity I take to be our cloudless skies. In Europe, where the sun does not shine more than half the number of days in the year which it does in America, they can build their town in a solid block with impunity; but here a constant sun produces too great an accumulation of heat to admit that. Ventilation is indispensably necessary. Experience has taught us that in the open air of the country the yellow fever is not only not generated, but ceases to be infectious. I cannot decide from the drawing you sent me, whether you have laid off streets round the squares thus: or only the diagonal streets therein marked. The former was my idea, and is, I imagine, most convenient.

You will receive herewith an answer to your letter as President of the Convention; and from the Secretary of War you receive from time to time information and instructions as to our Indian affairs. These communications being for the public records, are restrained always to particular objects and occasions; but this letter being unofficial and private, I may with safety give you a more extensive view of our policy respecting the Indians, that you may the better comprehend the parts dealt out to you in detail through the official channel, and observing the system of which they make a part, conduct yourself in unison with it in cases where you are obliged to act without instruction. Our system is to live in perpetual peace with the Indians, to cultivate an affectionate attachment from them, by everything just and liberal which we can do for them within the bounds of reason, and by giving them effectual protection against wrongs from our own people. The decrease of game rendering their subsistence by hunting insufficient, we wish to draw them to agriculture, to spinning and weaving. The latter branches they take up with great readiness, because they fall to the women, who gain by quitting the labors of the field for those which are exercised within doors. When they withdraw themselves to the culture of a small piece of land, they will perceive how useless to them are their extensive forests, and will be willing to pare them off from time to time in exchange for necessaries for their farms and families. To promote this disposition to exchange lands, which they have to spare and we want, for necessaries, which we have to spare and they want, we shall push our trading uses, and be glad to see the good and influential individuals among them run in debt, because we observe that when these debts get beyond what the individuals can pay, they become willing to lop them off by a cession of lands. At our trading houses, too, we mean to sell so low as merely to repay us cost and charges, so as neither to lessen nor enlarge our capital. This is what private traders cannot do, for they must gain; they will consequently retire from the competition, and we shall thus get clear of this pest without giving offence or umbrage to the Indians. In this way our settlements will gradually circumscribe and approach the Indians, and they will in time either incorporate with us as citizens of the United States, or remove beyond the Mississippi. The former is certainly the termination of their history most happy for themselves; but, in the whole course of this, it is essential to cultivate their love. As to their fear, we presume that our strength and their weakness is now so visible that they must see we have only to shut our hand to crush them, and that all our liberalities to them proceed from motives of pure humanity only. Should any tribe be foolhardy enough to take up the hatchet at any time, the seizing the whole country of that tribe, and driving them across the Mississippi, as the only condition of peace, would be an example to others, and a furtherance of our final consolidation.

Combined with these views, and to be prepared against the occupation of Louisiana, by a powerful and enterprising people, it is important that, setting less value on interior extension of purchases from the Indians, we bend our whole views to the purchase and settlement of the country on the Mississippi, from its mouth to its northern regions, that we may be able to present as strong a front on our western as on our eastern border, and plant on the Mississippi itself the means of its own defence. We now own from 31 to the Yazoo, and hope this summer to purchase what belongs to the Choctaws from the Yazoo up to their boundary, supposed to be about opposite the mouth of Acanza. We wish at the same time to begin in your quarter, for which there is at present a favorable opening. The Cahokias extinct, we are entitled to their country by our paramount sovereignty. The Piorias, we understand, have all been driven off from their country, and we might claim it in the same way; but as we understand there is one chief remaining, who would, as the survivor of the tribe, sell the right, it is better to give him such terms as will make him easy for life, and take a conveyance from him. The Kaskaskias being reduced to a few families, I presume we may purchase their whole country for what would place every individual of them at his ease, and be a small price to us,—say by laying off for each family, whenever they would choose it, as much rich land as they could cultivate, adjacent to each other, enclosing the whole in a single fence, and giving them such an annuity in money or goods forever as would place them in happiness; and we might take them also under the protection of the United States. Thus possessed of the rights of these tribes, we should proceed to the settling their boundaries with the Poutewatamies and Kickapoos; claiming all doubtful territory, but paying them a price for the relinquishment of their concurrent claim, and even prevailing on them, if possible, to cede, for a price, such of their own unquestioned territory as would give us a convenient northern boundary. Before broaching this, and while we are bargaining with the Kaskaskias, the minds of the Poutewatamies and Kickapoos should be soothed and conciliated by liberalities and sincere assurances of friendship. Perhaps by sending a well-qualified character to stay some time in Decoigne's village, as if on other business, and to sound him and introduce the subject by degrees to his mind and that of the other heads of families, inculcating in the way of conversation, all those considerations which prove the advantages they would receive by a cession on these terms, the object might be more easily and effectually obtained than by abruptly proposing it to them at a formal treaty. Of the means, however, of obtaining what we wish, you will be the best judge; and I have given you this view of the system which we suppose will best promote the interests of the Indians and ourselves, and finally consolidate our whole country to one nation only; that you may be enabled the better to adapt your means to the object for this purpose we have given you a general commission for treating. The crisis is pressing; what ever can now be obtained must be obtained quickly. The occupation of New Orleans, hourly expected, by the French, is already felt like a light breeze by the Indians. You know the sentiments they entertain of that nation; under the hope of their protection they will immediately stiffen against cessions of lands to us. We had better, therefore, do at once what can now be done.

I must repeat that this letter is to be considered as private and friendly, and is not to control any particular instructions which you may receive through official channel. You will also perceive how sacredly it must be kept within your own breast, and especially how improper to be understood by the Indians. For their interests and their tranquillity it is best they should see only the present age of their history. I pray you to accept assurances of my esteem and high consideration.

To Meriwether Lewis[2]

June 20, 1803

To Captain Meriwether Lewis esq. Capt. of the 1st regimt. of Infantry of the U.S. of A.

Your situation as Secretary of the President of the U.S. has made you acquainted with the objects of my confidential message of Jan. 18, 1803 to the legislature; you have seen the act they passed, which, tho' expressed in general terms, was meant to sanction those objects, and you are appointed to carry them into execution.

Instruments for ascertaining, by celestial observations, the geography of the country through which you will pass, have been already provided. Light articles for barter and presents among the Indians, arms for your attendants, say for from 10. to 12. men, boats, tents, & other travelling apparatus, with ammunition, medecine, surgical instruments and provisions you will have prepared with such aids as the Secretary at War can yield in his department; & from him also you will recieve authority to engage among our troops, by voluntary agreement, the number of attendants above mentioned, over whom you, as their commanding officer, are invested with all the powers the laws give in such a case.

As your movements while within the limits of the U.S. will be better directed by occasional communications, adapted to circumstances as they arise, they will not be noticed here. What follows will respect your proceedings after your departure from the United states.

Your mission has been communicated to the ministers here from France, Spain & Great Britain, and through them to their governments; & such assurances given them as to it's objects, as we trust will satisfy them. The country having been ceded by Spain to France, the passport you have from the minister of France, the representative of the present sovereign of the country, will be a protection with all it's subjects; & that from the minister of England will entitle you to the friendly aid of any traders of that allegiance with whom you may happen to meet.

The object of your mission is to explore the Missouri river, & such principal stream of it, as, by it's course and communication with the waters of the Pacific ocean, whether the Columbia, Oregan, Colorado or any other river may offer the most direct & practicable water communication across this continent for the purposes of commerce.

2. Meriwether Lewis (1774–1809), a Virginian of considerable intellectual accomplishments and an army officer, served as Jefferson's personal secretary from early in the new administration and lived in the White House with the president. As negotiations proceeded early in 1803 for what by April 30 became the Louisiana Purchase, Jefferson sent Lewis to Philadelphia to confer with leading scientists, including Benjamin Rush and Benjamin Barton Smith, in preparation for his responsibilities in leading the Corps of Discovery.

Beginning at the mouth of the Missouri, you will take observations of latitude & longitude, at all remarkeable points on the river, & especially at the mouths of rivers, at rapids, at islands, & other places & objects distinguished by such natural marks & characters of a durable kind, as that they may with certainty be recognised hereafter. The courses of the river between these points of observation may be supplied by the compass the log-line & by time, corrected by the observations themselves. The variations of the compass too, in different places, should be noticed.

The interesting points of the portage between the heads of the Missouri, & of the water offering the best communication with the Pacific ocean, should also be fixed by observation, & the course of that water to the ocean, in the same manner as that of the Missouri.

Your observations are to be taken with great pains & accuracy, to be entered distinctly & intelligibly for others as well as yourself, to comprehend all the elements necessary, with the aid of the usual tables, to fix the latitude and longitude of the places at which they were taken, and are to be rendered to the war-office, for the purpose of having the calculations made concurrently by proper persons within the U.S. Several copies of these as well as of your other notes should be made at leisure times, & put into the care of the most trust-worthy of your attendants, to guard, by multiplying them, against the accidental losses to which they will be exposed. A further guard would be that one of these copies be on the paper of the birch, as less liable to injury from damp than common paper.

The commerce which may be carried on with the people inhabiting the line you will pursue, renders a knolege of those people important. You will therefore endeavor to make yourself acquainted, as far as a diligent pursuit of your journey shall admit, with the names of the nations & their numbers;

the extent & limits of their possessions;

their relations with other tribes of nations;

their language, traditions, monuments;

their ordinary occupations in agriculture, fishing, hunting, war, arts, & the implements for these;

their food, clothing, & domestic accomodations;

the diseases prevalent among them, & the remedies they use;

moral & physical circumstances which distinguish them from the tribes we know;

peculiarities in their laws, customs & dispositions;

and articles of commerce they may need or furnish; & to what extent.

And, considering the interest which every nation has in extending & strengthening the authority of reason & justice among the people around them, it will be useful to acquire what knolege you can of the state of morality, religion, & information among them; as it may better enable those who may endeavor to civilize & instruct them, to adapt their measures to the existing notions & practices of those on whom they are to operate.

Other objects worthy of notice will be

the soil & face of the country, it's growth & vegetable productions, especially those not of the U.S.

the animals of the country generally, & especially those not known in the U.S.

the remains or accounts of any which may be deemed rare or extinct;

the mineral productions of every kind; but more particularly metals, limestone, pit coal, & saltpetre; salines & mineral waters, noting the temperature of the last, & such circumstances as may indicate their character;

volcanic appearances;

climate, as characterised by the thermometer, by the proportion of rainy, cloudy, & clear days, by lightning, hail, snow, ice, by the access & recess of frost, by the winds prevailing at different seasons, the dates at which particular plants put forth or lose their flower, or leaf, times of appearance of particular birds, reptiles or insects.

Altho' your route will be along the channel of the Missouri, yet you will endeavor to inform yourself, by enquiry, of the character & extent of the country watered by it's branches, & especially on it's Southern side. The North river or Rio Bravo[3] which runs into the gulph of Mexico, and the North river, or Rio colorado which runs into the gulph of California, are understood to be the principal streams heading opposite to the waters of the Missouri, and running Southwardly. Whether the dividing grounds between the Missouri & them are mountains or flat lands, what are their distance from the Missouri, the character of the intermediate country, & the people inhabiting it, are worthy of particular enquiry. The Northern waters of the Missouri are less to be enquired after, becaue they have been ascertained to a considerable degree, & are still in a course of ascertainment by English traders, and travellers. But if you can learn any thing certain of the most Northern source of the Missisipi, & of it's position relatively to the lake of the woods, it will be interesting to us.

Some account too of the path of the Canadian traders from the Missisipi, at the mouth of the Ouisconsing[4] to where it strikes the Missouri, & of the soil and rivers in it's course, is desireable.

In all your intercourse with the natives, treat them in the most friendly & conciliatory manner which their own conduct will admit; allay all jealousies as to the object of your journey, satisfy them of it's innocence, make them acquainted with the position, extent, character, peaceable & commercial dispositions of the U.S.[,] of our wish to be neighborly, friendly & useful to them, & of our dispositions to a commercial intercourse with them; confer with them on the points most convenient as mutual emporiums, and the articles of most desireable interchange for them & us. If a few of their influential chiefs, within practicable distance, wish to visit us, arrange such a visit with them, and furnish them with authority to call on our officers, on their entering the U.S. to have them conveyed to this place at the public expence. If any of them should wish to have some of their young people brought up with us, & taught such arts as may be useful to them, we will receive, instruct & take care of them. Such a mission, whether of influential chiefs or of young people, would give some security to your own party. Carry with you some matter of the kinepox;[5] inform those of them with whom you may be, of it's efficacy as a preservative from the smallpox; & instruct & encourage them in the use of it. This may be especially done wherever you winter.

As it is impossible for us to foresee in what manner you will be recieved by those people, whether with hospitality or hostility, so is it impossible to prescribe the exact degree of perseverance with which you are to pursue your journey. We value too much the lives of citizens to offer them to probable destruction. Your numbers will be sufficient to secure you against the unauthorised opposition of individuals or of small parties: but if a superior force, authorised, or not authorised, by a nation, should be arrayed against your fur-

3. Rio Grande.
4. Wisconsin.
5. Or cowpox, a relatively mild disease customarily used for inoculating against smallpox at this time.

ther passage, and inflexibly determined to arrest it, you must decline it's farther pursuit, and return. In the loss of yourselves, we should lose also the information you will have acquired. By returning safely with that, you may enable us to renew the essay with better calculated means. To your own discretion therefore must be left the degree of danger you may risk, and the point at which you should decline, only saying we wish you to err on the side of your safety, and to bring back your party safe even if it be with less information.

As far up the Missouri as the white settlements extend, an intercourse will probably be found to exist between them & the Spanish posts of St. Louis opposite Cahokia, or Ste. Genevieve opposite Kaskaskia. From still further up the river, the traders may furnish a conveyance for letters. Beyond that, you may perhaps be able to engage Indians to bring letters for the government to Cahokia or Kaskaskia, on promising that they shall there recieve such special compensation as you shall have stipulated with them. Avail yourself of these means to communicate to us, at seasonable intervals, a copy of your journal, notes & observations, of every kind, putting into cypher whatever might do injury if betrayed.

Should you reach the Pacific ocean inform yourself of the circumstances which may decide whether the furs of those parts may not be collected as advantageously at the head of the Missouri (convenient as is supposed to the waters of the Colorado & Oregan or Columbia) as at Nootka sound, or any other point of that coast; and that trade be consequently conducted through the Missouri & U.S. more beneficially than by the circumnavigation now practised.

On your arrival on that coast endeavor to learn if there be any port within your reach frequented by the sea-vessels of any nation, & to send two of your trusty people back by sea, in such way as shall appear practicable, with a copy of your notes: and should you be of opinion that the return of your party by the way they went will be eminently dangerous, then ship the whole, & return by sea, by the way either of cape Horn, or the cape of good Hope, as you shall be able. As you will be without money, clothes or provisions, you must endeavor to use the credit of the U.S. to obtain them, for which purpose open letters of credit shall be furnished you, authorising you to draw upon the Executive of the U.S. or any of it's officers, in any part of the world, on which draughts can be disposed of, & to apply with our recommendations to the Consuls, agents, merchants, or citizens of any nation with which we have intercourse, assuring them, in our name, that any aids they may furnish you, shall be honorably repaid, and on demand. Our consuls Thomas Hewes at Batavia in Java, Wm. Buchanan in the Isles of France & Bourbon & John Elmslie at the Cape of good Hope will be able to supply your necessities by draughts on us.

Should you find it safe to return by the way you go, after sending two of your party round by sea, or with your whole party, if no conveyance by sea can be found, do so; making such observations on your return, as may serve to supply, correct or confirm those made on your outward journey.

On re-entering the U.S. and reaching a place of safety, discharge any of your attendants who may desire & deserve it, procuring for them immediate paiment of all arrears of pay & cloathing which may have incurred since their departure, and assure them that they shall be recommended to the liberality of the legislature for the grant of a souldier's portion of land each, as proposed in my message to Congress: & repair yourself with your papers to the seat of government.

To provide, on the accident of your death, against anarchy, dispersion, &
the consequent danger to your party, and total failure of the enterprize, you
are hereby authorised, by any instrument signed & written in your own hand,
to name the person among them who shall succeed to the command on your
decease, and by like instruments to change the nomination from time to time
as further experience of the characters accompanying you shall point out
superior fitness: and all the powers and authorities given to yourself are, in
the event of your death, transferred to, & vested in the successor so named,
with further power to him, and his successors in like manner to name each
his successor, who, on the death of his predecessor, shall be invested with all
the powers & authorities given to yourself.

Given under my hand at the city of Washington this 20th day of June 1803.

TH: J. Pr. U.S. of A.

To General Horatio Gates[6]

DEAR GENERAL,—   WASHINGTON, July 11, '03.

I accept with pleasure, and with pleasure reciprocate your congratulations on the acquisition of Louisiana: for it is a subject of mutual congratulations as it interests every man of the nation. The territory acquired, as
it includes all the waters of the Missouri & Mississippi, has more than
doubled the area of the U. S. and the new part is not inferior to the old in
soil, climate, productions & important communications. If our legislature
dispose of it with the wisdom we have a right to expect, they may make it
the means of tempting all our Indians on the East side of the Mississippi to
remove to the West, and of condensing instead of scattering our population.
I find our opposition is very willing to pluck feathers from Monroe,
although not fond of sticking them into Livingston's coat.[7] The truth is both
have a just portion of merit and were it necessary or proper it could be
shewn that each has rendered peculiar service, & of important value. These
grumblers too are very uneasy lest the administration should share some
little credit for the acquisition, the whole of which they ascribe to the accident of war. They would be cruelly mortified could they see our files from
April 1801, the first organization of the administration, but more especially
from April 1802. They would see that tho' we could not say when war would
arise, yet we said with energy what would take place when it should arise.
We did not, by our intrigues, produce the war: but we availed ourselves of
it when it happened. The other party saw the case now existing on which
our representations were predicted, and the wisdom of timely sacrifice. But
when these people make the war give us everything, they authorize us to ask
what the war gave us in their day? They had a war. What did they make it
bring us? Instead of making our neutrality the grounds of gain to their country, they were for plunging into the war. And if they were now in place, they
would not be at war against the Alliests & disorganizers of France. They
were for making their country an appendage to England. We are friendly,
cordially and conscientiously friendly to England, but we are not hostile
to France. We will be rigorously just and sincerely friendly to both. I do

---

6. Horatio Gates (1727–1806), British-born American general, was a political ally of Jefferson's.
7. James Monroe was sent to France by Jefferson to negotiate for the purchase of West Florida and
New Orleans; along with Robert Livingston (1746–1813), Jefferson's minister to Napoleonic
France, Monroe secured the cession of the whole of Louisiana.

not believe we shall have as much to swallow from them as our predecessors had.

With respect to the territory acquired, I do not think it will be a separate government as you imagine. I presume the island of N. Orleans and the settled country on the opposite bank, will be annexed to the Mississippi territory. We shall certainly endeavor to introduce the American laws there & that cannot be done but by amalgamating the people with such a body of Americans as may take the lead in legislation & government. Of course they will be under the Governor of Mississippi. The rest of the territory will probably be locked up from American settlement, and under the self-government of the native occupants.

You know that every sentence from me is put on the rack by our opponents, to be tortured into something they can make use of. No caution therefore I am sure is necessary against letting my letter go out of your hands. I am always happy to hear from you, and to know that you preserve your health. Present me respectfully to Mrs. Gates, and accept yourself my affectionate salutations and assurances of great respect & esteem.

To John Tyler[8]

DEAR SIR,—   WASHINGTON, June 28, 1804.

Your favor of the 10th instant has been duly received. Amidst the direct falsehoods, the misrepresentations of truth, the calumnies and the insults resorted to by a faction to mislead the public mind, and to overwhelm those entrusted with its interests, our support is to be found in the approving voice of our conscience and country, in the testimony of our fellow citizens, that their confidence is not shaken by these artifices. When to the plaudits of the honest multitude, the sober approbation of the sage in his closet is added, it becomes a gratification of an higher order. It is the sanction of wisdom superadded to the voice of affection. The terms, therefore, in which you are so good as to express your satisfaction with the course of the present administration cannot but give me great pleasure. I may err in my measures, but never shall deflect from the intention to fortify the public liberty by every possible means, and to put it out of the power of the few to riot on the labors of the many. No experiment can be more interesting than that we are now trying, and which we trust will end in establishing the fact, that man may be governed by reason and truth. Our first object should therefore be, to leave open to him all the avenues to truth. The most effectual hitherto found, is the freedom of the press. It is therefore, the first shut up by those who fear the investigation of their actions. The firmness with which the people have withstood the late abuses of the press, the discernment they have manifested between truth and falsehood, show that they may safely be trusted to hear everything true and false, and to form a correct judgment between them. As little is it necessary to impose on their senses, or dazzle their minds by pomp, splendor, or forms. Instead of this artificial, how much surer is that real respect, which results from the use of their reason, and the habit of bringing everything to the test of common sense.

I hold it, therefore, certain, that to open the doors of truth, and to fortify the habit of testing everything by reason, are the most effectual manacles

8. John Tyler (1747–1813), Jefferson's fellow student at William and Mary and a vocal opponent of British authority in the Virginia legislature during the Revolution, had been appointed a state judge in 1788.

we can rivet on the hands of our successors to prevent their manacling the people with their own consent. The panic into which they were artfully thrown in 1798, the frenzy which was excited in them by their enemies against their apparent readiness to abandon all the principles established for their own protection, seemed for awhile to countenance the opinions of those who say they cannot be trusted with their own government. But I never doubted their rallying; and they did rally much sooner than I expected. On the whole, that experiment on their credulity has confirmed my confidence in their ultimate good sense and virtue.

I lament to learn that a like misfortune has enabled you to estimate the afflictions of a father on the loss of a beloved child.[9] However terrible the possibility of such another accident, it is still a blessing for you of inestimable value that you would not even then descend childless to the grave. Three sons, and hopeful ones too, are a rich treasure. I rejoice when I hear of young men of virtue and talents, worthy to receive, and likely to preserve the splendid inheritance of self-government, which we have acquired and shaped for them.

The complement of midshipmen for the Tripoline squadron, is full; and I hope the frigates have left the Capes by this time. I have, however, this day, signed warrants of midshipmen for the two young gentlemen you recommended. These will be forwarded by the Secretary of the Navy. He tells me that their first services will be to be performed on board the gun boats.

Accept my friendly salutations, and assurances of great esteem and respect.

To the Osages[1]

July 12, 1804

My Children. White hairs, Chiefs & Warriors of the Osage Nation.

I recieve you with great pleasure at the seat of the govmt. of the 17. United nations, and tender you a sincere welcome. I thank the Great Spirit who has inspired you with a desire to visit your new friends, & who has conducted you in safety to take us this day by the hand. The journey you have come is long, the weather has been warm & wet, & I fear you have suffered on the road, notwithstanding our endeavors for your accomodation. But you have come through a land of friends, all of whom I hope have looked on you kindly, & been ready to give you every aid and comfort by the way.

You are as yet fatigued with your journey. But you are under the roof of your fathers and best friends, who will spare nothing for your refreshment and comfort. Repose yourselves therefore, and recruit your health and strength, and when you are rested we will open the bottoms of our hearts more fully to one another. In the mean time we will be considering how we may best secure everlasting peace, friendship & commerce between the Osage nation, and the 17. United nations in whose name I speak to you, and take you by the hand.

TH: JEFFERSON

9. Jefferson's daughter Mary had died in April, Tyler's daughter Ann in 1803.
1. A. delegation of Osages from Missouri had arrived on July 11, 1804. In a speech on which Jefferson took hurried notes, their leader, Cheveux Blancs (White Hairs), said he had come to Washington on the advice of Meriwether Lewis. In a letter written the following day to Navy Secretary Robert Smith, the president wrote of this delegation, "They are the finest men we have ever seen" (*LLCE* 1:199).

To the Osages

July 16, 1804

My children. White-hairs, Chiefs & Warriors of the Osage nation.

I repeat to you assurances of the satisfaction it has given me to recieve you here. Besides the labour of such a journey, the confidence you have shown in the honor & friendship of my countrymen is peculiarly gratifying and I hope you have seen that your confidence was justly placed, that you have found yourselves, since you crossed the Missisipi, among brothers & friends, with whom you were as safe as at home.

My children. I sincerely weep with you over the graves of your chiefs & friends, who fell by the hands of their enemies lately descending the Osage river.[2] Had they been prisoners, & living, we would have recovered them: but no voice can awake the dead; no power undo what is done. On this side the Missisipi where our government has been long established, and our authority organised our friends visiting us are safe. We hope it will not be long before our voice will be heard and our arm respected, by those who meditate to injure our friends, on the other side of that river. In the mean time Governor Harrison will be directed to take proper measures to enquire into the circumstances of the transaction, to report them to us for consideration, and for the further measures they may require.

My children. By late arrangements with France & Spain, we now take their place as your neighbors, friends and fathers: and we hope you will have no cause to regret the change. It is so long since our forefathers came from beyond the great water, that we have lost the memory of it, and seem to have grown out of this land, as you have done. Never more will you have occasion to change your fathers. We are all now of one family, born in the same land, & bound to live as brothers; & the strangers from beyond the great water are gone from among us. The great Spirit has given you strength, and has given us strength; not that we might hurt one another, but to do each other all the good in our power. Our dwellings indeed are very far apart; but not too far to carry on commerce & useful intercourse. You have furs and peltries which we want, and we have clothes and other useful things which you want. Let us employ ourselves then in mutually accomodating each other. To begin this on our part it was necessary to know what nations inhabited the great country called Louisiana, which embraces all the waters of the Missisipi and Missouri, what number of peltries they could furnish, what quantities & kinds of merchandize they would require, where would be the deposits most convenient for them, and to make an exact map of all those waters. For this purpose I sent a beloved man, Capt. Lewis, one of my own household to learn something of the people with whom we are now united, to let you know we were your friends, to invite you to come and see us, and to tell us how we can be useful to you. I thank you for the readiness with which you have listened to his voice, and for the favor you shewed him in his passage up the Missouri. I hope your countrymen will favor and protect him as far as they extend. On his return we shall hear what he has seen & learnt, & proceed to establish trading houses where our red brethren shall think best, & to exchange commodities with them on terms with which they will be satisfied.

With the same views I had prepared another party to go up the Red river to it's source, thence to the source of the Arkansa, & down it to it's

---

2. Jefferson refers to a recent skirmish between the Osage and the Sac.

mouth.[3] But I will now give orders that they shall only go a small distance up the red river this season, and return to tell us what they have seen, and that they shall not set out for the head of that river till the ensuing spring, when you will be at home, and will I hope guide and guard them in their journey. I also propose the next year to send another small party up the river of the Kansas to it's source, thence to the head of the river of the Panis, and down to it's mouth; and others up the rivers on the North side of the Missouri. For guides along these rivers we must make arrangements with the nations inhabiting them.

My children. I was sorry to learn that a schism had taken place in your nation, and that a part of your people had withdrawn with the Great-track, to the Arkansa river. We will send an Agent to them and will use our best offices to prevail on them to return, and to live in union with you. We wish to make them also our friends, and to make that friendship, and the weight it may give us with them, useful to you and them.

We propose, my children, immediately to establish an Agent to reside with you, who will speak to you our words, and convey yours to us: who will be the guardian of our peace and friendship, convey truths from the one to the other, dissipate all falsehoods which might tend to alienate and divide us, and maintain a good understanding & friendship between us. As the distance is too great for you to come often and tell us your wants, you will tell them to him on the spot, and he will convey them to us in writing, so that we shall be sure that they come from you. Through the intervention of such an Agent we shall hope that our friendship will forever be preserved. No wrong will ever be done you by our nation, and we trust that yours will do none to us: and should ungovernable individuals commit unauthorised outrage on either side, let them be duly punished; or if they escape, let us make to each other the best satisfaction the case admits, and not let our peace be broken by bad men. For all people have some bad men among them whom no laws can restrain.

As you have taken so long a journey to see your fathers, we wish you not to return till you shall have visited our country & towns towards the sea coast. This will be new and satisfactory to you, and it will give you the same knowledge of the country on this side the Missisipi, which we are endeavoring to acquire of that on the other side, by sending trusty persons to explore them. We propose to do in your country only what we are desirous you should do in ours. We will provide accomodations for your journey, for your comfort while engaged in it, and for your return in safety to your own country, carrying with you those proofs of esteem with which we distinguish our friends, and shall particularly distinguish you. On your return tell your people that I take them all by the hand; that I become their father hereafter, that they shall know our nation only as friends and benefactors; that we have no views upon them but to carry on a commerce useful to them and us; to keep them in peace with their neighbors, that their children may multiply, may grow up & live to a good old age, and their women no longer fear the tomahawk of any enemy.

My children. These are my words. Carry them to your nation. Keep them in your memories, and our friendship in your hearts. And may the Great Spirit look down upon us, & cover us with the mantle of his love.

TH: JEFFERSON

3. Jefferson refers to the expedition under William Dunbar of Natchez in the fall of 1804, covering a small part of the Red River Valley. It originally was intended to be more ambitious.

To Constantin-François de Chasseboeuf,
Comte de Volney[4]

DEAR SIR,   Washington, February 18, 1805.
Your letter of November the 26th came to hand May the 14th; the books some time after, which were all distributed according to direction. The copy for the East Indies went immediately by a safe conveyance. The letter of April the 28th, and the copy of your work accompanying that, did not come to hand till August. That copy was deposited in the Congressional library. It was not till my return here from my autumnal visit to Monticello, that I had an opportunity of reading your work.[5] I have read it, and with great satisfaction. Of the first part I am less a judge than most people, having never travelled westward of Staunton, so as to know any thing of the face of the country; nor much indulged myself in geological inquiries, from a belief that the skin-deep scratches which we can make or find on the surface of the earth, do not repay our time with as certain and useful deductions, as our pursuits in some other branches. The subject of our winds is more familiar to me. On that, the views you have taken are always great, supported in their outlines by your facts; and though more extensive observations, and longer continued, may produce some anomalies, yet they will probably take their place in this first great canvass which you have sketched. In no case, perhaps, does habit attach our choice or judgment more than in climate. The Canadian glows with delight in his sleigh and snow, the very idea of which gives me the shivers. The comparison of climate between Europe and North America, taking together its corresponding parts, hangs chiefly on three great points. 1. The changes between heat and cold in America, are greater and more frequent, and the extremes comprehend a greater scale on the thermometer in America than in Europe. Habit, however, prevents these from affecting us more than the smaller changes of Europe affect the European. But he is greatly affected by ours. 2. Our sky is always clear; that of Europe always cloudy. Hence a greater accumulation of heat here than there, in the same parallel. 3. The changes between wet and dry are much more frequent and sudden in Europe than in America. Though we have double the rain, it falls in half the time. Taking all these together, I prefer much the climate of the United States to that of Europe. I think it a more cheerful one. It is our cloudless sky which has eradicated from our constitutions all disposition to hang ourselves, which we might otherwise have inherited from our English ancestors. During a residence of between six and seven years in Paris, I never, but once, saw the sun shine through a whole day, without being obscured by a cloud in any part of it: and I never saw the moment, in which, viewing the sky through its whole hemisphere, I could say there was not the smallest speck of a cloud in it. I arrived at Monticello, on my return from France, in January, and during only two months' stay there, I observed to my daughters, who had been with me to France, that twenty odd times within that term, there was not a speck of a cloud in the whole hemisphere. Still I do not wonder that an European should prefer his grey to our azure sky. Habit decides our taste in this, as in most other cases.

4. Constantin-François de Chasseboeuf, comte de Volney (1757–1820), French philosopher and writer. His *Les Ruines, ou méditations sur les révolutions des empires* (1791) was especially famous.
5. Jefferson refers here to Volney's *Tableau du climat et du sol des les Etats-Unis* (1803), based on his experience in the United States (1795–98), which was translated in 1804 by American novelist Charles Brockden Brown.

The account you give of the yellow fever, is entirely agreeable to what we then knew of it. Further experience has developed more and more its peculiar character. Facts appear to have established that it is originated here by a local atmosphere, which is never generated but in the lower, closer, and dirtier parts of our large cities, in the neighborhood of the water; and that, to catch the disease, you must enter the local atmosphere. Persons having taken the disease in the infected quarter, and going into the country, are nursed and buried by their friends, without an example of communicating it. A vessel going from the infected quarter, and carrying its atmosphere in its hold into another State, has given the disease to every person who there entered her. These have died in the arms of their families without a single communication of the disease. It is certainly, therefore, an epidemic, not a contagious disease; and calls on the chemists for some mode of purifying the vessel by a decomposition of its atmosphere, if ventilation be found insufficient. In the long scale of bilious fevers, graduated by many shades, this is probably the last and most mortal term. It seizes the native of the place equally with strangers. It has not been long known in any part of the United States. The shade next above it, called the stranger's fever, has been coeval with the settlement of the larger cities in the southern parts, to wit, Norfolk, Charleston, New Orleans. Strangers going to these places in the months of July, August or September, find this fever as mortal as the genuine yellow fever. But it rarely attacks those who have resided in them some time. Since we have known that kind of yellow fever which is no respecter of persons, its name has been extended to the stranger's fever, and every species of bilious fever which produces a black vomit, that is to say, a discharge of very dark bile. Hence we hear of yellow fever on the Alleganey mountains, in Kentucky, &c. This is a matter of definition only: but it leads into error those who do not know how loosely and how interestedly some physicians think and speak. So far as we have yet seen, I think we are correct in saying, that the yellow fever which seizes on all indiscrimately, is an ultimate degree of bilious fever never known in the United States till lately, nor farther south, as yet, than Alexandria, and that what they have recently called the yellow fever in New Orleans, Charleston and Norfolk, is what has always been known in those places as confined chiefly to strangers, and nearly as mortal *to them*, as the other is to *all* its subjects. But both grades are local: the stranger's fever less so, as it sometimes extends a little into the neighborhood; but the yellow fever rigorously so, confined within narrow and well defined limits, and not communicable out of those limits. Such a constitution of atmosphere being requisite to originate this disease as is generated only in low, close, and ill-cleansed parts of a town, I have supposed it practicable to prevent its generation by building our cities on a more open plan. Take, for instance, the chequer board for a plan. Let the black squares only be building squares, and the white ones be left open, in turf and trees. Every square of houses will be surrounded by four open squares, and every house will front an open square. The atmosphere of such a town would be like that of the country, insusceptible of the miasmata which produce yellow fever. I have accordingly proposed that the enlargements of the city of New Orleans, which must immediately take place, shall be on this plan. But it is only in case of enlargements to be made, or of cities to be built, that his means of prevention can be employed.

The *genus irritabile vatum*[6] could not let the author of the Ruins publish a new work, without seeking in it the means of discrediting that puzzling

---

6. The irritable genus of poets (or writers) (Latin).

composition. Some one of those holy calumniators has selected from your new work every scrap of a sentence, which, detached from its context, could displease an American reader. A cento[7] has been made of these, which has run through a particular description of newspapers, and excited a disapprobation even in friendly minds, which nothing but the reading of the book will cure. But time and truth will at length correct error.

Our countrymen are so much occupied in the busy scenes of life, that they have little time to write or invent. A good invention here, therefore, is such a rarity as it is lawful to offer to the acceptance of a friend. A Mr. Hawkins of Frankford, near Philadelphia, has invented a machine which he calls a polygraph, and which carries two, three, or four pens. That of two pens, with which I am now writing, is best; and is so perfect that I have laid aside the copying-press, for a twelve month past, and write always with the polygraph. I have directed one to be made, of which I ask your acceptance. By what conveyance I shall send it while Havre is blockaded, I do not yet know. I think you will be pleased with it, and will use it habitually as I do; because it requires only that degree of mechanical attention which I know you to possess. I am glad to hear that M. Cabanis is engaged in writing on the reformation of medicine. It needs the hand of a reformer, and cannot be in better hands than his. Will you permit my respects to him and the Abbé de la Roche to find a place here.

A word now on our political state. The two parties which prevailed with so much violence when you were here, are almost wholly melted into one. At the late Presidential election I have received one hundred and sixty-two votes against fourteen only. Connecticut is still federal by a small majority; and Delaware on a poise, as she has been since 1775, and will be till Anglomany with her yields to Americanism. Connecticut will be with us in a a short time. Though the people in mass have joined us; their leaders had committed themselves too far to retract. Pride keeps them hostile; they brood over their angry passions, and give them vent in the newspapers which they maintain. They still make as much noise as if they were the whole nation. Unfortunately, these being the mercantile papers, published chiefly in the sea ports, are the only ones which find their way to Europe, and make very false impressions there. I am happy to hear that the late derangement of your health is going off, and that you are reestablished. I sincerely pray for the continuance of that blessing, and with my affectionate salutations, tender you assurances of great respect and attachment.

TH: JEFFERSON.

P. S. The sheets which you receive are those of the copying pen of the polygraph, not of the one with which I have written.

To the Osage and Other Indians

January 4, 1806

My friends & children, Chiefs of the Osages, Missouris, Kanzas, Ottos, Panis, Ayowas, & Sioux.

I take you by the hand of friendship and give you a hearty welcome to the seat of the govmt. of the U.S. The journey which you have taken to visit your fathers on this side of our island is a long one, and your having undertaken

---

7. Patchwork (Latin).

it is a proof that you desired to become acquainted with us. I thank the great spirit that he has protected you through the journey and brought you safely to the residence of your friends, and I hope he will have you constantly in his safekeeping and restore you in good health to your nations and families.

My friends & children. We are descended from the old nations which live beyond the great water: but we & our forefathers have been so long here that we seem like you to have grown out of this land: we consider ourselves no longer as of the old nations beyond the great water, but as united in one family with our red brethren here. The French, the English, the Spaniards, have now agreed with us to retire from all the country which you & we hold between Canada & Mexico, and never more to return to it. And remember the words I now speak to you my children, they are never to return again. We are become as numerous as the leaves of the trees, and, tho' we do not boast, we do not fear any nation. We are now your fathers; and you shall not lose by the change. As soon as Spain had agreed to withdraw from all the waters of the Missouri & Missisipi, I felt the desire of becoming acquainted with all my red children beyond the Missipi, and of uniting them with us, as we have done those on this side of that river in the bonds of peace & friendship. I wished to learn what we could do to benefit them by furnishing them the necessaries they want in exchange for their furs & peltries. I therefore sent our beloved man Capt. Lewis one of my own family, to go up the Missouri river, to get acquainted with all the Indian nations in it's neighborhood, to take them by the hand, deliver my talks to them, and to inform us in what way we could be useful to them. Some of you who are here have seen him & heard his words. You have taken him by the hand, and been friendly to him. My children I thank you for the services you rendered him, and for your attention to his words. When he returns he will tell us where we should establish factories[8] to be convenient to you all, and what we must send to them. In establishing a trade with you we desire to make no profit. We shall ask from you only what every thing costs us, and give you for your furs & pelts whatever we can get for them again. Be assured you shall find your advantage in this change of your friends. It will take us some time to be in readiness to supply your wants, but in the mean while & till Capt. Lewis returns, the traders who have heretofore furnished you will continue to do so.

My friends & children. I have now an important advice to give you. I have already told you that you are all my children, and I wish you to live in peace & friendship with one another as brethren of the same family ought to do. How much better is it for neighbors to help than to hurt one another, how much happier must it make them. If you will cease to make war on one another, if you will live in friendship with all mankind, you can employ all your time in providing food & clothing for yourselves and your families. Your men will not be destroyed in war and your women & children will lie down to sleep in their cabins without fear of being surprised by their enemies & killed or carried away. Your numbers will be increased, instead of diminishing, and you will live in plenty & in quiet. My children, I have given this advice to all your red brethren on this side of the Missipi, they are following it, they are increasing in their numbers, are learning to clothe & provide for their families as we do, and you see the proofs of it in such of them as you happened to find here. My children, we are strong, we are numerous as the stars in the heavens, & we are all gun-men. Yet we live in peace with all nations; and all nations esteem & honour us because we are peaceable & just. Then let my

8. Trading posts.

red children then be peaceable & just also; take each other by the hand, and hold it fast. If ever bad men among your neighbors should do you wrong, and their nation refuse you justice, apply to the beloved man whom we shall place nearest to you; he will go to the offending nation, & endeavor to obtain right, & preserve peace. If ever bad men among yourselves injure your neighbors, be always ready to do justice. It is always honorable in those who have done wrong to acknolege & make amends for it; and it is the only way in which peace can be maintained among men. Remember then my advice, my children, carry it home to your people, and tell them that from the day that they have become all the same family, from the day that we became father to them all, we wish as a true father should do, that we may all live together as one household, and that before they strike one another, they should come to their father & let him endeavor to make up the quarrel.

My children. You are come from the other side of our great island, from where the sun sets to see your new friends at the sun rising. You have now arrived where the waters are constantly rising & falling every day, but you are still distant from the sea. I very much desire that you should not stop here, but go on and see your brethren as far as the edge of the great water. I am persuaded you have so far seen that every man by the way has recieved you as his brothers, and has been ready to do you all the kindnesses in his power. You will see the same thing quite to the sea shore; and I wish you therefore to go and visit our great cities in that quarter, & to see how many friends & brothers you have here. You will then have travelled a long line from West to East, and if you had time to go from North to South, from Canada to Florida, you would find it as long in that direction, & all the people as sincerely your friends. I wish you, my children to see all you can and to tell your people all you see; because I am sure the more they know of us, the more they will be our hearty friends. I invite you therefore to pay a visit to Baltimore, Philadelphia, New York, & the cities still beyond that if you should be willing to go further. We will provide carriages to convey you, & a person to go with you to see that you want for nothing. By the time you come back, the snows will be melted on the mountains, ice in the rivers broken up and you will be wishing to set out on your return home.

My children, I have long desired to see you. I have now opened my heart to you; let my words sink into your hearts & never be forgotten. If ever lying people or bad spirits should raise up clouds between us: let us come together as friends & explain to each other what is misrepresented or misunderstood. The clouds will fly away like the morning fog and the sun of friendship appear, & shine for ever bright & clear between us.

My children, it may happen that while you are here, occasion may arise to talk about many things which I do not now particularly mention. The Secretary at War will always be ready to talk with you: and you are to consider whatever he says as said by myself. He will also take care of you & see that you are furnished with all comforts here.

TH: JEFFERSON

To Constantin-François de Chasseboeuf, Comte de Volney

DEAR SIR,—   WASHINGTON, Feb. 11, 1806.
Since mine of Feb. 18 of the last year, I have received yours of July 2. I have been constantly looking out for an opportunity of sending your

Polygraph; but the blockade of Havre has cut off that resource, and I have feared to send it to a port from which there would be only land carriage. A safe conveyance now offering to Nantes, & under the particular care of Mr. Skipwith, who is returning to France, he will take care of it from Nantes by land if an easy carriage is found, or if not, then by the canal of Briare. Another year's constant use of a similar one attaches me more and more to it as a most valuable convenience. I send you also a pamphlet[9] published here against the English doctrine which denies to neutrals a trade in war not open to them in peace in which you will find it pulverized by a logic not to be controverted.

   Our last news of Captn Lewis was that he had reached the upper part of the Missouri, & had taken horses to cross the Highlands to the Columbia river. He passed the last winter among the Mandans 1610 miles above the mouth of the river. So far he had delineated it with as great accuracy as will probably be ever applied to it, as his courses & distances by mensuration were corrected by almost daily observations of latitude and longitude. With his map he sent us specimens or information of the following animals not before known to the northern continent of America. 1. The horns of what is perhaps a species of *Ovis Ammon*. 2. A new variety of the deer having a black tail. 3. An antelope. 4. The badger, not before known out of Europe. 5. A new species of marmotte. 6. A white weasel. 7. The magpie. 8. The Prairie hen, said to resemble the Guinea hen (peintade). 9. A prickly lizard. To these are added a considerable collection of minerals, not yet analyzed. He wintered in Lat. 47° 20' and found the maximum of cold 43° below the zero of Fahrenheit. We expect he has reached the Pacific, and is now wintering on the head of the Missouri, and will be here next autumn. Having been disappointed in our view of sending an exploring party up the Red river the last year, they were sent up the Washita, as far as the hot springs, under the direction of Mr. Dunbar. He found the temperature of the springs 150° of Fahrenheit & the water perfectly potable when cooled. We obtain also the geography of that river, so far with perfect accuracy. Our party is just at this time setting out from Natchez to ascend the Red river. These expeditions are so laborious, & hazardous, that men of science, used to the temperature & inactivity of their closet, cannot be induced to undertake them. They are headed therefore by persons qualified expressly to give us the geography of the rivers with perfect accuracy, and of good common knolege and observation in the animal, vegetable & mineral departments. When the route shall be once open and known, scientific men will undertake, & verify & class it's subjects. Our emigration to the western country from these states the last year is estimated at about 100,000. I conjecture that about one-half the number of our increase will emigrate westwardly annually. A newspaper paragraph tells me, with some details, that the society of agriculture of Paris had thought a mould-board of my construction worthy their notice & Mr. Dupont confirms it in a letter, but not specifying anything particular. I send him a model with an advantageous change in the form, in which however the principle is rigorously the same. I mention this to you lest he should have left France for America, and I notice it no otherwise lest there should have been any error in the information. Present my respectful salutations to Doctr. Cabanis & accept them yourself with assurances of my constant friendship & attachment.

9. Perhaps *An Examination of the British Doctrine* (1806), by Jefferson's friend James Madison.

To Joel Barlow[1]

Feb. 24, 06.

I return you the draft of the bill for the establishment of a National Academy & University at the city of Washington, with such alterations as we talked over the last night. They are chiefly verbal. I have often wished we could have a Philosophical society or academy so organized as that while the central academy should be at the seat of government, it's members dispersed over the states, should constitute filiated academies in each state, publish their communications, from which the central academy should select unpublished what should be most choice. In this way all the members wheresoever dispersed might be brought into action, and an useful emulation might arise between the filiated societies. Perhaps the great societies now existing might incorporate themselves in this way with the National one. But time does not allow me to pursue this idea, nor perhaps had we time at all to get it into the present bill. I procured an Agricultural society to be established (voluntarily) on this plan, but it has done nothing. Friendly salutations.

To John Norvell[2]

SIR,— WASHINGTON, June 14, 1807.

Your letter of May 9 has been duly received. The subject it proposes would require time & space for even moderate development. My occupations limit me to a very short notice of them. I think there does not exist a good elementary work on the organization of society into civil government: I mean a work which presents in one full & comprehensive view the system of principles on which such an organization should be founded, according to the rights of nature. For want of a single work of that character, I should recommend Locke on *Government*, Sidney, Priestley's *Essay on the first Principles of Government*, Chipman's *Principles of Government*, & the *Federalist*. Adding, perhaps, Beccaria on crimes & punishments, because of the demonstrative manner in which he has treated that branch of the subject. If your views of political inquiry go further, to the subjects of money & commerce, Smith's *Wealth of Nations* is the best book to be read, unless Say's *Political Economy* can be had, which treats the same subject on the same principles, but in a shorter compass & more lucid manner. But I believe this work has not been translated into our language.

History, in general, only informs us what bad government is. But as we have employed some of the best materials of the British constitution in the construction of our own government, a knolege of British history becomes useful to the American politician. There is, however, no general history of that country which can be recommended. The elegant one of Hume seems

---

1. Connecticut native Joel Barlow (1754–1812) was author of the American epic poem *The Vision of Columbus* (1787) and the radical tract *Advice to the Privileged Orders in the Several States of Europe* (1792–93). In 1806, he would publish *Prospectus for a National Institution, to Be Established in the United States*, calling for founding a national university and a research institute, favorite ideas of Jefferson.
2. John Norvell (1789–1850), seventeen-year-old son of an old Virginia family that moved to the district of Kentucky, wrote to President Jefferson asking for advice on his studies and on how to run a newspaper—as indeed he would do several times in his life, most notably as editor of an anti-Federalist paper in Philadelphia from 1816 to 1832. He later represented Michigan in the U.S. Senate.

intended to disguise & discredit the good principles of the government, and is so plausible & pleasing in it's style & manner, as to instil it's errors & heresies insensibly into the minds of unwary readers. Baxter has performed a good operation on it. He has taken the text of Hume as his ground work, abridging it by the omission of some details of little interest, and wherever he has found him endeavoring to mislead, by either the suppression of a truth or by giving it a false coloring, he has changed the text to what it should be, so that we may properly call it Hume's history republicanised. He has moreover continued the history (but indifferently) from where Hume left it, to the year 1800. The work is not popular in England, because it is republican; and but a few copies have ever reached America. It is a single 4to. volume. Adding to this Ludlow's *Memoirs*, Mrs. M'Cauley's & Belknap's histories, a sufficient view will be presented of the free principles of the English constitution.

To your request of my opinion of the manner in which a newspaper should be conducted, so as to be most useful, I should answer, "by restraining it to true facts & sound principles only." Yet I fear such a paper would find few subscribers. It is a melancholy truth, that a suppression of the press could not more compleatly deprive the nation of it's benefits, than is done by it's abandoned prostitution to falsehood. Nothing can now be believed which is seen in a newspaper. Truth itself becomes suspicious by being put into that polluted vehicle. The real extent of this state of misinformation is known only to those who are in situations to confront facts within their knolege with the lies of the day. I really look with commiseration over the great body of my fellow citizens, who, reading newspapers, live & die in the belief, that they have known something of what has been passing in the world in their time; whereas the accounts they have read in newspapers are just as true a history of any other period of the world as of the present, except that the real names of the day are affixed to their fables. General facts may indeed be collected from them, such as that Europe is now at war, that Bonaparte has been a successful warrior, that he has subjected a great portion of Europe to his will, &c., &c.; but no details can be relied on. I will add, that the man who never looks into a newspaper is better informed than he who reads them; inasmuch as he who knows nothing is nearer to truth than he whose mind is filled with falsehoods & errors. He who reads nothing will still learn the great facts, and the details are all false.

Perhaps an editor might begin a reformation in some such way as this. Divide his paper into 4 chapters, heading the 1st, Truths. 2d, Probabilities. 3d, Possibilities. 4th, Lies. The first chapter would be very short, as it would contain little more than authentic papers, and information from such sources as the editor would be willing to risk his own reputation for their truth. The 2d would contain what, from a mature consideration of all circumstances, his judgment should conclude to be probably true. This, however, should rather contain too little than too much. The 3d & 4th should be professedly for those readers who would rather have lies for their money than the blank paper they would occupy.

Such an editor too, would have to set his face against the demoralising practice of feeding the public mind habitually on slander, & the depravity of taste which this nauseous aliment induces. Defamation is becoming a necessary of life; insomuch, that a dish of tea in the morning or evening cannot be digested without this stimulant. Even those who do not believe these abominations, still read them with complaisance to their auditors, and instead of the abhorrence & indignation which should fill a virtuous mind, betray a secret pleasure in the possibility that some may believe them, tho they do not themselves. It seems to escape them, that it is not he who prints, but he who pays for printing a slander, who is it's real author.

These thoughts on the subjects of your letter are hazarded at your request. Repeated instances of the publication of what has not been intended for the public eye, and the malignity with which political enemies torture every sentence from me into meanings imagined by their own wickedness only, justify my expressing a solicitude, that this hasty communication may in nowise be permitted to find it's way into the public papers. Not fearing these political bull-dogs, I yet avoid putting myself in the way of being baited by them, and do not wish to volunteer away that portion of tranquillity, which a firm execution of my duties will permit me to enjoy.

I tender you my salutations, and best wishes for your success.

To Thomas Jefferson Randolph[3]

MY DEAR JEFFERSON,—   WASHINGTON, November 24, 1808.
I have just received the enclosed letter under cover from Mr. Bankhead which I presume is from Anne, and will inform you she is well. Mr. Bankhead has consented to go & pursue his studies at Monticello, and live with us till his pursuits or circumstances may require a separate establishment. Your situation, thrown at such a distance from us, & alone, cannot but give us all great anxieties for you. As much has been secured for you, by your particular position and the acquaintance to which you have been recommended, as could be done towards shielding you from the dangers which surround you. But thrown on a wide world, among entire strangers, without a friend or guardian to advise, so young too and with so little experience of mankind, your dangers are great, & still your safety must rest on yourself. A determination never to do what is wrong, prudence and good humor, will go far towards securing to you the estimation of the world. When I recollect that at 14 years of age, the whole care & direction of myself was thrown on myself entirely, without a relation or friend qualified to advise or guide me, and recollect the various sorts of bad company with which I associated from time to time, I am astonished I did not turn off with some of them, & become as worthless to society as they were. I had the good fortune to become acquainted very early with some characters of very high standing, and to feel the incessant wish that I could ever become what they were. Under temptations & difficulties, I would ask myself what would Dr. Small, Mr. Wythe, Peyton Randolph do in this situation? What course in it will insure me their approbation? I am certain that this mode of deciding on my conduct, tended more to its correctness than any reasoning powers I possessed. Knowing the even & dignified line they pursued, I could never doubt for a moment which of two courses would be in character for them. Whereas, seeking the same object through a process of moral reasoning, & with the jaundiced eye of youth, I should often have erred. From the circumstances of my position, I was often thrown into the society of horse racers, card players, fox hunters, scientific & professional men, and of dignified men; and many a time have I asked myself, in the enthusiastic moment of the death of a fox, the victory of

3. Thomas Jefferson Randolph (1792–1875), Jefferson's oldest grandson, was at school in Philadelphia at this time. His elder sister, Anne (1791–1826), to whom Jefferson refers in the opening of his letter, had married Charles Lewis Bankhead two months earlier.

a favorite horse, the issue of a question eloquently argued at the bar, or in the great council of the nation, well, which of these kinds of reputation should I prefer? That of a horse jockey? a fox hunter? an orator? or the honest advocate of my country's rights? Be assured, my dear Jefferson, that these little returns into ourselves, this self-catechising habit, is not trifling nor useless, but leads to the prudent selection & steady pursuit of what is right.

I have mentioned good humor as one of the preservatives of our peace & tranquillity. It is among the most effectual, and its effect is so well imitated and aided, artificially, by politeness, that this also becomes an acquisition of first rate value. In truth, politeness is artificial good humor, it covers the natural want of it, & ends by rendering habitual a substitute nearly equivalent to the real virtue. It is the practice of sacrificing to those whom we meet in society, all the little conveniences & preferences which will gratify them, & deprive us of nothing worth a moment's consideration; it is the giving a pleasing & flattering turn to our expressions, which will conciliate others, and make them pleased with us as well as themselves. How cheap a price for the good will of another! When this is in return for a rude thing said by another, it brings him to his senses, it mortifies & corrects him in the most salutary way, and places him at the feet of your good nature, in the eyes of the company. But in stating prudential rules for our government in society, I must not omit the important one of never entering into dispute or argument with another. I never saw an instance of one of two disputants convincing the other by argument. I have seen many, on their getting warm, becoming rude, & shooting one another. Conviction is the effect of our own dispassionate reasoning, either in solitude, or weighing within ourselves, dispassionately, what we hear from others, standing uncommitted in argument ourselves. It was one of the rules which, above all others, made Doctor Franklin the most amiable of men in society, "never to contradict anybody." If he was urged to announce an opinion, he did it rather by asking questions, as if for information, or by suggesting doubts. When I hear another express an opinion which is not mine, I say to myself, he has a right to his opinion, as I to mine; why should I question it? His error does me no injury, and shall I become a Don Quixote, to bring all men by force of argument to one opinion? If a fact be misstated, it is probable he is gratified by a belief of it, & I have no right to deprive him of the gratification. If he wants information, he will ask it, & then I will give it in measured terms; but if he still believes his own story, & shows a desire to dispute the fact with me, I hear him & say nothing. It is his affair, not mine, if he prefers error. There are two classes of disputants most frequently to be met with among us. The first is of young students, just entered the threshold of science, with a first view of its outlines, not yet filled up with the details & modifications which a further progress would bring to their knoledge. The other consists of the ill-tempered & rude men in society, who have taken up a passion for politics. (Good humor & politeness never introduce into mixed society, a question on which they foresee there will be a difference of opinion.) From both of those classes of disputants, my dear Jefferson, keep aloof, as you would from the infected subjects of yellow fever or pestilence. Consider yourself, when with them, as among the patients of Bedlam, needing medical more than moral counsel. Be a listener only, keep within yourself, and endeavor to establish with yourself the habit of silence, especially on politics. In the fevered state of our country, no good can ever result from any attempt to set one of these fiery zealots to rights, either in fact or principle. They are determined as to the facts they will believe, and the opinions on which they will act. Get by them, therefore, as you would by an angry bull; it is not for a man of sense to dispute the road with such an animal. You will be more exposed than others to have these animals shaking their horns at you, because of the relation in which you stand with me. Full of political venom, and willing to see me & to hate me as a chief in the antagonist party, your presence will be to them what the vomit grass is to the sick dog, a nostrum for producing ejaculation. Look upon them exactly with that eye, and pity them as objects to whom you can administer only occasional ease. My character is not within their power. It is in the hands of my fellow citizens at large, and will be consigned to honor or infamy by the verdict of the republican mass of our country, according to what themselves will have seen, not what their enemies and mine shall have said. Never, therefore, consider these puppies in politics as requiring any notice from you, & always show that you are not afraid to leave my character to the umpirage of public opinion. Look steadily to the pursuits which have carried you to Philadelphia, be very select in the society you attach yourself to, avoid taverns, drinkers, smokers, idlers, & dissipated persons generally; for it is with such that broils & contentions arise; and you will find your path more easy and tranquil. The limits of my paper warn me that it is time for me to close with my affectionate adieu.

P. S. Present me affectionately to Mr. Ogilvie, &, in doing the same to Mr. Peale, tell him I am writing with his polygraph, & shall send him mine the first moment I have leisure enough to pack it.

To John Hollins[4]

DEAR SIR,   Washington, February 19, 1809.

A little transaction of mine, as innocent an one as I ever entered into, and where an improper construction was never less expected, is making some noise,[5] I observe, in your city. I beg leave to explain it to you, because I mean to ask your agency in it. The last year, the Agricultural Society of Paris, of which I am a member, having had a plough presented to them, which, on trial with a graduated instrument, did equal work with half the force of their best ploughs, they thought it would be a benefit to mankind to communicate it. They accordingly sent one to me, with a view to its being made known here, and they sent one to the Duke of Bedford also, who is one of their members, to be made use of for England, although the two nations were then at war. By the Mentor, now going to France, I have given permission to two individuals in Delaware and New York, to import two parcels of Merino sheep from France, which they have procured there, and to some gentlemen in Boston, to import a very valuable machine which spins cotton, wool, and flax equally. The last spring, the Society informed me they were cultivating the cotton of the Levant and other parts of the Mediterranean, and wished to try also that of our southern States. I immediately got a friend to have two tierces of seed forwarded to me. They were consigned to Messrs. Falls and Brown, of Baltimore, and notice of it being given me, I immediately wrote to them to re-ship them to New York, to be sent by the Mentor. Their first object was to make a show of my letter, as something very criminal, and to carry the subject into

---

4. John Hollins was a merchant and shipowner in Baltimore and one of the partners in the Baltimore Water Company.
5. Derived from the embargo he had imposed on American shipping in December 1807, which his opponents could claim was violated by his own scientific shipments.

the newspapers. I had, on a like request, some time ago, (but before the embargo) from the President of the Board of Agriculture of London, of which I am also a member, to send them some of the genuine May wheat of Virginia, forwarded to them two or three barrels of it. General Washington, in his time, received from the same Society the seed of the perennial succory, which Arthur Young had carried over from France to England, and I have since received from a member of it the seed of the famous turnip of Sweden, now so well known here. I mention these things, to shew the nature of the correspondence which is carried on between societies instituted for the benevolent purpose of communicating to all parts of the world whatever useful is discovered in any one of them. These societies are always in peace, however their nations may be at war. Like the republic of letters, they form a great fraternity spreading over the whole earth, and their correspondence is never interrupted by any civilized nation. Vaccination has been a late and remarkable instance of the liberal diffusion of a blessing newly discovered. It is really painful, it is mortifying, to be obliged to note these things, which are known to every one who knows any thing, and felt with approbation by every one who has any feeling. But we have a faction to whose hostile passions the torture even of right into wrong is a delicious gratification. Their malice I have long learned to disregard, their censure to deem praise. But I observe, that some republicans are not satisfied (even while we are receiving liberally from others), that this small return should be made. They will think more justly at another day; but in the mean time, I wish to avoid offence. My prayer to you, therefore, is, that you will be so good, under the inclosed order, as to receive these two tierces of seed from Falls and Brown, and pay them their disbursements for freight, &c. which I will immediately remit you on knowing the amount. Of the seed, when received, be so good as to make manure for your garden. When rotted with a due mixture of stable manure or earth, it is the best in the world. I rely on your friendship to excuse this trouble, it being necessary I should not commit myself again to persons of whose honour, or the want of it, I know nothing.

Accept the assurances of my constant esteem and respect.

TH. JEFFERSON.

To Henri Grégoire[6]

SIR,   WASHINGTON, February 25, 1809.

I have received the favor of your letter of August 17th, and with it the volume you were so kind as to send me on the *Literature of Negroes*. Be assured that no person living wishes more sincerely than I do, to see a complete refutation of the doubts I have myself entertained and expressed on the grade of understanding allotted to them by nature, and to find that in this respect they are on a par with ourselves. My doubts were the result of personal observation on the limited sphere of my own State, where the opportunities for the development of their genius were not favorable, and those of exercising it still less so. I expressed them therefore with great hesitation; but whatever be their degree of talent it is no measure of their rights. Because Sir Isaac Newton was superior to others in understanding, he was not therefore lord of the person or property of others. On this subject they are gain-

6. The priest Baptiste-Henri Grégoire (1750–1831), a champion of minority rights, had published *De la Littérature des Nègres* in 1808.

ing daily in the opinions of nations, and hopeful advances are making towards their reestablishment on an equal footing with the other colors of the human family. I pray you therefore to accept my thanks for the many instances you have enabled me to observe of respectable intelligence in that race of men, which cannot fail to have effect in hastening the day of their relief; and to be assured of the sentiments of high and just esteem and consideration which I tender to yourself with all sincerity.

To Horatio G. Spafford[7]

SIR   Monticello May 14. [18]09.
I have duly recieved your favor of Apr. 3. with the copy of your General Geography, for which I pray you to accept my thanks. My occupations here have not permitted me to read it through, which alone could justify any judgment expressed on the work. indeed as it appears to be an abridgment of several branches of science, the scale of abridgment must enter into that judgment. different readers require different scales according to the time they can spare, & their views in reading; and no doubt that the view of the sciences which you have brought into the compass of a 12mo volume will be accomodated to the time & object of many who may wish for but a very general view of them.

In passing my eye rapidly over parts of the book, I was struck with two passages, on which I will make observations, not doubting your wish; in any future edition, to render the work as correct as you can. in page 186. you say the potatoe is a native of the US. I presume you speak of the Irish potatoe. I have enquired much into this question, & think I can assure you that plant is not a native of N. America. Zimmerman, in his Geographical Zoology, says it is a native of Guiana; & Clavigero, that the Mexicans got it from S. America, *it's native country.* the most probable account I have been able to collect is that a vessel of Sr Walter Raleigh's, returning from Guiana, put into the West of Ireland in distress, having on board some potatoes which they called earth apples. that the season of the year, & circumstance of their being already sprouted induced them to give them all out there, and they were no more heard or thought of, till they had been spread considerably into that island, whence they were carried over into England, & therefore called the Irish potatoe. from England they came to the US. bringing their name with them.

the other passage respects the description of the passage of the Potomac through the Blue ridge in the Notes on Virginia. you quote from Volney's account of the US. what his words do not justify. his words are 'on coming from Frederick town one does not see the rich perspective mentioned in the notes of Mr Jefferson. on observing this to him a few days after he informed me he had his information from a French engineer who, during the war of Independance ascended the height of the hills & I concieve that at that elevation the perspective must be as imposing as a wild country, whose horizon

7. Horatio Gates Spafford (1778–1832), a Vermont native who had emigrated to upstate New York, published the school text he sent Jefferson, *General Geography, and Rudiments of Useful Knowledge,* in 1809. His greatest fame came from his ambitious *Gazetteer of the State of New-York* (1813; rev. ed. 1825). He had written Jefferson an adulatory letter asking, if he approved of the earlier book, to "give it publicity." Alerting Jefferson that he might visit Virginia later in the year and would like to visit Monticello, he added, "May I expect that a *little Philosopher,* will be well received by the *greatest our country has yet to boast?*" (*PTJ:RS* 1:105).

has no obstacles, may present.' that the scene described in the Notes is not visible from any part of the road from Frederick town to Harper's ferry is most certain, that road passes along the valley. nor can it be seen from the tavern after crossing the ferry; & we may fairly infer that mr Volney did not ascend the height back of the tavern from which alone it can be seen, but that he pursued his journey from the tavern along the high road. yet he admits that at the elevation of that height the perspective may be as rich as a wild country can present. but you make him 'surprised to find by *a view of the spot*, that the description was *amazingly exaggerated.*' but it is evident that mr Volney did not ascend the hill to get *a view of the spot*, and that he supposes that that height may present a view as such a country admits. but mr Volney was mistaken in saying I told him I had recieved the description from a French engineer. by an error of memory he has misapplied to this scene what I mentioned to him as to the Natural bridge, I told him I recieved a *drawing* of that from a French engineer sent there by the Marquis de Chastellux, & who has published that drawing in his travels. I could not tell him I had the description of the passage of the Potomak from a French engineer, because I never heard any French man say a word about it, much less did I ever recieve a description of it from any mortal whatever. I visited the place myself in Oct. 1783. wrote the description some time after, & printed the work in Paris in 1784. & 1785. I wrote the description from my own view of the spot, stated no fact but what I saw, & can now affirm that no fact is exaggerated. it is true that the same scene may excite very different sensations in different spectators according to their different sensibilities. the sensations of some may be much stronger than those of others, and with respect to the Natural bridge, it was not a description, but a drawing only which I recieved from the French engineer. the description was written before I ever saw him. it is not from any merit which I suppose in either of these descriptions, that I have gone into these observations, but to correct the imputation of having given to the world as my own, ideas, & false ones too, which I had recieved from another. nor do I mention the subject to you with a desire that it should be any otherwise noticed before the public than by a more correct statement in any future edition of your work.

You mention having inclosed to me some printed letters announcing a design in which you ask my aid. but no such letters came to me. any facts which I possess & which may be useful to your views shall be freely communicated, & I shall be happy to see you at Monticello, should you come this way as you propose. you will find me engaged entirely in rural occupations, looking into the field of science but occasionally & at vacant moments.

I sowed some of the Benni seed the last year, & distributed some among my neighbors; but the whole was killed by the September frost. I got a little again the last winter, but it was sowed before I recieved your letter. Col° Few of New York recieves quantities of it from Georgia, from whom you may probably get some through the Mayor of N. York. but I little expect it can succeed with you. it is about as hardy as the Cotton plant, from which you may judge of the probability of raising it at Hudson.

I salute you with great respect.

TH: JEFFERSON

To John Wyche[8]

SIR   Monticello May 19. [18]09.
Your favor of March 19. came to hand but a few days ago and informs me of the establishment of the Westward mill library society, of it's general views & progress. I always hear with pleasure of institutions for the promotion of knolege among my countrymen. the people of every country are the only safe guardians of their own rights, and are the only instruments which can be used for their destruction. and certainly they would never consent to be so used were they not decieved. to avoid this they should be instructed to a certain degree. I have often thought that nothing would do more extensive good at small expence than the establishment of a small circulating library in every county to consist of a few well chosen books, to be lent to the people of the county under such regulations as would secure their safe return in due time. these should be such as would give them a general view of other history & particular view of that of their own country, a tolerable knolege of geography, the elements of Natural philosophy, of agriculture & mechanics. should your example lead to this, it will do great good. having had more favorable opportunities than fall to every man's lot of becoming acquainted with the best books on such subjects as might be selected, I do not know that I can be otherwise useful to your society than by offering them any information respecting these which they might wish. my services in this way are freely at their command, & I beg leave to tender to yourself my salutations & assurances of respect.

TH: JEFFERSON

To John W. Campbell[9]

SIR   Monticello Sep. 3. [18]09
Your letter of July 29 came to hand some time since, but I have not sooner been able to acknolege it. In answer to your proposition for publishing a compleat edition of my different writings, I must observe that no writings of mine, other than those merely official have been published, except the Notes on Virginia, & a small pamphlet under the title of a Summary view of the rights of British America. the Notes on Virginia I have always intended to revise & enlarge, & have from time to time laid by materials for that purpose. it will be long yet before other occupations will permit me to digest them; & observations & enquiries are still to be made which will be more correct in proportion to the length of time they are continued. it is not unlikely that

---

8. John Wyche (d. 1848), a surveyor and local official in Brunswick County, Virginia, and one of "the many thousands" of Jefferson's "great admirers," wrote to ask advice about a plan to establish a local library company in his community (*PTJ:RS*, 1:66–67). Wyche took Jefferson up on his offer to suggest books for inclusion in the library, and on October 4 Jefferson complied by sending a long list of titles with notes on which editions he would recommend and a calculation of likely costs. See *PTJ:RS* 1:508–509, 579–582.
9. John Wilson Campbell (1779–1842), bookseller of Petersburg, Virginia. His July letter to Jefferson sketched his plan to issue, through "the best publisher" in Philadelphia, "a complete Edition of your different writings, as far as they may be designed for the public; including the, 'Notes on Virginia.'" Campbell replied to Jefferson's skeptical answer that he nonetheless thought he could select enough material to fill "an Octavo Volume," a tentative list of which he included. On October 1, Jefferson encouraged Campbell and sent him copies of original publications, but the plan came to nought, and Campbell eventually returned the materials (*PTJ:RS* 1:385, 538–539, 569–570).

this may be through my life. I could not therefore at present offer any thing new for that work.

The Summary view was not written for publication. It was a draught I had prepared of a petition to the King, which I meant to propose in my place as a member of the Convention of 1774. being stopped on the road by sickness, I sent it on to the Speaker, who laid it on the table for the perusal of the members, it was thought too strong for the times & to become the act of the convention, but was printed by subscription of the members with a short preface written by one of them. if it had any merit it was that of first taking our true ground, & that which was afterwards assumed & maintained.

I do not mention the Parliamentary manual published for the use of the Senate of the US. because it was a mere compilation, into which nothing entered of my own, but the arrangement, & a few observations necessary to explain that & some of the cases.

I do not know whether your view extends to official papers of mine which have been published. many of these would be like old news papers, materials for future historians, but no longer interesting to the readers of the day. they would consist of Reports, correspondencies, messages, answers to addresses a few of my Reports while Secretary of State might perhaps be read by some as Essays on abstract subjects, such as the Report on Measures, weights & coins, on the mint, on the fisheries, on commerce, on the use of distilled sea-water E^{t}c. the correspondencies with the British & French ministers, Hammond and Genet, were published by Congress. the Messages to Congress, which might have been interesting at the moment, would scarcely be read a second time, and answers to addresses are hardly read a first time.

So that on a review of these various materials, I see nothing encouraging a printer to a republication of them. they would probably be bought by those only who are in the habit of preserving state-papers, & who are not many.

I say nothing of numerous draughts of reports, resolutions, declarations etc. drawn as a member of Congress or of the legislature of Virginia, such as the Declaration of Independance, Report on the money Unit of the US. the Act for religious freedom etc., etc. these having become the acts of public bodies, there can be no personal claim to them, and they would no more find readers now than the Journals & Statute books in which they are deposited.

I have presented this general view of the subjects which might have been within the scope of your contemplation, that they might be correctly estimated before any final decision. they belong mostly to a class of papers not calculated for popular reading, & not likely therefore to offer profit, or even indemnification to the republisher. submitting it to your consideration I tender you my salutations & respects.

TH: JEFFERSON

To Benjamin Smith Barton[1]

DEAR SIR   Monticello Sep. 21. [18]09.

I recieved last night your favor of the 14th and would with all possible pleasure have communicated to you any part or the whole of the Indian vocabularies which I had collected, but an irreparable misfortune has deprived me

1. Benjamin Smith Barton (1766–1815), botanist and ethnologist, had published *New Views of the Origin of the Tribes and Nations of America* in 1798 and, with a view to a new edition, had written Jefferson to ask for information about the linguistic discoveries of Meriwether Lewis. See *PTJ:RS* 1:520–521.

of them. I have now been thirty years availing myself of every possible opportunity of procuring Indian vocabularies to the same set of words: my opportunities were probably better than will ever occur again to any person having
the same desire. I had collected about 50. and had digested most of them in
collateral columns and meant to have printed them the last year of my stay in
Washington. but not having yet digested Capt Lewis's collection, nor having
leisure then to do it, I put it off till I should return home. the whole, as well
digest as originals were packed in a trunk of stationary & sent round by water
with about 30. other packages of my effects from Washington, and while
ascending James river, this package, on account of it's weight & presumed
precious contents, was singled out & stolen. the thief being disappointed on
opening it, threw into the river all it's contents of which he thought he could
make no use. among these were the whole of the vocabularies. some leaves
floated ashore & were found in the mud; but these were very few, & so defaced
by the mud & water that no general use can ever be made of them. on the
reciept of your letter I turned to them, & was very happy to find that the only
morsel of an original vocabulary among them was Capt Lewis's of the Pani[2]
language of which you say you have not one word. I therefore inclose it to you,
as it is, & a little fragment of some other, which I see is in his handwriting,
but no indication remains on it of what language it is. it is a specimen of the
condition of the little which was recovered. I am the more concerned at this
accident as of the 250 words of my vocabularies and the 130. words of the
great Russian vocabularies of the languages of the other quarters of the globe,
73. were common to both, and would have furnished materials for a comparison from which something might have resulted, altho I believe no general
use can ever be made of the wrecks of my loss, yet I will ask the return of the
Pani vocabulary when you are done with it. perhaps I may make another
attempt to collect, altho' I am too old to expect to make much progress in it.

I learn with pleasure your acquisition of the pamphlet on the astronomy
of the antient Mexicans.[3] if it be antient & genuine, or modern & rational it
will be of real value. it is one of the most interesting countries of our hemisphere, and merits every attention.

I am thankful for your kind offer of sending the original Spanish for my
perusal. but I think it a pity to trust it to the accidents of the post, & whenever you publish the translation, I shall be satisfied to read that which shall
be given by your translator, who is, I am sure, a greater adept in the language than I am. Accept the assurances of my great esteem & respect.

TH: JEFFERSON

To C. and A. Conrad and Company[4]

MESS^RS CONRAD & CO.   Monticello Nov. 23. [18]09.

On my return after an absence of a fortnight, I yesterday recieved your
letter of the 13th. Govr Lewis had in his lifetime apprized me that he had

2. Pawnee.
3. Antonio de León y Gama, *Descripción Histórica y Cronológica de los Piedras* (1792).
4. This Philadelphia printing and bookselling firm, already being operated by John Conrad as early as
1795, was expanded to include his brothers Cornelius and Andrew by 1807. It had contracted with
Meriwether Lewis to publish his narrative of the expedition to the Pacific, but first Lewis's death
in 1809 and then the firm's failure in 1812, before the narrative eventually prepared by Nicholas
Biddle and Paul Allen could be readied for the press, left the work to be picked up by another
Philadelphia firm, Bradford and Inskeep. John Conrad had written Jefferson on November 13,
when news first reached him of the tragic death of Lewis, apparently at his own hand, while traveling to Washington through Tennessee. See *PTJ:RS* 1:668–669.

contracted with you for the publication of his account of his expedition. I had written to him some time ago to know when he would have it ready & was expecting an answer when I recieved the news of his unfortunate end. James Neelly, the US. agent to the Chickasaws, writes me that "he has his two trunks of papers (at Nashville, I suppose, from whence his letter is dated) amongst which is said to be his travels to the Pacific ocean; that some days previous to his death he requested of him (Neely) in case any accident happened to him, to send his trunk, with the papers therein *to the President*, but he thinks it very probable he meant, *to me*, and wishes to be informed what arrangements may be considered best in sending on his trunks etc."⁵ I am waiting the arrival of Genˡ Clarke, expected here in a few days, to consult with him on the subject, his aid & his interest in the publication of the work may render him the proper depository to have it prepared & delivered over to you. but my present idea is (if he concurs) to order it on to the President, according to his literal desire, and the rather because it is said that there are in his trunks vouchers for his public accounts. be assured I shall spare no pains to secure the publication of his work, and when it may be within my sphere to take any definitive step respecting it, you shall be informed of it by, Gentlemen,

Your most obedᵗ servᵗ

TH: JEFFERSON

To James Madison

DEAR SIR   Monticello Nov. 26. [18]09.

Your letter of the 6ᵗʰ was recieved from our post office on the 24ᵗʰ after my return from Bedford. I now re-inclose the letters of Mʳ Short & Romanzoff, and with them a letter from Armstrong for your perusal, as there may be some matters in it not otherwise communicated. the infatuation of the British government & nation is beyond every thing imaginable. a thousand circumstances announce that they are on the point of being blown up, & they still proceed with the same madness & increased wickedness. with respect to Jackson.⁶ I hear of but one sentiment, except that some think he should have been sent off. the more moderate step was certainly more advisable. there seems to be a perfect acquiescence in the opinion of the Government respecting

---

5. James Neely, U.S. agent to the Chickasaw Nation, accompanied Lewis on his final trip east from Missouri. In addition to what Jefferson summarizes from Neely's report about the trunks of papers in Neely's possession, Neely wrote Jefferson from Nashville on October 18 the following about the circumstances of Lewis's demise: "It is with extreme pain that I have to inform you of the death of His Excellency Meriwether Lewis, Governor of upper Louisiana who died on the morning of the 11th instant and I am sorry to say by Suicide. . . . One days Journey after crossing Tennessee River & where we encamped we lost two of our horses. I remained behind to hunt them & Governor Lewis proceeded on, with a promise to wait for me at the first houses he came to that was inhabited by white people; he reached the house of a Mr. Grinder about sun set, the man of the house being from home, and no person there but a woman who discovering the governor to be deranged, gave him up the house & slept herself in one near it. His servant and mine slept in the stable loft some distance from the other houses. The woman reports that about three o'Clock she heard two pistols fire off in the Governors Room: the servants being awakened by her, came in but too late to save him. He had shot himself in the head with one pistol & a little below the Breast with the other— when his servant came in he says; I have done the business my good Servant give me some water. He gave him water, he survived but a short time. I came up some time after, & had him as decently Buried as I could in that place—if there is any thing wished for by his friends to be done to his grave I will attend to their Instructions." *LLCE*, 2:467–468.

6. Francis James Jackson (1770–1814), British minister to the United States, 1809–10, had a short and rough career in Washington.

Onis.[7] the public interest certainly made his rejection expedient; and as that is a motive which it is not pleasant always to avow, I think it fortunate that the contending claims of Charles & Ferdinand furnished such plausible embarrasment to the question of right: for, on our principles, I presume, the right of the Junta to send a minister could not be denied. La Fayette, in a letter to me expresses great anxiety to recieve his formal titles to the lands in Louisiana. indeed I know not why the proper officers have not sooner sent on the papers on which the grants might issue. it will be in your power to forward the grants or copies of them by some safe conveyance, as La Fayette says that no negotiation can be effected without them.

I inclose you a letter from Maj^r Neely, Chickasaw agent, stating that he is in possession of 2. trunks of the unfortunate Governor Lewis, containing public vouchers, the manuscripts of his Western journey, & probably some private papers. as he desired they should be sent *to the president*,[8] as the public vouchers render it interesting to the public that they should be safely recieved, and they would probably come most safely if addressed to you, would it not be advisable that Major Neely should recieve an order on your part to forward them to Washington addressed to you, by the stage, & if possible under the care of some person coming on? when at Washington, I presume, the papers may be opened & distributed, that is to say, the Vouchers to the proper offices where they are cognisable; the manuscript voyage etc. to Genl Clarke who is interested in it, and is believed to be now on his way to Washington; and his private papers if any to his administrator, who is John Marks, his half brother. it is impossible you should have time to examine & distribute them; but if mr Coles could find time to do it the family would have entire confidence in his distribution. the other two trunks which are in the care of Capt Russel at the Chickasaw bluffs, & which Pernier (Govr Lewis's serv^t) says contain his private property, I write to Capt Russel, at the request of mr Marks, to forward to mr Brown at N. Orleans to be sent on to Richmond under my address. Pernier says that Governor Lewis owes him 240.D. for his wages, he has received money from Neely to bring him on here, & I furnish him to Washington, where he will arrive pennyless, and will ask for some money to be placed to the Governor's account. he rides a horse of the Governor's, which with the approbation of the Administrator I tell him to dispose of & give credit for the amount in his account against the Governor. he is the bearer of this letter and of my assurances of constant & affectionate esteem & respect

TH: JEFFERSON

To General Tadeusz Kościuszko[9]

MY DEAR GENERAL & FRIEND   Monticello Feb. 26. [18]10.

I have rarely written to you; never but by safe conveyances; & avoiding every thing political, lest, coming from one in the station I then held, it might

7. Luis de Onis y Gonzales (1762–1827), Spanish representative in the United States during the rule of a junta installed by Bonaparte following the forced abdication of King Charles and his son and heir, Ferdinand.
8. Madison himself.
9. Andrzej Tadeusz Bonawentura Kościuszko (1746–1817), Polish and American military hero, was a native of a town now in Belarus. He served in the American Revolution from 1776, eventually becoming a brigadier general and having special responsibility for military engineering, at West Point among other sites. Returning to Poland in 1784, he became centrally involved in defending his homeland against the Russians. He returned to the United States in 1797–98 and spent much time with Jefferson, then vice president, in Philadelphia.

be imputed injuriously to our country, or perhaps even excite jealousy of you. hence my letters were necessarily dry. retired now from public concerns, totally unconnected with them, and avoiding all curiosity about what is done or intended, what I say is from myself only, the workings of my own mind, imputable to nobody else. The anxieties which I know you have felt, on seeing exposed to the justlings of a warring world, a country to which in early life you devoted your sword & services, when oppressed by foreign dominion, were worthy of your philanthropy & disinterested attachment to the freedom and happiness of man. altho' we have not made all the provisions which might be necessary for a war in the field of Europe, yet we have not been inattentive to such as would be necessary here. from the moment that the affair of the Chesapeake[1] rendered the prospect of war imminent, every faculty was exerted to be prepared for it, & I think I may venture to solace you with the assurance that we are in a good degree prepared. military stores for many campaigns are on hand, all the necessary articles (sulphur excepted) & the art of preparing them among ourselves abundantly, arms in our magazines for more men than will ever be required in the field, & 40,000. new stand[2] yearly added, of our own fabrication, superior to any we have ever seen from Europe; heavy artillery much beyond our need, an increasing stock of field pieces, several founderies casting one every other day, each; a military school of about 50. students which has been in operation a dozen years, and the manufacture of men constantly going on, and adding 40,000. young souldiers to our force every year that the war is deferred: at all our seaport towns of the least consequence we have erected works of defence, and assigned them gunboats, carrying one or two heavy pieces, either $18^s 24^s$ or 32 pounders, sufficient, in the smaller harbors to repel the predatory attacks of privateers or single armed ships, & proportioned in the larger harbors to such more serious attacks as they may probably be exposed to. all these were nearly completed, & their gunboats in readiness, when I retired from the government. the works of New York & New Orleans alone, being on a much larger scale, are not yet compleated. the former will be finished this summer, mounting 438. guns, & with the aid of from 50. to 100. gunboats will be adequate to the resistance of any fleet which will ever be trusted across the Atlantic; the works for N. Orleans are less advanced. these are our preparations. they are very different from what you will be told by newspapers, and travellers, even Americans. but it is not to them the government communicates the public condition. ask one of them if he knows the exact state of any particular harbour, and you will find probably that he does not know even that of the one he comes from. you will ask perhaps where are the proofs of these preparations for one who cannot go & see them. I answer, in the acts of Congress authorising such preparations, & in your knolege of me that, if authorised, they would be executed. two measures have not been adopted which I pressed on Congress repeatedly at their meetings. the one, to settle the whole ungranted territory of Orleans by donations of land to able bodied young men, to be engaged & carried there at the public expence, who would constitute a force always ready on the spot to defend New Orleans. the other was to class the militia according to the years of their birth, & make all those from 20. to 25. liable to be trained & called into service at a moment's warning. this would have given us a force of 300,000. young men,

---

1. In June 1807, in a dispute over American recruitment of British deserters and British impressment of American sailors, the British warship *Leopard* detained and then attacked the U.S.S. *Chesapeake* just outside the limits of American waters off the Virginia coast.
2. I.e., stand of arms, or a complete set of weapons and associated equipment for one soldier.

prepared by proper training for service in any part of the US. while those who had passed thro' that period would remain at home liable to be used in their own or adjacent states. these two measures would have compleated what I deemed necessary for the entire security of our country. they would have given me, on my retirement from the government, of the nation, the consolatory reflection that having found, when I was called to it, not a single seaport town in a condition to repel a levy of contribution by a single privateer or pirate, I had left every harbor so prepared by works & gunboats as to be in a reasonable state of security against any probable attack, the territory of Orleans acquired & planted with an internal force sufficient for it's protection, & the whole territory of the US. organised by such a classification of it's male force as would give it the benefit of all it's young population for active service, and that of a middle & advanced age for stationary defence. but these measures will, I hope, be compleated by my successor, who, to the purest principles of republican patriotism, adds a wisdom & foresight second to no man on earth.

So much as to my country. now a word as to myself. I am retired to Monticello, where, in the bosom of my family, & surrounded by my books, I enjoy a repose to which I have been long a stranger. my mornings are devoted to correspondence. from breakfast to dinner I am in my shops, my garden, or on horseback among my farms; from dinner to dark I give to society & recreation with my neighbors & friends; & from candlelight to early bed-time I read. my health is perfect; and my strength considerably reinforced by the activity of the course I pursue; perhaps it is as great as usually falls to the lot of near 67. years of age. I talk of ploughs & harrows, seeding & harvesting, with my neighbors, & of politics too, if they chuse, with as little reserve as the rest of my fellow citizens, & feel at length the blessing of being free to say & do what I please, without being responsible for it to any mortal. a part of my occupation, & by no means the least pleasing, is the direction of the studies of such young men as ask it. they place themselves in the neighboring village, and have the use of my library & counsel, & make a part of my society. in advising the course of their reading, I endeavor to keep their attention fixed on the main objects of all science, the freedom & happiness of man. so that coming to bear a share in the councils and government of their country, they will keep ever in view the sole objects of all legitimate government.

From this portion of my personal condition, I must turn to another of unpleasant hue, and apologize to you for what has given me much mortification, for some time before I retired from the government I anxiously endeavored to have all outstanding accounts called in, & no new ones contracted, that I might retire, at least without any embarrasment of debt. wholly occupied with the care of the public affairs, I was obliged to trust to others for that of my own: and in the last moments of my stay in Washington, notwithstanding my precautions, accounts came in in a mass so overwhelming as to exceed all my resources by ten or twelve thousand Dollars. a friend[3] accomodated me readily with a considerable part of the deficiency, to be reimbursed out of the first proceeds of my estate. while sunk in affliction as to the residue, mr Barnes suggested that the public were paying off the whole of the 8. percent stock, that he had not yet recieved yours of that description, or reinvested it in any other form: that he had thought of placing it in bank stock, but, he supposed, if I should pay you an interest equal to the dividends on bank stock, it would be indifferent to you from what hand your

3. James Madison.

profits came: & that the 4500.D. of yours then disengaged, would entirely relieve my remaining deficiency. the proposition was like a beam of light; & I was satisfied that were you on the spot to be consulted the kindness of your heart would be gratified, while recieving punctually the interest for your own subsistence, to let the principal be so disposed of for a time, as to lift a friend out of distress. I therefore gave mr Barnes a proper written acknolegement of the debt, & he applied your 8. percent principal to the closing of my affairs. I was the more encouraged to do this, because I knew it was not your intention to call your capital from this country during your life, & that should any accident happen to you, it's charitable destination, as directed by the paper you left with me, would not be at all delayed.⁴ I have set apart an estate of 3000.D. a year which I have at some distance from Monticello, & which is now engaged in reimbursing what was furnished by the friend I alluded to. it will be nearly accomplished by the close of this year. two more years will suffice for the residue of that, & yours; when this part of your funds can again be invested in some of the monied institutions. the diversion of it from them for 4. or 5. years, will in the mean time have saved me. but the affliction is a sore one, & needs the solace of your approbation. instead of the unalloyed happiness of retiring, unembarrased & independent, to the enjoiment of my estate, which is ample for my limited views, I have to pass such a length of time in a thraldom of mind never before known to me. except for this, my happiness would have been perfect. that yours may never know disturbance, & that you may enjoy as many years of life, health & ease as yourself shall wish, is the sincere prayer of your constant & affectionate friend.

TH: JEFFERSON

P.S. I put under cover herewith mr Barnes's letter with his annual account & a remittance of £200. sterl. the Duplicates shall follow by another occasion.

To Dr. Benjamin Rush⁵

DEAR SIR   Monticello Jan. 16. [18]11.
    I had been considering for some days whether it was not time, by a letter, to bring myself to your recollection, when I recieved your welcome favor of the 2ᵈ inst. I had before heard of the heart-rending calamity you mention, & had sincerely sympathised with your afflictions. but I had not made it the subject of a letter, because I knew that condolances were but renewals of grief. yet I thought, & still think, this is one of the cases wherein we should "not sorrow, even as others who have no hope."⁶ I have myself known so many cases of recovery from confirmed insanity, as to reckon it ever among the recoverable diseases. one of these was that of a near relation and namesake of mine, who after many years of madness of the first degree, became

---

4. In 1798, Kościuszko had left with Jefferson a document directing that, in the event of his death, the money and lands he had been given in the United States should be used to free and educate as many slaves as possible. Merchant and customs collector John Barnes (c. 1731–1826), long Jefferson's banker and friend, had oversight of Kościuszko's American property; with his approval Jefferson borrowed $4,500.00 to help defray his own debts.
5. Pennsylvania native Benjamin Rush (1745–1813), eminent physician and reformer, had played a key political role in the early years of the Revolution. He had written Jefferson in January to share the tragic story of his son, gunboat commander John Rush, who had killed another naval officer in a duel the previous October and since then had exhibited signs of serious mental distress. The younger Rush was institutionalized and died in the Pennsylvania Hospital twenty-four years later.
6. Thessalonians 4.13.

entirely sane, & amused himself to a good old age in keeping school; was an excellent teacher, & much valued citizen.

You ask if I have read Hartley?[7] I have not. my present course of life admits less reading than I wish, from breakfast, or noon at latest, to dinner, I am mostly on horseback, attending to my farms or other concerns, which I find healthful to my body, mind, & affairs: and the few hours I can pass in my cabinet, are devoured by correspondences; not those with my intimate friends, with whom I delight to interchange sentiments, but with others who, writing to me on concerns of their own in which I have had an agency, or from motives of mere respect and approbation, are entitled to be answered with respect and a return of good will. my hope is that this obstacle to the delights of retirement will wear away with the oblivion which follows that, and that I may at length be indulged in those studious pursuits, from which nothing but revolutionary duties would ever have called me.

I shall receive your proposed publication,[8] & read it, with the pleasure which every thing gives me from your pen. altho' much of a sceptic in the practice of medecine, I read with pleasure it's ingenious theories.

I receive with sensibility your observations on the discontinuance of friendly correspondence between mr Adams & myself, & the concern you take in it's restoration.[9] this discontinuance has not proceeded from me, nor from the want of sincere desire, and of effort on my part to renew our intercourse. you know the perfect co-incidence of principle, & of action, in the early part of the revolution which produced a high degree of mutual respect & esteem between mr Adams & myself. certainly no man was ever truer than he was, in that day, to those principles of rational republicanism which, after the necessity of throwing off our monarchy, dictated all our efforts in the establishment of a new government, and altho' he swerved afterwards towards the principles of the English constitution, our friendship did not abate on that account. while he was Vice-president, & I Secretary of state, I recieved a letter from President Washington then at Mount-Vernon, desiring me to call together the heads of departments, and to invite mr Adams to join us (which, by the bye, was the only instance of that being done) in order to determine on some measure which required dispatch: and he desired me to act on it, as decided, without again recurring to him. I invited them to dine with me, and after dinner, sitting at our wine, having settled our question, other conversation came on, in which a collision of opinion arose between mr Adams & Col° Hamilton, on the merits of the British constitution, mr Adams giving it as his opinion that, if some of it's defects & abuses were corrected, it would be the most perfect constitution of government ever devised by man. Hamilton, on the contrary asserted that, with it's existing vices, it was the most perfect model of government that could be formed; & that the

---

7. David Hartley (1705–1757), British philosopher, to whose *Observations on Man, His Frame, Duty, and Expectations* (1749) Rush referred in his letter.
8. Rush promised to send his *Sixteen Introductory Lectures, to Courses of Lectures upon the Institutes and Practice of Medicine* (1811), then in press.
9. Rush, who was instrumental in reviving the long-suspended friendship of the two ex-presidents, explained to Jefferson, "Your and my Old friend Mr. Adams now & then drops me a line from his Seat at Quincy. . . . When I consider your early Attachment to Mr. Adams, and his—to you—when I consider how much the liberties & Independance [sic] of the United States owe to the Concert of your principles and labors, and when I reflect upon the sameness of your Opinions at present, upon most of the Subjects of Government, and all the Subjects of legislation, I have ardently wished a friendly and epistolary intercourse might be revived between you before you take a final leave of the Common Object of your Affections" (*PTJ:RS* 3:278). In an 1809 letter to Adams, Rush had stated that he had dreamed that a "renewal of the friendship & intercourse" between Adams and Jefferson had occurred; Adams answered that he had "no other objection to your Dream, but that it is not History. It may be Prophecy" (quoted in *PTJ:RS* 4:389).

correction of it's vices would render it an impracticable government. and this you may be assured was the real line of difference between the political principles of these two gentlemen. another incident took place on the same occasion which will further delineate Hamilton's political principles. the room being hung around with a collection of the portraits of remarkable men, among them were those of Bacon, Newton & Locke. Hamilton asked me who they were. I told him they were my trinity of the three greatest men the world had ever produced, naming them. he paused for some time: "the greatest man, said he, that ever lived was Julius Caesar." Mr Adams was honest as a politician as well as a man; Hamilton honest as a man, but, as a politician, believing in the necessity of either force or corruption to govern men.—you remember the machinery which the federalists played off, about that time, to beat down the friends to the real principles of our constitution, to silence by terror every expression in their favor, to bring us into war with France and alliance with England, and finally to homologise our constitution with that of England. mr Adams, you know, was overwhelmed with feverish addresses, dictated by the fear, and often by the pen, of the *bloody buoy*,[1] and was seduced by them into some open indications of his new principles of government, & in fact was so elated as to mix, with his kindness, a little superciliousness towards me. even mrs Adams, with all her good sense & prudence, was sensibly flushed. and you recollect the short suspension of our intercourse, & the circumstance which gave rise to it, which you were so good as to bring to an early explanation, and have set to rights, to the cordial satisfaction of us all. the nation at length passed condemnation on the political principles of the Federalists by refusing to continue mr Adams in the presidency. on the day on which we learned in Philadelphia the vote of the city of New York, which it was well known would decide the vote of the state, and that again the vote of the Union, I called on mr Adams on some official business. he was very sensibly affected, and accosted me with these words. "Well, I understand that you are to beat me in this contest, & I will only say that I will be as faithful a subject as any you will have." "Mr Adams, said I, this is no personal contest between you & me. two systems of principles on the subject of government divide our fellow-citizens into two parties. with one of these you concur, & I with the other. as we have been longer on the public stage than most of those now living, our names happen to be more generally known. one of these parties therefore has put your name at it's head, the other mine. were we both to die to-day, tomorrow two other names would be in the place of ours, without any change in the motion of the machine. it's motion is from it's principle, not from you or myself." "I believe you are right, said he, that we are but passive instruments, and should not suffer this matter to affect our personal dispositions." but he did not long retain this just view of the subject. I have always believed that the thousand calumnies which the federalists, in bitterness of heart, & mortification at their ejection, daily invented against me, were carried to him by their busy intriguers, & made some impression, when the election between Burr & myself was kept in suspense by the federalists, and they were meditating to place the President of the Senate at the head of the government, I called on mr Adams with a view to have this desperate measure prevented by his negative, he grew warm in an instant, and said with a vehemence he had not used towards me before, "Sir, the event of the election is within your own

---

1. English emigrant William Cobbett published his *Bloody Buoy*, a highly partisan account of the excesses of the French Revolution, in Philadelphia in 1796.

power. you have only to say you will do justice to the public creditors, maintain the navy, and not disturb those holding offices, and the government will instantly be put into your hands. we know it is the wish of the people it should be so."—"mr Adams, said I, I know not what part of my conduct, in either public or private life, can have authorised a doubt of my fidelity to the public engagements. I say however I will not come into the government by capitulation. I will not enter on it but in perfect freedom to follow the dictates of my own judgment." I had before given the same answer to the same intimation from Gouverneur Morris. "then, said he, things must take their course." I turned the conversation to something else, & soon took my leave. it was the first time in our lives we had ever parted with any thing like dissatisfaction, and then followed those scenes of midnight appointment which have been condemned by all men. the last day of his political power, the last hours, & even beyond the midnight, were employed in filling all offices, & especially permanent ones, with the bitterest federalists, & providing for me the alternative either to execute the government by my enemies, whose study it would be to thwart & defeat all my measures, or to incur the odium of such numerous removals from office as might bear me down. a little time & reflection effaced in my mind this temporary dissatisfaction, with mr Adams, and restored me to that just estimate of his virtues & passions which a long acquaintance had enabled me to fix. and my first wish became that of making his retirement easy by any means in my power; for it was understood he was not rich. I suggested to some republican members of the delegation from his state the giving him, either directly, or indirectly, an office, the most lucrative in that state, and then offered to be resigned, if they thought he would not deem it affrontive. they were of opinion he would take great offence at the offer; and moreover that the body of republicans would consider such a step in the outset, as auguring very ill of the course I meant to pursue. I dropped the idea therefore but did not cease to wish for some opportunity of renewing our friendly understanding. two or three years after, having had the misfortune to lose a daughter, between whom & mrs Adams there had been a considerable attachment, she made it the occasion of writing me a letter, in which, with the tenderest expressions of concern at this event, she carefully avoided a single one of friendship towards myself, and even concluded it with the wishes "of her who *once* took pleasure in subscribing herself your friend Abigail Adams." unpromising as was the complexion of this letter, I determined to make an effort towards removing the clouds from between us. this brought on a correspondence which I now inclose for your perusal, after which be so good as to return it to me, as I have never communicated it to any mortal breathing before. I send it to you to convince you I have not been wanting, either in the desire, or the endeavor to remove this misundersta[nd]ing. indeed I thought it highly disgraceful to us both; as indicating minds not sufficiently elevated to prevent a public competition from affecting our personal friendship. I soon found from the correspondence that conciliation was desperate, and, yielding to an intimation in her last letter, I ceased from further explanation. I have the same good opinion of mr Adams which I ever had. I know him to be an honest man, an able one with his pen, and he was a powerful advocate on the floor of Congress. he has been alienated from me by belief in the lying suggestions contrived for electioneering purposes, that I perhaps mixed in the activity & intrigues of the occasion. my most intimate friends can testify that I was perfectly passive. they would sometimes indeed tell me what was going on; but no man ever heard me take part in such conversations; & none ever misrepresented mr Adams in my presence, without my asserting his just character. with very confidential persons I have doubtless disapproved of the principles & practices of his administration, this was unavoidable. but never with those with whom it could do him any injury. decency would have required this conduct from me, if disposition had not: and I am satisfied mr Adams's conduct was equally honorable towards me. but I think it a part of his character to suspect foul play in those of whom he is jealous, and not easily to relinquish his suspicions.

I have gone, my dear friend, into these details that you might know every thing which had passed between us, might be fully possessed of the state of facts and dispositions, and judge for yourself whether they admit a revival of that friendly intercourse for which you are so kindly solicitous. I shall certainly not be wanting in any thing on my part which may second your efforts; which will be the easier with me inasmuch as I do not entertain a sentiment of mr Adams, the expression of which could give him reasonable offence. and I submit the whole to yourself with the assurance that whatever be the issue, my friendship and respect for yourself will remain unaltered & unalterable.

TH: JEFFERSON

To Charles Willson Peale[2]

Pop. Forest. Aug. 20, 1811

It is long, my dear Sir, since we have exchanged a letter. our former correspondence had always some little matter of business interspersed; but this being at an end, I shall still be anxious to hear from you sometimes, and to know that you are well & happy. I know indeed that your system is that of contentment under any situation. I have heard that you have retired from the city to a farm, & that you give your whole time to that. does not the Museum suffer? and is the farm as interesting? here, as you know, we are all farmers, but not in a pleasing stile. we have so little labor in proportion to our land, that altho' perhaps we make more profit from the same labor we cannot give to our grounds that stile of beauty which satisfies the eye of the amateur. our rotations are Corn, wheat & clover, or corn wheat, clover & clover, or wheat, corn, wheat, clover & clover; preceding the clover by a plaistering. but some, instead of clover, substitute mere rest, and all are slovenly enough. we are adding the care of Merino sheep. I have often thought that if heaven had given me choice of my position & calling, it should have been on a rich spot of earth, well watered, and near a good market for the productions of the garden. no occupation is so delightful to me as the culture of the earth, & no culture comparable to that of the garden. such a variety of subjects, some one always coming to perfection, the failure of one thing repaired by the success of another, & instead of one harvest a continued one thro' the year. under a total want of demand except for our family table I am still devoted to the garden. but tho' an old man, I am but a young gardener. your application to whatever you are engaged in I

2. Charles Willson Peale (1741–1827), artist, collector, and museum proprietor, had actively supported the Revolution, serving both as a militia officer in Philadelphia and as a portrait painter for many of the new nation's leaders, including George Washington. Now retired to a farm in Germantown, he had long been Jefferson's friend and correspondent. In response to this effort at renewing their communication, he sent Jefferson a long letter about his farm, illustrated with several sketches, early the next month.

know to be incessant. but Sundays and rainy days are always days of writing for the farmer. think of me sometimes when you have your pen in hand, & give me information of your health and occupations; and be always assured of my great esteem & respect

TH: JEFFERSON

To John Adams[3]

DEAR SIR   Monticello Jan. 21. 1812.
   I thank you before hand (for they are not yet arrived) for the specimens of homespun you have been so kind as to forward me by post. I doubt not their excellence, knowing how far you are advanced in these things in your quarter. here we do little in the fine way, but in coarse & midling goods a great deal. every family in the country is a manufactory within itself, and is very generally able to make within itself all the stouter and midling stuffs for it's own cloathing & houshold use. we consider a sheep for every person in the family as sufficient to clothe it, in addition to the cotton, hemp & flax which we raise ourselves. for fine stuff we shall depend on your Northern manufactures. of these, that is to say, of company establishments, we have none. we use little machinery. the Spinning Jenny and loom with the flying shuttle can be managed in a family; but nothing more complicated the economy and thriftiness resulting from our houshold manufactures are such that they will never again be laid aside; and nothing more salutary for us has ever happened than the British obstructions to our demands for their manufactures. restore free intercourse when they will, their commerce with us will have totally changed it's form, and the articles we shall in future want from them will not exceed their own consumption of our produce.
   A letter from you calls up recollections very dear to my mind. it carries me back to the times when, beset with difficulties & dangers, we were fellow laborers in the same cause, struggling for what is most valuable to man, his right of self-government. laboring always at the same oar, with some wave ever ahead threatening to overwhelm us & yet passing harmless under our bark we knew not how, we rode through the storm with heart & hand, and made a happy port. still we did not expect to be without rubs and difficulties; and we have had them. first the detention of the Western posts: then the coalition of Pilnitz, outlawing our commerce with France, & the British enforcement of the outlawry. in your day French depredations: in mine English, & the Berlin and Milan decrees: now the English orders of council, & the piracies they authorise: when these shall be over, it will be the impressment of our seamen, or something else: and so we have gone on, & so we shall go on, puzzled & prospering beyond example in the history of man. and I do believe we shall continue to growl, to multiply & prosper until we exhibit an association, powerful, wise, and happy, beyond what has yet been seen by men. as for France & England, with all their preeminence in science, the one is a den of robbers, & the other of pirates. and if science produces no better fruits than tyranny, murder, rapine, and destitution of national morality,

3. John Adams had written Jefferson on New Year's Day 1812, "As you are a Friend to American Manufactures, . . . I take the Liberty of Sending you by the Post a Packett containing two Pieces of Homespun lately produced in this quarter by One who was honoured in his youth with Some of your Attention and much of your kindness" (PTJ:RS 4:390). As the packet had not arrived by the time Jefferson answered Adams in this letter, the Virginian mistook Adams's metaphor: the "Pieces of Homespun" sent by Adams were not textiles but rather the two-volume Lectures on Rhetoric and Oratory published in 1810 by his son, John Quincy Adams.

I would rather wish our country to be ignorant, honest & estimable as our neighboring savages are.—but whither is senile garrulity leading me? into politics, of which I have taken final leave. I think little of them, & say less. I have given up newspapers in exchange for Tacitus & Thucydides, for Newton & Euclid; & I find myself much the happier. sometimes indeed I look back to former occurrences, in remembrance of our old friends and fellow laborers, who have fallen before us. of the signers of the Declaration of Independance I see now living not more than half a dozen on your side of the Patomak, and, on this side, myself alone. you & I have been wonderfully spared, and myself with remarkable health, & a considerable activity of body & mind. I am on horseback 3. or 4. hours of every day; visit 3. or 4. times a year a possession I have 90 miles distant, performing the winter journey on horseback. I walk little however; a single mile being too much for me; and I live in the midst of my grandchildren, one of whom has lately promoted me to be a great grandfather. I have heard with pleasure that you also retain good health, and a greater power of exercise in walking than I do. but I would rather have heard this from yourself, & that, writing a letter, like mine, full of egotisms, & of details of your health, your habits, occupations & enjoiments, I should have the pleasure of knowing that, in the race of life, you do not keep, in it's physical decline, the same distance ahead of me which you have done in political honors & atchievements. no circumstances have lessened the interest I feel in these particulars respecting yourself; none have suspended for one moment my sincere esteem for you; and I now salute you with unchanged affections and respect.

TH: JEFFERSON

To John Adams

DEAR SIR					Monticello June 11. 1812.
By our post preceding that which brought your letter of May 21, I had recieved one from Mr. Malcolm on the same subject with yours, and by the return of the post had stated to the President my recollections of him.[4] But both of your letters were probably too late; as the appointment had been already made, if we may credit the newspapers.

You ask if there is any book that pretends to give any account of the traditions of the Indians, or how one can acquire an idea of them? Some scanty accounts of their traditions, but fuller of their customs and characters are given us by most of the early travellers among them. These you know were chiefly French. Lafitau, among them, and Adair[5] an Englishman, have written on this subject; the former two volumes, the latter one, all in 4to [quarto]. But unluckily Lafitau had in his head a preconcieved theory on the mythology, manners, institutions and government of the antient nations of Europe, Asia, and Africa, and seems to have entered on those of America only to fit them into the same frame, and to draw from them a confirmation

---

4. In his May 21, 1812, letter, Adams had asked Jefferson to write President Madison or James Monroe, secretary of state, in support of the naming of his own former secretary, Samuel B. Malcolm (1776–1815), to a judgeship in Utica, New York. As Jefferson indicates, Malcolm had already written him; he in turn had written Madison, saying he had little recollection of Malcolm except that he was "a strong federalist" (*AJL* 2:304).
5. James Adair (1709–1783), a native of Ireland who traded among the Chickasaw Indians for many years, published his *History of the American Indians* . . . in 1775. Joseph-François Lafitau (1681–1746), a French Jesuit missionary at Caughnawaga, above Montreal on the St. Lawrence, was author of *Moeurs des Sauvages Amériquains, Comparées aux Moeurs des Premiers Temps* (1724).

of his general theory. He keeps up a perpetual parallel, in all those articles, between the Indians of America, and the antients of the other quarters of the globe. He selects therefore all the facts, and adopts all the falsehoods which favor his theory, and very gravely retails such absurdities as zeal for a theory could alone swallow. He was a man of much classical and scriptural reading, and has rendered his book not unentertaining. He resided five years among the Northern Indians, as a Missionary, but collects his matter much more from the writings of others, than from his own observation.

Adair too had his kink. He believed all the Indians of America to be descended from the Jews: the same laws, usages; rites and ceremonies, the same sacrifices, priests, prophets, fasts and festivals, almost the same religion, and that they all spoke Hebrew. For altho he writes particularly of the Southern Indians only, the Catawbas, Creeks, Cherokees, Chickasaws and Choctaws, with whom alone he was personally acquainted, yet he generalises whatever he found among them, and brings himself to believe that the hundred languages of America, differing fundamentally every one from every other, as much as Greek from Gothic, have yet all one common prototype. He was a trader, a man of learning, a self-taught Hebraist, a strong religionist, and of as sound a mind as Don Quixot in whatever did not touch his religious chivalry. His book contains a great deal of real instruction on it's subject, only requiring the reader to be constantly on his guard against the wonderful obliquities of his theory.

The scope of your enquiry would scarcely, I suppose, take in the three folio volumes of Latin of De Bry.[6] In these fact and fable are mingled together, without regard to any favorite system. They are less suspicious therefore in their complexion, more original and authentic, than those of Lafitau and Adair. This is a work of great curiosity, extremely rare, so as never to be bought in Europe, but on the breaking up, and selling some antient library. On one of these occasions a bookseller procured me a copy, which, unless you have one, is probably the only one in America.

You ask further, if the Indians have any order of priesthood among them, like the Druids, Bards or Minstrels of the Celtic nations? Adair alone, determined to see what he wished to see in every object, metamorphoses their Conjurers into an order of priests, and describes their sorceries as if they were the great religious ceremonies of the nation. Lafitau calls them by their proper names, Jongleurs, Devins, Sortileges; De Bry praestigiatores, Adair himself sometimes Magi, Archimagi, cunning men, Seers, rain makers, and the modern Indian interpreters, call them Conjurers and Witches. They are persons pretending to have communications with the devil and other evil spirits, to foretel future events, bring down rain, find stolen goods, raise the dead, destroy some, and heal others by enchantment, lay spells etc. And Adair, without departing from his parallel of the Jews and Indians, might have found their counterpart, much more aptly, among the Soothsayers, sorcerers and wizards of the Jews, their Jannes and Jambres, their Simon Magus, witch of Endor, and the young damsel whose sorceries disturbed Paul so much; instead of placing them in a line with their High-priest, their Chief priests, and their magnificent hierarchy generally. In the solemn ceremonies of the Indians, the persons who direct or officiate, are their chiefs, elders and warriors, in civil ceremonies or in those of war; it is the Head of the Cabin, in their private or particular feasts or ceremonies; and sometimes the

6. Theodor de Bry (1528–1598), a native of the independent Prince-Bishopric of Liège, was a famous publisher of accounts of European exploration in the Americas. Jefferson had purchased an early edition of de Bry while in Europe in 1789.

Matrons, as in their Corn feasts. And, even here, Adair might have kept up his parallel, with ennobling his Conjurers. For the antient Patriarchs, the Noahs, the Abrahams, Isaacs and Jacobs, and, even after the consecration of Aaron, the Samuels and Elijahs, and we may say further every one for himself, offered sacrifices on the altars. The true line of distinction seems to be, that solemn ceremonies, whether public or private, addressed to the Great Spirit, are conducted by the worthies of the nation, Men, or Matrons, while Conjurers are resorted to only for the invocation of evil spirits. The present state of the several Indian tribes, without any public order of priests, is proof sufficient that they never had such an order. Their steady habits permit no innovations, not even those which the progress of science offers to increase the comforts, enlarge the understanding, and improve the morality of mankind. Indeed so little idea have they of a regular order of priests, that they mistake ours for their Conjurers, and call them by that name.

So much in answer to your enquiries concerning Indians, a people with whom, in the very early part of my life, I was very familiar, and acquired impressions of attachment and commiseration for them which have never been obliterated. Before the revolution they were in the habit of coming often, and in great numbers to the seat of our government, where I was very much with them. I knew much the great Outassete, the warrior and orator of the Cherokees. He was always the guest of my father, on his journeys to and from Williamsburg. I was in his camp when he made his great farewell oration to his people, the evening before his departure for England. The moon was in full splendor, and to her he seemed to address himself in his prayers for his own safety on the voyage, and that of his people during his absence. His sounding voice, distinct articulation, animated action, and the solemn silence of his people at their several fires, filled me with awe and veneration, altho' I did not understand a word he uttered. That nation, consisting now of about 2000. wariors, and the Creeks of about 3000. are far advanced in civilisation. They have good Cabins, inclosed fields, large herds of cattle and hogs, spin and weave their own clothes of cotton, have smiths and other of the most necessary tradesmen, write and read, are on the increase in numbers, and a branch of the Cherokees is now instituting a regular representative government. Some other tribes were advancing in the same line. On those who have made any progress, English seductions will have no effect. But the backward will yeild, and be thrown further back. These will relapse into barbarism and misery, lose numbers by war and want, and we shall be obliged to drive them, with the beasts of the forest into the Stony mountains. They will be conquered however in Canada. The possession of that country secures our women and children for ever from the tomahawk and scalping knife, by removing those who excite them: and for this possession, orders I presume are issued by this time; taking for granted that the doors of Congress will re-open with a Declaration of war. That this may end in indemnity for the past, security for the future, and compleat emancipation from Anglomany, Gallomany, and all the manias of demoralized Europe, and that you may live in health and happiness to see all this, is the sincere prayer of Yours affectionately.

TH: JEFFERSON

To Anne Louise Germaine Necker,
Madame de Staël-Holstein[7]

United States of America, May 24, 1813.

I received with great pleasure, my dear Madam and friend, your letter of November the 10th, from Stockholm, and am sincerely gratified by the occasion it gives me of expressing to you the sentiments of high respect and esteem which I entertain for you. It recals to my remembrance a happy portion of my life, passed in your native city, then the seat of the most amiable and polished society of the world, and of which yourself and your venerable father were such distinguished members. But of what scenes has it since been the theatre, and with what havoc has it overspread the earth! Robespiere met the fate, and his memory the execration, he so justly merited. The rich were his victims, and perished by thousands. It is by millions that Buonaparte destroys the poor, and he is eulogised and deified by the sycophants even of science. These merit more than the mere oblivion to which they will be consigned; and the day will come when a just posterity will give to their hero the only pre-eminence he has earned, that of having been the greatest of the destroyers of the human race. What year of his military life has not consigned a million of human beings to death, to poverty and wretchedness! What field in Europe may not raise a monument of the murders, the burnings, the desolations, the famines and miseries it has witnessed from him! And all this to acquire a reputation, which Cartouche[8] attained with less injury to mankind, of being fearless of God or man.

To complete and universalize the desolation of the globe, it has been the will of Providence to raise up, at the same time, a tyrant as unprincipled and as overwhelming, for the ocean. Not in the poor maniac George,[9] but in his government and nation. Buonaparte will die, and his tyrannies with him. But a nation never dies. The English government and its piratical principles and practices, have no fixed term of duration. Europe feels, and is writhing under the scorpion whips of Buonaparte. We are assailed by those of England. The one continent thus placed under the gripe of England, and the other of Buonaparte, each has to grapple with the enemy immediately pressing on itself. We must extinguish the fire kindled in our own house, and leave to our friends beyond the water that which is consuming theirs. It was not till England had taken one thousand of our ships and impressed into her service more than six thousand of our citizens; till she had declared, by the proclamation of her Prince Regent, that she would not repeal her aggressive orders *as to us*, until Buonaparte should have repealed his *as to all nations;* till her minister, in formal conference with ours, declared, that no proposition for protecting our seamen from being impressed, under colour of taking their own, was practicable or admissible; that, the door to justice and to all amicable arrangement being closed, and negotiation become both desperate and dishonourable, we concluded that the war she had been for years waging against us, might as well become a war on both sides. She takes fewer vessels from us since the declaration of war than before, because they venture

---

7. Anne Louise Germaine Necker Madame de Staël-Holstein (1766–1817), French-born Swiss intellectual and author, was the daughter of banker and political figure Jacques Necker. Having inspired the jealousy of Napoleon, she was still living in exile in Switzerland when Jefferson, whom she had come to know during his residence in France, wrote her this letter.
8. Louis Dominique Bourguignon (1693–1721), famous Parisian bandit.
9. England's King George III, notoriously unstable during this period of his life.

more cautiously; and we now make full reprisals where before we made none. England is, in principle, the enemy of all maritime nations, as Buonaparte is of the continental; and I place in the same line of insult to the human understanding, the pretension of conquering the ocean, to establish continental rights, as that of conquering the continent, to restore maritime rights. No, my dear Madam; the object of England is the *permanent dominion of the ocean*, and the *monopoly of the trade of the world*. To secure this she must keep a larger fleet than her own resources will maintain. The resources of other nations, then, must be impressed to supply the deficiency of her own. This is sufficiently developed and evidenced by her successive strides towards the usurpation of the sea. Mark them, from her first war after William Pitt the little[1] came into her administration. She first forbade to neutrals all trade with her enemies in time of war, which they had not in time of peace. This deprived them of their trade from port to port of the same nation. Then she forbade them to trade from the port of one nation to that of any other at war with her, although a right fully exercised in time of peace. Next, instead of taking vessels only *entering* a blockaded port, she took them over the whole ocean, if destined to that port, although ignorant of the blockade, and without intention to violate it. Then she took them returning from that port, as if infected by previous infraction of blockade. Then came her paper blockades, by which she might shut up the whole world without sending a ship to sea, except to take all those sailing on it, as they must, of course, be bound to some port. And these were followed by her orders of council, forbidding every nation to go to the port of any other, without coming first to some port of Great Britain, there paying a tribute to her, regulated by the cargo, and taking from her a license to proceed to the port of destination; which operation the vessel was to repeat with the return cargo on its way home. According to these orders, we could not send a vessel from St. Mary's to St. Augustine, distant six hours' sail, on our own coast, without crossing the Atlantic four times, twice with the outward cargo, and twice with the inward. She found this too daring and outrageous for a single step, retracted as to certain articles of commerce, but left it in force as to others which constitute important branches of our exports. And finally, that her views may no longer rest on inference, in a recent debate, her minister declared in open parliament, that the object of the present war is a *monopoly of commerce*.

In some of these atrocities, France kept pace with her fully in speculative wrong, which her impotence only shortened in practical execution. This was called retaliation by both; each charging the other with the initiation of the outrage. As if two combatants might retaliate on an innocent bystander, the blows they received from each other. To make war on both would have been ridiculous. In order, therefore, to single out an enemy, we offered to both, that if either would revoke its hostile decrees, and the other should refuse, we would interdict all intercourse whatever with that other; which would be war of course, as being an avowed departure from neutrality. France accepted the offer, and revoked her decrees as to us. England not only refused, but declared by a solemn proclamation of her Prince Regent, that she would not revoke her orders *even as to us*, until those of France should be annulled *as to the whole world*. We thereon declared war, and with abundant additional cause.

In the mean time, an examination before parliament of the ruinous effects of these orders on her own manufacturers, exposing them to the nation and

---

1. William Pitt the Younger (1759–1806), British prime minister from 1783 to 1801, and again from 1804 to his death.

to the world, their Prince issued a palinodial proclamation,[2] *suspending* the orders on certain conditions, but claiming to renew them at pleasure, as a matter of right. Even this might have prevented the war, if done and known here before its declaration. But the sword being once drawn, the expense of arming incurred, and hostilities in full course, it would have been unwise to discontinue them, until effectual provision should be agreed to by England, for protecting our citizens on the high seas from impressment by her naval commanders, through error, voluntary or involuntary; the fact being notorious, that these officers, entering our ships at sea, under pretext of searching for their seamen, (which they have no right to do by the law or usage of nations, which they neither do, nor ever did, as to any other nation but ours, and which no nation ever before pretended to do in any case,) entering our ships, I say, under pretext of searching for and taking out their seamen, they took ours, native as well as naturalized, knowing them to be ours, merely because they wanted them; insomuch that no American could safely cross the ocean, or venture to pass by sea from one to another of our own ports. It is not long since they impressed at sea two nephews of General Washington, returning from Europe, and put them, as common seamen, under the ordinary discipline of their ships of war. There are certainly other wrongs to be settled between England and us, but of a minor character, and such as a proper spirit of conciliation on both sides would not permit to continue them at war. The sword, however, can never again be sheathed, until the personal safety of an American on the ocean, among the most important and most vital of the rights we possess, is completely provided for.

As soon as we heard of her partial repeal of her orders of council, we offered instantly to suspend hostilities by an armistice, if she would suspend her impressments, and meet us in arrangements for securing our citizens against them. She refused to do it, because impracticable by any arrangement, as she pretends; but, in truth, because a body of sixty to eighty thousand of the finest seamen in the world, which we possess, is too great a resource for manning her exaggerated navy, to be relinquished, as long as she can keep it open. Peace is in her hand, whenever she will renounce the practice of aggression on the persons of our citizens. If she thinks it worth eternal war, eternal war we must have. She alleges that the sameness of language, of manners, of appearance, renders it impossible to distinguish us from her subjects. But because we speak English, and look like them, are we to be punished? Are free and independent men to be submitted to their bondage?

England has misrepresented to all Europe this ground of the war. She has called it a new pretension, set up since the repeal of her orders of council. She knows there has never been a moment of suspension of our reclamations against it, from General Washington's time inclusive, to the present day: and that it is distinctly stated in our declaration of war, as one of its principal causes. She has pretended we have entered into the war to establish the principle of "free bottoms, free goods," or to protect her seamen against her own right over them. We contend for neither of these. She pretends we are partial to France; that we have observed a fraudulent and unfaithful neutrality between her and her enemy. She knows this to be false, and that if there has been any inequality in our proceedings towards the belligerents, it has been in her favour. Her ministers are in possession of full proofs of this. Our accepting at once, and sincerely, the mediation of the virtuous Alexander,[3]

2. I.e., a recantation.
3. Czar Alexander I of Russia (1777–1825), at first an enthusiastic ally of Napoleon, later turned against him and welcomed the emperor's defeat before Moscow in 1812.

their greatest friend, and the most aggravated enemy of Buonaparte, sufficiently proves whether we have partialities on the side of her enemy. I sincerely pray that this mediation may produce a just peace. It will prove that the immortal character, which has first stopped by war the career of the destroyer of mankind, is the friend of peace, of justice, of human happiness, and the patron of unoffending and injured nations. He is too honest and impartial to countenance propositions of peace derogatory to the freedom of the seas.

Shall I apologise to you, my dear Madam, for this long political letter? But yours justifies the subject, and my feelings must plead for the unreserved expression of them; and they have been the less reserved, as being from a private citizen, retired from all connection with the government of his country, and whose ideas, expressed without communication with any one, are neither known, nor imputable to them.

The dangers of the sea are now so great, and the possibilities of interception by sea and land such, that I shall subscribe no name to this letter. You will know from whom it comes, by its reference to the date of time and place of yours, as well as by its subject in answer to that. This omission must not lessen in your view the assurances of my great esteem, of my sincere sympathies for the share which you bear in the afflictions of your country, and the deprivations to which a lawless will has subjected you. In return, you enjoy the dignified satisfaction of having met them, rather than be yoked with the abject, to his car; and that, in withdrawing from oppression, you have followed the virtuous example of a father, whose name will ever be dear to your country and to mankind. With my prayers that you may be restored to it, that you may see it re-established in that temperate portion of liberty which does not infer either anarchy or licentiousness, in that high degree of prosperity which would be the consequence of such a government, in that, in short, which the constitution of 1789 would have insured it, if wisdom could have stayed at that point the fervid but imprudent zeal of men, who did not know the character of their own countrymen, and that you may long live in health and happiness under it, and leave to the world a well educated and virtuous representative and descendant of your honoured father, is the ardent prayer of the sincere and respectful friend who writes this letter.

To Paul Allen[4]

Sir   Monticello Aug. 5. [18]13.

Not being able to go myself in quest of the information respecting Govr. Lewis which was desired in your letter of May 25. I have been obliged to wait the leisure of those who could do it for me. I could forward you within a few days a statement of what I have collected, but more time would improve it, if the impression of the work will not be delayed. I will ask the favor of you therefore to name the latest time which the progress of the other part will admit, by which time you shall not fail to recieve it. My matter may fill perhaps 20 8vo. pages, and as these may be paged independantly of the body of the work, I suppose it may be the last sheet printed.

---

4. Paul Allen (1775–1826), journalist and biographer, had inherited the task of readying for the press the narrative of the Lewis and Clark expedition that Philadelphian Nicholas Biddle had produced from the expedition's original materials. Allen, who had written Jefferson asking him to supply a biographical sketch of Lewis (see "To Paul Allen," August 18, 1813, p. 337), replied two weeks later with word that the Philadelphia firm of Bradford and Inskeep had agreed to delay publication of the work to accommodate Jefferson.

Of General Clarke I shall be able to give you nothing. He was indeed born within 2. miles of Charlottesvill, & 4. of the place of my birth in the county of Albermarle, but he was so much my junior, that before I could know him, his father removed to another part of the country. Accept the assurance of my great respect.

TH: JEFFERSON

To Paul Allen

Sir   Monticello Aug. 18. 1813.
   In compliance with the request conveyed in your letter of May 25. I have endeavored to obtain, from the relations & friends of the late Governor Lewis, information of such incidents of his life as might be not unacceptable to those who may read the Narrative of his Western discoveries. The ordinary occurrences of a private life, & those also while acting in a subordinate sphere in the army, in a time of peace, are not deemed sufficiently interesting to occupy the public attention; but a general account of his parentage, with such smaller incidents as marked early character, are briefly noted, and to these are added, as being peculiarly within my own knolege, whatever related to the public mission, of which an account is now to be published. The result of my enquiries & recollections, shall now therefore be offered, to be enlarged or abridged as you may think best, or otherwise to be used with the materials you may have collected from other sources.
   Meriwether Lewis late Govr. of Louisiana was born on the 18th of Aug. 1774. near the town of Charlottesville in the county of Albemarle in Virginia, of one of the distingished families of that state. John Lewis one of his father's uncles was a member of the King's council, before the revolution, another of them, Fielding Lewis, married a sister of Genl. Washington. His father Wm. Lewis was the youngest of 5. sons of Colo. Robert Lewis of Albemarle, the 4th of whom Charles was one of the early patriots who stepped forward in the commencement of the revolution, and commanded one of the regiments first raised in Virginia and placed on Continental establishment. Happily situated at home with a wife and young family, & a fortune placing him at ease, he left all to aid in the liberation of his country from foreign usurpations then first unmasking their ultimate end & aim. His good sense, integrity, bravery, enterprize & remarkable bodily powers marked him an officer of great promise; but he unfortunately died early in the revolution. Nicholas Lewis the 2d of his father's brothers commanded a regiment of militia in the successful expedition of 1776 against the Cherokee Indians, who, seduced by the agents of the British government to take up the hatchet against us, had committed great havoc on our Southern frontier, by murdering and scalping helpless women & children according to their cruel and cowardly principles of warfare. The chastisement they then recieved closed the history of their wars, prepared them for recieving the elements of civilisation which zealously inculcated by the present government of the U.S. have rendered them an industrious, peaceable and happy people. This member of the family of Lewises, whose bravery was so usefully improved on this occasion, was endeared to all who knew him by his inflexible probity, courteous disposition, benevolent heart, & engaging modesty & manners. He was the umpire of all the private differences of his county, selected always by both parties. He was also the guardian of Meriwether Lewis, of whom we are now to speak and who had lost his father at an early age. He

continued some years under the fostering care of a tender Mother, of the
respectable family of Meriwethers of the same county, and was remarkable
even in infancy for enterprize, boldness & discretion. When only 8. years
of age, he habitually went out in the dead of night alone with his dogs, into
the forest to hunt the raccoon & opossum, which, seeking their food in the
night, can then only be taken. In this exercise no season or circumstance
could obstruct his purpose, plunging thro' the winter's snows and frozen
streams in pursuit of his object. At 13. he was put to the Latin school and
continued at that untill 15. when he returned to his mother, and entered
on the cares of his farm, having, as well as a younger brother, been left by
his father with a competency for all the correct and comfortable purposes
of temperate life. His talent for observation which had led him to an accurate knolege of the plants & animals of his own country, would have distinguished him as a farmer; but at the age of 20. yeilding to the ardor of
youth and a passion for more dazzling pursuits, he engaged as a volunteer
in the body of militia which were called out by Genl. Washington, on occasion of the discontents produced by the Excise taxes in the Western parts
of the U.S. and from that situation he was removed to the regular service
as a lieutenant in the line. At 23. he was promoted to a Captaincy & always
attracting the first attention where punctuality & fidelity were requisite, he
was appointed paymaster to his regiment. About this time a circumstance
occurred which leading to the transaction which is the subject of this book,
will justify a recurrence to it's original idea. While I resided in Paris John
Ledyard[5] of Connecticut arrived there, well known in the U.S. for energy
of body & mind. He had accompanied Capt. Cook in his voyage to the
Pacific ocean, and distinguished himself on that voyage by his intrepidity.
Being of a roaming disposition, he was now panting for some new enterprize. His immediate object at Paris was to engage a mercantile company in
the fur-trade of the Western coast of America, in which however he failed.
I then proposed to him to go by land to Kamschatka, cross in some of the
Russian vessels to Nootka sound, fall down into the latitude of the Missouri, and penetrate to and thro' that to the U.S. He eagerly siesed the idea,
and only asked to be assured of the permission of the Russian government.
I interested in obtaining that M. de Simoulin M.P.[6] of the Empress at Paris,
but more especially the Baron de Grimm M.P. of Saxe-Gotha her more special agent & correspondent there in matters not immediately diplomatic.
Her permission was obtained & an assurance of protection while the
course of the voyage should be thro' her territories. Ledyard set out from
Paris & arrived at St. Petersbg. after the empress had left that place to pass
the winter (I think) at Moscow. His finances not permitting him to make
unnecessary stay at St. Petersburg he left it, with a passport from one of the
ministers, & at 200. miles from Kamschatka was obliged to take up his winter quarters. He was preparing in the spring to resume his journey, when he
was arrested by an officer of the Empress, who by this time had changed
her mind, and forbidden his proceeding. He was put into a close carriage &
conveyed day & night, without ever stopping, till they reached Poland where
he was set down & left to himself. The fatigue of this journey broke down
his constitution, and when he returned to Paris his bodily strength was

5. John Ledyard (1751–1789), American sailor who joined the Pacific expedition of Captain James
   Cook in 1776 and published *A Journal of Captain Cook's Last Voyage* in London in 1783. After
   unsuccessfully attempting expeditions of his own in Russia and the Pacific Basin, he died in Cairo
   where he had gone in an effort to explore the Niger River.
6. Minister plenipotentiary.

much impaired. His mind however remained firm and he after this undertook the journey to Egypt. I recieved a letter from him, full of sanguine hopes, dated at Cairo, the 15th of Nov. 1788. the day before he was to set out for the head of the Nile on which day however he ended his career and life. And thus failed the first attempt to explore the Western part of our Northern continent.

In 1792. I proposed to the A.P.S.[7] that we should set on foot a subscription to engage some competent person to explore that region in the opposite direction that is, by ascending the Missouri, crossing the Stony mountains, and descending the nearest river to the Pacific. Capt. Lewis being then stationed at Charlottesville on the recruiting service, warmly sollicited me to obtain for him the execution of that object. I told him it was proposed that the person engaged should be attended by a single companion only, to avoid exciting alarm among the Indians. This did not deter him. But Mr. André Michaux a professed botanist, author of the Flora Boreali-Americana, and of the histoire des chenes d'Amerique, offering his services, they were accepted. He recieved his instructions, and when he had reached Kentucky in the prosecution of his journey, he was overtaken by an order from the minister of France then at Philadelphia to relinquish the expedition, & to pursue elsewhere the Botanical enquiries on which he was employed by that government; and thus failed the 2d attempt for exploring that region.[8]

In 1803 the act for establishing trading houses with the Indian tribes being about to expire some modifications of it were recommended to Congress by a confidential message of Jan. 18. and an extension of it's views to the Indians on the Missouri. In order to prepare the way the message proposed the sending an exploring party to trace the Missouri to it's source, to cross the highlands and follow the best water communication which offered itself from thence to the Pacific ocean. Congress approved the proposition and voted a sum of money for carrying it into execution. Captain Lewis who had then been near two years with me as private secretary, immediately renewed his sollictations to have the direction of the party. I had now had opportunities of knowing him intimately. Of courage undaunted, possessing a firmness & perseverance of purpose which nothing but impossibilities could divert from it's direction, careful as a father of those committed to his charge, yet steady in the maintenance of order & discipline, intimate with the Indian character, customs & principles, habituated to the hunting life, guarded by exact observation of the vegetables & animals of his own country, against losing time in the description of objects already possessed, honest, disinterested, liberal, of sound understanding and a fidelity to truth so scrupulous that whatever he should report would be as certain as if seen by ourselves, with all these qualifications as if selected and implanted by nature in one body, for this express purpose, I could have no hesitation in confiding the enterprize to him. To fill up the measure desired, he wanted nothing but a greater familiarity with the technical language of the natural sciences, and readiness in the astronomical observations necessary for the geography of his route. To acquire these he repaired immediately to

7. American Philosophical Society.
8. At this point Jefferson wrote but then deleted the following: "When in 1803. Louisiana was ceded to the U.S. a knolege of the Missouri was no longer an object of mere geographical curiosity, but was become highly interesting to the nation, all the country covered by the waters running into the Misipi constituting the extent of their new acquisition in the upper country. Capt. Lewis was now become my private Secretary, and on the first mention of the subject he renewed his sollicitations to be the person employed. My knolege of him, now become more intimate, left no hesitation on my part. I had now had opportunity of knowing his character intimately" (*LLCE* 2:589).

Philadelphia, and placed himself under the tutorage of the distinguished professors of that place, who with a zeal & emulation, enkindled by an ardent devotion to science, communicated to him freely the information requisite for the purposes of the journey. While attending too, at Lancaster, the fabrication of the arms with which he chose that his men should be provided, he had the benefit of daily communication with Mr. Andrew Ellicot,[9] whose experience in Astronomical observation, and practice of it in the woods, enabled him to apprise Capt. Lewis of the wants & difficulties he would encounter, and of the substitutes & resources offered by a woodland and uninhabited country.

Deeming it necessary he should have some person with him of known competence to the direction of the enterprise, & to whom he might confide it, in the event of accident to himself he proposed William Clarke, brother of Genl. Geo. Rogers Clarke, who was approved, and with that view recieved a commission of captain.

In April 1803. a draught of his instructions was sent to Capt. Lewis & on the 20th of June they were signed in the following form.[1]

While these things were going on here, the country of Louisiana, lately ceded by Spain to France, had been the subject of negociation at Paris between us & this last power; and had actually been transferred to us by treaties executed at Paris on the 30th of April. This information recieved about the 1st day of July, increased infinitely the interest we felt in the expedition, & lessened the apprehensions of interruption from other powers. Every thing in this quarter being now prepared, Capt. Lewis left Washington on the 5th of July 1803 and proceeded to Pittsburg where other articles had been ordered to be provided for him. The men too were to be selected from the military stations on the Ohio. Delays of preparation, difficulties of navigation down the Ohio, & other untoward obstruction retarded his arrival at Cahokia until the season was so far advanced as to render it prudent to suspend his entering the Missouri before the ice should break up in the succeeding spring. From this time his journal, now published,[2] will give the history of his journey to and from the Pacific ocean, until his return to St. Louis on the 23d of Sep. 1806. Never did a similar event excite more joy thro' the United States. The humblest of it's citizens had taken a lively interest in the issue of this journey, and looked forward with impatience for the information it would furnish. Their anxieties too for the safety of the corps had been kept in a state of excitement by lugubrious rumors, circulated from time to time on uncertain authorities, and uncontradicted by letters or other direct information from the time they had left the Mandan towns on their ascent up the river in April of the preceding year 1805, until their actual return to St. Louis.

It was the middle of Feb. 1807. before Capt. Lewis with his companion Clarke reached the city of Washington where Congress was then in session. That body granted to the two chiefs and their followers, the donation of lands which they had been encouraged to expect in reward of their toils & dangers. Capt. Lewis was soon after appointed Governor of Louisiana, and Capt. Clarke a General of it's militia and agent of the U.S. for Indian affairs in that department.

---

9. Andrew Ellicott (1754–1820), surveyor and astronomer from Lancaster.
1. See "To Meriwether Lewis," June 20, 1803, p. 294.
2. The Biddle-Allen *History of the Expedition under the Command of Captains Lewis and Clark* (1814) relied on Lewis's journals, but was not a simple transcription of any of the original materials produced by members of the expedition.

A considerable time intervened before the Governor's arrival at St. Louis. He found the territory distracted by feuds & contentions among the officers of the government, & the people themselves divided by these into factions & parties. He determined at once, to take no side with either; but to use every endeavor to conciliate & harmonize them. The even-handed justice he administered to all soon established a respect for his person & authority, and perseverance & time wore down animosities and reunited the citizens again into one family.

Governor Lewis had from early life been subject to hypocondriac affections.[3] It was a constitutional disposition in all the nearer branches of the family of his name, & was more immediately inherited by him from his father. They had not however been so strong as to give uneasiness to his family. While he lived with me in Washington, I observed at times sensible depressions of mind, but knowing their constitutional source, I estimated their course by what I had seen in the family. During his Western expedition the constant exertion which that required of all the faculties of body & mind, suspended these distressing affections; but after his establishment at St. Louis in sedentary occupations they returned upon him with redoubled vigor, and began seriously to alarm his friends. He was in a paroxysm of one of these when his affairs rendered it necessary for him to go to Washington. He proceeded to the Chickasaw bluffs where he arrived on the 16th of Sep. 1809. with a view of continuing his journey thence by water. Mr. Neely, agent of the U.S. with the Chickasaw Indians arriving there two days after, found him extremely indisposed, and betraying at times some symptoms of a derangement of mind. The rumors of a war with England, & apprehensions that he might lose the papers he was bringing on, among which were the vouchers of his public accounts, and the journals & papers of his Western expedition, induced him here to change his mind and to take his course by land thro' the Chickasaw country. Altho' he appeared somewhat relieved, Mr. Neely kindly determined to accompany & watch over him. Unfortunately, at their encampment after having passed the Tennessee one day's journey, they lost two horses, which obliging Mr. Neely to halt for their recovery, the Governor proceeded under a promise to wait for him at the house of the first white inhabitant on his road. He stopped at the house of a Mr. Grinder, who not being at home, his wife alarmed at the symptoms of derangement she discovered, gave him up the house, and retired to rest herself in an outhouse;[4] the Governor's & Neely's servants lodging in another. About 3. oclock in the night he did the deed which plunged his friends into affliction and deprived his country of one of her most valued citizens whose valour & intelligence would have been now imployed in avenging the wrongs of his country and in emulating by land the splendid deeds which have honored her arms on the ocean. It lost too to the nation the benefit of recieving from his own hand the Narrative now offered them of his sufferings & successes in endeavoring to extend for them the boundaries of science, and to present to their knolege that vast & fertile country which their sons are destined to fill with arts, with science, with freedom & happiness.

To this melancholy close of the life of one whom posterity will declare not to have lived in vain I have only to add that all facts I have stated are either known to myself, or communicated by his family or others for whose truth

3. In the old sense of afflictions or symptoms.
4. Outbuilding.

I have no hesitation to make [myself][5] responsible: and I conclude with tendering you the assurances of my respect & consideration.

TH: JEFFERSON

To Nicholas Biddle[6]

Sir   Monticello Aug. 20. [18]13.
In a letter from Mr. Paul Allen of Philadelphia, I was informed that other business had obliged you to turn over to him the publication of Govr. Lewis's journal of his Western expedition; and he requested me to furnish him with any materials I could for writing a sketch of his life. I now inclose him such as I have been able to procure, to be used with any other information he may have recieved, or alone, if he has no other or in any way you & he shall think proper. The part you have been so good as to take in digesting the work entitles you to decide on whatever may be proposed to go out under it's auspice's; and on this ground I take the liberty of putting under cover to you, and for your perusal, my letter to Mr. Allen, which I will request you to seal & hand on to him. I am happy in this occasion of expressing my portion of the thanks all will owe you for the trouble you have taken with the interesting narrative, and the assurance of my sentiments of high esteem and respect.

TH: JEFFERSON

To John Adams

DEAR SIR   Monticello Oct. 28. [18]13.
According to the reservation between us, of taking up one of the subjects of our correspondence at a time, I turn to your letters of Aug. 16. and Sep. 2.[7]
The passage you quote from Theognis, I think has an Ethical, rather than a political object. The whole piece is a moral *exhortation*, παραίνεσις, and this passage particularly seems to be a reproof to man, who, while with his domestic animals he is curious to improve the race by employing always the finest male, pays no attention to the improvement of his own race, but intermarries with the vicious, the ugly, or the old, for considerations of wealth or ambition. It is in conformity with the principle adopted afterwards by the Pythagoreans, and expressed by Ocellus[8] in another form. Περι δε τῆς ἐκ

---

5. *Myself* is supplied to complete the apparent sense of Jefferson's sentence.
6. Nicholas Biddle (1786–1844), a wealthy, multitalented Philadelphian, had been approached to write the Narrative of the expedition by William Clark in February 1810. Clark had decided he could not do it himself, and he had had no luck trying to convince Virginian William Wirt to undertake it instead. Biddle at first declined as well, but then having changed his mind proceeded with great thoroughness. He visited Clark in Virginia later in 1810 and took lengthy notes on Clark's answers to his many questions, and by midsummer 1811 had completed his impressive draft. Financial difficulties that befell the contracted publisher, Conrad & Co., caused delay at that point, and then Biddle, having been elected to the Pennsylvania legislature, withdrew from the project in 1812, turning it over to Paul Allen.
7. The letters from John Adams had been more numerous over the summer: in fact, before penning this letter, Jefferson had last written his old friend on June 27 and August 22; Adams in that period had written him sixteen letters. Small wonder that, on August 22, Jefferson confessed, "Since my letter of June 27, I am in your debt for many." He had read all of them "with infinite delight" but had had trouble keeping up with his replies.
8. Ocellus Lucanus was an obscure Greek poet connected with the Pythagoreans. Jefferson quotes from a work called, in Thomas Taylor's 1831 translation, On the Nature of the Universe, ch. 4. Adams had quoted a similar precept from Theognis of Megara (fl. 544–548 B.C.E.).

τῶν αλληλων ανθρωπων γενεσεως etc.—ουχ ἡδονης ἑνεκα ἡ μιξις. Which, as literally as intelligibility will admit, may be thus translated. "Concerning the interprocreation of men, how, and of whom it shall be, in a perfect manner, and according to the laws of modesty and sanctity, conjointly, this is what I think right. First to lay it down that we do not commix for the sake of pleasure, but of the procreation of children. For the powers, the organs and desires for coition have not been given by god to man for the sake of pleasure, but for the procreation of the race. For as it were incongruous for a mortal born to partake of divine life, the immortality of the race being taken away, god fulfilled the purpose by making the generations uninterrupted and continuous. This therefore we are especially to lay down as a principle, that coition is not for the sake of pleasure." But Nature, not trusting to this moral and abstract motive, seems to have provided more securely for the perpetuation of the species by making it the effect of the oestrum implanted in the constitution of both sexes. And not only has the commerce of love been indulged on this unhallowed impulse, but made subservient also to wealth and ambition by marriages without regard to the beauty, the healthiness, the understanding, or virtue of the subject from which we are to breed. The selecting the best male for a Haram of well chosen females also, which Theognis seems to recommend from the example of our sheep and asses, would doubtless improve the human, as it does the brute animal, and produce a race of veritable αριστοι.[9] For experience proves that the moral and physical qualities of man, whether good or evil, are transmissible in a certain degree from father to son. But I suspect that the equal rights of men will rise up against this privileged Solomon, and oblige us to continue acquiescence under the Ἀμαυρωσις γενεος ἀστων[1] which Theognis complains of, and to content ourselves with the accidental aristoi produced by the fortuitous concourse of breeders. For I agree with you that there is a natural aristocracy among men. The grounds of this are virtue and talents. Formerly bodily powers gave place among the aristoi. But since the invention of gunpowder has armed the weak as well as the strong with missile death, bodily strength, like beauty, good humor, politeness and other accomplishments, has become but an auxiliary ground of distinction. There is also an artificial aristocracy founded on wealth and birth, without either virtue or talents; for with these it would belong to the first class. The natural aristocracy I consider as the most precious gift of nature for the instruction, the trusts, and government of society. And indeed it would have been inconsistent in creation to have formed man for the social state, and not to have provided virtue and wisdom enough to manage the concerns of the society. May we not even say that that form of government is the best which provides the most effectually for a pure selection of these natural aristoi into the offices of government? The artificial aristocracy is a mischievous ingredient in government, and provision should be made to prevent it's ascendancy. On the question, What is the best provision, you and I differ; but we differ as rational friends, using the free exercise of our own reason, and mutually indulging it's errors. You think it best to put the Pseudo-aristoi into a separate chamber of legislation where they may be hindered from doing mischief by their coordinate branches, and where also they may be a protection to wealth against the Agrarian and plundering enterprises of the Majority of the people. I think that to give them power

9. Aristocrats (Greek).
1. Decline of the human race (Greek).

in order to prevent them from doing mischief, is arming them for it, and increasing instead of remedying the evil. For if the coordinate branches can arrest their action, so may they that of the coordinates. Mischief may be done negatively as well as positively. Of this a cabal in the Senate of the U. S. has furnished many proofs. Nor do I believe them necessary to protect the wealthy; because enough of these will find their way into every branch of the legislation to protect themselves. From 15. to 20. legislatures of our own, in action for 30. years past, have proved that no fears of an equalisa-tion of property are to be apprehended from them.

I think the best remedy is exactly that provided by all our constitutions, to leave to the citizens the free election and separation of the aristoi from the pseudo-aristoi, of the wheat from the chaff. In general they will elect the real good and wise. In some instances, wealth may corrupt, and birth blind them; but not in sufficient degree to endanger the society.

It is probable that our difference of opinion may in some measure be produced by a difference of character in those among whom we live. From what I have seen of Massachusets and Connecticut myself, and still more from what I have heard, and the character given of the former by yourself, [vol. I. pa. III.][2] who know them so much better, there seems to be in those two states a traditionary reverence for certain families, which has rendered the offices of the government nearly hereditary in those families. I presume that from an early period of your history, members of these families hap-pening to possess virtue and talents, have honestly exercised them for the good of the people, and by their services have endeared their names to them.

In coupling Connecticut with you, I mean it politically only, not morally. For having made the Bible the Common law of their land they seem to have modelled their morality on the story of Jacob and Laban. But altho' this hereditary succession to office with you may in some degree be founded in real family merit, yet in a much higher degree it has proceeded from your strict alliance of church and state. These families are canonised in the eyes of the people on the common principle "you tickle me, and I will tickle you." In Virginia we have nothing of this. Our clergy, before the revolution, hav-ing been secured against rivalship by fixed salaries, did not give themselves the trouble of acquiring influence over the people. Of wealth, there were great accumulations in particular families, handed down from generation to generation under the English law of entails. But the only object of ambi-tion for the wealthy was a seat in the king's council. All their court then was paid to the crown and it's creatures; and they Philipised[3] in all collisions between the king and people. Hence they were unpopular; and that unpop-ularity continues attached to their names. A Randolph, a Carter, or a Bur-well must have great personal superiority over a common competitor to be elected by the people, even at this day.

At the first session of our legislature after the Declaration of Indepen-dance, we passed a law abolishing entails. And this was followed by one abolishing the privilege of Primogeniture, and dividing the lands of intes-tates equally among all their children, or other representatives. These laws, drawn by myself, laid the axe to the root of Pseudo-aristocracy. And had another which I prepared been adopted by the legislature, our work would have been compleat. It was a Bill for the more general diffusion of learn-

2. Jefferson's bracketed reference is to A Defence of the Constitutions of Government of the United States (1788–89), by Adams.
3. Sided with the ruler.

ing. This proposed to divide every county into wards of 5. or 6. miles square, like your townships; to establish in each ward a free school for reading, writing and common arithmetic; to provide for the annual selection of the best subjects from these schools who might recieve at the public expence a higher degree of education at a district school; and from these district schools to select a certain number of the most promising subjects to be compleated at an University, where all the useful sciences should be taught. Worth and genius would thus have been sought out from every condition of life, and compleatly prepared by education for defeating the competition of wealth and birth for public trusts.

My proposition had for a further object to impart to these wards those portions of self-government for which they are best qualified, by confiding to them the care of their poor, their roads, police, elections, the nomination of jurors, administration of justice in small cases, elementary exercises of militia, in short, to have made them little republics, with a Warden at the head of each, for all those concerns which, being under their eye, they would better manage than the larger republics of the county or state. A general call of ward-meetings by their Wardens on the same day thro' the state would at any time produce the genuine sense of the people on any required point, and would enable the state to act in mass, as your people have so often done, and with so much effect, by their town meetings. The law for religious freedom, which made a part of this system, having put down the aristocracy of the clergy, and restored to the citizen the freedom of the mind, and those of entails and descents nurturing an equality of condition among them, this on Education would have raised the mass of the people to the high ground of moral respectability necessary to their own safety, and to orderly government; and would have compleated the great object of qualifying them to select the veritable aristoi, for the trusts of government, to the exclusion of the Pseudalists: and the same Theognis who has furnished the epigraphs of your two letters assures us that "ουδεμιαν πω, Κυρν' ἀγαθοι πολιν ὤλεσαν ἀνδρες."[4] Altho' this law has not yet been acted on but in a small and inefficient degree, it is still considered as before the legislature, with other bills of the revised code, not yet taken up, and I have great hope that some patriotic spirit will, at a favorable moment, call it up, and make it the key-stone of the arch of our government.

With respect to Aristocracy, we should further consider that, before the establishment of the American states, nothing was known to History but the Man of the old world, crouded within limits either small or overcharged, and steeped in the vices which that situation generates. A government adapted to such men would be one thing; but a very different one that for the Man of these states. Here every one may have land to labor for himself if he chuses; or, preferring the exercise of any other industry, may exact for it such compensation as not only to afford a comfortable subsistence, but wherewith to provide for a cessation from labor in old age. Every one, by his property, or by his satisfactory situation, is interested in the support of law and order. And such men may safely and advantageously reserve to themselves a wholsome controul over their public affairs, and a degree of freedom, which in the hands of the Canaille of the cities of Europe, would be instantly perverted to the demolition and destruction of every thing public and private. The history of the last 25. years of France, and of the last 40.

4. Curnis, good men have never injured a city (Greek). Curnis is the man addressed in the maxim of Theognis quoted by Adams.

years in America, nay of it's last 200. years, proves the truth of both parts of this observation.

But even in Europe a change has sensibly taken place in the mind of Man. Science had liberated the ideas of those who read and reflect, and the American example had kindled feelings of right in the people. An insurrection has consequently begun, of science, talents and courage against rank and birth, which have fallen into contempt. It has failed in it's first effort, because the mobs of the cities, the instrument used for it's accomplishment, debased by ignorance, poverty and vice, could not be restrained to rational action. But the world will recover from the panic of this first catastrophe. Science is progressive, and talents and enterprize on the alert. Resort may be had to the people of the country, a more governable power from their principles and subordination; and rank, and birth, and tinsel-aristocracy will finally shrink into insignificance, even there. This however we have no right to meddle with. It suffices for us, if the moral and physical condition of our own citizens qualifies them to select the able and good for the direction of their government, with a recurrence of elections at such short periods as will enable them to displace an unfaithful servant before the mischief he meditates may be irremediable.

I have thus stated my opinion on a point on which we differ, not with a view to controversy, for we are both too old to change opinions which are the result of a long life of inquiry and reflection; but on the suggestion of a former letter of yours, that we ought not to die before we have explained ourselves to each other. We acted in perfect harmony thro' a long and perilous contest for our liberty and independance. A constitution has been acquired which, tho neither of us think perfect, yet both consider as competent to render our fellow-citizens the happiest and the securest on whom the sun has ever shone. If we do not think exactly alike as to it's imperfections, it matters little to our country which, after devoting to it long lives of disinterested labor, we have delivered over to our successors in life, who will be able to take care of it, and of themselves.

Of the pamphlet on aristocracy which has been sent to you, or who may be it's author, I have heard nothing but thro' your letter. If the person you suspect[5] it may be known from the quaint, mystical and hyperbolical ideas, involved in affected, new-fangled and pedantic terms, which stamp his writings. Whatever it be, I hope your quiet is not to be affected at this day by the rudeness of intemperance of scribblers; but that you may continue in tranquility to live and to rejoice in the prosperity of our country until it shall be your own wish to take your seat among the Aristoi who have gone before you. Ever and affectionately yours.

TH: JEFFERSON

P.S. Can you assist my memory on the enquiries of my letter of Aug. 22.?[6]

---

5. As Adams suspected, John Taylor (1753–1824), of Caroline County, Virginia, was the man who had attacked Adams's *Defence* in the work in question, *An Inquiry into the Principles and Policy of the Government of the United States* (1814).
6. Jefferson had asked Adams to confirm his recollection as to the authors of three Revolutionary-era pamphlets. See *AJL* 2:370.

To Alexander von Humboldt[7]

MY DEAR FRIEND AND BARON,—   December 6, 1813.

I have to acknowledge your two letters of December 20 and 26, 1811, by Mr. Correa, and am first to thank you for making me acquainted with that most excellent character. He was so kind as to visit me at Monticello, and I found him one of the most learned and amiable of men.[8] It was a subject of deep regret to separate from so much worth in the moment of its becoming known to us.

The livraison of your astronomical observations, and the 6th and 7th on the subject of New Spain, with the corresponding atlasses, are duly received, as had been the preceding cahiers.[9] For these treasures of a learning so interesting to us, accept my sincere thanks. I think it most fortunate that your travels in those countries were so timed as to make them known to the world in the moment they were about to become actors on its stage. That they will throw off their European dependence I have no doubt; but in what kind of government their revolution will end I am not so certain. History, I believe, furnishes no example of a priest-ridden people maintaining a free civil government. This marks the lowest grade of ignorance, of which their civil as well as religious leaders will always avail themselves for their own purposes. The vicinity of New Spain[1] to the United States, and their consequent intercourse, may furnish schools for the higher, and example for the lower classes of their citizens. And Mexico, where we learn from you that men of science are not wanting, may revolutionize itself under better auspices than the Southern provinces. These last, I fear, must end in military despotisms. The different casts of their inhabitants, their mutual hatreds and jealousies, their profound ignorance and bigotry, will be played off by cunning leaders, and each be made the instrument of enslaving others. But of all this you can best judge, for in truth we have little knowledge of them to be depended on, but through you. But in whatever governments they end they will be *American* governments, no longer to be involved in the never-ceasing broils of Europe. The European nations constitute a separate division of the globe; their localities make them part of a distinct system; they have a set of interests of their own in which it is our business never to engage ourselves. America has a hemisphere to itself. It must have its separate system of interests, which must not be subordinated to those of Europe. The insulated state in which nature has placed the American continent, should so far avail it that no spark of war kindled in the other quarters of the globe should be wafted across the wide oceans which separate us from them. And it will be so. In fifty years more the United States alone will contain fifty millions of inhabitants, and fifty years are soon gone over. The peace of 1763 is within that period. I was then twenty years old, and of course remember well all the transactions of the war preceding it. And you will live to see the epoch now equally ahead of us; and the numbers which will then be spread over the other parts of the

---

7. Alexander von Humboldt (1769–1859), German scientist and explorer, had traveled in South America from 1799 to 1804 and had begun publishing the important results of his work in 1805. After visiting Philadelphia while on his return to Europe in 1804, Humboldt, accompanied by Charles Willson Peale, made a two-week stay in Washington to converse with Jefferson on their shared interests in natural history and politics. The two had been occasional correspondents ever since.
8. See "To José Corrêa da Serra," April 26, 1816, p. 358.
9. Sections (French); i.e., of Humboldt's ongoing series of scientific publications on his American travels. "Livraison": part (French).
1. All of Spanish America.

American hemisphere, catching long before that the principles of our portion of it, and concurring with us in the maintenance of the same system. You see how readily we run into ages beyond the grave; and even those of us to whom that grave is already opening its quiet bosom. I am anticipating events of which you will be the bearer to me in the Elysian fields fifty years hence.

You know, my friend, the benevolent plan we were pursuing here for the happiness of the aboriginal inhabitants in our vicinities. We spared nothing to keep them at peace with one another. To teach them agriculture and the rudiments of the most necessary arts, and to encourage industry by establishing among them separate property. In this way they would have been enabled to subsist and multiply on a moderate scale of landed possession. They would have mixed their blood with ours, and been amalgamated and identified with us within no distant period of time. On the commencement of our present war, we pressed on them the observance of peace and neutrality, but the interested and unprincipled policy of England has defeated all our labors for the salvation of these unfortunate people. They have seduced the greater part of the tribes within our neighborhood, to take up the hatchet against us, and the cruel massacres they have committed on the women and children of our frontiers taken by surprise, will oblige us now to pursue them to extermination, or drive them to new seats beyond our reach. Already we have driven their patrons and seducers into Montreal, and the opening season will force them to their last refuge, the walls of Quebec. We have cut off all possibility of intercourse and of mutual aid, and may pursue at our leisure whatever plan we find necessary to secure ourselves against the future effects of their savage and ruthless warfare. The confirmed brutalization, if not the extermination of this race in our America, is therefore to form an additional chapter in the English history of the same colored man in Asia, and of the brethren of their own color in Ireland, and wherever else Anglo-mercantile cupidity can find a two-penny interest in deluging the earth with human blood. But let us turn from the loathsome contemplation of the degrading effects of commercial avarice.

That their Arrowsmith[2] should have stolen your Map of Mexico, was in the piratical spirit of his country. But I should be sincerely sorry if our Pike[3] has made an ungenerous use of your candid communications here; and the more so as he died in the arms of victory gained over the enemies of his country. Whatever he did was on a principle of enlarging knowledge, and not for filthy shillings and pence of which he made none from that work. If what he has borrowed has any effect it will be to excite an appeal in his readers from his defective information to the copious volumes of it with which you have enriched the world. I am sorry he omitted even to acknowledge the source of his information. It has been an oversight, and not at all in the spirit of his generous nature. Let me solicit your forgiveness then of a deceased hero, of an honest and zealous patriot, who lived and died for his country.

You will find it inconceivable that Lewis's journey to the Pacific should not yet have appeared; nor is it in my power to tell you the reason. The measures taken by his surviving companion, Clarke, for the publication, have

2. Aaron Arrowsmith (1750–1823), influential map publisher in London.
3. Zebulon M. Pike (1779–1813), American explorer born in New Jersey, published *An Account of Expeditions to the Sources of the Mississippi* . . . in 1810. In his own travel account, Humboldt soon complained that Pike's "maps of Mexico" were "reduced from my great map of New Spain, of which I left a copy, in 1804, at the secretary of state's office at Washington." Translated and quoted in Donald Jackson, ed., *The Journals of Zebulon Montgomery Pike, with Related Documents*, 2 vols. (Norman: University of Oklahoma Press, 1966), 2:378.

not answered our wishes in point of despatch. I think, however, from what I have heard, that the mere journal will be out within a few weeks in two volumes 8vo. These I will take care to send you with the tobacco seed you desired, if it be possible for them to escape the thousand ships of our enemies spread over the ocean. The botanical and zoological discoveries of Lewis will probably experience greater delay, and become known to the world through other channels before that volume will be ready. The Atlas, I believe, waits on the leisure of the engraver.

Although I do not know whether you are now at Paris or ranging the regions of Asia to acquire more knowledge for the use of men, I cannot deny myself the gratification of an endeavor to recall myself to your recollection, and of assuring you of my constant attachment, and of renewing to you the just tribute of my affectionate esteem and high respect and consideration.

To Edward Coles[4]

DEAR SIR,—   MONTICELLO. August 25th, [18]14
Your favour of July 31, was duly received, and was read with peculiar pleasure. The sentiments breathed through the whole do honor to both the head and heart of the writer. Mine on the subject of slavery of negroes have long since been in possession of the public, and time has only served to give them stronger root. The love of justice and the love of country plead equally the cause of these people, and it is a moral reproach to us that they should have pleaded it so long in vain, and should have produced not a single effort, nay I fear not much serious willingness to relieve them & ourselves from our present condition of moral & political reprobation. From those of the former generation who were in the fulness of age when I came into public life, which was while our controversy with England was on paper only, I soon saw that nothing was to be hoped. Nursed and educated in the daily habit of seeing the degraded condition, both bodily and mental, of those unfortunate beings, not reflecting that that degradation was very much the work of themselves & their fathers, few minds have yet doubted but that they were as legitimate subjects of property as their horses and cattle. The quiet and monotonous course of colonial life has been disturbed by no alarm, and little reflection on the value of liberty. And when alarm was taken at an enterprize on their own, it was not easy to carry them to the whole length of the principles which they invoked for themselves. In the first or second session of the Legislature after I became a member, I drew to this subject the attention of Col. Bland, one of the oldest, ablest, & most respected members, and he undertook to move for certain moderate extensions of the protection of the laws to these people. I seconded his motion, and, as a younger member, was more spared in the debate; but he was denounced as an enemy of his country, & was treated with the grossest indecorum. From an early stage of our revolution other & more distant duties were assigned to me, so that from that time till my return from Europe in 1789, and I may say till I returned to reside at home in 1809, I had little opportunity of knowing the progress of public sentiment here on this subject. I had always hoped that the younger generation receiving their early impressions after

4. Virginian Edward Coles (1786–1868), serving at the time as President James Madison's private secretary, had written Jefferson for advice on how to eliminate slavery. In 1815, Coles would move with his slaves to Illinois Territory and set them free, giving each emancipated family a 160-acre farm. He would win election as an antislavery governor of Illinois in 1822.

the flame of liberty had been kindled in every breast, & had become as it were the vital spirit of every American, that the generous temperament of youth, analogous to the motion of their blood, and above the suggestions of avarice, would have sympathized with oppression wherever found, and proved their love of liberty beyond their own share of it. But my intercourse with them, since my return has not been sufficient to ascertain that they had made towards this point the progress I had hoped. Your solitary but welcome voice is the first which has brought this sound to my ear; and I have considered the general silence which prevails on this subject as indicating an apathy unfavorable to every hope. Yet the hour of emancipation is advancing, in the march of time. It will come; and whether brought on by the generous energy of our own minds; or by the bloody process of St. Domingo, excited and conducted by the power of our present enemy, if once stationed permanently within our Country, and offering asylum & arms to the oppressed, is a leaf of our history not yet turned over. As to the method by which this difficult work is to be effected, if permitted to be done by ourselves, I have seen no proposition so expedient on the whole, as that of emancipation of those born after a given day, and of their education and expatriation after a given age. This would give time for a gradual extinction of that species of labour & substitution of another, and lessen the severity of the shock which an operation so fundamental cannot fail to produce. For men probably of any color, but of this color we know, brought from their infancy without necessity for thought or forecast, are by their habits rendered as incapable as children of taking care of themselves, and are extinguished promptly wherever industry is necessary for raising young. In the mean time they are pests in society by their idleness, and the depredations to which this leads them. Their amalgamation with the other color produces a degradation to which no lover of his country, no lover of excellence in the human character can innocently consent. I am sensible of the partialities with which you have looked towards me as the person who should undertake this salutary but arduous work. But this, my dear sir, is like bidding old Priam to buckle the armour of Hector "trementibus æquo humeris et inutile ferruncingi."[5] No, I have overlived the generation with which mutual labors & perils begat mutual confidence and influence. This enterprise is for the young; for those who can follow it up, and bear it through to its consummation. It shall have all my prayers, & these are the only weapons of an old man. But in the mean time are you right in abandoning this property, and your country with it? I think not. My opinion has ever been that, until more can be done for them, we should endeavor, with those whom fortune has thrown on our hands, to feed and clothe them well, protect them from all ill usage, require such reasonable labor only as is performed voluntarily by freemen, & be led by no repugnancies to abdicate them, and our duties to them. The laws do not permit us to turn them loose, if that were for their good: and to commute them for other property is to commit them to those whose usage of them we cannot control. I hope then, my dear sir, you will reconcile yourself to your country and its unfortunate condition; that you will not lessen its stock of sound disposition by withdrawing your portion from the mass. That, on the contrary you will come forward in the public councils, become the missionary of this doctrine truly christian; insinuate & inculcate it softly but steadily, through the medium

---

5. Andrew Burstein translates this passage as follows: "shoulders trembling from old age, he put on useless iron," noting it is "an abbreviated line from Vergil's *Aeneid* recalling the fall of Troy." Burstein, *Jefferson's Secrets: Death and Desire at Monticello* (New York: Basic Books, 2005), 137.

of writing and conversation; associate others in your labors, and when the phalanx is formed, bring on and press the proposition perseveringly until its accomplishment. It is an encouraging observation that no good measure was ever proposed, which, if duly pursued, failed to prevail in the end. We have proof of this in the history of the endeavors in the English parliament to suppress that very trade which brought this evil on us. And you will be supported by the religious precept, "be not weary in well-doing." That your success may be as speedy & complete, as it will be of honorable & immortal consolation to yourself, I shall as fervently and sincerely pray as I assure you of my great friendship and respect.

To Samuel H. Smith[6]

DEAR SIR,—   MONTICELLO, September 21, 1814.
I learn from the newspapers that the Vandalism of our enemy has triumphed at Washington over science as well as the arts, by the destruction of the public library with the noble edifice in which it was deposited. Of this transaction, as of that of Copenhagen, the world will entertain but one sentiment. They will see a nation suddenly withdrawn from a great war, full armed and full handed, taking advantage of another whom they had recently forced into it, unarmed, and unprepared, to indulge themselves in acts of barbarism which do not belong to a civilized age. When Van Ghent destroyed their shipping at Chatham, and De Ruyter rode triumphantly up the Thames, he might in like manner, by the acknowledgment of their own historians, have forced all their ships up to London bridge, and there have burnt them, the tower, and city, had these examples been then set. London, when thus menaced, was near a thousand years old, Washington is but in its teens.[7]
I presume it will be among the early objects of Congress to re-commence their collection. This will be difficult while the war continues, and intercourse with Europe is attended with so much risk. You know my collection, its condition and extent. I have been fifty years making it, and have spared no pains, opportunity or expense, to make it what it is. While residing in Paris, I devoted every afternoon I was disengaged, for a summer or two, in examining all the principal bookstores, turning over every book with my own hand, and putting by everything which related to America, and indeed whatever was rare and valuable in every science. Besides this, I had standing orders during the whole time I was in Europe, on its principal book-marts, particularly Amsterdam, Frankfort, Madrid and London, for such works relating to America as could not be found in Paris. So that in that department particularly, such a collection was made as probably can never again be effected, because it is hardly probable that the same opportunities, the same time, industry, perseverance and expense, with some knowledge of the bibliography of the subject, would again happen to be in concurrence. During the same period, and after my return to America, I was led to procure, also, whatever related to the duties of those in the high concerns of the nation. So that the collection, which I suppose is of between nine and ten thousand volumes, while it

---

6. Samuel Harrison Smith (1772–1845), a Pennsylvania-born printer with close ties to Jefferson during his presidency, when he published the official administration paper, the *National Intelligencer*, in Washington. Smith was serving as secretary of the treasury in 1814.
7. The British burned Washington, D.C., in August 1814, partly in retaliation for the American destruction of York (Toronto), the capital of Upper Canada, earlier in the war. Jefferson recalls the naval attacks on Britain during the war with the Dutch in 1667 as well as the more recent British attack on Copenhagen in 1807.

includes what is chiefly valuable in science and literature generally, extends more particularly to whatever belongs to the American statesman. In the diplomatic and parliamentary branches, it is particularly full. It is long since I have been sensible it ought not to continue private property, and had provided that at my death, Congress should have the refusal of it at their own price. But the loss they have now incurred, makes the present the proper moment for their accommodation, without regard to the small remnant of time and the barren use of my enjoying it. I ask of your friendship, therefore, to make for me the tender of it to the library committee of Congress, not knowing myself of whom the committee consists. I enclose you the catalogue, which will enable them to judge of its contents. Nearly the whole are well bound, abundance of them elegantly, and of the choicest editions existing. They may be valued by persons named by themselves, and the payment made convenient to the public. It may be, for instance, in such annual instalments as the law of Congress has left at their disposal, or in stock of any of their late loans, or of any loan they may institute at this session, so as to spare the present calls of our country, and await its days of peace and prosperity. They may enter, nevertheless, into immediate use of it, as eighteen or twenty wagons would place it in Washington in a single trip of a fortnight. I should be willing indeed, to retain a few of the books, to amuse the time I have yet to pass, which might be valued with the rest, but not included in the sum of valuation until they should be restored at my death, which I would carefully provide for, so that the whole library as it stands in the catalogue at this moment should be theirs without any garbling. Those I should like to retain would be chiefly classical and mathematical. Some few in other branches, and particularly one of the five encyclopedias in the catalogue. But this, if not acceptable, would not be urged. I must add, that I have not revised the library since I came home to live, so that it is probable some of the books may be missing, except in the chapters of Law and Divinity, which have been revised and stand exactly as in the catalogue. The return of the catalogue will of course be needed, whether the tender be accepted or not. I do not know that it contains any branch of science which Congress would wish to exclude from their collection; there is, in fact, no subject to which a member of Congress may not have occasion to refer. But such a wish would not correspond with my views of preventing its dismemberment. My desire is either to place it in their hands entire, or to preserve it so here. I am engaged in making an alphabetical index of the author's names, to be annexed to the catalogue, which I will forward to you as soon as completed. Any agreement you shall be so good as to take the trouble of entering into with the committee, I hereby confirm. Accept the assurance of my great esteem and respect.

To William Short, Esq.[8]

DEAR SIR,—   MONTICELLO, November 28, 1814.
    Yours of October 28th came to hand on the 15th instant only. The settlement of your boundary with Colonel Monroe, is protracted by circumstances which seem foreign to it. One would hardly have expected that the

8. William Short (1759–1849), Jefferson's secretary from 1785 to 1789, remained in Europe in the American diplomatic service until 1802 and returned there again from 1808 to 1810, before returning to the United States and settling in Philadelphia. Jefferson at this time was attempting to resolve a boundary dispute between Short and James Monroe, making use of the services of William Champe Carter, who had sold Short the parcel in question, but in December Jefferson declined to serve as an arbitrator.

hostile expedition to Washington could have had any connection with an operation one hundred miles distant. Yet preventing his attendance, nothing could be done. I am satisfied there is no unwillingness on his part, but on the contrary a desire to have it settled; and therefore, if he should think it indispensable to be present at the investigation, as is possible, the very first time he comes here I will press him to give a day to the decision, without regarding Mr. Carter's absence. Such an occasion must certainly offer soon after the fourth of March, when Congress rises of necessity, and be assured I will not lose one possible moment in effecting it.

Although withdrawn from all anxious attention to political concerns, yet I will state my impressions as to the present war, because your letter leads to the subject. The essential grounds of the war were, 1st, the orders of council; and 2d, the impressment of our citizens; (for I put out of sight from the love of peace the multiplied insults on our government and aggressions on our commerce, with which our pouch, like the Indian's, had long been filled to the mouth.) What immediately produced the declaration was, 1st, the proclamation of the Prince Regent that he would never repeal the orders of council as to us, until Bonaparte should have revoked his decrees as to all other nations as well as ours; and 2d, the declaration of his minister to ours that no arrangement whatever could be devised, admissible in lieu of impressment. It was certainly a misfortune that *they* did not know themselves at the date of this silly and insolent proclamation, that within one month they would repeal the orders, and that *we*, at the date of our declaration, could not know of the repeal which was then going on one thousand leagues distant. Their determinations, as declared by themselves, could alone guide us, and they shut the door on all further negotiation, throwing down to us the gauntlet of war or submission as the only alternatives. We cannot blame the government for choosing that of war, because certainly the great majority of the nation thought it ought to be chosen, not that they were to gain by it in dollars and cents; all men know that war is a losing game to both parties. But they know also that if they do not resist encroachment at some point, all will be taken from them, and that more would then be lost even in dollars and cents by submission than resistance. It is the case of giving a part to save the whole, a limb to save life. It is the melancholy law of human societies to be compelled sometimes to choose a great evil in order to ward off a greater; to deter their neighbors from rapine by making it cost them more than honest gains. The enemy are accordingly now disgorging what they had so ravenously swallowed. The orders of council had taken from us near one thousand vessels. Our list of captures from them is now one thousand three hundred, and, just become sensible that it is small and not large ships which gall them most, we shall probably add one thousand prizes a year to their past losses. Again, supposing that, according to the confession of their own minister in parliament, the Americans they had impressed were something short of two thousand, the war against us alone cannot cost them less than twenty millions of dollars a year, so that each American impressed has already cost them ten thousand dollars, and every year will add five thousand dollars more to his price. We, I suppose, expend more; but had we adopted the other alternative of submission, no mortal can tell what the cost would have been. I consider the war then as entirely justifiable on our part, although I am still sensible it is a deplorable misfortune to us. It has arrested the course of the most remarkable tide of prosperity any nation ever experienced, and has closed such prospects of future improvement as were never before in the view of any people. Farewell all hopes of extinguishing public debt! farewell all visions of applying surpluses of revenue to the improvements of peace rather than the ravages of war. Our enemy has indeed the consolation of Satan on removing our first parents from Paradise: from a peaceable and agricultural nation, he makes us a military and manufacturing one. We shall indeed survive the conflict. Breeders enough will remain to carry on population. We shall retain our country, and rapid advances in the art of war will soon enable us to beat our enemy, and probably drive him from the continent. We have men enough, and I am in hopes the present session of Congress will provide the means of commanding their services. But I wish I could see them get into a better train of finance. Their banking projects are like dosing dropsy with more water. If anything could revolt our citizens against the war, it would be the extravagance with which they are about to be taxed. It is strange indeed that at this day, and in a country where English proceedings are so familiar, the principles and advantages of funding should be neglected, and expedients resorted to. Their new bank, if not abortive at its birth, will not last through one campaign; and the taxes proposed cannot be paid. How can a people who cannot get fifty cents a bushel for their wheat, while they pay twelve dollars a bushel for their salt, pay five times the amount of taxes they ever paid before? Yet that will be the case in all the States south of the Potomac. Our resources are competent to the maintenance of the war if duly economized and skillfuly employed in the way of anticipation. However, we must suffer, I suppose, from our ignorance in funding, as we did from that of fighting, until necessity teaches us both; and, fortunately, our stamina are so vigorous as to rise superior to great mismanagement. This year I think we shall have learnt how to call forth our force, and by the next I hope our funds, and even if the state of Europe should not by that time give the enemy employment enough nearer home, we shall leave him nothing to fight for here. These are my views of the war. They embrace a great deal of sufferance, trying privations, and no benefit but that of teaching our enemy that he is never to gain by wanton injuries on us. To me this state of things brings a sacrifice of all tranquillity and comfort through the residue of life. For although the debility of age disables me from the services and sufferings of the field, yet, by the total annihilation in value of the produce which was to give me subsistence and independence, I shall be like Tantalus, up to the shoulders in water, yet dying with thirst. We can make indeed enough to eat, drink and clothe ourselves; but nothing for our salt, iron, groceries and taxes, which must be paid in money. For what can we raise for the market? Wheat? we can only give it to our horses, as we have been doing ever since harvest. Tobacco? it is not worth the pipe it is smoked in. Some say Whiskey; but all mankind must become drunkards to consume it. But although we feel, we shall not flinch. We must consider now, as in the revolutionary war, that although the evils of resistance are great, those of submission would be greater. We must meet, therefore, the former as the casualties of tempests and earthquakes, and like them necessarily resulting from the constitution of the world. Your situation, my dear friend, is much better. For, although I do not know with certainty the nature of your investments, yet I presume they are not in banks, insurance companies, or any other of those gossamer castles. If in groundrents, they are solid; if in stock of the United States, they are equally so. I once thought that in the event of a war we should be obliged to suspend paying the interest of the public debt. But a dozen years more of experience and observation on our people and government, have satisfied me it will never be done. The sense of the necessity of public credit is so universal and so deeply rooted, that no other necessity will prevail against it; and I am glad to see that while the former eight millions are steadfastly applied to the sinking of the old debt, the Senate have lately insisted on a sinking fund for the new. This is the dawn of that improvement in the management of our finances which I look to for salvation; and I trust that the light will continue to advance, and point out their way to our legislators. They will soon see that instead of taxes for the whole year's expenses, which the people cannot pay, a tax to the amount of the interest and a reasonable portion of the principal will command the whole sum, and throw a part of the burthens of war on times of peace and prosperity. A sacred payment of interest is the only way to make the most of their resources, and a sense of that renders your income from our funds more certain than mine from lands. Some apprehend danger from the defection of Massachusetts. It is a disagreeable circumstance, but not a dangerous one. If they become neutral, we are sufficient for one enemy without them, and in fact we get no aid from them now. If their administration determines to join the enemy, their force will be annihilated by equality of division among themselves. Their federalists will then call in the English army, the republicans ours, and it will only be a transfer of the scene of war from Canada to Massachusetts; and we can get ten men to go to Massachusetts for one who will go to Canada. Every one, too, must know that we can at any moment make peace with England at the expense of the navigation and fisheries of Massachusetts. But it will not come to this. Their own people will put down these factionists as soon as they see the real object of their opposition; and of this Vermont, New Hampshire, and even Connecticut itself, furnish proofs.

You intimate a possibility of your return to France, now that Bonaparte is put down. I do not wonder at it, France, freed from that monster, must again become the most agreeable country on earth. It would be the second choice of all whose ties of family and fortune gives a preference to some other one, and the first of all not under those ties. Yet I doubt if the tranquillity of France is entirely settled. If her Pretorian bands are not furnished with employment on her external enemies, I fear they will recall the old, or set up some new cause.

God bless you and preserve you in bodily health. Tranquillity of mind depends much on ourselves, and greatly on due reflection "how much pain have cost us the evils which have never happened." Affectionately adieu.

To John Adams

DEAR SIR   Monticello Apr. 8. [18]16.

I have to acknolege your two favors of Feb. 16. and Mar. 2. and to join sincerely in the sentiment of Mrs. Adams, and regret that distance separates us so widely. An hour of conversation would be worth a volume of letters. But we must take things as they come.

You ask if I would agree to live my 70. or rather 73. years over again? To which I say Yea. I think with you that it is a good world on the whole, that it has been framed on a principle of benevolence, and more pleasure than pain dealt out to us. There are indeed (who might say Nay) gloomy and hypocondriac minds, inhabitants of diseased bodies, disgusted with the present, and despairing of the future; always counting that the worst will happen, because it may happen. To these I say How much pain have cost us the evils which have never happened? My temperament is sanguine. I steer my bark with Hope in the head, leaving Fear astern. My hopes indeed sometimes fail; but not oftener than the forebodings of the gloomy. There are, I acknolege, even in the happiest life, some terrible convulsions, heavy set-offs against the opposite page of the account. I have often wondered for what good end the sensations of Grief could be intended. All our other passions, within proper bounds, have an useful object. And the perfection of the moral character is, not in a Stoical apathy, so hypocritically vaunted, and so untruly too, because impossible, but in a just equilibrium of all the passions. I wish the pathologists then would tell us what is the use of grief in the economy, and of what good it is the cause, proximate or remote.

Did I know Baron Grimm[9] while at Paris? Yes, most intimately. He was the pleasantest, and most conversible member of the diplomatic corps while I was there: a man of good fancy, acuteness, irony, cunning, and egoism: no heart, not much of any science, yet enough of every one to speak it's language. His fort was Belles-lettres, painting and sculpture. In these he was the oracle of the society, and as such was the empress Catharine's private correspondent and factor in all things not diplomatic. It was thro' him I got her permission for poor Ledyard to go to Kamschatka, and cross over thence to the Western coast of America, in order to penetrate across our continent in the opposite direction to that afterwards adopted for Lewis and Clarke: which permission she withdrew after he had got within 200. miles of Kamschatska, had him siesed, brought back and set down in Poland. Altho' I never heard Grimm express the opinion, directly, yet I always supposed him to be of the school of Diderot, D'Alembert, D'Holbach, the first of whom committed their system of atheism to writing in "Le bon sens," and the last in his "Systeme de la Nature." It was a numerous school in the Catholic countries, while the infidelity of the Protestant took generally the form of Theism. The former always insisted that it was a mere question of definition between them, the hypostasis of which on both sides was "Nature" or "the Universe:" that both agreed in the order of the existing system, but the one supposed it from eternity, the other as having begun in time. And when the atheist descanted on the unceasing motion and circulation of matter thro' the animal vegetable and mineral kingdoms, never resting, never annihilated, always changing form, and under all forms gifted with the power of reproduction; the Theist pointing "to the heavens above, and to the earth beneath, and to the waters under the earth," asked if these did not proclaim a first cause, possessing intelligence and power; power in the production, and intelligence in the design and constant preservation of the system; urged the palpable existence of final causes, that the eye was made to see, and the ear to hear, and not that we see because we have eyes, and hear because we have ears; an answer obvious to the senses, as that of walking across the room was to the philosopher demonstrating the nonexistence of motion. It was in D'Holbach's[1] conventicles that Rousseau imagined all the machinations against him were contrived; and he left, in his Confessions the most biting anecdotes of Grimm. These appeared after I left France; but I have heard that poor Grimm was so much afflicted by them, that he kept

9. Friedrich Melchior, baron von Grimm (1723–1807), served as an agent in France for Empress Catherine of Russia and, in that capacity, helped Jefferson make preliminary arrangements for John Ledyard's planned transit through her domain. Grimm's *Correspondence*, to which Adams referred in asking Jefferson about Grimm in his letter of March 2, appeared in Paris in sixteen volumes in 1812–13.
1. Paul-Henri Thiry, baron d'Holbach (1723–1789), a wealthy Paris intellectual and famous atheist who published *Système de la Nature* in 1770 and, during Jefferson's Paris years, regularly hosted the compilers of the *Encyclopédic* at his salon.

his bed several weeks. I have never seen these Memoirs of Grimm. Their volume has kept them out of our market.

I have been lately amusing myself with Levi's book[2] in answer to Dr. Priestley. It is a curious and tough work. His style is inelegant and incorrect, harsh and petulent to his adversary, and his reasoning flimsey enough. Some of his doctrines were new to me, particularly that of his two resurrections: the first a particular one of all the dead, in body as well as soul, who are to live over again, the Jews in a state of perfect obedience to god, the other nations in a state of corporeal punishment for the sufferings they have inflicted on the Jews. And he explains this resurrection of bodies to be only of the original stamen of Leibnitz, or the homunculus in semine masculino,[3] considering that as a mathematical point, insusceptible of separation, or division. The second resurrection a general one of souls and bodies, eternally to enjoy divine glory in the presence of the supreme being. He alledges that the Jews alone preserve the doctrine of the unity of god. Yet their god would be deemed a very indifferent man with us: and it was to correct their Anamorphosis of the deity that Jesus preached, as well as to establish the doctrine of a future state. However Levi insists that that was taught in the old testament, and even by Moses himself and the prophets. He agrees that an anointed prince was prophecied and promised: but denies that the character and history of Jesus has any analogy with that of the person promised. He must be fearfully embarrassing to the Hierophants of fabricated Christianity; because it is their own armour in which he clothes himself for the attack. For example, he takes passages of Scripture from their context (which would give them a very different meaning) strings them together, and makes them point towards what object he pleases; he interprets them figuratively, typically, analogically, hyperbolically; he calls in the aid of emendation, transposition, ellipsis, metonymy, and every other figure of rhetoric; the name of one man is taken for another, one place for another, days and weeks for months and years; and finally avails himself of all his advantage over his adversaries by his superior knolege of the Hebrew, speaking in the very language of the divine communication, while they can only fumble on with conflicting and disputed translations. Such is this war of giants. And how can such pigmies as you and I decide between them? For myself I confess that my head is not formed tantas componere lites. And as you began your Mar. 2. with a declaration that you were about to write me the most frivolous letter I had ever read, so I will close mine by saying I have written you a full match for it, and by adding my affectionate respects to Mrs. Adams, and the assurance of my constant attachment and consideration for yourself.

Th: Jefferson

2. David Levi (1740–1799), a Jewish controversialist born in London, published his *Letters to Dr. Priestley* (1787) in response to Priestley's *Letters to the Jews, Inviting them to an Amicable Discussion of the Evidences of Christianity* (1787). He later attacked Thomas Paine's *Age of Reason*.
3. The little man in the male seed (Latin). Jefferson humorously links the resurrected souls of Levi to the preformationist ideas associated with Gottfried Wilhelm Leibniz (1646–1716), the German polymath to whom we owe the botanical concept of the stamen. Leibniz's theory of monads held that the universe is composed of irreducible dimensionless entities.

To José Corrêa da Serra[4]

Dear Sir   Poplar Forest April 26. [18]16.
Your favor of Mar. 29. was recieved just as I was setting out for this place.
I brought it with me to be answered hence. Since you are so kind as to inter-
est yourself for Capt. Lewis's papers, I will give you a full statement of them.

1. Ten or twelve such pocket volumes, Morocco bound, as that you
describe, in which, in his own hand writing, he had journalised all
occurences, day by day, as he travelled. They were small 8vos and opened at
the end for more convenient writing. Every one had been put into a separate
tin case, cemented to prevent injury from wet. But on his return the cases, I
presume, had been taken from them, as he delivered me the books uncased.
There were in them the figures of some animals drawn with the pen while on
his journey. The gentlemen who published his travels must have had these
Ms. volumes, and perhaps now have them, or can give some account of them.

2. Descriptions of animals and plants. I do not recollect whether there
was such a book or collection of papers, distinct from his journal; altho' I am
inclined to think there was one: because his travels as published, do not contain all the new animals of which he had either descriptions or specimens.
Mr. Peale, I think, must know something of this, as he drew figures of some
of the animals for engraving, and some were actually engraved. Perhaps
Conrad, his bookseller, who was to have published the work, can give an
account of these.

3. Vocabularies. I had myself made a collection of about 40. vocabularies
of the Indians on this side of the Missisipi, and Capt. Lewis was instructed
to take those of every tribe beyond, which he possibly could: the intention
was to publish the whole, and leave the world to search for affinities between
these and the languages of Europe and Asia. He was furnished with a number of printed vocabularies of the same words and form I had used, with
blank spaces for the Indian words. He was very attentive to this instruction,
never missing an opportunity of taking a vocabulary. After his return, he
asked me if I should have any objection to the printing his separately, as
mine were not yet arranged as I intended. I assured him I had not the least;
and I am certain he contemplated their publication. But whether he had put
the papers out of his own hand or not, I do not know. I imagine he had not:
and it is probable that Doctr. Barton, who was particularly curious on this
subject, and published on it occasionally, would willingly recieve and take
care of these papers after Capt. Lewis's death, and that they are now among
his papers.

4. His observations of longitude and latitude. He was instructed to send
these to the war-office, that measures might be taken to have the calcula-

2. José Corrêa da Serra (1751–1823), Portuguese botanist and diplomat, relocated to the United
States in 1812 but was to return to Portugal in 1820. In the interval, he and Jefferson spent much
time together. Jefferson had confided to him on January 1 that his anxiety over the whereabouts
and condition of the papers of Meriwether Lewis had been revived by the death of Dr. Benjamin
S. Barton, who had agreed to prepare the desired natural history reports on the 1803–06 expedition. After receiving Jefferson's letter, Corrêa da Serra visited Barton's widow, only to find that "The
Dr. has left such an immense heap of papers, and in such disorder" that it was hard to identify
Lewis's. At the very end of March, Corrêa da Serra could finally write, "Mrs. Barton has sent me a
little morocco bound volume, part of Capt. Lewis journal," adding that he hoped further items
would surface. In the meantime, he asked Jefferson to help by sending him a description of the
"external appearance" and size of the individual volumes (LLCE 2:607–609).

tions made. Whether he delivered them to the war-office, or to Dr. Patter-son,[5] I do not know; but I think he communicated with Dr. Patterson concerning them. These are all-important: because altho', having with him the Nautical almanacs, he could & did calculate some of his latitudes, yet the longitudes were taken merely from estimates by the log-line, time and course. So that it is only as to latitudes that his map may be considered as tolerably correct; not as to its longitudes.

5. His Map. This was drawn on sheets of paper, not put together, but so marked that they could be joined together with the utmost accuracy; not as one great square map, but ramifying with the courses of the rivers. The scale was very large, and the sheets numerous, but in perfect preservation. This was to await publication, until corrected by the calculations of longitude and latitude. I examined these sheets myself minutely, as spread on the floor, and the originals must be in existence, as the Map published with his travels must have been taken from them.

These constitute the whole. They are the property of the government, the fruits of the expedition undertaken at such expense of money and risk of valuable lives. They contain exactly the whole of the information which it was our object to obtain for the benefit of our own country and of the world. But we were willing to give to Lewis and Clarke whatever pecuniary benefits might be derived from the publication, and therefore left the papers in their hands, taking for granted that their interests would produce a speedy publication, which would be better if done under their direction. But the death of Capt. Lewis, the distance and occupations of General Clarke, and the bankruptcy of their bookseller, have retarded the publication, and rendered necessary that the government should attend to the reclamation & security of their papers. Their recovery is now become an imperious duty. Their safest deposit as fast as they can be collected, will be the Philosophical Society, who no doubt will be so kind as to receive and preserve them, subject to the orders of government; and their publication, once effected in any way, the originals will probably be left in the same deposit. As soon as I can learn their present situation, I will lay the matter before the government to take such order as they think proper. As to any claims of individuals to these papers, it is to be observed that, as being the property of the public, we are certain neither Lewis nor Clarke would undertake to convey away the right to them, and that they could not convey them, had they been capable of intending it. Yet no interest of that kind is meant to be disturbed, if the individual can give satisfactory assurance that he will promptly & properly publish them. Otherwise they must be restored to the government, & the claimant left to settle with those on whom he has any claim. My interference will, I trust, be excused, not only from the portion which every citizen has in whatever is public, but from the peculiar part I have had in the design and execution of this expedition.

To you, my friend, apology is due for involving you in the trouble of this inquiry. It must be found in the interest you take in whatever belongs to science, and in your own kind offers to me of aid in this research. Be assured always of my affectionate friendship and respect.

TH: JEFFERSON

---

5. Robert Patterson (1743–1824), professor of mathematics at the University of Pennsylvania, was one of the men with whom Lewis consulted in Philadelphia before the start of the expedition.

To Peter S. Du Ponceau[6]

DEAR SIR,—   MONTICELLO, November 7, 1817.

A part of the information of which the expedition of Lewis and Clarke was the object, has been communicated to the world by the publication of their journal; but much and valuable matter yet remains uncommunicated. The correction of the longitudes of their map is essential to its value; to which purpose their observations of the lunar distances are to be calculated and applied. The new subjects they discovered in the vegetable, animal, and mineral departments, are to be digested and made known. The numerous vocabularies they obtained of the Indian languages are to be collated and published. Although the whole expense of the expedition was furnished by the public, and the information to be derived from it was theirs also, yet on the return of Messrs. Lewis and Clarke, the government thought it just to leave to them any pecuniary benefit which might result from a publication of the papers, and supposed, indeed, that this would secure the best form of publication. But the property in these papers still remained in the government for the benefit of their constituents. With the measures taken by Governor Lewis for their publication, I was never acquainted. After his death, Governor Clarke put them, in the first instance, into the hands of the late Dr. Barton, from whom some of them passed to Mr. Biddle, and some again, I believe, from him to Mr. Allen. While the MS. books of journals were in the hands of Dr. Barton, I wrote to him, on behalf of Governor Lewis' family, requesting earnestly, that, as soon as these should be published, the originals might be returned, as the family wished to have them preserved. He promised in his answer that it should be faithfully done. After his death, I obtained, through the kind agency of Mr. Correa, from Mrs. Barton, three of those books, of which I knew there had been ten or twelve, having myself read them. These were all she could find. The rest, therefore, I presume, are in the hands of the other gentlemen. After the agency I had had in effecting this expedition, I thought myself authorized, and, indeed, that it would be expected of me, that I should follow up the subject, and endeavor to obtain its fruits for the public. I wrote to General Clarke, therefore, for authority to receive the original papers. He gave it in the letters to Mr. Biddle and to myself, which I now enclose. As the custody of these papers belonged properly to the War Office, and that was vacant at the time, I have waited several months for its being filled. But the office still remaining vacant, and my distance rendering any effectual measures, by myself, impracticable, I ask the agency of your committee, within whose province I propose to place the matter, by making it the depository of the papers generally. I therefore now forward the three volumes of MS. journals in my possession, and authorize them, under General Clarke's letters, to inquire for and to receive the rest. So also the astronomical and geographical papers, those relating to zoological, botanical, and mineral subjects, with the Indian vocabularies, and statistical tables relative to the Indians. Of the astronomical and geographical papers, if the committee will be so good as to give me a statement, I will, as soon as a Secretary of War is appointed, propose to him to have made, at the public expense, the requisite calculations, to have the map corrected in its

---

6. French native Pierre-Etienne du Ponceau (1760–1844), lawyer and writer, came to America in 1777 to serve in the Revolution, after which he became the country's leading expert on international law. At the time of Jefferson's letter, du Ponceau was chair of the Historical and Literary Committee of the American Philosophical Society.

longitudes and latitudes, engraved and published on a proper scale; and I will ask from General Clarke the one he offers, with his corrections. With respect to the zoological and mineralogical papers and subjects, it would perhaps be agreeable to the Philosophical Society, to have a digest of them made, and published in their transactions or otherwise. And if it should be within the views of the Historical Committee to have the Indian vocabularies digested and published, I would add to them the remains of my collection. I had through the course of my life availed myself of every opportunity of procuring vocabularies of the languages of every tribe which either myself or my friends could have access to. They amounted to about forty, more or less perfect. But in their passage from Washington to this place, the trunk in which they were was stolen and plundered, and some fragments only of the vocabularies were recovered. Still, however, they were such as would be worth incorporation with a larger work, and shall be at the service of the Historical Committee, if they can make any use of them. Permit me to request the return of General Clarke's letter, and to add assurances of my respect and esteem.

P. S. With the volumes of MS. journal, Mrs. Barton delivered one by mistake I suppose, which seems to have been the journal of some botanist. I presume it was the property of Dr. Barton, and therefore forward it to you to be returned to Mrs. Barton.

To John Adams

Monticello Nov. 13. 1818.
The public papers, my dear friend, announce the fatal event of which your letter of Oct. 20. had given me ominous foreboding.[7] Tried myself, in the school of affliction, by the loss of every form of connection which can rive the human heart, I know well, and feel what you have lost, what you have suffered, are suffering, and have yet to endure. The same trials have taught me that, for ills so immeasurable, time and silence are the only medecines. I will not therefore, by useless condolances, open afresh the sluices of your grief nor, altho' mingling sincerely my tears with yours, will I say a word more, where words are vain, but that it is of some comfort to us both that the term is not very distant at which we are to deposit, in the same cerement, our sorrows and suffering bodies, and to ascend in essence to an ecstatic meeting with the friends we have loved and lost and whom we shall still love and never lose again. God bless you and support you under your heavy affliction.

TH: JEFFERSON

To John Holmes[8]

MONTICELLO, April 22, 1820.
I thank you, dear Sir, for the copy you have been so kind as to send me of the letter to your constituents on the Missouri question. It is a perfect

---

7. Abigail Adams died of typhoid fever on October 28, 1818.
8. Antislavery politician John Holmes (1773–1843), had been a congressman from Massachusetts and was senator-elect from the new state of Maine at the time Jefferson wrote him.

justification to them. I had for a long time ceased to read newspapers, or pay any attention to public affairs, confident they were in good hands, and content to be a passenger in our bark to the shore from which I am not distant. But this momentous question, like a fire bell in the night, awakened and filled me with terror. I considered it at once as the knell of the Union. It is hushed, indeed, for the moment. But this is a reprieve only, not a final sentence. A geographical line, coinciding with a marked principle, moral and political, once conceived and held up to the angry passions of men, will never be obliterated; and every new irritation will mark it deeper and deeper. I can say, with conscious truth, that there is not a man on earth who would sacrifice more than I would to relieve us from this heavy reproach, in any *practicable* way. The cession of that kind of property, for so it is misnamed, is a bagatelle which would not cost me a second thought, if, in that way, a general emancipation and *expatriation* could be effected; and gradually, and with due sacrifices, I think it might be. But as it is, we have the wolf by the ears, and we can neither hold him, nor safely let him go. Justice is in one scale, and self-preservation in the other. Of one thing I am certain, that as the passage of slaves from one State to another, would not make a slave of a single human being who would not be so without it, so their diffusion over a greater surface would make them individually happier, and proportionally facilitate the accomplishment of their emancipation, by dividing the burthen on a greater number of coadjutors. An abstinence too, from this act of power, would remove the jealousy excited by the undertaking of Congress to regulate the condition of the different descriptions of men composing a State. This certainly is the exclusive right of every State, which nothing in the constitution has taken from them and given to the General Government. Could Congress, for example, say, that the non-freemen of Connecticut shall be freemen, or that they shall not emigrate into any other State?

I regret that I am now to die in the belief, that the useless sacrifice of themselves by the generation of 1776, to acquire self-government and happiness to their country, is to be thrown away by the unwise and unworthy passions of their sons, and that my only consolation is to be, that I live not to weep over it. If they would but dispassionately weigh the blessings they will throw away, against an abstract principle more likely to be effected by union than by scission, they would pause before they would perpetrate this act of suicide on themselves, and of treason against the hopes of the world. To yourself, as the faithful advocate of the Union, I tender the offering of my high esteem and respect.

To John Adams

DEAR SIR   Monticello. Oct. 12. [18]23.

I do not write with the ease which your letter of Sep. 18. supposes.[9] Crippled wrists and fingers make writing slow and laborious. But, while writing to you, I lose the sense of these things, in the recollection of antient times, when youth and health made happiness out of every thing. I forget for a while the hoary winter of age, when we can think of nothing but how to

---

9. Adams had written on September 18, "As you write so easy, and so well, I pray you to write me as often as possible, for nothing revives my spirits so much as your letters except the society of my son and his Family . . ." (*AJL* 2:599).

keep ourselves warm, and how to get rid of our heavy hours until the friendly hand of death shall rid us of all at once. Against this tedium vitae[1] however I am fortunately mounted on a Hobby, which indeed I should have better managed some 30. or 40. years ago, but whose easy amble is still sufficient to give exercise and amusement to an Octogenary rider. This is the establishment of an University, on a scale more comprehensive, and in a country more healthy and central than our old William and Mary, which these obstacles have long kept in a state of languor and inefficiency. But the tardiness with which such works proceed may render it doubtful whether I shall live to see it go into action.

Putting aside these things however for the present, I write this letter as due to a friendship co-eval with our government, and now attempted to be poisoned, when too late in life to be replaced by new affections. I had for some time observed, in the public papers, dark hints and mysterious innuendoes of a correspondence of yours with a friend, to whom you had opened your bosom without reserve, and which was to be made public by that friend, or his representative. And now it is said to be actually published.[2] It has not yet reached us, but extracts have been given, and such as seemed most likely to draw a curtain of separation between you and myself. Were there no other motive than that of indignation against the author of this outrage on private confidence, whose shaft seems to have been aimed at yourself more particularly, this would make it the duty of every honorable mind to disappoint that aim, by opposing to it's impression a seven-fold shield of apathy and insensibility. With me however no such armour is needed. The circumstances of the times, in which we have happened to live, and the partiality of our friends, at a particular period, placed us in a state of apparent opposition, which some might suppose to be personal also; and there might not be wanting those who wish'd to make it so, by filling our ears with malignant falsehoods, by dressing up hideous phantoms of their own creation, presenting them to you under my name, to me under your's, and endeavoring to instill into our minds things concerning each other the most destitute of truth. And if there had been, at any time, a moment when we were off our guard, and in a temper to let the whispers of these people make us forget what we had known of each other for so many years, and years of so much trial, yet all men who have attended to the workings of the human mind, who have seen the false colours under which passion sometimes dresses the actions and motives of others, have seen also these passions subsiding with time and reflection, dissipating, like mists before the rising sun, and restoring to us the sight of all things in their true shape and colours. It would be strange indeed if, at our years, we were to go an age back to hunt up imaginary, or forgotten facts, to disturb the repose of affections so sweetening to the evening of our lives. Be assured, my

---

1. Or *taedium vitae*, weariness of life (Latin).
2. Jefferson refers to *Correspondence between the Hon. John Adams, Late President of the United States, and the Late Wm. Cunningham, Esq., beginning in 1803, and ending in 1813* (1823). Adams had corresponded with Cunningham, a distant cousin and an opponent of Jefferson during the election campaign of 1804, at Cunningham's request, insisting that the letters not be published until after his own death. However, the suicide of Cunningham in 1823 threw the letters into the hands of his son, who issued them in violation of that agreement—and, ironically, in hope that John Adams's frankness in the letters would discredit his son John Quincy Adams, whose campaign for the presidency in the 1824 election the young Cunningham opposed. Adams replied to Jefferson's worried letter by calling the Cunningham book "a blunder-buss . . . which was loaded by a miserable melancholy man, out of his wits, and left by him to another to draw the trigger. . . . The peevish and fretful effusions of politicians in difficult and dangerous conjunctures from the agony of their hearts are not worth remembering, much less laying to heart" (*AJL* 2:601). Nonetheless, Jefferson wrote only a short note of introduction to Adams across the following fifteen months.

dear Sir, that I am incapable of recieving the slightest impression from the effort now made to plant thorns on the pillow of age, worth, and wisdom, and to sow tares between friends who have been such for near half a century. Beseeching you then not to suffer your mind to be disquieted by this wicked attempt to poison it's peace, and praying you to throw it by, among the things which have never happened, I add sincere assurances of my unabated, and constant attachment, friendship and respect.

TH: JEFFERSON

To James Monroe[3]

DEAR SIR,—   MONTICELLO, October 24, 1823.

The question presented by the letters you have sent me, is the most momentous which has ever been offered to my contemplation since that of Independence. That made us a nation, this sets our compass and points the course which we are to steer through the ocean of time opening on us. And never could we embark on it under circumstances more auspicious. Our first and fundamental maxim should be, never to entangle ourselves in the broils of Europe. Our second, never to suffer Europe to intermeddle with cis-Atlantic affairs. America, North, and South, has a set of interests distinct from those of Europe, and peculiarly her own. She should therefore have a system of her own, separate and apart from that of Europe. While the last is laboring to become the domicil of despotism, our endeavor should surely be, to make our hemisphere that of freedom. One nation, most of all, could disturb us in this pursuit; she now offers to lead, aid, and accompany us in it. By acceding to her proposition, we detach her from the bands, bring her mighty weight into the scale of free government, and emancipate a continent at one stroke, which might otherwise linger long in doubt and difficulty, Great Britain is the nation which can do us the most harm of any one, or all on earth; and with her on our side we need not fear the whole world. With her then, we should most sedulously cherish a cordial friendship; and nothing would tend more to knit our affections than to be fighting once more, side by side, in the same cause. Not that I would purchase even her amity at the price of taking part in her wars. But the war in which the present proposition might engage us, should that be its consequence, is not her war, but ours. Its object is to introduce and establish the American system, of keeping out of our land all foreign powers, of never permitting those of Europe to intermeddle with the affairs of our nations. It is to maintain our own principle, not to depart from it. And if, to facilitate this, we can effect a division in the body of the European powers, and draw over to our side its most powerful member, surely we should do it. But I am clearly of Mr. Canning's opinion, that it will prevent instead of provoking war. With Great Britain withdrawn from their scale and shifted into that of our two continents, all Europe combined would not undertake such a war. For how would they propose to get at either enemy without superior fleets? Nor is the occasion to be slighted which this proposition offers, of declaring our protest against the atrocious violations of the rights of nations, by the interference of any one in the internal affairs of

---

3. On October 17, President Monroe had written Jefferson for advice on the policy that would come to be known as the Monroe Doctrine. He enclosed dispatches from London, including letters from British foreign Secretary George Canning, who was endeavoring to restrict the influence of the Holy Alliance (Prussia, Russia, and Austria) in South America and for that purpose requested the cooperation of the United States.

another, so flagitiously begun by Bonaparte, and now continued by the equally lawless Alliance, calling itself Holy.

But we have first to ask ourselves a question. Do we wish to acquire to our own confederacy any one or more of the Spanish provinces? I candidly confess, that I have ever looked on Cuba as the most interesting addition which could ever be made to our system of States. The control which, with Florida Point, this island would give us over the Gulf of Mexico, and the countries and isthmus bordering on it, as well as all those whose waters flow into it, would fill up the measure of our political well-being. Yet, as I am sensible that this can never be obtained, even with her own consent, but by war; and its independence, which is our second interest, (and especially its independence of England,) can be secured without it, I have no hesitation in abandoning my first wish to future chances, and accepting its independence, with peace and the friendship of England, rather than its association, at the expense of war and her enmity.

I could honestly, therefore, join in the declaration proposed, that we aim not at the acquisition of any of those possessions, that we will not stand in the way of any amicable arrangement between them and the mother country; but that we will oppose, with all our means, the forcible interposition of any other power, as auxiliary, stipendiary, or under any other form or pretext, and most especially, their transfer to any power by conquest, cession, or acquisition in any other way. I should think it, therefore, advisable, that the Executive should encourage the British government to a continuance in the dispositions expressed in these letters, by an assurance of his concurrence with them as far as his authority goes; and that as it may lead to war, the declaration of which requires an act of Congress, the case shall be laid before them for consideration at their first meeting, and under the reasonable aspect in which it is seen by himself.

I have been so long weaned from political subjects, and have so long ceased to take any interest in them, that I am sensible I am not qualified to offer opinions on them worthy of any attention. But the question now proposed involves consequences so lasting, and effects so decisive of our future destinies, as to rekindle all the interest I have heretofore felt on such occasions, and to induce me to the hazard of opinions, which will prove only my wish to contribute still my mite towards anything which may be useful to our country. And praying you to accept it at only what it is worth, I add the assurance of my constant and affectionate friendship and respect.

To Ellen W. Coolidge[4]

MONTICELLO, August 27, 1825.

Your affectionate letter, my dear Ellen, of the 1st inst. came to hand in due time. The assurances of your love, so feelingly expressed, were truly soothing to my soul, and none were ever met with warmer sympathies. We did not know until you left us what a void it would make in our family. Imagination had illy sketched its full measure to us; and, at this moment, everything around serves but to remind us of our past happiness, only consoled by the addition it has made to yours. Of this we are abundantly assured by the most excellent and amiable character to which we have committed your future well-being, and by the kindness with which you have been received

4. Ellen Wayles Randolph Coolidge (1796–1876), Jefferson's granddaughter.

by the worthy family into which you are now engrafted. We have no fear but that their affections will grow with their growing knowledge of you, and the assiduous cultivation of these becomes the first object in importance to you. I have no doubt you will find also the state of society there more congenial with your mind than the rustic scenes you have left although these do not want their points of endearment. Nay, one single circumstance changed, and their scale would hardly be the lightest. One fatal stain deforms what nature had bestowed on us of her fairest gifts.

I am glad you took the delightful tour which you describe in your letter. It is almost exactly that which Mr. Madison and myself pursued in May and June, 1791. Setting out from Philadelphia, our course was to New York, up the Hudson to Albany, Troy, Saratoga, Fort Edward, Fort George, Lake George, Ticonderoga, Crown Point, penetrated into Lake Champlain, returned the same way to Saratoga, thence crossed the mountains to Bennington, Northampton, along Connecticut River to its mouth, crossed the Sound into Long Island, and along its northern margin to Brooklyn, recrossed to New York, and returned. But from Saratoga till we got back to Northampton was then mostly desert. Now it is what thirty-four years of free and good government have made it. It shows how soon the labor of men would make a paradise of the whole earth, were it not for misgovernment, and a diversion of all his energies from their proper object—the happiness of man,—to the selfish interests of kings, nobles, and priests.

Our University goes on well. We have passed the limit of 100 students some time since. As yet it has been a model of order and good behavior, having never yet had occasion for the exercise of a single act of authority. We studiously avoid too much government. We treat them as men and gentlemen, under the guidance mainly of their own discretion. They so consider themselves, and make it their pride to acquire that character for their institution. In short, we are as quiet on that head as the experience of six months only can justify. Our professors, too, continue to be what we wish them. Mr. Gilmer accepts the Law chair, and all is well.

My own health is what it was when you left me. I have not been out of the house since, except to take the turn of the Roundabout twice; nor have I any definite prospect when it will be otherwise.

I shall not venture into the region of small news, of which your other correspondents of the family are so much better informed. I am expecting to hear from Mr. Coolidge on the subject of the clock for the Rotunda. Assure him of my warmest affections and respect, and pray him to give you ten thousand kisses for me, and they will still fall short of the measure of my love to you. If his parents and family can set any store by the esteem and respect of a stranger, mine are devoted to them.

To Dr. James Mease[5]

DEAR SIR,—   MONTICELLO, September 26, 1825.
It is not for me to estimate the importance of the circumstances concerning which your letter of the 8th makes inquiry. They prove, even in their minuteness, the sacred attachments of our fellow citizens to the event of which the paper of July 4th, 1776, was but the declaration, the genuine

---

5. Mease (1771–1846), of Philadelphia, who was interested in geology, had written inquiring where the Declaration of Independence had been written.

effusion of the soul of our country at that time. Small things may, perhaps, like the relics of saints, help to nourish our devotion to this holy bond of our Union, and keep it longer alive and warm in our affections. This effect may give importance to circumstances, however small. At the time of writing that instrument, I lodged in the house of a Mr. Graaf, a new brick house, three stories high, of which I rented the second floor, consisting of a parlor and bed-room, ready furnished. In that parlor I wrote habitually, and in it wrote this paper, particularly. So far I state from written proofs in my possession. The proprietor, Graaf, was a young man, son of a German, and then newly married. I think he was a bricklayer, and that his house was on the south side of Market street, probably between Seventh and Eighth streets, and if not the only house on that part of the street, I am sure there were few others near it. I have some idea that it was a corner house, but no other recollections throwing light on the question, or worth communication. I am ill, therefore only add assurance of my great respect and esteem.

To Roger C. Weightman[6]

RESPECTED SIR,—   MONTICELLO, June 24, 1826.
The kind invitation I receive from you, on the part of the citizens of the city of Washington, to be present with them at their celebration on the fiftieth anniversary of American Independence, as one of the surviving signers of an instrument pregnant with our own, and the fate of the world, is most flattering to myself, and heightened by the honorable accompaniment proposed for the comfort of such a journey. It adds sensibly to the sufferings of sickness, to be deprived by it of a personal participation in the rejoicings of that day. But acquiescence is a duty, under circumstances not placed among those we are permitted to control. I should, indeed, with peculiar delight, have met and exchanged there congratulations personally with the small band, the remnant of that host of worthies, who joined with us on that day, in the bold and doubtful election we were to make for our country, between submission or the sword; and to have enjoyed with them the consolatory fact, that our fellow citizens, after half a century of experience and prosperity, continue to approve the choice we made. May it be to the world, what I believe it will be, (to some parts sooner, to others later, but finally to all,) the signal of arousing men to burst the chains under which monkish ignorance and superstition had persuaded them to bind themselves, and to assume the blessings and security of self-government. That form which we have substituted, restores the free right to the unbounded exercise of reason and freedom of opinion. All eyes are opened, or opening, to the rights of man. The general spread of the light of science has already laid open to every view the palpable truth, that the mass of mankind has not been born with saddles on their backs, nor a favored few booted and spurred, ready to ride them legitimately, by the grace of God. These are grounds of hope for others. For ourselves, let the annual return of this day forever refresh our recollections of these rights, and an undiminished devotion to them.
I will ask permission here to express the pleasure with which I should have met my ancient neighbors of the city of Washington and its vicinities,

6. Roger Chew Weightman (1787–1876), mayor of Washington, D.C., had written to invite Jefferson to take part in the July 4 celebration on the fiftieth anniversary of the Declaration of Independence. Jefferson's answer is the last letter from his hand. Weightman went on to chair the national memorial committee organized to honor Jefferson and Adams.

with whom I passed so many years of a pleasing social intercourse; an inter-course which so much relieved the anxieties of the public cares, and left impressions so deeply engraved in my affections, as never to be forgotten. With my regret that ill health forbids me the gratification of an acceptance, be pleased to receive for yourself, and those for whom you write, the assur-ance of my highest respect and friendly attachments.

CONTEXTS

A Declaration by the Representatives of the United Colonies of *North-America*, Now Met in General Congress at *Philadelphia*, Seting forth the Causes and Necessity of Their Taking Up Arms.[1]

If it was possible for men, who exercise their reason to believe, that the Divine Author of our existence intended a part of the human race to hold an absolute property in, and an unbounded power over others, marked out by his infinite goodness and wisdom, as the objects of a legal domination, never rightfully resistible, however severe and oppressive, the Inhabitants of these Colonies might at least require from the Parliament of Great-Britain, some evidence, that this dreadful authority over them has been granted to that body. But a reverence for our great Creator, principles of humanity, and the dictates of common sense, must convince all those who reflect upon the subject, that government was instituted to promote the welfare of mankind, and ought to be administered for the attainment of that end. The legislature of Great-Britain, however stimulated by an inordinate passion for a power not only unjustifiable, but which they know to be peculiarly reprobated by the very constitution of that kingdom, and desperate of success in any mode of contest, where regard should be had to truth, law, or right, have at length, deserting those, attempted to effect their cruel and impolitic purpose of enslaving these Colonies by violence, and have thereby rendered it necessary for us to close with their last appeal from Reason to Arms.—Yet, however blinded that assembly may be, by their intemperate rage for unlimited domination, so to slight justice and the opinion of mankind, we esteem ourselves bound by obligations of respect to the rest of the world, to make known the justice of our cause.

Our forefathers, inhabitants of the island of Great-Britain, left their native land, to seek on these shores a residence for civil and religious freedom. At the expence of their blood, at the hazard of their fortunes, without the least charge to the country from which they removed, by unceasing labor and an unconquerable spirit, they effected settlements in the distant and inhospitable wilds of America, then filled with numerous and warlike nations of barbarians.—Societies or governments, vested with perfect legislatures, were formed under charters from the crown, and an harmonious intercourse was established between the colonies and the kingdom from which they derived their origin. The mutual benefits of this union became in a short time so extraordinary, as to excite astonishment. It is universally confessed, that the amazing increase of the wealth, strength and navigation of the realm, arose from this source; and the minister who so wisely and successfully directed the measures of Great-Britain in the late war, publicly declared, that these colonies enabled her to triumph over her enemies.—Towards the conclusion of that war, it pleased our sovereign to make a change in his counsel.—From that fatal moment, the affairs of the British empire began to fall into confusion, and gradually sliding from the summit of glorious prosperity to which they had been advanced by the virtues and abilities of one man, are at length

---

1. This declaration, written by John Dickinson of Pennsylvania and by Jefferson, was approved by the Continental Congress on July 6, 1775. It was published in Philadelphia in July 1775 and soon was being widely reprinted in both the colonies and England. The text is taken from the first edition.

distracted by the convulsions, that now shake it to its deepest foundations—
The new ministry finding the brave foes of Britain, though frequently
defeated, yet still contending, took up the unfortunate idea of granting them
a hasty peace, and of then subduing her faithful friends.

These devoted colonies were judged to be in such a state, as to present victories without bloodshed, and all the easy emoluments of statuteable
plunder.—The uninterrupted tenor of their peaceable and respectful behaviour from the beginning of colonization, their dutiful, zealous and useful services during the war, though so recently and amply acknowledged in the
most honorable manner by his Majesty, by the late king, and by Parliament,
could not save them from the meditated innovations.—Parliament was
influenced to adopt the pernicious project, and assuming a new power over
them, have in the course of eleven years given such decisive specimens of
the spirit and consequences attending this power, as to leave no doubt concerning the effects of acquiescence under it. They have undertaken to give
and grant our money without our consent, though we have ever exercised an
exclusive right to dispose of our own property; statutes have been passed for
extending the jurisdiction of courts of Admiralty and Vice-Admiralty beyond
their ancient limits: for depriving us of the accustomed and inestimable privilege of trial by jury in cases affecting both life and property; for suspending
the legislature of one of the colonies; for interdicting all commerce of
another; and for altering fundamentally the form of government established
by charter, and secured by acts of its own legislature solemnly confirmed by
the crown; for exempting the "murderers" of colonists from legal trial, and
in effect, from punishment; for erecting in a neighbouring province,
acquired by the joint arms of Great-Britain and America, a despotism dangerous to our very existence; and for quartering soldiers upon the colonists
in time of profound peace It has also been resolved in parliament, that
colonists charged with committing certain offences, shall be transported to
England to be tried.

But why should we enumerate our injuries in detail? By one statute it is
declared, that parliament can "of right make laws to bind us IN ALL CASES
WHATSOEVER."[2] What is to defend us against so enormous, so unlimited a
power? Not a single man of those who assume it, is chosen by us; or is subject to our controul or influence: but on the contrary, they are all of them
exempt from the operation of such laws, and an American revenue, if not
diverted from the ostensible purposes for which it is raised, would actually
lighten their own burdens in proportion, as they increase ours. We saw the
misery to which such despotism would reduce us. We for ten years incessantly and ineffectually besieged the Throne as supplicants; we reasoned,
we remonstrated with parliament in the most mild and decent language.
But Administration sensible that we should regard these oppressive measures as freemen ought to do, sent over fleets and armies to enforce them.
The indignation of the Americans was roused it is true; but it was the indignation of a virtuous, loyal, and affectionate people. A Congress of Delegates
from the united colonies was assembled at Philadelphia, on the fifth day of
last September. We resolved again to offer an humble and dutiful petition
to the King, and also addressed our fellow subjects of Great-Britain. We
have pursued every temperate, every respectful measure, we have even pro-

2. The Declaratory Act, passed by Parliament on March 7, 1766, made this claim.

ceeded to break off our commercial intercourse with our fellow subjects, as the last peaceable admonition, that our attachment to no nation upon earth should supplant our attachment to liberty.—This, we flattered ourselves, was the ultimate step of the controversy: But subsequent events have shewn, how vain was this hope of finding moderation in our enemies.

Several threatening expressions against the colonies were inserted in his Majesty's speech; our petition, though we were told it was a decent one, that his Majesty had been pleased to receive it graciously, and to promise laying it before his Parliament, was huddled into both houses amongst a bundle of American papers, and there neglected. The Lords and Commons in their address, in the month of February, said, that "a rebellion at that time actually existed within the province of Massachusetts bay; and that those concerned in it, had been countenanced and encouraged by unlawful combinations and engagements, entered into by his Majesty's subjects in several of the other colonies; and therefore they besought his Majesty, that he would take the most effectual measures to inforce due obedience to the laws and authority of the supreme legislature"—Soon after the commercial intercourse of whole colonies, with foreign countries and with each other, was cut off by an act of Parliament; by another, several of them were intirely prohibited from the fisheries in the seas near their coasts, on which they always depended for their sustenance; and large re-inforcements of ships and troops were immediately sent over to General Gage.

Fruitless were all the entreaties, arguments and eloquence of an illustrious band of the most distinguished Peers and Commoners, who nobly and strenuously asserted the justice of our cause, to stay or even to mitigate the heedless fury with which these accumulated and unexampled outrages were hurried on—Equally fruitless was the interferrence of the city of London, of Bristol, and many other respectable towns in our favour. Parliament adopted an insidious manœuvre calculated to divide us, to establish a perpetual auction of taxations where colony should bid against colony, all of them uninformed what ransom would redeem their lives, and thus to extort from us at the point of the bayonet, the unknown sums that should be sufficient to gratify, if possible to gratify, ministerial rapacity, with the miserable indulgence left to us of raising in our own mode the prescribed tribute. What terms more rigid and humiliating could have been dictated by remorseless victors to conquered enemies? In our circumstances to accept them would be to deserve them.

Soon after the intelligence of these proceedings arrived on this continent, General Gage, who, in the course of the last year, had taken possession of the town of Boston, in the province of Massachusett's-Bay, and still occupied it as a garrison, on the 19th day of April, sent out from that place a large detachment of his army, who made an unprovoked assault on the inhabitants of the said province, at the town of Lexington, as appears by the affidavits of a great number of persons, some of whom were officers and soldiers of that detachment, murdered eight of the inhabitants, and wounded many others. From thence the troops proceeded in warlike array to the town of Concord, where they set upon another party of the inhabitants of the same province, killing several and wounding more, until compelled to retreat by the country people suddenly assembled to repel this cruel aggression. Hostilities thus commenced by the British troops, have been since prosecuted by them without regard to faith or reputation.—The inhabitants of Boston being confined within that town by the General their Governor, and having in order to procure their dismission, entered into a treaty with him, it was stipulated that the said inhabitants having deposited their arms with their own magistrates, should have liberty to depart, taking with them their other effects. They accordingly delivered up their arms, but in open violation of honor, in defiance of the obligation of treaties, which even savage nations esteem sacred, the Governor ordered the arms deposited as aforesaid, that they might be preserved for their owners, to be seized by a body of soldiers; detained the greatest part of the inhabitants in the town, and compelled the few who were permitted to retire, to leave their most valuable effects behind.

By this perfidy, wives are seperated from their husbands, children from their parents, the aged and the sick from their relations and friends, who wish to attend and comfort them; and those who have been used to live in plenty, and even elegance, are reduced to deplorable distress.

The General further emulating his ministerial masters, by a proclamation bearing date on the 12th day of June, after venting the grossest falsehoods and calumnies against the good people of these colonies, proceeds to "declare them all either by name or description to be rebels and traitors, to supersede the course of the common law, and instead thereof to publish and order the use and exercise of the law martial."[3]—His troops have butchered our countrymen; have wantonly burnt Charles-Town,[4] besides a considerable number of houses in other places; our ships would not permit us to be called into this severe controversy, until we were grown up to our present strength, had been previously exercised in warlike operations, and possessed of the means of defending ourselves.—With hearts fortified with these animating reflections, we most solemnly, before GOD and the world declare, that, exerting the utmost energy of those powers, which our beneficient Creator hath graciously bestowed upon us, the arms we have been compelled by our enemies to assume, we will, in defiance of every hazard, with unabating firmness and perseverance, employ for the preservation of our liberties, being with one mind resolved, to dye Free-men rather than to live Slaves.

Lest this declaration should disquiet the minds of our friends and fellow subjects in any part of the empire, we assure them, that we mean not to dissolve that Union which has so long and so happily subsisted between us, and which we sincerely wish to see restored.—Necessity has not yet driven us into that desperate measure, or induced us to excite any other nation to war against them.—We have not raised armies with ambitious designs of separating from Great-Britain, and establishing independant states.—We fight not for glory or for conquest. We exhibit to mankind the remarkable spectacle of a people attacked by unprovoked enemies, without any imputation, or even suspicion, of offence. They boast of their privileges and civilization, and yet proffer no milder conditions than servitude or death.— ships and vessels are seized; the necessary supplies of provisions are intercepted, and he is exerting his utmost power to spread destruction and devastation around him.

We have received certain intelligence, that General Carleton, the Governor of Canada, is instigating the people of that province and the Indians to

3. On that date, General Thomas Gage issued a proclamation in Boston that, among other things, declared the colony to be under martial law.
4. During the Battle of Bunker Hill, on June 17.

fall upon us; and we have but too much reason to apprehend, that schemes have been formed to excite domestic enemies against us. In brief a part of these colonies now feels, and all of them are sure of feeling, as far as the vengeance of administration can inflict them, the complicated calamities of fire, sword and famine.[5]—We are reduced to the alternative of chusing an unconditional submission to the tyranny of irritated ministers, or resistance by force—The latter is our choice.—We have counted the cost of this contest, and find nothing so dreadful as voluntary slavery.—Honor, justice, and humanity forbid us tamely to surrender that freedom which we received from our gallant ancestors, and which our innocent posterity have a right to receive from us. We cannot endure the infamy and guilt of resigning succeeding generations to that wretchedness which inevitably awaits them, if we basely entail hereditary bondage upon them.

Our cause is just. Our union is perfect. Our internal resources are great, and if necessary, foreign assistance is undoubtedly attainable.—We gratefully acknowledge, as signal instances of the Divine favour towards us, that his Providence would not permit us to be called into this severe controversy, until we were grown up to our present strength, had been previously exercised in warlike operations, and possessed of the means of defending ourselves.—With hearts fortified with these animating reflections, we most solemnly, before GOD and the world declare, that, exerting the utmost energy of those powers, which our beneficient Creator hath graciously bestowed upon us, the arms we have been compelled by our enemies to assume, we will, in defiance of every hazard, with unabating firmness and perseverance, employ for the preservation of our liberties, being with one mind resolved, to dye Free-men rather than to live Slaves.

Lest this declaration should disquiet the minds of our friends and fellow subjects in any part of the empire, we assure them, that we mean not to dissolve that Union which has so long and so happily subsisted between us, and which we sincerely wish to see restored.—Necessity has not yet driven us into that desperate measure, or induced us to excite any other nation to war against them.—We have not raised armies with ambitious designs of separating from Great-Britain, and establishing independent states.—We fight not for glory or for conquest. We exhibit to mankind the remarkable spectacle of a people attacked by unprovoked enemies, without any imputation, or even suspicion, of offence. They boast of their privileges and civilization, and yet proffer no milder conditions than servitude or death.—

In our own native land, in defence of the freedom that is our birthright, and which we ever enjoyed till the late violation of it—for the protection of our property, acquired solely by the honest industry of our fore-fathers and ourselves, against violence actually offered, we have taken up arms. We shall lay them down when hostilities shall cease on the part of the aggressors, and all danger of their being renewed shall be removed, and not before.

With an humble confidence in the mercies of the supreme and impartial Judge and Ruler of the universe, we most devoutly implore his divine goodness to conduct us happily through this great conflict, to dispose our adver-

---

5. The remainder of this *Declaration,* from this point on, was drafted by Jefferson.

saries to reconciliation on reasonable terms, and thereby to relieve the empire from the calamities of civil war.

> By Order of CONGRESS,
> JOHN HANCOCK, PRESIDENT.
> Attested,
> CHARLES THOMSON, SECRETARY.

PHILADELPHIA,
JULY 6th, 1775.

THOMAS PAINE

From Common Sense[1]

Thoughts, on the Present State of American Affairs

In the following pages I offer nothing more than simple facts, plain arguments, and common sense: and have no other preliminaries to settle with the Reader, than that he will divest himself of prejudice and prepossession, and suffer his reason and his feelings to determine for themselves: that he will put *on* or rather that he will not put *off* the true character of a man, and generously enlarge his views beyond the present day.

Volumes have been written on the subject of the struggle between England and America. Men of all ranks have embarked in the controversy, from different motives, and with various designs; but all have been ineffectual, and the period of debate is closed. Arms as the last resource decide the contest: the appeal was the choice of the King, and the Continent has accepted the challenge.

It hath been reported of the late Mr. Pelham[2] (who tho' an able minister was not without his faults) that on his being attacked in the House of Commons on the score that his measures were only of a temporary kind, replied, *"they will last my time."* Should a thought so fatal and unmanly possess the Colonies in the present contest, the name of ancestors will be remembered by future generations with detestation.

The Sun never shined on a cause of greater worth. 'Tis not the affair of a City, a County, a Province or a Kingdom; but of a Continent—of at least one eighth part of the habitable Globe. 'Tis not the concern of a day, a year, or an age; posterity are virtually involved in the contest, and will be more or less affected even to the end of time by the proceedings now. Now is the seed time of Continental union, faith and honour. The least fracture now, will be like a name engraved with the point of a pin on the tender rind of a young oak; the wound will enlarge with the tree, and posterity read it in full grown characters.

By referring the matter from argument to arms, a new æra for politics is struck—a new method of thinking hath arisen. All plans, proposals, &c. prior

---

1. Thomas Paine, an English native, had been in America for little more than a year by late 1775, when he was urged to write this pamphlet by the Philadelphia physician and radical Benjamin Rush. It first appeared in Philadelphia on January 10, 1776, and was widely reprinted throughout the colonies and in England in the months following. The text is derived from *The Writings of Thomas Paine*, ed. Moncure Daniel Conway (1894–1896), with corrections from the first edition.
2. Henry Pelham (1694–1754) served as British prime minister from 1743 to his death.

to the 19th of April, *i.e.* to the commencement of hostilities,[3] are like the almanacks of the last year; which tho' proper then, are superceded and useless now. Whatever was advanced by the advocates on either side of the question then, terminated in one and the same point, viz. a union with Great Britain; the only difference between the parties was the method of effecting it; the one proposing force, the other friendship; but it hath so far happened that the first hath failed, and the second hath withdrawn her influence.

As much hath been said of the advantages of reconciliation, which, like an agreeable dream, hath passed away and left us as we were, it is but right, that we should examine the contrary side of the argument, and enquire into some of the many material injuries which these Colonies sustain, and always will sustain, by being connected with, and dependant on Great-Britain. To examine that connection and dependance on the principles of nature and common sense, to see what we have to trust to if separated, and what we are to expect if dependant.

I have heard it asserted by some, that as America hath flourished under her former connection with Great Britain, that the same connection is necessary towards her future happiness and will always have the same effect—Nothing can be more fallacious than this kind of argument:—we may as well assert that because a child has thrived upon milk, that it is never to have meat, or that the first twenty years of our lives is to become a precedent for the next twenty. But even this is admitting more than is true, for I answer, roundly, that America would have flourished as much, and probably much more had no European power taken any notice of her. The commerce by which she hath enriched herself are the necessaries of life, and will always have a market while eating is the custom of Europe.

But she has protected us says some. That she hath engrossed us is true, and defended the Continent at our expense as well as her own is admitted; and she would have defended Turkey from the same motive viz. for the sake of trade and dominion.

Alas! we have been long led away by ancient prejudices and made large sacrifices to superstition. We have boasted the protection of Great Britain, without considering, that her motive was *interest* not *attachment;* and that she did not protect us from *our enemies* on *our account* but from *her enemies* on *her own account,* from those who had no quarrel with us on any *other account,* and who will always be our enemies on the *same account.* Let Britain waive her pretensions to the continent, or the continent throw off the dependance, and we should be at peace with France and Spain were they at war with Britain. The miseries of Hanover[4] last war ought to warn us against connections.

It hath lately been asserted in parliament, that the colonies have no relation to each other but through the Parent Country, *i. e.* that Pennsylvania and the Jerseys[5] and so on for the rest, are sister Colonies by the way of England; this is certainly a very round-about way of proving relationship, but it is the nearest and only true way of proving enemyship, if I may so call it.

---

3. I.e., the battle of Lexington and Concord.
4. The electorate of Hanover, in modern Germany, suffered during the Seven Years' War (1755–63) owing to its links to England, then ruled by the house of Hanover.
5. The state of New Jersey was originally composed of two colonies, and even in Paine's day had two capitals, Burlington and Perth Amboy.

France and Spain never were, nor perhaps ever will be our enemies as *Americans,* but as our being the *subjects of Great Britain.*

But Britain is the parent country says some. Then the more shame upon her conduct. Even brutes do not devour their young, nor savages make war upon their families; wherefore the assertion if true, turns to her reproach; but it happens not to be true, or only partly so, and the phrase *parent* or *mother country,* hath been jesuitically adopted by the King and his parasites, with a low papistical design of gaining an unfair bias on the credulous weakness of our minds. Europe and not England is the parent country of America. This new World hath been the asylum for the persecuted lovers of civil and religious liberty from *every part* of Europe. Hither have they fled, not from the tender embraces of the mother, but from the cruelty of the monster; and it is so far true of England, that the same tyranny which drove the first emigrants from home, pursues their descendants still.

In this extensive quarter of the globe, we forget the narrow limits of three hundred and sixty miles (the extent of England) and carry our friendship on a larger scale; we claim brotherhood with every European Christian, and triumph in the generosity of the sentiment.

It is pleasant to observe by what regular gradations we surmount the force of local prejudice as we enlarge our acquaintance with the World. A man born in any town in England divided into parishes, will naturally associate most with his fellow parishioners (because their interests in many cases will be common) and distinguish him by the name of *neighbour;* if he meet him but a few miles from home, he drops the narrow idea of a street, and salutes him by the name of *townsman;* if he travel out of the county and meet him in any other, he forgets the minor divisions of street and town and calls him *countryman,* i. e. *countyman:* but if in their foreign excursions they should associate in France, or any other part of *Europe,* their local remembrance would be enlarged into that of *Englishmen.* And by a just parity of reasoning, all Europeans meeting in America, or any other quarter of the globe, are *countrymen;* for England, Holland, Germany, or Sweden, when compared with the whole, stand in the same places on the larger scale, which the divisions of street, town, and county do on the smaller ones; Distinctions too limited for Continental minds. Not one third of the inhabitants, even of this province,[6] are of English descent. Wherefore, I reprobate the phrase of parent or mother country applied to England only, as being false, selfish, narrow and ungenerous.

But admitting that we were all of English descent, what does it amount to? Nothing. Britain being now an open enemy, extinguishes every other name and title: and to say that reconciliation is our duty, is truly farcical. The first king of England, of the present line (William the Conqueror) was a Frenchman, and half the Peers of England are descendants from the same country; wherefore, by the same method of reasoning, England ought to be governed by France.

Much hath been said of the united strength of Britain and the Colonies, that in conjunction, they might bid defiance to the world: But this is mere presumption, the fate of war is uncertain, neither do the expressions mean any thing; for this Continent would never suffer itself to be drained of inhabitants, to support the British Arms in either Asia, Africa, or Europe.

6. I.e., Pennsylvania, where Paine lived and wrote.

Besides, what have we to do with setting the world at defiance. Our plan is commerce, and that well attended to, will secure us the peace and friendship of all Europe, because it is the interest of all Europe to have America a *free port*. Her trade will always be a protection, and her barrenness of gold and silver secure her from invaders.

I challenge the warmest advocate for reconciliation, to shew, a single advantage that this Continent can reap, by being connected with Great Britain. I repeat the challenge, not a single advantage is derived. Our corn will fetch its price in any market in Europe, and our imported goods must be paid for buy them where we will.

But the injuries and disadvantages which we sustain by that connection, are without number, and our duty to mankind at large, as well as to ourselves, instruct us to renounce the alliance: Because any submission to, or dependance on Great Britain, tends directly to involve this Continent in European wars and quarrels. As Europe is our market for trade, we ought to form no political connection with any part of it. 'Tis the true interest of America, to steer clear of European contentions, which she never can do, while by her dependance on Britain, she is made the make-weight in the scale of British politics.

Europe is too thickly planted with Kingdoms, to be long at peace, and whenever a war breaks out between England and any foreign power, the trade of America goes to ruin, *because, of her connection with Britain*. The next war may not turn out like the last, and should it not, the advocates for reconciliation now, will be wishing for separation then, because neutrality in that case, would be a safer convoy than a man of war. Every thing that is right or reasonable pleads for separation. The blood of the slain, the weeping voice of nature cries, 'TIS TIME TO PART. Even the distance at which the Almighty hath placed England and America, is a strong and natural proof, that the authority of the one over the other, was never the design of Heaven. The time likewise at which the Continent was discovered adds weight to the argument, and the manner in which it was peopled encreases the force of it.—The Reformation was preceded by the discovery of America; As if the Almighty graciously meant to open a sanctuary to the persecuted in future years, when home should afford neither friendship nor safety.

The authority of Great Britain over this Continent, is a form of government which sooner or later must have an end: And a serious mind can draw no true pleasure by looking forward, under the painful and positive conviction that what he calls "the present constitution," is merely temporary. As parents, we can have no joy, knowing that *this government* is not sufficiently lasting to ensure any thing which we may bequeath to posterity: And by a plain method of argument, as we are running the next generation into debt, we ought to do the work of it, otherwise we use them meanly and pitifully. In order to discover the line of our duty rightly, we should take our children in our hand, and fix our station a few years farther into life; that eminence will present a prospect, which a few present fears and prejudices conceal from our sight.

Though I would carefully avoid giving unnecessary offence, yet I am inclined to believe, that all those who espouse the doctrine of reconciliation, may be included within the following descriptions. Interested men who are not to be trusted, weak men who *cannot* see, prejudiced men who *will not* see, and a certain set of moderate men who think better of the European world than it deserves; and this last class, by an ill judged deliberation, will be the cause of more calamities to this continent, than all the other three.

It is the good fortune of many to live distant from the scene of present sorrow; the evil is not sufficiently brought to *their* doors to make *them* feel the precariousness with which all American property is possessed. But let our imaginations transport us a few moments to Boston; that seat of wretchedness will teach us wisdom, and instruct us for ever to renounce a power in whom we can have no trust. The inhabitants of that unfortunate city who but a few months ago were in ease and affluence, have now no other alternative than to stay and starve, or turn out to beg. Endangered by the fire of their friends if they continue within the city, and plundered by government if they leave it. In their present condition they are prisoners without the hope of redemption, and in a general attack for their relief, they would be exposed to the fury of both armies.

Men of passive tempers look somewhat lightly over the offences of Britain, and still hoping for the best are apt to call out, "*Come, come, we shall be friends again for all this.*" But examine the passions and feelings of mankind: bring the doctrine of reconciliation to the touchstone of nature, and then tell me, whether you can hereafter love, honour, and faithfully serve the power that hath carried fire and sword into your land? if you cannot do all these, then are you only deceiving yourselves, and by your delay bringing ruin upon posterity. Your future connection with Britain whom you can neither love nor honour, will be forced and unnatural, and being formed only on the plan of present convenience, will in a little time, fall into a relapse more wretched than the first. But if you say, you can still pass the violations over, then I ask, Hath your house been burnt? Hath your property been destroyed before your face? Are your wife and children destitute of a bed to lie on, or bread to live on? Have you lost a parent or a child by their hands, and yourself the ruined and wretched survivor? If you have not, then are you not a judge of those who have. But if you have, and can still shake hands with the murderers, then are you unworthy the name of husband, father, friend, or lover, and whatever may be your rank or title in life, you have the heart of a coward, and the spirit of a sycophant.

This is not inflaming or exaggerating matters, but trying them by those feelings and affections which nature justifies, and without which, we should be incapable of discharging the social duties of life, or enjoying the felicities of it. I mean not to exhibit horror for the purpose of provoking revenge, but to awaken us from fatal and unmanly slumbers, that we may pursue determinately some fixed object. 'Tis not in the power of Britain or of Europe to conquer America, if she doth not conquer herself by *delay* and *timidity*. The present winter is worth an age if rightly employed, but if lost or neglected, the whole continent will partake of the misfortune; and there is no punishment which that man doth not deserve, be he, who, or what, or where he will, that may be the means of sacrificing a season so precious and useful.

'Tis repugnant to reason, to the universal order of things, to all examples from former ages, to suppose that this continent can long remain subject to any external power. The most sanguine in Britain doth not think so. The utmost stretch of human wisdom cannot at this time, compass a plan, short of separation, which can promise the continent even a year's security. Reconciliation is *now* a fallacious dream. Nature hath deserted the connection, and Art cannot supply her place. For as Milton wisely expresses "never can true reconcilement grow where wounds of deadly hate have pierced so deep."[7]

Every quiet method for peace hath been ineffectual. Our prayers have been rejected with disdain; and hath tended to convince us that nothing flatters vanity or confirms obstinacy in Kings more than repeated petitioning— and nothing hath contributed more, than that very measure to make the Kings of Europe absolute. Witness Denmark and Sweden. Wherefore, since nothing but blows will do, for god's sake let us come to a final separation, and not leave the next generation to be cutting throats under the violated unmeaning names of parent and child.

To say, they will never attempt it again is idle and visionary; we thought so at the repeal of the stamp-act, yet a year or two undeceived us; as well may we suppose that nations which have been once defeated will never renew the quarrel.

As to government matters 'tis not in the power of Britain to do this continent justice: The business of it will soon be too weighty and intricate to be managed with any tolerable degree of convenience, by a power so distant from us, and so very ignorant of us; for if they cannot conquer us, they cannot govern us. To be always running three or four thousand miles with a tale or a petition, waiting four or five months for an answer, which when obtained requires five or six more to explain it in, will in a few years be looked upon as folly and childishness—There was a time when it was proper, and there is a proper time for it to cease.

Small islands not capable of protecting themselves, are the proper objects for government to take under their care; but there is something very absurd, in supposing a Continent to be perpetually governed by an island. In no instance hath nature made the satellite larger than its primary planet, and as England and America with respect to each other reverses the common order of nature, it is evident they belong to different systems. England to Europe: America to itself.

I am not induced by motives of pride, party, or resentment to espouse the doctrine of Separation and independance, I am clearly, positively, and conscientiously persuaded that 'tis the true interest of this continent to be so; that every thing short of *that* is mere patchwork, that it can afford no lasting felicity,—that it is leaving the sword to our children, and shrinking back at a time when, a little more, a little further, would have rendered this continent the glory of the earth.

As Britain hath not manifested the least inclination towards a compromise, we may be assured that no terms can be obtained worthy the acceptance of the continent, or any ways equal to the expence of blood and treasure we have been already put to.

The object contended for, ought always to bear some just proportion to the expense. The removal of North, or the whole detestable junto,[8] is a matter unworthy the millions we have expended. A temporary stoppage of trade was an inconvenience, which would have sufficiently ballanced the repeal of all the acts complained of, had such repeals been obtained; but if the whole

---

7. John Milton (1608–1674), *Paradise Lost*, bk. 4, lines 97–98.
8. Frederick North (1732–1792) was prime minister of Great Britain, 1770–82. In 1772 Paul Revere published an engraving of "A Certain Cabinet Junto" that captured American suspicion that the British government was being run by North and his coterie of favorites, including the Earl of Bute, a former prime minister, and the Earl of Mansfield, currently lord chief justice.

Continent must take up arms, if every man must be a soldier, 'tis scarcely worth our while to fight against a contemptible ministry only. Dearly, dearly do we pay for the repeal of the acts, if that is all we fight for; for, in a just estimation, 'tis as great a folly to pay a Bunker-hill price for law as for land. As I have always considered the independancy of this Continent, as an event which sooner or later must arrive, so from the late rapid progress of the Continent to maturity, the event cannot be far of[f]: Wherefore, on the breaking out of hostilities, it was not worth the while to have disputed a matter which time would have finally redressed, unless we meant to be in earnest: otherwise it is like wasting an estate on a suit at law, to regulate the trespasses of a tenant, whose lease is just expiring. No man was a warmer wisher for a reconciliation than myself, before the fatal 19th of April 1775 but the moment the event of that day was made known, I rejected the hardened, sullen tempered Pharaoh of England for ever; and disdain the wretch, that with the pretended title of FATHER OF HIS PEOPLE can unfeelingly hear of their slaughter, and composedly sleep with their blood upon his soul.

*   *   *

To conclude, however strange it may appear to some, or however unwilling they may be to think so, matters not, but many strong and striking reasons may be given, to shew, that nothing can settle our affairs so expeditiously as an open and determined declaration for independance. Some of which are,

First.—It is the custom of Nations when any two are at war, for some other powers not engaged in the quarrel, to step in as Mediators, and bring about the preliminaries of a Peace: but while America calls herself the Subject of Great Britain, no power however well disposed she may be, can offer her mediation. Wherefore, in our present state we may quarrel on for ever.

Secondly.—It is unreasonable to suppose, that France or Spain will give us any kind of assistance, if we mean only, to make use of that assistance for the purpose of repairing the breach, and strengthening the connection between Britain and America; because, those powers would be sufferers by the consequences.

Thirdly.—While we profess ourselves the Subjects of Britain, we must, in the eyes of foreign Nations be considered as Rebels. The precedent is somewhat dangerous to *their peace,* for men to be in arms under the name of Subjects: we on the spot can solve the paradox; but to unite resistance and subjection, requires an idea much too refined for common understanding.

Fourthly.—Were a manifesto to be published, and dispatched to foreign Courts, setting forth the miseries we have endured, and the peaceful methods which we have ineffectually used for redress, declaring at the same time, that not being able any longer to live happily or safely, under the cruel disposition of the British Court, we had been driven to the necessity of breaking off all connections with her; at the same time, assuring all such Courts, of our peaceable disposition towards them, and of our desire of entering into trade with them: such a memorial would produce more good effects to this Continent, than if a ship were freighted with petitions to Britain.

Under our present denomination of British Subjects, we can neither be received nor heard abroad: the custom of all Courts is against us, and will be so, until by an Independance we take rank with other Nations.

These proceedings may at first seem strange and difficult, but, like all other steps which we have already passed over, will in a little time become familiar and agreeable: and until an Independance is declared, the Continent will feel itself like a man who continues putting off some unpleasant business from day to day, yet knows it must be done, hates to set about it, wishes it over, and is continually haunted with the thoughts of it's necessity.

Manuscript Notes on Resolutions of Congress[1]

[June 7, 1776][2]

Resolved
That these United Colonies are, and of right ought to be, free and independent States, that they are absolved from all allegiance to the British Crown, and that all political connection between them and the State of Great Britain is, and ought to be, totally dissolved.

That it is expedient forthwith to take the most effectual measures for forming foreign Alliances.

That a plan of confederation be prepared and transmitted to the respective Colonies for their consideration and approbation.

[June 10, 1776]

Resolved that it is the opinion of this Com tha[t] the first Resolution be postponed to this day three weeks and that in the mean time[3] a committee be appointed to prepare a Declaration to the effect of the said first resolution.

[July 4, 1776]

Ordered That the declaration be authenticated & printed
That the committee appointed to prepare the declaration superintend & correct the press.

That copies of the declaration be sent to the several assemblies, conventions & committees or councils of safety and to the several commanding officers of the continental troops that it be proclaimed in each of the united states & at the head of the army.

FRANÇOIS BARBÉ-MARBOIS

Queries Concerning American States[1]

[Before 30 November 1780]
Articles of which you are requested to give some details

1. The Charters of your State.
2. The present Constitution.

---

1. These brief manuscript notes are reprinted from Robert Ginsberg, ed., *A Casebook on the Declaration of Independence* (1967).
2. This entry is in the hand of Richard Henry Lee, Jefferson's associate from Virginia.
3. At this point, the original entry contains the following note: "Least [i.e., lest] any time shd. be lost in case the Congress agree to this resolution."
1. This copy of the queries, in the hand of Joseph Jones, a Virginia delegate to Congress, is reprinted from *PTJ*, 4:166–167. It preserves the original order of the queries, later altered by Jefferson in *Notes on the State of Virginia*.

 3. An exact description of its limits and boundaries.
 4. The Memoirs published in its name, in the time of its being a
    Colony and the pamphlets relating to its interior or exterior affairs
    present or ancient.
 5. The History of the State.
 6. A notice of the Counties Cities Townships Villages Rivers Rivulets
    and how far they are navagible. Cascades Caverns Mountains Pro-
    ductions Trees Plants Fruits and other natural Riches.
 7. The number of its Inhabitants.
 8. The different Religions received in that State.
 9. The Colleges and public establishments. The Roads Buildings &c.
10. The Administration of Justice and a description of the Laws.
11. The particular Customs and manners that may happen to be
    received in that State.
12. The present State of Manufactures Commerce interior and exte-
    rior Trade.
13. A notice of the best Sea Ports of the State and how big are the ves-
    sels they can receive.
14. A notice of the commercial productions particular to that State
    and of those objects which the Inhabitants are obliged to get from
    Europe and from other parts of the World.
15. The weight measures and the currency of the hard money. Some
    details relating to the exchange with Europe.
16. The public income and expences.
17. The measures taken with regard of the Estates and Possessions of
    the Rebels commonly called Tories.
18. The condition of the Regular Troops and the Militia and their pay.
19. The marine and Navigation.
20. A notice of the Mines and other subterranean riches.
21. Some Samples of these Mines and of the extraordinary Stones. In
    short a notice of all what can increase the progress of human
    Knowledge.
22. A description of the Indians established in the State before the Eu-
    ropean Settlements and of those who are still remaining. An indi-
    cation of the Indian Monuments discovered in that State.

JOHN SULLIVAN

To Jefferson, with John McDuffee's Answers to Queries Concerning the Moose[1]

SIR   Durham March 12th. 1784
    I have now the honor to inclose answers to your Queries respecting the
Moose, and beg you will excuse the long delay. It was late in February when

1. John Sullivan (1740–1795), member of the Continental Congress and one of the original generals
of the American army, was then attorney general of New Hampshire. Having compiled his own brief
answers to the queries of Barbé-Marbois, Sullivan, a celebrated frontier fighter, was a natural
source of information on the moose, a key species in Jefferson's argument against Buffon's theories. Sullivan later was enlisted by Jefferson, then in France, to secure the skin, skeleton, and horns
of a moose to aid in convincing Buffon of his errors.

I arrived at Durham and being deeply impressed with the necessity of having your Queries answered with the greatest exactness I wrote to persons in various parts of the Country but have as yet received no answers but the inclosed. My principal reliance was on the Gentleman who signs the inclosed; and upon a Clergyman one of my friends settled in one of the Frontier Towns in the Province of Maine; in whose parish lives one Jonathan Door taken by the Indians when an Infant, and remained with them thirty Years became one of them and has hunted with them in every part of America North of the Ohio. He was with difficulty prevailed upon to return to his Friends about the Year 1764 and has since become a regular sober and Industrious Citizen. I have requested the Clergyman to procure from him and forward answers to all your Queries which I will transmit as soon as they come to hand.

Colo. McDuffee who signs the inclosed followed the business of hunting for many years in the Early part of his life, was a Captain of the Rangers in the last French War; has been in every part of Canada and Nova Scotia, and in many other parts of America, was a Colonel in our service this War and is now settled in a Town (but a few Years since) one of the frontier Towns of New Hampshire; in which Town there are many persons who have been brought up in the business of hunting. The Colonel is himself a man of observation and of strict veracity. I therefore suppose you may rely with great safety upon Every thing he has said on the subject. I shall however forward the other answers as they come to hand. General Whipple has not as yet given me an answer whether he can procure the Skeletons of a Moose as he waits to see his brother. When he does if it should be in the Negative I will endeavor to procure one myself and lest a disappointment should take place from him have already wrote my friends in the frontier settlements to procure me one if possible.

I had the pleasure to see Colo. McDuffee yesterday who desired me to add to his observations "That in the summer season the Moose wades into the ponds and Rivers pulls up and Eats the Roots of Pond Lilleys and other water Flowers, and that the Indians by lying in ambush kill more of them in such places in the summer season than in any other way." You will be so obliging as to make my most respectful Compliments to Doctor Lee and inform him that when I go to April Court in the Province of Main I will make the proper inquiries respecting the unappropriated Lands in the Eastern Quarter and give him the Earliest information. The subjects of Natural history you may depend on as soon as they can be procured and the rivers (which are now frozen) will admit of their being sent on.

I have the honor to be with the most Lively sentiments of Esteem & respect sir Your most obedt & very humble servant,

JNO SULLIVAN

ENCLOSURE

John McDuffee to John Sullivan, with Answers to [Jefferson's] Queries concerning the Moose

Rochester March 5th. 1784

1. Is not the Caribou and the Black Moose one and the same Animal? The Carabou Calevan or Indian Shovler is an Animal very different from the Moose. His hoofs are like a Horses his Horns are short and have no prongs, is about the bigness of a small Horse, lives in Heaths

and Swamps, feeds chiefly on Roots which he digs up with his feet, is seldom seen in this quarter of the Country.

2. Is not the grey Moose and the Elk one and the same Animal and quite different from the former?

The Elk is Deer of a large size and is known by the name of the Newfoundland Deer.

The Black and Grey Moose are one and the same Animal. The Black are mostly found to the Eastward, the Grey to the Southward.

3. What is the heighth of the grey Moose at the weathers, its length from the Ears in the root of the Tail, and its circumference where largest?

One of the largest is about 8½ feet high at the weathers, 8½ or 9 feet long, behind his fore legs is about 7 feet in circumference.

[4.] Has it a Sollid or Cloven Hoof? Cloven.

5. Do their feet make a loud ratling as they run? They do.

6. Is the under part of the Hoof covered with Hair? It is not.

7. Are they a Swift Animal? They trott exceeding fast and have no other gait.

8. Do they sweat when hard run or only drip at the tongue? Only drip at the Tongue.

9. At what season do they shed their Horns, and when recover them? They shed their Horns in January, push'd off by the succeeding Horns and recover them gradually 'till push'd off again by Succession.

10. Has the Doe Horns as well as the Buck? They have not.

11. How many young does She produce at a time? She has but one the first time, ever after two.

12. What is their Food? Brouse and Bark of Trees chiefly of Maple.

13. How far southward are they known? No farther than Hudsons River, to the southward of that the Moose are grey.

14. Have they ever been tamed and used to any purpose? They are Easily tamed, but can bear no labour.

15. Are the Horns of the Elk Palmated, or are they round and pointed? The Horns are the same as a Deers only flatted at the topp.

16. Has the Elk always or ever a white spot a foot in Diameter round the root of the Tail? I never saw but one; that had none.

SIR

The above answers are the best I am able to give to your Queries, would only observe that there is a Moose's Horn in one of the Pig-wackett Towns so large that is Used for a Cradle to rock the Children in. Am Sir with due Respects Your Most Humble Servant,

JOHN McDUFFEE

WILLIAM WHIPPLE

To Jefferson, with Answers to Queries Concerning the Moose[1]

DEAR SIR   Portsmouth the 15th March 1784

The only Apology I have to make for not sooner answering Your favor of the 12th Jany. is, that I have been expecting more satisfactory information on the subject of the Moose; but dispairing of speedily obtaining the satisfaction I wish; I now inclose you such answers to Your questions as I have been able to procure, also a small parcel of the hair of the Moose sent me by a Gentleman of whom I have been making inquiry respecting that Animal.

I have never heard of but one kind of Moose in this Country, whether that is the Black or Grey Moose I will not undertake to decide but it differs greatly in size from the Black Moose described by the Naturalists of Europe. Some Years ago I saw one of these Animals which was a female said to be one Year Old and was then judged to be four feet and a half high but was not Measured when I saw it. The Caribou is found in Nova-Scocia and is a very different animal from the Moose of this Country. It is much smaler and as it has been described to me answers the description of the Reindeer of Lapland. I have seen the skin of a Caribou, the Colour of the hair is something darker than that of the Moose and as thick and fine as that of the Bear.

I have taken Measures to procure a complete skeleton, which if I fail in I have no doubt of procuring in the course of the summer a pair of Horns and some of the principal Bones which probably may be sent to Virginia or Maryland if You should prefer having them at either of those places to Philadelphia.

The Gentleman who furnished me with the inclosed answers to Your questions informs me that he never measured a Moose tho' he has seen many. I am inclined to think he is somthing mistaken in the size. I have heard some hunters say they have seen them more than six feet high.

The Pleasure I receive from this Communication will be in proportion to the satisfaction it affords You.

I am with very great Esteem & Respect Dr. Sir Your Most obedt. & Very Humle Servt,

WM. WHIPPLE

ENCLOSURE[2]

[Before 15 March 1784]

The Moose found in this country I suppose to be a different annimal from the Caribou.

The Orignal, the Elk are unknown to me.

The Moose is 4½ to 5½ feet high at the weathers when full grown. Its length from the ears to the root of the tail about 5½ feet. Its circumference just behind the weathers about 5 feet.

The hoof is cloven like the Cow and Ox, but rather longer.

1. William Whipple (1730–1785) of New Hampshire, member of the Continental Congress and signer of the Declaration of Independence, had served as a general, part of the time under John Sullivan, during the Revolution. His letter, like Sullivan's, exemplifies both the care Jefferson used in gathering information and the emergence of scientific discourse in America at large.
2. Compare the answers passed on by Whipple with Jefferson's queries as they are recorded in McDuffee's answers, on p. 385–86.

The Doe has no horns.
The time of shedding the horns I cannot at present ascertain.
When Surpriz'd they go off on a trott with long steps proportion'd to the length of the leg and at the rate of 20 or More Miles [per] hour.
I never heard of a rattling of the feet as they run nor of the hairs appearing on the under part of the hoof.
Their Sweating when pursu'd, or only dripping at the tongue cannot be now answer'd.
Browse is their common food. When tam'd they will eat Bread or any thing offerd them.
When taken young they Soon become very tame and continue so when grown up. When attemps have been made to employ them in the reins or harness, they are Sulky and not to be prevaild on to move. This may probably be owing to want of skill in the Managers.
They are known in New Hampshire and Massachusetts. Cannot say whether farther Southward.

JOHN SULLIVAN

To Jefferson, with Memoranda on the Moose

SIR   Durham New Hampshire June 22. 1784
   I was some time since honored with your favor of the 27th of April and postponed my answer in order to obtain Mr. Dores answer to your Queries respecting the Moose. I now inclose you Mr. Hasseys answer to my Letter with answers to your Queries taken by him from Mr. Dore and the other Hunters in that Quarter. I also send you answers from Gilbert Warren a famous hunter in the province of Main. He once took a pair of those Animals alive and sold them to Governor Wentworth, who sent them to the Marquiss of Rockingham. I have conversed with him in person and he assures me that there are no Grey Moose except females though the Buck is not always Black, yet is ever Darker than the Doe and sometimes almost Black which is never the Case with the Doe. I have procured from the head of the province of Main a Large pair of Mooses horns and a pr. of the Calibous, together with a pair of our Largest Deers horns and will send them to Philadelphia agreably to your directions by the first vessel that sails from hence. This will Demonstrate the great difference between these Animals. The Caribous horns are much smaller than either and differently formed. His hoofs and his manner of Living differs so much from the Moose that it cannot be supposed that they are the same Animal. I fear I shall not be able to obtain the skeletons of a Moose untill the next winter though if I had seasonably known that General Whipple would not have done it I should have procured one last Winter. I am convinced that the Elk the Kenne and the Deer are the same Animal Though the two former are of the Larger Size and more Especially the first.
   I congratulate Your Excellency on your Late appointment, and more sincerly wish that the success of your Endeavors while in that important office may equal the zeal which you have ever shown in the Cause of your Country.
   Permit me to assure you that, the permission which your Excellency has given me of keeping up a correspondence affords me the highest pleasure

and while on my part I make use of the Licence I beg you to believe that a Line from Your Excellency will at all times be deemed an honor. I have the honor to be with the most perfect Esteem & respect Your Excellencys most obedient & very humble servant,

JNO SULLIVAN

P.S. I was informed that the shortness of the Moose Neck and the Length of his Legs were such that he could not feed upon Grass or even drink without wading into the water which occasioned in the answers some observations upon that subject as I had mentioned it in my Letter to Mr. Hassey and requested him to inform me respecting the truth of it. J:S:

ENCLOSURE I

Isaac Hasey to John Sullivan, together with Memoranda on the Moose[1]

SIR

A Pardon for your Freedom in applying to me for Answers to certain Queries I shall readily grant Sensible that I Stand in much more Need of one from you for not Sending them myself immediately. I feel the utmost Readiness to gratify my good Friends. I paid Attention to your Request directly. I depended upon a certain Gentleman to furnish you with Answers. I conclude he did not do it by your asking me whether I had Thot upon the Subject of Your Letter. I have Now inclosed you Answers and Some Account of the Moose Elk and Caribou. I believe it to be nearly Just, collected from Persons who have been well acquainted with those Creatures by your extreamly oblidged Most Obedient and very humble Servant,

ISAAC HASEY

The black Moose divides the Hoofs, the Caribou has a Solid and flat Hoof. The Savages call this Creature Cattivoo the Eastern Hunters call him the Shoveler from the Manner of his pawing away the Snow in Winter in order to get at Moss and Roots which he lives upon. In Size he is about middle way between the Moose and Deer has flat and forked Horns not so long but rather more Spreading than Deer.

The black and grey Moose differ only in Colour. The grey Moose and Elk are very difrent from the Caribou and from each other. The Elk nearly resembles the Deer; is Taller, some say as tall as an Horse and very Swift. Moose Elk and Deer have divided Hoofs, have no Hair upon the under Parts of their Hoofs, only between them by means of which their Tracks are scented by Dogs in Pursuit of them.

The Black Moose when full grown is about Ten Feet high Eight Feet in Circumference where largest and of proportionable Length with a Tail 3 or 4 Inches long curling upwards. Upon a Trot which is the common Gate of a Moose tis supposed that he will go Eight Miles in an Hour. He makes no more ratling with his Hoofs than an Ox would in runing.

Hunters Say they never observed that a Moose Sweat but only loll'd or drip'd at the Tongue like a Dog.

---

1. The Reverend Isaac Hasey (1742–1812), a graduate of Harvard, served as the original congregational minister at Lebanon, district of Maine. Like Whipple's unnamed source, both of Hasey's (Lebanon residents John Dore and Gilbert Warren) also followed Jefferson's queries.

They Shed their Horns in Month of Jany: they begin to Sprout in March and get to be about a Foot long in April.

Their Horns are palmated and Forked and Sometimes so Spreading as to have Eight Feet between their Extremities as a Gentleman told me Who found a Pair of very large Horns on an Head between two Small maple Trees which joind at their Roots and gradualy widened upwards. Between these, as he was browsing upon them, he Sliped his Head in Such a Manner that he coud not free himself and so lost his Life. The Doe never has any Horns. She commonly brings forth two Young ones at a Time.

Their Food is Browse of any kind in Winter and any Kind of Leaves in Summer tho the Shortness of their Necks and length of their legs woud not prevent their Eating Grass did they Choose it nor hinder them from drinking without wading into the water. There is a Small Tree or Bush with us commonly called Moose Wood. The Extremities of the Limbs are of a pulpous nature. Of these the Moose may eat occasionally but are not confind to them.

Travelers and Hunters tell me they have not Seen Moose further Southward than Hudsons River.

They have been tamed but are utterly unfit for any kind of domestic Service.

Hunters from Shapleigh or Washington or Limerick coud procure the Skeleton or Horns of a Moose without Much Difficulty.

ENCLOSURE II

Gilbert Warren's Replies to Questions concerning the Moose

1. Is not the Carribou and the Black-Moose one and the same Animal? No. The Carribou is between a Moose and Deer.
2. Is not the Grey-moose and the Elk one and the same animal? and quite different from the former? They are very different Animals.
3. What is the height of the Moose? Eighteen hands.
4. What is the difference between the black and the grey Moose? The black is the Male and grey the female of the same species. Have they a solid or cloven hoof? Cloven.
5. Do their feet make a loud ratling as they run? They do.
6. Is the under part of their hoof covered with hair? It is not.
7. Are they a swift animal? Not very swift.
8. Do they sweat when hard run or only drip at the tongue? They do not sweat.
9. At what season do they shed their horns? In November. And when recover them? In May.
10. Has the Doe horns as well as the Buck? No.
11. How many young does she produce at a time? Two.
13. [sic] How far southward are they known? I know not.
14. Have they ever been tamed and used for any purpose? They have been tamed, but not used. I have seen a young one suck a Cow as gently and kindly as her calf.
15. Are the horns of the Elk Palmated, viz. flatted at the top, or are they round and pointed? Flattened at the top.
16. Has the Elk always or ever a white spot a foot in diameter round the root of the Tail? I never saw one.

FRANÇOIS-JEAN DE BEAUVOIR, CHEVALIER DE CHASTELLUX

From Travels in North America in the Years 1780, 1781, and 1782[1†]

Visit to Mr. Jefferson at Monticello

APRIL 13, 1782: BOSWELL'S TAVERN—MONTICELLO

I set out the next morning at eight o'clock, having learned nothing in this house worthy of remark, except that notwithstanding the hale and robust appearance of Mr. and Mrs. Boswell, not one of their fourteen children had attained the age of two. We were now approaching a chain of mountains of considerable height, called the South-west Mountains, because they are the first you meet in traveling westward before reaching the chain known in France as the Appalachians and in Virginia as the Blue Ridge, North Ridge [North Mountain], and Alleghany Mountains. As the country is heavily wooded, we seldom had a view of them. I traveled a long time without seeing any habitation, and was at a loss to know which of the many crossroads to take. At last I overtook a traveler who had preceded us and he not only served as my guide, but also made the journey seem less long by his company. He was an Irishman, who though but lately arrived in America, had served in several campaigns and had received a considerable wound in his thigh. He told me that they had never been able to extract the bullet, but he was none the less in good health and spirits. I got him to tell me about his military exploits, and particularly asked him for details about the country where he now lives, for he had told me that he was settled in North Carolina, upwards of eighty miles from Catawba and more than 300 from the seacoast. These new settlements are of special interest as they are remote from all trade and thus wholly dependent on agriculture; I mean that patriarchal agriculture which consists in producing only what is sufficient for the owner's consumption, without hope of either sale or barter. These settlers must therefore be self-sufficient. It is easy to conceive that there is soon no deficiency of food, but it is also necessary that their own flocks and their own fields supply them with clothing; they must manufacture their own wool and flax into cloth and linen, they must prepare the hides to make shoes, etc., etc. As for drink, they are obliged to content themselves with milk and water, until their apple trees are large enough to bear fruit, or until they have been able to procure themselves stills, to distill their grain. It would be difficult in Europe to imagine that the article which the new settlers are most in need of, in these difficult days, is nails, for the axe and saw can supply every other want. They contrive however to erect fences and to construct roofs without nails, but the work thus takes much longer and it is obvious what this costs in time and

† Translated by Howard C. Rice Jr. Copyright © 1963 by the University of North Carolina Press; renewed 1991 by Mrs. Howard C. Rice Jr. Published for the Omohundro Institute of Early American History and Culture. Used by permission of the publisher.
1. Chastellux published *Voyages de m. le marquis de Chastellux dans l'Amérique Septentrionale* in Paris in 1786. The present text is derived from the eighteenth-century translation of George Grieve (1787), as substantially revised and corrected by Howard C. Rice, *Travels in North America in the Years 1780, 1781, and 1781*, 2 vols. (Chapel Hill, 1963), 2:389–396, 448–456.

labor. It was a natural question to ask this farmer what could take him four hundred miles from home, and I learned that he was carrying on the only trade possible in his country and by which the people who are the best off seek to increase their income—that of selling horses. Indeed, these animals multiply very fast in regions where there is abundant pasturage; and as they can be driven with no expense, by letting them graze along the way, they are the most convenient article of exportation for localities distant from the main roads and from the trading centers.

The conversation continued between us and brought us imperceptibly to the foot of the mountains. We had no difficulty in recognizing on one of the summits the house of Mr. Jefferson, for it may be said that "it shines alone in this secluded spot."[2] He himself built it and chose the site, for although he already owned fairly extensive lands in the neighborhood, there was nothing, in such an unsettled country, to prevent him from fixing his residence wherever he wanted to. But Nature so contrived it, that a Sage and a man of taste should find on his own estate the spot where he might best study and enjoy Her. He called this house *Monticello* (in Italian, Little Mountain), a very modest name indeed, for it is situated upon a very high mountain, but a name which bespeaks the owner's attachment to the language of Italy and above all to the Fine Arts, of which Italy was the cradle and is still the resort.

As I had no further occasion for a guide, I parted ways with my Irishman, and after continuing uphill for more than half an hour by a rather good road, I arrived at Monticello. This house, of which Mr. Jefferson was the architect, and often the builder, is constructed in an Italian style, and is quite tasteful, although not however without some faults; it consists of a large square pavilion, into which one enters through two porticoes ornamented with columns. The ground floor consists chiefly of a large and lofty *salon*, or drawing room, which is to be decorated entirely in the antique style; above the *salon* is a library of the same form; two small wings, with only a ground floor and attic, are joined to this pavilion, and are intended to communicate with the kitchen, offices, etc. which will form on either side a kind of basement topped by a terrace. My object in giving these details is not to describe the house, but to prove that it resembles none of the others seen in this country; so that it may be said that Mr. Jefferson is the first American who has consulted the Fine Arts to know how he should shelter himself from the weather. But it is with him alone that I should concern myself.

Let me then describe to you a man, not yet forty, tall, and with a mild and pleasing countenance, but whose mind and attainments could serve in lieu of all outward graces; an American, who, without ever having quitted his own country, is Musician, Draftsman, Surveyor, Astronomer, Natural Philosopher, Jurist, and Statesman; a Senator of America, who sat for two years in that famous Congress which brought about the Revolution and which is never spoken of here without respect—though with a respect unfortunately mingled with too many misgivings; a Governor of Virginia, who filled this difficult station during the invasions of Arnold, Phillips, and Cornwallis; and finally a Philosopher, retired from the world and public business, because he loves the world only insofar as he can feel that he is useful, and because the temper of his fellow citizens is not as yet prepared either to face the truth or to suffer contradiction. A gentle and amiable wife, charming children whose

2. Rice speculates (2:574, n. 2) that Chastellux was here quoting from some favorite poem.

education is his special care, a house to embellish, extensive estates to improve, the arts and sciences to cultivate—these are what remain to Mr. Jefferson, after having played a distinguished role on the stage of the New World, and what he has preferred to the honorable commission of Minister Plenipotentiary in Europe.

APRIL 14–16, 1782: AT MONTICELLO

The visit which I made Mr. Jefferson was not unexpected, for he had long since invited me to come and spend a few days in his company, that is, amid the mountains. Nevertheless I at first found his manner grave and even cold; but I had no sooner spent two hours with him than I felt as if we had spent our whole lives together. Walking, the library—and above all, conversation which was always varied, always interesting, always sustained by that sweet satisfaction experienced by two persons who in communicating their feelings and opinions invariably find themselves in agreement and who understand each other at the first hint—all these made my four days spent at Monticello seem like four minutes.

This conformity of feelings and opinions, on which I dwell because it was a source of satisfaction to me and because egotism must now and then appear, this conformity, I repeat, was so perfect that not only our tastes were similar, but our predilections also—those predilections or partialities which cold and methodical minds hold up to ridicule as mere "enthusiasm," but which men of spirit and feeling take pride in calling by this very name of "enthusiasm." I recall with pleasure that as we were conversing one evening over a "bowl of punch," after Mrs. Jefferson had retired, we happened to speak of the poetry of Ossian.[3] It was a spark of electricity which passed rapidly from one to the other; we recalled the passages of those sublime poems which had particularly struck us, and we recited them for the benefit of my traveling companions, who fortunately knew English well and could appreciate them, even though they had never read the poems. Soon the book was called for, to share in our "toasts": it was brought forth and placed beside the bowl of punch. And, before we realized it, book and bowl had carried us far into the night. At other times, natural philosophy was the subject of our conversations, and at still others, politics or the arts, for no object has escaped Mr. Jefferson; and it seems indeed as though, ever since his youth, he had placed his mind, like his house, on a lofty height, whence he might contemplate the whole universe.

The only stranger who visited us during our stay at Monticello was Colonel Armand[4] whom I have mentioned in my first journal. As my friends know, he went to France last year [1781] with Colonel [John] Laurens, but returned in time to be present at the siege of Yorktown, where he marched as a volunteer in the attack on the redoubts. His object in going to France was to purchase clothing and complete equipment for a legion that he had already commanded, but which had been broken up in the southern campaigns, so that it was necessary to form it anew. He himself advanced the

3. The legendary poet whose supposed works were translated by James Macpherson (1736–1796). See "To Charles McPherson," February 25, 1773, p. 210.
4. Charles-Armand Tuffin, marquis de la Rouërie (1751–1793), known during his service in the Revolution simply as Charles Armand, made many friends in America before returning to France for good in 1784.

necessary funds to Congress, which agreed to provide the men and the horses. Charlottesville, a rising little town situated in a valley two leagues from Monticello, is the headquarters assigned for assembling this legion. Colonel Armand invited me to dine with him the next day; I went there with Mr. Jefferson, and found the legion under arms. It is to be composed of 200 horse and 150 foot. The cavalry was almost complete and fairly well mounted; the infantry was still much below full strength, but the whole was well clothed, well armed, and made a very good appearance. We dined at Colonel Armand's with all the officers of his regiment, and with his wolf, for he has made a pastime of raising a wolf, which is now ten months old, and is as familiar, mild, and gay as a young dog. The wolf never leaves his master, and even has the privilege of sharing his bed. I hope that he will still reflect his good upbringing and not revert to his natural character when he has come to wolf's estate. He is not quite of the same kind as ours, for his coat is almost black and very smooth; so that there is nothing fierce about his head, and were it not for his upright ears and pendant tail, one might easily take him for a dog. Perhaps he owes the singular advantage of not exhaling a bad smell to the care which is taken of his toilet, for I noticed that the dogs were not in the least afraid of him and that when they crossed his track they paid no attention to it. Now it is difficult for me to believe that all the cleanliness possible can deceive the instinct of these animals, which have such a dread of wolves, that they have been observed at the *Jardin du Roi* in Paris to bristle up and howl at the mere smell of two mongrels born of a dog and a she-wolf. I am inclined therefore to believe that this peculiarity belongs only to the species of black wolf, for you also see in America species similar to ours. It may be that we also have in Europe something like the American black kind; one might at least so conclude from the common saying, "*il a peur de moi comme du loup gris* (he is as much afraid of me as of a grey wolf)," which would imply that there were also black wolves.

Since I am on the subject of animals, I shall mention here some observations which Mr. Jefferson enabled me to make upon the only wild animals which are common in this country. I was long in doubt whether they should be called *chevreuils* (roe deer), *cerfs* (hart), or *daims* (deer), for in Canada they are known by the first name, in the eastern provinces by the second, and in the south by the third. Besides, in America, nomenclatures are so inexact, and observations so rare, that no information can be acquired by querying the people of the country. Mr. Jefferson having amused himself by raising a score of these animals in a park, they soon become very tame, which happens to all American animals, which are in general much more easily tamed than those of Europe. He enjoys feeding them with Indian corn, of which they are very fond, and which they eat out of his hand. I followed him one evening into a deep valley where they are accustomed to assemble towards the close of the day. I watched them walk, run, and bound; and the more I examined their paces, the less I was inclined to annex them to any European species: they are of absolutely the same color as the *chevreuil*, and this color never varies from one individual to another, even when they are tamed, as often happens with our *daims*. Their horns, which are never more than a foot and a half long, and never have more than three or four branches on each side, are more open and broader than those of the *chevreuil* and slant forward; their tail is from eight to ten inches long, and when they leap they carry it almost upright like our *daims*, which they further resemble not only in their proportions, but in the form of their head, which is longer and less frizzled than that of the *chevreuil*. They differ also from the *chevreuil* in that they never go in pairs, but gather in herds as do our *cerfs* and *daims*. From my own observations, in short, and from all I have been able to collect on the subject, I am convinced that this species is peculiar to America, and that it may be considered as somewhere in between the *daim* and the *chevreuil*.

Mr. Jefferson being no sportsman, and never having crossed the seas, could have no definite opinion on this point of natural history; but he has not neglected the other branches. I saw with pleasure that he had applied himself in particular to meteorological observation, which, in fact, of all the branches of natural philosophy, is the most appropriate for Americans to cultivate, because the extent of their country and the variety of sites give them in this particular a great advantage over us, who in other respects have so many over them. Mr. Jefferson has made, with Mr. Madison,[5] a well-informed professor of mathematics, some corresponding observations on the prevailing winds at Williamsburg and at Monticello; and although these two places are only fifty leagues distant from each other and are not separated by any chain of mountains, the difference between the results was that for 127 observations of the northeast wind at Williamsburg there were only 32 at Monticello, where the northwest wind in general took the place of the northeast. This latter appears to be a seawind, easily counteracted by the slightest obstacle, insomuch that twenty years ago it was scarcely ever felt beyond West Point, that is, beyond the confluence of the Pamunkey and the Mattaponi which unite to form the York River about thirty-five miles from its mouth. Since the progress of population and agriculture has considerably cleared the woods, this northeast wind penetrates as far as Richmond, which is thirty miles further inland. It may thus be observed, first, that the winds vary greatly in their obliquity and in the height of their regions; and, secondly, that nothing is more important than the manner in which the clearing of a country is undertaken, for the salubrity of the air, even the order of the seasons, may depend on the access allowed to the winds and the direction given to them. It is a generally accepted opinion in Rome that the air there is less healthy since the cutting of a large forest which used to be situated between that city and Ostia and which protected it from the winds known in Italy as the *Scirocco* and the *Libico*. It is also believed in Spain that the excessive droughts, of which the Castilians complain more and more, are occasioned by the cutting down of the woods, which used to stop and break up the clouds. There is still another very important consideration upon which I thought fit to call to the attention of the learned in this country, whatever diffidence I may have of my own knowledge in natural philosophy, as in every other subject. The greatest part of Virginia is very low and flat, and so divided by creeks and great rivers, that it appears in fact redeemed from the sea and entirely of very recent creation; it is therefore swampy, and can be dried only by cutting down many woods; but as on the other hand it can never be so drained as not still to abound in mephitic exhalations;[6] and of whatever nature these exhalations may be, whether partaking of fixed or inflammable air, it is certain that vegetation absorbs them equally, and that trees are the most proper to accomplish this object. It therefore appears

5. The Reverend James Madison (1749–1812), president of the College of William and Mary.
6. Poisonous fumes.

equally dangerous either to cut down or to preserve a great quantity of wood; so that the best manner of proceeding to clear the country would be to disperse the settlements as much as possible, and always to leave some groves of trees standing between them. In this manner the ground inhabited would always be made healthy; and as there will still remain considerable marshes which cannot be drained, there will be no risk of admitting too easily the winds which blow the exhalations from them.

APRIL 17, 1782: DEPARTURE FROM MONTICELLO

But I perceive that my journal is something like the conversation I had with Mr. Jefferson. I pass from one object to another, and forget myself as I write, as it happened not unfrequently in his society. I must now take leave of the Friend of Nature, but not of Nature herself, for she expects me in all her splendor at the goal of my journey—I refer to that famous "rock bridge" which joins two mountains, the greatest curiosity that I have ever beheld, because it is the one most difficult to account for. Mr. Jefferson would most willingly have taken me there, although this wonder with which he is perfectly acquainted is more than eighty miles from his home; but his wife was expecting her confinement at any moment,[7] and he is as good a husband as he is a philosopher and citizen. He therefore only acted as my guide for about sixteen miles, as far as the crossing of the little Mechum River. Here we parted, and I presume to believe that it was with mutual regret.[8]

* * *

Description of the Natural Bridge, called Rocky Bridge in Virginia

On my return from my journey in Upper Virginia, I still regretted not having been able to take proper measurements of the Natural Bridge. I was anxious that some person, who was both a draftsman and a surveyor, should make the journey to the Appalachians for this sole purpose, and that he should be provided with the instruments necessary for doing it accurately. No one was more capable of this than Baron de Turpin,[9] Captain in the Royal Engineer Corps (*Corps Royal du Génie*), for he possesses all that theoretical knowledge, which is carried to such a high degree in the Corps to which he belongs, combined with the skill of drawing with as much facility as precision; he was furthermore well enough acquainted with the English language to dispense with an interpreter. I therefore proposed to the Comte de Rochambeau to entrust him with this errand, which I was sure he would undertake with pleasure. The General thought that he could render another service to the Americans by making known one of the natural wonders

---

7. Martha Wayles Jefferson gave birth to a daughter, Lucy, on May 8, 1782, three weeks after Chastellux took his leave from Monticello. The mother died late that year, and the child in October 1784.
8. Chastellux crossed paths with Jefferson on several later occasions, most particularly following their reunion in France in 1784, when the Frenchman helped arrange for the placement of the American's eldest daughter in school at the Abbaye de Pentemont. They also corresponded frequently (three of Jefferson's letters to Chastellux are reprinted herein).
9. Charles Joseph Antoine Soualhat de Frontalard, baron de Turpin, remains a shadowy figure. His visit to the Natural Bridge is mentioned in the contemporary journal of the comte de Clermont-Crèvecoeur, an artillery officer. See Howard C. Rice Jr. and Anne S. K. Brown, eds. and trans., *The American Campaigns of Rochambeau's Army, 1780, 1781, 1782, 1783*, 2 vols. (Princeton and Providence, 1972), 1:67–68.

which shed luster upon their country, and that it would even be rather droll for people to see that the French had been the first to describe it with precision and publish a correct plan of it.[1] Baron de Turpin set out, therefore, at the beginning of May, and in three weeks brought me back five plans, three of which have been engraved and are annexed to this book. Two of these plans give perspectives, taken from the two sides of the Natural Bridge and from the bottom of the valley whence it rises. The third is a bird's-eye view, and shows a part of the surrounding country. The two others being only imaginary sections of this bridge at the spots where it holds to the bank and which may be considered its abutments, I have not seen fit to have them engraved, in order not to increase the number of plates that have to be added to this work. As for the measurements, here are those given me by M. de Turpin:

The Natural Bridge forms a vault fifteen *toises*[2] long, of the type known as a *corne de vache* (cow's horn). The chord of this vault is seventeen *toises* on the upstream side, and nine on the downstream side, and the arc is a semi-ellipse so flattened that its minor axis is only a twelfth of the major axis. The solid mass of rock and stone which loads this vault is 49 feet high on the crown of the big arch, and 37 on the small one; and as about the same difference is found in the slope of the hill, it may be supposed that the roof of the vault itself is on a level the whole length of the crown. It is worth noting that the living rock extends over the whole span of the vault, which is only 25 feet wide at its greatest width and gradually becomes narrower.

The whole vault seems to form but a single stone, for the sort of seams which one notices on the upstream face are the result of lightning which struck this part in 1779; the other face has not the least vein, while the intrados[3] is so smooth that the martins, which flutter about in great numbers, can get no hold on it. The abutments, which have a slight talus, are quite entire, and without being absolutely smooth, have all the polish which a current of water would give to rough stone after a certain time. The four cliffs adjacent to the abutments seem to be perfectly homogeneous and to have very little rock debris at their base. The two cliffs on the right bank of the stream rise 200 feet above the water; the two on the left bank, 180 feet; the intrados of the vault is 150 feet above the stream.

If we consider this bridge simply as a picturesque object, we are struck by the majesty with which it towers in the valley. The white oaks which grow on its soil seem to rear their lofty tops to the clouds, while the same trees growing along the stream appear but as shrubs. As for the Naturalist, he must content himself with such observations as may guide a bolder Philosopher to form some conjecture on the probable origin of this extraordinary mass.

From all parts of the vault and from its supporting piers, cubic pieces of rock measuring three or four lines were taken; these were placed successively

---

1. Chastellux here added a footnote that ran in part: "So interesting an object could not have escaped the curiosity and observations of Mr. Jefferson. He had measured the height and width of the Natural Bridge, and has mentioned it in an excellent memoir which he composed in 1781, and of which he had several copies printed last year [i.e., 1785] under the modest title of *Notes on the state* [sic] *of Virginia*, or rather with no title, for this work has not been made public. We hope, however, that the precious documents on natural philosophy as well as politics included in this work will not be lost to the public."
2. An old French *toise* was equivalent to about six English feet.
3. The interior curve of an arch.

in the same aqua fortis. The first ones dissolved in less than half an hour; the others required more time, but this difference must be attributed to the weakening of the acid, which lost its activity as it became progressively saturated.

It will be seen that these rocks, being of a calcareous nature, exclude any idea of a volcano, which furthermore could not be reconciled with the form of the Bridge and all its adjacent parts. If one wants to believe that this astonishing arch is the result of a current of water, it must then be supposed that this current had enough force to take with it and carry to a great distance a mass of 5000 cubic *toises*, for there remains close by no trace of such an operation. The blocks found beneath the vault and a little below it have their former places still visible on the overhanging walls on the downstream side, and come from no other demolition than that of the Bridge itself, which is said to have been a third wider than it is now.

The depression of eight or ten inches hollowed out at the foot of the arch on the left bank of the stream extends this base into the form of a *bec de corbin*, or claw. This wearing away, and some other parts which are flaking off, give reason to believe that this surprising edifice will one day become the victim of time, which has destroyed so many others.

Such are the observations that Baron de Turpin brought back and which he was pleased to favor me with. As their accuracy may be relied on, it would perhaps be sufficient to transcribe them here and let the reader form his own opinions about the causes which could have produced this sort of prodigy. This was in fact what I had intended when, abandoned to my own powers, which I quite properly mistrusted, I was writing up for myself alone, at Williamsburg, the journal of my recent excursion. But it was then that a Spanish work, which fell into my hands, confirmed me in the opinion that I had at first entertained, that it was to the action of the waters alone that we owed the magnificent construction of the Natural Bridge.[4] The opinion of Comte de Buffon, whom I have since consulted, has left me no further doubt. His sublime ideas on the different Epochs of Nature should have been sufficient to put me on the right path; but the disciple who is aware of his own limitations is timid, even in applying his master's principles. Nevertheless, anyone who has traveled in America becomes a witness entitled to depose in favor of that genius whose oracles too frequently find contradictors. If it were necessary to justify what the Montesquieus, the Humes, the Voltaires have said about the baleful effects heretofore produced by superstition, ignorance, and prejudice, we might still, in surveying Europe, find peoples which could display to us the picture of what we were like 300 years ago, nations which are, so to speak, the contemporaries of past ages, and thus the truth of historical facts could be confirmed by those which we might ourselves witness. The same holds true for America, as far as the Epochs of Nature and all documents of natural history are concerned. In traveling through this part of the world, you might think yourself carried backwards in time for a whole epoch: the lowlands and the plains are watered by such large rivers and so intersected by creeks, the coasts are so frequently indented by gulfs and arms of the sea—which seem to carry the ocean into

---

4. Here (and more overtly later on) Chastellux refers, as does Jefferson in the *Notes on the State of Virginia*, to Antonio de Ulloa's *Noticias Americanas* (1772).

the very heart of the land and to the very foot of the mountains—that it is impossible not to be persuaded that all this part of the continent is of recent creation, and is simply the product of successive alluviums. On the other hand, if we observe that all the high mountains form long chains parallel to each other, and almost always in a north-south direction; that most of the rivers which flow into the ocean have their source in the narrow valleys which separate these mountains, and that after following the direction of the valleys for a considerable distance, they suddenly turn towards the east, pierce the mountains, and at length reach the sea, acquiring magnitude as they proceed—we shall believe ourselves, if not coeval with, at least not far removed from that Epoch of Nature when the waters, collected to an extraordinary height and confined in the valleys, were seeking to break through their dikes, still uncertain of the means they would take to make their escape. We shall further be inclined to believe that the motion of the earth on its axis, or the westerly winds, which in North America correspond to the trade winds of the tropics, and are perhaps a result of them, have at length determined the motion of the waters towards the east. In which case, one of two things happened: either the waters, having exceeded the height of the least lofty summits which opposed their passage, formed some sort of gutters, through which the surplus escaped; or being unable to reach the height of these mountains, they found some softer parts in the greater mass itself, which they first undermined, and then entirely pierced. In the first case, if the declivity was very steep, and the rock which served as the bed was very hard, the waters would have formed a cataract, but where the slope was less steep, and the soil less compact, the waters would not only have formed the gutter which served as a passage, but would have loosened and carried along with them the lands, forming them into long slopes, which would finally merge into the plains. Thus the Hudson River, the Delaware, the Potomac, the James River, and many others, have opened channels for themselves to the sea by piercing the mountains at more or less right angles, and forming more or less spacious valleys. In the second case, the waters unable to pierce the mountains except below the summits, must have left above them a sort of *calotte*, or roof, similar to that of the Natural Bridge. But how many chances there were that these arches would eventually crumble, especially when, as the river-beds gradually deepened, the load became too heavy, and they thus lost their support!

   If we still doubt the probability of this hypothesis and still want more striking tokens, more obvious traces of the action of the waters, let us continue our travels in America; let us go to the vicinity of the Ohio, to the banks of the "Kentucke River." Here is what we may observe there, or rather what the recent historian of that region has written:

>   Amongst the natural curiosities of this country, the winding banks, or rather precipices of Kentucke, and Dick's Rivers, deserve the first place. The astonished eye there beholds almost every where three or four hundred feet of a solid perpendicular lime-stone rock; in some parts a fine white marble, either curiously arched, pillared or blocked up into fine building stones. These precipices, as was observed before, are like the sides of a deep trench, or canal; the land above being level, except where creeks set in, and crowned with fine groves of red cedar. It is only at particular places that this river can be crossed, one of which is worthy of admiration; a great road large enough for waggons made by

buffaloes, sloping with an easy descent from the top to the bottom of a very large steep hill, at or near the river above Lees-town [Frankfort].[5]

Or let us consult Don Joseph [Antonio] de Ulloa, already so famous for his travels; he is the author of the Spanish book which I have mentioned above, a book entitled *Noticias Americanas,* in which he gives very curious and detailed descriptions of all Spanish America. In the article I am about to translate, he begins by pointing out a very noticeable difference between the mountains in America situated below the torrid zone, and those we observe in other parts of the world; for although the height of the latter is often very considerable, nevertheless, as the ground rises gradually and as their combined summits cover immense expanses, those who inhabit them may be ignorant of their elevation in relation to sea level; whereas these American mountains being separated, and, so to speak, cloven through their whole height, continually give evidence, and even the measure of their prodigious altitudes. De Ulloa then continues:

> In these high regions the land is dissected by deep gorges or *quebradas,* as they are called, of considerable width; they form the boundary between the plains and mountains on either side, and some are more than two leagues across when seen from above. They are broader where they are deepest. The rivers flow through the middle and deepest parts of these valleys, leaving plains of about the same width on either side. What is remarkable is that the angles and bends made by the rivers correspond exactly to those of the two walls, so that if these could be fitted together they would match perfectly and form a solid mass with no breaks. The rivers continue their courses through these canyons until they reach the low country, and thence to the sea. But the channels they cut in the latter part of their courses are not very deep nor much above sea level. Thus it may in general be said that the higher the mountain ranges, the deeper the gorges of the rivers. . . .

> Among the many natural wonders to be found in the province of Angaraez, and which are more varied and remarkable here than in larger and more extensive countries, there is one of unique interest. This province, which is a dependency of the government of Guancavelica [Huancavelica], is divided into several *doctrinas* or departments, in one of which, called Conaica, there is a little village called Viñas.[6] The distance between it and Conaica, the capital, is nine leagues; at a distance of five of these leagues there is a hill called Corosunta. Below it there is an opening through which flows the river called the Chapllancas. For a distance of about a half a league this river flows through a canyon about 6 to 8 *varas*[7] wide and more than 40 *varas* high, the width being not perceptibly more at the upper than at the lower part. By this route, where the stream in the narrow parts fills the whole width, goes the road leading from Viñas to the town of Conaica. The river can only be followed through the places where the opening is 8 *varas* wide, as has been said, and it must be crossed nine times, at those spots, generally at the bends, where it flows away from the banks a bit, for when it flows straight it completely fills the gap. This canyon is cut through the bedrock with

---

5. Chastellux is quoting from John Filson, *The Discovery, Settlement and Present State of Kentucke* (1784).
6. These localities are in modern Peru.
7. A Spanish *vara* (yard) was equivalent to 2.8 English feet.

such precision that the recesses or indentures on one side correspond to the projections on the other, as if the mountain had parted on purpose, with its windings and turnings, to make a passage for the waters between the two high walls. They are so similar that if they were joined they would fit exactly together with no space in between. There is no danger in traveling this road, for the rock is too solid to crumble and the river is not so swift as to be dangerous. Nevertheless, one is seized with fear and trembling when entering into this narrow gorge with its high and perpendicular sides, so perfectly matched that they seem ready at any moment to snap back together again.

This opening is an example in miniature of what the great *quebradas* were originally like, when their depth was no greater than this one and when their banks, which now slope away, were perpendicular, or nearly so, as in this instance. It was only after the waters had cut the channels deeper that there were landslides above and that the upper walls, unable to maintain themselves perpendicular, gradually crumbled to their present shape. In the same manner the passage of time and the effects of rain, frost, and sun are abrading the Chapllancas canyon, so that it too will eventually lose the even width from top to bottom that it now has, and which it has retained more than others because the rock is hard and not interbedded with easily eroded veins of earth. Everything thus leads us to believe that the waters alone have worn away this channel to its present form and that the waters will by the same process continue to widen it in its upper part, inasmuch as time suffices to reduce the hardest and most solid rocks to sand, and as evidences of this are already apparent in the fragments of stone in the river-bed here and where it leaves the canyon in the mountain and broadens out on to the plain.

But whether we attribute the origin of this deep channel to the action of the waters which have worn it down to its present state, or whether we suppose that an earthquake rent asunder the mountain to give a new course to the river which had previously taken another direction, there can be no doubt that this opening was formed at some time after the Deluge had receded, and from this example, that the *quebradas* frequently met with throughout the higher parts of South America were formed by the gradual wearing of the waters, for it can be observed, on the one hand, that the force of their current is capable of wrenching off rocks of extraordinary size, and, on the other hand we have manifest proofs of the continuing effort of the waters to deepen their bed, traces of which are seen in the huge blocks shaped like dice or cubes which they have formed wherever the rocks have offered too great an obstacle to allow them to split them and clear away the whole extent of the channel. In the Iscuchaca River, near the place of the same name, there is one such rock which looks exactly like a die, about 12 *varas* square and rising out of low water to a distance of 7 or 8 *varas*. Such large formations and the smaller ones found in the river beds must have been left standing there after the waters had eaten away the surrounding rocks and sand, but they will remain only until such time as the deepening rivers find some soluble material at their bases, penetrate it, destroy it, and weaken its substance. Put in motion by great floods, these masses of rock will go crashing against others, and be broken into smaller pieces which will roll more easily. Such is doubtless the origin of all the stones seen beneath the waters or along the banks, some very small and others so enormous that human strength could not move them. To give some idea of the depth of these *quebradas* or valleys in relation to the habitable areas of South America certain experiments may be cited as evidence. The town of Huancavelica was founded in one of the valleys among the various chains of mountains. Here the mercury in the barometer tube remains at 18 *pulgadas* (inches), 1½ *líneas* (lines), this being the average between the two extremes of 1¼ and 1¾ lines. The elevation above sea level is accordingly 1949 *toesas* or 4536 ⅔ *varas*. At the summit of the mountain where the mercury mine is located—which is still habitable and which is surrounded by other mountains as high again as this one is above Huancavelica—the barometer marks exactly 16 inches, which makes its altitude above sea level 2337 ⅔ *toesas* or 5448 *varas*, and its height above Huancavelica 912 ⅔ *varas*. This latter figure thus represents the depth to which the Huancavelica valley has been cut since the time of the Deluge by the action of the different rivers which take their rise in another region called Icho and join to form the Huancavelica River.

After so many observations concerning the extraordinary action of the waters and the astonishing effects resulting from it, are we not justified in supposing that the Natural Bridge is also the work of the waters, and should we not regard it as a sort of *quebrada?* When the valleys of the Appalachians were only great lakes, in which the waters were imprisoned, the little valley now spanned by the Bridge may have formed a special reservoir in which the waters remained even after they had escaped from the larger valleys. The mass of the rock out of which the Natural Bridge was hollowed may have served as a barrier to them; but whether the height of the waters did not reach the summit of this rock, or whether they more easily succeeded in undermining its lower part, they would in either case have left subsisting the immense *calotte,* or roof, which forms the arch of the Bridge as we now see it. It would be useless, and perhaps rash, to attempt to explain in detail how the curve of this vault was so regularly drawn; but once the cause is known, all the effects, however varied, and however astonishing they may appear, must be attributed to it. We may further observe that the largest arc of this vault bears a relation to the angle formed by the valley at this place, inasmuch as the rock seems to have been most hollowed out there where the force of the waters was greatest. However this may be, I leave every one free to form any conjecture he pleases, and as I have said above, my design has been less to explain this prodigy of Nature than to describe it with enough accuracy to enable the learned to form an opinion about it.

LUTHER MARTIN

To the Honorable Thomas Jefferson, Esq. Vice-President of the United States[1]

SIR,   Baltimore, June 24th, 1797.

IN your notes on Virginia, combating certain sentiments of the celebrated Buffon, you have given us an eulogium of the *North American Savages,* and,

---

1. Maryland Federalist Luther Martin (1748–1826), the son-in-law of Cresap, intensified his political battles with Jefferson by publishing this letter, and an earlier one, attacking the account of Logan (and the text of Logan's speech) as given in *Notes on the State of Virginia.* A decade later, Jefferson would refer to Martin as an "unprincipled & impudent federal bulldog" (quoted by Peden, 300). The text of this letter is transcribed from the *Federal Gazette and Baltimore Daily Advertiser,* July 22, 1797.

to establish their eminence in oratory, have introduced the *speech* of Logan (whom *you* have dubbed a Mingo chief) to lord Dunmore, when governor of Virginia—a morsel of eloquence, in your opinion, not to be excelled by *any* passage in the orations of Demosthenes, Cicero, or any more eminent orator, if Europe has furnished more eminent. And, that your reader might be the better enabled to distinguish all its superiority of lustre, you have given him the following preliminary statement of incidents: "In the spring of the year 1774, (you say) a robbery and murder were committed on an inhabitant of the frontiers of Virginia, by two Indians of the Shawanese tribe. The neighboring whites, according to their custom, undertook to punish this outrage in a summary way. Col. Cresap, a man *infamous* for the *many murders* he had committed on those much injured people, collected a party and proceeded down the Kanaway, in quest of vengeance. Unfortunately, a canoe of women and children, with one man only, was seen coming from the opposite shore, unarmed, and unsuspecting an hostile attack from the whites. Cresap and his party concealed themselves on the bank of the river, and the moment the canoe reached the shore, singled out their objects, and at one fire killed every person in it. This happened to be the family of Logan, who had long been distinguished as the friend of the whites. This unworthy return provoked his vengeance. He accordingly signalized himself in the war which ensued. In the autumn of the same year, a decisive battle was fought, at the mouth of the Great Kanhaway, between the collected forces of the Shawanese, Mingoes and Delawares, and a detachment of the Virginia militia. The Indians were defeated, and sued for peace. Logan, however, disdained to be seen among the supplicants. But left the sincerity of a treaty should be distrusted, from which so distinguished a chief absented himself, he sent by a messenger the following speech to be delivered to lord Dunmore[.]"

This story and *that speech* of Logan, having been selected by mr. Fennel in his readings and recitations, moral, critical and entertaining, induced me to address to that gentleman a letter on the subject, which perhaps you may not have *seen*, for I know not whether you are in the habit of reading the newspapers; but that you may, if you please, have an *opportunity of seeing* it, permit me to refer you to the 26th number of Porcupine's Gazette, printed in the city of Philadelphia, in which paper a copy of my letter was published.[2]

To the world at large, and to every individual interested, *you*, as an historian, *must* be considered *answerable*, that the *speech* of Logan is *genuine*, *unadulterated*, and not a *fiction*. And as, that the beauty and excellency of that speech might be the more clearly perceived, you thought good to enter into a detail of facts. To the world, and to every person interested, *you must*, as an historian, be considered answerable for the *truth* of those facts.

I *first* became acquainted with col. Cresap in the year 1772. I was then on a journey to Fort Pitt. Col. Cresap was at that time living at his seat by Old-Town. He was *never* on the west side of the Allegany mountains from that day until his death. Nor was Logan's family killed on the Kanhaway, but at the mouth of Yellow Creek, on the east side of the Ohio river, and about forty or fifty miles above Fort Wheelan. And as you have so much mistaken the *place* where the transactions happened, which, by the by, is a little remarkable in an *enlightened* historian, volunteering on events which happened in the state where he lived, and those too of so recent a date, it is not,

---

2. The letter in question, dated March 29, 1797, was addressed to James Fennell, editor of the *Federal Gazette and Baltimore Daily Advertiser*.

very improbable, that you have been equally mistaken in the *person*, or in the *title* of the person, whom you have fixed on as the principal personage in those transactions. Although the Cresaps all lived within a few hundred yards of your state,[3] and the north branch of the Patowmac, one of its boundaries, ran through their possessions; I will therefore take no advantage of any error you may have made in the designatio personæ,[4] but will give you full liberty to select, out of the *whole family*, the individual on whom you with to fix the charge.

And now, sir, to lay the proper foundation for the further investigation of this subject, permit me to request, and not only to request, but to *expect*, your answer to the following questions.

1st, From what document did you copy the speech of Logan; or from whom did you receive your information of that speech, and of its contents?

2d, What person was meant to be designated by the *title* and *name* of col. Cresap, as used by *Logan* in his *speech*, and by *yourself*, in your *statement of the incidents* necessary for the better understanding that speech?

3d, Whence did you procure your information that col. Cresap, or *or any person of that name*, was "infamous for the many murders he had committed on the much injured Indians?" When and where were those murders committed? and who of those "much injured people" were the victims?

It is not in the human heart to feel that I need an apology for proposing to you these questions; but, if an apology was wanting I have it;—In two amiable daughters, a parent may at least be pardoned for thinking them such, who are directly descended from *that man*, whose character your pen, I hope from no worse motive than to support a philosophical hypothesis, has endeavored to stigmatise with *indelible infamy!* a variety of circumstances have combined to give an *unmerited* celibrity, and extensiveness of diffusion to an *unfounded calumny*. This calumny I *will efface*.

The letter I have written on this subject to Mr. Fennel; the letter I now address to you, and all those which I shall hereafter address to you on the same subject, I shall transmit to the authors of the annual register in Great-Britain, by them to be published; and to the Rev. Mr. Morse, to Mr. Lendrum, and to every other author, by whom the speech and story of Logan may have been copied from your *notes*, will I also send *the same* to be hereafter inserted by them in a republication of their works.

If my directions are complied with, this will be delivered to you immediately on the rising of congress; for I would not wish to take off your attention one single moment from the concerns of the public, while congress is in session.

With *due* respect, I am, Sir,

Your obedient servant,
LUTHER MARTIN.

---

3. At the time of the murders in question, the boundaries of Virginia ran as far west as the Ohio Valley.
4. Identification of persons (Latin).

CRITICISM

Early Responses to Jefferson and His Writings, 1802–1896

THOMAS KENNEDY

Ode to the Mammoth Cheese[1]

Presented to Thomas Jefferson, President of the United States, by the Inhabitants of Cheshire, Massachusetts,

January 1, 1802.

Most Excellent—far fam'd and far fetch'd CHEESE!
Superior far in smell, taste, weight and size,[2]
To any ever form'd 'neath foreign skies,
And highly honour'd—thou wert made to please,
The man belov'd by all—but stop a trice,
Before he's praised—I too must have a slice.

II.

Rich too thou art, and pleasant tho' so large
As any Millstone—or a North-west Moon;
To measure thee 'twould take an afternoon—
Few tables can support the pond'rous charge,
Into what cupboard Mammoth[3] canst thou enter,
And where's the knife can cut clean thro' thy centre.

III.

'Twould take a Gallatin[4] to ascertain
How many meals for Congress—clerks and all

---

1. This humorous poem by Thomas Kennedy (1776–1832), a Scots Presbyterian immigrant living in Baltimore, celebrated the gift of a very large cheese to President Jefferson by the citizens of Cheshire, in western Massachusetts. The text is derived from the broadside edition of 1802.
2. The cheese, which was more than four feet in diameter and weighed 1,235 pounds, had been made from the milk of nine hundred certifiably "Republican cows." Federalists mocked the present (for which Jefferson in fact paid the producers, as he had a strict ethical rule against such gifts). It lay on display in an unfinished room of the executive mansion until July 4, 1803, when it was cut into and tasted in celebration of the Louisiana Purchase. Fifteen years later, John Adams humorously told Jefferson to settle a philosophical problem they were debating by putting the question to "a Mite, in the center of your Mammoth Cheese," but cheese and mite had long since vanished by then. See Merrill Peterson, *Thomas Jefferson and the New Nation: A Biography* (New York, 1970), 722–723; AJL, 2:465.
3. The use of the term *Mammoth* in conjunction with the gift was intended to make a jovial defense of Jefferson's interest in recovering authenticated bones of the legendary mammoth as part of his ongoing attempts to correct the errors of Buffon and others regarding the powers of nature in the Americas.
4. Albert Gallatin (1761–1849), a Swiss native, served as Jefferson's secretary of the treasury from 1801 on.

The supernumeraries about their Hall,
Thy spacious limits actually contain:
What number of WELSH RABBITS, thou wouldst make
How many thousand loaves there's cause to bake.

IV.

For cent'ries past—in Europe—sometimes here,
Placemen were said to share the *loaves* and *fishes*,
(And where's the man that for a share ne'er wishes)
But now Americans have better cheer,
And to their worthy servants 'stead of these,
They've wisely substituted—LOAVES and CHEESE.

V.

Cheese is the attendant of a New-Year's day,
Cheese is the Blithe-meat[5] when a bairn is born,
Cheese, may those taste thee ne'er, who tasting scorn,
Cheese—still proceeding from the milky way,
Is nature's purest, plain and simple food;
Cheese is a lux'ry, when like this 'tis good.

VI.

God bless the Cheese—and kindly bless the makers,
The givers—generous—good and sweet and fair,
And the receiver—great beyond compare,
All those who shall be happy as partakers;
O I may no traitor to his country's cause
E'er have a bit of thee between his jaws.

VII.

Some folks may sneer, with envy in their smiles,
And with low wit at ridicule endeavour,
Their sense and breeding's shewn by their behaviour,
Well—let them use Aristocratic wiles,
Do what they can—and say just what they please,
RATS love to nibble at good Cheshire Cheese.

VIII.

'Tis a good New-Year's Gift I think indeed,
But the Cheese-Master must be on his guard,
And against *longing women* be prepar'd,
Once they begin to eat—do pray take heed;
Once they begin—when they may stop's unknown,
Perhaps they will not till the whole is gone.

5. In Scotland [Kennedy's note].

IX.

To othcrs leaving wealth, and place and pow'r,
    I'll to my home and to my HARRIS hie,
    Our wants are few—those industry supply;
All that we want or wish for in life's hour,
    Heavcn still will grant us—they are only those,
    Poetry—Health—Peace—Virtue—Bread and *Cheese*.

JAMES T. CALLENDER

From The President Again[1]

It is well known that the man, *whom it delighteth the people to honour*, keeps, and for many years past has kept, as his concubine, one of his own slaves. Her name is SALLY. The name of her eldest son is TOM.[2] His features are said to bear a striking although sable resemblance to those of the president himself. The boy is ten or twelve years of age. His mother went to France in the same vessel with Mr. Jefferson and his two daughters.[3] —The delicacy of this arrangement must strike every person of common sensibility. What a sublime pattern for an American ambassador to set before the eyes of two young ladies

If the reader does not feel himself *disposed to pause* we beg leave to proceed. Some years ago, this story had once or twice been hinted at in Rind's Federalist.[4] At that time, we believed the surmise to be an absolute calumny. One reason for thinking so was this. A vast body of the people wished to debar Mr. Jefferson from the presidency. *The establishment of this single fact* would have rendered his election impossible. We reasoned thus; that if the allegation had been true, it was sure to have been ascertained and advcrtised by his enemies, in every corner of the continent. The suppression of so decisive an enquiry serves to show that the common sense of the federal party was overruled by divine providence.—It was the predestination of the supreme being that they should be turned out; that they should be expelled from office by the popularity of a character, which, at that instant, was lying fettered and gagged, consumed and extinguished at their feet!

---

1. Jefferson, who relished the attacks of Scottish-born gossipmonger and political radical James T. Callender (1758–1803) on Alexander Hamilton and other Federalists, at one time looked on the journalist with considerable favor. However, once the mercurial Callender fell on hard times and Jefferson, then president, refused Callender's preposterous demand that Jefferson appoint him postmaster of Richmond (or suffer the consequences), the journalist turned on the president, giving fresh exposure to preexisting rumors about Jefferson's relationship with one of his female slaves, Sally Hemings. This brief newspaper report, with a follow-up published a month later, turned the rumors into a political scandal whose repercussions are still being felt today. It is reprinted from the Baltimore *Republican; or Anti-Democrat* for September 6, 1802.
2. It remains doubtful that Sally Hemings had such a son. Furthermore, when the results of DNA tests conducted on male descendents of Hemings, Jefferson's brother, and other related individuals were published in 1999, they indicated that the Woodson family (which claimed descent from "Tom") had no close genetic ties to the Hemingses or the Jeffersons.
3. It is clear, to the contrary, that Sally Hemings accompanied Jefferson's second surviving daughter, Maria, to France in 1787.
4. The editor of the *Virginia Federalist*, William Rind, hinted at the story as early as June 1800, and it was circulating otherwise in the press when Callender published this piece.

We do not wish to give wanton offence to many very good kind of people. Concerning a certain sort of connexions, we have already stated that, "of boys and batchelors, we have said nothing, and we have nothing to say." They will be pleased, therefore to stand out of the way. When the king of Prussia was on the point of fighting the great and decisive battle of Lissa, he assembled his principal officers, and, under the penalty of his utmost contempt, exhorted them to bravery. In the midst of this address, an old veteran dissolved into tears. "My dear general," said Frederick, "I did not refer to *you.*"—Some of our acquaintances are, upon the same principle, requested to believe that we do not, in this allusion, refer to *them.* We have formerly stated that *superem-inent pretensions to chastity are always suspicious.* This hint was sufficient plain to shew that the Recorder does not desire to set up a manufacture of wry faces. The writer of this essay does not bear the stamp of a Scots presbyterian parson of the last century. But still, we all know that some things may be overlooked, which can hardly be excused, and which it is impracticable either to praise or even to vindicate. Such is human nature, and such is human life. One of our correspondents very justly observes that "there is nobody, of whom something disagreeable may not be said."

By the wench Sally, our president has had several children. There is not an individual in the neighbourhood of Charlottesville who does not believe the story; and not a few who know it.

If Duane[5] fees this account, he will not prate any more about the treaty between Mr. Adams and Toussaint. Behold the favorite, the first born of republicanism! the pinnacle of all that is good and great! in the open consummation of an act which tends to subvert the policy, the happiness, and even the existence of this country!

'Tis supposed that, at the time when Mr. Jefferson wrote so smartly concerning negroes, when he endeavoured so much to belittle the African race, he had no expectation that the chief magistrate of the United States was to be the ringleader in shewing that his opinion was erroneous; or, that he should chuse an African stock whereupon he was to engraft his own descendants.

Duane and Cheetham[6] are not worth asking whether this is a lie or not? But censor Smith is requested to declare whether the statement is a *federal misrepresentation?* Mute! Mute! Mute! Yes very mute! will all those republican printers of political biographical be upon this point. Whether they stir, or not, they must feel themselves like a horse in a quicksand. They will plunge deeper and deeper, until no assistance can save them.

The writer of this piece has been arraigned as capable of selling himself to a British ambassador.[7] The impeachment was made by a printer, who is in the confidence of Mr. Jefferson. The president had the utmost reason to believe that the charge was an utter fiction. This charge was met in a decisive stile. We, at once, selected and appealed to the testimony, or belief, of five persons,

5. William Duane (1760–1835), editor of the *Philadelphia Aurora,* was one of Callender's enemies and Jefferson's avid supporters. In a recent article, he had claimed that Callender had infected his wife with venereal disease and then, as she lay dying, had sat in a nearby room getting drunk.
6. James Cheetham (1772–1810), an English radical, had immigrated to New York in 1798 and begun a journalistic career.
7. Although this legal broil is not strictly relevant to the question of Jefferson's behavior, its inclusion here helps give a savor of Callender's character as a man and writer, and he actually does make some use of it once he returns to the subject in hand.

who were intimately acquainted with the situation of Callender. at the period of the pretended project of sale. These were Mr. Israel Israel, Dr. James Reynolds, Mr. John Beckley, Mr. John Smith, federal marshal of Pennsylvania, and Mr. Matthew Carey, whose name has been heard of in every county and corner of the United States. This appeal harmonized with the feelings of innocence and defiance. If the friends of Mr. Jefferson are convinced of his innocence, they will make an appeal of the same sort. If they resist in silence, or if they content themselves with resting upon a *general denial,* they cannot hope for credit. The allegation is of a nature too black to be suffered to remain in suspence. We should be glad to hear of its refutation. We gave it to the world under the firmest belief that such a refutation *never can be made.* The African Venus is said to officiate, as house keeper at Monticello.—When Mr. Jefferson has read this article, he will find leisure to estimate how much has been lost or gained by so many unprovoked attacks upon

J. T. CALLENDER.

ABRAHAM BISHOP

From Oration, in Honor of the Election of President Jefferson, and the Peaceable Acquisition of Louisiana[1]

We are not convened to do homage to a tyrant, nor to parade the virtues of *a President and Senate for life,* nor to bow before a First Consul, nor to bend the knee before a host of privileged orders; but we have assembled to pay our annual respects to a President, whom the voice of his country has called to the head of the freest and happiest nation on earth.

While Providence is giving to Britons a solemn commentary on the burning of our towns and the murder of our brethren, we are enjoying the fruits of a glorious defence against the passive obedience, which her insatiate court attempted to impose on us, as a punishment for the high misdemeanors of having descended from themselves, of having sought liberty of mind and conscience in this new world, and of having resolved to be free.

While France is learning, under awful impressions, the danger of delegating power without limit, and of trusting to ambition and the sword what ought to remain in the sacred deposit of peace and legislative counsel, the people of most of our States enjoy the full benefit of free elections, and derive from them all the blessings, which the best state of society admits.

While symptoms of death have seized on the governments of the eastern continent, and are hurrying them to that grave, which has buried all the ancient empires, we are in youth, advancing to maturity rapidly, as a sound constitution well guarded, and the best nourishment well administered can advance us.

---

1. The prominent Connecticut republican Abraham Bishop (1763–1844) was a staunch supporter of Jefferson. His speech on the president's behalf, delivered at a "National Festival" in his home state on May 11, 1804, at a time when the Napoleonic Wars were raging in Europe, is reprinted from the first edition (Hartford, 1804).

ABRAHAM BISHOP

The history of the world teaches that nations, like men, must decay. Ours will not forever escape the fate of others. Wealth, luxury, vice, aristocracies will attack us in our decline: these are evils of society, never to be courted, but to be put to as distant a day as possible.—The season of national youth, of vigor, of pure principles and fair prospects is peculiarly a season of joy.—We have lived at a period, more eventful than any which can recur. Having passed the dark season of our revolution, having witnessed the birth of our empire, having combated the tendency of an administration,[2] which fought to rank us with nations, whose systems of eternal war and debt we abhorred, which publicly approved the doctrines of the old school, and in every measure sounded our retreat to the ruins of the old world, we have lived to see a real republic, combining all the blessings for which our fathers professed to embrace this country, and distressing none but the enemies of civil and religious liberty.

* * *

Uniform respect for the sovereign people and for peace has characterized our President: his ears have been open to the voice of the people, who called him to his high office, and he has waited till that voice was distinctly expressed. In the present case the southern people called loudly for the acquisition, republicans were united in sentiment, and federalists declared that Louisiana was worth the price of blood.—To kings and the lovers of a President and Senate for life be it left to shed blood for territory; our President saw in amicable negotiation a prospect of gaining the desired possession.—He might have marshalled armies and bid defiance to the mighty power of France—the blood of your sons and brothers might have flown like the waters of the Ohio and reddened the Missisippi, and this would have been the only export ever acquired—the banks of that majestic river would have furnished another scene of whitened bones, and this would have been the only right of deposit ever secured! Louisiana would have remained the proud possession of France, a land of citadels, from which all the southern world would have been successfully annoyed. The wilderness, now blossoming as the rose, and filled with the shouts of republican husbandmen, would have been restored to beasts of prey. The price of blood would indeed have been paid, but the object forever defeated!

By our revolution, which cost more than an hundred millions, beside much shedding of blood and years of anxious suspence, the Atlantic states of this continent were redeemed from the dominion of an island. By the skilful negociation of Livingston and Monroe[3] was purchased, at an expence of 15 millions, a territory equal in extent to these states. Had the rivers Connecticut, Hudson and Delaware been owned by France and gained by government at any price, we should have felt the immediate profit and have acknowledged it a cheap purchase; but to us as a nation the acquisition of Louisiana as important as would have been the surrendry of those rivers. To the rapidly increasing and fruitful regions of the south it is equal to the possession of the Atlantic by these northern states.

* * *

2. Of President John Adams, 1797–1801.
3. Future president James Monroe (1758–1831), special envoy to France at the time of the Louisiana Purchase in 1803. New York jurist Robert Livingstone (1746–1813), U. S. minister to France.

To federalists this territory, for which they would have shed blood, now seems a barren waste, where no verdure quickens; but to us it appears fruitful, abounding in broad rivers and streams, producing whatever is necessary to our commerce with foreign nations. We see in Louisiana an assurance of long life to our cause. The Atlantic states, as they advance to that condition of society, where wealth and luxury tend to vice and aristocracies, will yield to that country accessions of enterprizing men. The spirit of faction, which tends to concentrate, will be destroyed by this diffusion. We see in this acquisition the enterprize, which it excites, the fraternity which it promises, an asylum for the oppressed of all nations, without fear of an alien act, destroying the germs of war and opening the spring of that century of seasons, which exhibits the whole western continent detached from the wars of the eastern, from its kings, its first consuls, and nobles, from vast plans of dominion by conquest, a country producing the best and making it the interest of all nations to trade with us, promising a rich addition of revenue to expedite a legal oblivion to a detested funding system.

Such a President, such a distinguished acquisition and such an immense host of Connecticut Republicans convened to rejoice! This coincidence must present to our minds this moment, as combining events important to ourselves, our children, our country and the world, never to be forgotten. A President advancing with the olive branch, while other potentates exchange no civilities but at the point of the sword—peaceable acquisition perched on the ruins of conquest, and our rejoicing rising like a Phœnix from the ashes of federalism.

* * *

JOHN QUINCY ADAMS

On the Discoveries of Captain Lewis[1]

Good people, listen to my tale,[2]
'Tis nothing but what true is;
I'll tell you of the mighty deeds
Atchiev'd by Captain Lewis—
How starting from the Atlantick shore
By fair and easy motion,
He journied, *all the way by land,*
Until he met the ocean.

1. As a young man of seventeen in France with his parents, John Quincy Adams had been an admirer of Jefferson. By the time of Jefferson's election to the presidency, however, he joined in the Federalist mockeries of the philosopher-politician, as is evident in this satire on Meriwether Lewis. Along the way, Adams also takes shots at the Jeffersonian poet Joel Barlow's celebratory "Ode" on Meriwether Lewis, read at a public dinner for Lewis in Washington on February 14, 1807. When, during his own campaign for the presidency in 1824, his satire was unearthed and reprinted, Adams expressed regrets that he had ever written it. Reprinted from the *Monthly Anthology*, 4 (1807). All notes are by the present editor unless otherwise specified.
2. There are *some* understandings, graduated on such a scale, that it may be necessary to inform them, that our intention is not to depreciate the merits of Captain Lewis's publick services. We think highly of the spirit and judgment, with which he has executed the duty undertaken by him, and we rejoice at the rewards bestowed by congress upon him and his companions. But we think with Mr. John Randolph, that there is a bombast in Politicks, as well as in Poetry; and Mr. Barlow's "elegant and glowing stanzas" have the advantage of combining both [Adams's note].

Heroick, sure, the toil must be
    To travel through the woods, sir;
And never meet a foe, yet save
    His person and his goods, sir!
What marvels on the way he found
    He'll tell you, if inclin'd, sir—
But *I* shall only now disclose
    The things he *did not* find, sir.

He never with a Mammoth met,
    However you may wonder;
Nor even with a Mammoth's bone,
    Above the ground or under—
And, spite of all the pains he took
    The animal to track, sir,
He never could o'ertake the hog
    With navel on his back, sir.

And from the day his course began,
    Till even it was ended,
He never found an Indian tribe
    From Welchmen straight descended:
Nor, much as of Philosophers
    The fancies it might tickle:
To season his adventures, met
    A Mountain, sous'd in pickle.

He never left this nether world[3]—
    For still he had his reason—
Nor once the waggon of the sun
    Attempted he to seize on.
To bind a *Zone* about the earth
    He knew he was not able—
THEY SAY he did—but, ask himself,
    He'll tell you 'tis a fable.

He never dreamt of taming *tides*,[4]
    Like monkeys or like bears, sir—

3.   "With the same soaring genius, thy Lewis ascends,
                    "And *seizing the Car of the Sun*,
                "O'er the sky-propping hills, and high-waters he bends,
                    "And gives the proud earth *a new zone.*"

Thus sweetly sings the soaring genius of Barlow. He has in this stanza obtained an interesting victory over verse. He has brought *zone* and *sun* to rhyme together; which is more than ever was attempted by his great predecessor in psalmody, Sternhold [Adams's note]. In 1562, Thomas Sternhold played a major role in the production of an English psalter or psalm book that was infamous for its rough meter.

4.   "His long curving course has completed the belt,
                    "And tamed the last tide of the West.

                "Then hear the loud voice of the nation proclaim,
                    "And all ages resound the decree,
                "Let our Occident stream bear the young hero's name,
                    "Who *taught him his path to the sea.*"
                                                    BARLOW's *Stanzas*

A *school,* for teaching floods to flow,
    Was not among his cares, sir—
Had rivers ask'd of him their path,
    They had but mov'd his laughter—
They knew their courses, all, as well
    Before he came as after.

And must we then resign the hope
    These Elements of changing?
And must we still, alas! be told
    That after all his ranging,
The Captain could discover nought
    But Water in the Fountains?
Must Forests still be form'd of Trees?
    Of rugged Rocks the Mountains?

We never will be so fubb'd off,
    As sure as I'm a sinner!
Come—let us all subscribe, and ask
    The HERO to a dinner—
And Barlow stanzas shall indite—
    A bard, the tide who tames, sir—
And if we cannot alter *things,*
    By G—, we'll change their *names,* sir!

Let old Columbus be once more
    Degraded from his glory;
And not a river by his name
    Remember him in story—
For what is *old* Discovery
    Compar'd to that which new is?
Strike—strike *Columbia* river out,
    And put in—*river Lewis!*

Let dusky Sally henceforth bear
    The name of Isabella;
And let the mountain, all of salt,
    Be christen'd Monticella—
The hog with navel on his back
    Tom Pain may be when drunk, sir—
And *Joël* call the Prairie-dog,
    Which once was call'd a Skunk, sir.

Here the young HERO is exhibited in the interesting character of schoolmaster to a river; and the proposition, that the river should take his name by way of payment for his tuition, appears so modest and reasonable, that we should make no objection, were it not that the wages must be deducted from the scanty pittance of poor Columbus. He has already been so grossly defrauded by the name of this hemisphere, that we cannot hear with patience a proposal to strip him of that trifling substitute of a river, which had so late and so recently been bestowed upon him.

We invite the attention of the reader to the *rare* modesty of Mr. Barlow himself, who, in committing this *spoliation* upon the fame of Columbus, does not even allow him the chance of an adjudication, . . but undertakes, by self-created authority, to make proclamation for the whole nation, and to pronounce the decree for all ages [Adams's note].

And when the wilderness shall yield[5]
To bumpers, bravely brimming,
A nobler victory than men;—
While all our heads are swimming,
We'll dash the bottle on the wall
And name (the thing's agreed on)
Our first-rate-ship United States,
The flying frigate *Fredon*.[6]

True—Tom and Joël now, no more
Can overturn a nation;
And work, by butchery and blood,
A great regeneration;—
Yet, still we can turn inside out
Old Nature's Constitution,
And bring a Babel back of *names*—
Huzza! for REVOLUTION!

WILLIAM CULLEN BRYANT

From The Embargo; or, Sketches of the Times[1]

Look where we will, and in whatever land,
Europe's rich soil, or Afric's burning sand;
Where the wild savage hunts his wilder prey,
Or art and science pour their brightest day;
The monster vice appears before our eyes,
In naked impudence or gay disguise.

BUT quit the lesser game, indignant Muse,
And to thy country turn thy nobler views.
Ill-fated clime! condemn'd to feel th' extremes
Of a weak ruler's philosophic dreams;
Driv'n headlong on to ruin's fateful brink,
When will thy Country feel, when will she think!

WAKE Muse of Satire, in the cause of trade,
Thou scourge of miscreants who the laws evade!
Dart thy keen glances, knit thy threat'ning brows,
And hurl thine arrows at fair Commerce's foes!

MUCH injur'd Commerce! 'tis thy falling cause,
Which, from obscurity, a stripling draws;

5. "Victory over the wilderness, which is more *interesting*, than that over men."—*Barlow's Toast at the Dinner* [Adams's note].
6. Fredonia was proposed by New Yorker Samuel Latham Mitchell as a term for America. It was generally met with ridicule from Federalist quarters, although Barlow endorsed the coinage.
1. Bryant, the son of an active Federalist in western Massachusetts, was only thirteen at the time he penned this attack on Jefferson's infamous embargo, imposed in December 1807 on all foreign trade. The poem is reprinted from the first edition (Boston, 1808).

And were his powers but equal to his zeal,
Thy dastard foes his keen reproach should feel.
Curse of our Nation, source of countless woes,
From whose dark womb unreckon'd misery flows;
Th' embargo rages like a sweeping wind,
Fear low'rs before, and famine stalks behind.
What words, oh, Muse! can paint the mournful scene,
The saddening street, the desolated green;
How hungry labourers leave their toil and sigh,
And sorrow droops in each desponding eye!

    SEE the bold sailor from the ocean torn,
His element, sink friendless and forlorn!
His suffering spouse the tear of anguish shed,
His starving children cry in vain for bread!

    THE farmer, since supporting trade is fled,
Leaves the rude joke, and cheerless hangs his head;
Misfortunes fall, an unremitting shower,
Debts follow debts, on taxes, taxes pour.
See in his stores his hoarded produce rot,
Or sheriff sales his profits bring to naught;
Disheartening cares in thronging myriads flow,
Till down he sinks to poverty and woe!

    OH, ye bright pair, the blessing of mankind!
Whom time has sanction'd, and whom fate has join'd,
COMMERCE, that bears the trident of the main,
And AGRICULTURE, empress of the plain;
Who hand in hand, and heav'n-directed, go
Diffusing gladness through the world below;
Whoe'er the wretch, would hurl the flaming brand,
Of dire disunion, palsied be his hand!
Like "Cromwell damn'd to everlasting fame,"[2]
Let unborn ages execrate his name!
Dark is the scene, yet darker prospects threat,
And ills may follow unexperienc'd yet!
Oh Heaven! defend, as future seasons roll,
This western world from Buonaparte's control,
Preserve our *Freedom*, and our rights secure,
While truth subsists, and virtue shall endure!

               *   *   *

    WE, who seven years erst brav'd Britannia's power,
By Heaven supported in the gloomiest hour;
For whom our Sages plann'd, our Heroes bled,
Whom WASHINGTON, our pride and glory led;

---

2. "See Cromwell, damn'd to everlasting fame," Alexander Pope, *Essay on Man*, IV:281. Oliver
Cromwell (1599–1658), a military leader of the radical Puritan army during the English Civil War,
served as lord protector of England from 1653 to his death.

Till Heaven, propitious did our efforts crown,
With freedom, commerce, plenty, and renown!

WHEN shall this land, some courteous angel say,
Throw off a weak, and erring ruler's sway?
Rise, injur'd people, vindicate your cause!
And prove your love of Liberty and laws;
Oh wrest, sole refuge of a sinking land,
The sceptre from the slave's imbecile hand!
Oh ne'er consent, obsequious, to advance
The *willing vassal* of imperious France!
Correct that suffrage you misus'd before,
And lift your voice above a Congress' roar?
And thou, the scorn of every patriot name,
Thy country's ruin, and her council's shame!
Poor servile thing! derision of the brave!
Who erst from Tarleton fled to Carter's cave;[3]
Thou, who, when menac'd by perfidious Gaul,
Didst prostrate to her whisker'd minion fall;
And when our cash her empty bags supplied,
Didst meanly strive the foul disgrace to hide;
Go, wretch, resign the presidential chair,
Disclose thy secret measures foul or fair,
Go, search, with curious eye, for horned frogs,
'Mongst the wild wastes of Louisianian bogs;
Or where Ohio rolls his turbid stream,
Dig for huge bones, thy glory and thy theme;
Go scan, Philosophist; thy [Sally's] charms,
And sink supinely in her sable arms;
But quit to abler hands, the helm of state,
Nor image ruin on thy country's fate!

                    *   *   *

RISE then, Columbians! heed not France's wiles,
Her bullying mandates, her seductive smiles;
Send home Napolean's slave, and bid him say,
No arts can lure us, and no threats dismay;
Determin'd yet to war with whom we will,
Choose our own allies or be neutral still.

YE merchants, arm! the pirate Gaul repel,
Your prowess shall the naval triumph swell;
Send the marauders shatter'd, whence they came,
And Gallia's cheek suffuse with crimson shame.
But first select, our councils to direct,
One whose true worth entitles to respect;
In whom concentrates all that men admire.
The sage's prudence, and the soldier's fire;

---

3. Bryant refers to Jefferson's retreat from British forces under Banastre Tarleton, which raided the
   Charlottesville, Virginia, area in the summer of 1781.

Who scorns ambition, and the venal tribe,
And neither offers, nor receives a bribe;
Who firmly guards his country's every right,
And shines alike in council or in fight.

THEN on safe seas the merchant's barque shall fly,
Our waving flag shall kiss the polar sky;
On canvass wings our thunders shall be borne,
Far to the west, or tow'rd the rising morn;
Then may we dare a haughty tyrant's rage,
And gain the blessings of an unborn age.

'TIS done, behold the cheerful prospects rife!
And splendid scenes the startled eye surprise;
Lo! busy commerce courts the prosperous main;
And peace and plenty glad our shores again!
Th' industrious swain sees nature smile around
His fields with fruit, with flocks, his pastures crown'd.[4]

* * *

WASHINGTON IRVING

From A History of New York[1]

Book IV. Containing the Chronicles of the reign of William the Testy[1]

Chap. I. * * * the universal acquirements of William the Testy * * *

Such were the personal endowments of William the Testy, but it was the sterling riches of his mind that raised him to dignity and power. In his youth he had passed with great credit through a celebrated academy at the Hague, noted for producing finished scholars, with a dispatch unequalled, except by certain of our American colleges, which seem to manufacture bachelors of arts, by some patent machine. Here he skirmished very smartly on the frontiers of several of the sciences, and made such a gallant inroad into the dead languages, as to bring off captive a host of Greek nouns and Latin verbs, together with divers pithy saws and apothegms, all which he constantly paraded in conversation and writing, with as much vain glory as would a triumphant general of yore display the spoils of the countries he

4. After the second edition of 1809, Bryant never reprinted *The Embargo* (which he came to regard as "a very foolish thing") and eventually came to admire Jefferson; see Parke Godwin, *A Biography of William Cullen Bryant* (New York, 1883), 1:75. Late in life, he called Jefferson "one of the wisest political philosophers of his time,—wiser, I think, than any who lived in the times before him— one who saw deeper into the principles of government than his contemporaries knew." W. C. Bryant II and Thomas G. Voss, eds., *The Letters of William Cullen Bryant*, 6 vols. (New York, 1975–92), 4:102–103.
1. The text is from the first edition of *A History of New York* (1809), as edited by Stanley Williams and Tremaine McDowell (New York, 1927). William the Testy was Irving's nickname for Wilhelm Kieft (c. 1600–1647), the fifth director-general of the Dutch West India Company's colony of New Netherland. It is evident from a variety of details in the portrait of Kieft that Irving, who had Federalist leanings, was using Kieft as a vehicle for attacking then-president Jefferson.

had ravaged. He had moreover puzzled himself considerably with logic, in which he had advanced so far as to attain a very familiar acquaintance, by name at least, with the whole family of syllogisms and dilemmas; but what he chiefly valued himself on, was his knowledge of metaphysics, in which, having once upon a time ventured too deeply, he came well nigh being smothered in a slough of unintelligible learning—a fearful peril, from the effects of which he never perfectly recovered.—In plain words, like many other profound intermeddlers in this abstruse bewildering science, he so confused his brain, with abstract speculations which he could not comprehend, and artificial distinctions which he could not realize, that he could never think clearly on any subject however simple, through the whole course of his life afterwards. This I must confess was in some measure a misfortune, for he never engaged in argument, of which he was exceeding fond, but what between logical deductions and metaphysical jargon, he soon involved himself and his subject in a fog of contradictions and perplexities, and then would get into a mighty passion with his adversary, for not being convinced gratis.

It is in knowledge, as in swimming, he who ostentatiously sports and flounders on the surface, makes more noise and splashing, and attracts more attention, than the industrious pearl diver, who plunges in search of treasures to the bottom. The "universal acquirements" of William Kieft, were the subject of great marvel and admiration among his countrymen—he figured about at the Hague with as much vain glory, as does a profound Bonze at Pekin,[2] who has mastered half the letters of the Chinese alphabet; and in a word was unanimously pronounced an *universal genius!*—I have known many universal geniuses in my time, though to speak my mind freely I never knew one, who, for the ordinary purposes of life, was worth his weight in straw—but, for the purposes of government, a little sound judgment and plain common sense, is worth all the sparkling genius that ever wrote poetry, or invented theories.

Strange as it may sound therefore, the *universal acquirements* of the illustrious Wilhelmus, were very much in his way, and had he been a less learned little man, it is possible he would have been a much greater governor. He was exceedingly fond of trying philosophical and political experiments; and having stuffed his head full of scraps and remnants of ancient republics, and oligarchies, and aristocracies, and monarchies, and the laws of Solon and Lycurgus and Charondas, and the imaginary commonwealth of Plato, and the Pandects of Justinian, and a thousand other fragments of venerable antiquity, he was forever bent upon introducing some one or other of them into use; so that between one contradictory measure and another, he entangled the government of the little province of Nieuw Nederlandts in more knots during his administration, than half a dozen successors could have untied.

No sooner had this bustling little man been blown by a whiff of fortune into the seat of government, than he called together his council and delivered a very animated speech on the affairs of the province. As every body knows what a glorious opportunity a governor, a president, or even an emperor has, of drubbing his enemies in his speeches, messages and bulletins, where

2. A Buddhist monk at Peking (or Beijing).

he has the talk all on his own side, they may be sure the high mettled William Kieft did not suffer so favourable an occasion to escape him, of evincing that gallantry of tongue, common to all able legislators. Before he commenced, it is recorded that he took out of his pocket a red cotton handkerchief, and gave a very sonorous blast of the nose, according to the usual custom of great orators. This in general I believe is intended as a signal trumpet, to call the attention of the auditors, but with William the testy it boasted a more classic cause, for he had read of the singular expedient of that famous demagogue Caius Gracchus, who when he harangued the Roman populace, modulated his tones by an oratorical flute or pitch-pipe—"which", said the shrewd Wilhelmus, "I take to be nothing more nor less, than an elegant and figurative mode of saying—he previously blew his nose."

This preparatory symphony being performed, he commenced by expressing a humble sense of his own want of talents—his utter unworthiness of the honour conferred upon him, and his humiliating incapacity to discharge the important duties of his new station—in short, he expressed so contemptible an opinion of himself, that many simple country members present, ignorant that these were mere words of course, always used on such occasions, were very uneasy, and even felt wrath that he should accept an office, for which he was consciously so inadequate.

He then proceeded in a manner highly classic, profoundly erudite, and nothing at all to the purpose, being nothing more than a pompous account of all the governments of ancient Greece, and the wars of Rome and Carthage, together with the rise and fall of sundry outlandish empires, about which the assembly knew no more than their great grand children who were yet unborn. Thus having, after the manner of your learned orators, convinced the audience that he was a man of many words and great erudition, he at length came to the less important part of his speech, the situation of the province—and here he soon worked himself into a fearful rage against the Yankees, whom he compared to the Gauls who desolated Rome, and the Goths and Vandals who overran the fairest plains of Europe—nor did he forget to mention, in terms of adequate opprobrium, the insolence with which they had encroached upon the territories of New Netherlands, and the unparalleled audacity with which they had commenced the town of New Plymouth, and planted the onion patches of Weathers-field under the very walls, or rather mud batteries of Fort Goed Hoop.[3]

Having thus artfully wrought up his tale of terror to a climax, he assumed a self satisfied look, and declared, with a nod of knowing import, that he had taken measures to put a final stop to these encroachments—that he had been obliged to have recourse to a dreadful engine of warfare, lately invented, awful in its effects, but authorized by direful necessity. In a word, he was resolved to conquer the Yankees—by proclamation!

3. I.e., Good Hope, a Dutch outpost near the present site of Hartford, Connecticut, which had been established in 1633. According to the original grant to the Dutch West India Company, the boundaries of New Netherland included some portions of modern Connecticut, including the valley of the Connecticut River, which the Dutch called the Varsche (or Fresh) River. Irving recounts in exaggerated form the long skirmishes between the Yankees of New England and the Dutch that eventually led to the conquest of the latter in 1664 and the redrawing of the boundaries to their present position.

For this purpose he had prepared a tremendous instrument of the kind ordering, commanding and enjoining the intruders aforesaid, forthwith to remove, depart and withdraw from the districts, regions and territories aforesaid, under pain of suffering all the penalties, forfeitures, and punishments in such case made and provided, &c. This proclamation he assured them, would at once exterminate the enemy from the face of the country, and he pledged his valour as a governor, that within two months after it was published, not one stone should remain on another, in any of the towns which they had built.

The council remained for some time silent, after he had finished; whether struck dumb with admiration at the brilliancy of his project, or put to sleep by the length of his harangue, the history of the times doth not mention. Suffice it to say, they at length gave a universal grunt of acquiescence—the proclamation was immediately dispatched with due ceremony, having the great seal of the province, which was about the size of a buckwheat pancake, attached to it by a broad red ribband. Governor Kieft having thus vented his indignation, felt greatly relieved—adjourned the council *sine die*[4]—put on his cocked hat and corduroy small clothes, and mounting a tall raw boned charger, trotted out to his country seat, which was situated in a sweet, sequestered swamp, now called Dutch street, but more commonly known by the name of Dog's Misery.

Here, like the good Numa, he reposed from the toils of legislation, taking lessons in government, not from the Nymph Egeria, but from the honoured wife of his bosom;[5] who was one of that peculiar kind of females, sent upon earth a little after the flood, as a punishment for the sins of mankind, and commonly known by the appellation of *knowing women*. In fact, my duty as an historian obliges me to make known a circumstance which was a great secret at the time, and consequently was not a subject of scandal at more than half the tea tables in New Amsterdam, but which like many other great secrets, has leaked out in the lapse of years—and this was, that the great Wilhelmus the Testy, though one of the most potent little men that ever breathed, yet submitted at home to a species of government, neither laid down in Aristotle, nor Plato; in short, it partook of the nature of a pure, unmixed tyranny, and is familiarly denominated *petticoat government*.—An absolute sway, which though exceedingly common in these modern days, was very rare among the ancients, if we may judge from the rout made about the domestic economy of honest Socrates; which is the only ancient case on record.

The great Kieft however, warded off all the sneers and sarcasms of his particular friends, who are ever ready to joke with a man on sore points of the kind, by alledging that it was a government of his own election, which he submitted to through choice; adding at the same time that it was a profound maxim which he had found in an ancient author—"he who would aspire to *govern*, should first learn to *obey*."

---

4. Without day (Latin), i.e., without naming a day to reconvene.
5. The legendary second king of Rome, Numa Pompilius (d. 673 B.C.E), took the water nymph Egeria as his second wife and counselor.

CHAP.II.

In which are recorded the sage Projects of a Ruler of universal Genius.—The art of Fighting by Proclamation,—and how that the valiant Jacobus Van Curlet came to be foully dishonoured at Fort Goed Hoop.

Never was a more comprehensive, a more expeditious, or, what is still better, a more economical measure devised, than this of defeating the Yankees by proclamation—an expedient, likewise, so humane, so gentle and pacific; there were ten chances to one in favour of its succeeding,—but then there was one chance to ten that it would not succeed—as the ill-natured fates would have it, that single chance carried the day! The proclamation was perfect in all its parts, well constructed, well written, well sealed and well published—all that was wanting to insure its effect, was that the Yankees should stand in awe of it; but, provoking to relate, they treated it with the most absolute contempt, applicd it to an unseemly purpose, which shall be nameless, and thus did the first warlike proclamation come to a shameful end—a fate which I am credibly in formed, has befallen but too many of its successors.

It was a long time before Wilhelmus Kieft could be persuaded by the united efforts of all his counsellors, that his war measure had failed in producing any effect.—On the contrary, he flew in a passion whenever any one dared to question its efficacy; and swore, that though it was slow in operating, yet when once it began to work, it would soon purge the land from these rapacious intruders. Time however, that tester of all experiments both in philosophy and politics, at length convinced the great Kieft, that his proclamation was abortive; and that notwithstanding he had waited nearly four years, in a state of constant irritation, yet he was still further off than ever from the object of his wishes. His implacable adversaries in the east became more and more troublesome in their encroachments, and founded the thriving colony of Hartford close upon the skirts of Fort Goed Hoop. They moreover commenccd the fair settlement of Newhaven (alias the Red Hills) within the domains of their high mightinesses—while the onion patches of Pyquag[6] were a continual eye sore to the garrison of Van Curlet. Upon beholding therefore the inefficacy of his measure, the sage Kieft like many a worthy practitioner of physic, laid the blame, not to the medicine, but the quantity administered, and resolutely resolved to double the dose.

In the year 1638 therefore, that being the fourth year of his reign, he fulminated against them a second proclamation, of heavier metal than the former; written in thundering long sentences, not one word of which was under five syllables. This, in fact, was a kind of non-intercourse bill,[7] forbidding and prohibiting all commerce and connexion, between any and every of the said Yankee intruders, and the said fortified post of Fort Goed Hoop, and ordering, commanding and advising all his trusty, loyal and well-beloved subjects, to furnish them with no supplies of gin, gingerbread or sour crout; to buy none of their pacing horses, meazly pork, apple brandy, Yankee rum, cyder water, apple sweetmeats, Weathersfield onions or wooden bowls but to starve and exterminate them from the face of the land.

6. Wethersfield.
7. A reference to the early 1809 act of this name, a successor the 1807 Embargo.

Another pause of a twelve month ensued, during which the last proclamation received the same attention, and experienced the same fate as the
first—at the end of which term, the gallant Jacobus Van Curlet dispatched his
annual messenger, with his customary budget of complaints and entreaties.
Whether the regular interval of a year, intervening between the arrival of Van
Curlet's couriers, was occasioned by the systematic regularity of his movements, or by the immense distance at which he was stationed from the seat
of government is a matter of uncertainty. Some have ascribed it to the slow-
ness of his messengers, who, as I have before noticed, were chosen from the
shortest and fattest of his garrison, as least likely to be worn out on the road;
and who, being pursy, short winded little men, generally travelled fifteen
miles a day, and then laid by a whole week, to rest. All these, however, are
matters of conjecture; and I rather think it may be ascribed to the immemo-
rial maxim of this worthy country—and which has ever influenced all its public transactions—not to do things in a hurry.

The gallant Jacobus Van Curlet, in his dispatches respectfully represented, that several years had now elapsed, since his first application to his
late excellency, the renowned Wouter Van Twiller:[8] during which interval, his
garrison had been reduced nearly one-eighth, by the death of two of his most
valiant, and corpulent soldiers, who had accidentally over eaten themselves
on some fat salmon, caught in the Varsche rivier. He further stated that the
enemy persisted in their inroads, taking no notice of the fort or its inhabitants; but squatting themselves down, and forming settlements all around it;
so that, in a little while, he should find himself enclosed and blockaded by the
enemy, and totally at their mercy.

But among the most atrocious of his grievances, I find the following still
on record, which may serve to shew the bloody minded outrages of these savage intruders. "In the meanetime, they of Hartford have not onely usurped
and taken in the lands of Connecticott, although unrighteously and against
the lawes of nations, but have hindered our nation in sowing theire owne purchased broken up lands, but have also sowed them with corne in the night,
which the Netherlanders had broken up and intended to sowe: and have
beaten the servants of the high and mighty the honored companie, which
were labouring upon theire master's lands, from theire lands, with sticks and
plow staves in hostile manner laming, and amongst the rest, struck Ever
Duckings[9] a hole in his head, with a stick, soe that the blood ran downe very
strongly downe upon his body!"

But what is still more atrocious——

"Those of Hartford sold a hogg, that belonged to the honored companie,
under pretence that it had eaten of theire grounde grass, when they had not
any foot of inheritance. They profered the hogg for 5s. if the commissioners would have given 5s. for damage; which the commissioners denied,
because noe man's owne hogg (as men used to say) can trespasse upon his
owne master's grounde."[1]

---

8. Wouter van Twiller (1606–1654) had administered New Netherland before Kieft; under his rule,
   Dutch West India Company employee Jacob van Curler (not Curlet) had established Fort Good
   Hope.
9. This name is no doubt misspelt. In some old Dutch MSS. of the time, we find the name of Evert
   Duyckingh, who is unquestionably the unfortunate hero above alluded to [Irving's note]. Evert
   Duyckinck (d. 1833) was a prominent New York City publisher at the time Irving wrote his book.
1. Haz. Col. State Pass [Irving's note].

The receipt of this melancholy intelligence incensed the whole community—there was something in it that spoke to the full comprehension, and touched the obtuse feelings even of the puissant vulgar, who generally require a kick in the rear, to awaken their slumbering dignity. I have known my profound fellow citizens bear without murmur, a thousand essential infringements of their rights, merely because they were not immediately obvious to their senses—but the moment the unlucky Pearce[2] was shot upon our coasts, the whole body politic was in a ferment—so the enlighted Nederlanders, though they had treated the encroachments of their eastern neighbours with but little regard, and left their quill valiant[3] governor, to bear the whole brunt of war, with his single pen—yet now every individual felt his head broken in the broken head of Duckings——and the unhappy fate of their fellow citizen the hog; being impressed,[4] carried and sold into captivity, awakened a grunt of sympathy from every bosom.

The governor and council, goaded by the clamours of the multitude, now set themselves earnestly to deliberate upon what was to be done. Proclamations had at length fallen into temporary disrepute; some were for sending the Yankees a tribute, as we make peace offerings to the petty Barbary powers, or as the Indians sacrifice to the devil. Others were for buying them out, but this was opposed, as it would be acknowledging their title to the land they had seized. A variety of measures were, as usual in such cases, proposed, discussed and abandoned, and the council had at last, to adopt the means, which being the most common and obvious, had been knowingly overlooked—for your amazing acute politicians, are for ever looking through telescopes, which only enable them to see such objects as are far off, and unattainable; but which incapacitates them to see such things as are in their reach, and obvious to all simple folk, who are content to look with the naked eyes, heaven has given them. The profound council, as I have said, in their pursuit after Jack-o'-lanterns, accidentally stumbled on the very measure they were in need of; which was to raise a body of troops, and dispatch them to the relief and reinforcement of the garrison. This measure was carried into such prompt operation, that in less than twelve months, the whole expedition, consisting of a serjeant and twelve men, was ready to march; and was reviewed for that purpose, in the public square, now known by the name of the Bowling Green. Just at this juncture the whole community was thrown into consternation, by the sudden arrival of the gallant Jacobus Van Curlet; who came straggling into town at the head of his crew of tatterdemalions, and bringing the melancholy tidings of his own defeat, and the capture of the redoubtable post of Fort Goed Hope by the ferocious Yankees.

The fate of this important fortress, is an impressive warning to all military commanders. It was neither carried by storm, nor famine; no practicable breach was effected by cannon or mines; no magazines were blown up by red hot shot, nor were the barracks demolished, or the garrison destroyed, by the bursting of bombshells. In fact, the place was taken by a stratagem

---

2. In 1806, a sailor from Maryland, John Pierce, was killed by British cannon fire while standing at the helm of a merchant vessel entering New York waters. The subsequent outrage electrified patriotic sentiment in the city.
3. I.e., quill-valiant, courageous at writing out his proclamations.
4. The forced enlistment (or impressment) of American sailors into the British navy in the early years of the nineteenth century was one cause for the ensuing War of 1812.

no less singular than effectual; and one that can never fail of success, whenever an opportunity occurs of putting it in practice. Happy am I to add, for the credit of our illustrious ancestors, that it was a stratagem, which though it impeached the vigilance, yet left the bravery of the intrepid Van Curlet and his garrison, perfectly free from reproach.

It appears that the crafty Yankees, having learned the regular habits of the garrison, watched a favourable opportunity and silently introduced themselves into the fort, about the middle of a sultry day; when its vigilant defenders having gorged themselves with a hearty dinner and smoaked out their pipes, were one and all snoring most obstreperously at their posts; little dreaming of so disasterous an occurrence. The enemy most inhumanly seized Jacobus Van Curlet, and his sturdy myrmidons by the nape of the neck, gallanted them to the gate of the fort, and dismissed them severally, with a kick on the crupper, as Charles the twelfth dismissed the heavy bot-tomed Russians, after the battle of Narva—only taking care to give two kicks to Van Curlet, as a signal mark of distinction.

A strong garrison was immediately established in the fort; consisting of twenty long sided, hard fisted Yankees; with Weathersfield onions stuck in their hats, by way of cockades and feathers—long rusty fowling pieces for muskets—hasty pudding, dumb fish, pork and molasses for stores; and a huge pumpkin was hoisted on the end of a pole, as a standard—liberty caps not having as yet come into fashion.

*   *   *

JAMES FENIMORE COOPER

From The Letters and Journals of James Fenimore Cooper

To the New-York Patriot, June 17, 1823[1]

[24 April–17 June? 1823]

While we were at the Point[2] it rained much of the time, and as M[athews] was quite unwell, he had a charming fit of the "blues." Two or three of the intelligent men that I found here spoke so confidently of the merits of a pic-ture that they had, of Jefferson, by Sully, that I thought I would relieve both M— and myself by a visit to the library. You know my antipathies, as you please to call them, to Mr. Jefferson. I was brought up in that school where his image seldom appeared, unless it was clad in red breeches, and where it was always associated with the idea of infidelity and political heresy.[3]

---

1. Cooper, having published his first three books by early 1823, was returning to New York City in April after escorting the British actor Charles Matthews through a brief tour upstate. Although this letter, published in June in a newspaper edited by an old associate of Cooper's, was unsigned, its contents are completely consistent with Cooper's recent activities and early life. Reprinted from *The Letters and Journals of James Fenimore Cooper*, ed. James F. Beard, 6 vols. (Cambridge, Mass., 1960–68), 1:94–95.
2. I.e., the U.S. Military Academy at West Point, where Thomas Sully's full-length portrait of Jeffer-son had recently been hung.
3. Cooper was the youngest son of the fiercely partisan Federalist developer, judge, and congressman, William Cooper (1754–1809), founder of Cooperstown, New York. By 1823, however, the novelist

Consequently I would have gone twice as far to see the picture of almost any other man. The moment I entered the library and cast my eyes on the picture, I desired the gentlemen with me to wait, until I could go for M—. I am no judge of paintings, though I have seen hundreds of celebrated ones both here and in Europe; and M— is a collector, and by his sensible remarks, I believe a very respectable critic. However, I determined he should rouse himself and see the picture of Jefferson. After some difficulty I succeeded, and persuaded him to follow me to the library. I shall dispose of M— by merely saying, that he pronounced it one of the finest portraits he had ever beheld, and that he would never have forgiven me if I had let it escape his notice. But you will smile when I tell you its effects on myself. There was a dignity, a repose, I will go further, and say a loveliness, about this painting, that I never have seen in any other portrait. With respect to its merit as a painting, to me it seemed more easy and natural by far than Lawrence's West, though its colouring might not, possibly, be so splendid. They said something about a mistake in the perspective, which could be easily altered, &c. I saw none of it. In short I saw nothing but Jefferson, standing before me, not in red breeches and slovenly attire, but a gentleman, appearing in all republican simplicity, with a grace and ease on the canvas, that to me seemed unrivalled. It has really shaken my opinion of Jefferson as a man, if not as a politician; and when his image occurs to me now, it is in the simple robes of Sully, sans red breeches, or even without any of the repulsive accompaniments of a political "sans culotte."[4]

To Charles Wilkes, April 9, 1830[5]

* * *

I think you must own Mr. Jackson has sent a very good message to Congress. I do assure you it has done, both him and us credit, all over Europe. I deem it sound, constitutional, democratic and intelligible. I am much inclined to believe, we did well, in changing. What do you think of Jefferson's letters? Have we not had a false idea of that man? I own he begins to appear to me, to be the greatest man, we ever had. His knowledge of Europe was of immense service to him. Without it, no American is fit to speak of the institutions of his own Country, for as nothing human is perfect, it is only by comparison, that we can judge of our own advantages.

* * *

had shunned the old Federalists and attached himself to the party forming around New York Republican DeWitt Clinton.
4. A lower-class radical during the French Revolution. The term is a reference to the simple trousers worn by the commoners, instead of the knee britches fashionable among the upper classes.
5. Having gone to Europe for an extended visit earlier in 1826, Cooper was out of the country on July 4, when both Jefferson and his old friend John Adams died. By then he had, like his mentor DeWitt Clinton, become a supporter of Andrew Jackson, who bore the mantle of the old Jeffersonian Democratic-Republicans. Still abroad in 1830, Cooper sought out the newly published *Memoirs, Correspondence, and Miscellanies, from the Papers of Thomas Jefferson,* edited by Jefferson's grandson, T. J. Randolph (Charlottesville, 1829), and read the volumes with keen interest. He wrote of his response to his old friend Charles Wilkes, a New York City banker. The text is reprinted from Beard, ed., *Letters and Journals,* 1:411.

GEORGE HENRY EVANS

The Working Men's Declaration of Independence[1]

"When, in the course of human events, it becomes necessary" for one class of a community to assert their natural and unalienable rights in opposition to other classes of their fellow men, "and to assume among" them a political "station of equality to which the laws of nature and of nature's God," as well as the principles of their political compact, "entitle them; a decent respect to the opinions of mankind," and the more paramount duty they owe to their own fellow citizens, "requires that they should declare the causes which impel them" to adopt so painful, yet so necessary, a measure.

"We hold these truths to be self evident, that all men are *created equal;* that they are endowed by their creator with certain unalienable rights; that among these are *life, liberty,* and the *pursuit of happiness;* that to secure these rights" against the undue influence of other classes of society, prudence, as well as the claims of self defence, dictates the necessity of the organization of a party, who shall, by their representatives, prevent dangerous combinations to subvert these indefeasible and fundamental privileges. "All experience hath shown, that mankind" in general, and *we as a class in particular,* "are more disposed to suffer, while evils are sufferable, than to right themselves," by an opposition which the pride and self interest of unprincipled political aspirants, with more unprincipled zeal or religious bigotry, will wilfully misrepresent. "But when a long train of abuses and usurpations" take place, all invariably tending to the oppression and degradation of one class of society, and to the unnatural and iniquitous exaltation of another by political leaders, "it is their right, it is their duty," to use every constitutional means to *reform* the abuses of such a government, and to provide new guards for their future security. The history of the political *parties* in this state, is a history of political *iniquities,* all tending to the enacting and enforcing oppressive and unequal laws. To prove this, let facts be submitted to the candid and impartial of our fellow citizens of all parties.

1. The laws for levying taxes are all based on erroneous principles, in consequence of their operating most oppressively on one class of society, and being scarcely felt by the other.

2. The laws regarding the duties of jurors, witnesses, and militia trainings, are still more unequal and oppressive.

3. The laws for private incorporations are all partial in their operations; favoring one class of society to the expense of the other, who have no equal participation.

4. The laws incorporating religious societies have a pernicious tendency, by promoting the erection of magnificent places of public worship, by the rich, excluding others, and which others cannot imitate; consequently engendering spiritual pride in the clergy and people, and thereby creating odious distinctions in society, destructive to its social peace and happiness.

1. The English-born George Henry Evans (1805–1856) immigrated to the United States when he was fourteen. After being apprenticed to a printer in Ithaca, New York, he became an editor and organizer of the New York Working Men's Party in 1829, for which he drew up this radical parody of Jefferson's Declaration of Independence. It is reprinted here from *We, the Other People,* Philip S. Foner, ed. (Chicago, 1976), 48–50.

5. The laws establishing and patronizing seminaries of learning are unequal, favoring the rich, and perpetuating imparity, which natural causes have produced, and which judicious laws ought, and can, remedy.

6. The laws and municipal ordinances and regulations, generally, besides those specially enumerated, have heretofore been ordained on such principles, as have deprived nine tenths of the members of the body politic, who are *not* wealthy, of the *equal means* to enjoy *"life, liberty, and the pursuit of happiness,"* which the *rich* enjoy exclusively; but the federative compact intended to secure to all, indiscriminately. The lien law in favor of landlords against tenants, and all other honest creditors, is one illustration among innumerable others which can be adduced to prove the truth of these allegations.

We have trusted to the influence of the justice and good sense of our political leaders, to prevent the continuance of these abuses, which destroy the natural bands of equality so essential to the attainment of moral happiness, "but they have been deaf to the voice of justice and of consanguinity."

Therefore, we, the working class of society, of the city of New York, "appealing to the supreme judge of the world," and to the reason, and consciences of the impartial of all parties, "for the rectitude of our intentions, do, in the spirit, and by the authority," of that political liberty which has been promised to us equally with our fellow men, solemnly publish and declare, and invite all under like pecuniary circumstances, together with every liberal mind, to join us in the declaration, "that we are, & of right ought to be," entitled to EQUAL MEANS to obtain equal moral happiness, and social enjoyment, and that all lawful and constitutional measures ought to be adopted to the attainment of those objects. "And for the support of this declaration, we mutually pledge to each other" our faithful aid to the end of our lives.

ELIZABETH CADY STANTON

Declaration of Sentiments[1]

When, in the course of human events, it becomes necessary for one portion of the family of man to assume among the people of the earth a position different from that which they have hitherto occupied, but one to which the laws of nature and of nature's God entitle them, a decent respect to the opinions of mankind requires that they should declare the causes that impel them to such a course.

We hold these truths to be self-evident: that all men and women are created equal; that they are endowed by their Creator with certain inalienable rights; that among these are life, liberty, and the pursuit of happiness; that to secure these rights governments are instituted, deriving their just powers

1. Elizabeth Cady Stanton (1815–1902) had been active in the abolitionist movement before organizing the first Women's Rights Convention in Seneca Falls, New York, in the summer of 1848. In a deft parody that turns the offending "He" of Jefferson's original (i.e., King George III) into an iconic figure of patriarchal authority in the United States, she prepared this famous "Declaration of Sentiments," along with a series of "Resolutions" that the convention adopted. The "Declaration" is reprinted here from *We, the Other People*, Philip S. Foner, ed. (Chicago, 1976), 78–81.

from the consent of the governed. Whenever any form of government becomes destructive of these ends, it is the right of those who suffer from it to refuse allegiance to it, and to insist upon the institution of a new government, laying its foundation on such principles, and organizing its powers in such form, as to them shall seem most likely to effect their safety and happiness. Prudence, indeed, will dictate that governments long established should not be changed for light and transient causes; and accordingly all experience hath shown that mankind are more disposed to suffer, while evils are sufferable, than to right themselves by abolishing the forms to which they were accustomed. But when a long train of abuses and usurpations, pursuing invariably the same object evinces a design to reduce them under absolute despotism, it is their duty to throw off such government, and to provide new guards for their future security. Such has been the patient sufferance of the women under this government, and such is now the necessity which constrains them to demand the equal station to which they are entitled.

The history of mankind is a history of repeated injuries and usurpations on the part of man toward woman, having in direct object the establishment of an absolute tyranny over her. To prove this, let facts be submitted to a candid world.

He has never permitted her to exercise her inalienable right to the elective franchise.

He has compelled her to submit to laws, in the formation of which she had no voice.

He has withheld from her rights which are given to the most ignorant and degraded men—both natives and foreigners.

Having deprived her of this first right of a citizen, the elective franchise, thereby leaving her without representation in the halls of legislation, he has oppressed her on all sides.

He has made her, if married, in the eye of the law, civilly dead.

He has taken from her all right in property, even to the wages she earns.

He has made her, morally, an irresponsible being, as she can commit many crimes with impunity, provided they be done in the presence of her husband. In the covenant of marriage, she is compelled to promise obedience to her husband, he becoming, to all intents and purposes, her master—the law giving him power to deprive her of her liberty, and to administer chastisement.

He has so framed the laws of divorce, as to what shall be the proper causes, and in case of separation, to whom the guardianship of the children shall be given, as to be wholly regardless of the happiness of women—the law, in all cases, going upon a false supposition of the supremacy of man, and giving all power into his hands.

After depriving her of all rights as a married woman, if single, and the owner of property, he has taxed her to support a government which recognizes her only when her property can be made profitable to it.

He has monopolized nearly all the profitable employments, and from those she is permitted to follow, she receives but a scanty remuneration. He closes against her all the avenues to wealth and distinction which he considers most honorable to himself. As a teacher of theology, medicine, or law, she is not known.

He has denied her the facilities for obtaining a thorough education, all colleges being closed against her.

He allows her in Church, as well as State, but a subordinate position, claiming Apostolic authority for her exclusion from the ministry, and, with some exceptions, from any public participation in the affairs of the Church.

He has created a false public sentiment by giving to the world a different code of morals for men and women, by which moral delinquencies which exclude women from society, are not only tolerated, but deemed of little account in man.

He has usurped the prerogative of Jehovah himself, claiming it as his right to assign for her a sphere of action, when that belongs to her conscience and to her God.

He has endeavored, in every way that he could, to destroy her confidence in her own powers, to lessen her self-respect, and to make her willing to lead a dependent and abject life.

Now, in view of this entire disfranchisement of one-half the people of this country, their social and religious degradation—in view of the unjust laws above mentioned, and because women do feel themselves aggrieved, oppressed, and fraudulently deprived of their most sacred rights, we insist that they have immediate admission to all the rights and privileges which belong to them as citizens of the United States.

In entering upon the great work before us, we anticipate no small amount of misconception, misrepresentation, and ridicule; but we shall use every instrumentality within our power to effect our object. We shall employ agents, circulate tracts, petition the State and National legislatures, and endeavor to enlist the pulpit and the press in our behalf. We hope this Convention will be followed by a series of Conventions embracing every part of the country.

*   *   *

MADISON HEMINGS

Memoirs[1]

I never knew of but one white man who bore the name of Hemings. He was an Englishman and my great grandfather. He was captain of an English whaling vessel which sailed between England and Williamsburg, Va., then quite a port. My [great-]grandmother was a fullblooded African, and possibly a native of that country. She was the property of John Wales, a Welchman. Capt. Hemings happened to be in the port of Williamsburg at the time my grandmother was born, and acknowledging her fatherhood he tried to purchase her of Mr. Wales who would not part with the child, though he was offered an extraordinarily large price for her. She was named Elizabeth Hemings. Being thwarted in the purchase, and determined to own his own

---

1. Madison Hemings (1805–1877) was the son of Sally Hemings and, DNA tests conducted in 1998 make clear, a male of the Jefferson family. Even before the publication of his story in a Ohio newspaper in 1873, it was widely known in his community, Huntington Township, Ross County, that he was (as the federal census enumerator for 1870 put it) "the son of Thos. Jefferson." His memoir is reprinted from Fawn Brodie, *Thomas Jefferson: An Intimate History* (1974), 471–476, where the comment from the census population schedule is also quoted.

flesh and blood he resolved to take the child by force or stealth, but the knowledge of his intention coming to John Wales' ears, through leaky fellow servants of the mother, she and the child were taken into the "great house" under their master's immediate care. I have been informed that it was not the extra value of that child over other slave children that induced Mr. Wales to refuse to sell it, for slave masters then, as in later days, had no compunctions of conscience which restrained them from parting mother and child of however tender age, but he was restrained by the fact that just about that time amalgamation began, and the child was so great a curiosity that its owner desired to raise it himself that he might see its outcome. Capt. Hemings soon afterwards sailed from Williamsburg, never to return. Such is the story that comes down to me.

Elizabeth Hemings grew to womanhood in the family of John Wales, whose wife dying she (Elizabeth) was taken by the widower Wales as his concubine, by whom she had six children—three sons and three daughters, viz: Robert, James, Peter, Critty, Sally and Thena. These children went by the name of Hemings.

Williamsburg was the capital of Virginia, and of course it was an aristocratic place, where the "bloods" of the Colony and the new State most did congregate. Thomas Jefferson, the author of the Declaration of Independence, was educated at William and Mary College, which had its seat at Williamsburg. He afterwards studied law with Geo. Wythe, and practiced law at the bar of the general court of the Colony. He was afterwards elected a member of the provincial legislature from Albemarle county. Thos. Jefferson was a visitor at the "great house" of John Wales, who had children about his own age. He formed the acquaintance of his daughter Martha (I believe that was her name, though I am not positively sure,) and an intimacy sprang up between them which ripened into love, and they were married. They afterwards went to live at his country seat Monticello, and in course of time had born to them a daughter whom they named Martha. About the time she was born my mother, the second daughter of John Wales and Elizabeth Hemings was born. On the death of John Wales, my grandmother, his concubine, and her children by him fell to Martha, Thomas Jefferson's wife, and consequently became the property of Thomas Jefferson, who in the course of time became famous, and was appointed minister to France during our revolutionary troubles, or soon after independence was gained. About the time of the appointment and before he was ready to leave the country his wife died, and as soon after her interment as he could attend to and arrange his domestic affairs in accordance with the changed circumstances of his family in consequence of this misfortune (I think not more than three weeks thereafter) he left for France, taking his eldest daughter with him.[2] He had had sons born to him, but they died in early infancy, so he then had but two children— Martha and Maria. The latter was left at home, but was afterwards ordered to follow him to France. She was three years or so younger than Martha. My mother accompanied her as her body servant. When Mr. Jefferson went to France Martha was a young woman grown, my mother was about her age, and

2. Although Jefferson at first planned to go to France shortly after his wife's death in the fall of 1782, bad weather delayed his departure and then it was canceled when word of the tentative peace treaty with Britain arrived in America. He eventually left for Europe in 1784. In the following sentence, Hemings overlooks the third Jefferson daughter, who was born in 1782 and died in 1784.

Maria was just budding into womanhood. Their stay (my mother's and Maria's) was about eighteen months. But during that time my mother became Mr. Jefferson's concubine, and when he was called back home she was *enciente*[3] by him. He desired to bring my mother back to Virginia with him but she demurred. She was just beginning to understand the French language well, and in France she was free, while if she returned to Virginia she would be re-enslaved. So she refused to return with him. To induce her to do so he promised her extraordinary privileges, and made a solemn pledge that her children should be freed at the age of twenty-one years. In consequence of his promises, on which she implicitly relied, she returned with him to Virginia. Soon after their arrival, she gave birth to a child, of whom Thomas Jefferson was the father. It lived but a short time. She gave birth to four others, and Jefferson was the father of all of them. Their names were Beverly, Harriet, Madison (myself), and Eston—three sons and one daughter. We all became free agreeably to the treaty entered into by our parents before we were born. We all married and have raised families.

Beverly left Monticello and went to Washington as a white man. He married a white woman in Maryland, and their only child, a daughter, was not known by the white folks to have any colored blood coursing in her veins. Beverly's wife's family were people in good circumstances.

Harriet married a white man in good standing in Washington City, whose name I could give, but will not, for prudential reasons. She raised a family of children, and so far as I know they were never suspected of being tainted with African blood in the community where she lived or lives. I have not heard from her for ten years, and do not know whether she is dead or alive. She thought it to her interest, on going to Washington, to assume the role of a white woman, and by her dress and conduct as such I am not aware that her identity as Harriet Hemings of Monticello has ever been discovered.

Eston married a colored woman in Virginia, and moved from there to Ohio, and lived in Chillicothe several years. In the fall of 1852 he removed to Wisconsin, where he died a year or two afterwards. He left three children.

As to myself, I was named Madison by the wife of James Madison, who was afterwards President of the United States. Mrs. Madison happened to be at Monticello at the time of my birth, and begged the privilege of naming me, promising my mother a fine present for the honor. She consented, and Mrs. Madison dubbed me by the name I now acknowledge, but like many promises of white folks to the slaves she never gave my mother anything. I was born at my father's seat of Monticello, in Albemarle county, Va., near Charlottesville, on the 19th day of January, 1805. My very earliest recollections are of my grandmother Elizabeth Hemings. That was when I was about three years old. She was sick and upon her death bed. I was eating a piece of bread and asked her if she would have some. She replied: "No; granny don't want bread any more." She shortly afterwards breathed her last. I have only a faint recollection of her.

Of my father, Thomas Jefferson, I knew more of his domestic than his public life during his life time. It is only since his death that I have learned much of the latter, except that he was considered as a foremost man in the land, and held many important trusts, including that of President. I learned

---

3. I.e., *enceinte*, pregnant (French).

to read by inducing the white children to teach me the letters and some-thing more; what else I know of books I have picked up here and there till now I can read and write. I was almost 21 years of age when my father died on the 4th of July, 1826.

About his own home he was the quietest of men. He was hardly ever known to get angry, though sometimes he was irritated when matters went wrong, but even then he hardly ever allowed himself to be made unhappy any great length of time. Unlike Washington he had but little taste or care for agricultural pursuits. He left matters pertaining to his plantations mostly with his stewards and overseers. He always had mechanics at work for him, such as carpenters, blacksmiths, shoemakers, coopers, &c. It was his mechanics he seemed mostly to direct, and in their operations he took great interest. Almost every day of his later years he might have been seen among them. He occupied much of the time in his office engaged in cor-respondence and reading and writing. His general temperament was smooth and even; he was very undemonstrative. He was uniformly kind to all about him. He was not in the habit of showing partiality or fatherly affection to us children. We were the only children of his by a slave woman. He was affectionate toward his white grandchildren, of whom he had fourteen, twelve of whom lived to manhood and womanhood. His daughter Martha married Thomas Mann Randolph by whom she had thirteen children. Two died in infancy. The names of the living were Ann, Thomas Jefferson, Ellen, Cornelia, Virginia, Mary, James, Benj. Franklin, Lewis Madison,[4] Septemia and Geo. Wythe. Thos. Jefferson Randolph was Chairman of the Democratic National Convention in Baltimore last spring which nominated Horace Greeley for the Presidency, and Geo. Wythe Randolph was Jeff. Davis' first Secretary of War in the late "unpleasantness."

Maria married John Eppes, and raised one son—Francis.

My father generally enjoyed excellent health. I never knew him to have but one spell of sickness, and that was caused by a visit to the Warm Springs in 1818. Till within three weeks of his death he was hale and hearty, and at the age of 83 years he walked erect and with stately tread. I am now 68, and I well remember that he was a much smarter man physically, even at that age, than I am.

When I was fourteen years old I was put to the carpenter trade under the charge of John Hemings, the youngest son of my grandmother. His father's name was Nelson, who was an Englishman. She had seven children by white men and seven by colored men—fourteen in all. My brothers, sister Harriet and myself, were used alike. They were put to some mechanical trade at the age of fourteen. Till then we were permitted to stay about the "great house," and only required to do such light work as going on errands. Harriet learned to spin and to weave in a little factory on the home planta-tion. We were free from the dread of having to be slaves all our lives long, and were measurably happy. We were always permitted to be with our mother, who was well used. It was her duty, all her life which I can remember, up to the time of our father's death, to take care of his chamber and wardrobe, look after us children and do such light work as sewing, &c. Provision was made in the will of our father that we should be free when we arrived at the age of 21 years. We had all passed that period when he died but Eston, and

4. Meriwether Lewis Randolph. James was James Madison Randolph.

he was given the remainder of his time shortly after. He and I rented a house and took mother to live with us, till her death, which event occurred in 1835.

In 1834 I married Mary McCoy. Her grandmother was a slave, and lived with her master, Stephen Hughes, near Charlottesville, as his wife. She was manumitted by him, which made their children free born. Mary McCoy's mother was his daughter. I was about 28 and she 22 years of age when we married. We lived and labored together in Virginia till 1836, when we voluntarily left and came to Ohio. We settled in Pebble township, Pike county. We lived there four or five years and during my stay in that county I worked at my trade on and off for about four years. Joseph Sewell was my first employer. I built for him what is now known as Rizzleport No. 2 in Waverly. I afterwards worked for George Wolf Senior, and I did the carpenter work of the brick building now owned by John J. Kellison in which the Pike County Republican is printed. I worked for and with Micajab Hinson. I found him to be a very clever man. I also reconstructed the building on the corner of Market and Water streets from a store to a hotel for the late Judge Jacob Row.

When we came from Virginia we brought one daughter (Sarah) with us, leaving the dust of a son in the soil near Monticello. We have born to us in this State nine children. Two are dead. The names of the living, besides Sarah, are Harriet, Mary Ann, Catharine Jane, William Beverly, James Madison and Ellen Wales. Thomas Eston died in the Andersonville prison pen, and Julia died at home. William, James and Ellen are unmarried and live at home, in Huntington township, Ross county. All the others are married and raising families. My post-office address is Pee Pee, Pike county Ohio.

MOSES COIT TYLER

The Declaration of Independence in the Light of Modern Criticism[1]

I.

It can hardly be doubted that some hindrance to a right estimate of the Declaration of Independence is occasioned by either of two opposite conditions of mind, both of which are often to be met with among us: on the one hand, a condition of hereditary, uncritical awe and worship of the American Revolution, and of that state paper as its absolutely perfect and glorious expression; on the other hand, a later condition of cultivated distrust of the Declaration, as a piece of writing lifted up into inordinate renown by the passionate and heroic circumstances of its origin, and ever since then extolled beyond reason by the blind energy of patriotic enthusiasm. Turning from the former state of mind, which obviously calls for no further comment, we may note, as a partial illustration of the latter, that American confidence in the

1. Moses Coit Tyler (1835–1900) is best known for his two studies of early American writing, *History of American Literature during the Colonial Time, 1607–1765* (1878) and *The Literary History of the American Revolution, 1763–1783* (1897). This piece, which was to be included in the latter work, is reprinted from its first version in the *North American Review*, 163 (1896): 1–16, with corrections from the version in Tyler's book.

supreme intellectual merit of this all-famous document received a serious
wound some forty years ago from the hand of Rufus Choate, when, with a
courage greater than would now be required for such an act, he characterized it as made up of "glittering and sounding generalities of natural right."[2]
What the great advocate then so unhesitatingly suggested, many a thought-
ful American since then has at least suspected—that our great proclamation,
as a piece of political literature, cannot stand the test of modern analysis; that
it belongs to the immense class of over-praised productions; that it is, in fact,
a stately patchwork of sweeping propositions of somewhat doubtful validity;
that it has long imposed upon mankind by the well-known effectiveness of
verbal glitter and sound; that, at the best, it is an example of florid political
declamation belonging to the sophomoric period of our national life, a period
which, as we flatter ourselves, we have now outgrown.

Nevertheless, it is to be noted that whatever authority the Declaration of
Independence has acquired in the world, has been due to no lack of criticism, either at the time of its first appearance, or since then; a fact which
seems to tell in favor of its essential worth and strength. From the date of
its original publication down to the present moment, it has been attacked
again and again, either in anger, or in contempt, by friends as well as by
enemies of the American Revolution, by liberals in politics as well as by con-
servatives. It has been censured for its substance, it has been censured for
its form, for its misstatements of fact, for its fallacies in reasoning, for its
audacious novelties and paradoxes, for its total lack of all novelty, for its repetition of old and threadbare statements, even for its downright plagiarisms;
finally, for its grandiose and vaporing style.

II.

One of the earliest and ablest of its assailants was Thomas Hutchinson,
the last civil governor of the colony of Massachusetts, who, being stranded
in London by the political storm which had blown him thither, published
there, in the autumn of 1776, his "Strictures Upon the Declaration of the
Congress at Philadelphia,"[3] wherein, with an unsurpassed knowledge of the
origin of the controversy, and with an unsurpassed acumen in the discussion of it, he traverses the entire document, paragraph by paragraph, for the
purpose of showing that its allegations in support of American Independence are "false and frivolous."[4]

A better-written, and, upon the whole, a more plausible and a more powerful arraignment of the great Declaration was the celebrated pamphlet by
Sir John Dalrymple, "The Rights of Great Britain Asserted against the
Claims of America: Being an Answer to the Declaration of the General
Congress,"—a pamphlet scattered broadcast over the world at such a rate
that at least eight editions of it were published during the last three or four
months of the year 1776.[5] Here, again, the manifesto of Congress is sub-

2. Letter of Rufus Choate to the Whigs of Maine, 1856 [Tyler's note].
3. His pamphlet is dated October 15, 1776 [Tyler's note].
4. "*Strictures*," etc., 3 [Tyler's note].
5. While Tyler is correct about the many reprints of the pamphlet, we now believe it was written by
James Macpherson (the "translator" of the Ossian poems), and in fact was first published in 1775,
being an answer not to the Declaration of Independence but to the *Declaration by the Representatives of the United Colonies . . . Setting forth the Causes and Necessity of Their Taking Up Arms* (see
p. 371 herein).

jected to a searching examination, in order to prove that "the-facts are either wilfully or ignorantly misrepresented, and the arguments deduced from premises that have no foundation in truth."[6] It is doubtful if any disinterested student of history, any competent judge of reasoning, will now deny to this pamphlet the praise of making out a very strong case against the historical accuracy and the logical soundness of many parts of the Declaration of Independence.

Undoubtedly, the force of such censures is for us much broken by the fact that they proceeded from men who were themselves partisans in the Revolutionary controversy, and bitterly hostile to the whole movement which the Declaration was intended to justify. Such is not the case, however, with the leading modern English critics of the same document, who, while blaming in severe terms the policy of the British Government toward the Thirteen Colonies, have also found much to abate from the confidence due to this official announcement of the reasons for our secession from the empire. For example, Earl Russell, after frankly saying that the great disruption proclaimed by the Declaration of Independence was a result which Great Britain had "used every means most fitted to bring about," such as "vacillation in council, harshness in language, feebleness in execution, disregard of American sympathies and affections," also pointed out that "the truth of this memorable Declaration" was "warped" by "one singular defect," namely, its exclusive and excessive arraignment of George the Third "as a single and despotic tyrant," much like Philip the Second to the people of the Netherlands.[7]

This temperate criticism from an able and a liberal English statesman of the present century may be said to touch the very core of the problem as to the historic justice of our great indictment of the last King of America; and there is deep significance in the fact that this is the very criticism upon the document, which, as John Adams tells us, he himself had in mind when it was first submitted to him in committee, and even when, shortly afterward, he advocated its adoption by Congress. After mentioning certain things in it with which he was delighted, he adds:

> "There were other expressions which I would not have inserted if I had drawn it up—particularly that which called the King tyrant. I thought this too personal; for I never believed George to be a tyrant in disposition and in nature. I always believed him to be deceived by his courtiers on both sides of the Atlantic, and in his official capacity only cruel. I thought the expression too passionate, and too much like scolding, for so grave and solemn a document; but, as Franklin and Sherman were to inspect it afterwards, I thought it would not become me to strike it out. I consented to report it."[8]

6. "The Rights," etc., 1–2. The copy used by me is the seventh edition, London, 1776 [Tyler's note].
7. Lord John Russell, "Memorials and Correspondence of Charles James Fox," I., 151–162 [Tyler's note].
8. "The Works of John Adams," ii., 514. note. The distinction here made by John Adams between the personal and the official character of George III. is quite pointless in its application to the Declaration of Independence; since it is of the King's official character only that the Declaration speaks. Moreover, John Adams's testimony in 1822 that he "never believed George to be a tyrant in disposition and nature." is completely destroyed by John Adams's own testimony on that subject as recorded at an earlier period of his life. For example, in 1780, in a letter to M. Dumas, he thus speaks of George III. under the name of "White Eyes": "Europe, in general, is much mistaken in that character; it is a pity that he should be believed to be so amiable; the truth is far otherwise. Nerone neronior is nearer the truth." Ibid., vii., 327 [Tyler's note].

A more minute and a more poignant criticism of the Declaration of Independence has been made in recent years by still another English writer of liberal tendencies, who, however, in his capacity as critic, seems here to labor under the disadvantage of having transferred to the document which he undertakes to judge much of the extreme dislike which he has for the man who wrote it, whom, indeed, he regards as a sophist, as a demagogue, as quite capable of inveracity in speech, and as bearing some resemblance to Robespierre "in his feline nature, his malignant egotism, and his intense suspiciousness, as well as in his bloody-minded, yet possibly sincere, philanthropy."[9] In the opinion of Prof. Goldwin Smith, our great national manifesto is written "in a highly rhetorical strain";[1] "it opens with sweeping aphorisms about the natural rights of man, at which political science now smiles, and which . . . might seem strange when framed for slave-holding communities by a publicist who himself held slaves";[2] while, in its specifications of fact, it "is not more scrupulously truthful than are the general utterances"[3] of the statesman who was its scribe. Its charges that the several offensive acts of the king, besides "evincing a design to reduce the colonists under absolute depotism," "all had as their direct object the establishment of an absolute tyranny," are simply "propositions which history cannot accept."[4] Moreover, the Declaration "blinks the fact that many of the acts, styled steps of usurpation, were measures of repression, which, however unwise or excessive, had been provoked by popular outrage."[5] "No government could allow its officers to be assaulted and their houses sacked, its loyal lieges to be tarred and feathered, or the property of merchants sailing under its flag to be thrown by lawless hands into the sea."[6] Even "the preposterous violence and the manifest insincerity of the suppressed clause" against slavery and the slave trade "are enough to create suspicion as to the spirit in which the whole document was framed."[7]

III.

Finally, as has been already intimated, not even among Americans themselves has the Declaration of Independence been permitted to pass on into the enjoyment of its superb renown, without much critical disparagement at the hands of statesmen and historians. No doubt Calhoun had its preamble in mind when he declared that "nothing can be more unfounded and false" than "the prevalent opinion that all men are born free and equal"; for "it rests upon the assumption of a fact which is contrary to universal observation."[8] Of course, all Americans who have shared to any extent in Calhoun's doctrines respecting human society could hardly fail to agree with him in regarding as fallacious and worthless those general propositions in the Declaration which seem to constitute its logical starting point, as well as its ultimate defence.

9. Goldwin Smith, in *The Nineteenth Century*, No. 131, January, 1888, p. 109 [Tyler's note].
1. "*The United States: An Outline of Political History*," 88 [Tyler's note].
2. "*The United States*," etc., 87–88 [Tyler's note].
3. *The Nineteenth Century*, No. 131, p. 111 [Tyler's note].
4. "*The United States*," etc., 88.
5. *Ibid.*, 88 [Tyler's note].
6. *The Nineteenth Century*, No. 131, p. 111 [Tyler's note].
7. *Ibid* [Tyler's note].
8. "A Disquisition on Government" in "*The Works of John C. Calhoun*," I., 57 [Tyler's note].

Perhaps, however, the most frequent form of disparagement to which Jefferson's great state paper has been subjected among us is that which would minimize his merit in composing it, by denying to it the merit of originality. For example, Richard Henry Lee sneered at it as a thing "copied from Locke's *Treatise on Government.*"[9] The author of a life of Jefferson, published in the year of Jefferson's retirement from the presidency, suggests that the credit of having composed the Declaration of Independence "has been perhaps more generally, than truly, given by the public" to that great man.[1] Charles Campbell, the historian of Virginia, intimates that some expressions in the document were taken without acknowledgment from Aphra Behn's tragi-comedy, "The Widow-Ranter, or the History of Bacon in Virginia."[2] John Stockton Littell describes the Declaration of Independence as "that enduring monument at once of patriotism, and of genius and skill in the art of appropriation"—asserting that "for the sentiments and much of the language" of it, Jefferson was indebted to Chief Justice Drayton's charge to the grand jury of Charleston, delivered in April, 1776, as well as to the Declaration of Independence said to have been adopted by some citizens of Mecklenburg County, North Carolina, in May, 1775.[3] Even the latest and most critical editor of the writings of Jefferson calls attention to the fact that a glance at the Declaration of Rights, as adopted by Virginia on the 12th of June, 1776, "would seem to indicate the source from which Jefferson derived a most important and popular part" of his famous production.[4] By no one, however, has the charge of a lack of originality been pressed with so much decisiveness as by John Adams, who took evident pleasure in speaking of it as a document in which were merely "recapitulated" previous and well-known statements of American rights and wrongs,[5] and who, as late as in the year 1822, deliberately wrote:

"There is not an idea in it but what had been hackneyed in Congress for two years before. The substance of it is contained in the declaration of rights and the violation of those rights, in the Journals of Congress, in 1774. Indeed, the essence of it is contained in a pamphlet, voted and printed by the town of Boston, before the first Congress met, composed by James Otis, as I suppose, in one of his lucid intervals, and pruned and polished by Samuel Adams."[6]

IV.

Perhaps nowhere in our literature would it be possible to find a criticism brought forward by a really able man against any piece of writing less applicable to the case, and of less force and value, than is this particular criticism by John Adams and others, as to the lack of originality in the Declaration of Independence. Indeed, for such a paper as Jefferson was commissioned to write, the one quality which it could not properly have had, the one quality which would have been fatal to its acceptance either by the American

---

9. "*The Writings of Thomas Jefferson,*" H. A. Washington ed., vii., 39 [Tyler's note].
1. Stephen Cullen Carpenter, "*Memoirs of Thomas Jefferson,*" i., 11 [Tyler's note].
2. "*History of . . . . . . Virginia,*" 317 [Tyler's note].
3. Grayden's "*Men and Times of the American Revolution,*" 323, note [Tyler's note].
4. Paul Leicester Ford, "*The Writings of Thomas Jefferson,*" I Introd. xxvi [Tyler's note].
5. "*The Works of John Adams,*" ii., 377 [Tyler's note].
6. *Ibid.*, 514, note [Tyler's note].

Congress or by the American people—is originality. They were then at the culmination of a tremendous controversy over alleged grievances of the most serious kind—a controversy that had been steadily raging for at least twelve years. In the course of that long dispute, every phase of it, whether as to abstract right or constitutional privilege or personal procedure, had been presented in almost every conceivable form of speech. At last, they had resolved, in view of all this experience, no longer to prosecute the controversy as members of the empire; they had resolved to revolt, and, casting off forever their ancient fealty to the British crown, to separate from the empire, and to establish themselves as a new nation among the nations of the earth. In this emergency, as it happened, Jefferson was called upon to put into form a suitable statement of the chief considerations which prompted them to this great act of revolution, and which, as they believed, justified it. What, then, was Jefferson to do? Was he to regard himself as a mere literary essayist, set to produce before the world a sort of prize-dissertation—a calm, analytic, judicial treatise on history and politics with a particular application to Anglo-American affairs—one essential merit of which would be its originality as a contribution to historical and political literature? Was he not, rather, to regard himself as, for the time being, the very mouthpiece and prophet of the people whom he represented, and as such required to bring together and to set in order, in their name, not what was new, but what was old; to gather up into his own soul, as much as possible, whatever was then also in their souls, their very thoughts and passions, their ideas of constitutional law, their interpretations of fact, their opinions as to men and as to events in all that ugly quarrel, their notions of justice, of civic dignity, of human rights; finally, their memories of wrongs which, seemed to them intolerable, especially of wrongs inflicted upon them during those twelve years by the hands of insolent and brutal men, in the name of the King, and by his apparent command?

    Moreover, as the nature of the task laid upon him made it necessary that he should thus state, as the reasons for their intended act, those very considerations both as to fact and as to opinion which had actually operated upon their minds, so did it require him to do so, to some extent, in the very language which the people themselves, in their more formal and deliberate utterances, had all along been using. In the development of political life in England and America, there had already been created a vast literature of constitutional progress—a literature common to both portions of the English race, pervaded by its own stately traditions, and reverberating certain great phrases which formed, as one may say, almost the vernacular of English justice, and of English aspiration for a free, manly and orderly political life. In this vernacular the Declaration of Independence was written. The phraseology thus characteristic of it is the very phraseology of the champions of constitutional expansion, of civic dignity and progress, within the English race ever since Magna Charta; of the great state papers of English freedom in the seventeenth century, particularly the Petition of Right in 1629, and the Bill of Rights in 1689; of the great English Charters for colonization in America; of the great English exponents of legal and political progress—Sir Edward Coke, John Milton, Sir Philip Sidney, John Locke; finally, of the great American exponents of political liberty, and of the chief representative bodies, whether local or general, which had convened in America from the time of Stamp Act Congress until that of the Congress which resolved upon our independence. To say, therefore, that the official declaration of that resolve is a paper made up of the very opinions, beliefs, unbeliefs, the very sentiments, prejudices, passions, even the errors in judgment and the personal misconstructions—if they were such—which then actually impelled the American people to that mighty act, and that all these are expressed in the very phrases which they had been accustomed to use, is to pay to that state-paper the highest tribute as to its fitness for the purpose for which it was framed.

Of much of this, also, Jefferson himself seems to have been conscious; and perhaps never does he rise before us with more dignity, with more truth, than when, late in his lifetime, hurt by the captious and jangling words of disparagement then recently put into writing by his old comrade, to the effect that the Declaration of Independence "contained no new ideas, that it is a commonplace compilation, its sentences hackneyed in Congress for two years before, and its essence contained in Otis's pamphlet," Jefferson quietly remarked that perhaps these statements might "all be true: of that I am not to be the judge. . . . Whether I had gathered my ideas from read-ing or reflection, I do not know. I know only that I turned to neither book nor pamphlet while writing it. I did not consider it as any part of my charge to invent new ideas altogether and to offer no sentiment which had ever been expressed before."[7]

Before passing from this phase of the subject, however, it should be added that, while the Declaration of Independence lacks originality in the sense just indicated, in another and perhaps in a higher sense, it possesses originality—it is individualized by the character and by the genius of its author. Jefferson gathered up the thoughts and emotions and even the char-acteristic phrases of the people for whom he wrote, and these he perfectly incorporated with what was already in his mind, and then to the music of his own keen, rich, passionate, and enkindling style, he mustered them into that stately and triumphant procession wherein, as some of us still think, they will go marching on to the world's end.

There were then in Congress several other men who could have written the Declaration of Independence, and written it well—notably Franklin, either of the two Adamses, Richard Henry Lee, William Livingston, and, best of all, but for his own opposition to the measure, John Dickinson; but had any one of these other men written the Declaration of Independence, while it would have contained, doubtless, nearly the same topics and nearly the same great formulas of political statement, it would yet have been a wholly different composition from this of Jefferson's. No one at all familiar with his other writings, as well as with the writings of his chief contempo-raries, could ever have a moment's doubt, even if the fact were not already notorious, that this document was by Jefferson. He put into it something that was his own, and that no one else could have put there. He put him-self into it—his own genius, his own moral force, his faith in God, his faith in ideas, his love of innovation, his passion for progress, his invincible enthusiasm, his intolerance of prescription, of injustice, of cruelty; his sym-pathy, his clarity of vision, his affluence of diction, his power to fling out great phrases which will long fire and cheer the souls of men struggling against political unrighteousness.

7. "The Writings of Thomas Jefferson," H. A. Washington ed., vii., 305 [Tyler's note].

And herein lies its essential originality, perhaps the most precious, and, indeed, almost the only, originality ever attaching to any great literary product that is representative of its time. He made for himself no improper claim, therefore, when he directed that upon the granite obelisk at his grave should be carved the words: "Here was buried Thomas Jefferson, author of the Declaration of Independence."[8]

V.

If the Declaration of Independence is now to be fairly judged by us, it must be judged with reference to what it was intended to be, namely, an impassioned manifesto of one party, and that the weaker party, in a violent race-quarrel; of a party resolved, at last, upon the extremity of revolution, and already menaced by the inconceivable disaster of being defeated in the very act of armed rebellion against the mightiest military power on earth. This manifesto, then, is not to be censured because, being avowedly a statement of its own side of the quarrel, it does not also contain a moderate and judicial statement of the opposite side; or because, being necessarily partisan in method, it is likewise both partisan and vehement in tone; or because it bristles with accusations against the enemy so fierce and so unqualified as now to seem in some respects overdrawn; or because it resounds with certain great aphorisms about the natural rights of man, at which, indeed, political science cannot now smile, except to its own discomfiture and shame—aphorisms which are likely to abide in this world as the chief source and inspiration of heroic enterprises among men for self-deliverance from oppression.

Taking into account, therefore, as we are bound to do, the circumstances of its origin, and especially its purpose as a solemn and piercing appeal to mankind on behalf of a small and weak nation against the alleged injustice and cruelty of a great and powerful one, it still remains our duty to enquire whether, as has been asserted in our time, history must set aside either of the two central charges embodied in the Declaration of Independence.

The first of these charges affirms that the several acts complained of by the colonists evinced "a design to reduce them under absolute despotism," and had as their "direct object the establishment of an absolute tyranny" over the American people. Was this, indeed, a groundless charge, in the sense intended by the words "despotism" and "tyranny"—that is, in the sense commonly given to those words in the usage of the English-speaking race? According to that usage, it was not an Oriental despotism that was meant, nor a Greek tyranny, nor a Roman, nor a Spanish. The sort of despot, the sort of tyrant, whom the English people, ever since the time of King John and especially during the period of the Stuarts, had been accustomed to look for and to guard against, was the sort of tyrant or despot that could be evolved out of the conditions of English political life. Furthermore, he was not by them expected to appear among them at the outset in the fully developed shape of a Philip or an Alva in the Netherlands. They were able to recognize him, they were prepared to resist him, in the earliest and most incipient stage of his being—at the moment, in fact, when he should make his first attempt to gain all power over his people, by assuming the single

8. Randall, "*The Life of Thomas Jefferson*," iii., 563 [Tyler's note].

power to take their property without their consent. Hence it was, as Edmund Burke pointed out in the House of Commons only a few weeks before the American Revolution entered upon its military phase, that:

"The great contests for freedom . . . were from the earliest times chiefly upon the question of taxing. Most of the contests in the ancient commonwealths turned primarily on the right of election of magistrates, or on the balance among the several orders of the state. The question of money was not with them so immediate. But in England it was otherwise. On this point of taxes the ablest pens and most eloquent tongues have been exercised, the greatest spirits have acted and suffered. . . . They took infinite pains to inculcate, as a fundamental principle, that in all monarchies the people must in effect, themselves, mediately or immediately, possess the power of granting their own money, or no shadow of liberty could subsist. The colonies draw from you, as with their life-blood, these ideas and principles. Their love of liberty, as with you, fixed and attached on this specific point of taxing. Liberty might be safe or might be endangered in twenty other particulars without their being much pleased or alarmed. Here they felt its pulse, and as they found that beat, they thought themselves sick or sound."[9]

Accordingly, the meaning which the English race on both sides of the Atlantic were accustomed to attach to the words "tyranny" and "despotism," was a meaning to some degree ideal; it was a meaning drawn from the extraordinary political sagacity with which that race is endowed, from their extraordinary sensitiveness as to the use of the taxing-power in government, from their instinctive perception of the commanding place of the taxing-power among all the other forms of power in the state, from their perfect assurance that he who holds the purse with the power to fill it and to empty it, holds the key of the situation—can maintain an army of his own, can rule without consulting Parliament, can silence criticism, can crush opposition, can strip his subjects of every vestige of political life; in other words, he can make slaves of them, he can make a despot and a tyrant of himself. Therefore, the system which in the end might develop into results so palpably tyrannic and despotic, they bluntly called a tyranny and a despotism in the beginning. To say, therefore, that the Declaration of Independence did the same, is to say that it spoke good English. Of course, history will be ready to set aside the charge thus made in language not at all liable to be misunderstood, just so soon as history is ready to set aside the common opinion that the several acts of the British government, from 1764 to 1776, for laying and enforcing taxation in America, did evince a somewhat particular and systematic design to take away some portion of the property of the American people without their consent.

The second of the two great charges contained in the Declaration of Independence, while intimating that some share in the blame is due to the British Parliament and to the British people, yet fastens upon the king himself as the one person chiefly responsible for the scheme of American tyranny therein set forth, and culminates in the frank description of him as "a prince whose character is thus marked by every act which may define a

9. "Speech on moving his Resolutions for Concilition with the Colonies," March 22, 1775. *"The Works of Edmund Burke,"* ii., 120–121 [Tyler's note].

tyrant." Is this accusation of George the Third now to be set aside as unhistoric? Was that king, or was he not, chiefly responsible for the American policy of the British government between the years 1764 and 1776? If he was so, then the historic soundness of the most important portion of the Declaration of Independence is vindicated.

Fortunately, this question can be answered without hesitation, and in a few words; and for these few words, an American writer of to-day, conscious of his own bias of nationality, will rightly prefer to cite such words as have been uttered upon the subject by the ablest English historians of our time. Upon their statements alone it must be concluded that George the Third ascended his throne with the fixed purpose of resuming to the crown many of those powers which, by the constitution of England, did not then belong to it, and that in this purpose, at least during the first twenty-five years of his reign, he substantially succeeded—himself determining what should be the policy of each administration, what opinions his ministers should advocate in Parliament, and what measures Parliament itself should adopt. Says Sir Erskine May:

> "The king desired to undertake personally the chief administration of public affairs, to direct the policy of his ministers, and himself to distribute the patronage of the crown. He was ambitious not only to reign, but to govern." "Strong as were the ministers, the king was resolved to wrest all power from their hands, and to exercise it himself." "But what was this in effect but to assert that the king should be his own minister? . . . The king's tactics were fraught with danger, as well to the crown itself as to the constitutional liberties of the people."[1]

Already, prior to the year 1778, according to Lecky, the king had "laboriously built up" in England a "system of personal government"; and it was because he was unwilling to have this system disturbed that he then refused,

> "In defiance of the most earnest representations of his own minister and of the most eminent politicians of every party . . . to send for the greatest of living statesmen at the moment when the empire appeared to be in the very agonies of dissolution. . . . Either Chatham or Rockingham would have insisted that the policy of the country should be directed by its responsible ministers and not dictated by an irresponsible sovereign."

This refusal of the king to pursue the course which was called for by the constitution, and which would have taken the control of the policy of the government out of his hands, was, according to the same great historian, an act "the most criminal in the whole reign of George the Third; . . . as criminal as any of those acts which led Charles the First to the scaffold."[2]

Even so early as the year 1768, according to John Richard Green,

> "George the Third had at last reached his aim . . . In the early days of the ministry" (which began in that year) "his influence was felt to be predominant. In its later and more disastrous days it was supreme;

---

1. These sentences occur in the chapter on the "The Influence of the Crown during the Reign of George III.," in Sir Erskine May's "*Constitutional History of England*," i., 11, 12, 14–15 [Tyler's note].
2. Lecky, "*A History of England in the Eighteenth Century*," iv., 457–458 [Tyler's note].

for Lord North, who became the head of the ministry on Grafton's retirement in 1770, was the mere mouthpiece of the king. 'Not only did he direct the minister,' a careful observer tells us, 'in all important matters of foreign and domestic policy, but he instructed him as to the management of debates in Parliament, suggested what motions should be made or opposed, and how measures should be carried. He reserved for himself all the patronage, he arranged the whole cast of the administration, settled the relative place and pretensions of ministers of state, law officers, and members of the household, nominated and promoted the English and Scotch judges, appointed and translated bishops and deans, and dispensed other preferments in the church. He disposed of military governments, regiments, and commissions, and himself ordered the marching of troops. He gave and refused titles, honors, and pensions'. All this immense patronage was steadily used for the creation of a party in both houses of Parliament attached to the king himself . . . George was, in fact, sole minister during the fifteen years which followed; and the shame of the darkest hour of English history lies wholly at his door."[3]

Surely, until these tremendous verdicts of English history shall be set aside, there need be no anxiety in any quarter as to the historic soundness of the two great accusations which together make up the principal portion of the Declaration of Independence. In the presence of these verdicts also, even the passion, the intensity of language, in which those accusations are uttered, seem to find a perfect justification. Indeed, in the light of the most recent and most unprejudiced expert testimony, the whole document, both in its substance and in its form, seems to have been the logical response of a nation of brave men to the great words of the greatest of English statesmen, as spoken in the House of Commons precisely ten years before:

"This kingdom has no right to lay a tax on the colonies.[4] Sir, I rejoice that America has resisted. Three millions of people, so dead to all the feelings of liberty as voluntarily to submit to be slaves, would have been fit instruments to make slaves of the rest."[5]

VI.

Thus, ever since its first announcement to the world, and down almost to the present moment, has the Declaration of Independence been tested by criticism of every possible kind—by criticism intended and expected to be destructive. Apparently, however, all this criticism has failed to accomplish its object.

It is proper for us to remember, also, that what we call criticism is not the only valid test of the genuineness and worth of any piece of writing of great practical interest to mankind: there is, in addition, the test of actual use and service, in direct contact with the common sense and the moral sense of large masses of men, under various conditions, and for a long period. Probably no writing which is not essentially sound and true has ever survived this test.

3. "A Short History of the English People," 736, 737 [Tyler's note].
4. "The Celebrated Speech of a Celebrated Commoner," London, 1776, p. 5 [Tyler's note].
5. Ibid., 12 [Tyler's note].

Neither from this test has the great Declaration any need to shrink. As to the immediate use for which it was sent forth—that of rallying and uniting the friends of the Revolution, and bracing them for their great task—its effectiveness was so great and so obvious that it has never been denied. During the century and a quarter since the Revolution, its influence on the political character and the political conduct of the American people has been great beyond calculation. For example, after we had achieved our own national deliverance, and had advanced into that enormous and somewhat corrupting material prosperity which followed the adoption of the constitution and the development of the cotton-interest and the expansion of the Republic into a trans-continental power, we fell under an appalling temptation—the temptation to forget, or to repudiate, or to refuse to apply to the case of our human brethren in bondage, the principles which we had once proclaimed as the basis of every rightful government. The prodigious service rendered to us in this awful moral emergency by the Declaration of Independence was, that its public repetition, at least once every year, in the hearing of vast throngs of the American people in every portion of the Republic, kept constantly before our minds, in a form of almost religious sanctity, those few great ideas as to the dignity of human nature, and the sacredness of personality, and the indestructible rights of man as mere man, with which we had so gloriously identified the beginnings of our national existence. It did at last become very hard for us to listen each year to the preamble of the Declaration and still to remain the owners and users and catchers of slaves; still harder, to accept the doctrine that the righteousness and prosperity of slavery was to be accepted as the dominant policy of the nation. The logic of Calhoun was as flawless as usual, when he concluded that the chief obstruction in the way of his system was the preamble of the Declaration of Independence. Had it not been for the inviolable sacredness given by it to those sweeping aphorisms about the natural rights of man, it may be doubted whether Calhoun might not have won over an immense majority of the American people to the support of his compact and plausible scheme for making slavery the basis of the Republic. It was the preamble of the Declaration of Independence which elected Lincoln, which sent forth the Emancipation Proclamation, which gave victory to Grant, which ratified the Thirteenth Amendment.

We shall not here attempt to delineate the influence of this state paper upon mankind in general. Of course, the emergence of the American Republic as an imposing world-power is a phenomenon which has now for many years attracted the attention of the human race. Surely, no slight effect must have resulted from the fact that, among all civilized peoples, the one American document best known is the Declaration of Independence,[6] and that thus the spectacle of so vast and beneficent a political success has been everywhere associated with the assertion of the natural rights of man. "The doctrines it contained," says Buckle, "were not merely welcomed by a majority of the French nation, but even the government itself was unable to withstand the general feeling."[7] "Its effect in hastening the approach of the French Revolution . . . was indeed most remarkable."[8] Elsewhere, also, in many lands,

6. The editor of the latest edition of "The Writings of Thomas Jefferson." i., Introd. xxv., does not shrink from calling it "the paper which is probably the best known that ever came from the pen of an individual [Tyler's note]."
7. "History of Civilization in England," 846 [Tyler's note].
8. "Ibid., 847 [Tyler's note].

among many peoples, it has been cited again and again as an inspiration to political courage, as a model for political conduct; and if, as the brilliant historian just alluded to has affirmed, "that noble Declaration. . . . ought to be hung up in the nursery of every king, and blazoned on the porch of every royal palace,"[9] it is because it has become the classic statement of political truths which must at last abolish kings altogether, or else teach them to identify their existence with the dignity and happiness of human nature.

9. Buckle, "*History of Civilization in England*," 846 [Tyler's note].

Modern Analysis and Criticism

H. TREVOR COLBURN

From Thomas Jefferson and the Rights of Expatriated Men[†]

The earth Belongs always to the living generation," Jefferson reminded James Madison.[1] Thomas Jefferson is perhaps best known for his commitment to this belief. Dedicated to the proposition that man had a right to happiness and fulfillment in this world Jefferson strove to emancipate the present from the tyranny of the past. The dead hand of custom and habit were not for Jefferson.

It was to the tyranny of the past that Jefferson was opposed, not to the past itself. He rejected oppressive custom, but not custom. Convinced of the intrinsic virtue of his fellow man, Jefferson searched for an explanation for the seeming corruption of that virtue. He saw history as an extension of political experience, as a guide to a perfectible future through a heightened awareness of the blemished past.

I

Jefferson probably read his first history book in the modest library of his father. In Peter Jefferson's collection young Thomas found Rapin's *History of England* in a two-volume folio edition, and he never ceased singing its praises.[2] When he started buying books for himself, history soon emerged as his favorite category. The *Virginia Gazette* Day Books show Jefferson purchasing in March 1764 his first copy of David Hume's *History of England* (which he soon learned to detest), along with William Robertson's *History of Scotland*. Between 1762 and 1767 Jefferson studied law under the wise tutelage of George Wythe, gaining familiarity with works which combined historical and legal scholarship. When admitted to the bar he was well advanced in his studies of the *Reports* of Salkeld and Raymond and the *Institutes* of Coke.[3]

---

† From *The Lamp of Experience: Whig History and the Intellectual Origins of the American Revolution* (Chapel Hill: University of North Carolina Press, 1965), pp. 158–67. All numbered notes are Colburn's.

1. Jefferson to James Madison, Sept. 6, 1789, Boyd *et al.*, eds., *Jefferson Papers*, XV, 396.
2. Jefferson to George Washington Lewis, Oct. 25, 1825, Lipscomb and Bergh, eds., *Writings of Jefferson*, XVI, 125. The inventory of Peter Jefferson's property (including his library), filed after his death in Aug. 1757, is in the Albemarle County Will Book No. 2 which Marie Kimball cites in *Jefferson: The Road to Glory*, 13.
3. The *Virginia Gazette* Day Books disclose considerable book buying by Jefferson between 1764 and 1766; they are transcribed in William Peden's *Thomas Jefferson: Book Collector*. See also Peden's

But his reading had indeed barely begun. By 1771, when he advised young Robert Skipwith on his book buying, Jefferson was able to include Sidney's *Discourses*, Bolingbroke's *Political Works*, Rollin's *Ancient History*, Stanyan's *Grecian History*, the Gordon translations of Tacitus and Sallust, as well as works by Clarendon, Hume, and Robertson. Into his Commonplace Book went passages from Dalrymple's *Essay on Feudal Property*, Spelman's *De Terminis Juridicis*, Kames' *Historical Law Tracts*, Sullivan's *Feudal Laws*, Blackstone's *Commentaries*, Molesworth's *Account of Denmark*, and the (to Jefferson) anonymously written *Historical Essay on the English Constitution*.[4] He had his own copies of William Petyt's *Ius Parliamentum*, Thornhagh Gurdon's *History of Parliament*, and Anthony Ellis' *Tracts on Liberty*.[5] Later he acquired copies of Henry Care's *English Liberties*, Rushworth's *Historical Collections*, Acherley's *Britannic Constitution*, Atkyn's *Power of Parliament*, Catherine Macaulay's popular *History of England*, Trenchard and Gordon's *Cato's Letters*, and—of course—Burgh's *Political Disquisitions*.[6] The list is not quite endless. But it is extraordinary for the representation Jefferson accorded the "True Whigs." These were books Jefferson bought not once, but twice, or three times, books he found essential to his political existence, books which served him beyond the realm of his practice of law. These books by introducing him to the mysteries of feudalism and constitutionalism led to a personal (but not unique) perspective on the rights of the American colonies and the Englishmen residing there.

In the 1760's and early 1770's the political content of his reading mounted sharply; indeed Jefferson's studies reflect his growing sensitivity to, and involvement in his political environment. While studying law with Wythe in Williamsburg Jefferson breathed the air of the political controversy swirling about the bustling Virginia capital. He stood in the lobby of the Capitol building and heard Patrick Henry attack the Stamp Act in 1765. He knew, firsthand, the anger of the Burgesses at the Townshend Acts in 1767. When he secured election in 1769 as Burgess for Albemarle County, Jefferson brought experience as well as learning to his new responsibilities. He was ready to participate in Virginia's Non-Importation Resolutions in 1769 and was fully alert to the challenge presented by the Coercive Acts in 1774. When he learned of the oppressive measures directed at his Boston compatriots, Jefferson and Charles Lee "cooked up" (as Jefferson so nicely phrased it) some resolutions calling for a general day of fasting and prayer on the day the Boston Port Act took effect. He hoped this would "give us one heart and one mind to oppose, by all just means, every injury

---

"Some Notes concerning Thomas Jefferson's Libraries," *Wm. and Mary Qtly.*, 3d Ser., 1 (1944), 265–74. Marie Kimball, by analysis of Jefferson's changing handwriting and identification of the "Pro Patria" paper used in his commonplacing, has deduced that the first 174 entries were made in 1766; see Kimball, *Jefferson: The Road to Glory*, 85–88.

4. Jefferson to Robert Skipwith, with a List of Books for a Private Library, Aug. 3, 1771, Boyd *et al.*, eds., *Jefferson Papers*, I, 76–81. Jefferson's notes are in Chinard, ed., *Commonplace Book*, as follows: Dalrymple: 135–62; Spelman: 186–87, 189; Kames: 95–135; Sullivan: 233–34, 236–57; Blackstone: 193, 364–68; Molesworth: 213, 225–26; Hulme's *Historical Essay*: 296–98.

5. These books were invoiced by Perkins, Buchanan, and Brown, Oct. 2, 1769, Boyd *et al.*, eds., *Jefferson Papers*, I, 34.

6. Jefferson owned two copies of Care, and had *English Liberties* included in the University of Virginia library; Jefferson's initaled copy of Rushworth survives in the Lib. Cong., as does Acherley, Atkyns, Macaulay, Trenchard and Gordon, and Burgh. See Sowerby, ed., *Catalogue of Jefferson's Library*. See also, my "Thomas Jefferson's Use of the Past," *Wm. and Mary Qtly.*, 3d Ser., 15 (1958), 60–65.

to American Rights."⁷ In the process of preparing his resolves Jefferson demonstrated his historical approach. He thought of the similarity of his own times to the days of the Puritan Revolution in seventeenth-century England and turned to John Rushworth's *Historical Collections* for help. In the pages of Rushworth Jefferson "rummaged over for the revolutionary precedents and forms of the Puritans of that day."⁸ While Jefferson found Rushworth interesting, Governor Dunmore did not, and he dissolved the House of Burgesses. Before breaking up, the Burgesses held a lively meeting of their own at the Raleigh Tavern and issued a call for a Continental Congress to discuss the new British oppression.⁹

This move brought from Jefferson one of his most notable contributions to the literature of the American Revolution. He prepared a series of resolutions to present to a special Virginia convention meeting in August 1774; the resolutions would, if adopted, become instructions for the Virginia delegates to the forthcoming Congress in Philadelphia. Taken ill, Jefferson was unable to attend, but he sent two copies of his resolutions to Williamsburg. The convention took no official notice of his effort, but several members read the resolutions with enthusiasm. Without Jefferson's knowledge they had the manuscript published with the title *A Summary View of the Rights of British America.*¹ The *Summary View* laid the foundation of Jefferson's revolutionary reputation and was his most cogent and detailed examination of colonial rights before 1776.

In some ways, the *Summary View* is more representative of Jefferson's political thinking than the Declaration of Independence; it is a more personal expression of Jefferson's concept of Anglo-American relations. There has been criticism of the *Summary View* for the intemperance of its language and its lack of historical precision;² some scholars have commented on the lack of attention paid to the natural rights philosophy which Jefferson later expressed in the superbly simple opening paragraphs of the Declaration.³ And yet the *Summary View* was an instant popular success with colonial patriots and sympathetic English whigs⁴ because Jefferson was telling men what they wanted to believe and arguing the American cause in language immediately familiar. He assumed a working knowledge of history and did not seriously misjudge his unexpected audience; he took for granted the doctrine of natural rights, which was part and parcel of the eighteenth-century political atmosphere. He did not attempt to justify the colonial position with philosophy, but instead undertook an historical appraisal of the colonial case. In the process Jefferson, unlike a revolutionary, identified the good with the ancestral rather than with the purely rational.

7. Malone, *Jefferson the Virginian*, 92; Virginia Nonimportation Resolutions, 1769, Boyd et al., eds., *Jefferson Papers*, I, 27–31; John Pendleton Kennedy, ed., *Journals of the House of Burgesses of Virginia, 1773–1776* . . . (Richmond, 1905), 124.
8. Autobiography, Ford, ed., *Writings of Jefferson*, I, 10.
9. See Kimball, *Jefferson: The Road to Glory*, 234–37.
1. The best account of the political and biographical background to the *Summary View* is in Malone, *Jefferson the Virginian*, 180–81. For an interesting discussion of "Jefferson's *Summary View* as a Chart of Political Union" by Anthony M. Lewis, see *Wm. and Mary Qtly.*, 3d Ser., 5 (1948), 34–51.
2. Malone, *Jefferson the Virginian*, 182–84.
3. For example, see Carl L. Becker, *The Declaration of Independence; A Study in the History of Political Ideas* (N. Y., 1922), 278.
4. There is an excellent account of the reception given the *Summary View* in Boyd et al., eds., *Jefferson Papers*, I, 671–76.

In the *Summary View*, Jefferson supplied a most persuasive and felici-
tously phrased argument for resistance to British tyranny, and at the same
time he provided a graphic illustration of the political uses of his careful
reading of history. He established the tone of his essay at the outset. After
a polite opening address to the King as "chief magistrate of the British
Empire," the *Summary View* reminded George III of a history he seemed
to have forgotten. Jefferson went back to his "Saxon ancestors" to point out
how they "left their native wilds and woods in the North of Europe, [and]
had possessed themselves of the island of Britain." These ancient forefathers, he observed, had enjoyed the right of leaving their native land to establish new societies in the new world of England.[5] The transplanted Saxons
had carried their free customs and political democracy with them, establishing in England "that system of laws which has so long been the glory and
protection of that country." Jefferson noted that there was never any question of these Saxon settlers being subject to any form of allegiance or control by the mother country from which they had emigrated. These
forefathers had "too firm a feeling of the rights derived to them from their
ancestors to bow down the sovereignty of their state before such visionary
pretensions." Jefferson declared pointedly that "no circumstance has
occurred to distinguish materially the British from the Saxon emigration."

If the Saxon origins of English and American history held political lessons
of merit, so too did the Saxon land system translated from ancient Germany
to new settlements in England. Like the majority of the whig historians he
consulted, Jefferson believed that in Saxon England "feudal holdings were
certainly altogether unknown, and very few if any had been introduced at the
time of the Norman conquest." His Saxon ancestors had held their lands and
personal property "in absolute dominion, disencumbered with any superior,
[and] answering nearly to the nature of those possessions which the Feu-
dalist term Allodial." The responsibility for the obvious and tragic change in
England Jefferson placed squarely upon "William the Norman"—just as did
such favorite writers as Sir Henry Spelman and Sir John Dalrymple. Consequently Jefferson could and did insist that "feudal holdings were, therefore, but the exceptions out of the Saxon law of possession, under which all
lands were held in absolute right." Feudalism for Jefferson was an alien
thing, Norman in nature, established and maintained by force. A Norman
conquest may have inflicted feudalism upon the bewildered and betrayed
Saxons in England, but Jefferson saw no reason why their modern descendants in America should suffer a similar fate. The ancient Saxons had made
their settlements at their own expense, with no aid from the mother country, and thus were under no obligation. And so it was with the offspring of
these same Saxons when they came to America: in both cases, argued Jefferson, "for themselves they fought, for themselves they conquered, and for
themselves alone they have a right to hold."

An apparent weakness in Jefferson's appeal to whig history lay in the current, if temporary, fact of American submission to the British Crown, a
weakness rather reminiscent of general whig embarrassment over the Norman conquest. The ancient Saxons had not indulged their Germanic forefathers so generously as to pretend to be politically dependent upon them;
but, Jefferson explained, the early American colonists were "laborers, not

5. All references to the *Summary View* are to the text in *ibid.*, 121–35.

lawyers,"[6] who had "thought proper to adopt that system of laws under which they had hitherto lived in the mother country." Therefore, the early Americans had graciously consented to continue a form of union with the mother country by submitting themselves to a common monarchy, which became the "central link connecting the several parts of the empire thus newly multiplied." Engrossed in winning existence from a strange and hostile land, the colonists had then been misled by crafty Crown lawyers into thinking that all American lands really did belong to the King. Accordingly, Americans had fallen into the grievous error of assuming they took their holdings from the British Crown, and as long as administration was mild, there was no occasion for the historic reality to be discovered. But recent efforts, begun in 1763, to restrict land grants and confine American settlements demonstrated that the time had come for fraud to be exposed, for a firm declaration that the King "has no right to grant lands of himself."

However, the issue of feudalism and land tenure was only one instance of the perils of historical ignorance, and Jefferson employed the *Summary View* as an instrument of whig enlightenment. He found the history of the British empire full of examples of similar invasions by both Crown and Parliament of the colonial rights so dearly acquired with the "lives, the labors and the fortunes of individual adventurers." And the list of British iniquities compiled by Jefferson was long indeed, demonstrating a continuous effort to reduce America to a modern version of feudal slavery. In each instance Jefferson reviewed the historical background and injustice involved, and with a fine impartiality indicted both British Crown and Parliament for an unrelieved record of arbitrary acts.

He blamed the Crown for continually authorizing the dissolution of colonial legislatures, a crime, Jefferson noted, for which the traitorous advisers of Richard II had suffered death. Jefferson recalled that since 1688, when the British constitution was supposedly restored "on it's free and antient principles," this power of dissolution had been rarely practiced in England. Since colonists were Englishmen equally entitled to ancient privileges, they were equally entitled to respect for their representative institutions.

Naturally the same argument applied to the suspension of the New York legislature over the recent Quartering Act controversy, although on this issue Jefferson chose to attack Parliament and denounced that body for an unwarranted assumption of authority. After all, as any well-read colonist knew, Parliament was now both corrupt and unrepresentative; if Americans submitted to the pretensions of the House of Commons, "we should suddenly be found the slaves, not of one, but of 160,000 tyrants," the limited electorate in Britain. Most of the recent acts of oppression Jefferson laid at Parliament's door and suggested that the King was influenced by "the partial representations of a few worthless ministerial dependents, whose constant office it has been to keep that government embroiled, and who by their treacheries hope to obtain the dignity of the British knighthood." The Administration of Justice Act, the Coercive Act which permitted trial of colonists in England, served to illustrate Jefferson's alarm at "parliamentary tyranny." Measures such as this were completely contrary to Magna Charta, since the accused American would be "stripped of his privilege of trial by peers, of his vicinage."

---

6. *Ibid.*, 133. Jefferson first wrote "farmers, not lawyers," see *ibid.*, 137, note no. 35.

What made Jefferson's indignation at the contemporary condition of English politics so impressive in the *Summary View* was his recollection of past difficulties. British interference with colonial trade and industry was not new; its history was painfully long and familiar, reaching back to the despotic Stuarts. Here was "a family of princes . . . whose treasonable crimes against their people brought on them afterwards the exertion of those sacred and sovereign rights of punishment, reserved in the hands of the people for cases of extreme necessity." But the execution of Charles I had not brought freedom for colonial trade; the Commonwealth Parliament proved equally capable of arbitrary acts, which were tragically maintained when Charles II was restored to the British throne. Once more American rights fell "a victim to arbitrary power."

For Jefferson, this record of Crown and Parliament presented an obvious message: "History has informed us that bodies of men as well as individuals are susceptible of the spirit of tyranny." And history also demonstrated to Jefferson that the British nation had so succumbed: "Single acts of tyranny may be ascribed to the accidental opinion of a day; but a series of oppressions, begun at a distinguished period, and pursued unalterably thro' every change of ministers, too plainly prove a deliberate, systematical plan of reducing us to slavery."

Jefferson even found danger in apparently harmless measures: setting up a colonial post office in Queen Anne's reign became just another device "for accommodating his majesty's ministers and favorites with the sale of a lucrative and easy office." This fitted perfectly with Jefferson's conclusions about England's political decline from the glory of Saxon times. The day had now arrived "when the representative body have lost the confidence of their constituents, when they have notoriously made sale of their most valuable rights, when they have assumed to themselves powers which the people never put into their hands."

If the British had forgotten that "the whole art of government consists in the art of being honest,"[7] Jefferson had not. The colonists were standing upon their historical rights as transplanted Englishmen; "expatriated men"[8] was Jefferson's later phrase claiming liberties sadly forgotten in the mother country. Clearly George III would not be permitted the role of another William the Norman and allowed to fasten a similar tyranny upon the Saxon emigrant in America. Jefferson concluded with an earnest plea to the King: "Let not the name of George III be a blot in the page of history."[9] In Jefferson's view, the King already had much for which to answer.

The warnings of Jefferson offered in his *Summary View* went unheeded. Indeed the King himself seemed bent upon destroying the empire, pursuing beliefs and policies that could only end in disaster. Jefferson was deeply disturbed by George III's address to Parliament in October 1775, a speech in which the King claimed for Britain complete credit for the establishment and survival of the American colonies.[1] Drawing upon Hakluyt and Raleigh for corroboration, Jefferson reviewed the colonization efforts of Gilbert and Raleigh. The historical record showed "no assistance from the crown," and

7. *Ibid.*, 134.
8. Jefferson to Judge Tyler, June 17, 1812, H. A. Washington, ed., *The Writings of Thomas Jefferson*, 9 vols. (N. Y., 1855), VI, 65.
9. *Summary View*, Boyd et al., eds., *Jefferson Papers*, I, 134.
1. Quoted in *ibid.*, 284 *n.*

any claim to the contrary was a "palpable untruth." Jefferson knew only contempt for "a king who can adopt falsehood." One might pity and even pardon error. But flagrant misstatements of historical fact Jefferson found intolerable. The King, his "weak ministers," and "wicked favorites" now joined Parliament as objects of Jefferson's scorn.[2] American separation from England had become a necessity.

* * *

FAWN M. BRODIE

Sally Hemings[†]

The earth belongs to the living, and not to the dead.
Jefferson to Madison, September 6, 1789[1]

Sally Hemings' third son, Madison, born at Monticello in 1805, wrote explicitly of the beginnings of his mother's relationship with Jefferson:

> Their stay (my mother and Maria's) was about eighteen months. But during that time my mother became Mr Jefferson's concubine, and when he was called home she was *enciente* by him. He desired to bring my mother back to Virginia with him but she demurred. She was just beginning to understand the French language well, and in France she was free, while if she returned to Virginia she would be re-enslaved. So she refused to return with him. To induce her to do so he promised her extraordinary privileges, and made a solemn pledge that her children should be freed at the age of twenty-one years. In consequence of his promises, on which she implicitly relied, she returned with him to Virginia. Soon after their arrival, she gave birth to a child, of whom Thomas Jefferson was the father.[2]

Actually Sally Hemings was in Paris not eighteen but almost twenty-six months. Born in 1773, she was between fourteen and fifteen when she arrived, and between sixteen and seventeen when she went back to Virginia. She was certainly lonely in Paris, as well as supremely ready for the first great love of her life, and she was living daily in the presence of a man who was by nature tender and gallant with all women. For any slave child at Monticello Jefferson was a kind of deity. Since her own father John Wayles had died in the year of her birth, Jefferson was perhaps as close to being a parental figure as anyone she had ever known.[3]

---

2. "Refutation of the Argument that the Colonies Were Established at the Expense of the British Nation" [after Jan. 19, 1776], *ibid.*, 277–84. If Jefferson planned to publish this investigation, his intentions were not realized.
† From *Thomas Jefferson: An Intimate History* (New York: Norton, 1974), pp. 228–45. Copyright © 1974 by Fawn M. Brodie. Used by permission of W. W. Norton & Company, Inc. Numbered notes are Brodie's.
1. Jefferson to Madison, September 6, 1789, *Papers*, Boyd, XV, 396.
2. *Pike County Republican*, March 13, 1873.
3. Her father, John Wayles, had died May 28, 1773, as recorded in Jefferson's account book on May 31. Born the year of his death, Sally had lived for a time at the Elkhill plantation (*Farm Book*, 18), and had come with her mother to Monticello before 1776. The *Farm Book* frequently lists Sally's name with the year of her birth, '73, after it.

In December of 1787 he had said goodbye to a woman he adored, but who had turned out to be guilt-ridden and ill equipped for adultery. He was bewildered, angered, and somewhat disenchanted, but he did not at once cease loving her, or needing her. Now, living under his roof, was a swiftly maturing young woman who represented all that had been alluring and forbidden in the world of his childhood. In his *Notes on the State of Virginia* he had described blacks as more "ardent" than whites, a preconception that could have served only to heighten his dilemma of the moment. He had an important model in the person of his father-in-law, who had turned to a slave woman after the death of the last of his three white wives. And Sally Hemings, too, had a model in her own mother, that same Betty Hemings who had apparently dominated the private life and passions of John Wayles until his death.

The first evidence that Sally Hemings had become for Jefferson a special preoccupation may be seen in one of the most subtly illuminating of all his writings, the daily journal he kept on a seven-week trip through eastern France, Germany, and Holland in March and April of 1788. He went to Amsterdam, where with John Adams he completed negotiations for a Dutch loan to the United States, and arranged for a further loan in the years 1789 and 1790. Then he took off as a tourist. He visited Strasbourg, Metz, Saarbrücken, Mannheim, Heidelberg, Frankfurt, Cologne, and Düsseldorf. Not normally a diary keeper, he did write an almost daily account of his travels. Anyone who reads with care these twenty-five pages must find it singular that in describing the countryside between these cities he used the word "mulatto" eight times.

> The road goes thro' the plains of the Maine, which are mulatto and very fine. . . .
> It has a good Southern aspect, the soil a barren mulatto clay. . . .
> It is of South Western aspect, very poor, sometimes gray, sometimes mulatto. . . .
> These plains are sometimes black, sometimes mulatto, always rich. . . .
> . . . the plains are generally mulatto. . . .
> . . . the valley of the Rhine . . . varies in quality, sometimes a rich mulatto loam, sometimes a poor sand. . . .
> . . . the hills are mulatto but also whitish. . . .
> Meagre mulatto clay mixt with small broken stones. . . . [4]

In marked contrast is the journal Jefferson had kept while touring southern France in the spring of 1787, just before Sally Hemings' disturbing mulatto presence had come to trouble him. In that account, covering forty-eight printed pages, he used the word "mulatto" only twice, otherwise describing the hills, plains, and earth as dark, reddish-brown, gray, dark brown, and black.[5]

Another quotation in Jefferson's Holland journal is also illuminating. It follows ruminations about the proper shape of a plow, stimulated by the

---

4. "Notes of a Tour through Holland and the Rhine Valley," *Papers*, Boyd, XIII, 8–33. See especially 17, 19–20, 22, 24–25, 28–29.
5. "Notes of a Tour into the Southern Parts of France, &c," *Papers*, Boyd, XI, 415–63. Freud noted that many landscapes in dreams, especially wooded hills, were often symbols for the female body. *Complete Psychological Works*, V (1900–1901), part 2, 356.

sight of the badly designed moldboard plows he saw in the fields of eastern France. In his travel journal he drew a design and wrote details of the exact construction of a superior model—later developed at Monticello into his famous "plough of least resistance." Considering the ancient symbolism of the plow, it is not surprising, perhaps, that writing about the ideal shape of this ancient and basic agricultural tool led him immediately to observations about the women he had seen in the fields who followed close behind it.

> The women here . . . do all sorts of work. While one considers them as useful and rational companions, one cannot forget that they are also objects of our pleasures. Nor can they ever forget it. While employed in dirt and drudgery some tag of ribbon, some ring or bit of bracelet, earbob or necklace, or something of that kind will shew that the desire of pleasing is never suspended in them. . . . They are formed by nature for attentions and not for hard labour.[6]

This is all very tender, and suggests that he was thinking not at all about the splendidly dressed Maria Cosway when he wrote it.

Jefferson later was extremely proud of his moldboard plow, which was awarded a prize by the Agricultural Society of the Seine. "The plough," he would write, "is to the farmer what the wand is to the Sorcerer, its effect is really like sorcery."[7] He told Robert Fulton his own model was "the finest plough which has ever been constructed in America," and kept a model on display at Monticello. He designed improvements on his original model, writing in 1798, ". . . if the plough be in truth the most useful of all instruments known to man, it's perfection cannot be an idle speculation."[8]

Upon his return to Paris on April 23, 1788, Jefferson found a letter from Maria Cosway reproaching him in mixed rage and anguish for not writing to her for three months. "Your long silence is impardonable. . . . My war against you is of such a Nature that I cannot even find terms to express it. . . . my intention was only to say, *nothing*, send a blank paper; as a Lady in a Passion is not fit for Any thing."[9] Jefferson's reply is a great curiosity. He described briefly his trip to Germany, with a glowing description of the art gallery at Düsseldorf. Here, in describing the painting that excited him above all others, he betrayed, inadvertently as a man often does to an old love, that he had been captured by a new one.

> At Dusseldorp I wished for you much. I surely never saw so precious a collection of paintings. Above all things those of Van der Werff affected me the most. His picture of Sarah delivering Agar to Abraham is delicious. I would have agreed to have been Abraham though the consequence would have been that I should have been dead five or six thousand years. . . . I am but a son of nature, loving what I see and feel, without being able to give a reason, nor caring much whether there be one.[1]

---

6. "Notes of a Tour through Holland and the Rhine Valley, *Papers*, Boyd, XIII, 27. Freud noted the phallic symbolism, in dreams, of "ploughs, hammers, rifles, revolvers, daggers, etc." *Complete Psychological Works*, V, part 2, 356.
7. Jefferson to Charles Willson Peale, April 17, 1813 (film, University of Virginia, Case M, Reel 50 B).
8. Jefferson to Robert Fulton, April 16, 1810, *Writings*, L. and B., XIX, 173. Jefferson to St. John Sinclair, March 23, 1798, *Garden Book*, 653.
9. Maria Cosway to Jefferson, March 6, 1788, *Papers*, Boyd, XII, 645.
1. Jefferson to Maria Cosway, April 24, 1788, *Papers*, Boyd, XIII, 103–4. Trumbull had urged Jefferson to visit the Düsseldorf gallery, though he held Adriaen van der Werff's paintings in contempt,

"Agar"—Hagar the Egyptian—it will be remembered, was Abraham's concubine, given to him by his wife Sarah when she could not bear a child, and destined to become the legendary mother of the Arab peoples. In this painting she is pictured as very young, partly nude, but seductive in a fashion that is innocence itself. She is blond, with long straight hair down her back. Abraham, though bearded, is far from old, with the nude shoulders and chest of a young and vigorous giant. The round "bull's-eye" windows in the conventional Dutch interior are very like those Jefferson later installed in his own bedroom in Monticello, after remodeling it in 1797.[2]

Although Jefferson included tender passages in this letter to Maria Cosway—"At Dusseldorp I wished for you much. . . . At Heidelberg I wished for you too. In fact I led you by the hand thro' the whole garden"—he confessed callously that he had found it impossible to write a letter to her on the whole seven-week journey. "At Strasbourg I sat down to write to you," he admitted. "But for my soul I could think of nothing at Strasbourg but the promontory of noses, of Diego, of Slawkenburgius his historian, and the procession of the Strasburgers to meet the man with the nose. Had I written to you from thence it would have been a continuation of Sterne upon noses."[3]

Anyone not familiar with Sterne's *Tristram Shandy* would find this passage incomprehensible. Maria Cosway was not only baffled but enraged:

> How could you led me by the hand all the way, think of me, have Many things to say, and not find One word to write, *but on Noses?*[4]

In *Tristram Shandy* there is a great deal about noses, including a formal discussion on the hierarchy of caste among men based on their length and shape. Jefferson was specifically referring to the ironic tale told by Slawkenburgius about a Spaniard named Diego whose nose was so long he needed a specially large bedroom in the inn. Diego's visit to Strasbourg had set the city atwitter with argument as to its cause, and on the day he was due to return the whole populace trooped outside the walls in a procession to greet him. Whereupon the French troops, who had been waiting to capture the city, moved in and occupied it without firing a shot.

Even if one understands all this, one may well echo Maria Cosway's queston, "Why Noses?" As we have already asked, "Why mulatto?" Jefferson's bemusement with the one may well have been related to the other. If Sally Hemings, though "mighty near white," retained a suggestion of her grandmother's physical heritage in the shape of her nose, it could be that Jefferson, caught up in a new passion, was cursing the world's insistence on caring about such matters. Though his preoccupation with this girl of mixed blood did not cost him a city, as did the preoccupation of the Strasbourgers with a nose, it would eventually threaten to cost him the presidency.

---

describing them as "mere monuments of labor, patience, and want of genius." Trumbull, *Autobiography*, 137. A copy of the Düsseldorf museum catalogue may be seen today among Maria Cosway's papers in the library of the Collegio di Maria SS. Bambina, Lodi, Italy.
2. When I first pointed out the relationship between "Agar" and Sally Hemings in "The Great Jefferson Taboo," *American Heritage*, XXIII (June 1972), 53–54, John Maass traced the present location of the Adriaen van der Werff painting to a museum in Franconia, Bavaria. It was he who first pointed out the similarity in hair styles between that of Hagar and Sally Hemings, and the similarity in window styles between those in the painting and those at Monticello. See Maass, "Postscripts to History," *American Heritage*, XXIV (December, 1972), 111.
3. Jefferson to Maria Cosway, April 24, 1788, *Papers*, Boyd, XIII, 104.
4. Maria Cosway to Jefferson, April 29, 1788, *Papers*, Boyd, XIII, 115.

During the succeeding months after his return to Paris, similar otherwise inexplicable curiosities continued to surface in Jefferson's letters. In the severe cold of January 1789, when the Seine was frozen so solid carriages could cross on the ice, and the Parisian poor perished by the hundreds for want of heat and shelter, Jefferson wrote to Maria Cosway, "Surely it was never so cold before. To me who am an animal of a warm climate, a mere Oran-ootan, it has been a severe trial."[5] In 1789 the word "orangutan" meant for most people not one of the great apes but "wild man of the woods," the literal translation of the Malay words from which it is derived. There was much confusion about the relation of the great apes to man; even the gorilla was as yet unknown in Europe and America. Jefferson had doubtless read Buffon's chapter, "The Orang-Outang, or the Pongo, and the Jocko," in his *Histoire naturelle*, where the French naturalist contributed mightily to the mythology that the great apes ravished women, and himself confused the orangutan, which he had never seen, with the chimpanzee of Africa, which he had seen and which he greatly admired for its capacity to learn some of the habits of men. Buffon also insisted that pygmies were apes, and that some apes were intelligent enough to serve as servants in Africa.[6]

We do not know exactly what Jefferson conceived an "Oran-ootan" to be, but we do know that in his *Notes on the State of Virginia*, published only a few months before Sally Hemings' arrival, he had indiscreetly written that blacks preferred whites over their own species, just as "the Oran-ootan" preferred "the black woman over those of his own species."[7] That he may now suddenly have become uneasy about what he had written concerning this mysterious man of nature, or man of the woods, is suggested by the fact that on October 2, 1788, when he sent away to his London bookdealer a list of books for purchase, he included E. Tyson's *Oran-outang; or, An Anatomy of a Pigmy* (1699), one of the earliest scholarly volumes which had tried to clarify the whole classification problem. Jefferson had good reason to be uncomfortable. For when the Federalist press in America later heard rumors about his slave paramour, the editors needled him cruelly on this very passage in his *Notes*.[8]

There is also what one might call hard evidence as well as psychological evidence that Jefferson in Paris treated Sally Hemings with special consideration. On November 6, 1787, he paid 240 francs to a Dr. Sutton for Sally's smallpox inoculation, a very great sum. Shortly after her arrival a French tutor was hired, whose services lasted at least twenty months. A letter from this Monsieur Perrault to Jefferson on January 9, 1789, makes clear that he was tutoring "gimme" (Jimmy), Sally's brother [who had accompanied Jefferson to Paris in 1784], and one could expect that Sally would likely have been included. Perrault had come to the kitchen to ask for his pay; there had been an altercation, and the tutor complained bitterly to Jefferson of "*mauvais traitemens de gimme*" and "*Sotisses les plus durs*," which suggests that Jimmy Hemings was quick of temper and anything but the stereotype of the docile slave.[9] By January 1788,

5. Jefferson to Maria Cosway, January 14, 1789, *Papers*, Boyd, XIV, 446.
6. Buffon, *Natural History*, 10 vols. in 5 (London, 1792), IX, 149–77. Buffon described the confusion of scholars such as Linnaeus, M. Noel, M. de la Broff, and Edward Tyson as to whether the orangutan was a great ape or a wild man, but himself added to the wild inaccuracies of the period.
7. *Notes on the State of Virginia*, 138.
8. *Frederick-Town Herald*, reprinted in the *Richmond Recorder*, September 29, 1802. See p. 352.
9. Julian Boyd summarized the letter and reproduced most of it in the original French, *Papers*, XIV, 426. The Missouri Historical Society kindly furnished me a copy.

Jefferson had begun to pay this slave youth wages, 24 francs a month, with "*étrennes*," an additional gift of 12 francs for the New Year holiday. Sally received 36 francs in the same month, but did not get regular wages until December 1788. The French servants received 50 to 60 francs per month.[1]

There is a curious item in Jefferson's account book for April 29, 1789:

> pd Dupre 5 weeks board of Sally   105" [i.e., francs]
> washing &c   41–9
> 146–9[2]

This suggests the possibility that when Jefferson went to Holland and Germany he saw to it that Sally was properly chaperoned in a French home and not left as prey to the French servants at the ministry on the Champs Elysées.

Did he write to her when he was away? Was there ever even a brief note, wishing her well in her study of French? The one record that might illuminate this, the letter-index volume recording Jefferson's incoming and outgoing letters for this critical year of 1788, has disappeared. It is the only volume missing in the whole forty-three-year epistolary record. Julian Boyd tells us that "entries once existed but cannot now be found."[3] Also missing are any letters Jefferson may have written to his daughters on this seven-week trip. On his previous trip to southern France in the spring of 1787 Jefferson had written Patsy five letters, and he had taken his small letter-copying press with him so that copies are extant as well as some originals. This letter press he took with him again to Holland,[4] but even the copies of whatever letters he wrote to his daughters have mysteriously vanished. This raises the question whether or not someone at some time went through Jefferson's papers systematically eliminating every possible reference to Sally Hemings. Letters from Jefferson to Sally's brothers, and from her brothers to him, are extant.[5] But no letters or notes exchanged between Sally Hemings and Thomas Jefferson have as yet ever found their way into the public record.

His account books were preserved intact, however, and here occasional references to Sally during the Paris years provide a slight but important illumination of a record that seems to have been kept as secret as possible. In April 1789, for example, Jefferson began to spend a surprising amount of money on Sally Hemings' clothes. There is an item for 96 francs for "clothes for Sally" on April 6, 72 francs on April 16, and an itemized 23 francs on April 26 for "making clothes for servts." May 25 has another item, "pd making clothes for Sally 25# 2." The money Jefferson spent for Patsy's clothes is several times that of her maid during roughly the same period. Still, if one knows that a pair of gloves could be had for two francs, the expenditure of 216 francs for Sally in seven weeks plus her monthly salary of 24 francs would seem to be considerable, especially when compared with the total lack of specific expenditures on her behalf in the earlier months.

---

1. Account book, 1788–89.
2. James A. Bear, Jr., who transcribed the account books at the University of Virginia, describes Madame Dupré in his index as "Sally Hemings's Paris landlady." The delay of a year in making the payment was not unusual for Jefferson.
3. *Papers*, Boyd, VI, viii.
4. *Papers*, Boyd, XII, 655n. One example of a letter to Patsy which exists in the original and in the press copy, May 21, 1787, may be seen in *Papers*, Boyd, XI, 370.
5. There are eleven letters from John Hemings to Jefferson presently in the University of Virginia Library.

Both Sally and James Hemings knew they were free if they chose to make an issue of it,[6] and Jefferson knew from his earliest months in Paris that even his diplomatic status did not give him the right to hold slaves against their will. When another American in Paris wrote asking him the legal status of a slave boy he had brought with him, Jefferson replied, "The laws of France give him freedom if he claims it, and . . . it will be difficult, if not impossible, to interrupt the course of the law." He added cautiously, and apparently without guilt, "Nevertheless I have known an instance where a person bringing in a slave, and saying nothing about it, has not been disturbed in his possession. I think it will be easier in your case to pursue the same plan, as the boy is so young that it is not probable he will think of claiming freedom."[7]

It will be seen that for a man theoretically intent upon emancipation of all slaves, Jefferson was extremely possessive about his own. When he received a letter from Edward Bancroft asking him pointedly his opinion on the value of Quaker experiments in Virginia where owners freed and then hired their own slaves, Jefferson replied with notable lack of enthusiasm, "As far as I can judge from the experiments which have been made, to give liberty to, or rather, to abandon persons whose habits have been formed in slavery is like abandoning children." And he went on to describe in rather vague terms what was essentially a sharecropping experiment he hoped to carry out on his return, dividing his farms into 50 acres each, importing about as many Germans as he had slaves, and settling them together "intermingled," with the same education "in habits of property and foresight"— all this without emancipation.[8]

Still, Jefferson had under his roof in Paris two slaves who were learning to speak French, who counted themselves free, and were thinking of becoming expatriates. James Hemings, who had served as an apprentice under the cook of the Prince de Conde, and also with a *pâtissier*, was now an experienced chef, and could easily command a salary in Paris.[9] Freeing him would hardly have been "abandoning" a child. In using such an argument against emancipation Jefferson was falling back into a pattern of thinking that had already long been a cliché in Virginia. Whence this sudden backing away from his old zeal for emancipation? In these same months he could on the one hand spend hours translating the Marquis de Condorcet's passionate indictment of slavery, and yet refuse to lend his name to a new organization in France agitating for an end simply to the slave trade.[1] So he was locked in a conflict that was in a sense old, and which had been with him from childhood—but which was now new and compellingly personal.

Jefferson's letter to Bancroft marks the first time in all his writings that he moved backward, however slightly, to defend slavery, just as his failure to free James and Sally Hemings in Paris marks a decisive watershed in his zeal for emancipation. To free them was to lose them, and Jefferson was an extraordinarily possessive man. He did free James Hemings. Faced with the threat of his staying in Paris, Jefferson agreed to emancipate him in Virginia

---

6. According to Madison Hemings. See Appendix I.
7. Jefferson to Paul Bentalou, August 25, 1786, *Papers*, Boyd, X, 296.
8. Jefferson to Edward Bancroft, January 26, 1789, *Papers*, Boyd, XIV, 492–93, mistakenly dated 1788. It is a reply to Bancroft's letter of September 16, 1788.
9. *Papers*, Boyd, XI, 98n, 99n, 297–98.
1. See "Jefferson's Notes from Condorcet on Slavery," January 1789, *Papers*, Boyd, XIV, 494–98; Jefferson to Brissot de Warville, February 11, 1788, *Papers*, Boyd, XII, 577–78.

once James had taught someone else at Monticello to cook French style. Jefferson kept his word, but not before seven years had passed. The reasons for not freeing Sally Hemings would complicate the rest of his life.

What meanwhile, during these successive interludes of the heart, had been happening to Jefferson's eldest daughter [Martha or Patsy]? By April 1789 she had been in the convent school five years, and was now seventeen. Though the nuns were kind and motherly, they watched her rigorously and forbade her to leave the school for any purpose without her father's written permission.[2] In America, when father and daughter had been separated, it had been Jefferson who begged for letters from her. But when Jefferson spent thirteen weeks in southern France in 1787, it was she who had chided him for not writing every week, as he had promised, adding, as he had so often written to her, "you are never a moment absent from my thoughts."[3] He replied from Aix-en-Provence with his old tenderness: "No body in this world can make me so happy, or so miserable as you. Retirement from public life will ere long become necessary for me. To your sister and yourself I look to render the evening of my life serene and contented. It's morning has been clouded by loss after loss till I have nothing left but you."[4]

Still, his letters indicate that he continued to treat Patsy very much as he had done when she was eleven. He gave her the same repetitious homiletic advice—never be angry—never be idle—"Be good and be industrious, and you will be what I shall most love in this world."[5] He did not respond, at least in his letters, to her attempts to discuss anything other than her schoolwork, ignoring comments on French scandals and politics, and her rampant abolitionism which burst out in a letter of May 3, 1787—"I wish with all my soul the poor negroes were all freed. It grieves my heart."[6] She told him what he most wanted to hear, "Believe me to be for life your most tender and affectionate child,"[7] and he seemed largely unaware that she was no longer a child and was tormented with longings the nature of which she did not herself understand.

William Short, more astute than Jefferson in this matter, sensed that Patsy was jealous of both Maria Cosway and Angelica Church. He wrote secretly to John Trumbull, who had painted portraits of Jefferson for both these women, suggesting that to make a third for Martha Jefferson would be a "very clever gallant thing," to do, and exacting secrecy concerning his own role in the matter. Trumbull followed the suggestion, and we thus have three separate miniatures of Jefferson, all based on the portrait made in the larger *Signing of the Declaration of Independence*. The one made for Martha is the most youthful, the most endearing, with an unusual suggestion of a smile.[8]

Sometime in 1788 Jefferson learned to his consternation that Patsy was considering becoming a nun. The papal nuncio in Paris, Comte Dugnani, who knew Jefferson, wrote to John Carroll of Baltimore on July 5, "The eldest seems to have tendencies toward the Catholic religion. She is only sixteen.

2. See Martha Jefferson to Jefferson, April 9, 1787, *Family Letters*, 37.
3. Martha Jefferson to Jefferson, March 25, 1787, *Family Letters*, 34.
4. Jefferson to Martha Jefferson, March 28, 1787, *Family Letters*, 35.
5. Jefferson to Martha Jefferson, May 21, 1787, *Family Letters*, 41–42.
6. Martha Jefferson to Jefferson, May 3, 1787, *Family Letters*, 39.
7. *Ibid.*
8. *Papers*, Boyd, XIV, xxxvi. Boyd reproduces the portrait made for Martha Jefferson in XIV, 328. The portraits made for Maria Cosway and Angelica Church are reproduced in X, 467.

Her father, without absolutely opposing her vocation, has tried to distract her."⁹ Henry Randall, who had access to Jefferson family gossip, wrote by way of explanation that "the daring and flippant infidelity now rife in French society, disgusted the earnest, serious, naturally reverential girl."¹ But the "daring and flippant infidelity" of Paris had caught up her own beloved parent. She could hardly have missed his new *joie de vivre* in the autumn of 1786 when he first fell in love with Maria Cosway and joined what may well have seemed to her the giddy and lascivious turmoil of the artist colony. She had written to her father in April 1787, "There was a gentleman, a few days ago, that killed himself because he thought his wife did not love him. They had been married ten years. I believe that if every husband in Paris was to do as much there would be nothing but widows left."² If she was subtly warning her father to beware of married women as they were all wanton, he did not heed the message.

Jefferson was sufficiently alarmed by Patsy's possible conversion that he thought of taking his daughters home in the summer of 1788. But he delayed. "I wished Polly to perfect her French," he explained to Elizabeth Eppes.³ Still, in September he formally petitioned for a leave of absence the following spring, planning to take his daughters home in April 1789, arrange for their schooling, and return in the autumn. Though Jefferson complained that the prospect of returning without his daughters was indeed dreary, the fact that he could even consider the separation seems to have been for Patsy a shattering knowledge.

For Jefferson Paris in 1788 was becoming an increasingly exciting political experience. The growing threat of revolution delighted him, and he eagerly became a quiet, even secret, participant, consulting with Lafayette on several papers pertinent to the ever deepening crisis between the King and the Estates-General, which was to be convened in May 1789, the first time since 1614. There has been a great deal of astute analysis of Jefferson's somewhat conservative role in the beginnings of the French Revolution. While the stream of his letters back to the United States in 1788, particularly to Madison, reflect what would seem to be an almost total absorption in the beginnings of the potentially momentous social experiment, they also show that he expected it to move with a good deal more rationality and less upheaval than it did.⁴ So, indeed, did everyone else.

There are also letters which offer important clues to Jefferson's personal life in this great year of ferment, clues to intimate conflicts which exploded in a small but crucial fashion in the spring of 1789, just as Paris itself exploded into revolutionary violence. To Anne W. Bingham, an American friend who had recently returned home from Paris, he wrote on May 11, 1788:

---

9. The original source, Melville, *John Carroll of Baltimore*, gives the date of the Dugnani letter as July 5, 1787. But since he speaks of Jefferson's planning to take both daughters home, and gives Patsy's age as sixteen, the letter could have been written only in 1788. Polly did not arrive in Paris until July 15, 1787. See *Papers*, Boyd, XIV, 356n, who gives a portion of the original letter.
1. Randall, *Jefferson*, I, 538.
2. Martha Jefferson to Jefferson, April 9, 1787, *Family Letters*, 37–38. Martha may have been especially impressed by this story because her own father had been married just ten years.
3. Jefferson to Elizabeth Eppes, December 15, 1788, *Papers*, Boyd, XIV, 355.
4. See especially Peterson, *Jefferson and the New Nation*, 370–89, Malone, *Jefferson and the Rights of Man*, 180–237.

The gay and thoughtless Paris is now become a furnace of Politics. All the world is run politically mad. Men, women, children talk nothing else; and you know that naturally they talk much, loud and warm. Society is spoilt by it, at least for those who, like myself, are but lookers on—You too, have had your political fever. But our good ladies, I trust, have been too wise to wrinkle their foreheads with politics. They are contented to soothe and calm the minds of their husbands returning ruffled from political debate. They have the good sense to value domestic happiness above all other, and the art to cultivate it beyond all others. There is no part of the earth where so much of this is enjoyed as in America.[5]

Thus Jefferson, who in 1785 had delighted in sparring with the sharp intellect of Abigail Adams, and who in 1786 and 1787 had listened with admiration to Madame Helvétius, Madame Necker, and Madame de Staël, now sang the virtues of the totally domestic woman who lived only to soothe and calm her husband. To an old Virginia friend he wrote on February 7, 1788, "No attachments soothe the mind so much as those contracted in early life. . . . I had rather be shut up in a very modest cottage, with my books, my family and a few old friends, dining on simple bacon, and letting the world roll on as it liked, than to occupy the most splendid post which any human power can give."[6] And he, who had devotedly followed Maria Cosway from gallery to gallery, and who had ordered copies of paintings by the score and the sculptures of busts of notable Europeans and Americans, now turned even against the artists. In a paper he drew up in 1788 for the use of American travelers in Europe, *Hints on European Travel*, he urged his countrymen to study agriculture, gardens, architecture, and politics. But for "Painting and Statuary" he wrote, with a trace of contempt, "Too expensive for the state of wealth among us. It would be useless and therefore preposterous for us to endeavor to make ourselves connoisseurs in those arts. They are worth seeing, but not studying."[7]

In his letter to Anne Bingham he had also written, "Recollect the women of this capital, some on foot, some on horses, and some in carriages hunting pleasure in the streets, in routs and assemblies, and forgetting that they have left it behind them in their nurseries; compare them with our countrywomen occupied in the tender and tranquil amusements of domestic life, and confess that it is a comparison of Amazons and Angels."[8]

If the political woman—the Amazon—remained a threat, and the domestic woman—the Angel—had now triumphed, still the Angel who was apparently at present providing the "tender and tranquil amusements" in his own domestic life was in the most crucial sense a fallen angel, and forbidden. It is not surprising that he wrote to Maria Cosway on May 21, 1789, "All is politics in this capital. Even love has lost it's part in conversation. This is not well, for love is always a consolatory thing. I am going to a country where it is felt in its sublimest degree."[9] In 1786 and 1787 Jefferson could talk about his affection for Maria Cosway at least within a limited circle, including Trumbull, d'Hancarville, William Short, and possibly Angelica Church. But

5. Jefferson to Anne Willing Bingham, May 11, 1788, *Papers*, Boyd, XIII, 151.
6. Jefferson to A. Donald, February 7, 1788, *Papers*, Boyd, XII, 572.
7. *Papers*, Boyd, XIII, 269.
8. Jefferson to Anne Willing Bingham, May 11, 1788, *Papers*, Boyd, XIII, 152.
9. Jefferson to Maria Cosway, May 21, 1789, *Papers*, Boyd, XV, 142–43.

in 1788 he could share his delight in his new love with no one, and had to be content with the glowing generalizations about American angels such as we find in his letter to Mrs. Bingham. There was only one advantage for Jefferson in this new attachment without marriage, as against a new marriage to a woman he could love as much, and that advantage may for Jefferson have been preëminent. The slave girl, unlike a wife, could never be a rival to his old and continuing mistress, politics. Nor need she ever become a threat to any decision-making on his part that had to do with his political life.

We know from his account books that Jefferson in September 1788 went to his old haunts—St. Germain and Marly, and that he went back to the "Desert" in May 1789. Was it Sally Hemings who accompanied him? Conceivably it could have been his daughters. We know that he bought a "watch for Patsy" on January 5, 1789, costing 554 francs, and on June 30 a "ring for Patsy" costing 48 francs. Was it for Sally Hemings, on September 30, 1788, that he paid 40 francs for "a locket"? If so, Jefferson even here was too discreet to leave a trace. Still, only the most naïve of men could have believed that he could continue to keep a liaison with the slave girl secret, especially from his daughters. One wonders if it ever occurred to him that Patsy upon coming home from school on Sunday would look upon the spectacle of her maid newly dressed in stylish Parisian clothes with absolute incomprehension. Perhaps it didn't happen that way. But there is the coincidence that it was in early April that Jefferson spent almost two hundred francs on "clothes for Sally," and that on April 18 Jefferson was appalled to get a note from Patsy formally requesting his permission to let her become a nun. However affectionate the pressures may have been by the motherly nuns, or however Martha may have convinced herself that the life of a nun was her true vocation, the act was one of enormous hostility to her father. One has only to read the letters of the papal nuncio to see with what satisfaction he would have looked upon the conversion of the daughter of a man whose suspicion of priestcraft and contempt for organized religion was known all over Europe.[1]

Randall, who learned of Martha's request to join the nunnery from her children, reported what happened afterward:

> For a day or two she received no answer. Then his carriage rolled up to the door of the Abbaye, and poor Martha met her father in a fever of doubts and fears. Never was his smile more benignant and gentle. He had a private interview with the Abbess. He then told his daughters he had come for them. They stepped into his carriage—it rolled away—and Martha's school life was ended.[2]

Jefferson's account book provides fascinating additional details. On April 19, the day before he went to the convent school, he recorded a purchase of "linen for Patsy," costing 274 francs. On the twentieth Patsy herself was permitted to buy "lawn and cambrick" amounting to 332 francs. The explosion of clothes buying continued into May, with 229 francs for silks, 106 francs for shoes, and 84 francs for stays, and shortly afterward an important

---

1. See *Papers*, Boyd, XIV, 356n.
2. Randall, *Jefferson*, I, 538. Jefferson's account book for April 20, 1789, reads, "paid at Panthemont in full 625–15–2."

symbolic purchase—48 francs for "a ring for Patsy." The 12 francs he paid for "a whip for Patsy" on May 7 suggests that he was now taking her horseback riding. And it may have been at this time that he arranged to have her portrait painted by Joseph Boze.[3]

That Jefferson's control over his daughters was implicit rather than explicit, and that he chose what should and should not be discussed, even in this important crisis, is suggested by Sarah Randolph, Jefferson's great-granddaughter, who added a significant footnote to the whole story. "No word in allusion to the subject [of Patsy's becoming a nun] ever passed between father and daughter, and it was not referred to by either of them until years afterwards, when she spoke of it to her children."[4] This is the kind of control many parents succeed in imposing who rule exclusively by love. Where annoyance or even hatred is explicit, the child has the advantage of being able to reply in kind, and the hatred can often be exorcised in the heated exchange. This was not permitted to Martha Jefferson. And one suspects that the same kind of control was employed by Jefferson in the fall of 1789, when it could no longer be kept a secret that Sally Hemings was pregnant.[5]

There had been plenty of political crises in Jefferson's life during the previous months—a serious bread shortage in Paris because of the bad harvest of 1788, a riot among Paris workmen which took a hundred lives in April, and finally on July 14 the fall of the Bastille, which astonished and delighted him. He went to watch the demolition of what he called a "fortification of infinite strength . . . which in other times had stood several sieges, and had never been taken,"[6] and noted in his account book a contribution of 60 francs on August 21 for the widows of the men who had been slain capturing it. He wrote to Madison on July 22, 1789, of "this astonishing train of events as will be forever memorable in history," concluding with a classic understatement, "Indeed this scene is too interesting to be left at present."[7]

The mob violence and decapitations that accompanied the Bastille destruction did not trouble him, and even as an old man he wrote with satisfaction that when the Duc de la Rochefoucauld-Liancourt forced his way into the King's bedchamber and told him the Bastille's Governor, Lieutenant Governor, and *Prévôt des Marchands* had had their heads chopped off and their bodies dragged through the streets of Paris, the King "went to bed fearfully impressed."[8] Even two years earlier Jefferson had written in defense of Shays' Rebellion, a brief armed revolt of Massachusetts farmers against heavier taxes, which had frightened John and Abigail Adams into believing the United States was threatened with anarchy:

> What country before ever existed a century and half without a rebellion? And what country can preserve it's liberties if their rulers are not warned from time to time that their people preserve the spirit of resistance? Let them take arms. The remedy is to set them right as to facts,

3. Julian Boyd dates this charming portrait, which shows Martha Jefferson at seventeen, with reddish hair, blue eyes, and cream-colored dress, as having been made in the spring of 1789. There are no letters to Boze, and the account book indicates no payment to him. The portrait is reproduced by Boyd in *Papers*, XIV, 361. See also XIV, xli.
4. Sarah Randolph, *Domestic Life*, 146.
5. See Appendix I.
6. *Autobiography*, 108.
7. Jefferson to Madison, July 22, 1789, *Papers*, Boyd, XV, 299–300.
8. *Autobiography*, 108.

pardon and pacify them. What signify a few lives lost in a century or two? The tree of liberty must be refreshed from time to time with the blood of patriots and tyrants. It is it's natural manure.[9]

With the revolutionary fervor spreading among French intellectuals Jefferson had become, finally, what Franklin had been before him, a kind of hero in Paris. American inventor James Rumsey, writing home on March 20, 1789, described him as "the most popular Embassador at the french Court." "American principles," he said, "are bursting forth in Every quarter: it must give pleasure to the feeling mind, to see millions of his fellow Creatures Emerging from a state not much better than Slavery."[1] Jefferson had gone daily to Versailles to hear the debates of the Estates-General, and had helped Lafayette draft his Declaration of the Rights of Man, which was presented to the National Assembly on July 11.[2] Though almost no one knew of this special collaboration, the indebtedness of Lafayette's famous document at least to the Declaration of Independence was secret to no one in the French government, and Jefferson could hardly have lived through these weeks without an exciting sense of involvement, a recognition that if not a father he was at least one of the patron saints of the new revolution.

He hoped for a peaceful evolution into a constitutional monarchy, with the King giving "freedom of the press, freedom of religion, freedom of commerce and industry, freedom of persons against arbitrary arrests, and modification if not total prohibition of military agency in civil cases." And with his characteristic optimism he wrote to John Mason on July 17, "I have not a single doubt of the sincerity of the king, and that there will not be another disagreeable act from him."[3]

There is every indication that when Jefferson finally received congressional permission to return to America he was loath to go, and eager to return quickly to Paris. For the first time he seemed willing to be free of his daughters, and he told Trumbull he expected to come back for several years. Whether he planned to take James and Sally Hemings back with him and return with them again to Paris is unknown; that they were agitating to stay in Paris as free citizens at this point is suggested by the reminiscences of Madison Hemings.

Maria Cosway, learning that Jefferson was returning to America, peppered him with letters begging him to visit her in England en route. "Pray write, pray write," she said, "and dont go to America without coming to England."[4] This request he dodged with pleasantries, suggesting that she and Angelica Church come to America on the same boat, but in the same breath warning her how "furiously displeased" was Madame de Brehan with America a gentle warning that the United States was not Arcadia, like Paris.[5] Late in May he wrote cruelly that he might be traveling across the Atlantic with Angelica Church. "We shall talk a great deal of you. . . . Adieu, my dear friend. Be

9. Jefferson to William Stephens Smith, Adams' son-in-law, November 13, 1787, Papers, Boyd, XII, 356.
1. Rumsey to Benjamin West, March 20, 1789, Rumsey to Charles Morrow, March 27, 1789, quoted in Papers, Boyd, XV, 81n, 82n.
2. See Jefferson to Lafayette, June 3, 1789, and his "Draft of a Charter of Rights," Papers, Boyd, XV, 165–68.
3. Jefferson to Willliam Carmichael, August 9, 1789; Jefferson to John Mason, July 17, 1789, Papers, Boyd, XV, 338, 278.
4. Maria Cosway to Jefferson, December 23, 1788, Papers, Boyd, XIV, 372.
5. Jefferson to Maria Cosway, January 14, 1789, Papers, Boyd, XIV, 446.

our affections unchangeable, and if our little history is to last beyond the grave, be the longest chapter in it that which shall record their purity, warmth and duration."[6] Still, he found it difficult to let go even of this dying love, and told Maria in a letter from the Isle of Wight (he embarked for America this close to London), "The ensuing spring might give us a meeting at Paris with the first swallow. . . . remember me and love me."[7]

The knowledge that he might never return to Paris came to Jefferson stealthily in September, six weeks before he left. He had received a letter from Madison on August 6 with an ominous query: "I have been asked whether any appointment at home would be agreeable to you."[8] Jefferson recognized at once that this was a tacit bid to join the government under the new constitution, with Washington as president, and he replied with as firm a no as he could muster: "You ask me if I would accept any appointment on that side of the water? You know the circumstances which led me from retirement, step by step and from one nomination to another, up to the present. My object is a return to the same retirement. Whenever therefore I quit the present, it will not be to engage in any other office, and most especially any one which would require a constant residence from home."[9]

But could he say no directly to Washington? On the first of September he made a final list of what to take with him and what to leave behind in Paris. Patsy's harpsichord and guitar were to go, along with clocks, beds, mattresses, and clothes, boxes of books specially packed for Franklin, Washington, and Madison, as well as wine, cheese, tea, pictures, busts, and his old phaeton. The list included also two cork oaks, four melon apricots, one white fig, five larch trees, four Cresanne pears, three Italian poplars, and numerous other small trees and plants.[1] So the nostalgia for Monticello showed its power, and underlined the fundamental precariousness of his will to return to France. On September 2 he said goodbye to John Trumbull, whom he had asked to become his secretary should William Short decide to return to America.[2] One hour after Trumbull left for London Jefferson was in bed seriously ill. The old migraine was back for the first time since he had set foot on French soil. It lasted six days,[3] Again it was triggered, it would seem, by a sense of loss. He was losing friends, artists, scholars, scientists, Paris—all of Europe—to say nothing of a place in the new French Revolution, possibly for a few months but probably forever.

How Sally Hemings figured in this agonized conflict is simply non-recoverable. We know only what her son later wrote, that she was pregnant and refused to return to America with Jefferson till he promised to free her children at age twenty-one. We know, too, Jefferson waited to a surprisingly late date—September 16, sixteen days after completing the baggage list and eight days after his recovery—before writing to James Maurice in London the exact specifications for cabins on the boat he was taking: "three master births (for himself and two daughters of 17. and 11. years of age) and births [surely an odd misspelling, under the circumstances] for a man and woman servant, the latter convenient to that of my daughters: A use of the cabbin in common

6. Jefferson to Maria Cosway, May 21, 1789, *Papers*, Boyd, XV, 143.
7. Jefferson to Maria Cosway, October 14, 1789, *Papers*, Boyd, XV, 521.
8. Madison to Jefferson, May 27, 1789, *Papers*, Boyd, XV, 153.
9. Jefferson to Madison, August 29, 1789, *Papers*, Boyd, XV, 369.
1. "List of Baggage Shipped by Jefferson from France," *Papers*, Boyd, XV, 375.
2. Jefferson to Trumbull, May 21, 1789, *Papers*, Boyd, XV, 143–44.
3. Jefferson to Trumbull, September 9, 1789, *Papers*, Boyd, XV, 407.

with the others, and not exclusive of them which serves only to render me odious to those excluded."[4] So he insisted that on shipboard he be close to all three young females, from whom he would not—and could not—in the end be separated.

☆   ☆   ☆

JOHN C. MILLER

From Slavery and the Declaration of Independence[†]

Thomas Jefferson was intimately associated with slavery from the cradle to the grave. His first memory was of being carried on a pillow by a slave; and a slave carpenter made the coffin in which he was buried at Monticello. The labor of black slaves made possible Jefferson's cultivation of the arts; the building of Monticello and the Virginia State Capitol, his principal architectural monuments; the acquisition of the books which made his library one of the largest private libraries in the United States (and which eventually formed the nucleus of the Library of Congress); the accumulation of choice wines and the fine food prepared by a French chef, both of which made dinner at the President's House a notable event in the lives of congressmen; and the leisure which he devoted to science, philosophy, and politics. Even Jefferson's salaries as Secretary of State, Vice-President and President were indirectly paid in large part by slaves: their labor provided the tobacco, cotton, and sugar, the export of which stimulated Northern shipping, manufacture, banking, and insurance and enabled the United States to make remittances for imported manufactured goods and to attract the foreign investment capital vital to the agricultural, industrial, and commercial development of the Republic. Next to land, slaves constituted the largest property interest in the country, far larger than manufacturing and shipping combined. Truly, one of the main pillars of the world of Thomas Jefferson was black slavery.

This pillar Jefferson was resolved to destroy. As he saw it, the eradication of slavery was to be the crowning achievement of the American Revolution; that revolution could not be considered complete, he insisted, until this ugly scar, a vestige of the colonial period, had been removed. Compared with many of his fellow patriots, Jefferson was a radical revolutionary: revolutions, he said, were not made with rose water, and the purpose of a revolution was not to dispense sweetness and light but to effect needed changes in the existing social, political, and economic structure. He never supposed that the American Revolution consisted merely of the severance of the political ties that united the colonies to Great Britain or that it was an effort to maintain liberties already enjoyed in full plenitude by Americans. Among other things, Jefferson proposed to destroy in Virginia the last vestiges of "artificial aristocracy" based upon wealth and family connections and to

---

4. Jefferson to James Maurice, September 16, 1789, *Papers*, Boyd, XV, 433.
† From *The Wolf by the Ears: Thomas Jefferson and Slavery* (New York: The Free Press, 1977), pp. 1–11. Copyright © 1991 by the Rector and Visitors of the University of Virginia and the Thomas Jefferson Memorial Foundation. Reprinted with permission of the University of Virginia Press. Numbered notes are Miller's.

bring to the fore the talents and virtues that lay submerged and fallow in the lower strata of society. Even though he was born into the aristocracy, Jefferson put his hope of a new order in "the plebeian interest." Without the abolition of slavery, Jefferson realized that the attainment of a society based upon freedom and equality of opportunity would forever elude the American people.

Although nineteen "Negars" had been brought to Virginia as early as 1619 by Dutch traders, the black population had increased slowly during the seventeenth century. By 1700, there were only between six thousand and ten thousand black slaves in the Old Dominion; but thereafter, partly as a result of the curtailment of the flow of white immigrants, most of whom came as indentured servants, and also because the Indians, despite the best efforts of the whites, failed to make satisfactory slaves, large numbers of Africans were imported to work the plantations of Tidewater Virginia and, later, of the Piedmont. By 1776, Virginia contained more than two hundred thousand blacks, over half the entire colored population of the United States.[1]

As a result, slaves were ubiquitous in the society in which Jefferson was reared and in which he came to his majority. Especially in the privileged circles of society in which Jefferson moved, it was difficult to find anyone who did not own slaves. His father was a slaveowner from whom Thomas inherited both land and slaves; all the Randolphs, to whom he was related through his mother, held slaves; and when he went to Williamsburg in 1760 to attend the College of William and Mary he took with him a personal slave, "Jupiter," whom he later made his coachman. Jefferson's wife's dowry consisted of 132 slaves and many thousands of acres of land. Like other Virginia patricians, he reckoned his wealth principally in slaves and land. By the time he wrote the Declaration of Independence he had become, by inheritance, purchase, and marriage, one of the principal slaveowners and one of the wealthiest men in Virginia.

Jefferson's perception of slavery was determined by several ambivalent circumstances: he was a planter-slaveowner, a Virginian whose strongest allegiance, when the test came, was to his state and section, and withal a man of the eighteenth century Enlightenment. This circumstance created in Jefferson's mind an ambiguity and a dissonance which he never succeeded in resolving to his own satisfaction. While Jefferson regarded slavery as a "hideous evil," the bane of American society, and wholly irreconcilable with his ideal of "republican virtue," he was never able wholly to cast aside the prejudices and the fears which he had absorbed from his surroundings toward people of color; he did not free himself from dependence upon slave labor; and, in the end, he made the expansion of slavery into the territories a constitutional right, and a *conditio sine qua non* of the South's adherence to the Union.

* * *

Without exception, the men of the Enlightenment condemned slavery as a vestige of barbarism, an offense against the moral law, and a flagrant violation of the rights of man derived from the Creator. It was agreed that all men received from Nature, by virtue of their common humanity, an absolute right to the fruit of their labor and to the freedom of their persons

1. See Elkins 1963, pp. 37–52, and E. S. Morgan 1975, pp. 295–331.

of which they could not lawfully be deprived. Where human rights were concerned, the Enlightenment studiously ignored skin coloration.

As a student at the College of William and Mary, Jefferson was introduced to Enlightenment ideas by his mentors: Dr. William Small, a professor at the college; Edmund Pendleton and George Wythe, two of the leading lawyers of the province; and Lord Francis Fauquier, the Royal Governor of Virginia. The direction given Jefferson's thinking by these men was reinforced by his wide reading in history, philosophy, and the classics; he found in Stoic philosophy and in Cicero and Seneca conclusive evidence that many Enlightenment ideas had pedigrees that could be traced to classical Greece and Rome. At a relatively early age (when he wrote the Declaration of Independence he was thirty-three) Jefferson became one of the principal exponents of the ideals and attitudes of the Enlightenment in the American colonies and subsequently in the new American Republic. But Jefferson was never content merely to expound ideas: he conceived of the United States as the proving ground where Enlightenment ideas were to demonstrate that they could serve as the basis for a rational and morally perfected political and social order.

Among those ideas, Jefferson always included the Enlightenment's uncompromising rejection of slavery. Even while asserting the rights of white colonists against the British government, he did not forget the rights of the slaves—a position which set him apart from most of his contemporaries. When he was elected to the Virginia House of Burgesses in 1769, one of his first acts was to attempt to make the manumission of slaves easier for owners. For half a century, manumission had been permitted only with the consent of the governor and council; Jefferson sought to give every slaveowner the right to free his slaves if he so desired.

Characteristically, Jefferson chose to work through others to effect this reform. One of the more revealing stories told of his boyhood is the account of how, when a pupil at a plantation school taught by the Reverend Mr. Douglas, Jefferson decided that some changes in the curriculum were needed. Instead of going directly to Mr. Douglas, young Thomas persuaded one of his fellow students to go in his place. For his temerity, the hapless accomplice was roundly rebuked by the clergyman-pedagogue while Jefferson himself remained undetected and unscathed. Jefferson, one of the great managers of men, began his career as a manager of children.

In 1769, his boyhood aversion to personal confrontations having hardened into a settled habit, he induced his cousin Richard Bland, a longtime member of the House of Burgesses, to introduce a bill facilitating manumission—Jefferson's role being confined to that of seconding the motion. Bland, a respected defender of colonial rights against Great Britain, found himself "treated with the grossest indecorum" and denounced as an enemy of the province. Because of his youth and inexperience (he was twenty-six years old) Jefferson escaped most of the censure so liberally bestowed upon Richard Bland.[2]

As a lawyer (he was admitted to the Virginia bar in 1769), Jefferson took several cases dealing with slavery. In 1770, he drew up without charge a brief in support of the claim of the grandson of a mulatto woman and a

2. See Davis 1970, p. 7; Hawke 1964, p. 54; Parton 1889, pp. 97–98; Robinson 1970, pp. 81–82; and Virginia Magazine 80, p. 146.

black slave who was suing for his freedom. Jefferson had a weak case; for while the law was specific in providing that the child of a white woman and a black slave father was to go free after serving until the age of thirty years as a slave, it made no exception in the case of the children or grandchildren of a mulatto woman. In contrast to Latin America, no mulatto class existed in Virginia or, indeed, in any British colony: a mulatto was a "black" or a "Negro" and, unless his or her mother were white, a slave for life. No one was free in colonial Virginia merely by virtue of the possession of white genes: to be valid they had to be derived specifically from the maternal side. The law declared that any person with one-eighth African "blood" was a mulatto; it was not possible to "pass" into the white community until all obvious physical traces of African ancestry had disappeared.[3]

In 1770, with the facts against his client, Jefferson had no choice but to try to move the case beyond the law of Virginia which, in these matters, was usually strictly interpreted. He did so by asserting that "under the law of nature, all men are born free, and every one comes into the world with a right to his own person, which includes the liberty of moving and using it at his own will." Unless this natural right to freedom were recognized, Jefferson declared, the status of the mulatto grandmother would be transmitted not merely to her grandchild but to her latest posterity.[4]

Among Jefferson's friends, the idea of the natural equality and freedom of man occasioned no sense of shock; in this particular, both Christians and Enlightenment rationalists agreed in holding that all men had been created free and equal. Edmund Pendleton, George Wythe (although he served as counsel for the defendant in this case), and George Mason did not take exception to the proposition boldly advanced by Jefferson. But as Jefferson was quickly given to understand, the idea of the natural equality and freedom of man was not to be applied to blacks or mulattoes in a Virginia courtroom. The judge dismissed the case not, however, because Jefferson had appealed to a higher law but because he had failed to prove that his client was the descendant of a free woman and was therefore entitled to freedom.

In 1770, Jefferson had not contended that the slaves held in Virginia had the right to instant, unqualified freedom because they had been born free. The law of Virginia described slaves as chattel property; as such, they could be bought, sold, mortgaged, seized for debt, and devised by will. Jefferson recognized that the emancipation of the slaves waited upon the voluntary act of their owners or upon the will of the majority as expressed in statute law. Until and unless either of these conditions was fulfilled, the legal status of slaves could not be changed—as Jefferson himself implicitly recognized when in 1769 he advertised for the return of a slave who had stolen a horse and run away.[5]

Abortive as this case of 1770 proved to be, it revealed Jefferson's propensity for relating human rights to the laws of nature. In the struggle for American freedom against Great Britain, Jefferson habitually rationalized American rights by reference to the laws of nature which, his English adversaries complained, always worked in favor of Americans—leaving the only possible conclusion that the Great Lawgiver himself must be an American.

3. See Fogel and Engerman 1 (1974), pp. 131–133, and Macleod 1974, p. 82.
4. See P. L. Ford 1, p. 380; Hawke 1964, pp. 53–54; and Malone 1948, pp. 121–122.
5. See Cotterill 1 (1926), pp. 90–92, and Brodie 1974, pp. 90–92.

In 1772, Jefferson was appointed by the court as counsel to a mulatto suing for freedom, an assignment which suggests that he was acquiring a reputation as a defender of the rights of mulattoes. But his client died before judgment could be rendered, and two years later Jefferson abandoned the practice of law in order to devote himself to the management of his estate and to the cause of American freedom. Only on one occasion thereafter did he briefly espouse the cause of mulattoes and of free blacks. The American Revolution, while it enhanced his determination to abolish slavery, marked the end of his efforts to advance the cause of black freedom without simultaneously providing for the removal of the blacks themselves from the territory of the United States.

Jefferson delivered his first attack in print upon slavery in 1774, when he published a pamphlet entitled A Summary View of the Rights of British America. Intended to serve as a policy guide to the Virginia House of Burgesses in its controversy with the British government, A Summary View took the radical ground that Americans owed no allegiance whatever to the British Parliament, a position not assumed by the Continental Congress until 1775. Although Jefferson's handiwork was rejected by the House of Burgesses, it helped create a favorable opinion of his literary ability and called attention to his advanced views in the matter of colonial rights. Had it not been for the publication of A Summary View, it is unlikely that Jefferson would have been designated in June 1776 to write the Declaration of Independence.

In the Summary View, Jefferson assailed slavery where it was most vulnerable: the traffic in human beings by which slaves were transported from Africa to the slave barracoons of the New World. Perhaps nowhere in the world were the rights of man by which the Enlightenment set inestimable store more flagrantly violated than on the Middle Passage between Africa and the western hemisphere. Since 1671, when the Royal African Company was founded with King Charles II and James, Duke of York, among the principal stockholders, British and American slave-traders had carried over a million black Africans across the Atlantic.

Yet Jefferson was not content merely to deplore this evil: he converted it into an indictment of the British government and, specifically, of King George III. Jefferson declared that the abolition of slavery was "the great object of desire in these colonies" and that the American people had been thwarted in this objective by the king, thereby proving the existence not only of a "deliberate, systematical plan of reducing us to slavery" but of an equally sinister plan of compelling Americans who asked to be free of the "detestable" institution of slavery to keep in servitude men, women, and children of another race.

Jefferson based this arraignment of the British monarch upon the fact that many colonial assemblies had imposed duties—in some instances virtually prohibitive—upon the importation of African slaves. Most of these acts of the colonial legislatures, especially those which seriously impeded the traffic in slaves, had been disallowed by the Royal Privy Council on the ground that they interfered with the free flow of "a considerable article of British commerce." On the strength of these abortive attempts by the colonial legislatures to tax the importation of slaves, Jefferson laid it down as an incontestable truth that the American people had set their hearts upon abolishing slavery and that they had been prevented from accomplishing that objective by the malice, greed, and inhumanity of George III.

In his draft of the Declaration of Independence, Jefferson amplified the charge that the King was responsible for the perpetuation of slavery and the slave trade. Among the twenty-seven crimes and misdemeanors of which the Declaration accused the British monarch, none was more important in Jefferson's opinion than George III's complicity in foisting slavery upon the American people. And he deliberately presented this charge as the concluding article of his indictment of George III, obviously intending that it should serve as the capstone of his catalogue of royal misdeeds. On the subject of slavery, Jefferson could not restrain his righteous indignation against his late sovereign. By negating the salutary laws against the slave trade enacted by the colonial assemblies, Jefferson declared, George III had "waged cruel war against human nature itself, violating the most sacred right of life and liberty in the persons of a distant people who never offended him, captivating and carrying them into slavery in another hemisphere, or to incur miserable death in their transportation thither"—and this crime against humanity was committed merely in order to enrich a few African corsairs by keeping open the markets "where Men should be bought and sold."

There was a compelling reason for Jefferson's efforts to fix the responsibility for the perpetuation of slavery upon the British monarch. Jefferson and other American patriots had repeatedly accused the British government of trying to reduce them to "slavery." If it could be shown that white Americans— the very citizenry who had taken up arms in defense of freedom—had, for their own profit, reduced hundreds of thousands of Africans to a real state of slavery, the appeal to a candid world might fall very flat indeed. Already, Dr. Samuel Johnson had, in fact, raised the embarrassing question: "How is it," he asked, "that we hear the loudest yelps for liberty from the drivers of Negroes?"[6] Therefore, by placing the burden of guilt wholly upon George III, Jefferson rhetorically relieved the American people of any culpability for the existence of an institution so utterly abhorrent, as he saw it, to their humanitarian instincts and to the ideals of the Enlightenment. If it could be made to appear that the slave trade and slavery itself had been forced upon a virtuous, virginal, and moral people who yearned to be free of this detestable institution, Jefferson would succeed in exalting his fellow countrymen into champions of freedom at the same time that he held up George III to the execration of his subjects and of the world.[7]

To Jefferson's mortification, the Continental Congress struck out this climactic passage from the Declaration of Independence, thereby putting Jefferson in the position of a prosecuting attorney who finds the culprit in the dock held not guilty on the main charge. Jefferson attributed the "mutilation" of his original draft (Congress made many more deletions, emendations, and additions) to the influence of Northern slavetraders who, having profited from the slave trade, did not wish to see it condemned and to the

---

6. In his *Observations Concerning the Distinction of Ranks in Society* (1771), John Millar, the Scottish philosopher and sociologist, remarked that "it offers a curious spectacle to observe, that the same people who talk in so high a strain of political liberty, and who consider the privilege of imposing their own taxes as one of the inalienable rights of mankind, should make no scruple of reducing a great proportion of the inhabitants into circumstances by which they are not only deprived of property, but almost of every right whatsoever." Jefferson was familiar with Millar's work. See Harris 1968, pp. 51–52.
7. See Brown and Brown 1964, p. 284.

"avarice" of some Southerners, especially South Carolinians and Georgians, whose demand for slaves remained unsatisfied. Even though John Adams considered the arraignment of the king on the charge of collusion with slave traders to be the best part of the Declaration, Congress was, however, well advised to eliminate it. More aware than was Jefferson—who was obviously carried away by his zeal for pillorying the king—of the dangers of propagandistic overkill, Congress wisely took the position that the monarch, already burdened by Jefferson with culpability for "murder," "piratical warfare," and inflicting "miserable death," could not be held accountable for all the evil extant in the British Empire.[8] Moreover, the inclusion of Jefferson's strictures on slavery and the slave trade would have committed the United States to the abolition of slavery once the tyrannical yoke of George III had been thrown off—a commitment few Southerners were willing to undertake at this time. Finally, in presenting facts to a candid world, Congress felt that these facts had to be historically verifiable. In the case of the laws enacted by the colonial assemblies levying duties upon the importation of African slaves adduced in A Summary View as irrefutable proof of Americans' abhorrence of slavery and their desire to rid themselves of the institution, the facts were clearly at variance with his postulate. These acts were designed to raise revenue, enhance the price of slaves, prevent the glutting of the slave market, and, especially in the case of Virginia, to keep the slave population within manageable bounds—everything, in short, except to prepare the way for the abolition of slavery. At least in this regard, Jefferson had obviously thought too well of his countrymen, especially those who had a financial stake in slavery and who were dependent upon it for their labor supply.[9]

Similarly, the Royal Privy Council, in disallowing the acts of colonial legislatures imposing high duties upon the importation of African slaves, was acting less out of solicitude for slavery itself than in consequence of the fact that the slave trade had become "big business" and was too powerful and too important to the British economy to be successfully challenged by the government. About two thousand British and American ships were regularly engaged in transporting forty to fifty thousand Africans annually to the western hemisphere; of these slave ships, over a hundred were based in Liverpool, the British seaport most heavily involved in this traffic. The slavetraders, allied with the mercantile, shipping, and manufacturing interests, constituted a powerful lobby in Parliament, and the British government was inclined to proceed upon the assumption that what was good for the slave trade was good for the empire.[1]

But Jefferson had not done with George III; indeed, he never tired of inveighing against the iniquities of his one-time sovereign. Ten years after writing the Declaration of Independence, Jefferson met George III face to

8. Even John Adams who, as Jefferson said, fought "fearlessly for every word" of the Declaration as written by Jefferson and who especially approved of holding George III responsible for the slave trade, privately felt that Jefferson had gone too far in his arraignment of the British monarch. In Adams's opinion, George III was not a born tyrant: "I always believed him to be deceived by his courtiers on both sides of the Atlantic and in his official capacity, only, cruel. . . . I thought the expression (as it came from Jefferson's pen) too passionate and too much like scolding, for so grave and solemn a document." See Lipscomb and Berg 15 (1903), p. 463 and the Virginia Magazine 31, p. 299.
9. See Virginia Magazine 80, pp. 146–150.
1. See Mullin 1972, pp. 130–132, and Schachner 1953, p. 134.

face in London. That brief encounter did not persuade Jefferson that he had done His Britannic Majesty an injustice: "the ulcerations in the narrow mind of that mulish being" indicated to Jefferson that the warmest feeling of the monarch's heart was his undying hatred of the United States and of the freedom for which it stood.

Under the firm conviction that there was nothing to which George III would not stoop to crush the American revolt, Jefferson, in his draft of the Declaration of Independence, sought to compound the numerous crimes of which the king already stood accused by charging him with attempting to foment a slave insurrection and thereby inflict the horrors of racial war upon Americans; which people were already exposed, by the express orders of the sovereign, to the incursions of merciless, bloodthirsty Indians in whose massacres and scalping he presumably took a vicarious delight.

In November 1775, Lord Dunmore, the Royal Governor of Virginia, issued from the British man-of-war on which he had taken refuge from the patriots a proclamation promising freedom to all slaves belonging to rebels who joined "His Majesty's Troops . . . for the more speedily reducing the Colony to a proper sense of their duty to His Majesty's Crown and dignity." On the strength of this promise of freedom, about a thousand slaves rallied to the British standard; some of them wore the emblem "Liberty to Slaves." But Dunmore had little force at his command and he and his black allies were easily routed by the Virginia militia, whereupon the governor and the British fleet left Virginia waters carrying with them the "property" of the patriots.[2]

Even though the slave uprising had been crushed, Jefferson used the event to blacken further the reputation of His Britannic Majesty. He pictured the king, from the security of Whitehall, engaged in "exciting these very people to rise up in arms among us, and to purchase that liberty of which *he* deprived them, by murdering the people upon whom he also intruded them; thus paying off former crimes committed against the *liberties* of one *people*, which crimes he urges them to commit against the *lives* of another." Here again Jefferson rehearsed the familiar litany: Americans wished to abolish slavery; they were prevented from doing so by the intervention of the Crown; and now the king was inciting *his* slaves to murder freedom-loving white Americans who, had they been free of royal control, would have abolished slavery of their own accord.[3]

Jefferson made Lord Dunmore's proclamation the final, damning proof that a conspiracy against American freedom existed at the highest levels of the British government. Only men bent upon establishing despotism, Jefferson argued, would seek to foment a racial, servile war. The Declaration of Independence, as revised by the Continental Congress, did not go that far: although the members adopted the view that the king himself was behind the effort to use black slaves to impose "slavery" upon white Americans, they did not see fit to mention in the Declaration that a slave insurrection had occurred in Virginia—and, indeed, *that* might have been difficult to explain to a candid world. Instead, the Declaration merely accuses the king of "exciting insurrections against us." In 1776, "insurrections" signified to the

---

2. See D. B. Davis 1975, pp. 73, 76, 80.
3. See Malone 1954, pp. 85–88.

American people the Loyalist uprising in North Carolina and, above all, Lord Dunmore's efforts to stir up racial war in Virginia.[4]

Thus, the Declaration of Independence, in sum, while it asserts the right of white Americans to rebel against attempts to reduce them to "slavery," denies inferentially, in the context of the events of 1775–1776, the right of black slaves to rebel against their masters in order to attain freedom. It is accounted a major crime against American freedom for the king to have incited an insurrection among a people whose experience of the tyranny of slavery was real and palpable against those whites who, in the words of Edmund Burke, merely "snuffed tyranny in every tainted breeze" and who rebelled even before they actually felt the lash.

JAY FLIEGELMAN

From Jefferson's Pauses[†]

Mostly silent in debate and preferring to express himself in writing, Jefferson was throughout his career an anxious orator. When he began to speak in public his voice, as eulogist William Wirt put it, "sank into his throat" and became "guttural and inarticulate."[1] John Adams recollected, "During the whole time I sat with him in Congress, I never heard him utter three sentences together."[2] Indeed, hoping that his Summary View of the Rights of British America would be read by the infinitely more talented orator, Patrick Henry, Jefferson became "conveniently ill" with dysentery on his way to the Virginia Convention in the summer of 1774.[3] Even in his youthful prepolitical career as a lawyer (which consisted mostly of delivering petitions relating to land titles to the same seven members of the governor's council), Jefferson was described as a formalist speaker "enumerating" arguments, quite in contrast to Henry, who "spoke powerfully from his heart."[4] And as president, more than a quarter century later, Jefferson not only delivered his first Inaugural address at such a whisper that most in attendance could not hear a word he said, but violated his predecessors' practice of addressing Congress in person by communicating his State of the Union messages in writing.[5] Throughout his two terms, "the early president known most for his democratic views, spoke the least to the public directly."[6]

But on June 28, 1776, as chairman of the drafting committee, Jefferson was expected to rise to the oratorical task of reading the text of the Declaration of Independence aloud to the assembled Continental Congress, a

---

4. See Hawke 1971, p. 160.
† From Declaring Independence: Jefferson, Natural Language, and the Culture of Performance. Copyright © 1993 by the Board and Trustees of the Leland Stanford Jr. University. All rights reserved. Used with the permission of Stanford University Press. Numbered notes are Fliegelman's.
1. William Wirt, Sketches of the Life and Character of Patrick Henry (Richmond, 1817), p. 23.
2. John Adams, Diary and Autobiography, ed. L. H. Butterfield, 4 vols. (New York, 1964), 3: 335. Adams speculates that Jefferson was put on the Committee on Style charged with drafting the Declaration in part because the famed orator "Mr Richard Henry Lee was not beloved by the most of his Colleagues from Virginia and Mr. Jefferson was sett up to rival and supplant him. This could be done only by the Pen, for Mr. Jefferson could stand no competition with him or any one else in Elocution and public debate." (Diary and Autobiography, 3:336.)
3. Garry Wills, Inventing America: Jefferson's Declaration of Independence (New York, 1978), p. 16.
4. Frank L. Dewey, Thomas Jefferson, Lawyer (Charlottesville, Va., 1986), p. 98.
5. Alf J. Mapp, Thomas Jefferson: A Strange Case of Mistaken Identity (New York, 1987), p. 397.
6. Jeffrey K. Tulis, The Rhetorical Presidency (Princeton, N. J., 1987), pp. 70–71.

body that would dramatically alter his draft in ways Jefferson would later bitterly term "mutilations."[7] Whether he actually read it, or once again succeeded in passing the burden of public performance onto someone else, is unrecorded. There nevertheless is compelling evidence that he thought deeply about how it should be read and heard. Though the fact has received virtually no attention since Julian Boyd first noted it in 1976, a part of Jefferson's still-surviving rough draft of the Declaration, on which the now-missing final reading copy was based, is marked with what appear to be diacritical accents. Boyd speculated that the marks were used to assist Jefferson in his reading of the Declaration. They were, he suggested, comparable to those advised by John Rice in his 1765 *Introduction to the Art of Reading with Energy and Propriety*, one of several books Jefferson owned on the subject of effective public speaking, and to the accents Jefferson used to scan poetic meter in his essay "Thoughts on Prosody" (1786).[8]

Indeed, a unique proof copy of John Dunlap's official broadside printing of the Declaration, set hastily from Jefferson's original reading copy, which he had corrected with Congress's extensive revisions and deletions, is full of seemingly inexplicable quotation marks in the opening two paragraphs. Boyd ingeniously concluded that these quotation marks can only be explained as a printer's misreading of Jefferson's reading marks, marks that also appear in a surviving manuscript of the second Inaugural.[9]

An examination of both the one "marked" section of the rough draft of the Declaration and the relevant section of the second Inaugural manuscript clearly shows, however, that the marks Boyd understood to indicate emphasis make no sense as such. For example, in the marked section of the Declaration, accents appear to fall on the last syllables of "oppressions," "injuries," and "compass," syllables that would in no reasonable reading ever be accented. A closer look indicates that in clear contrast to the metrical accents in "Thoughts on Prosody," the marks in the printed and manuscript Declaration fall less on particular syllables of words than immediately before and immediately after words. All this suggests that the marks indicate not emphases but pauses.

In discussing the beauties of Homer's Greek in his "Thoughts on Prosody," Jefferson printed a verse passage from the *Iliad* as if it were prose and argued that the rhythms of the verse remain perfectly audible to the reader because Homer had "studied the human ear."

> He has discovered that in any rhythmical composition the ear is pleased to find at certain regular intervals a pause where it may rest, by which it may divide the composition into parts, as a piece of music is divided into bars. He contrives to mark this division by a pause in the sense or at least by an emphatical word which may force the pause so that the ear may feel the regular return of the pause. The interval

7. John H. Hazelton, *The Declaration of Independence and Its History* (New York, 1906), p. 178.
8. Julian Boyd, "The Declaration of Independence: The Mystery of the Lost Original," *Pennsylvania Magazine of History and Biography*, 100 (1976): 458. On Jefferson's early ownership of Rice's *Art of Reading*, see Millicent Sowerby, *Catalogue of the Library of Thomas Jefferson*, 5 vols. (Charlottesville, Va., 1983), 1: 51. Jefferson assembled several libraries during his lifetime. Using the physical evidence of the surviving books from those libraries, as well as Jefferson's manuscript catalogues, invoices, and references in his letters, especially those recommending reading to friends, Sowerby's heavily annotated work tries to establish when Jefferson was in possession of a particular book and what edition he possessed.
9. Boyd, "Declaration," p. 458.

between these regular pauses constitutes a verse. . . . A well-organized ear makes the pause regularly whether it be printed as verse or as prose.[1]

The locations of the marks on the rough draft of the Declaration as well as the locations of the "quotation marks" on the proof copy of the Dunlap broadside represent not breath or punctuational pauses but precisely what Jefferson discusses: rhythmical pauses of emphatical stress that divide the piece into units comparable to musical bars or poetic lines. These marks are identical to ones suggested by the influential Irish rhetorician Thomas Sheridan in his *Lectures on the Art of Reading* (1775). Sheridan uses a "small inclined line, thus /," to indicate a short "pause marking an incomplete sense" and a double line, //, for a pause "double the time of the former." Thus, in Sheridan's example: "thy kingdom / come // thy will / be done//."[2]

Below I have printed the one marked passage from the rough draft of the Declaration with single or short pauses (' in the manuscript) indicated by diagonal lines and double or full pauses (" in the manuscript) indicated by new lines. The passage can now be read as Jefferson rhythmically set it forth:

in every stage / of these oppressions
we have petitioned for redress / in the most humble terms;
our repeated petitions / have been answered only by repeated injuries.
a prince whose character is thus marked / by every act which may define
   a tyrant,
is unfit to be the ruler / of a free people who mean to be free.
future ages will scarce believe / that the hardiness of one man
adventured within the short compass / of twelve years to build
a foundation / so broad and undisguised,
for tyranny

Because the Dunlap "quotation" marks do not distinguish between single and double pauses, here is the opening paragraph of the broadside Declaration with each pause indicated by a new line:

When in the Course of human Events, it becomes necessary for one
   People
to dissolve the Political Bands which have connected them with another
and to assume among the Powers of the Earth, the separate and equal
   Station
to which the Laws of nature and of nature's God entitle them,
a decent Respect to the Opinions of Mankind requires
that they should declare the causes which impel them to the Separation.

In Sheridan's earlier, more theoretical work, *Lectures on Elocution* (1762), a book Jefferson purchased in the mid 1760's as part of his preparation for a career in law, the author argued that because of the false assumption that pauses correlate exclusively and merely with punctuation "there is no article

1. Thomas Jefferson, "Thoughts on Prosody," in *The Complete Jefferson*, ed. Saul Padover (New York, 1943), p. 846.
2. Thomas Sheridan, *The Art of Reading; First Part: Containing The Art of Reading Prose* (London, 1765), pp. 181, 210.

in reading more difficult, than that of observing a due proportion of stops."[3] The "truth is that the modern art of punctuation was not taken from the art of speaking." Instead, punctuation was and is "in a great measure regulated by the rules of grammar; that is, certain parts of speech are kept together, and others divided by stops."[4]

In contrast to the formalism of punctuation, rhetorical pauses indicate the "matter of the discourse and the disposition of the mind of the speaker"— and thus express both text and speaker. They mark sense, create rhythm, are accompanied by infinitely various changes in tone that indicate "the kind of pause it is," and thereby "inform the mind what to expect from them," such as whether "the sense is still to be continued in the same sentence or not." They are also a mode of direct emphasis, and thus are part of a larger cultural code. If a proposition or sentiment is preceded "by a longer pause than usual," Sheridan argued, it will "rouze attention and give more weight when delivered."[5] Indeed, Edmund Randolph would say of Patrick Henry that "his pauses, which for their length might sometimes be feared to dispel the attention, riveted it the more by raising the expectation."[6] But if pauses are too numerous, or too much "liberty" is taken in elongating them, Sheridan concluded, they "disgust."[7] The entire second half of Sheridan's *Art of Reading* is printed with pause marks and accentual stresses to indicate the precise phrasing of every sentence in the text.

Finally, Jefferson's pauses make a crucial link between oratory and music, which according to Sheridan is "also distributed by phrase, demi-phrase and measures." Such a link clearly interested Jefferson, who not only was interested in how Homer rhythmically measured his language "as a piece of music is divided into bars," but who in a 1773 letter to a law student recommended John Mason's *Essay on the Power and Harmony of Prosaic Numbers*, a volume that described at length how prose, no less than poetry, could profit from being written "in measured Cadences." In addition, Jefferson, who devoted (in his words) "no less than *three hours* a day" to the practice of the violin (an instrument he brought with him to the Continental Congress), owned a number of books on musical theory that explicitly addressed the connections between oratory and music.[8]

One such volume, Francesco Geminiani's *The Art of Playing the Violin* (1751), not only defined "the perfect tone of the violin" as the one that rivals

---

3. Thomas Sheridan, *A Course of Lectures on Elocution* (1762; Menston, York., 1968), p. 79. On Jefferson's purchase of Sheridan, see Marie Kimball, *Jefferson: The Road to Glory, 1743–1776* (New York, 1943), p. 83.
4. Sheridan, *Lectures on Elocution*, pp. 79–80.
5. Ibid., p. 77.
6. Randolph is quoted in Wills, *Inventing America*, p. 9.
7. Sheridan, *Lectures on Elocution*, p. 77.
8. The letter recommending Mason's volume is reproduced in Morris L. Cohen, "Thomas Jefferson Recommends a Course of Law Study," *University of Pennsylvania Law Review* 119 (1971): 823–844. John Mason, *Essay on the Power and Harmony of Prosaic Numbers* (1749; Menston, York., 1967), p. 2. Jefferson is quoted in Henry S. Randall, *The Life of Thomas Jefferson*, 3 vols. (Philadelphia, 1865) 1: 131. The works on musical theory that appear in Jefferson's 1783 book catalogue are conveniently listed in Helen Cripe, *Thomas Jefferson and Music* (Charlottesville, Va., 1974), p. 97. She describes his traveling violin on pp. 14–15. Several months before his 1761 legal arguments against the Writs of Assistance set the stage for future challenges to British authority, the incendiary lawyer James Otis published *The Rudiments of Latin Prosody with . . . the Principles of Harmony in Poetic and Prosaic Composition* (Boston, 1760). Drawing heavily on "Mason on Pronunciation," Otis's first published work used the subject of prosody—pronunciation informed by a knowledge of the "spirit, accent, and qualities of words"—to address what was a social and political question as much as a literary one: how best to "convey the passions of the speaker into the breasts of the audience" (pp. 2, 66).

"the most perfect human Voice," but insisted that "all good music should be composed in imitation of a Discourse," with forte and pianissimo producing "the same Effects that an Orator does by raising and falling his Voice." Or, as John Holden put it in his *Essay Towards a Rational System of Music* (1770), another of the half dozen books on music theory listed in the earliest surviving catalogue of Jefferson's library, "the particular manners and modulations of the voice," which naturally obey "the custom of a particular country," and which "accompany the emotions . . . of common speech," are "the subject given to music." Irresistibly leading the listener "to distribute a tune into proper measure," music is the inflected and infinitely expressive speech and voice of a "particular country."[9]

Playing an instrument, like speaking, involved the expression of private feelings, yet at the same time demanded conformity to the social and musical etiquette of measured regularity and an articulation of the character and conventions of "common speech." Eighteenth-century public speaking, that is, involved a drama of competing understandings of orality. In one view orality was "an inner voice of emotion" and an expression of subjectivity. In another it was "public-oriented oratorical communication," a mode of expression in which national values and a common sensibility were to be articulated and reinforced or (if romanticized as preliterate) recovered.[1] Jefferson addressed such conflicting obligations toward self-expression and self-effacement by insisting that the document he authored constituted not an expression of his mind but "an expression of the American mind" and "the common sense of the subject."[2]

Let us now return to John Rice's *Art of Reading*, the book that served Jefferson as an early guide to the mechanics and character of public speaking, for another perspective on the significance of the Declaration's marks. In his long section on pauses (which along with cadence, tone, and gesture are treated as "natural" modes of emphasis), Rice argues, following his mentor Abbé Batteux, that their primary function is to allow

> the Objects of a Discourse . . . to be all represented distinct and without Confusion . . . separated by some Kind of Interval. Let us consider them as they are found in Nature, or in a Picture; not one but has its Line of Circumscription, which bounds it and separates it from every other Object . . . in the most exact and regular Manner. . . . Like a Painter, it draws its Strokes one after another, whence they must necessarily be separated from one another by some Kind of Space or Interval.[3]

Like architectural columns or the geometrical grid Jefferson would later impose on the Western territories, the pauses (whether heard by an auditor or by "the well-organized ear" of the silent reader) are a mode of framing, of dividing a discourse into units that can be engaged and absorbed. In *Elements of Criticism*, a book Jefferson enthusiastically recommended to

9. Francesco Geminiani, *The Art of Playing the Violin*, ed. David Boyden (1751; Oxford, n. d.), p. v. Published in 1769 in Boston, Geminiani's volume was the first book on the subject printed in America; John Holden, *Essay Towards a Rational System of Music* (London, 1770), p. 35.
1. John Bender and David E. Wellbery, "Rhetoricality," in Bender and Wellberry, eds., *The Ends of Rhetoric* (Stanford, Calif., 1990) p. 21.
2. Jefferson to Henry Lee, May 8, 1825, in Andrew A. Lipscomb and Albert E. Bergh, eds., *The Writings of Thomas Jefferson*, 20 vols. (Washington, D.C., 1903–1904), 16: 118.
3. John Rice, *An Introduction to the Art of Reading* (1765; Menston, York., 1969), pp. 236–37.

his nephew Robert Skipwith in 1771, the Scottish aesthetician, lawyer, and historian, Lord Kames, insisted that because "the eye is the best avenue to the heart," the successful poet must represent "every thing as passing before our sight; and from readers and hearers transform us . . . into spectators." In a related fashion, Thomas Paine declares in the first of his *Crisis Papers*, written in December of 1776, that he will "in language as plain as A, B, C, hold up truth to your eyes."[4] Because the visual is associated in the human mind with reality, and the will and passions operate largely in response to images, Kames argued, whatever serves to enhance the visual or material character of a spoken text, whatever transforms a text into a drama that one "beholds," both strengthens the illusion of an immediate engagement with truth and more effectively influences future behavior. By dividing a spoken text into what Rice called "multiple objects" of a discourse circumscribed and differentiated by painterly lines, by seeming to confer on the spoken text the palpable dramatic presence of the orator, Jefferson's pauses turn the text itself into units of self-evidence: we [be]hold these truths to be self-evident.

Jefferson's pause marks also suggest the degree to which music, which he called in 1778 "the favorite passion of my soul," was simultaneously an expression of personal sentiments and a mechanistic science.[5] A notational language based on precise mathematical relations, music was spirit and passion rooted not in transcendental feeling but in a materialist base, the actualization of fixed tonal relations. Thus, inscribing pauses in the Declaration that were like musical measures also manifested Jefferson's preoccupation with accounting, scientific measurement, and a lifetime habit of dividing virtually everything into mathematical units. For Jefferson, proportionality (as in his 1779 draft bill for "proportioning crimes and punishments") was a moral concept. Even in advising a new law student in 1773 on a course of reading, Jefferson divided the reading day into five distinct intervals, with different subjects appropriate to different times ("From Dark to Bed-time, Belles lettres, Criticism, Rhetoric, Oratory"), and with specific books given to be read in a specific order.[6]

While at the second Continental Congress, Jefferson purchased a thermometer to take and record the daily temperature, for in his view the precise recording of information not only permitted the past to be compared with the present but allowed patterns in nature and human nature to be seen and understood in a fashion that held out the seductive possibility of predictive value for the future. The keeping of records extended to the private sphere as well. For example, Jefferson recorded his Philadelphia purchases on the blank leaves of his *Timothy Telescope's Almanack for 1776*. On the page that records his accounts from June 20 to July 6, however, the anxious period of his writing and presenting the Declaration, Jefferson forgot that June has 30 rather than 31 days. He left out June 29 and entered purchases on a nonexistent June 31, making clear that the "scientific" record was always subject to the psychological preoccupation of the scientist.

4. Henry Home, Lord Kames, *Elements of Criticism* (1762; New York, 1854), p. 404; Jefferson to Skipwith, *PTJ* 1: 79; Thomas Paine, *The Thomas Paine Reader*, ed. Michael Foot and Isaac Kramnick (New York, 1987), p. 123.
5. Jefferson to (name missing in original letter), June 28, 1778, in Eleanor D. Berman, *Thomas Jefferson Among the Arts* (New York, 1947), p. 172.
6. Morris L. Cohen, "Thomas Jefferson Recommends," p. 824.

Though, like many, he was, in his word, "charmed" by the new instrument of the pianoforte, with its full stroke-responsive capacity to express and interpret human emotions (he ordered a piano for his wife Martha in 1771), Jefferson's interest in music had as much to do with measure as with expression. As minister to Paris in the mid 1780's, Jefferson improved Renaudin's recent invention of a new mechanical metronome, further fixing the precise numerical relations between pendulum swings and vibrations for largo, adagio, and so on.[7] If playing, like public speaking, involved an expression of character and personal feelings, in addition to the presentation of the character and arguments of a composition, the stress on regularity in music and speech suggested a complementary impulse to contain, restrain, and order that expression.

Discussing the difficulty of reading poetry out loud in his "Thoughts on Prosody," Jefferson concluded that "no two persons will accent the same passage alike. No person but a real adept would accent it twice alike." Even when cast in regular meters, poetic texts are fluid, and reading is an art not a science. "I suppose that in those passages of Shakespeare, for example, no man but Garrick ever drew their full tone out of them, if I may borrow an expression from music." Tone, for Jefferson, was both a feature of the speaker's voice and a feature of the printed text that sounded "an author's sentiments or revealed his character." Jefferson's mention of Garrick, the premier actor of the age, also suggests a new standard of professional theatrical performance by which anxious public speakers were to be judged by a public given a new franchise to be critical. Jefferson's defensive remark about his ability to accent poetry so as to elicit its full tone—"Let those who are disposed to criticise . . . try a few experiments themselves"—suggests his sensitivity to criticism. The mention of Garrick also extends to public speaking the theatrical problem of whether acting should involve the artful representation of feelings or the "natural" expression of those immediately felt. As we shall see, this was a major source of an oratorical anxiety shared by many more than Jefferson.[8]

When John Dunlap, the Declaration's printer, realized his error and removed the misread quotation marks that survive in the proof copy from the rest of the broadside's print run, the words in the opening paragraphs were not respaced, thereby leaving an awkward, unbalanced appearance. Thus, even after they were eliminated the markers of the Declaration's fundamentally oral character left their trace presence in the deformation of the printed text. No subsequent printed transcription of Jefferson's original version of the Declaration—from the one Jefferson provided in his own *Autobiography* to the one in the Jefferson *Papers* to those available in textbooks and literary anthologies—reproduces those marks. But as part of the original text of the Declaration and as unique registers of the self-consciousness and protocols of public speaking that defined the conditions of its verbal production, those accents are crucial to its meaning.

In opposition to the spoken Declaration, whose speaker illuminated, elicited, and partially created its meaning in the context of a larger social interaction, the printed Declaration, experienced as it is today in the indi-

7. Cripe, *Jefferson and Music*, p. 69.
8. *The Complete Jefferson*, p. 846.

vidualistic context of a silent reading largely untuned to the performative dimension of the text, is radically cut off from its original rhetorical context. It appears fixed in its visual field, and by the mystique of print is made to seem permanent and immutable, an analogue to what it calls the "perpetual" league sought by a people "fixed" in immutable principles of freedom. Its visual self-evidence is total—independent of a complex interpretive performance wherein a speaker's skill and sincerity are judged by a critical audience.

This separation of the printed document from its context of rhetorical performance has helped enable the cultural appropriation of the document as a primary text in America's civic religion. Though the famous painting by John Trumbull shows the Declaration's presentation to John Hancock, then president of Congress, the moment that has become culturally appropriated is the signatory moment (an event delayed until August, in part to avoid accountability for treason), in which the 56 members of the second Continental Congress are transformed into "the signers." That moment suggests authorization, consensus, and, by falsely equating the Declaration to formal legislation, legality and permanence.

In what probably is an early 1770's entry in his commonplace book, Jefferson, seeking to disprove the proposition that "Christianity is part of the Common Law," succeeded in tracing the absorption of ecclesiastical law into English common law (with what he saw as its heinous consequences) to a seventeenth-century English mistranslation of a French treatise on Anglo-Norman law. The phrase "en ancien scripture," he argued, had been falsely rendered as "holy Scripture" rather than laws in "ancient writing."[9] Once in print, the error was perpetuated by dozens of subsequent treatises, all relying on the translator's original codification. The close interplay between "holy Scripture" and "ancient writing" would, of course, come to characterize the status of the printed Declaration itself and speak to the dangers of the independent historical status and agency of print.

By viewing the Declaration as a text meant to be read silently rather than to be heard as performance we have lost sight of crucial mid-eighteenth-century assumptions about speakers and personal expression, about rhetoric and the art of reading (a phrase that, as in John Rice's title, still had the primary sense of reading aloud), assumptions necessary to a full understanding of Revolutionary American culture. Recovering those assumptions allows us to see the rhetoric of the Revolution as participating not only in a political revolution but in a revolution in the conceptualization of language, a revolution that sought to replace artificial language with natural language and to make writing over in the image of speaking. Once a decorous, rule-governed, and class-specific behavior that articulated the public virtues of civic humanism—the honor of the office and the public good—public speaking became reconceptualized in the mid eighteenth century as an occasion for the public revelation of a private self. Such a private self would then be judged by private rather than public virtues: prudence, temperance, self-control, honesty, and, most problematically, sincerity.[1] American independence

9. Thomas Jefferson, *The Commonplace Book*, ed. Gilbert Chinard (Baltimore, 1926), p. 351.
1. For an intellectual and cultural history of sincerity with particular reference to changing notions of personal identity, see Lionel Trilling, *Sincerity and Authenticity* (Cambridge, 1970). On sincerity in eighteenth-century English letters, see Leon Guilhamet, *The Sincere Ideal: Studies on Sincerity in Eighteenth-Century English Literature* (Montreal, 1974).

occurred at a historical moment when the speaking voice was seen as a register of the speaker's subjectivity in ways that required a new set of rhetorical prescriptions and expectations in order to regulate the vagaries of that subjectivity. The narrative of America's "declaring independence" has hitherto emphasized the drama of the second term at the expense of the drama of the first, the drama suggested by the oratorical stresses felt as well as marked by Jefferson.

* * *

ANDREW BURSTEIN

From Jefferson and the Familiar Letter†

Despite the widely held view that Thomas Jefferson was a hard man to know intimately, it is possible to probe his thoughts by understanding the nature of self-expression in mid-eighteenth-century familiar letters and the particular influences Jefferson received through his early exposure to, and long fondness for, classical learning. Familiar letter-writing was a lifeline for Jefferson, a means of expression that was, if filled with anxiety, emotionally satisfying and, for us, ultimately revealing.

The world in which Jefferson reached maturity could not sustain reliable communications across distances. People like Jefferson and John Adams, whose aspirations extended beyond what local society could provide, ached to become acquainted with like-minded people for intellectual male companionship. Noted a young John Adams: "We are seldom so happy, as to find Company much inclined to Speculation, and as some of us, can find no Company at all, the only Method left, is that of Correspondences." He maintained that letters had "all the Advantages of Conversation, with the Additional ones of searching deeper into subjects."[1] The pursuit of knowledge required careful attention and frequent stimulation, whether one was training as a young lawyer in Massachusetts or Virginia.

By the outbreak of the American Revolution, letter-writing had become many things: a political necessity for those who wished to achieve united action, a social form for elites seeking to maintain and expand valuable connections, and a personal form to carry news to friends and loved ones to announce births, marriages, deaths, journeys, and changes of heart. Letters, of course, framed Jefferson's day and affected his state of mind. Throughout the years, he yearned for a regular and reliable postal service and had reason to despair during much of his public life over a lack of security in the mail.

To clear up confusion arising from undelivered letters, regular correspondents were careful to acknowledge letters received and sometimes reiterated their most recent letter before proceeding. The manner in which

---

† From *Journal of the Early Republic* 14 (1994): 195–220. Reprinted with permission of the University of Pennsylvania Press. Numbered notes are Burstein's.
1. Adams to Robert Treat Paine, Dec. 6, 1759, cited in Richard D. Brown, *Knowledge is Power: The Diffusion of Information in Early America, 1700–1865* (New York 1989), 90. Brown notes that in his twenties the yet unheralded Adams, of moderate means, sought a genteel identity through conversational prowess, that he might make a favorable impression on more cosmopolitan professionals, the elders of the community. Establishing "quasi-fraternal networks" through letters stimulated personal growth and political advancement.

Jefferson and his family communicated in 1792–1793, when they could not find any trustworthy acquaintance setting off on a journey to deliver messages, is instructive. He began a letter to his daughter Martha from Philadelphia on the last day of 1792:

> I received three days ago Mr. Randolph's [Thomas Mann Randolph, Martha's husband] letter of the 14th. from Richmond. . . . I apprehend from an expression in his letter that some of mine may have miscarried. I have never failed to write every Thursday or Friday. Percieving [sic] by the Richmond paper that the Western post now leaves that place on Monday, I change my day of writing also to Sunday or Monday.

Two weeks later he advised her, "Mr. Randolph's letter of December 20, from Richmond is the only one to come to hand from him or you since your's from Bizarre of two months ago." Waiting just two days after this, Martha replied, "With infinite pleasure I date once more from Monticello tho for the third time since my return. But from the negligence of the servant that carried the letters once and the great hurry of the post another time they never got farther than Charlottesville." In the same letter she referred to "4 or 5 other Letters of yours which had been detained by some accident." Finally, she noted that Jefferson's nephew, Peter Carr, had written from Richmond. To all this Jefferson replied that he had received Martha's of January 16 on January 24 but that he had not received Carr's at all. Exhausted, he wrote to his daughter on February 11, "The hour of the Post is come and a throng of business allows me only to inform you we are well. . . ."[2]

Sensitive contents required special arrangements. In 1764, exchanging confidences with his college chum John Page of Rosewell, Jefferson proposed, "We must fall on some scheme of communicating our thoughts to each other, which shall be totally unintelligible to every one but to ourselves. I will send you some of these days Shelton's Tachygraphical Alphabet, and directions." This would not have seemed excessive to Page, for the same letter had begun:

> I received your letter of Wednesday the 18th instant; in that, of this day, you mention one which you wrote last Friday, and sent by the Secretary's boy; but I have neither seen nor heard of such a one. God send, mine of Jan. 19 to you may not have shared the same fate; for, by your letter, I am uncertain whether you have received it or not. . . . My letter of Jan. 19, may have been opened, and the person who did it may have been further incited by curiosity. . . . [3]

From the Continental Congress a decade later, Jefferson demonstrated a charming sense of irony as he reflected on the ways of the post. "I have set apart nearly one day in every week since I came here to write letters," he wrote Page. "Notwithstanding this I never had received a scrip of a pen from any mortal breathing. I should have excepted two lines from Mr. Pendleton to desire me to buy him 24 lb. of wire from which I concluded he was alive." In

2. Jefferson to Martha Randolph, Dec. 31, 1792, Jan. 14, 26, Feb. 11, 1793, Martha Randolph to Jefferson, Jan. 16, 1793, in *The Family Letters of Thomas Jefferson*, ed. Edwin Morris Betts and James Adam Bear, Jr. (Charlottesville 1966), 108–111.
3. Jefferson to Page, Jan. 23, 1764, in *The Papers of Thomas Jefferson*, ed. Julian P. Boyd, Lyman H. Butterfield, *et al.* (25 vols., Princeton 1950–1992), I, 14–15. Shelton's method of "short and swift writing," Boyd notes, was published in London in 1646.

1777 when war had intensified, he queried John Adams from Virginia about postal regulations earlier passed by Congress that required riders "to travel night and day, and to go their several stages three times a week. The speedy and frequent communication of intelligence is really of great consequence. . . . Our people merely for want of intelligence which they may rely on are becoming lethargick and insensible of the state they are in." Adams replied that a Committee on the Post office, too, had found, "a thousand difficulties. . . . It is not easy to get faithfull [sic] riders, to go oftener."[4]

During Jefferson's first week as governor of Virginia in 1779, when the British or their sympathizers might have intercepted mail, he wrote from Williamsburg to the Virginia delegation in Philadelphia, "I put no name to this letter, because letters have miscarried, and if it goes safely you know the hand." Well after independence had been won, Jefferson remained acutely aware of the problem. When he and James Madison corresponded on political matters, they wrote in cipher or else in expectation of interception. Partisan politics made it all too tempting for the unprincipled to violate the privacy of communications. Jefferson found the same drawbacks to carefree writing during his five years in France as the American minister. To Richard Henry Lee he cautioned that while letters came "most speedily by the French packet," they were "read indeed if not confided to the care of a passenger; but that is an evil they incur in whatever way they come."[5] Whenever possible, he would travel to meet in person with allies or rely on personal messengers, rather than entrust sensitive or coded correspondence to the post office.

Eighteenth-century Americans were surrounded by news of death and disease, and letters quite often contained word of someone's passing or ill health. Constant breaks in mail delivery resulted in tremendous anticipation of follow-up news and anxiety over what that news would be. Philip Fithian's Virginia diary mourned the passing of a young woman of his recent acquaintance:

> For soon after her return to Town the disorder fixed, & in a few Months destroy'd a wise, useful, religious Girl—Her death surely was untimely, since she took with her all her virtues, which, with great pleasure & Sincerity She used to diffuse among her giddy Equals!—I am at a Loss to express my feeling for the Death of a young Lady, with whom I had only a short, yet a beneficial Intimacy. . . . We commenced a Litterary [sic] Correspondence, of which I only say that She always express'd herself with so much Truth, Ease, & Humour as to make me read her Letters with eagerness and satisfaction. . . . [6]

While letter-writing was instrumental in maintaining political ties among the American revolutionaries who banded together to form committees of correspondence, the best understood and most personal impact of letters in everyone's life issued from news of loved ones. During the aforementioned exchange of letters between Jefferson and his daughter Martha, the most conspicuous theme was Jefferson's concern for the health of Anne, his

4. Jefferson to Page, Oct. 31, 1775, Jefferson to Adams, May 16, 1777, Adams to Jefferson, May 26, 1777, *ibid.*, 251, II, 19, 21.
5. Jefferson to William Fleming, June 8, 1779, Madison to Jefferson, Oct. 17, 1784, Jefferson to Richard Henry Lee, Feb. 7, 1785, *ibid.*, 289, VII, 444–452, 644.
6. Hunter Dickinson Farish, ed., *Journal and Letters of Philip Vickers Fithian, 1773–1774: A Plantation Tutor of the Old Dominion* (1943; rep., Williamsburg 1957), journal entry of Aug. 17, 1774.

first grandchild, not quite two years old. He fretted on October 26 that "having not received a letter by yesterday's post, and that of the former week from Mr. Randolph having announced dear Anne's indisposition, I am under much anxiety." On December 6 he begged Martha not to "destroy the powers of [Anne's] stomach with medicine." Finally, on the last day of 1792 he exulted, "I received [Mr. Randolph's letter] with great joy as it informed me of the re-establishment of dear Anne's health."[7]

A more extreme example of this recurrent, anxiety-producing condition is the manner in which Jefferson learned of the illness and subsequent death of his daughter Lucy Elizabeth (tragically, it was as a result of Lucy's birth two years earlier that he had lost his wife). Jefferson, in Paris since August 1784, first received word of the situation on January 26, 1785, from the recently returned Marquis de Lafayette, who bore a September 16 letter from Francis Eppes, announcing that the child had fallen ill with whooping cough. Lafayette, however, was also carrying a November 20 letter from Jefferson's friend, Richmond doctor James Currie, who related the final outcome of the disease. "I was called too late to do any thing but procrastinate the settled fate of the poor Innocent," Currie lamented. On February 5, Jefferson wrote Eppes that "it is in vain to describe the situation of my mind." Having waited so long for news, the saddened father went on to advise that Eppes only send mail by the "French packet," with instructions how to route it through a Mr. Jamieson in New York. Fearing only European postmasters' over eager eyes, Jefferson added, "Should there at any time be anything which ought not to be read by any other, it will be necessary to desire Mr. Jamieson to confide it to some passenger who will put it into my own hands." Finally, on May 6, 1785, Jefferson received Eppes's letter of October 14 of the previous year, lamenting that Lucy had suffered a painful death sometime earlier.[8] Obviously, then, the effect of letters was great not only for the palpable friendship and affection that might be expressed within, but for the weight of gloomy news that could be expected as well.

Familiar letter-writing already had a considerable history by this time, and it is essential to understand how Jefferson and his intimates actively applied its inherited conventions. Rhetoric and the epistolary form owe their origin to Cicero, Quintilian, Seneca, and Pliny, whose works Jefferson owned in Latin and in translation and repeatedly turned to throughout his life. In Notes on Virginia, he wrote, "The learning of Greek and Latin, I am told, is going into disuse in Europe. I know not what their manners and occupations may call for: but it would be very ill-judged in us to follow their example in this instance."[9] Enlightenment intellects on both sides of the Atlantic consciously modeled their efforts after accomplished classical writers who had published their uncensored (if sometimes carefully self-edited) thought—moral and philosophical exposition disguised, as it were, in familiar correspondence.

For Jefferson, the foremost authority was Cicero, who linked masculine virtue, self-control, self-improvement, and the dignified expression of

---

7. Jefferson to Martha Jefferson Randolph, Oct. 26, Dec. 6, Dec. 31, 1792, in Betts and Bear, eds., Family Letters, 105, 107, 108.
8. Francis Eppes to Jefferson, Oct. 14, 1784, James Currie to Jefferson, Nov. 20, 1784, Jefferson to Eppes, Feb. 5, 1785, in Boyd, Butterfield, et al., eds., Papers of Jefferson, VII, 441–442, 538–539, 635–636. Lucy's guardian during Jefferson's absence, Eppes was the husband of Elizabeth Wayles Eppes, half-sister of the late Martha Wayles Jefferson. They lived in Chesterfield County, Virginia.
9. Thomas Jefferson, Notes on the State of Virginia, ed. William Peden (Chapel Hill 1954), 147.

character through epistolary eloquence.[1] After a youth devoted to study of the classics, Jefferson claimed to have reread entirely Cicero's many volumes of letters during his retirement at Monticello. Writing John Adams, Jefferson described Cicero as "able," "learned," and "honest," the "first master" of style.[2]

In the *Epistolae ad Atticum*, Cicero wrote his beloved friend Atticus through times of personal and political trial. "Who can prefer speaking to writing?" he asked. "How much more did I learn from your letters, than from [the letter-bearer's] conversation . . . ?" Going into exile, Cicero offered a profound illustration of how expressive words can enrich friendship and support one's public reputation at the same time. "All I beg of you is, that as you have ever loved me personally, you will continue in the same affections," he implored Atticus. "I am still the same man. My enemies have robbed me of all external comforts but not of my internal peace and satisfaction."[3]

Similarly in 1781, during his troubled governorship, Jefferson was personally and politically wounded when Virginians accused him of cowardice in evading capture by the British. He attempted gracefully to uphold this Ciceronian ethos shortly thereafter in a letter to his friend and protégé James Monroe, in which he explained his decision to leave politics:

> Before I ventured to declare to my countrymen my determination to retire from public employment I examined well my heart to know whether it were thoroughly cured of every principle of political ambition, whether no lurking particle remained which might leave me uneasy when reduced within the limits of mere private life. I became satisfied that every fibre of that passion was thoroughly eradicated.[4]

Jefferson combined sensuous language and statement of principle to fortify outer dignity and restore inner ease. As he continued to express his thoughts to Monroe, Jefferson curiously crossed out the word "esteem" and substituted the more personal "affection" in declaring what it was that he sought from his countrymen. At the hands of the "well-meaning but uninformed," Jefferson insisted that he had been

> suspected and suspended in the eyes of the world without the least hint then or afterwards made public which might restrain them from supposing I stood arraigned for treasons of the heart and not mere weaknesses of the head. And I felt that these injuries, for such they have been since acknowledged, had inflicted a wound on my spirit which will only be cured by the all-healing grave.[5]

Though anxiety over his wife's final illness merged with these revelations of self-image, a hearty expression of reciprocal friendship was not lost in the composition. In closing, he invited Monroe to visit Monticello, "It will give

1. Karl Lehmann, *Thomas Jefferson, American Humanist* (1947; rep., Charlottesville 1985), 60. Full treatment can be found in James M. May, *Trials of Character: The Eloquence of Ciceronian Ethos* (Chapel Hill 1988).
2. Jefferson to Adams, July 5, 1814, in *The Adams-Jefferson Letters: The Complete Correspondence Between Thomas Jefferson and Abigail and John Adams*, ed. Lester J. Cappon (2 vols. Chapel Hill 1959), II, 433.
3. *Cicero's Epistles to Atticus: With Notes Historical, Explanatory and Critical*, trans. William Guthrie (3 vols., London, Eng. 1806), I, 124; *ibid.*, 174–175.
4. Jefferson to Monroe, May 20, 1782, in Boyd, Butterfield, *et al.*, eds., *Papers of Jefferson*, VI, 184.
5. *Ibid.*, 185

me great pleasure to see you here whenever you can favor us with your company. . . . You will find me to retain a due sense of your friendship. . . ." [6]
The dignity of great writing could be expressed no more convincingly than in friends' letters. In the preface to his 1751 translation of *Epistolae ad Atticum*, William Guthrie revealed how the mid-eighteenth century incorporated the ancient into its own evolving world view. He and his contemporaries were searching for greater personal intimacy:

> They [the Epistles] are written in the language of friendship, a language which friends alone understand. If there is any material difference between human nature in that age and this, it lies in the conception of virtue. The following pages evince, there was a time, when friendship in the human breast could rise into a passion strong as their love, and sacred as their religion, but without the impurities that sometimes debased the one, and the superstitions that always polluted the other. The friendship of our author for Atticus, is full of nice suspicions, delicate jealousies, kind fears, and fond endearments. It has every characteristic of violent, but virtuous, passion. It breathes every tender grace that delights the mind, and awakens every soft emotion that affects the heart.

Guthrie recognized that the greatness of letters lay in the unintended revelation of human nature "in all its beauties, and with all its blemishes; with all its virtue, and with all its weaknesses." Cicero's love of Atticus "triumphs in his soul; sparkling amidst his affections, and unextinguished by his calamities."[7] This is the height to which Jefferson and his contemporaries aspired in emulation of the masters of eloquence.

Pliny's letters offered Jefferson another classical model of epistolary craft demonstrating friendship, honor, and social advancement. Recommending a friend for a military position, Pliny wrote, "Our friendship began with our studies, and we were early united in the closest intimacy. . . . In his conversation, and even in his very voice and countenance, there is the most amiable sweetness. . . . He has so happy a turn for epistolary writing, that were you to read his letters, you would imagine they had been dictated by the Muses themselves."[8] William Melmoth, the eighteenth-century translator-editor of Pliny's letters, noted below that text comments of John Locke that he deemed instructive to his audience. "The writing of letters enters so much into all the occasions of life, that no gentleman can avoid shewing himself in compositions of this kind," Locke observed. "Occurrences will daily force him to make this use of his pen, which lays open his breeding, his sense, and his abilities, to a severer examination than any oral discourse."[9]

Without insisting that a candidate's letter-writing talent was always the key to advancement, we can still point to the sentiment and style of Pliny's example in the laudatory letters of introduction that travelers and office-seekers carried in the new American republic. Typical is Jefferson's on behalf of his protégé William Short, the law student who would later become his secretary in Paris:

6. *Ibid.*, 186
7. *Cicero's Epistles to Atticus*, I, viii–ix, xiii, xvi.
8. *The Letters of Pliny the Consul: with Occasional Remarks*, ed. William Melmoth (2 vols., London, Eng. 1757), 1, 96–97.
9. From Locke's *Treatise on Education*, cited *ibid.*, 97n.

The bearer Mr. William Short purposing to Philadelphia for the prosecution of his studies, I do myself the honor under authority of the acquaintance I had the pleasure of forming with you in Philadelphia, of introducing him to your notice, persuaded that should you give him an opportunity of being known to you, you will think it a circumstance not merely indifferent to add to the number of your well wishers a gentleman of very uncommon genius, erudition and merit.[1]

* * *

Naturally, as a product of his times, Jefferson was influenced as well by the letter-writing manner of his contemporaries. Perhaps none of these was so absorbed in the transforming power of the familiar letter as the English novelist Samuel Richardson, who referred to letter-writing as "the cement of friendship . . . friendship avowed under hand and seal."[2] He achieved tremendous popularity with his epistolary novels *Pamela* (1740) and *Clarissa* (1747). With Richardson, the nature of reading had come to be understood "not as a substitute for experience but a primary emotional experience itself, a constituent of identity, a way of understanding and making one's self."[3] Richardson saw the medium of the letter as a precipitant to dramatic action. It was something to comment on and solicit comments about, a document that demanded care and time and, he might say, formed the heart of life's activities. Just as his characters were absorbed in contemplation and production of soulful personal letters, Richardson himself wrote an admiring lady in 1748 that letter-writing was friendship "more pure, yet more ardent, and less broken in upon, than personal conversation can be amongst the most pure, because of the deliberation it allows, from the very preparation to, and action of writing."[4]

In Jefferson's familiar letters, Richardson's injunctions are borne out: letter-writing that was personal and contemplative demanded particular care if it was to strike profoundly.

* * *

The controversial English clergyman and novelist Laurence Sterne was [another] important influence on Jefferson, one whose work helped release emotions and urged the introspective self into the process of familiar letter-writing. His *Sermons* stressed the individual's obligation both to self and to others. His manic, digressive, Rabelaisian nine-volume *Tristram Shandy* (1759–1767) was a novel of self-discovery, an investigation of how people communicated, a gossipy picture of intimate life which gave to otherwise ordinary words rich texture and fuller meaning.[5] Sterne's purpose was to celebrate the individual's capacity for compassionate understanding. He wrote

1. Jefferson to Thomas McKean, Sept. 30, 1781, in Boyd, Butterfield, *et al.*, eds., *Papers of Jefferson*, VI, 123.
2. Richardson to Sophia Westcomb, [1746], cited in Bruce Redford, *The Converse of the Pen: Acts of Intimacy in the Eighteenth Century Familiar Letter* (Chicago 1986), 1.
3. Fliegelman, *Declaring Independence* (Stanford, Calif. 1993), 58. In the list he prepared in 1771 for Robert Skipwith, Jefferson personally recommended both of these works. See Jefferson to Robert Skipwith, Aug. 3, 1771, in Boyd, Butterfield, *et al.*, eds., *Papers of Jefferson*, I, 76–80:
4. Malvin R. Zirker, Jr., "Richardson's Correspondence: The Personal Letter as Private Experience," in Howard Anderson, Philip B. Daghlian, and Irvin Ehrenpreis, eds., *The Familiar Letter in the Eighteenth Century* (Lawrence, Kan. 1966), 74–78.
5. Max Byrd, *Tristram Shandy* (London, Eng. 1985). This is critical theory relating to the novel. See also Valerie Grosvenor Meyer, ed., *Laurence Sterne: Riddles and Mysteries* (London, Eng. 1984).

in detail and with nuance, to suggest that "between perfunctory clichés and ridiculous elaboration" was an advanced awareness of character.[6] Jefferson frequently acknowledged his fascination with Sterne. He had acquired Sterne's *Sermons* as a young attorney in 1765; living in the President's House in 1804, he was still purchasing new editions of Sterne's works. As early as 1771 and as late as 1822, Jefferson referred to Sterne in letters, calling his writing in 1787 "the best course of morality that ever was written."[7] Earlier the same year, he had ordered the pocket-sized works of Sterne from a London bookseller, with special reference to *A Sentimental Journey*, to carry with him on his own "sentimental journey" through the south of France. He had then adopted Sterne's narrative style in letters to such correspondents as the Marquis de Lafayette and Parisian artist Madame de Tott.[8]

If Richardson presented a psychological world of letter-writing, Sterne elevated the art of feeling and reveled in compassionate emotion. Feelings augmented a man's strength, pushing the self out; by reaching out, a person gained consciousness of himself. As his avid readers all knew, Sterne was battling tuberculosis all the while he wrote his masterpieces. Sterne did not like endings. The comic spirit he relied on was but a diversion; the tension surrounding the unavoidable dilemma of mortality common to all explains why *Tristram Shandy*, a novel whose action takes place in consciousness only, in effect has no ending.[9] Tellingly, the single passage from Sterne inscribed by Jefferson in his *Literary Commonplace Book* is the tragic adieu that became the shared sentiment of Jefferson and his wife Patty on her deathbed in 1782, and a written legacy the widower kept at his bedside, perusing regularly over the next forty-four years.[1] Sentimentalism, as expressed in Sterne's writing, joined self-consciousness to the desire to understand, in general, the human mind. Sterne made Jefferson sensitive to the suggestiveness of language when creatively used. Sterne perhaps also helped imbue him with a duty toward the living, inviting a nostalgic feeling for life ever drifting toward death.

Hugh Blair, Scottish clergyman and professor of rhetoric at Edinburgh University, published a series of his lectures in 1783 that became the preeminent text on rhetoric and belles-lettres in Great Britain and America for at least the next half century. Jefferson repeatedly recommended this author to students. Blair's work is representative of that part of Jefferson's education as a stylist of words that was not strictly classical or legal.[2]

6. William V. Holtz, *Image and Immortality: A Study of Tristram Shandy* (Providence, R.I. 1970), 39, 58–59 (quotation at 58).
7. Jefferson to Peter Carr, Aug. 10, 1787, in Boyd, Butterfield, *et al.*, eds., *Papers of Jefferson*, XII, 15. See also Jefferson to Robert Skipwith, Aug. 3, 1771, *ibid.*, I, 76–81; Jefferson to John B. Garland, Feb. 27, 1822, *The Writings of Thomas Jefferson*, ed. Albert Ellery Bergh and Andrew A. Lipscomb (20 vols., Washington, D.C. 1903–1905), XV, 353. References to incidents in *Tristram Shandy* appear in Jefferson's letters to Maria Cosway, Oct. 12, 1786, Apr. 24, 1788, and July 27, 1788, in Boyd, Butterfield, *et al.*, eds., *Papers of Jefferson*, X, 450–451, XIII, 103–104, 423–424. Also see Garry Wills, *Inventing America: Jefferson's Declaration of Independence* (Garden City, N.Y. 1978), 273–280.
8. Compare Jefferson to Lafayette, Apr. 11, 1787, in Boyd, Butterfield, *et al.*, eds., *Papers of Jefferson*, XI, 284–285, with Sterne's chapters "The Supper" and "The Grace" in *A Sentimental Journey through France and Italy* (London, Eng. [1767]); also compare Jefferson to Madame de Tott, Apr. 5, 1787, in Boyd, Butterfield, *et al.*, eds., *Papers of Jefferson*, XI, 271, beginning with the phrase, "A traveller, said I, retired at night to his chamber in an Inn, all his effects contained in a single trunk . . ." with Sterne's opening scene at the Calais inn.
9. See Holtz, *Image and Immortality*, 138–143.
1. Douglas L. Wilson, ed., *Jefferson's Literary Commonplace Book* (Princeton, N.J. 1989), 62, 182–184; Henry S. Randall, *Life of Thomas Jefferson* (3 vols., New York 1858), I, 384.
2. Jefferson to John Minor, Aug. 30, 1814, copying a letter he sent years earlier to Bernard Moore, in Bergh and Lipscomb, eds., *Writings of Jefferson*, XIX, 104; Jefferson to John Garland Jefferson,

Blair said of his age, "wherein improvements in every part of science, have been prosecuted with ardour," none of the liberal arts had been more favored than "the beauty of language, and the grace and elegance of every kind of writing. The public ear is become refined." Style in writing, "the peculiar manner in which a man expresses his conceptions," was something beyond mere choice of words. No two words conveyed precisely the same idea. For example, the word "custom" meant "frequent repetition of the same act," and "habit," generally considered its synonym, in fact meant "the effect which that repetition produces on the mind or body." "To abhor" indicated "strong dislike"; "To detest" added "strong disapprobation." And beyond such distinctions, Blair cited the importance of sound, the musicality of words used to "facilitate certain emotions." To avoid monotony, short sentences were to be mixed with "long and swelling ones, to render discourse sprightly." Yet, to apply too much effort to producing harmony was to exceed "proper bounds." Blair settled for moderation. "Sense has its own harmony, as well as sound; and where the sense of a period is expressed with clearness, force and dignity, it will seldom happen but that the words will strike the ear agreeably." Late in life, Jefferson wrote to the Bostonian Edward Everett, a Unitarian minister who would soon be serving in Congress, "I readily sacrifice the niceties of syntax to euphony and strength."[3]

Blair believed, as Jefferson later did, that the Roman masters were worthy of study as stylists of language but insufficient in imagination for the eighteenth-century mind. "Language is become a vehicle by which the most delicate and refined emotions of one's mind can be transmitted, or, if we may so speak, transfused into another."[4] Ultimately, nature endowed the writer with ability, so that method and rule—even Blair's own—were of secondary importance. No figure of speech could bring beauty or elegance to a composition that lacked those qualities. Merit lay in animation, what at one point he called "spirited conciseness."

Blair extolled the epistolary medium. "Even if there should be nothing very considerable in the subject," he wrote, "yet if the spirit and turn of the correspondence be agreeable; if they be written in a sprightly manner, and with native grace and ease, they may still be entertaining." He also presented a qualified view of the contents of letters. "It is childish indeed to expect, that in letters we are to find the whole heart of the author unveiled," Blair observed. "Concealment and disguise take place, more or less, in all human intercourse. But still, as letters from one friend to another make the

---

Apr. 14, 1793, *ibid.*, XI, 420–426. In 1784, when James Madison requested that Jefferson procure a copy of Blair's *Lectures* for him, Jefferson used this request as a launching point to declare, "I shall take care to . . . attend to your presumed wishes whenever I meet with any thing rare and of worth." Madison to Jefferson, Feb. 11, 1784, Jefferson to Madison, Feb. 20, 1784, in Boyd, Butterfield, *et al.*, eds., *Papers of Jefferson*, VI, 537–538, 544 (quotation). Blair's *Lectures* were delivered from 1759, coinciding with Jefferson's college years. Jefferson's teachers, like Blair, were imbued with the thinking of the Scottish Enlightenment. Jefferson knew of Blair by 1762, when the latter wrote his *A Critical Dissertation of the Poems of Ossian*, epic verse which Jefferson, too, praised throughout his life. If Blair was not in the strictest sense a part of Jefferson's early education, his perspective surely had an impact on Jefferson's appreciation of style in writing after 1783.
3. Hugh Blair, *Lectures on Rhetoric and Belles-Lettres* (1783; rep., Philadelphia 1833), 12, 101–112, 134–142; Jefferson to Edward Everett, Feb. 24, 1823, in Bergh and Lipscomb, eds., *Writings of Jefferson*, XV, 414. Compare with Jefferson's line-by-line evaluation of rhythm and accent in his "Thoughts on English Prosody," 1786, in Bergh and Lipscomb, eds., *Writings of Jefferson*, XVII, 415–451. Also see the discussion of intended pauses and musicality in Fliegelman, *Declaring Independence*, 4–15.
4. Blair, *Lectures on Rhetoric and Belles-Lettres*, I, 58b.

nearest approach to conversation, we may expect to see more of a character displayed in these than in other productions, which are studied for public view."[5]

This latter observation helps explain why it is difficult to perceive Jefferson's personality as readily as we might wish. Yet unlike many of his distinguished contemporaries, Jefferson had no desire to publish his personal letters, and he had a limited audience in mind when he wrote them.[6] For Jefferson, more than most prodigious letter-writers of the eighteenth century, the act of writing contained an implied trust. Perhaps the best way to characterize his craft is part history, part art, intention, and invention. Minimally, his letters show the range of his interests, the amount of time he spent in reflection, and the quality of what emerged. Those designed to enlarge civic activity and to influence were more self-conscious and less emotionally revealing. Even in his most personal letters, Jefferson did not "gush." Bernard Bailyn has offered the opinion that Jefferson's form of writing was remarkable not for having introduced anything radically new, but for having raised prose to a higher power without departing from eighteenth-century conventions.[7] But * * * his personal letters, being for the most part absent of political posturing, retained a spontaneous spirit and especially effusive expression.

Jefferson believed that "style in writing or speaking is formed very early in life while the imagination is warm, and impressions are permanent."[8] To judge from this statement, we must assume that Jefferson considered the greatest influences on his style to have been the ancients, Laurence Sterne, and not insignificantly, the English rationalist Henry St. John, Lord Viscount Bolingbroke, whom Jefferson in his late years compared to the "lofty, rhythmical, full-flowing eloquence of Cicero. Periods of just measure, their members proportioned, their close full and round. . . . His writings are certainly the finest samples in the English language. . . ."[9]

It was only much later, as an ex-president constantly sought out for advice or assistance, that he began to "suffer . . . under the persecution of letters. . . ." He had already earlier complained to Adams of "drudging at

---

5. *Ibid.*, 414.
6. In his seventies, writing to John Adams, he was still complaining of a lack of privacy: "I presume that our correspondence has been observed at the post offices. . . . Would you believe that a printer has had the effrontery to propose to me the letting him publish it?" Jefferson termed his correspondence "secret" and "sacred" and resisted publication. Jefferson to Adams, Aug. 10, 1815, in Cappon, ed., *The Adams-Jefferson Letters*, II, 453. Six years later, he wrote, "The abuse of confidence by publishing my letters has cost me more than all other pains, and makes me afraid to put pen to paper in a letter of sentiment." Jefferson to Charles Hammond, Aug. 18, 1821, in Bergh and Lipscomb, eds., *Writings of Jefferson*, XV, 332–333. Not every student of Jefferson's writing takes such protestations at face value. To Douglas L. Wilson, Jefferson was "incapable of showing off" by publishing in his own lifetime, but Wilson also points to contrivances, leaving open the possibility that Jefferson, a great organizer and collector, copied and kept letters that he could expect to be published after his death. He believes that "Thoughts on English Prosody" was intended for publication, despite Jefferson's having modestly conveyed it to the Marquis de Chastellux as a "tribute" to their friendship. See Wilson, "Thomas Jefferson and the Republic of Letters," in Peter S. Onuf, ed., *Jeffersonian Legacies* (Charlottesville 1993), 50–76 (quotations at 67, 63).
7. Bernard Bailyn, "Boyd's Jefferson: Notes for a Sketch," *New England Quarterly*, 33 (Sept. 1960), 392.
8. Jefferson to John Banister, Jr., Oct. 15, 1785, in Boyd, Butterfield, *et al.*, eds., *Papers of Jefferson*, VIII, 637.
9. See entries of the late 1750s and early 1760s in Wilson, ed., *Jefferson's Literary Commonplace Book, passim*. Reconstruction of undated entries is clarified in Appendix B. On Bolingbroke, see Jefferson to Francis Wayles Eppes, Jan. 19, 1821, in Betts and Bear, eds., *Family Letters*, 438. The "Periods" in "Periods of just measure" means full sentences.

the writing table." But even in this final period of his life, he became animated putting forth freewheeling ideas about creative word usage, which he
had culled from a lifetime of writing. Jefferson maintained:

> Dictionaries are but the depositories of words already legitimated by
> usage. Society is the work-shop in which new ones are elaborated. When
> an individual uses a new word, if ill-formed it is rejected by society, if
> wellformed, adopted, and, after due time, laid up in the depository of
> dictionaries. And if, in this process of sound neologisation, our transat-
> lantic brethren shall not choose to accompany us, we may furnish, after
> the Ionians, a second example of a colonial dialect improving on it's [sic]
> primitive.[1]

Jefferson and the Enlightenment *philosophes* from whom he drew so
much of his state of mind if not his style all profited from the epistolary tradition. They were aided by the expansion of a discriminating reading public. Men of letters no longer required * * * prominent people to serve as
patrons, and ideas circulated more freely. In part owing to political events
for which Jefferson's pen was a beacon, man was gaining control of his
moral universe and was now freer to cultivate himself through the creative
use of words.

There is no question that Jefferson knew the familiar letter as intimate
conversation, in addition to an instrument of Ciceronian ethos, and knew
its emotive power well. To his lifelong friend John Page, nineteen-year-old
Jefferson wrote on Christmas Day 1762 of the tediousness of legal studies
and his frustration in seeking the affection of one Rebecca Burwell: "Is
there any such thing as happiness in this world? No[.]" He protested his station in life: "And as for admiration I am sure the man who powders most,
parfumes [sic] most, embroiders most, and talks most nonsense, is most
admired. Though to be candid, there are some who have too much good
sense to esteem such monkey-like animals as these. . . ." Toward the end of
the letter, Jefferson acknowledged his anxiety: loneliness. He thus wrote to
Page to feel close. "My mind has been so taken up with thinking of my
acquaintances," he mused, "that till this moment I almost imagined myself
in Williamsburgh talking to you in our old unreserved way. . . ."[2]

The following month, Jefferson seemed broken by his isolation from the
social scene he craved, and he was about to give up on the young lady whom
he had been trying to impress. To Page once again he complained, "All
things here appear to me to trudge on in one and the same round: we rise
in the morning that we may eat breakfast, dinner and supper and go to bed
again that we may get up the next morning and do the same. . . . How does
R.B. [Rebecca Burwell] do? What do you think of my affair, or what would
you advise me to do?" Anticipating that he would receive his "sentence, and
be no longer in suspense" upon his return from Albemarle to Williamsburg,
he proposed that Page join him in an as yet unconstructed vessel (which he
planned to name the *Rebecca*) to sail to Europe and be "cured of love."[3]

*   *   *

1. Jefferson to Adams, June 27, 1822, Jan. 11, 1817, Jefferson to John Adams, Aug. 15, 1820, in Cappon, ed., *The Adams-Jefferson Letters*, II, 580, 505, 567.
2. Jefferson to John Page, Dec. 25, 1762, in Boyd, Butterfield, *et al.*, eds., *Papers of Jefferson*, I, 5, 6.
3. *Ibid.*, 7, 8.

It was his need for family and concern about family matters that best evinces Jefferson's emotional dependence upon letters. Amidst the bitter struggle that preceded the election of 1800, the then vice president wrote from Philadelphia to his elder daughter Martha in Virginia:

> I ought oftener, my dear Martha, to recieve [sic] your letters, for the very great pleasure they give me, and especially when they express your affections for me. For though I cannot doubt them, yet they are among those truths which tho' not doubted we love to hear repeated. Here too they serve like gleams of light, to chear [sic] a dreary scene where envy, hatred, malice, revenge, and all the worse passions of men are marshalled to make one another as miserable as possible.

Through letter-writing, Jefferson found many instances to resolve matters that caused emotional unease, and he did so with an unmistakable dramatic effect. He inaugurated the Monticello cemetery in 1773 with the burial of his inseparable companion and brother-in-law, Dabney Carr and subsequently took in his children. Before setting out for France a decade later, he appealed to James Madison to assume responsibility as guardian for his teenage nephew: "I have a tender legacy to leave you on my departure. I will not say it is the son of my sister, tho her worth would justify my resting it on that ground; but it is the son of my friend, the dearest friend I knew, who, had fate reversed our lots, would have been the father to my children."[4]

In 1785, secure in Paris, he wrestled with the problem of exposing Maria, the young daughter he left behind, to an ocean voyage. But he could not be without her. Writing Elizabeth Wayles Eppes, the relative with whom Maria was living, he confronted his dilemma: "No event in your life has put it into your power to conceive how I feel when I reflect that such a child, and so dear to me, is to cross the ocean, is to be exposed to all the sufferings and risks, great and small, to which a situation on board a ship exposes every one. I drop my pen at the thought—but she must come." Jefferson, figuratively dropping his pen, presents an image of a man who regularly brought his heart to his writing desk. Indeed, one month earlier he had written of his "present anxiety" over Maria to Eliza House Trist, the Philadelphian in whose home he and Madison had previously boarded. "My wishes are fixed, but my resolution is wavering."[5]

To a select few, Jefferson let down his guard and let loose his imagination. A preoccupation with the natural and supernatural and the "far away and long ago" suggests that he was capable of spontaneity of feeling when he wrote. The dark and desolate world of Ossian enchanted Jefferson throughout his life, much as the provocative wit of Sterne did. Ossian, the reputed Celtic bard of the third century A.D., used a mystical backdrop of "grey torrents" and "noisy streams" to introduce a world filled with sentimental suffering in which readers could find compassion and benevolence. Jefferson inscribed a volume of Ossianic poetry to his granddaughter decades after these works had been proven a fraudulent contemporary production.[6]

4. Jefferson to Martha Randolph, Feb. 8, 1798, in Betts and Bear, eds., *Family Letters*, 155; Jefferson to Madison, May 8, 1784, in Boyd, Butterfield, *et al.*, eds., *Papers of Jefferson*, VII, 233.
5. Jefferson to Elizabeth Wayles Eppes, Sept. 22, 1785, Jefferson to Eliza House Trist, Aug. 18, 1785, *ibid.*, VIII, 539–540, 404.
6. Fiona J. Stafford, *The Sublime Savage: A Study of James Macpherson and The Poems of Ossian* (Edinburgh, Scot. 1988). The 1783 edition of *Temora* inscribed to Anne Carey Randolph remains in the collection of Monticello today. Jefferson was apparently unruffled by the revelation that the works were not genuine.

ANDREW BURSTEIN

As absorbed as he was with the political reality of his day, he could paint energetic pictures that combined an appreciation of past glory with a primitivist's conception of the Virginia idyll. The famous dialogue between his Head and Heart raised the sublime (heights of nature and heights of feeling) in the description of his own private mountain:

> our own dear Monticello, where has nature spread so rich a mantle under the eye? mountains, forests, rocks, rivers. With what majesty do we there ride above the storms! How sublime to look down into the workhouse of nature, to see her clouds, hail, snow, rain, thunder, all fabricated at our feet! And the glorious Sun, when rising as if out of a distant water, just gilding the tops of the mountains, and giving life to all nature!

Jefferson's familiar letters thus show him to be both a classical scholar and a sensitive, modern friend. Such letters as those to Page and to his own family reveal a vulnerability and softness of expression with which he was as comfortable as the cleverly contrived turns of phrase for which the public Jefferson was best known. A letter of 1770 to Page containing news of Dabney Carr was presented with a sensitivity hard to miss. "He speaks, thinks, and dreams of nothing but his young son," Jefferson observed. "This friend of ours, Page, in a very small house, with a table, half a dozen chairs, and one or two servants, is the happiest man in the universe."[7]

In "My Head and My Heart," the Head persisted in trying to rein in his emotion with such injunctions as: "Everything in this world is matter of calculation. Advance then with caution." Surely Jefferson did. And yet the Heart, free to express what lay outside mere intellectual pleasures, declared boldly, in the longest uninterrupted passage of the twelve page letter, that the "sublimated philosopher" was an object of pity. "Their supreme wisdom is supreme folly: and they mistake for happiness the mere absence of pain," he wrote. "Had they ever felt the solid pleasure of one generous spasm of the heart, they would exchange for it all the frigid speculations of their lives. . . ."[8] This, too, describes the real Thomas Jefferson, who was demonstrating to the recipient that he had come to regard the familiar letter as both an exercise of emotional release and a testament to his desire for intimacy.

A portrait of Thomas Jefferson emerges from his letters that moves beyond the more common characterizations of the bookish planter, the contentious political thinker, reticent about self-exposure. Inside the man whom most contemporaries described only in terms of the "mild and pleasant" countenance they saw, was a heart easily aroused.[9] Jefferson was a soft-spoken man who could not still his thoughts. He may have had, as Wilson Carey McWilliams observed, "a character which seems to be made up of warring antitheses." And, he may have been, as James A. Bear, Jr., characterized, "a very reserved individual who believed that his private life was his own." But Jefferson, while so clearly connected to the learned Romans, also honored the Greeks "for the freedom they granted their thinkers in pursuit of truth and their artists in search of beauty."[1]

7. Jefferson to Maria Cosway, Oct. 12, 1786, Jefferson to Page, Feb. 21, 1770, in Boyd, Butterfield, et al., eds., *Papers of Jefferson*, X, 447–448, I, 36.
8. Jefferson to Maria Cosway, Oct. 12, 1786, *ibid.*, X, 448, 450.
9. This was the characterization made by Jefferson's longtime overseer, Edmund Bacon. See James A. Bear, Jr., ed., *Jefferson at Monticello* (Charlottesville 1967), 71. Similarly, La Rochefoucauld described "a mild, easy and obliging temper," cited in Randall, *The Life of Thomas Jefferson*, II, 306.
1. Wilson Carey McWilliams, *The Idea of Fraternity in America* (Berkeley 1973), 208; Bear, ed., *Jefferson at Monticello*, xi; Dumas Malone "Foreward" in Lehmann, *Thomas Jefferson: American Human-*

He may be known best for noble principles, for preserving order and promoting rationality, rather than for spontaneity. For this sensibility Jefferson is, at least in part, indebted to his Latin and legal studies. Certainly he exercised tremendous self-control and inner strength reflective of those classical values which the mid-eighteenth century in general upheld. But he was also a man who required emotional fulfillment and employed his talents as a writer as much toward that end as toward the loftier political tracts, which, in his words, represented a "dry and dreary waste . . . into which I have been impressed by the times on which I happened."[2]

Jefferson kept a 656-page "Epistolary Record," noting by date (and during some of the early years by correspondent) all that he sent and received from 1783 until his death in 1826.[3] The careful maintenance of such a system testifies to the importance he placed on his correspondence. Jefferson surely recognized that language, spoken or written, is the means by which all people become conscious of their behavior, assess the past and present, and endeavor to shape the future. His craft allowed his natural judgment and reasoning, invention and versatility to coexist. In the act of writing, whether a public or private document, he found fortitude, inspiration—an inner meaning that was, for this unreligious man, something just short of salvation. By writing in the manner he did, he showed that he placed importance on the individual conscience. In other words, in grasping the limitations of systems of order contrived by the Head, he accepted that the Heart must experience repeated bouts with anxiety, for which letters served as a temporary balm.

ANNETTE GORDON-REED

From Thomas Jefferson and Sally Hemings:
An American Controversy[†]

Jefferson the Gentleman and the Problem of Miscegenation

Consider first the argument that Jefferson's status as a gentleman would have precluded a liaison of this nature. This contention is most often framed in terms of disbelief at the idea that Thomas Jefferson would have "overreached" himself in this fashion. Engaging in a sexual relationship with a slave was an abuse of power by the master (a curious concept, that), and Jefferson was not known as an "abusive" individual.[1]

---

ist, x. Greek, not Latin, was Jefferson's favorite language for its "fancy," that is, its vitality and capacity for creative expression. Lehmann makes this point most convincingly. *Ibid.*, 148–155.

2. Jefferson to Dr. Casper Wistar, June 21, 1807, in Bergh and Lipscomb, eds., *Writings of Jefferson*, XI, 248.
3. The original Summary Journal of Letters is at the Library of Congress and a photocopy may be found in the Alderman Library, University of Virginia.
† From *Thomas Jefferson and Sally Hemings: An American Controversy*. Copyright © 1997 by the Rector and Visitors of the University of Virginia. Reprinted with permission of the Univesity of Virginia Press. Numbered notes are Gordon-Reed's.
1. Merrill D. Peterson, *Thomas Jefferson and the New Nation: A Biography* (New York, 1970), 707; W. S. Randall, *Thomas Jefferson: A Life* (New York, 1993), 477.

This line of argument promotes at least two questionable theses. The first is that the type of overreaching involved in a sexual liaison with a slave actually was, and was thought at the time to be, vastly different—and worse—than the other types of overreaching that were also part and parcel of the slave system. The claim that southern gentlemen saw and were able to maintain a clear demarcation between the types of exploitation involved in starting a sexual relationship with a slave and, say, making that slave work from sunrise to sundown for nothing or selling that slave's children must be viewed with some skepticism given the extent of violations of this item in the code of honor. It may have been necessary to the maintenance of order in society— to avoid giving offense to white women and to make sure that white women would not take a sauce for the goose approach to miscegenation—for southern gentlemen to say that this demarcation was clear and rigid. There is much evidence, however, that the many components of the slave system, which included miscegenation, could not be so easily compartmentalized.[2]

In Jefferson's case it is by no means obvious that a man who owned people, bought and sold them, gave them away as wedding presents, and impressed them into the armed services to put themselves at risk in a war for other people's freedom would believe that having sex with one of the people so used would amount to overreaching so great as to be beyond his contemplation. His contradictory statements about the nature of freedom and slavery and of black people suggest that his ability to draw absolute lines on these matters was not as refined as some would allege.

On one hand, Jefferson wrote that slavery was an abomination. On the other hand, he seldom freed slaves. On the one hand, he argued that slaves could not be freed because they were like children. On the other hand, he saw to it that many slaves on his plantation became skilled craftsmen. This was done to suit Jefferson's purposes, but the end result was the creation of adults who could have worked to support themselves. On one hand, Jefferson seems to have been revolted by the notion of amalgamation and social relations with blacks. On the other hand, he took products of amalgamation and made them favored members of his household. He also maintained cordial relations with some blacks and encouraged one black family to send their children to the local white school in Charlottesville. The truth is that Thomas Jefferson can be cited to support almost any position on slavery and the race question that could exist.[3]

This part of the character defense also posits that what Jefferson was accused of doing amounts to an act so heinous that it could only have been carried out by a depraved individual.[4] In keeping with this idea, the picture

2. Winthrop Jordan, *White over Black: American Attitudes Toward the Negro, 1550–1812* (Chapel Hill, 1968), 136–78; Eugene Genovese, *Roll Jordan Roll: The World the Slaves Made* (New York, 1972), 413–31.
3. Dumas Malone, *Jefferson and His Time*, 6 vols. (Boston, 1948–1981), 1:265, 3:208, 4:496; Jack McLaughlin, *Jefferson and Monticello: Biography of a Builder* (New York, 1988), 102–4, 106, 121–23; John C. Miller, *The Wolf by the Ears: Thomas Jefferson and Slavery* (New York, 1977), 207. See also Frederick M. Binder, *The Color Problem in Early National America as viewed by John Adams, Jefferson, and Jackson* (Paris: 1968), 48, noting that "the phenomenon of having exponents of all sides of a question claim Jefferson's support is a tribute to the great man's prestige, but, to say the least, it causes considerable confusion among the uncommitted and those seeking the truth. The color problem is an example of this. Racists and integrationist, abolitionists, and states righters have claimed Jefferson as their own."
4. Peterson, *Thomas Jefferson and the New Nation*, 707; Miller, *Wolf by the Ears*, 164.

painted of what any Jefferson-Hemings relationship necessarily would have been like is almost invariably something along the lines of forcible rape or, by some commentators, child molestation. "What you're saying then is that Thomas Jefferson was a rapist." "What you're saying then is that Thomas Jefferson had sex with an eight-year-old girl."

This immediately brings to mind a picture of Thomas Jefferson knocking down a woman's door and dragging her by her hair to his bedroom, precisely the image that defenders want to project because they know that most people who have ever read anything about Jefferson would discount that scenario. The goal is to make any conception of Jefferson's actions so bad that no one would, or would want to, believe that it could be true.

Actually, characterizing a Jefferson-Hemings relationship as thirty-eight years' worth of nights of "Come here gal!" is a sophisticated technique. It presents the proponent of the idea as enlightened and forward thinking with regard to the nature of slavery, even as that individual promotes a cardboard version of the system. It is all the more seductive because the idea is not without merit. The slave system was inherently coercive. Therefore, one could argue, every act of sex between a master and slave was the equivalent of nonconsensual sex, in other words, rape.

We may know this is true in the theoretical sense, but something should tell us that it cannot have been true in every situation, under every circumstance, that existed from the early 1600s until emancipation. Do we really believe that over the entire course of slavery in the United States, no master and slave woman ever experienced a mutual sexual or emotional attachment to one another? Can we really believe that a slave woman confronted with a master whom she knew, or reasonably believed, would desist if she refused his advances was in the same position as a woman whose master would knock down the door and drag her off to his bedroom? Both women would have existed in a state of relative powerlessness. But we instinctively feel that there is a difference. In the former situation the woman would have had a small but important individualized bit of power even as she existed in a state of general powerlessness. The power was, of course, to say yes or no. In the latter situation her powerlessness would have been total.

The idea of total powerlessness on the part of all slaves is attractive to both whites and blacks for different reasons. For some whites, even as they denounce the barbarity of slavery, the fantasy of white omnipotence may remain secretly appealing. Their presentation of slaves as having been totally helpless evinces sympathy for blacks, but it also imagines a time when whites allegedly had the power to rule blacks, mind, body, and soul. To admit that there might have been some instances when blacks exercised a degree of free will interrupts the dream of omnipotence and forces consideration of the ways in which that will may have been exercised and what effect it may have had upon whites.

It is especially hard (and unpleasant) for some to think that a black woman might have exercised her will, circumscribed as it was, by saying yes to Thomas Jefferson and, in doing so, have been able to exercise some influence over him. Scholars have scoffed at the notion that Sally Hemings, no matter how beautiful or appealing, could have had enough power to extract a promise from Jefferson to free her children and then over the years hold

him to that promise.[5] Jefferson, the personification of America, simply cannot be put in that position. The actions he took with respect to Hemings's
children, for example, must be seen as a product of Jefferson's will alone.
It should not be considered for a moment that he may have been acting
under the influence of so insignificant a person as a black female slave.

The notion of total powerlessness has appeal to some blacks because it
seems to make the slave system worse, as if that were possible. Saying that
there were instances where blacks had room to maneuver can be taken as
an attempt to minimize the horror of the slave system. This is not the case.
The idea brings forth the truth that there were two sets of human beings
involved in that sorry state of affairs, not one race of all powerful gods and
another race of totally dominated submortals. While it is true that the balance of power dramatically favored whites, it is not true that blacks were
unable to influence the lives of whites on an individual and societywide
basis. No matter what amount of short-term gain may be achieved by focusing on black powerlessness (to trigger white guilt), it can never be in the
long-term interests of blacks to accept so limited and distorted a version of
history.

THE CHARACTER DEFENSE AT ALL COSTS

It has not been enough to evoke the vision of the totally powerless slave
for use as a weapon in the arsenal of Jefferson defenders; the vulnerability
of children has been deployed as well. In considering this campaign in the
battle of perceptions, the saying "All's fair in love and war" seems especially
appropriate. The writings of historians Alf E. Mapp, Jr., and Willard Sterne
Randall come the most quickly to mind in this regard. Both historians'
defenses of Jefferson depend, in part, upon telling readers that to believe
in the truth of the Hemings story is to believe that Thomas Jefferson had
designs upon a prepubescent girl.

Mapp wrote of the Hemings allegation:

> Some with imaginations less restrained than Mrs. Brodie's have sug-
> gested that Jefferson had Sally accompany his daughter to Europe so
> that he might consummate his passion for the slave girl. Since Sally
> was fourteen or fifteen when she arrived in France in 1787 and Jeffer-
> son had not seen her for more than three years, one is asked to believe
> that even amid the caresses of the cultivated belles of Paris he pined
> for an ignorant serving girl whose eleven or twelve year old charms
> were indelibly burnt into his brain.[6]

Mapp did not identify who had made such suggestions. One would think
that the name or names of anyone who made so outrageous a charge—and
the context in which they made it—should have been exposed. If any historian had said this, Mapp's readers should have been alerted so that they
would know in the future to view that scholar's other claims with suspicion.

Willard Sterne Randall created his own variation on Mapp's theme,
reducing Hemings's age at the time of her alleged seduction and thus rais-

5. Douglass Adair, *Fame and the Founding Fathers*, ed. Trevor Colbourn (New York, 1974) 176; Clif-
ford Hogan, "How Not to Write a Biography: A Critical Look at Fawn Brodie's *Thomas Jefferson*,"
Social Science Journal 14 (1977): 132–133.
6. Alf Mapp, Jr., *Thomas Jefferson: A Strange Case of Mistaken Identity* (New York, 1987), 264.

ing the stakes for belief in the Hemings story. He discussed Fawn Brodie's attempt to draw a relationship between what she thought was Jefferson's excessive use of the term *mulatto* in his descriptions of the terrain of certain European countries and his interest in Sally Hemings. Randall seized upon this admittedly problematic contention and said that because Hemings was not yet in France at the time Jefferson took this trip, he would have to be remembering Hemings from the last time he had spent much time around her, which was when she was eight years old. Several reviewers of Randall's book picked up on this aspect of his analysis, and trumpeted the claim that Brodie had accused Jefferson of starting his affair with Hemings when she was eight years old.[7]

However, Jefferson took two trips through the European countryside, one before Hemings arrived and one after. Brodie made it explicit—indeed it was the whole point of the passage—that she was contrasting the number of times he used the term in the descriptions of the terrain before Hemings got to Paris and the number of times he used it afterward. She was clear that she believed the liaison began sometime after Sally Hemings accompanied Jefferson's daughter to Paris.[8] Hemings, who was born in 1773, would have been between fourteen and fifteen at the time she arrived there and between sixteen and seventeen when she left. Yet, even for those who did not further distort Randall's reading of Brodie, Hemings's youth relative to Jefferson's age has been invoked to suggest that Brodie's thesis amounted to a charge of child molestation on the part of Jefferson.[9]

But did Thomas Jefferson, and other men and women of the eighteenth century, think of teenaged girls in the same way that we think of them today? One particular circumstance from the life of one of Jefferson's closest friends, and his direct involvement in the situation, suggests that they did not. The great love of James Madison's life (before he met and married Dolley) was a fifteen-year-old girl named Catherine Floyd. Madison was thirty-one years old at the time. Jefferson, who was awaiting instructions for his trip to France, actively encouraged the relationship. He went so far as to speak with the young girl about Madison, becoming in the words of Madison's biographer Irving Brant, "an energetic matchmaker." When he was certain of her affection for his friend, Jefferson wrote to Madison assuring him that a marriage between the two would "render you happier than you can possibly be in a single state." Madison and Floyd got to the point of setting a date for their marriage, but Kitty eventually broke Madison's heart by casting him aside for another teenager. Jefferson wrote a sympathetic letter counseling Madison that if reconciliation proved impossible, he would eventually find other "resources of happiness."[1]

7. W. S. Randall, *Thomas Jefferson: A Life*, 476; *New York Times*, Sept. 6, 1993, Herbert Mitgang, "For Jefferson, the Presidency Held Second Place"; *San Diego Union*, Aug. 22, 1993, Peter Rowe, "Books Help the Undecided Judge Jefferson"; *Star Tribune* (Minneapolis-St. Paul), Nov. 14, 1993, Dennis Watley, "New Book on Jefferson Hardly Overcritical."
8. Thomas M. Morris and Persephone Weene, *Thomas Jefferson's European Travel Diaries* (Ithaca, N.Y., 1987), 40, 106; Malone, *Jefferson and His Time* 2:xxvi, xxvi; Fawn Brodie, *Thomas Jefferson: An Intimate History* (New York: 1974), 228–30.
9. See, e.g., Adair, *Fame and the Founding Fathers*, 182; Virginius Dabney, *Jefferson Scandals: A Rebuttal* (New York, 1981), 48; Miller, *Wolf by the Ears*, 164; *Virginian-Pilot* (Norfolk), April 17, 1995.
1. James M. Smith, ed., *The Republic of Letters: The Correspondence between Thomas Jefferson and James Madison, 1776–1826* (New York, 1995), 228–29, 242, 264; Irving Brant, *James Madison* 6 vols. (Indianapolis, 1941–1953), 2:283.

If Brodie was correct, Jefferson was in his mid-forties and Hemings was either fifteen or sixteen when their alleged relationship began. He was older than Madison. But child molestation is not judged by the age of the adult who is said to engage in it, it is judged by the age of the child. If the forty-four-year-old Thomas Jefferson could be characterized as something on the order of a child molester for having allegedly started a relationship with a female who was either fifteen or sixteen, then one must also question the activities of his friend the adult James Madison who courted a female of the same age.

Ultimately, this argument against the notion of a Jefferson-Hemings liaison is problematic, not only because it distorts Jefferson's views about the appropriateness of sexual relations with fifteen-year-olds (we can presume he thought that Madison and Floyd would consummate their marital relationship), but because it gives readers an incorrect impression of eighteenth-century standards and practices. Females of Hemings's age at the time of her stay in France were thought eligible for relationships with men.

HISTORIANS AND THE PROBLEM OF MISCEGENATION

What are black Americans to make of all this? Do the people who frame their responses to this allegation in these desperate ways know or even care how they might sound? Why should the thought that a white president may have had a long-term relationship with a black person be the source of such a venomous reaction? When I have discussed this issue with blacks, they almost instantly and invariably see the reaction to the story in the same way. They say that the belief that having sex with a slave was the most base activity in which whites could engage has its origins in the discomfort and fear that some whites felt and still feel at the thought of miscegenation—whatever has been the actual practice. It is that fear, rather than any concern about the abuse of the power held over blacks, that is the driving force behind the response. For what other reason would modern commentators forgive Jefferson for all the other things he is known to have done to blacks but view this particular story as something so awful that they recoil in horror at the very thought that it might be true? The horror is not at the thought of the defilement of Sally Hemings but at the thought of Thomas Jefferson defiling himself by lying with Sally Hemings. By doing so, Jefferson would have hurt himself and, by extension, other whites. That particular sin would be unforgivable.

That is the most reasonable conclusion that can be drawn when one considers the posture in which this issue resurfaced with the appearance of Fawn Brodie's biography of Jefferson. The Jefferson-Hemings story and the alleged details of the relationship have had two major public airings. The first was given by James Callender and the second by Brodie. The two writers had completely different takes on the matter. Callender was offended by the charge that Jefferson had slept with a slave woman because he was revolted by miscegenation and what he saw as the too casual acceptance of the practice in the South. He was appalled that the vehemence of white southerners' rhetoric against miscegenation did not seem to match their actual practices. Callender's charges against Jefferson were designed to play into that society's purported equation of miscegenation with bestiality. He drew a picture of Sally Hemings as being so low a creature that only an equally low individual would have had anything to do with her. His hysteria on this point stemmed from his own racism.

Fawn Brodie's depiction of the nature of the Jefferson-Hemings relationship was markedly different than Callender's. She saw Jefferson's actions with regard to Sally Hemings and her children from a vantage point that Callender did not, and would not have wanted to, view it. Brodie was not the enemy of Jefferson. Her view led her to conclude that Jefferson had done the following things. He had engaged in a thirty-eight-year liaison with a woman who was a slave. The length of the relationship suggested to her that both parties derived some satisfaction from it, because it would have taken a monster to have forced his attentions on a woman for so long a period. Because she did not think Jefferson a monster, it was likely to her that this was a case of mutual affection. Brodie accepted the claim in Madison Hemings's statement that Jefferson promised to free Sally Hemings's children when they attained majority. The fact that all of those children went free at that time suggested that Jefferson cared enough about Hemings to keep his promise, even though he knew that his actions could cause problems. She then said that Jefferson arranged to have Sally Hemings freed a discrete length of time after his death, to protect both his white family and his slave family.

One wonders why people writing in the twentieth century should view this scenario with such disgust. After all, if this is what happened, it is not the depiction of deviance and depravity that James Callender was making it out to be. If Brodie was correct, this was, rather, a tragic story of people trapped by the circumstances of their times into doing the best that they could do, a scenario that played itself out in other households across the Old South. For no matter how strenuously some may resist believing it, there were slave masters who had long liaisons with slave mistresses and who freed the children from these unions and the women as well.

A FANTASY OF THE 1970S

It has been suggested that in constructing her theory about the nature of the Jefferson-Hemings relationship, Fawn Brodie was imposing twentieth-century notions onto the eighteenth century or, in other words, engaging in presentism. Douglas Wilson made this point in an essay on Thomas Jefferson's character. Wilson defined *presentism* as "applying contemporary or otherwise inappropriate standards to the past." Wilson said that Brodie was compelled to present a vision of the Jefferson-Hemings relationship that would be palatable to Americans, who wanted to view the liaison in a romantic light.[2]

Wilson's reading of Brodie ignores the fact that she reached her conclusion about the likely nature of the Jefferson-Hemings relationship by looking at facts and drawing inferences from those facts. The pattern of Sally Hemings's conceptions and the freeing of all of her children by Jefferson are facts that belong to the time in which they occurred. The inferences Brodie drew from those facts must be the focus of any inquiry into the charge of presentism. One must ask whether Brodie's inferences would be unique to the time in which they were drawn, the early 1970s.

They would not be. The fact that Jefferson freed Hemings's children and the ways in which he did it might lead in any age to an inference that he cared something for her. It may be an incorrect inference (not to be confused with

---

2. Douglas Wilson, "Thomas Jefferson and the Character Issue," *Atlantic Monthly* 270 (Nov. 1992), 58.

an unreasonable inference, the mistake to which presentism is addressed), but it is, in fact, an inference that draws upon sensibilities that would exist in any era. The length of time that had elapsed between the alleged promise of freedom and the fulfillment of the promise; the fact that an important event (Callender's exposé) occurred in the intervening years that made fulfillment of the alleged promise substantially more difficult; the fact that it was nevertheless carried out and done so under circumstances that could cause great distress to people whom Jefferson loved, all might lead at any point in history to an inference that the man in question cared about the feelings of the woman to whom he had made the promise.

A historian in any era who believed a subject to have been extremely sensitive, disinclined to engage in open conflict, inclined to make deep and lasting attachments, and fearful of rejection might infer that such a man would not have been in a thirty-eight-year relationship with a woman unless she welcomed him. A man with those characteristics would not be able to ignore the woman's suffering, which would be readily apparent at so close a range. He would also be too thin-skinned to take the humiliation of continually presenting himself for body-to-body contact when he knew he was not wanted. This would be particularly true if the liaison was one to which other loved ones might be hostile, since their disapproval would have given him an additional excuse to exit the relationship.

That Sally Hemings conceived no children during Jefferson's long absences from Monticello suggests monogamy on her part and also might suggest in any era that she felt something for him. It is not as though she had no other option. Sally Hemings was, by accounts of her, a remarkably attractive woman. During the years that Jefferson was often away from Monticello, she was between seventeen and thirty-six years old. She could have attracted, and been attracted to, other men. Drawing from these facts the inference that the two probably had affection for one another does not amount to engaging in presentism. Brodie's inferences may not have been correct, but they were inferences that could be reasonably drawn in any age.

PRESENTISM TO A DIFFERENT END

Just as it is possible to use presentism to idealize a Jefferson-Hemings liaison, it is also possible to use presentism to demonize it. It seems that Wilson in his brief analysis of the situation did the latter. He wrote:

> If he [Jefferson] did take advantage of Hemings and father her children over a period of twenty years, he was acting completely out of character and violating his own standards of honor and decency. For a man who took questions of morality and honor seriously, such a hypocritical liaison would have been a constant source of shame and guilt. For his close-knit family, who worshipped him and lived too near him to be ignorant of such an arrangement it would have been a moral tragedy of no small dimensions.[3]

Well, what was "slavery time" (as southern blacks sometimes refer to it) but a series of "moral traged[ies] of no small dimensions"? Why should Jefferson's family have not known some of the "moral tragedies" that grew out of the sys-

3. Ibid., 62.

tem of which they were so intimately a part? Why would we assume for a moment that the Jeffersons and Randolphs could live in the midst of the slave system and not be touched by some of the more common circumstances that it spawned?

Families all over the South had fathers, brothers, grandfathers who had relationships and children with black women, just as southern families, including Jefferson's, had emotionally disturbed relatives, wastrel nephews, granddaughters who were physically abused, and ne'er-do-well relatives. These things were part of life. To write of this alleged circumstance as though it would have amounted to some special horror unknown in the annals of southern history misleads as to the extent of the contradictions and complexities of antebellum southern life. It also seems an attempt to rescue the Jeffersons and Randolphs from their immersion in a way of life that now embarrasses us—to suggest that they were somehow in that slave system but not really of it, when it is clear that they were both.

As to Jefferson and his personal code of honor and the turmoil that a relationship with Sally Hemings would have caused within him, an answer may be found by examining closely Jefferson's attitudes about slaves and slavery. Historians tend to divorce Jefferson's ownership of slaves from his personal needs. His attitudes about this subject are most often analyzed in terms of what he thought it meant for society as a whole. In this view Jefferson remained a slave owner, not for himself, but just because he could not see society's way out of the system. He was afraid of what would happen to the slaves if they were freed, because they were like children. At the same time he was afraid of what free blacks would mean for American civilization. As a result, he adopted a posture of saying something on the order of, "It's a tough job, but somebody has got to do it."

Thomas Jefferson kept slaves primarily because he needed them to help him live the way he wanted to live. He knew very well the moral issues at stake with respect to slavery. As a lifetime participant in that system, he had to make rationalizations every day of his life about how he could be a part of it and remain honorable, decent, and moral. If he could do this for all the other aspects of the slave system, why would he have been incapable of making similar rationalizations about another inevitable part of the system: sexual contacts between masters and slaves?

It is difficult for us at this remove to understand how people could cope with such situations, even though we know that many southerners did. But we are seeing this through the eyes of a society solidly rooted in modern bourgeois value and sensibilities, where our more equalized vision of relationships between men and women and parents and children would militate against such behavior. This is presentism of the highest order. There are so many things about a society built upon slavery that are difficult for us to reconcile or imagine. The accommodations that had to be made—the mode of thinking that people had to adopt in order to keep the system going—often pass all understanding: Blacks are dirty and subhuman, but I will put my infant child to the breast of a black woman. Black men are infantile, but they are sexual predators who must be kept away from our women. Black women are animals, but I will have sex with them.

The world of the antebellum southern planter was not the world of the late twentieth-century bourgeoisie. There is no way to assess the capabilities, beliefs, and professed moral standards of the individuals who lived in that society without keeping that fact in mind. Jefferson, for all his understanding of and stated appreciation for democratic institutions, was a despot in his own realm. He may have been a benign despot, but he was a despot nevertheless. Women and children were cherished and indulged, friends were deeply appreciated, but in the final analysis they did not rule; he did.

The evidence indicates that other than the times when forces beyond his control had the upper hand, death and disease for example, Thomas Jefferson did pretty much what he wanted to do and had things pretty much as he wanted them. Two of his most often cited characteristics were his ability to speak only of those things of which he wanted to speak and his capacity to will his vision of how matters would proceed upon even those whom he loved. To say that it would have been impossible for Jefferson to have carried on a liaison with Sally Hemings would be to assume that he voluntarily allowed himself to be ruled by others in a matter as intensely personal as his sexual life. It is by no means clear that he would have allowed this.

At one point, when Jefferson realized that he was in terrible financial straits, he sat down to draw up a long-term financial plan for ridding himself of his debts. He projected that his farm would operate in the black for each successive year until all debts were retired, even though his operations had never operated in the black.[4] This is only one example of many that reveal the extent to which Jefferson could see the world in exactly the way he chose to see it despite all evidence to the contrary. Indeed, this ability is a useful, if not essential, trait for a visionary to possess.

Why could he not bring this trait to bear on the alleged relationship with Sally Hemings? Jefferson had been widowed at a young age, and there is evidence that he felt himself bound to a promise to his dying wife not to remarry. Almost nine months to the day after he married Martha Wayles Skelton, his first child was born.[5] Thereafter, Martha, who was sick during much of their marriage, was pregnant every two years until her death. Jefferson must have known that he had no problems with fertility. With what type of white woman could he have developed a long-term relationship and not fear that a circumstance might develop that would require him to marry? If he needed companionship, and his dalliance with Maria Cosway is evidence that Martha Jefferson's death had not killed his desire for the company of women, where could he turn to find it? Why could Thomas Jefferson not—as he did in so many other contexts—turn to a slave from Monticello for an answer to his predicament?

It is illustrative of the depth of passion that this topic excites, that some scholars—with an almost audible sigh of relief—have suggested that Jefferson solved his dilemma by seeking attachments to women who were already married.[6] To them, the thought of Jefferson perhaps cuckolding one of his neighbors and running the great risk of having small Jeffersons living under the roof of an unsuspecting husband is more comforting than the notion that the widowed Thomas Jefferson would have bound himself to the unmarried but inconveniently one-quarter black Sally Hemings. The former transgression would be understandable (and forgivable), the latter not so.

---

4. James A. Bear Jr., and Lucia C. Stanton, eds., Jefferson's Memorandum Books, 1393–94, Monticello Research Library.
5. Malone, Jefferson and His Time 1:153, 434.
6. Adair, Fame and the Founding Fathers, 182.

There is evidence from a man whom Malone described as Jefferson's friend that he did turn to a slave woman to satisfy his desire for companionship. John Hartwell Cocke, who worked closely with Jefferson as a founder of the University of Virginia and who served as one of the original members of its Board of Visitors, spoke of this matter in two entries of his diary. Writing in 1853 Cocke bemoaned the fact that many slave owners had children by slave women on their plantations. He went on to say that there was no wonder that this should be so when "Mr. Jefferson's notorious example is considered." In an 1859 entry Cocke complained about what he said was the common practice of unmarried slave owners keeping a slave woman "as a substitute for a wife." "In Virginia," he wrote, "this damnable practice prevails as much as anywhere—probably more—as Mr. Jefferson's example can be pleaded for its defense."[7]

Although Cocke expressed his disdain for what he said was this particular feature of Jefferson's life, there is ample evidence of his overall high regard for his colleague on the board. Edmund Bacon remembered that Cocke was often at Monticello during Jefferson's retirement. Against significant opposition Cocke was one of the key figures in helping Jefferson persuade the legislature to let him sell some of his land by lottery to avoid losing all of his estates. Even though Cocke, under the influence of religion, had become a fervent opponent of slavery by the time he wrote of Jefferson's liaison with a slave woman, to assume that having become an abolitionist, he also became a liar would be unfair. There were many other ways for Cocke to express his displeasure at Jefferson's involvement with slavery than making passing references in his private diary to Jefferson's having had a slave mistress.[8]

It seems that most Jefferson defenders have chosen to respond to the presentation of the Jefferson-Hemings liaison that was made in 1802, and not to the presentation made of it in the 1970s. By taking this tack they are falsely equating Fawn Brodie with James Callender, and they are also implicitly accepting as true Callender's depiction of the basic nature of this alleged relationship. In their view none of the events that happened in the years between 1802 and 1873 that shed additional light on this matter should be considered. Only James Callender's framing of the issue counts. Commentaries on this subject carry a tone of outrage that implies that the commentators themselves believe that Thomas Jefferson is being charged with something on the order of bestiality. This view of the allegation has affected their judgment and, consequently, their ability to present and assess the evidence in a fair or even a coherent fashion.

Jefferson and His "Very Snow-Broth" Blood

A variation on the theme that Thomas Jefferson's character would not have allowed a liaison with Sally Hemings centers, not on how the code of the southern gentleman would have shaped Jefferson's attitudes regarding such a liaison, but on how Jefferson's personal eccentricities would have made a relationship (especially one with a component of affection), if not impossible, at least improbable. This view is premised on the belief that

7. Excerpts from the journal of John Hartwell Cocke, Jan. 26, 1853, April 23, 1859, Monticello Research Library.
8. James A. Bear, Jr., *Jefferson at Monticello* (Charlottesville, Va., 1967), 61; Malone, *Jefferson and His Time* 6:142, 477.

while Jefferson had a great capacity for platonic love, he had no strong interest in expressing love in a romantic or sexual way.

Before looking at the substance of the argument, it is important to consider why it has been necessary to make it. In most historical writings the boundaries of Thomas Jefferson's sexual life have been firmly set as starting with his marriage to Martha Wayles and ending upon her death. As sexuality is, for most people, thought to be a normal part of human life, the question naturally arises about what Jefferson may or may not have been doing with respect to that issue over the forty-five years he lived after Martha Wayles died. There are no serious allegations of his sexual involvement with any woman over the course of that period but Sally Hemings. Because most scholars have been unwilling even to consider the possible truth of that story, they have had to put forth an explanation for the apparent absence of sexual activity on Jefferson's part.

The idea that Thomas Jefferson was a man lacking in sexual passion has been the most often cited explanation, and it is one of long standing. At the time the Sally Hemings story broke, one writer in a Federalist newspaper took extreme delight in expressing his surprise that the "solemn, the grave, and the didactic Mr. Jefferson" would have had a mistress. The writer was indicating that Jefferson's demeanor and his reputation for having a philosophical bent implied that his blood was "very snow-broth."[9] Of course, this enemy of Jefferson was having a bit of sport at the president's expense, and one would not expect much depth of insight from that quarter. To equate being solemn, grave, and didactic with being without sexual passion is, at best, a simplistic formulation. It is a caricature of the human personality which fits nicely with the goal of ridiculing Thomas Jefferson. The writer of those words was presenting a literary cartoon.

Surprisingly, this way of viewing Jefferson has leached into the scholarly writing about him as well. For some scholars Jefferson's fastidiousness, his attachment to reason and rationality, his zeal for exactitude, his obsession with orderliness, all signal that he was without a real capacity for romantic involvement or sexual passion.[1] What one makes of the fact that an individual possesses some or all of these characteristics is a function of one's own values and experiences and, of course, one's personal view of what it takes to be sexual or romantic. People who are compulsive about making lists have no interests in sex or romance. People who hold their emotions severely in check have no interest in sex or romance. People who are extremely clean have no interest in sex or romance. None of this follows. It is not even remotely a fact that a person who possesses all of these traits—even in abundance—is without sexual passion or romantic yearnings.

One could just as easily look to other aspects of Jefferson's activities and tastes to come to an opposite conclusion. He was a physical man, riding horses some great number of miles a day, gaining his slave artisans' admiration for his ability to make metal tools, pitting himself against much younger men in competitions designed to test strength and sometimes winning. Jefferson was also a man oriented to the senses. He had a stated appreciation for beauty in women, music, and art. He loved good food and

9. *Frederick-Town Herald*, reprinted in the *Richmond Recorder*, Sept. 29, 1802.
1. *PTJ* 10:453; Nathan Schachner, *Thomas Jefferson: A Biography*, 2 vols. (New York, 1951), 323; Garry Wills, "Uncle Thomas's Cabin," *New York Review of Books* 21 (April 18, 1974): 26

good wine. Even if individual character traits were reliable indicators of a person's level of sexual passion (a claim that requires the employment of stereotypes and extremely subjective judgments), it would be wrong to seize upon some aspects of Jefferson's character to draw inferences about the likely state of his sexual drive to the exclusion of other aspects. Malone described Jefferson as "a half dozen men rolled into one."[2] While one of those men may have been Jefferson the cerebral engineer (a specimen who hardly qualifies for presumptive asexuality), another of them was most certainly Jefferson the sybarite.

Even Jefferson's youthful romantic misadventure with Rebecca Burwell, in which he pined somewhat pathetically for a young woman who decided to marry another, has been employed to suggest that Jefferson's emotional development was abnormal. Certainly, some variation of Jefferson's experience with Burwell while he was a student in Williamsburg has happened to almost everyone, particularly in their youth. Jefferson's crush, which came when he was in his early twenties, has been treated as an event of singular importance that shaped his sexual profile over the sixty years that followed. It was long thought that the youthful and disappointed Jefferson placed misogynistic clippings in his Literary Commonplace Book in reaction to the Burwell affair, as though the event so traumatized him that he shunned women until he met Martha Wayles. But Douglas Wilson, the most recent editor of the Literary Commonplace Book, has demonstrated that the quotations were gathered well before Jefferson even met Burwell.[3] Jefferson's attraction to Burwell and, later, to Martha Wayles suggests that whatever negative feelings he may have had about women as group, he remained susceptible to the attractions of individual women.

Jefferson's written response to being thrown over by Rebecca Burwell has only rarely been considered. Jack McLaughlin noted it as one of Jefferson's few references to his attitude about sex. After he discovered that Burwell was lost to him, Jefferson wrote to friend: "Many and great are the comforts of a single state, and neither of the reasons you urge can have any influence with an inhabitant and a young inhabitant too of Wmsburgh. For St. Paul only says that it is better to be married than to burn. Now I presume that if that apostle had known that providence would at an after day be so kind to any particular set of people as to furnish them with other means of extinguishing the fire than those of matrimony, he would have earnestly recommended them to their practice."[4]

Jefferson was saying, in this extremely convoluted fashion, that he was glad that one does not have to be married in order to have sex. To paraphrase Jack McLaughlin's very perceptive question about this quote, who were the "particular set of people" whom "providence" had given the "means of extinguishing the fire" that St. Paul suggested should be extinguished through the marital bed? Loose women in Williamsburg? Prostitutes? One could argue that these words were the idle boast of a young man attempting to hide his pain. On the other hand, Jefferson may not only have been hurt, he may also have been serious about what he wrote. If so, this would

---

2. Malone, *Jefferson and His Time* 3:452.
3. Douglas Wilson, ed., *Thomas Jefferson's Literary Commonplace Book* (Princeton, N.J., 1989), 16.
4. McLaughlin, *Jefferson and Monticello*, 148; TJ. to William Fleming, March 10, 1764, *PTJ*, 1:16.

indicate that Jefferson considered sex with females to be a natural part of life, his life in particular. Scholars also have employed the Rebecca Burwell episode along with Jefferson's clumsy attempt as a young bachelor to seduce Mrs. Walker, his friend's wife, as evidence that he was awkward and shy with women, once again using incidents that occurred in his youth to define him at all stages of his extremely long life. Even if Jefferson continued to be awkward and shy with women all of his life, does that state necessarily indicate that he was without sexual passion or sexual partners? For all his alleged awkwardness, at least some of the women of Jefferson's era adored him. The correspondence of Eliza House Trist and the memoirs of Margaret Bayard Smith demonstrate that both were smitten with Jefferson. These two women's very warm responses were registered at two different periods in Jefferson's life, when he was in his forties and in his sixties. He spent his thirties as a married man. This all suggests that Jefferson knew very well how to make himself attractive to women and that the desire to do so was a basic feature of his personality.[5]

JEFFERSON'S HEAD AND HEART

Jefferson himself contributed to the view that he lacked the capacity for erotic passion by giving historians a handy phrase to use as a guidebook to his psyche. The title of Jefferson's love letter to the artist Maria Cosway, "My Head and Heart," has served as an all-purpose way of explaining him. Put simply, the argument goes, Thomas Jefferson's head always ruled over his heart.[6] This view of Jefferson has been useful to his worshipers and detractors alike. It allows worshipers of Jefferson to portray him as a man of supreme intellect, which can, of course, be seen as a good thing. Jefferson detractors can take that same belief and portray him as having been emotionally unbalanced; after all, what healthy person always does what his head tells him to do?

Certainly, "My Head and My Heart" was effective as a literary device, and it was self-revelatory. Jefferson was telling Cosway of the conflict that existed within him about their relationship. The problem arises when one lifts that phrase out of its very specific context and attempts to use it to explain or analyze other situations. Scholars who see Jefferson through the prism (and, it turns out, prison) of his literary device fail to understand its inherent limitations as a means for conducting a serious analysis of an individual's personality.

What matters are of "the head," and what matters are of "the heart"? Who decides? The historian? Jefferson? Are the head and heart always in opposition to one another? Don't they, in fact, usually work together in some combination? It is common for people whose hearts are deeply committed to something to see the matter as one of the head and, on other occasions, to take calculated (headlike) actions and then convince themselves that those acts arose from their sincere feelings (their hearts). Given that reality, historians who insist upon taking the "head and heart" vehicle seriously must

5. Margaret Bayard Smith, *The First Forty Years of Washington Society* (New York, 1906), 55–59; Eliza House Trist to TJ, April 13, 1784, *PTJ* 7:97.
6. *PTJ* 10:453; Jordan, *White over Black*, 461–62.

negotiate some difficult mental terrain. That is not an impossible task; it does, however, require the historian to try to know and consider with great care what Jefferson knew and considered at the time he took a particular action. The scholarly writing on the Hemings story gives no hint that such an attempt has been made.

Historians have taken it for granted that if Jefferson was involved with Sally Hemings, it would have been an instance in which the head failed to do its duty, because Jefferson would have made himself vulnerable politically were it widely known that he had a slave mistress. Jefferson might have seen matters differently than historians writing in the twentieth century. He existed in a society where a slave master taking a slave as a mistress, though frowned upon, was not unheard of. All that was required was discretion on the part of those involved and those who knew of it. James Callender's injection of this issue into the public domain undoubtedly was taken by southerners as further proof of that journalist's low status. Even if Jefferson's fellow countrymen believed the charge, they may have felt more anger at the one who exposed Jefferson than at Jefferson himself. Northerners seemed to view the matter as just another example of the strange things that went on in the South.

Of course, Jefferson's political enemies used the Hemings story as they would have used any other tool they thought would hurt him. It was to no avail, either because a critical mass of voters did not believe the charge— which seems unlikely given the story's persistence over the years—or it didn't matter. Jefferson's greatness outstripped whatever meaning could be derived from the Hemings allegation. Why couldn't Jefferson, one of the most astute politicians the country has produced, have used some combination of his head and heart to realize that he could weather whatever storm might arise by keeping his mouth shut, staying above the fray, and letting his enemies reveal themselves for the small men they were?

While Andrew Burstein's portrait of Jefferson moves beyond the simple head and heart formula, he fell back on the device when discussing Sally Hemings. Burstein's employment of the formula as a way of debunking the Hemings story is illustrative. He argued, based upon the prevailing view of scholars, that Jefferson "would have been uncharacteristically imprudent to be responsible for giving Sally the two children she bore after [Callender's] charges surfaced, while he remained president."[7] Burstein's analysis is a product of his virtual certainty that the Jefferson-Hemings relationship was not real. It is not very useful to think of the Hemings allegation only in terms of its being false. One must also consider the state of affairs that would have obtained if it was true.

Think of Burstein's argument and ask, If the story was true, how would Jefferson have responded to the Callender crisis? Before he was a lawyer, politician, president, or any of the other roles he played, Thomas Jefferson was a slave owner. It was the one role that he was born to. Is it so clear that Jefferson would not reasonably see Callender's attacks as touching, not only upon his political life, but upon his life as the master of Monticello as well? If so, would the master of Monticello alter his living arrangements because of a scandal created from the outside? That would mean, in Jefferson's eyes and

---

7. Andrew Burstein, *The Inner Jefferson: Portrait of a Grieving Optimist* (Charlottesville, Va. 1995), 231.

those of everyone else at Monticello, that a group of newspaper columnists, not he, ran the plantation. Jefferson would not have been inclined to let this happen.

What would have been the state of affairs between Jefferson and Hemings in 1802 if Madison Hemings's account is accurate? The relationship would have begun fourteen years before Callender's articles appeared. By that time Hemings would have borne him five children, three who died as infants. How would Jefferson have extricated himself from the relationship? Would Thomas Jefferson, portrayed in Burstein's book as an extremely sensitive man who made deep connections to others and held fast to those connections, have summarily abandoned a young woman who had placed her faith in him by giving up her chance for freedom and who had suffered for him in childbirth and in lost children? If so, this would be more than just a case of a man who used his head more than his heart; it would be Thomas Jefferson, a man with little heart and not a shred of honor or decency.

Perhaps the strangest thing of all about the view of Jefferson as a man ill-equipped for women and romance is that there is such obvious evidence against the proposition. Jefferson successfully courted and married a woman. Did his heart tell him to do this or his head? To be sure, Martha Wayles's father was a very wealthy man, but Jefferson's actions and others' accounts of their relationship show that he truly loved Martha. He loved one woman; why couldn't he have loved another? If reason always reigned supreme for Jefferson, how could he have put his beloved wife through the rigors of frequent childbearing when reason should have told him that she was unsuited to that particular task?

No matter what Jefferson's youthful statement to his friend suggests about the importance of female companionship, no matter what his courtship and marriage say about his ability to be touched by and to touch women, no matter what the Cosway-Jefferson affair demonstrates about his continuing interest in doing that, and no matter what evidence exists to support the notion that Jefferson's sexuality was expressed through a relationship with a woman on his plantation, those who believe that Jefferson had no great interest in sex rely on their already formulated and entrenched opinion and refuse to consider anything that suggests otherwise. Jefferson can never be let out of whatever box the given historian has chosen to place him in.

Ironically, historians who fasten upon the Burwell and Walker encounters and the phrase "head and heart" to make definitive statements about Jefferson's personality are engaging in psychological analyses every bit as tenuous as any of Fawn Brodie's Freudian speculations. Brodie's mistake was to be open about the fact that she was, at points, analyzing Thomas Jefferson according to the dictates of a particular school of psychology. The more traditional scholars who use the above-cited tools to make pronouncements about Jefferson's sexuality, or lack thereof, are doing the same thing but obscuring it by presenting their assertions in matter-of-fact declarative statements. They are using the tenets of their own method of psychoanalysis to construct their version of Thomas Jefferson.

The better approach would be to have some humility about one's capacity to know an individual with whom one has never interacted. Caution is certainly required when making judgments about an aspect of human life—sexuality—that is so personal and likely to be influenced by a myriad of hidden subtleties and nuances. Even when one knows another personally, making a judgment about that individual's level of sexual drive, or when or how it can be triggered, is risky.

For Thomas Jefferson historians must rely upon documents or circumstances to give guidance. That is all that is left to us, and those sources of information have limitations. Despite the existence of a voluminous body of Jefferson's personal letters, very little is known about his private life that could tell us about his sexuality. In his own writings Jefferson managed, as very private people often do, to impart a great deal of personal information without being particularly informative.

The views of Jefferson's daughters and grandchildren are important but must be taken with a grain of salt. They loved him. It is to be expected that there might be some bias in their assessments and that they would have had no interest in discussing examples of his sexuality even if they knew any. The all too widespread practice of cannibalizing one's family members for public consumption is largely a late twentieth-century sport. Therefore, they would not have left for posterity any thoughts they might have had about his sexual nature. Even if the Jefferson grandchildren could have presented totally unbiased remembrances of him, the Jefferson they knew was in his sixties, seventies, and eighties. A man at those stages of life could present himself in a very different guise than a man in his forties, the age at which Jefferson allegedly became involved with Sally Hemings.

In any case, one should be wary of the notion that Thomas Jefferson can be known by devouring the large body of documents that he and his family left for our perusal. Jefferson knew that he would be considered by posterity to have been a great man. Being familiar with the classical tradition, he also knew some of the ways in which posterity handles the lives of great men. The writings of, and about, the great man are pored over, analyzed, and discussed with the aim of discovering the source of his greatness. The basic nature of the great man is always of interest.

When Thomas Jefferson destroyed the letters that had passed between himself and Martha Wayles Jefferson, he was most likely destroying the best source of insight into who he really was. He would have been with her as he was with no one else. When he took similar actions on other occasions, asking correspondents to return his letters or to destroy them, the end result was the same: some important aspect of his true self was hidden from the world. What is left when one considers the remaining body of Jeffersonian documents, then, is generally a road map for how Thomas Jefferson wanted people to think of him. This does not mean that Jefferson's correspondence contains no insight into his character. He was not omnipotent. He could not hide everything. It does suggest that whatever certainty about the nature of his character one forms from such a body of documents must be tempered by the knowledge that key documents are missing and they are missing because of Jefferson's deliberate action.

The day-to-day Thomas Jefferson may have been, not the opposite of, but perhaps very different than, the Jefferson who appears in his self-consciously constructed documentary legacy. If one gets the impression that Thomas Jefferson's blood was snow-broth from his extant letters and the actions and thoughts described in them, it may well be that for some reason Jefferson wanted to be thought of in that way, whether he was actually that way or not. When Jefferson destroyed, or asked others to destroy, letters, it may have been precisely because they showed him to have been in some material respects different than the image he wanted to project to posterity. If that is the case, and it seems a reasonable one to make, then it is unwise to think that a complete picture of his character or aspects of his character like his sexuality can be drawn from the extant documents. Those who feel that the character reconstructed from this incomplete file would have precluded a liaison with Sally Hemings must confront the possibility that aspects of the character that could have been gleaned from the deliberately discarded pieces (indeed, the very fact that certain pieces were discarded) indicate otherwise.

✳   ✳   ✳

ANDREW BURSTEIN

From The Seductions of Thomas Jefferson†

We do not have to venerate Thomas Jefferson the man in order to recognize that an adroitness with the English language made him an essential force in extending—if he was not the foremost progenitor behind—America's romantic self-image. Now he is found to have been the most likely progenitor of a diverse family of Americans as well. What does this say about Jefferson? Can we avoid choosing to like or dislike him?

Presuming to know Jefferson's "real" personality has always seemed to raise issues. In his lifetime, aside from the many like Margaret Bayard Smith who marveled at his candor and "manner and voice almost femininely soft and gentle," there was the occasional Abigail Adams, who went from describing him as "one of the choice ones of the earth" to suspecting him of deceptions and personal vindictiveness. He irked some Federalists who reacted viscerally against his political schemes and at the same time found him excruciatingly likable in private conversation. After his death, Jefferson's idealism (as preserved in texts that grew more and more beloved) long diverted attention from his partisan methods. His imagined charm long obscured his parochial limitations. So is it a shame for recent generations of historians to have been equally seduced by Thomas Jefferson's perfectly crafted moralisms? No, but that does not let us off the hook either. Or, I should say, it does not let me off the hook.

In writing The Inner Jefferson: Portrait of a Grieving Optimist (1995), I noted how hard it has been for scholars to credit Jefferson with passion, despite the emotional resonance of his language. I concluded from his self-fashioned literary and epistolary personality that Jefferson, personally and politically tormented, wrestled with his passion while ever insisting on the

---

† From Journal of the Early Republic 19 (1999): 499–509. Reprinted with permission of the University of Pennsylvania Press. Burstein writes in the wake of the publication of results of DNA tests conducted by a team of researchers led by Eugene Foster in the United Kingdom and The Netherlands. These results indicated a genetic tie between male descendents of Thomas Jefferson's uncle Field Jefferson and of Sally Hemings. The results also ruled out, as suspected fathers of Hemings's children, Jefferson's nephews, Peter and Samuel Carr, and showed that Thomas Woodson (claimed to be Hemings's first son, "Tom") was unrelated to the Carrs, the Jeffersons, or other Hemingses. The test did not, however, conclusively prove that Thomas Jefferson was the sexual partner of Sally Hemings or the father of any of her children. See Annette Gordon-Reed, Thomas Jefferson and Sally Hemings, "Authors Note" to the paperback edition, May 1999.

importance of moderation, restraint, and self-control. In the wake of the DNA solution—albeit a partial and tentative conclusion—to the mystery of Jefferson's post-marital sex life and his contradictory attitude toward slavery and race, I have been obliged to look again at the evidence present in the texts he produced. I have to ask, what led me to detect passion, and yet conjecture that he was, in the end, too cautious, deliberative, and consumed with public reputation to prefer a liaison with Sally Hemings to the more predictable, morally safe, and financially prudent choice of a wife belonging to the planter class? To call him a hypocrite is overly simplistic; it is to determine that he is not worth understanding as a complex individual who did not escape complex cultural times.

I placed my brief discussion of the Hemings charges in the context of Jefferson's varied responses to political attacks. (Most scholars relate the controversy to racist vocabulary in *Notes on Virginia* and sexual dynamics within the institution of slavery.) To my dismay, reviewers of the book tended to open their comments with some statement on where, in the two and one-half pages allotted, I stood on this sensational issue. My expertise lies in Jefferson's use of language, his literary sentimentalism, and so that is how I choose to address the questions that loom in the wake of the new scientific evidence.

First, I must question why I did not accord more weight to the oral history of Sally Hemings's son Madison. The simple answer is that in carrying out a study of Jefferson-as-Jefferson-saw-himself (vulnerable, brooding, sincere, and generous, all at once), I ultimately privileged his letter-writing persona over other evidence. His epistolary world tells a great deal about Jefferson's impulses, but clearly it does not tell everything.

I was not seduced by Jefferson's political vocabulary. He professed to be a harmonizer while he in fact harbored an intense fear of perceived enemies, toward whom (through his vocal allies) he directed a militant energy. But I was seduced by the consistent moral-philosophical rigidity in his texts to accept the explanation, implicit in an abundance of directives across decades, that he would not succumb to carnal temptation: for example, addressing nephew Peter Carr on how to act when faced with a moral decision, he urged in words that summon now with an almost ghostly pathos, "ask yourself how you would act were all the world looking at you." His most personal documents ring with phrases like "virtuous dispositions," "good sense and prudence," "most chaste honour," and "innocent intentions." Jefferson's protégé and private secretary in Paris, William Short, himself involved in a torrid love affair with a married duchess, remarked on Jefferson's almost prudish aversion to sexual humor. The simple lesson is that no historian or biographer can claim to know the entirety of his or her subject's character, because most people prefer to hide their inner urges and present cleansed, crafted versions of who they are for the judgments of others. Those who do not are either called eccentric or mad.

In the course of researching and writing, I frequently labored over Carl Becker's legitimate old plaint: "Felicity of expression, certainly Jefferson had that; but one wonders whether he did not have too much of it." Becker saw Jefferson as alarmingly complacent, giving forth light but no heat. My answer to Becker was to cull from a lifetime of epistolary modesty the anguish that a palpable struggle between private and public obligations produced. Indeed, Jefferson ignited politics with his passionate concern for what he defined as liberty (and what in his retirement sounded more like states' rights). With all his passion, though, the letter-writing Jefferson closely controlled his output, gauged what turns of phrase and metaphorical images would put his correspondents most at ease—in short, he knew exactly what he was saying and doing at all times.

That is what is so remarkable about the adult Jefferson: private and public inclinations frequently clash, but the expressive writer always maintains a clear conscience. His epistolary disposition is as composed and consistent over time as his low, rounded, flourish-free handwriting. The personal flaw he most often remarked upon was that of being subject to remorse or confusion or heightened feeling, owing to a compassionate commitment to friendship or community—that which his moral constitution dictated. It was a fairly conventional gentlemanly protestation, and certainly not a real "flaw." The clear impression that we get from those who best knew Jefferson instructs us that he was, furthermore, an emotionally balanced individual, a constant friend and good companion. With a consistency and guiltlessness comparable to his epistolary productions, he imposed order on his voluminous personal accounts, aware of the "facts" of his financial plight while optimistically projecting their resolution, as Herbert Sloan so persuasively details in his *Principle and Interest: Thomas Jefferson and Debt*. As far as we know, stress manifest[ed] itself only through "periodical" migraines. So I have to wonder, did this artful communicator and painstaking record-keeper really ever question the propriety of any part of his regime? Did he lose sleep over his sleeping with Sally Hemings?

Seducers, slaveowners, and slave-owning seducers grow comfortable with the exercise of power. Indeed, they manipulate power in order to gratify private desires. Americans of color, with agonizing appreciation for what such impulses mean, were neither surprised nor shocked by the DNA findings. Their historical experience has made clear that the white man's fine words often disguised vulgar motives. In lacking this kind of historic memory, others in this country, even first generation immigrants, were more easily persuaded by the textual Jefferson, the gifted humanist revolutionary, and not the common slaveholding revolutionary, whom Annette Gordon-Reed recently termed a "garden-variety version of a white man."

White America has tended to be more readily (and willingly) seduced by the clarity and apparent naturalness of Jefferson's language, wanting to see Jefferson in the best light, because doing so has served its psychic need for moral solutions to immediate problems. Jefferson could fight the Nazis (the Jefferson Memorial was constructed during World War II) and symbolize pure patriotism and a pure love of freedom; he has lent power to many a just cause. Jefferson's generation similarly, and for the most part ecstatically, uncritically, marveled at the outstanding humanity of the poets and intellects of antiquity. It is human, if terribly conventional, to find solace in the enhancement of patriotic legend. When a diametric opposite is needed, a usable past is found.

Over the past thirty years the uncomfortable facts of American racism have been amplified by employing a different Jefferson image. He has become a hypocrite for us, possibly deserving the full force of this judgment, possibly not; but in any case, the expansive, quotable Jefferson is a most opportune target, because in our minds the embarrassing persistence of social inequality in this "more perfect union" has to have roots, and he could have done more to challenge Southern conventions. Thus he symbolizes the nation's tolerance for moral stagnation amid so much self-congratulation for its "progress." But it was never just Jefferson. It was everyone who belonged to the power structure. Power invites abuses and, because it becomes comfortable, power produces widespread rationalizations for those abuses.

Yes, he seduced posterity with public documents that still feed the need to define the nation through beautiful sentiments, and so we are heartened by his humanism. A few months before Jefferson's death in 1826, in the United States Senate, the irritable John Randolph mocked his humanist language as a "fanfaronade of abstractions." He was not seduced. He was also called mad. But did Jefferson, this master of control, seduce his slaves as well into believing that they were better off working for him than freed, cast off on their own in a society that would not grant them the rights of citizenship? Living within the moral margins of eighteenth-century Virginia, did he feel any real urge to grieve over his complicity in slavery? Not knowing that this was to be the issue on which posterity would judge him most harshly, did he simply fail to protect himself? Would he not have written and preserved more seductive texts, had he been able to anticipate us? Clearly, I mean to critique America here, far more than Jefferson.

Non-African Americans (and many African Americans) who have sought to protect Jefferson have done so because he is an essential part of the dominant narrative of the American past. Nothing can change the fact that the hopeful origins of this nation were written on "sacred" parchment by white men, whose principles were better than they were. We can disregard the imagined power of political correctness, because the founders cannot be replaced by those who came later—by a Lucretia Mott, a Frederick Douglass—no matter how persuasive these later narratives might be in the histories of those now seeking a counter-narrative which amplifies the voices of true social justice. Jefferson exists on a larger scale. We want to be seduced by him. He is the emotional hero and intellectual defender of an indestructible narrative. It was a white male passion for white liberty that was enshrined in the Declaration of Independence, even if it was not only white blood that was shed in the Boston Massacre and throughout the Revolutionary War. To distrust Jefferson completely is to distrust the generous emotion that he conveyed and the decent principles that he espoused. It is a jarring prospect. Few are comfortable assailing the symbolic philosopher-king, the pillar of American humanism. He embodies America's moral self-regard.

So what do we make of the "real" Jefferson hidden behind his apparently deceptive texts? Even the wonderful dialogue "between my Head and my Heart" directed to Anglo-Italian artist Maria Cosway in 1786 (before Sally entered the picture) was pure fondness. It lacked passionate commitment to anything beyond a sympathetic spiritual communion. In Mrs. Cosway he found a woman of prominence and aesthetic affinity. They visited museums, attended theater, rode in carriages over appealing landscapes, and picnicked together. "The power of his imagination," I wrote of our seducer, "brought him to the verge of satisfying his physical needs, but the power of his conscience likely constrained him from realizing his private fantasy. Or, if he did indeed succumb to a few moments of unrestrained passion, the consciousness of these acts must have riddled him with guilt, as he returned to a friendship marked by controlled passion." Indeed, that is certainly how things appeared as I examined subsequent months and years of the Jefferson-Cosway correspondence.

Here is how he did it: in private correspondence, he enlarged the proportions of world events while reducing the proportions of his own actions as an emotional being. In a world that was unrestrained, with forces of nature operating on an immense scale, the enlightened gentleman stood in awe while remaining personally self-restrained. This was the only way, the literary Jefferson is informing us, that humans had any chance of exerting their collective reason to tame an otherwise out of control universe of emotions.

While still wary of all psycho-biographical approaches, I am now left to ponder whether guilt was even possible for Thomas Jefferson, and in that case, whether he gave much thought to his exertion of power over one particular woman whom he owned. Sexual repression appears consistent in his literary personality, and management of the passions his abiding spirit. I made much of his decades-long fondness for the writings of Laurence Sterne, whose protagonist in *Tristram Shandy* alludes often to sexual feeling but does not consummate; the author wants to arouse, but there is no real sex. I meant to suggest that Jefferson was the same. It seems clear that he wanted to convey such a posture. After all, the libidinous Sterne was also a moralist, and, like the more self-revealing Englishman, Jefferson's conscience was always clear in every text he produced—whether the prescription was for family or public consumption. In political economy he might appear the visionary, or be labeled a misguided experimenter; but in moral economy he always knew the ground on which he stood. Here his reading was complete, here he excelled.

If some southern patriarchs loved and lived openly with women they owned, and others plainly raped their slaves, what should be the moral and emotional margins within which Jefferson's actions are to be categorized? This remains a difficult problem for scholars. In so many letters to those under his charge, Jefferson urged charm along with moral rectitude. To his eldest grandson, Thomas Jefferson Randolph, he prescribed good humor and amiability as the only qualities of mind more important than integrity. Was Jefferson forthcoming with his family? Or was nothing said? But should it be at all odd that his one surviving daughter, Martha, protected her politically vulnerable father on all accounts? Without a son who could inherit, Jefferson raised her to be strong and competent, and unafraid. Typical of her dutiful posture, she wrote her father before he retired from the presidency, "It is truly the happiness of my life to think that I can dedicate the remainder of it to promote yours." Thus Martha Jefferson Randolph and her son were groomed to maintain a sturdy public demeanor much like the politically embattled Jefferson himself. If we assume that they knew the truth about Sally Hemings (and this must remain an assumption only), they appear to have behaved like Jefferson himself by absolving themselves from possible guilt through complicity in a "coverup." Were repression and control "Jefferson" qualities spanning the three immediate generations? This is another of those presumably indeterminate aspects of the story.

Americans most resistant to recasting historical "truth," jaded citizens of our day grown suspicious of all evidence, have already begun to point out the technicalities involved in the DNA study: A male relative of Jefferson could have had sexual relations with Sally Hemings. Little is known about Jefferson's violin-playing younger brother Randolph beyond his having fiddled in the slave quarters at Monticello. He shares his brother's DNA and had several sons. Plantations were inbred communities where race mixing was frequent.

Others, of course, ponder whether Jefferson might have loved Sally and whether she loved him. As DNA reveals paternity but not emotion, we most likely will never know. Yet this scenario must appear unlikely given Jefferson's ease in exercising power: Could he have overcome that governing dynamic? Construing love seems entirely the wishful thinking of modern romantics, who reflect the presumption that a virile president's sexual activity is less objectionable if the female is young and can be "made over" (as fiction writers and filmmakers have rendered Sally) into one who is physically appealing and acts from her own volition. In fact, though, once James T. Callender's politically inspired charges appeared in print in 1802, even Jefferson's most sarcastic detractors saw fit only to mock his irregular passion for a "low woman" and did not perceive any more significant transgression against the public morality—nor imagine the connection as companionate love.

Sadly, then, the renewed interest in Jefferson's sex life reflects ideological confusion and unresolved race-activated insecurities within American political culture in the 1990s. It denies the greater value of comprehending the moral and philosophical boundaries of Jeffersonian democracy. To most Americans, Jefferson's inspiring words are easily taken at face value, and the partisan, parochial southerner, is imagined only as a genial and enlightened cosmopolitan; here his epistolary personality continues to charm. Better to see him in the context of his personal and political alliances, to trace his interactions with other ambitious minds in the lively republic of letters. That way, we don't have to like or dislike him for what he did in order to find him an intriguing historical actor.

Approaching my own Jefferson project, I had vowed that I would not end up as devoted Jefferson scholars Dumas Malone and Merrill Peterson, the latter of whom wrote of Jefferson's "glasslike surface" and finally determined that his subject "concealed his feelings behind an almost impenetrable wall of reserve." Bernard Bailyn insisted in the early 1960s that Jefferson's real personality had vanished in history. John Dewey before that said that Jefferson was too atypical to be compared to any norm, and that, in any case, he did not want to be known. I had thought to challenge these images by studying what Jefferson read and how he responded to it. Enthusiastically, I announced that "the letter-writing Jefferson accentuated certain images, modified the uses of certain words, supplied individuality to his eloquence. Thus he is penetrable." I still believe that to call him a "sphinx" is a cop-out. Just because, like all people, he hid aspects of his thought and behavior does not mean he resists any analysis other than the psycho-historical. He manipulated language, was canny and convincing; this is what propelled him to the head of the first opposition party in American politics—and to the presidency—while eloquently asserting, as he did to John Adams in 1796, that politics was "a subject I never loved, and now hate."

* * *

Jefferson's ability to rationalize his angry politics might have suggested to me the possibility that he could as easily rationalize taking liberties with the enslaved woman. One reviewer was shocked that in what appeared an otherwise sympathetic treatment, I could assert that "Jefferson found himself blameless in all things" and "consistently assigned blame to sources outside himself." I recognized this in his political correspondence but saw, of course, how he unerringly avoided any such expression in his mild and appealing personal writings. Ah, the seductions of Thomas Jefferson. It makes sense that a man of extraordinary belletristic talents who tightly controlled his literary output, the compassionate friend who wrote warm letters to charm married women while scrupulously maintaining outward propriety, one who I surmised was sexually repressed—could have been in fact both sexually repressed and sexually active. In the texts he left, he refused to acknowledge himself as a sexual being.

Importantly, this does not vindicate every aspect of Fawn Brodie's analysis of Jefferson's character, though her conclusion can no longer be ignored. Her *Thomas Jefferson: An Intimate History* is still marred by frequent misreadings of language and over-interpretations of Jefferson's unconscious thoughts. For instance, the eighteenth-century letter writer's use of words like "ardour" or "appetite" does not necessarily indicate the "unmistakable flavor of sexuality," as she insisted. Annette Gordon-Reed's *Thomas Jefferson and Sally Hemings: An American Controversy* goes far in chastising adoring biographers for a single-minded acceptance of Jefferson's superior moral values; but it intends to introduce other possibilities, not other certainties. We do not now turn about and privilege African-American oral histories over Euro-American authored texts—the supposed pregnancy of Sally Hemings in France, testified to by Madison Hemings, remains unclear insofar as the alleged offspring, Thomas Woodson, did not share Jefferson's gene structure. Thus we must examine all evidence carefully, while recognizing that no one escapes ideology; all people have private motives.

In the historian's language of "likelihood," a variant of lawyer Gordon-Reed's recitation of circumstantial evidence, Thomas Jefferson has suddenly become the *most likely* father of Hemings's children. However, to prevent a new absolute from taking over, I wish to present a bit of countervailing evidence to remind us of the uncertainties inherent in what we do as scholars: Randolph Jefferson, of whom we know (and care about) far less than we do his famous older brother, was widowed at an indeterminate date and remarried in 1809, after which Hemings stopped conceiving. Randolph lived on the nearby plantation of Snowden and was as likely as brother Thomas to give Randolph family names—Beverly, Eston—to offspring. This, of course, does not explain why Madison Hemings, in his now heralded interview, would not have identified his father as *Randolph* Jefferson. Still, the cautionary note seems necessary, even if the "likelihood" remains with Thomas Jefferson.

Jefferson will never go on television to apologize that "I was wrong. I had an inappropriate relationship with Ms. Hemings." The unfathomable questions that remain are even more numerous than before the DNA tests. Among the most disquieting are these: How did Jefferson's family ultimately come to direct posterity to Peter and Samuel Carr as the most likely fathers of Sally's children? Why did Jefferson show no apparent tenderness, let alone acknowledge, his relationship to Sally's children, and how might this have affected Sally herself? In his testimony, Madison Hemings referred to his own mother as a "concubine"—no love is implied in that designation—and he never suggested that she was a good mother. Samuel Johnson's *Dictionary* defines concubine as "a woman kept in fornication; a whore." On the other hand, Madison may have been thinking dispassionately in the Biblical sense of a woman with whom a man shared a bed and shared feelings but not an empowering social legitimacy. In late eighteenth-century Latin America, concubinage was a common practice among elite men and lower class, racially mixed women. We may need to refocus on this element in interpreting southern United States slave culture. In any event, making sense of the emotional in what happened between this particular master and his slave will continue to be the principal mystery in the aftermath of the DNA findings.

I will conclude this exercise in re-engagement with the inner Jefferson by repeating one particular statement I made: "Embracing a concept of man's virtuous potential relieved his troubled soul. . . . Jefferson built and grew things and expanded his network of friends to preserve and maximize control over life that was fleeting." He needed others. He needed others to imagine a national political consensus, to realize a political vision which was often assailed and which he fought for with a ferocity the likes of which he brought to bear in no other cause; nearly to his dying day Jefferson projected that Federalism was merely dormant and was threatening to reconstitute and resurface. And, in a comparable way, he needed others to fortify the optimism he consistently (privately and publicly) expressed in his self-sustaining epistolary world.

His literary imagination, tapping human dramas from the Greek and Roman classics to Sterne, undergirded every other purpose in his emotional life. Here where Jefferson was most energetic and intense, we can continue to chart his activities and describe him, should his sexual imagination and his feelings about Sally Hemings and her/their children prove impossible to know. As a complex individual, Jefferson displayed a tendency to invite controversy and apparently denied responsibility for having done so. That is a good place to start.

ROBERT M. S. McDONALD

From Thomas Jefferson's Changing Reputation as Author of the Declaration of Independence†

Americans who cheered Thomas Jefferson as the author of the Declaration of Independence dumbfounded John Adams. He, too, had sat on the committee assigned by the Continental Congress to compose the treasonous tract. The committee approved it, and then so did Congress, but only after subjecting it to "severe Criticism, and striking out several of the most oratorical Paragraphs. . . ." The Declaration was a group project and not, as Jefferson's admirers claimed, a solitary performance. "Was there ever a *coup de théâtre* that had so great an effect as Jefferson's penmanship of the Declaration of Independence?" Adams wondered in 1805. "The Declaration of Independence I always considered as a theatrical show," he said six years later. "Jefferson ran away with all the stage effect . . . and all the glory of it."[1]

† From *Journal of the Early Republic* 19 (1999): 169–95. Reprinted with permission of the University of Pennsylvania Press. Numbered notes are McDonald's.

1. John Adams, "Autobiography," Oct. 5, 1802 [ca. June 7, 1805], in *Diary and Autobiography of John Adams*, ed. L.H. Butterfield (4 vols., Cambridge, MA, 1961), III, 337; Adams to Benjamin Rush, Sept. 30, 1805, in *The Spur of Fame: Dialogues of John Adams and Benjamin Rush, 1805–1813*, ed. John A. Schultz and Douglass Adair (San Marino, CA, 1966), 43; Adams to Rush, June 21, 1811, *ibid.*, 182.

Adams's resentment resulted from confusion as much as jealousy. When he was young, an author was an authorizer, and Congress, not Jefferson, had authorized the Declaration. Few people had known that Jefferson drafted the document, and even fewer people cared. Now, however, the meaning of authorship was shifting in ways that Adams did not yet grasp. For increasing numbers of Americans, authorship was an individual act of creation and, since the 1790s, Jeffersonian Republicans had told them that Jefferson did more than any other individual to create the Declaration. Adams still thought of him as the Declaration's penman, but they had come to exalt him as its author.

Two recent studies begin to explain this phenomenon. Pauline Maier's *American Scripture*, the first book-length monograph to examine critically how the Declaration gained its high status, shows that it "was at first forgotten almost entirely" by Americans. Then, for political reasons, Republicans "recalled and celebrated" it, and later elevated it "into something akin to a holy writ."[2] Meanwhile, Jay Fliegelman's *Declaring Independence* situates the Declaration and the literary craftsmanship of its principal draftsman within "eighteenth-century theories and practices of rhetoric." Fliegelman explains that Jefferson, who borrowed ideas and words from previous writers, did not anticipate "the changing nature of authorship— from a view that sees the editorial and authorial functions as versions of one another to one that stresses the primacy and originality of imagination." Taken together, these books represent the most important revision of our knowledge of the Declaration since Carl Becker and Julian Boyd issued their classic appraisals of the document many decades ago.[3]

But neither Maier's acknowledgment of the Declaration's partisan usefulness nor Fliegelman's cultural contextualization addresses the seemingly natural question: How did Jefferson, initially anonymous as penman of the Declaration, gain renown as its author? Apparently unaware of Jefferson's early obscurity as draftsman, Fliegelman ignores the issue. Maier notes that Jefferson's "authorship was not yet common knowledge" even in the 1780s; but like other scholars cognizant of this fact, she does not explain why.[4] Tracing the Declaration's stature within evolving political and literary landscapes, this essay argues that between 1776 and 1826 the text's usefulness

2. Pauline Maier, *American Scripture: Making the Declaration of Independence* (New York, 1997), 154. The final chapter of Maier's book updates and expands on the notable article by Philip F. Detweiler, "The Changing Reputation of the Declaration of Independence: The First Fifty Years," *The William and Mary Quarterly*, 19 (Oct. 1962), 557–74, from which this essay derives its title. The engaging new book by Len Travers, *Celebrating the Fourth: Independence Day and the Rites of Nationalism in the Early Republic* (Amherst, MA, 1997), chaps. 3–6, while focusing less on the Declaration than on Fourth of July festivities, also describes how partisanship played a role in the document's promotion.

3. Jay Fliegelman, *Declaring Independence: Jefferson, Natural Language and the Culture of Performance* (Stanford, CA, 1993), 1, 3 (quotations); Carl Becker, *The Declaration of Independence: A Study in the History of Political Ideas* (New York, 1922); "The Declaration of Independence," [June 11-July 4, 1776], in *PTJ*, I, 413–33; Julian P. Boyd, *The Declaration of Independence: The Evolution of the Text as Shown in Facsimiles of Various Drafts by its Author, Thomas Jefferson* (Princeton, 1945). Fliegelman's book incorporates ideas from Jacques Derrida's paper on the Declaration's "authority," delivered in 1976 at the University of Virginia and published in English as Derrida, "Declarations of Independence," *New Political Science*, 15 (Summer 1986), 7–17.

4. Maier, *American Scripture*, 162. For other acknowledgments of Jefferson's initial obscurity as the Declaration's author, see Detweiler, "The Changing Reputation of the Declaration of Independence," 560; *PTJ*, XV, 241n; and Joseph J. Ellis, *American Sphinx: The Character of Thomas Jefferson* (New York, 1997), 243. One recent Jefferson biography, though correctly observing that "it was years [after 1776] before most people knew Thomas Jefferson wrote the Declaration of Independence" erroneously dates the first public revelation of his authorship to 1800—seventeen years too late; see Willard Sterne Randall, *Thomas Jefferson: A Life* (New York, 1993), 272 (quotation), 279, 544.

hinged on Americans' initial ignorance and then gradual recognition of Jefferson's authorship.

* * *

Jefferson's draftsmanship remained obscure during the Revolution and throughout the 1780s. Americans who celebrated the Fourth of July as the anniversary of independence paid scant attention to the Declaration and even less to its writer. Dignitaries at a 1785 Independence Day dinner in New York, for example, toasted Washington, soldiers who died in combat, European allies, and "Liberty, peace and happiness to all mankind." But no one raised a glass to Jefferson. The earliest chroniclers of the nation's history, moreover, displayed similar indifference about the Declaration and its authorship. Philip Mazzei, Jefferson's long-time friend, mentioned only incidentally in his history of American politics that the Virginian had served as scribe of independence. William Gordon's history of war and independence, published in 1789, termed the Declaration an "act of separation from the crown of Great-Britain" and identified Jefferson only as one member of the committee that wrote it. Similarly, David Ramsay's *History of the American Revolution*, published the same year, ignored Jefferson and dryly described the Declaration as the "act of the united colonies for separating themselves from the government of Great-Britain." It was a means to an end of British rule, not a powerfully-penned beginning of American government.[5]

Beginning in the 1790s, after faction polarized the newly constituted United States government and Jefferson won recognition as a prominent political figure, partisans found new uses for the document. In 1792, while Jefferson as secretary of state endured an unprecedented barrage of Federalist opprobrium, his image as scribe of independence gained great currency. A *National Gazette* writer sought public support for "Tom Jefferson" by noting that "he composed the Declaration of Independence" and claiming that he "moved for it first in Congress." Apparently, this failed to impress William Loughton Smith, a leader of Alexander Hamilton's faction, for his 1792 pamphlet, *The Politicks and Views of a Certain Party, Displayed*, excoriated Jefferson as a self-promoting demagogue but mentioned, in passing, that he had served as "Chairman of the Committee who drew up the Declaration of Independence." Republicans, however, realized that by linking Jefferson with the Declaration they could increase his popularity, enhancing their chances for electoral success. At Fourth of July festivities, they bolstered their ties to America's revolutionary legacy by heaping praise upon the Declaration, which, they frequently informed audiences, Jefferson had drafted. Federalists, in various ways, rebuffed their rivals' assertions and minimized the Virginian's contribution.[6] Although politics spurred the protracted debate, it hinged on semantic

5. *Connecticut Courant* (Hartford), July 11, 1785; Filippo Mazzei, *Researches on the United States*, ed. and trans. Constance D. Sherman (1788; rep., Charlottesville, 1976), 157; David Ramsay, *The History of the American Revolution* (2 vols., Philadelphia, 1789), I, 340–41; William Gordon, *The History of the Rise, Progress, and Establishment of the Independence of the United States of America* (3 vols., New York, 1789), II, 92, 105. On the unimportance of the Declaration during this period, see Maier, *American Scripture*, 154, 160, 168–69. For a thorough account of the early historiography of the Declaration, see Detweiler, "The Changing Reputation of the Declaration of Independence," 563–66.
6. "Kibrothnataavah," *National Gazette* (Philadelphia), 12 Sept. 1792; [William Loughton Smith], *The Politicks and Views of a Certain Party, Displayed* (Philadelphia, 1792), 28. Republican efforts to connect Jefferson with the Declaration began in earnest after his inauguration as vice president. See, for example, toasts made in his honor at Republican Fourth of July banquets, printed in the

qualifications reflecting a tenuous, uneasy shift in traditional conceptions of authorship and authority. As such, Independence Day orators and patriotic toast-givers addressed not only the issue of who had written the Declaration, but also the question of who deserved credit for the thoughts it voiced.

The earliest known public reference to Jefferson's role as draftsman attributed the Declaration's sentiments to all Americans. "Jefferson," [Ezra] Stiles told the Connecticut General Assembly, "poured the soul of the continent into the monumental act of Independence."[7] The May 8, 1783, sermon, published in New Haven by Thomas and Samuel Green and then two years later by Isaiah Thomas in Worcester, Massachusetts, constitutes the first printed account of Jefferson's service as the framer of independence. With hundreds of copies sold in New England, Stiles's pronouncement about the origins of the Declaration resonated far beyond the walls of the Hartford statehouse.[8] A few months later a Boston newspaper, noting Jefferson's arrival in town to embark on a diplomatic mission to France, observed that "the memorable declaration of American Independence is said to have been penned by him."[9]

The recording in print of Jefferson's contribution hastened the dispersal of the information, which formerly had passed through conversations. Stiles, for example, recorded in his diary in 1777 that he had "Dined in Company with Col. [John] Langdon formerly of the Continental Congress. He says Mr. Jeffries of Virginia drafted the Declaration of Independency." Stiles's confusion about Jefferson's name probably resulted from the fact that Langdon, too, was a second-hand source. Although Langdon left the Congress in 1775, he was a close friend of William Whipple, who had replaced him in the New Hampshire delegation and signed the Declaration the following year. Jefferson's authorship may even have been known to most members of Connecticut's legislature. Stiles's brief reference to "Jefferson, who poured the soul of the continent into" Congress's "monumental act," reads like a reminder, not an announcement. Besides Stiles, however, the small and slowly growing number of Americans who knew of Jefferson's service had found no reason to consider it important.[1]

Now, however, they found a compelling one. As an embittered Federalist noted in 1802, Republicans employed America's seminal charter "as a weapon in favor of the election of a man to the first office under our government."[2] But while the dozens of wordsmiths who spread news of Jeffer-

---

Aurora (Philadelphia), July 7, 12, 13, 1797; and in the *Gazette of the United States* (Philadelphia), July 12, 15, 1797. Federalists appropriated the Declaration to enhance the fame of Adams and John Hancock, their own political heroes. See *Gazette of the United States*, July 4, 1792; and Jacob Fisher, *An Oration, Pronounced at Kennebunk, on the Fourth day of July, 1799; Being the Anniversary of American Independence* (Portland, ME, 1799), 5.

7. Ezra Stiles, *The United States elevated to glory and honor* (New Haven, 1783), 46.
8. Previous investigations have also failed to uncover an earlier public reference to Jefferson as author of the Declaration. See Detweiler, "The Changing Reputation of the Declaration of Independence," 560; and *PTJ* XV, 241n.
9. *The Massachusetts Centinel and the Republican Journal* (Boston), June 30, 1784. See also Merrill D. Peterson, *Thomas Jefferson and the New Nation: A Biography* (New York, 1970), 294–95, which quotes the *Centinel* tribute and notes that it "suggests Jefferson's rising fame as the author of the Declaration of Independence as well as his reputation, even before the publication of the *Notes on the State of Virginia*, for philosophy."
1. *The Literary Diary of Ezra Stiles*, ed. Franklin Bowditch Dexter (3 vols., New York, 1901), II, 155; William A. Robinson, "William Whipple" in Dumas Malone, ed., *The Dictionary of American Biography* (10 vols., 8 supplements, New York, 1928–88), X, part 2, 71.
2. "A Buckskin," *Virginia Gazette*, Sept. 10, 1802.

son's congressional role held in common a desire to promote him for office, they revealed subtle differences in how they viewed his contribution. All agreed that Jefferson had performed the physical act of drafting the Declaration. Toasts at Republican Fourth of July banquets in Washington, D.C., for example, described him as "the penman of the declaration of Independence" and noted that his was the "hand that drew the declaration of Independence."[3] As printers' frequent capitalization of "Independence" after their lowercasing of the word "declaration" suggests, during the first decade of the nineteenth century, the revolutionary idea of national autonomy still remained above and apart from Jefferson's decree.

Thus in 1801 the proadministration *National Intelligencer* distinguished between Jefferson's singular action and the Continental Congress's shared assertion when it reported the "patriotic gratitude" that an enthusiastic Independence Day crowd showered upon the "first magistrate . . . whose pen had traced, whose councils had recommended, and whose firmness and talents had co-operated to establish the declaration of Independence." Similarly, members of New York's zealously Republican Tammany Society heard the Fourth of July address in 1800 of Matthew Davis, who praised "the capacious mind and nervous pen of Jefferson," who produced a "Manly and energetic" text distinguished by a "Solemn and impressive . . . sound." Davis pointed out, however, that Jefferson's words communicated "the voice of a free, united and indignant people." Hundreds of miles south, at St. Philip's Church in Charleston, orator John Pringle extolled "JEFFERSON, in whose perspicuous and energetic language is expressed that sublime memorial of the rights, and the spirit of free-born Americans." James Kennedy, a year later at the same site (and displaying an uncommon spirit of nonpartisanship), lauded "that celebrated declaration, penned by the enlightened, dignified and patriotic Jefferson, and advocated by the firm, honest and sagacious Adams." In sum, the young Virginian drew, penned, traced, and phrased the Declaration; the act of independence itself, however, required the cooperation, embodied the will, and depended on the advocacy of others.[4]

Not all Republicans drew such distinctions. A number of them granted to Jefferson the much greater status of "author" and reified his text by conflating the Declaration as document, to which they imparted a more formalized title, with American autonomy as fact. At a Boston gathering of "Young Democratic Republicans" on July 4, 1805, for example, Ebenezer French praised the president as "the immortal author of the DECLARATION OF AMERICAN INDEPENDENCE"; twelve months later, he focused the attention of an assembly of Maine Republicans on "the glorious instrument written by the illuminous JEFFERSON, called the '*Declaration of American Independence.*'" Although other speechmakers merely credited Jefferson's hand for drawing up the document, these claimed that his thoughts had conceived it. Two years later, Levi Lincoln, Jr. of Massachusetts applauded Jefferson, "the sublimity of whose mind first ken'd American Independence and whose pen impressed the solemn Declaration." Three years later, Georgia's Steele White

3. *National Intelligencer* (Washington, DC), July 6, 1805; *ibid.*, July 16, 1804.
4. *Ibid.*, July 6, 1801; Matthew Livingston Davis, *An Oration, Delivered in St. Paul's Church, on The Fourth of July, 1800* (New York, 1800), 11–12; John J. Pringle, *An Oration, Delivered in St. Philip's Church, Before the Inhabitants of Charleston, South-Carolina, on the Fourth of July, 1800* (Charleston, 1800), 16; James Kennedy, *An Oration, Delivered in St. Philip's Church, Before the Inhabitants of Charleston, South-Carolina, on the Fourth of July, 1801* (Charleston, 1801), 21.

marveled at the skill with which the Virginian's "illumined mind could pen a 'Declaration of Independence'."[5]

* * *

Although earlier the exact nature of Jefferson's role as framer of the Declaration hardly mattered to the public, the apotheosis of his text now made crucial the issue of authorship. In 1802, a pseudonymous Federalist, who called himself "A Buckskin," lashed out at proud Republicans on the pages of the *Virginia Gazette*. He asserted that, despite "repeated and positive assertions to the contrary," Jefferson "was not the draftsman of the declaration of American independence." Instead, he claimed, the Virginian merely sat on a Congressional committee charged with composing a statement of autonomy. After "an instrument to that effect had been drawn by *the committee*, not by Mr. Jefferson," Congress made "essential alterations" of the document's language. Citing as his source first-hand testimony "from the mouths of two of the venerable sages and patriots who composed that congress," this writer attributed the "elegant form" that the Declaration "at last assumed" to "the handsome amendments proposed by a gentleman who has since become the victim of jacobinical slanders" but not to "any brilliancy of talents on the part of Mr. Thomas Jefferson."[6]

Although this writer strived to deprive the president of any special claim to the Declaration's substance and style, his assertions confirmed that the Declaration as a text had begun to assume a position of importance rivalling that of Congress's collective declaration. Though a number of Republican statements already corroborated the accuracy of this implicit recognition, the 1806 murder of George Wythe, Jefferson's friend and mentor, set off a chain of events that attracted additional attention to the issue of authorship. Wythe, who drank the poison of an estranged grandnephew, left an estate that included a copy of the draft of the Declaration of Independence that Jefferson, apparently, had given him thirty years earlier.[7] Thanks to the estate's executor and the editor of the Richmond *Enquirer*, Jefferson's "*original* Declaration of our Independence" subsequently gained a wide audience within the Old Dominion. The nationally-important *Intelligencer* reprinted it as well, adding its own recognition of the president as the "distinguished author" of this "splendid composition" to the *Enquirer*'s claim:

5. Ebenezer French, *An Oration, Pronounced July 4th, 1805, Before the Young Democratic Republicans, of the Town of Boston, in Commemoration of the Anniversary of American Independence* (Boston, 1805), 18; French, *An Oration, Pronounced Before the Republican Inhabitants, of Portland, on the Fourth of July, 1806, Being the Thirtieth Anniversary of American Independence* (Portland, ME, 1806), 6; Levi Lincoln, Jr., *An Oration, Pronounced at Brookfield, Upon the Anniversary of American Independence, on the Fourth of July, 1807; Before a Numerous Assembly of the Republicans of the County of Worcester* (Worcester, 1807), 13; Steele White, *An Oration, Commemorative of American Independence, Delivered on this Fourth of July, 1810* (Savannah, 1810), 14. See also *National Intelligencer*, July 11, 1804; and Adrian Hegeman, *An Oration, Delivered on the Fourth of July, 1801, in the Township of Oyster-Bay, in Queen's County, Before a Number of Republican Citizens Assembled to Celebrate the Anniversary of our National Independence* (New York, 1801), 14.
6. "A Buckskin," *Virginia Gazette*, Sept. 10, 1802, reprinted in the *Richmond Recorder*, Sept. 29, 1802.
7. Although Wythe's surviving correspondence with Jefferson does not reveal how he came to possess a copy of Jefferson's final draft of the Declaration, Jefferson later wrote of the "rough drafts I sent to distant friends who were anxious to know what was passing." Although "to whom" Jefferson sent his version he could "not recollect," it seems likely that Wythe, who led Virginia's Continental Congress delegation but had absented himself to tend to business in Williamsburg while Jefferson penned the document, was one of them. See Jefferson to John Vaughn, Sept. 16, 1825, in Paul Leicester Ford, ed., *Writings of Thomas Jefferson*, 10 vols. (New York, 1892–99), X, 345. On the provenance of the Wythe copy, see Boyd, *The Declaration of Independence*, 43–45. For a full examination of Wythe's demise, see Julian P. Boyd, "The Murder of George Wythe," *William and Mary Quarterly*, 12 (Oct. 1955), 513–42.

The federal assertion that Mr. Jefferson was not the author of this celebrated declaration, has long since been refuted or else these papers would have furnished the most abundant refutation. What now will become of the no less unfounded assertion, that this paper as it was adopted by Congress, owes much of its beauty and its force to the committee appointed to draft it? The world will see that not only were very few *additions* made by the committee, but that they even struck out two of the most forcible and striking passages in the whole composition.[8]

✻   ✻   ✻

✻ ✻ ✻ In 1821, when [Jefferson] penned the history of his life up until his service as secretary of state, he took care to affirm that in 1776, as a member of the committee appointed by the Continental Congress to "prepare a declaration of independence," his colleagues "desired me to do it. It was accordingly done, and being approved by them, I reported it to the house on Friday the 28th of June." Because "the sentiments of men are known not only by what they receive, but what they reject also," Jefferson included in his autobiography not only the draft approved by Congress but also the "parts struck out" by its members "& those inserted by them." Since "erroneous statements of the proceedings on the declaration of independence" had appeared "before the public in latter times," he emphasized that his lengthy description of the Declaration's development came from notes taken on the spot. Jefferson intended his autobiography, he wrote at the start, "for my own more ready reference & for the information of my family." That he made this claim at all, however, suggests an assumption—perhaps a hope—that a larger audience would someday read his account. Certainly, it included none of the personal recollections that he liked to share with loved ones, none of the stories of friendship and family devotion that his granddaughter, Sarah Randolph, later weaved into her *Domestic Life of Thomas Jefferson*. And if Jefferson truly wrote his autobiography solely for himself and his relatives, then why did Thomas Jefferson Randolph, the grandson to whom he entrusted his papers, rush it into publication as part of *The Memoirs, Correspondence and Private Papers of Thomas Jefferson*, which appeared only three years after his death?[9]

Beyond a few paragraphs of genealogical information, the autobiography constituted a record of his career as Jefferson saw it and wanted it remembered. The fact that he had labored as the Declaration's draftsman he wanted nobody to forget. This, after all, was the man who had hung copies of the Declaration and an engraving of John Trumbull's 1820 depiction of its signing on the walls of his much-visited mountain-top home, near

8. Richmond *Enquirer*, June 20, 1806, reprinted in the *National Intelligencer*, July 2, 1806. The argument that Congressional editing improved the Declaration did not vanish, however; nearly two decades later, Timothy Pickering wrote that "to those 'critics' Mr. Jefferson is indebted for much of the applause which has been bestowed upon him as AUTHOR of the Declaration." See Timothy Pickering, *A Review of the Correspondence Between the Hon. John Adams, Late President of the United States, and the Late William Cunningham, Esq., Beginning in 1803, and Ending in 1812* (2d ed., Salem, MA, 1824), 139.

9. Jefferson, "Autobiography," [6 Jan. 1821–29 July 1821], in *The Political Writings of Thomas Jefferson*, ed. Merrill D. Peterson (Charlottesville, 1993), 17–24, 3; Sarah N. Randolph, *The Domestic Life of Thomas Jefferson* (New York, 1871); Thomas Jefferson Randolph, ed., *The Memoirs, Correspondence and Private Papers of Thomas Jefferson* (4 vols., London, UK, 1829), I, 1–89. For provocative analyses of Jefferson's memoirs, see Andrew Burstein, *The Inner Jefferson: Portrait of a Grieving Optimist* (Charlottesville, 1995), 235–37; and James M. Cox, "Recovering Literature's Lost Ground Through Autobiography," in James Olney, ed., *Autobiography: Essays Theoretical and Critical* (Princeton, 1980), 123–45.

treasured maps, moose antlers, mastodon bones, and American Indian arti-
facts.[1] Even so, Jefferson stopped short of publicly claiming status as the
Declaration's author, if only because to do so would make him appear as a
self-promoter, inviting counter claims along the lines of those tendered by
Lee and Pickering. Instead, he crafted his history as a documentary record
that, given the precepts of the literary culture in which he had been raised,
possessed more authority than such a naked assertion. Readers could trust
it as a disinterested account. Why, after all, would he inflate his role before
the children and grandchildren who already adored him? Why, in notes
made in 1776, long before the Declaration of Independence had assumed
its honored place in the American memory, would he lie to himself?[2]

✳ ✳ ✳

PETER S. ONUF

From "We shall All Be Americans"†

✳ ✳ ✳

Philanthropy

Jefferson did not hate Indians. Instead, he hated their degraded condition
under the pernicious influence of America's antirepublican enemies; it was
George III, after all, who turned the natives into savages. After his inauguration in 1801, the new president rarely expressed hostile sentiments
toward the Indians. The balance of power now decisively favored the Americans; with European powers no longer offering critical support, dwindling
numbers of Indians were no match for the rapidly growing American population. "You see that we are as numerous as the leaves of the trees," Jefferson told one Indian leader in 1808, "strong enough to fight our own battles,
and too strong to fear any enemy."[1]

The Americans' numerical preponderance was so great that the Indians
would never again be able to intervene in the new nation's conflicts with
neighboring imperial powers. Toward the end of his second term, when
chronic conflict over maritime rights threatened war with England, Jefferson told the northwestern Indians that though the English were "strong on
the water," they were "weak on the land." The Indians should play no role

---

1. Susan R. Stein, *The Worlds of Thomas Jefferson at Monticello* (New York, 1993), 69, 162, 193–95.
2. On how the supposedly private and documentary nature of Jefferson's autobiography enhanced its
credibility within the republican literary aesthetic, see Fliegelman, *Declaring Independence*, 121,
123–25; and Larzar Ziff, *Writing in the New Nation: Prose, Print, and Politics in the Early United
States* (New Haven, 1991), 112–13.
† Reprinted courtesy of the *Virginia Magazine of History and Biography*. Numbered notes are Onuf's.
1. TJ to Kitchao Geboway, 27 Feb. 1808, in Andrew A. Lipscomb and Albert E. Bergh, eds., *The Writings of Thomas Jefferson*, 20 vols. (Washington, D.C., 1903–1904), 16:425–27, at 426. My understanding of "philanthropy" is indebted to Bernard Sheehan: ultimately, "hating Indians could not
be differentiated from hating Indianness": "philanthropy had in mind the disappearance of an
entire race" (Sheehan, *The Seeds of Extinction: Jeffersonian Philanthropy and the American Indian*
(Chapel Hill, N.C., 1973), 277, 278). See Ralph Lerner, "Reds and Whites: Rights and Wrongs,"
in Lerner, *The Thinking Revolutionary: Principle and Practice in the New Republic* (Ithaca, N.Y.,
1987), 166–70. For a critical account of TJ's Indian policy during his presidency, see Francis G.
Hutchins, *Constitution and the Tribes* (Manuscript in authors possession), chap. 6.

in this looming conflict: "We do not ask you to spill your blood in our quarrels," nor, he added ominously, "do we wish to be forced to spill it with our own hands." His meaning could not be mistaken: "The tribe which shall begin an unprovoked war against us, we will extirpate from the earth, or drive to such a distance as that they shall never again be able to strike us." Jefferson's chilling warning recalled his Revolutionary rage against the "Savages" and undoubtedly betrayed similar anxieties. But the message's tone was calculated and confident, with professions of friendship balancing threats. Jefferson presented a stark choice to his native "children" so that they would learn an important lesson: Indians must abandon war if they ever hoped for the peace, prosperity, and population growth that would make them a "great nation."[2]

The British were responsible for chronic warfare in the Northwest, Jefferson told another group of chiefs. "While we were under that government," before independence, "we were constantly kept at war with the red men our neighbors." Then many tribes fought against us in the Revolution, leaving a legacy of "ill blood . . . after we had made peace with the English," and the English had abandoned their Indian allies; "it was not till the treaty of Greeneville that we could come to a solid peace and perfect good understanding with all our Indian neighbors," he wrote.[3] According to Jefferson, wars between Indians and Americans were unnatural; they could only be explained by outside interference. Their British allies and patrons were not the Indians' true friends, for they fomented the chronic conflicts that led directly to the depopulation and demoralization of their communities. "Now, my children," the paternalistic president exhorted, "if we wanted to diminish our numbers, we would give up the culture of the earth, pursue the deer and buffalo, and be always at war; this would soon reduce us to be as few as you are, and if you wish to increase your numbers you must give up the deer and buffalo, live in peace, and cultivate the earth."[4]

Constant warfare led to a massive sacrifice of Indian peoples, not only of the young warriors wasted in battle but of future generations as well. Indians need only look across the frontier, to the rising tide of white settlement, to see the future they were forfeiting by holding fast to their savage way of life. "What a brilliant aspect is offered to your future history, if you give up war and hunting," exclaimed Jefferson, and "adopt the culture of the earth and raise domestic animals; you see how from a small family you may become a great nation by adopting the course which from the small beginning you describe has made us a great nation."[5] Jefferson invoked two related themes as he urged his native "children" on toward civilization. Only by turning to agriculture would Indians be able to sustain an enduring relation to their country, "the earth which covers the bones of your fathers," and therefore to their own past; only

2. TJ to the Chiefs of the Wyandots, Ottawas, Chippewas, Powtewatamies, and Shawanese, 10 Jan. 1809, Lipscomb and Bergh, *Writings*, 16:461–65, at 462–63; TJ to Captain Hendrick, the Delawares, Mohicans, and Munries, 21 Dec. 1808, ibid., 450–54, at 453.
3. TJ to the Chiefs of the Ottawas, Chippewas, Powtowatamies, Wyandots, and Senecas of Sandusky, 22 April 1808, ibid., 428–32, at 428.
4. TJ to Captain Hendrick, the Delawares, Mohicans, and Munries, 21 Dec. 1808, ibid., 450–54, at 451.
5. Ibid., at 453. See also TJ to the Chiefs of the Shawanee Nation, 19 Feb. 1807, ibid., 421–25, at 424: "When the white people first came to this land, they were few, and you were many: now we are many, and you few; and why? because, by cultivating the earth, we produce plenty to raise our children, while yours, during a part of every year, suffer for want of food, are forced to eat unwholesome things, are exposed to the weather in your hunting camps, get diseases and die. Hence it is that your numbers lessen."

by making farms, by growing instead of wasting children, could they hope for a future.[6] The choice lay with the present generation and its leaders:

> It depends on yourselves alone to become a numerous and great people. . . . Nothing is so easy as to learn to cultivate the earth; all your women understand it, and to make it easier, we are always ready to teach you how to make ploughs, hoes, and necessary utensils. If the men will take the labor of the earth from the women they will learn to spin and weave and to clothe their families. In this way you will also raise many children, you will double your numbers every twenty years, and soon fill the land your friends have given you, and your children will never be tempted to sell the spot on which they have been born, raised, have labored and called their own.[7]

If the Indians rejected Jefferson's advice, they would "disappear from the earth."[8] Demographic disaster was the real enemy, not American armies or the legions of white settlers that followed in their wake. And if the Indians should succumb to this enemy, if these refractory "children" should spurn their father's teaching, it would be their own responsibility.

Jefferson's presidential addresses to the Indians offered a righteous justification for an expansionist territorial policy that would set the stage, within less than two generations, for Andrew Jackson's removal policy. The inexorable progress of civilization—self-evidently a good thing—absolved Americans of agency or moral responsibility for the displacement of indigenous peoples; in stark contrast, the Indians did face choices and were responsible for their own fate. Professing solicitude for the welfare of his red children, the white father could offer them little protection from the expansion of settlements and the penetration of market forces. Jefferson argued that Indian peoples could only benefit by submitting to the discipline of the market, paying their debts to merchant creditors, exchanging portions of their vast land reserves for the capital needed to make farms. White settlers' land hunger thus was not a threat but a resource Indians should exploit. "Our people multiply so fast that it will suit us to buy as much as you wish to sell," Jefferson told the Chickasaw chiefs in 1805, and "if at this time you think it will be better for you to dispose of some of them to pay your debts, and to help your people to improve the rest, we are willing to buy on reasonable terms."[9]

The self-serving logic of these addresses provided the ideological rationale for an expansive republican empire. But Jefferson did not consciously seek to deceive or defraud his native charges, and if he was manipulative in his dealings with them, he was equally so with his own children.[1] Everything

---

6. TJ to the Chiefs of the Wyandots, Ottawas, Chippewas, Powtewatamies and Shawanese, 10 Jan. 1809, ibid., 461–65, at 463.

7. TJ to Captain Hendrick, the Delawares, Mohicans, and Munries, 21 Dec. 1808, ibid., 450–54, at 452.

8. TJ to the Chiefs of the Ottawas, Chippewas, Powtowatamies, Wyandots, and Senecas of Sandusky, 22 April 1808, ibid., 428–32, at 429.

9. TJ to My Children, Chiefs of the Chickasaw Nation, Mingkey, Mataha, and Tishohanta, 7 March 1805, ibid., 410–12, at 411–12. See also TJ to the Chiefs of the Ottawas, Chippewas, Powtowatamies, Wyandots, and Senecas of Sandusky, 22 April 1808, ibid., 428–32, at 429: "Whenever you find it your interest to dispose of a part to enable you to improve the rest, and to support your families in the meantime, we are willing to buy, because our people increase fast."

1. TJ sought to accelerate the liquidation of Indians' property rights by promoting their indebtedness. See TJ to Governor William H. Harrison, 27 Feb. 1803, ibid., 10:368–73, at 370: "When these debts get beyond what the individuals can pay, they become willing to lop them off by a cession of lands"; "they will in time either incorporate with us as citizens of the United States, or remove beyond the Mississippi." Modern commentators understandably find this strategy abhorrent. (Hutchins, *Constitution and the Tribes*, chap. 6, charges that "Jefferson advocated debt ensnarement, to place

he said in his messages to the Indians was meant for their own good: by giving up land they could not use, they might improve and secure the remainder. Becoming good husbands, Indian men would reap bountiful harvests of crops and father many children; learning to live under laws of their own making, Indian communities would become true republics, ultimately merging with white Americans in a single "great nation." If all of these adaptations to republican civilization served the interests of land-hungry white farmers, this was only as it should be in a peaceful and harmonious union of peoples. After all, Jefferson insisted, the assumption of a natural enmity between Indians and white settlers was false, an ugly image from the old regime fostered by generations of imperial warfare and diplomacy. The New World, purged of Old World corruption that had fostered Indian savagery, presented a different picture. If they did not disappear from view altogether, the Indians would be a part of this picture. This was Jefferson's promise to Captain Hendrick, an Indian leader, in December 1808: "Unite yourselves with us, join in our Great Councils and form one people with us, and we shall all be Americans; you will mix with us by marriage, your blood will run in our veins, and will spread with us over this great island."[2]

Jefferson knew that the choice would be difficult. "Are you prepared for this?" he asked the Upper Cherokees when they sought assistance in civilizing themselves. "Have you the resolution to leave off hunting for your living, to lay off a farm for each family to itself, to live by industry, the men working that farm with their hands, raising stock, or learning trades as we do, and the women spinning and weaving clothes for their husbands and children?"[3] For Jefferson the choice itself, not federal patronage, was crucial. The real American Revolution would come to Indian country when Indian men renounced their "aristocratic" prerogatives, elevated women to their naturally equal position, and provided for the welfare of future generations. The first challenge was to have children at all: Indian men should know that their savage way of life was a form of generational murder against unborn children, a criminal waste of the male potency and female fertility Jefferson celebrated in his *Notes on Virginia*.

Jefferson's addresses to the Indians revealed powerful emotions. Far from cynical productions of a manipulative diplomacy, these addresses were heartfelt testimonials to the principles on which, he believed, the new American regime was founded. As they asserted their rights and declared their independence, Americans acted as moral agents, following the precepts of natural law. The Revolution was lawful, not licentious; republicanism represented the high achievement of a civilized people, not a regression to savagery. Jefferson and his fellow patriots had provided freedom and

the Creeks under the exploitative control of the U.S. government.") But TJ's Indian messages did not disguise the mechanism at work, nor could he escape the discipline of debt in his own private life and public career. On debt, see Herbert Sloan, *Principle and Interest: Thomas Jefferson and the Problem of Debt* (New York, 1995); on TJ as manipulator, see: Jan Lewis, "'The Blessings of Domestic Society,'" in Peter S. Onuf, ed., *Jeffersonian Legacies* (Charlottesville, Va., 1993), 109–146.'"

2. TJ to Captain Hendrick, the Delawares, Mohicans, and Munries, 21 Dec. 1808, in Lipscomb and Bergh, *Writings*, 16:450–54, at 452. TJ made the same suggestion to the Cherokee in 1803, through Benjamin Hawkins, the U.S. agent: "In truth, the ultimate point of rest and happiness for them is to let our settlements and theirs meet and blend together, to intermix, and become one people" (TJ to Benjamin Hawkins, 18 Feb. 1803, ibid., 10:360–65, at 363).

3. TJ to the Chiefs of the Upper Cherokees, 4 May 1808, ibid., 16:432–35, at 434. For the context of this message, see William G. McCloughlin, "Jefferson and The Beginning of Cherokee Nationalism," *William and Mary Quarterly* 32 (1975): 564–65.

prosperity for future generations by liberating a great continent from monarchy and aristocracy. This great boon, "our country," had required great sacrifices in years of bloody warfare. Indians who would share in this magnificent legacy had to change themselves into civilized republicans and good Americans. Their arduous progress; recapitulating the progress of civilization itself, must begin at home.

"Your Blood Will Mix with Ours"

Jefferson's sentimental republicanism also began at home, in the idealized domesticity constituted by consensual conjugal union. In his most extravagantly optimistic moments, he could envision unions of unions, spreading circle upon circle, layer upon layer, until the whole enlightened world was transformed and redeemed. This republican millennium would be both the culminating moment in the progress of world history and a return to the wholeness and perfection of the family circle. The same pattern of thought can be traced through Jefferson's Indian addresses. When he imagined the reconciliation of the races, the merging of nations into "one people," the old language of Indian diplomacy took on new life for him: Jefferson was no longer a "father" by courtesy or convention, nor were the Indians "children" who would opportunistically adopt and dispose of "fathers" as the balance of forces in Indian country changed. Instead, Jefferson foresaw white Americans and their "red brethren" forming a single great family, connected by the most intimate ties of consanguinity. For the Indians this merging of the races would be at once the moment of their restoration—"peace and agriculture will raise you up to be what your forefathers were"—and their rebirth as Americans. Once "you . . . possess property" and "live under regular laws," Jefferson told the Indians, they would be prepared "to join us in our government, to mix with us in society, and your blood and ours united will spread again over the great island."[4]

In becoming Americans, the Indians would regain the continent that their forefathers had recklessly forfeited. Through this same process the new nation's title to its imperial domain would become perfect: any lingering misgivings about the Americans' claims to their country would be allayed. When, for instance, Jefferson told the Mandan that "we consider ourselves no longer of the old nations beyond the great water, but as united in one family with our red brethren here" or declared to the Osage that "it is so long since our forefathers came from beyond the great water, that we have lost the memory of it, and seem to have grown out of this land, as you have done," he acknowledged that native peoples had a prior, and in some sense more legitimate, claim to the land.[5] But as the two peoples merged into one, their common patrimony would be a bond of union, not a source of strife.

It is tempting to dismiss Jefferson's vision of interracial nationhood. Invoking his own experience and observation of Indian culture and politics, he emphasized the formidable obstacles to its fulfillment in his Indian

---

4. TJ to the Miamis, Powtewatamies, Delawares, and Chippeways, 21 Dec. 1808, in Lipscomb and Bergh, *Writings*, 16:438–40, at 439. On the mixing of whites and Indians, see Lerner, "Reds and Whites: Rights and Wrongs," 163–64, and Winthrop Jordan, *White over Black, American Attitudes toward the Negro, 1550–1812* (Chapel Hill, N.C., 1968), 477–81.
5. TJ to the Wolf and People of the Mandan Nation, 30 Dec. 1806, *Jefferson Writings*, ed. Merrill D. Peterson (New York, 1984), 564–66, at 564; TJ to My Children, White-hairs, Chiefs, and Warriors of the Osage Nation, 16 July 1804, in Lipscomb and Bergh, *Writings*, 16:405–10, at 406.

addresses. Perhaps Jefferson was simply setting the stage for experiments that he knew were bound to fail; he was full of "commiseration" for the Indians but free of any sense of moral responsibility. Yet Jefferson's Indian addresses did speak powerfully to some of the central concerns of his public career and private life. How could the Americans justify their claim to being a distinct people? By what right did they claim the continent as their own? How did native peoples figure in his understanding of the American Revolution? What place could these peoples claim for themselves in the new republican empire?

Jefferson never betrayed feelings of guilt about the fate of the Indians. He was more likely to be righteously enraged at their savagery or, in times of peace, philosophically resigned to their cultural resistance. But running through all of his responses was a sense of personal identification, the "attachment and commiseration" evoked by childhood memories that were still vivid in his old age. Perhaps, reasonable men would be inclined to agree, the Indians were doomed to "disappear from the earth." The wish for a different fate for the Indians, the fantasy of a "great island" redeemed from European corruption and the savagery it fostered, and nostalgia for lost childhood innocence—all were palpable in Jefferson's romantic image of the millennial moment when, he told the Indians, "your blood will mix with ours" and a truly new nation would emerge.

DOUGLAS L. WILSON

From The Evolution of Jefferson's
Notes on the State of Virginia†

In May 1784, Thomas Jefferson arrived in Philadelphia from Annapolis, where he had spent a miserable winter, much of the time in ill health, attending the fitful and dispiriting sessions of the American Congress. He carried with him the manuscript of a work that would soon become famous as *Notes on the State of Virginia*. It had started out as the response to a questionnaire circulated by François de Marbois, the secretary of the French legation, to representatives of all the American states in 1780, but by the time he had submitted his answers to Marbois in December 1781, Jefferson's interest in the scientific and political implications of his subject had been thoroughly engaged. Now, nearly two and a half years later, as he was preparing to assume his new diplomatic assignment in France, he intended to have the much-expanded manuscript privately printed so that he could oblige friends who had asked for a copy.

But his plans had hit a snag. On 21 May, he addressed a letter to his closest adviser in the two-and-a-half year enterprise, the secretary of Congress, Charles Thomson, who was still in Annapolis. "My matter in the printing way is dropped," he wrote Thomson, who had been promised a copy. "Aitken [the Philadelphia printer] had formerly told me he would print it for £4. a sheet. He now asked £5–10 which raised the price from £48 to £66. but

† Reprinted courtesy of the *Virginia Magazine of History and Biography*. Numbered notes are Wilson's.

what was a more effectual and insuperable bar was that he could not complete it under three weeks, a time I could not wait for it. . . . Perhaps I may have a few copies struck off in Paris if there be an English printer there."[1]

After Jefferson himself, Thomson had been the first to see the possibilities of what might come from matching Jefferson's particular talents and interests with this kind of inquiry. When Jefferson had sent Marbois his answers from Virginia in December 1781, he had written at the same time to Thomson, asking him to call on Marbois and look them over. He wanted Thomson to advise him on the possibility of further developing some of the answers for presentation to the American Philosophical Society. Jefferson professed to know little about the society, to which he had been elected earlier in the year, but he doubtless had a sense of its animating force. In the apt characterization of Daniel P. Boorstin, "its scope, its publications, and its discussions were shaped by the novel openness of the New World and the host of unfamiliar phenomena in nature and among the native peoples."[2]

To Jefferson's December inquiry about presenting to the APS, Thomson replied with enthusiasm:

> This Country opens to the philosophic view an extensive, rich and unexplored field. It abounds in roots, plants, trees and minerals, to the virtues and uses of which we are yet strangers. . . . The human mind seems just awakening from a long stupor of many ages to the discovery of useful Arts and inventions. Our governments are yet unformed and capable of great improvements in police, finance and commerce. The history, manners and customs of the Aborigines are but little known. These and a thousand other subjects which will readily suggest themselves open an inexhaustible mine to men of a contemplative and philosophical turn.[3]

Thomson knew his man, for his reply focused on the very things that had excited Jefferson about this project. Thomson probably also understood its timeliness for Jefferson, whose performance as governor of Virginia had been unfairly called into question and who was eager to turn his back on the thankless endeavors of public life and plunge into something more congenial. "And therefore though I regret your retiring from the busy anxious scenes of politics, yet I congratulate posterity on the Advantages they may derive from your philosophical researches."[4]

Marbois's queries, surely a routine chore for most who answered them,[5] had evoked from Jefferson a response that surprised and delighted the Frenchman.

> I cannot express to you how grateful I am for the trouble you have taken to draft detailed responses to the questions I had taken the liberty of addressing to you. The Philosophy which has inspired them, the understanding they give me of one of the most important states of the

1. Thomas Jefferson (hereafter cited as TJ) to Charles Thomson, 21 May 1784, *PTJ*, 7:282.
2. Daniel J. Boorstin, *The Seekers: The Story of Man's Continuing Quest to Understand His World* (New York, 1998), p. 172.
3. Charles Thomson to TJ, 8 Mar. 1782, *PTJ*, 6:163–64.
4. Ibid.
5. Respondents in various states who answered Marbois's queries, such as John Sullivan in New Hampshire and John Witherspoon of New Jersey, are identified in *PTJ* 4:167n. Sullivan's reply to Marbois, dated Philadelphia, 10 December 1780, is in the Huntington Library and has been printed in Otis G. Hammond, ed., *Letters and Papers of Major-General John Sullivan, Continental Army* (3 vols.; Concord, N.H., 1930–39), 3:229–39.

union and the circumstances in which you have taken the trouble to write about them, created the most valuable work that I could take from this country.[6]

But more importantly, the exercise appealed to what Jefferson thought of as his natural bent for what he called literary and scientific "objects." Marbois's queries, which addressed mainly factual matters such as naming and enumeration, had stimulated him to study further and had motivated him to pursue some of their scientific and philosophical implications.

Jefferson's career has been intensively studied, but the course of his research on this project and the process by which results were gathered, assimilated, and cast in their final form as *Notes on the State of Virginia* have always remained somewhat obscure. In these circumstances, the difficulty with the printer tells an instructive part of the story. In the six months that passed after Jefferson received an estimate from Aitken in November of 1783, the expanded size and complexity of the manuscript had necessitated a drastic increase in the printing cost (37.5 percent), as well as in the time required to print it. This indicates that the manuscript had been considerably transformed during those six months and suggests in tangible terms something of the magnitude of that transformation. But the progress and development of the project can be traced in much greater detail, and that process, when fully delineated, will have much to tell us about the nature of the work itself.[7] What follows is a preliminary attempt to describe the evolution of what became *Notes on the State of Virginia* by focusing on the evidence of its manuscript.

Students of the origin and history of Jefferson's *Notes* have not been well served by their principal source of information, its author. It is not so much that he set out deliberately to deceive his readers and correspondents about his work, but rather that he persisted in telling the story of its inception and execution in the disingenuous language of excessive modesty and self-deprecation. To any number of correspondents, he gave the impression that *Notes* was little more than the product of a few weeks' idleness, while he recovered from a fall from his horse. Thus he wrote Giovanni Fabbroni in 1785, shortly after the work was first printed: "They were written at the sollicitation of Monsr. de Marbois secretary of the French legation in America, while our country was wasting under the ravages of a cruel enemy, and whilst the writer was confined to his room by an accidental decrepitude. Less than this added to his want of talents would account for their errors and defects."[8] A few years later Jefferson wrote his future son-in-law, Thomas Mann Randolph, then a student at the University of Edinburgh:

> In the year 1781. while confined to my room by a fall from my horse, I wrote some Notes in answer to the enquiries of M. de Marbois as to the Natural and Political state of Virginia. They were hasty and indigested: yet as some of these touch slightly on some objects of it's natural history, I will take the liberty of asking the society to accept a copy of them.[9]

6. Marbois to TJ, 22 Apr. 1782, *PTJ*, 6:177–78. For this translation, I am indebted to Derry E. Voysey and Lucia Stanton.
7. The discussion here anticipates the appearance of the long-awaited definitive edition, to be published in the second series of *PTJ*. This is the primary sense in which these findings are referred to as "preliminary" in the next sentence.
8. TJ to Giovanni Fabbroni, 23 May 1785, *PTJ*, 27:745.
9. TJ to Thomas Mann Randolph, Jr., 6 July 1787, *PTJ*, 11:558–59.

This communication, while vastly understating the effort that went into *Notes*, reveals that its author was nonetheless sufficiently proud of the result to present a copy to the Edinburgh Natural History Society, which had recently honored him with a diploma, presumably for his authorship of that very work.[1]

The reports to Fabbroni and Randolph were nearly contemporaneous with the writing and publication of *Notes*, but there are others that have the appearance of authority but prove to be erroneous or misleading because of their distance in time from the events in question. In his abortive attempt at autobiography, for example, Jefferson had tried to recall, at the age of seventy-eight, the circumstances in which, forty years earlier, he had composed his only published book:

> Before I had left America, that is to say in the year 1781. I had received a letter from M. de Marbois, of the French legation in Philadelphia, informing me he had been instructed by his government to obtain such statistical accounts of the different states of our Union, as might be useful for their information; and addressing to me a number of queries relative to the state of Virginia. I had always made it a practice whenever an opportunity occurred of obtaining any information of our country, which might be of use to me in any station public or private, to commit it to writing. These memoranda were on loose papers, bundled up without order, and difficult of recurrence when I had occasion for a particular one. I thought this a good occasion to embody their substance, which I did in the order of Mr. Marbois' queries, so as to answer his wish and to arrange them for my own use. Some friends to whom they were occasionally communicated wished for copies; but their volume rendering this too laborious by hand, I proposed to get a few printed for their gratification. I was asked such a price however as exceeded the importance of the object. On my arrival at Paris I found it could be done for a fourth of what I had been asked here. I therefore corrected and enlarged them, and had 200. copies printed, under the title of Notes on Virginia.[2]

Although unobjectionable as a general outline of what Jefferson had done—that he had written at the prompting of the French legation, that he had employed existing memoranda, and that he had "corrected and enlarged" his original responses before having them printed in Paris—these recollections are a classic example of how memories can mislead. As we shall see, contemporary documents show that Jefferson was not approached directly by Marbois, who had actually submitted his questionnaire to Joseph Jones, a Virginia member of Congress, who in turn had passed the assignment on to Governor Jefferson. Moreover, the evidence is strong that Jefferson was able to make relatively little use of his accumulated memoranda in replying to Marbois. The evidence seems equally clear that though he extensively "corrected and enlarged" the answers he sent to Marbois before having them printed, when he did make use of his memoranda, very little of this revision was performed, as the autobiography states, in Paris.

What is most notable in Jefferson's varying accounts, as a study of the manuscript and materials relating to the composition of *Notes* amply shows,

---

1. The diploma sent to Jefferson by the society is in the Coolidge Collection of Thomas Jefferson Manuscripts, Massachusetts Historical Society, Boston, and is dated 22 February 1787.
2. "Autobiography, 1743–1790," Paul Leicester Ford, ed., *The Works of Thomas Jefferson*, 12 vols., (New York, 1905), 1:93–94.

is what they leave out. For example, he had, indeed, substantially "corrected and enlarged" the text he sent to Marbois, but this was carried out during the two and a half years between the time he sent Marbois his answers in December 1781 and his departure for Paris in July 1784. Other factors have contributed to the confusion about the dating of Jefferson's book. It was first published in English in London in 1787, but it had been privately printed by Jefferson in Paris two years earlier in 1785. That edition, however, confused matters further by carrying on its title page an even earlier date, MDCCLXXXII (1782), a date that, having the appearance of a publication date, understandably found its way into many accounts. This date, however, was intended to refer to the composition of the work, not its printing, as is explained by the notation that follows the title: "written in the year 1781, somewhat corrected and enlarged in the winter of 1782, for the use of a Foreigner of distinction."[3] But like so much of what Jefferson wrote about the composition of *Notes*, this turns out to be quite misleading, for his letters make it clear that he was actively gathering information for his "corrected and enlarged" version in the late fall of 1783 and during the early months of 1784.[4] As a result of these additions and alterations, the printer, as we have seen, had to revise his estimate of the printing cost upwards by more than a third.

The story of Jefferson's involvement in Marbois's questionnaire actually begins in 1780. When Marbois approached members of the Congress with his list of questions about their states, responsibility for Virginia's response was passed on to Jefferson, who was well known as a student of Virginia's political and natural history.[5] That he relished the opportunity to perform this work is clear from his remark to a French correspondent in November 1780:

> I am at present busily employed for Monsr. Marbois without his knowing it; and have to acknolege to him the mysterious obligation for making me much better acquainted with my own country than I ever was before. His queries as to this country put into my hands by Mr. Jones I take every occasion which presents itself of procuring answers to. Some of them however can never be answered till I shall [have] leisure to go to Monticello where alone the materials exist which can enable any one to answer them.[6]

When Marbois learned that Jones had transferred responsibility for his questions, he wrote to Jefferson, who replied on 4 March 1781: "Mr. Jones did put into my hands a paper containing sundry enquiries into the present state of Virginia, which he informed me was from yourself, some of which I meant to do myself the honour of answering. Hitherto it has been in my power to collect a few materials only, which my present occupations disable me from completing."[7] Jefferson's "present occupations" were, of course, his central

---

3. *Notes on the State of Virginia.* This privately printed edition, in Paris in 1785, combines the title page with a table of contents; no author or place is given.
4. Jefferson's correspondence for this period shows information being sought and obtained from Archibald Cary, Dr. Thomas Walker, Isaac Zane, William Whipple, John Sullivan, Henry Skipwith, Rev. James Madison, James Madison of Montpelier, Thomas Hutchins, George Rogers Clark, Charles Carter, and others.
5. Jefferson's copy of the Marbois questions in Jones's hand is printed in *PTJ*, 4:166–67.
6. TJ to D'Anmours, 30 Nov. 1780, *PTJ*, 4:168. This letter is evidence that Jefferson may have been resorting to his previously collected information before he had his papers removed from Monticello for safekeeping.
7. TJ to Marbois, 4 Mar. 1781, *PTJ*, 5:58.

involvement as governor in Virginia's frantic and largely ineffective attempts to deal with an invasion by the British army. What he was counting on by way of relief was not the defeat of the British but the merciful termination of his second term as governor in early June. "I mean however, shortly, to be in a condition which will leave me quite at leisure to take them up, when it shall certainly be one of my first undertakings to give you as full information as I shall be able to do on such of the subjects as are within the sphere of my acquaintance." At the same time, he offered one reservation: "On some of them however I trust Mr. Jones will engage abler hands, those in particular which relate to the commerce of the state, a subject with which I am totally unacquainted, and which is probably the most important in your plan."[8]

The much-anticipated end of Jefferson's gubernatorial term coincided with his near capture on 4 June by British dragoons under Banastre Tarleton at Charlottesville, where the governor and members of the Virginia legislature had retreated when the capital city of Richmond was overrun. Escaping with his family to his Bedford County plantation, Poplar Forest, Jefferson was injured late in June by the fall from his horse and confined for three to four weeks.[9] It was apparently during this brief period that most of the drafting of Jefferson's answers to Marbois's questions was done. He could not have had access to most of his books and previously collected memoranda, as these had been earlier sent for safekeeping across the Blue Ridge to Augusta County sometime before the arrival of Tarleton's dragoons.[1] And there is little evidence of further research in the succeeding months beyond the information Jefferson said he solicited from members of the Virginia legislature.[2]

On 20 December 1781, Jefferson wrote to Marbois from Richmond:

> I now do myself the honour of inclosing you answers to the quaeries which Mr. Jones put into my hands. I fear your patience has been exhausted in attending them, but I beg you to be assured there has been no avoidable delay on my part. I retired from the public service in June only, and after that the general confusion of our state put it out of my power to procure the informations necessary till lately. Even now you will find them very imperfect and not worth offering but as a proof of my respect for your wishes.[3]

The manuscript Jefferson sent to Marbois has never been found and may no longer exist; nor, more surprisingly, has Jefferson's retained copy been located. From lack of evidence to the contrary, it seems likely that the answers supplied to Marbois, while no doubt ripe with Jefferson's extensive personal knowledge and impressions, were not the result of extensive research, but were rather, as Jefferson frequently said, mainly the product of his three-to-four-week confinement at Poplar Forest in June and July of 1781. Having pre-

8. Ibid.
9. TJ recalled being injured in a fall from his horse "On a ride into the farm [Poplar Forest] about the end of the month [June]" (ibid., 4:261). This is confirmed by an entry for 30 June 1781, in his Memorandum Books: "Pd Dr. Brown 2. visits £600" (James A. Bear, Jr., and Lucia C. Stanton, eds., *Jefferson's Memorandum Books: Accounts with Legal Records and Miscellany,* 1767–1826 [2 vols.; Princeton, 1997], 1:511). Jefferson left Poplar Forest on 23 July (Bear and Stanton, eds., Memorandum Books, 1:512).
1. See TJ to James Madison, 24 Mar. 1782: "These ['antient M.S.S. which I have been able to collect'] with my other papers and books however had been removed to Augusta to be out of danger from the enemy and have not yet been brought back" (*PTJ,* 6:170).
2. TJ to Marbois, 24 Mar. 1782, *PTJ,* 6:171–72.
3. TJ to Marbois, 20 Dec. 1781, *PTJ,* 6:141–42.

viously warned Marbois in his 4 March letter that he did not regard himself as competent to answer some of the queries, it is even possible that the material he sent in December was restricted to a subset of Marbois's questions.[4]

What the student of the evolution of *Notes on the State of Virginia* must bear in mind is that, though this December 1781 submission of answers to Marbois's questions is often treated by its author as synonymous, or virtually synonymous, with the final published version, the two were very different. Just as he apparently felt compelled to minimize the value and significance of his work, Jefferson likewise tended to minimize greatly the effort he had put into it, particularly the work that went into the revision of the original version. As we have seen, the title page for the Paris edition says "somewhat corrected and enlarged in the winter of 1782," but the manuscript of that title page shows that Jefferson had originally written "the winter of 1782–1783."[5] We can only speculate why he struck out "1783," but it is possible that it suggested more time and effort than he cared to acknowledge. Nonetheless, the manuscript, the materials he collected that relate to it, and both sides of his surviving correspondence all combine to show clearly that even what Jefferson had written first had been an understatement, for he had labored over this revision not one but three winters in succession.

In spite of its being the basis of one of the most notable documents in early American history, the manuscript of Thomas Jefferson's *Notes on the State of Virginia* has never been studied intensively or in detail. Though it is often assumed that William Peden's durable "reader's edition" of *Notes* (1955) was based on a thorough study of the manuscript, such was not the case.[6] Peden's own correspondence and notes make clear that he was steered away from such a course by Lyman Butterfield, who had recruited him as editor, and by Julian P. Boyd, then editor of the Papers of Thomas Jefferson.[7] Both Butterfield and Boyd assumed (erroneously, as it turned out) that an intensive examination of the manuscript would be performed in the near future for the definitive edition of *Notes* that would appear under Boyd's editorship in the second series of The Papers of Thomas Jefferson. Peden thus never examined the actual manuscript and, working from an incomplete microfilm version, only pointed out in his edition "occasional representative examples of Jefferson's revisions in the manuscript."[8]

Peden seems to have been aware that the microfilm of the manuscript he consulted excluded a considerable amount of text as a result of having been filmed in ignorance of its very unusual makeup.[9] The manuscript of

4. Although this must be noted as a possibility, there is no evidence that this was the case.
5. The manuscript of the title page, which also served as a table of contents, was written after the rest of the manuscript had been set in print, as evidenced by the presence of the correct page numbers for each chapter, or query (*Notes* manuscript, in Coolidge Collection).
6. Thomas Jefferson, *Notes on the State of Virginia*, ed. William Peden (Chapel Hill, 1955), pp. vi, vii. Peden credits Marie Kimball with a "full discussion of this manuscript" (p. 265), but she may not have examined it at all. Her reasons for believing that the manuscript is an unfinished draft cannot be reconciled with the state of the actual document and can perhaps only be explained as having been based on a misleading microfilm or photostatic copy. See Marie Goebel Kimball, *Jefferson: War and Peace, 1776–1784* (New York, 1947), pp. 382–83.
7. See the letter from Lyman Butterfield, then director of the Institute of Early American History and Culture, to William Peden, 9 Sept. 1952; and Julian P. Boyd to William Peden, 5 Feb. 1953 (second letter of that date); Papers of William Harden Peden, mss 6833, Special Collections Department, University of Virginia Library, Charlottesville.
8. Peden, p. 265.
9. See Boyd to Peden, 5 Feb. 1953 (second letter of that date), Peden Papers. Responding to Peden's suggestion that the manuscript would have to be refilmed, Boyd wrote "to refilm the MS, on the

Jefferson's *Notes*, like the work itself, took on a unique form and is therefore difficult to picture or to describe. When completed, it consisted of a set of primary leaves on which a draft text had been written out fair on both sides (two pages per leaf); in revision, some leaves were subsequently added to the original set and some deleted; also, as part of the revision process, some of the original text was stricken and additions were made, either interlineated or written on smaller leaves, or tabs. The tabs were then attached to the primary leaves and, in some cases, onto other tabs. The resulting manuscript, which Jefferson eventually had bound, was thus a curious conglomeration of leaves that had to be read not only by turning pages horizontally, in the conventional way, but by frequent vertical unfoldings of the tabs.

The past tense is employed here not because the manuscript no longer exists, but because it has been disassembled, so that its leaves and tabs are no longer in their original configuration.[1] Its owner, the Massachusetts Historical Society, embarked in 1997 on a long-contemplated project to conserve the manuscript, a process that began with extensive photography followed by a careful and painstaking disassembly. Whether the manuscript will be reassembled is yet to be decided. The loss of the manuscript's unique constitution has resulted in an unmistakable gain for scholarship, for as Julian P. Boyd realized, the disassembling of the manuscript makes possible a scrutiny of its makeup and contents not otherwise possible. Some of the tabs had been attached by Jefferson so as to display text on both sides, while others were pasted down flat with text visible only on one side. Detaching the tabs makes it possible to reconstruct almost all of the original text underneath, including more than 2,000 words that have been hidden from view since 1783 or 1784.[2]

Of particular value is the recovery of the text that formed the basis of the revision, a fair copy draft that first ran to 88 pages and was later extended to 104 pages.[3] We can be reasonably certain it is a fair copy, rather than a composition draft, because there are almost no changes visible that are clearly contemporaneous with the writing, whereas Jefferson's composition drafts, a great many of which survive, are typically replete with contemporaneous additions and changes. By contrast, nearly all the changes and additions to the fair copy draft of *Notes* were made later, as shown by the differences in ink and handwriting and, occasionally, by the sentence structure.[4] Although certainly not the earliest form of the work, the fair copy draft undoubtedly

---

contrary, would lead to an almost unanswerable question short of the ultimate treatment—what will be the limit of research once you prepare the MS and refilm it? The MS needs to have its pasteons removed and many other things done before a refilming is necessary, and even this preparatory work could not be done before September." Unlike its predecessor, the microfilm version currently available at the Massachusetts Historical Society, which owns the manuscript, is an updated version and does show the text sent to the printer in full.

1. The manuscript was unbound and disassembled in 1997–98. I had the privilege of examining the manuscript and its constituent parts before, during, and after disassembly.
2. One should note, however, that much of the newly uncovered text turns out to be material that has been incorporated into the revised text.
3. A "fair copy draft" is one that incorporates the changes made in previous compositional drafts and whose text thus represents the current state of the narrative. In this case, the draft that Jefferson copied out fair in the summer of 1783 from earlier writing is discernable by the uniformity of its ink, line spacing, and placement of the strikeouts. Changes appear as interlineations, as marginal insertions, as deleted pages, and on tabs.
4. The sentence structure is often indicative because, in a composition draft, the changes a writer makes often reflect decisions made in mid-sentence, whereby one sentence structure is abandoned and another adopted. By contrast, changes in a fair copy text are made to sentences that are already present in their entirety.

represents a significant stage in the revision of the answers to Marbois and is an invaluable baseline against which to track subsequent changes.

It is useful to begin with the question of when the fair copy draft, the basic core of the existing manuscript, was written out. Fortunately, its text contains an anecdote concerning a Mr. Stanley,[5] who was captured by Indians and carried into the far West, an anecdote that was sent to Jefferson by Arthur Campbell in a letter dated 29 November 1782.[6] This provides a terminus post quern, or indication that the fair copy draft could not have been written before this date. Jefferson probably received Campbell's letter just before setting out in December 1782 for Philadelphia, where he hoped to embark for France on his first diplomatic assignment to Paris. This plan was frustrated when, before he could sail, preliminary news of the peace treaty was received, and Congress cancelled his mission. Jefferson had considerable time on his hands in the early months of 1783, both in Philadelphia and Baltimore, where he waited in vain nearly a month to sail. Although the project was never far from his mind, his correspondence yields no clue that he was actively drafting his revision of the Marbois answers in either place.[7]

His diplomatic assignment having been cancelled, Jefferson left Philadelphia in April and arrived home at Monticello on 15 May. Passing through Richmond while the Virginia legislature was in session, he believed from what he had seen and heard that the time was possibly ripe for a new constitution for Virginia. A month later he sent James Madison a draft of such a constitution, written on paper with a distinctive watermark that rarely occurs in his manuscripts. That the same paper was used for the first twenty-two pages of his fair copy draft of *Notes* is perhaps the best indication of when he began work on it. As evidence that his mind was then on the project, he wrote the same day to his friend and scientific informant, Isaac Zane, about his plan to visit him on the way to Philadelphia in the fall, most likely to gather information for *Notes*. Another indication that Jefferson was at work on the revision of his manuscript during the summer of 1783 is his composition draft of a letter dated 29 July, a recycled sheet of paper that also contains a list of Indian tribes that corresponds closely with the first table in query 11 of *Notes*. By 25 September, the fair copy draft of the revised work may well have been complete, for he wrote on that date to his longtime friend and neighbor, Dr. Thomas Walker: "The inclosed are part of some papers I wrote in answer to certain queries sent me by Monsr. de Marbois in 1781. Another foreigner of my acquaintance, now beyond the

---

5. This reference is found on page 24 of the *Notes* manuscript. Without disassembling the manuscript, one might mistakenly conclude that this information had been added only later, for it appears on a tab pasted over the original passage in the fair copy. But the Campbell anecdote actually appears in the original passage, as well as on the tab.

6. Arthur Campbell to TJ, 29 Nov. 1782, *PTJ*, 6:208; query 6, Peden, p. 44. Though Peden's has long been the standard edition for both scholars and general readers, the more recent version edited by Frank Shuffelton is a worthy alternative, offering a somewhat different approach to the text and presenting the work in a way that better addresses the concerns and expectations of contemporary readers. Whereas Peden's edition incorporates Jefferson's subsequent changes and additions directly into the text and substitutes English translations for all foreign language quotations, Shuffelton preserves the text that was read in Jefferson's lifetime and prints all changes, additions, and translations in the endnotes. Shuffelton also examined the manuscript and reports in his editorial notes on such major alterations and revisions as could be observed prior to the manuscript's disassembly. See Thomas Jefferson, *Notes on the State of Virginia*, ed. Frank Shuffelton (New York, 1999), p. 44.

7. Memoranda in Jefferson's hand that relate to the research and writing for his *Notes* are numerous. A substantial number in the Massachusetts Historical Society are identified as such, but many others have been found in the Jefferson manuscript collections at the Library of Congress, the Huntington Library, and the Pierpont Morgan Library.

water, having asked a copy of them, I undertook to revise and correct them in some degree."[8]

Before he left Monticello to return to Philadelphia in October, Jefferson met with Walker, who gave him some notes he had made on reading Jefferson's draft. These notes are still in the "loose papers" Jefferson compiled in working on Notes, and they reveal that Walker's information, where incorporated into the manuscript, always appears in the form of a change or addition to the fair copy text.[9] Another letter of this period, this one sent to Jefferson from Col. Archibald Cary on 12 October, presents a similar case. It is clear from Cary's letter that Jefferson had recently written to him for information about the weights of animals. Cary's letter gives many details about the comparative sizes of American and European animals. Having lived and hunted abroad, Cary offers a number of specific weights based on his own experience and that of other informants.[1]

Leaving for Philadelphia on 16 October 1783, Jefferson traveled far out of his way so as to visit sites in the Shenandoah Valley, such as Madison's Cave near Staunton and Isaac Zane's Marlboro ironworks near Winchester. It was on this trip that he made his only visit to Harpers Ferry and observed a scene memorably described in Notes, the juncture of the Shenandoah and Potomac rivers.[2] All of the data collected from informants and from personal observation on this thirteen-day trip and appearing in the manuscript of Notes are clear-cut additions or modifications to the fair copy text. And this is true for all information that came to Jefferson from the time he left Monticello to the first printing in May 1785. The upshot of all these circumstances would seem to indicate that Jefferson probably began the fair copy draft in the spring or early summer, possibly in June of 1783, and completed it before leaving home four months later on 16 October.

To bring into focus the major theme in the transformation of the revised version of Notes, it is necessary to backtrack in time to consider the involvement in this process of another Frenchman, the marquis de Chastellux, who was the "foreigner of my acquaintance, now beyond the water" mentioned in the letter to Thomas Walker. Chastellux was a well-known savant and member of the French Academy who had fought in the Revolutionary War and had paid a memorable visit to Jefferson at Monticello in April 1782.[3] While there, he had either seen or heard about Jefferson's answers to Marbois, and in the months immediately following his visit, Chastellux sent his host reminders of a promise to share these answers with him.[4] Jefferson's delay in complying may at first have been because of the need to correct and revise his answers. Keeping a close watch over his wife's declin-

8. TJ to Thomas Walker, 25 Sept. 1783, PTJ, 7:339. The other foreigner beyond the water will be discussed later.
9. According to his memorandum books, TJ settled his accounts with Walker on 10 Oct. (Bear and Stanton, eds., Memorandum Books, 1:536). Memoranda in Walker's hand bearing information on American Indians, birds, and animals are in the Massachusetts Historical Society, as part of the "loose papers" (Jefferson's term) associated with Notes, numbered xl7 and x28.
1. Archibald Cary to TJ, PTJ, 6:342–45. In addition to his own testimony, Cary conveyed information gleaned from three others, whose names are given as Col. Gist, Col. Tucker, and Gen. Green.
2. For autobiographical details of Jefferson's visit to Harpers Ferry, see TJ to Horatio G. Spafford, 14 May 1809, Andrew A. Lipscomb and Albert Ellery Bergh, eds., The Writings of Thomas Jefferson (20 vols.; Washington, D.C., 1907), 12:279–81.
3. Chastellux visited Monticello 13–16 April 1782. See marquis de Chastellux, Travels in North America in the Years 1780, 1781, and 1782, ed. Howard C. Rice, Jr. (2 vols.; Chapel Hill, 1963), 2:389–96.
4. See Chastellux's letters of 10 June and 30 June (PTJ, 6:190, 193), and the letter of his traveling companion, François-Ignace, chevalier d'Oyré, to TJ, PTJ, 6:191.

ing health during the following summer, he was reported by his daughter as being absorbed in only two tasks: "When not at her bed side he was writing in a small room which opened immediately at the head of her bed."[5] The assiduous attention to his wife, and her death in September 1782, effectively suppressed his correspondence for several months, so the writing in which he had been engaged during this period may well have been connected with revising the answers to Marbois.

Chastellux had proved to be a kindred spirit, and although Jefferson's hope of sailing to France with him in December 1782 was to be frustrated, their paths apparently did cross briefly in Philadelphia.[6] That Jefferson delivered the long-promised copy of his answers at that time is implied by his letter of 26 November 1782, which looked forward to their meeting: "This will give me full Leisure to learn the result of your observations on the Natural bridge, to communicate to you my answers to the queries of Monsr. de Marbois, to receive edification from you on these and on other subjects of science, considering chess too as a matter of science."[7]

Chastellux's keen interest in Jefferson's answers to Marbois was no doubt gratifying and surely gave impetus to work on the revision, but it also provided Jefferson with a convenient excuse for taking great pains with its details. Just as Marbois's questionnaire could stand as grounds for having embarked on such a project, so Chastellux's interest offered a rationale for Jefferson's exertions. And there was by this time an element in the equation that probably did not figure prominently, if at all, in the answers sent to Marbois, but that would have been of special interest to Chastellux: Jefferson's response to European theories about the natural environment of the New World. For like Jefferson, Chastellux was acutely interested in the differences and similarities observable between American and European animals, something that is readily evident in his account of his North American travels.[8]

In his letters to Walker and Cary in September 1783, Jefferson pointedly asked for specific information on American animals, and from Walker, who had extensive experience in the wilderness, he also solicited further information, as well as criticism of what he had already written, on American Indians. His letter to Cary is missing, but he wrote Walker:

> That part particularly which relates to the positions of Monsr. de Buffon I would wish to have very correct in matters of fact. You will observe in the table of animals that the American columns are almost entirely blank. I think you can better furnish me than any body else with the heaviest weights of our animals which I would ask the favour of you to do from the mouse to the mammoth as far as you have known them actually weighed, and where not weighed, you can probably conjecture pretty nearly.[9]

That he appealed to Cary on a similar basis is evident in Cary's response:

5. *PTJ*, 6:196.
6. Jefferson arrived in Philadelphia on 26 Dec. 1783 (Bear and Stanton, eds., *Memorandum Books*, 2:525). Chastellux was waiting to embark from Annapolis on 8 Jan. 1784, having just come from Philadelphia (*Travels in North America*, 2:660). This makes it reasonably certain that their stays in Philadelphia must have overlapped by at least a few days.
7. TJ to Chastellux, 26 Nov. 1782, *PTJ*, 6:203.
8. See, for example, the appendices of his *Travels in North America*, 2:457–68.
9. TJ to Thomas Walker, 25 Sept. 1783, *PTJ*, 6:339–40.

It proceeds from Vanaty in the European Gentlemen who not only think our anamals Less than theirs but assume as Great a superiority to their Minds as they do to the sise of their anamals. Would to heaven we had the same oppartunaty of Cultivating the Mind as they have and I veryly believe we should Exceed them as much as the People of Attaca did those of Beotia.[1]

What was at issue, of course, was the contention of leading European authorities—the celebrated comte de Buffon in particular—that the environment of the New World was physically debilitating, and that, as a result, its animals were inferior in size to their European counterparts. To subject this hypothesis to an empirical test, Jefferson was, as he wrote to Walker, preparing a comparative chart of animal weights. If the chart in September 1783 was, as Jefferson says, nearly empty, this would indicate that he had not attempted, in his original answers to Marbois, to oppose the European claims by a detailed, empirical refutation, as was to be the case in the revision. But what is especially telling in this regard is that nowhere in Marbois's list of questions is there any mention of animals.[2]

It is well recognized that Jefferson reordered Marbois's questions and deftly construed them for his own purposes, but animals would seem to have presented a special case; to get them into the purview of the questions at all required some doing.[3] He might have employed the catch-all question with which Marbois concluded his list—"In short a notice of all what can increase the progress of human Knowledge"[4]—which would have served very well as a rubric for a response aimed at correcting a widespread scientific misconception. But it seems certain that by the time he decided to make a serious issue of animal size, he had already appropriated this question as the basis for query 7, which he dedicated to his own favorite subject of research, Virginia's climate.

The first question posed by the decision to respond to the European authorities, then, was where Jefferson would insert it. If we assume that the query numbers and rubrics remained the same in the revision, there were no very propitious locations, including query 6, where it finally appeared. Modern readers are accustomed to editions in which this query (or chapter) is headed "Productions Mineral, Vegetable and Animal," which is the way it is listed in the table of contents of both the Paris and London (Stockdale) editions. But in both those editions, as in the manuscript, the chapter begins with a rubric that turns out to be Jefferson's own dexterous unpacking and reconstruction of two Marbois questions: "6. A notice of the Counties Cities Townships Villages Rivers Rivulets and how far they are navagible. Cascades Caverns Mountains Productions Trees Plants Fruits and other natural Riches" and "20. A notice of the Mines and other subterranean riches."[5] From these, Jefferson fashioned this: "Qu. 6. a notice of

---

1. Col. Archibald Cary to TJ, 12 Oct. 1783, *PTJ*, 6:344.
2. For the list of Marbois's questions that Jefferson received, see *PTJ*, 4:166–67.
3. For suggestive discussions of Jefferson's ordering of the queries, see Robert A. Ferguson, "Mysterious Obligation: Jefferson's Notes on the State of Virginia," in *Law and Letters in American Culture* (Cambridge, Mass., 1984), pp. 34–58; and Pamela Regis, "Jefferson and the Department of Man," in *Describing Early America: Bartram, Jefferson, Crèvecoeur, and the Rhetoric of Natural History* (Dekalb, Ill., 1992), pp. 79–105.
4. *PTJ*, 4:166. This is actually the next to last item; the last was likely an afterthought.
5. Ibid.

the mines & other subterraneous riches, it's trees, plants, fruits &c."[6] The clear indication is that Jefferson's discussion of animal size in his revised manuscript had no other warrant than his own creative "&c."

What this probably indicates is that, when he wrote or copied out this rubric for query 6, in the spring or early summer of 1783, Jefferson had not yet decided to include an extensive discussion of American animals, which in turn suggests that he had not previously contemplated a forceful refutation of European theories. The evidence of the manuscript—in particular, the paper stock and the revised pagination—suggests that the discussion of American animals and the response to Buffon and other European authorities existed in Jefferson's revision in at least three identifiable versions.[7] All that survives of the earliest version is the first 800-plus words, a passage that addresses the question of whether the massive fossil bones attributed to the American mammoth are those of an elephant.[8] Whatever originally followed this brief beginning was subsequently discarded and replaced by a second version that carried the discussion of American animals forward. Of this version we can discern somewhat more, because we know its length (eight pages), and because four of the original eight pages survive.[9] Knowing the length of the second version and about half of its contents make[s] it possible, to a limited extent, to compare it with the final version, which was expanded to twenty-two pages. Further study should tell us more about the nature of these revisions, but there can be little doubt that each successive version was more ambitious than the last.

In spite of suppositions to the contrary, the evidence makes it clear that the manuscript of Jefferson's *Notes on the State of Virginia* at the Massachusetts Historical Society served as the setting copy for the French printers who produced the 1785 Paris edition. For example, it includes bracketed notes in Jefferson's hand to the printer, such as "¶ wherever this mark is placed, begin a new line"; "This table must be put into one page"; and "This table to be placed between pa. 168. and 169." Moreover, the page numbers on the manuscript's table of contents page (which also serves as the title page) correspond to those of the Paris edition. And certain passages marked by Jefferson on the Paris printer's proof sheets for correction are found only in this manuscript. Most of these are minor, but a few are more substantive

---

6. *Notes* manuscript, p. 14.
7. The evidence for the existence of at least three successive versions of this part of the manuscript is as follows:

    1. "A" paper version. The distinctively watermarked paper ("A") on which the first eleven leaves, or twenty-two pages, of the fair copy was written contains the beginning of the discussion of American animals, and this fair copy text ends on page 22 in mid-sentence. This, together with the switch to another paper ("B") for succeeding pages, indicates that the surviving text on pages 21 and 22 belongs to an earlier version but gives no indication of how extensive it might have been.

    2. First "B" paper version. After the first eleven leaves ("A" paper), the "B" paper was used for the balance of the surviving draft, which originally numbered eighty-eight pages. But the pages written on "B" paper that first continued the discussion begun on pages 21 and 22 are missing, except for a fugitive discarded leaf containing the beginning of query 7. The perfect articulation of the text on this leaf with that on succeeding pages indicates quite clearly that this version of the discussion of American animals began on page 21 and ended on page 28.

    3. Second "B" paper version. This is the version that, after changes and corrections, was sent to the printer. Like the other two versions, it begins on the pages originally numbered 21 and 22 ("A" paper) and then proceeds entirely on "B" paper, concluding on a page numbered 42.

8. Peden, pp. 43–47; *Notes on the State of Virginia*, ed. Shuffelton (1999), pp. 44–48.
9. These are 21–22 and 27–28 (original numbers).

and indicative. Such a change was made in his discussion of the Virginia constitution, which Jefferson persisted in arguing was not properly enacted by a specially elected body and was nothing more than an act of the Virginia legislature. He had written: "But they might as well have voted that a square inch of linen should be sufficient to make them a shirt, and walk into public view in confidence of being covered by it. Nor would it make the shirt bigger, that they could get no more linen." Jefferson apparently decided at the last minute to eliminate this vivid figure, which was perhaps too revealing of his own irritation and likely to provoke the same in others. On the proof sheet, he crossed out everything after "But" and substituted less colorful language: "this danger could not authorize them to call that a house which was none: and if they may fix it at one number, they may at another, till it loses it's fundamental character of being a representative body."[1]

What do these and other revisions in the manuscript of Jefferson's *Notes* tell us? In general, they indicate that he went to a great deal of trouble to enhance and improve his text. He took great pains in assembling the requisite facts and details, and he was equally attentive to matters of style and tone. After working on the project by fits and starts since the fall of 1780, he completed a fair copy of eighty-eight pages of his revised version in summer or early fall of 1783, which was surely longer than the version sent to Marbois. He then substantially expanded query 6, which increased the size of his draft to 104 pages. He then sent parts of it to Thomas Walker, Archibald Cary, and possibly others, for correction, comment, and additional information. In the succeeding months, through his travels and his correspondence, he assiduously sought additional information on such matters as limestone caves, the American moose, the flood times of the great rivers, and "albino negroes," duly incorporating the results into his manuscript. By January 1784, realizing that his work had been greatly altered, if not transformed, he wrote to the marquis de Chastellux, "I must caution you to distrust information from my answers to Monsr. de Marbois' queries. I have lately had a little leisure to revise them. I found some things should be omitted, many corrected, and more supplied and enlarged. They are swelled nearly to treble bulk."[2] If "treble bulk" refers to the extended length of the manuscript, it suggests that the version sent to Marbois in December 1781, or perhaps a somewhat revised version given to Chastellux a year later, was most likely some thirty-five to forty pages long. It is also a rare acknowledgement on Jefferson's part that the work had, in fact, become more ambitious, ranging well beyond the scope of his answers to Marbois.

Some examples of Jefferson's revisions to his fair copy draft may serve to illustrate how his text evolved and perhaps indicate the kinds of new information and insights that further study of the manuscript may yield. At least a few of the revisions reveal interesting new facts about Jefferson's life. None is more notable, perhaps, than the light shed on his famous archaeological excavation. His account in the published *Notes* of digging up an Indian barrow, or burial mound, along the Rivanna River, has earned him acclaim as an

1. Proof sheets for the Paris edition of *Notes on the State of Virginia* were in the New York [State Library] before its great fire in 1911. Fortunately, the changes Jefferson made on these sheets were reported in great detail in the nineteenth century. See E. B. O'Callaghan, "The Revised Proofs of Jefferson's Notes on Virginia," *The Historical Magazine*, 2d ser., 3 (1868): 96–98.
2. TJ to Chastellux, 16 Jan. 1784, *PTJ*, 6:467.

American pioneer in scientific excavation, but the date and circumstances under which he performed it have remained elusive.

Jefferson's account of his dig appears on a long tab that was pasted onto a primary leaf and is thus a sizable addition to the fair copy draft. This tells us that he probably wrote the account after 16 October 1783, but it says nothing about when he excavated the barrow. The text that was added by way of the long tab replaced several lines of the fair copy draft, which were stricken. These stricken lines, which can readily be retrieved, describe the two barrows that Jefferson then claimed personally to have seen:

> the one in the lowgrounds of the South branch of Shenando, where it is crossed by the road leading from the Rockfish gap to Staunton: the other on the lowground of the Rivanna near its principal fork above the mountains, these as well as I recollect them are spherical hillocks [or mounds?] of about 10. feet height & 40 feet diameter at the base, round the base was a large excavation of about 5 feet depth & width from whence the earth was taken of which the mound was formed, digging a few inches into them human bones are found, and in some places they stick out from the surface, the mounds having been often superficially disturbed by the curiosity of those who have visited them. they have generally been considered as being the bones of those who have fallen in battles fought on the spot of interment, but this supposition is disproved if [stricken word] it be true, as I have heard, that the bones of infants have been sometimes taken out.[3]

Here it is apparent that, unlike the detailed description of the Rivanna barrow in the revised text, Jefferson does not claim close familiarity with either barrow. His phrase "as well as I recollect them" suggests that he has not seen them recently enough to remember them distinctly, just as the phrase "as I have heard" clearly indicates that, contrary to what he says in the revised text, he has not personally seen infant bones in a barrow. When we compare this vague account of the barrows with the vivid first-person description of the dig in the revised text, it become clear that Jefferson must have performed the excavation of the Rivanna mound after he wrote the fair copy draft. Since Jefferson did not return to Virginia until 1789, the conclusion is unavoidable that the dig must have been performed after Jefferson had completed his fair copy draft in the summer or early fall of 1783 and before he left for Philadelphia on 16 October.

What this further suggests is that Jefferson, having raised the question of the purpose of the burial mounds in his fair copy draft, took to the field in order to resolve the issue of their function, so as to include his findings in his manuscript. But appearances can be deceiving, for though the dig may well have been prompted by the questions he himself raised in composing his draft, his decision to include a description of it seems to have been prompted by something else. A critical juncture in the revision process was the close scrutiny given Jefferson's manuscript near the end of the project by Charles Thomson. Although he may have conferred with Jefferson from time to time about the project during the fall and winter in Annapolis, Thomson wrote out an extensive commentary on the manuscript in late

---

3. *Notes* manuscript, pp. 57–58.

March or April 1784.[4] Jefferson thought so highly of Thomson's commentary that he included a large sampling of it as an appendix to the printed edition of *Notes*. But a comparison of Thomson's page references and Jefferson's manuscript shows that the account of the barrows that Thomson read and commented on was the one Jefferson had first written in the fair copy draft, not the revised version that described the dig. The implication is unavoidable that Jefferson was prompted to describe his dig, many months after the dig itself by Thomson's spring 1784 commentary.

Jefferson had a high regard for Thomson's learning and judgment, which is evident not only in the material he appropriated for his appendix but also in the way he responded to and followed many of Thomson's suggestions for revising the manuscript. But some things they saw differently. For example, Thomson objected to Jefferson's famous passage describing the effect of viewing "one of the most stupendous scenes in nature," the coming together of the Potomac and Shenandoah rivers at Harpers Ferry. Jefferson had first written exuberantly: "it is impossible to contemplate this scene a moment without being hurried by your senses into an opinion that this earth has been created in time, that the mountains were formed first, that the rivers began to flow afterwards."[5] Thomson soberly objected: "This I confess is a reflection which did not occur to me on viewing this stupendous object.[6] As a result, Jefferson toned down the rhetoric, though he retained the basic claim for the experience of the sublime.

Nothing could be more consequential for Jefferson's reputation and the standing of his Notes in our own time than his failure to heed Thomson's warning on the subject of race. Commenting on the long passage on blacks and slavery in query 14, Thomson offered shrewd advice. He began with Jefferson's having introduced into his discussion of slavery the Roman Cato's practice of exacting commissions from his female slaves who earned money with their "favours." The reflections on Cato's conduct are not worthy a place here—I wd. therefore propose to expunge them & a great part of p. 70—because many people encourage & comfort themselves in keeping slaves because they do not treat them as bad as others have done. And though I am much pleased with the dissertation on the difference between the Whites and blacks & am inclined to think the latter a race lower in the scale of being yet for that very reason & because such an opinion might seem to justify slavery I should be inclined to leave it out.[7]

Thomson's admonitions were not strident, but his tactics were canny and his suggestions quite radical. He seized upon the Cato incident as an advantageous entry point, about which he could be quite blunt. He then proceeded to argue more diplomatically for the suppression of most of what comes after the Cato incident (p. 70) on the grounds that it lends comfort to those who rationalize their treatment of slaves. Finally, he suggested the

---

4. The Thomson commentary (in the Coolidge Collection) was written sometime after Jefferson returned from Virginia in the fall of 1783, as all of Jefferson's changes that were suggested by Thomson are alterations of the fair copy draft, written prior to Jefferson's departure. A reference by Thomson on page 10 to "the late Doct Bond" (Thomas Bond), whose death occurred on 26 March 1784, further narrows the time frame, for Jefferson left Annapolis, where he and Thomson were staying, on 11 May (Bear and Stanton, eds., *Memorandum Books*, 1:548). Thus, late March or April 1784 seems the likely date for Thomson's commentary.
5. *Notes* manuscript, p. 9 (tab).
6. Thomson commentary, p. 4.
7. Ibid., pp. 32–33.

suppression of much of what comes before the Cato incident, the now notorious discussion of racial differences between blacks and whites. Thomson's
advice was, in effect, to eliminate virtually the whole of this section from
the work. His expressed grounds were not disagreement with what Jefferson had to say about racial differences, but that the discussion "might seem
to justify slavery." Thomson thus showed a greater sensitivity to the racial
issue than most people of his day, including Jefferson.

Jefferson did respond. He made a number of changes in his text, some of
which were additions, some deletions, the overall effect of which was to
soften somewhat his harsh treatment of blacks. For example, he added a
mitigating passage that included this: "Whether further observation will or
will not verify the conjecture that Nature has been less bountiful to them
in the endowments of the head, I believe that in those of the heart she will
be found to have done them equal justice."[8] But he ignored Thomson's
advice to pass over the subject on grounds of discretion.

Here the revisions in Jefferson's manuscript begin to take on historic significance. Had Jefferson followed Thomson's suggestions on the treatment of
blacks and slavery, his *Notes on the State of Virginia* would no doubt have
occupied a very different standing and played a different role in subsequent
discussions of the vexing subject of race in America. The result, however,
would have been to mask Jefferson's views, not alter them. It would then have
remained, as it does now, for scholars to study his manuscript to recover and
weigh what he had originally proposed to say on the subject, and how and why
he was persuaded to change. One can readily see how Jefferson's exchange
with Thomson might have had a bearing on past analyses of Jefferson and
race, and it seems certain that it will figure importantly in many future discussions.[9]

As students of the period are well aware, there are very few extant manuscripts for eighteenth-century books, as they tended to be consumed by
the process of putting them through the press. This makes the survival of
Jefferson's manuscript of *Notes on the State of Virginia* all the more remarkable and its disassembly and conservation all the more important. Given the
range and complexity of its contents, together with the richness of supporting primary materials, it is clear that there is much to be learned by further study of this extraordinary manuscript.

8. *Notes* manuscript, p. 86 (tab).
9. For example, Jean Yarborough, "Race and the Moral Foundation of the American Republic: Another
Look at the Declaration and the *Notes on Virginia*," *Journal of Politics* 53 (1991): 90–106; and
Alexander O. Boulton, "The American Paradox: Jeffersonian Equality and Racial Science," *American Quarterly* 47 (1995): 467–92.

Thomas Jefferson: A Chronology

1743   Born on April 11 at Shadwell, Virginia, in present-day Albemarle County, the first son and third of ten children of landowner and surveyor Peter Jefferson and Jane Randolph, member of a prominent Virginia family.

1745–51   The family relocates for six years to a Randolph family property, Tuckahoe plantation, on the James River upstream from Richmond. From 1748 on, Jefferson attends school on the plantation.

1752   The family returns to Shadwell, where Thomas enters the Latin school of William Douglas, a Scottish clergyman.

1757   Jefferson's father dies.

1758–60   Jefferson relocates to Fredericksville to finish his schooling under the Reverend James Maury.

1760–62   Jefferson attends the College of William and Mary, in Williamsburg, where he is especially influenced by mathematics professor William Small.

1762–67   Jefferson studies the law with George Wythe, also in Williamsburg. He is admitted to the bar and begins his practice.

1769   Having inherited twenty-seven hundred acres of land from his father's estate on coming of age in 1764, Jefferson designs and starts building Monticello, on a mountain included in the bequest. Elected to the Virginia House of Burgesses from Albemarle County, Jefferson will continue serving until the Revolution forces its closure in 1776.

1772   Jefferson marries Martha Wayles Skelton, a young widow of independent wealth. September 27, at Monticello, their first child, Martha (Patsy), is born.

1774   At the request of the House of Burgesses, Jefferson writes the instructions for the colony's delegates to the first Continental Congress in Philadelphia. The legislature has the document published in Williamsburg as *A Summary View of the Rights of British America*.

1775–76   As a member of the Virginia delegation to the Continental Congress, Jefferson drafts the Declaration of Independence in June 1776. Here Jefferson meets John Adams, a Massachusetts delegate.

1776–79   Jefferson serves as a member of the new Virginia House of Delegates for Albemarle County, drafting a bill for religious freedom and a proposed constitution, both of which are rejected. Undertakes revision of Virginia laws.

1779–81   Jefferson serves two terms as governor of Virginia.

1781   Jefferson is chased from Monticello by British troops on June 4, two days after his second term as governor expires. He spends the remainder of the year preparing his answers to the queries of François Marbois, secretary of the French legation, regarding Virginia. In their first form, they are submitted in December.

1782   Martha Wayles Jefferson dies on September 6, several months after the birth of her sixth child, Lucy, in May. (Only three daughters survived her.). Jefferson agrees to serve as one of the American commissioners seeking to negotiate a treaty with Britain, but his departure for France is delayed until after news of a provisional agreement arrives in America.

1783–84   Jefferson, a Virginia delegate in Congress, submits a plan of government for the Western territories in March 1784, the basis for the nation's future expansion. In May 1784, Jefferson is chosen to join John Adams and Benjamin Franklin in France for the purpose of negotiating treaties with European states. Leaves from Boston on July 5, with his oldest daughter, Martha. Daughter Lucy dies in Virginia.

1785   Jefferson replaces Franklin as minister to France. In Paris, oversees the private printing of his answers to Marbois, now called *Notes on the States of Virginia*.

1786   The Virginia legislature enacts Jefferson's Statute for Religious Freedom in January. In March and April, Jefferson tours English gardens with John Adams, American minister to England. Jefferson meets the English artist Maria Cosway in Paris.

1787   Jefferson travels in the south of France and Italy from March to June. In July, his other daughter, Polly, joins him in Paris with fifteen-year-old slave Sally Hemings, his dead wife's half-sister. That same month, London bookseller John Stockdale issues, with Jefferson's approval, the first public edition of *Notes on the State of Virginia*.

1788   Jefferson visits Holland and the Rhine valley in March and April.

1789   Jefferson, having observed the opening events of the French Revolution, leaves Europe in October in the hope of retiring from public life. Sally Hemings, who is technically free in France, resists returning to America with him until Jefferson promises to free her children when they reach adulthood.

1790   Jefferson's daughter Patsy marries her cousin Thomas Mann Randolph in February. Having been named secretary of state in Washington's first administration the previous fall, Jefferson reluctantly agrees to serve, beginning his duties in the temporary capital, New York, on March 21. Sally Hemings gives birth to her first child, which dies.

1794–96   Having served as secretary of state until the end of 1793, Jefferson retires to Monticello for a period of long-delayed rest. In 1795, Harriet (I), the daughter of Sally Hemings, is born there.

1796–1800   Jefferson, defeated by John Adams in the presidential election in the fall of 1796, becomes vice president on March 4 (one day after he is installed as president of the American

Philosophical Society in Philadelphia). During the Adams administration, political hysteria generated in response to the political upheavals in France causes the formation of the first American parties. Jefferson becomes the leader of the Democratic-Republicans, Adams, of the Federalists. In 1798, another child, William Beverley Hemings, is born to Sally Hemings; the first printed references to the relationship between Jefferson and Hemings appear in 1799.

1801–03 Having run for president in the fall 1800 elections, but tied in the electoral college with Aaron Burr, Jefferson is chosen the winner in the House of Representatives on the thirty-sixth ballot the following February. He is inaugurated on March 4. His correspondence with Adams, carried on since 1777, ceases from now until it is revived in 1812. Harriet Hemings (II) is born to Sally Hemings in 1801.

1803 Jefferson's envoys, James Madison and Robert R. Livingston, succeed in purchasing the whole of Louisiana Territory from France. Jefferson had already begun planning a western expedition under his former private secretary, army captain Meriwether Lewis, who departs for Missouri that summer.

1804 Polly Jefferson, who had married her cousin John Wayles Eppes in 1797, dies in April of this year. Jefferson is reelected with a landslide in December.

1805–09 Jefferson's second term is marked by his attempts to avoid entanglement in the widening circle of war in Napoleonic Europe. The Non-Importation Act of 1806 is replaced by the more sweeping Embargo Act of December 1807, which plunges the economy into real distress. One of Jefferson's last acts, on March 1, 1809, is to sign an act repealing the Embargo. James Madison Hemings is born to Sally Hemings in 1805, followed by her last child, Thomas Eston Hemings, in 1808. Jefferson retires to Monticello following the inauguration of James Madison in March 1805. In October, Meriwether Lewis commits suicide in Tennessee while en route to Washington to settle his account with the government.

1812 In response to the intermediary efforts of Philadelphia physician and intellectual Benjamin Rush, Jefferson and Adams resume their correspondence.

1813–14 Jefferson, deeply involved in efforts to see that Meriwether Lewis's plan of writing an account of the expedition he commanded is carried out, assists it by preparing a sketch of Lewis's life. After more delays, the two-volume *History of the Expedition* appears in Philadelphia in 1814, with the sketch included. Following the British attack on Washington, D.C., that summer, Jefferson sells his extensive personal library to replace the destroyed Library of Congress.

1815–19 Among his many other interests, Jefferson publicly advocates for the establishment of the University of Virginia, for which he will design the "academical village" in 1817 (the university will open in March 1825).

1820–22   In 1820, Jefferson privately denounces the Missouri Compromise, which allows for the extension of slavery into the new states. Beverley and Harriet Hemings leave Monticello to live as whites in 1821; that year, Jefferson writes his brief *Autobiography* (published 1829), which includes his account of the writing of the Declaration of Independence together with a record of its revisions by the Continental Congress.

1823–25   In his final years, Jefferson remains engaged with public questions, advising President Monroe on what will become the Monroe Doctrine (which forbids Europe from meddling in the Western Hemisphere) and entertaining the marquis de Lafayette, an old friend, during the latter's triumphal tour of the country in 1824–25.

1826   In February, facing a load of debt he fears will deprive his heirs of Monticello, Jefferson secures the right to hold a raffle of his property, but the raffle is never held. In his March will, he emancipates five more slaves, including the two remaining children of Sally Hemings. He dies on July 4, the same day as John Adams in Massachusetts.

1831   Monticello is sold to cover Jefferson's debts.

Selected Bibliography

Thomas Jefferson is fortunate in having a massive editing project under way that promises to make virtually all of his published writings, public documents, and correspondence available in superbly prepared form. Begun under the supervision of Julian P. Boyd, *The Papers of Thomas Jefferson* (Princeton, N.J.: Princeton University Press, 1950–present) now comprises thirty-six volumes and covers Jefferson's life up to the beginning of 1802. A *Retirement Series*, ed. J. Jefferson Looney et al. (Princeton, N.J.: Princeton University Press, 2005–07), now includes six volumes covering from the time he left the presidency in 1809 to the beginning of 1813. For periods not yet included in this edition, there are several alternative resources. Jefferson's grandson produced the first collection of writings: *Memoir, Correspondence, and Miscellanies, from the Papers of Thomas Jefferson*, ed. T. J. Randolph, 4 vols. (Charlottesville, Va.: F. Carr, 1829). Heavily edited, in keeping with standards of the period, it is now chiefly of interest for historical reasons. A better and more inclusive collection that appeared twenty-five years later, *The Writings of Thomas Jefferson*, ed. H. A. Washington, 9 vols. (Washington, D.C.: Library of Congress, 1853–54), was produced after the U.S. government acquired a significant body of Jefferson's papers. But the best of the early editions of Jefferson's writings is that of Paul Leicester Ford, also titled *The Writings of Thomas Jefferson*, 10 vols. (New York: G. P. Putnam's Sons, 1892–99). Ford carefully studied surviving manuscripts and applied scrupulous editorial principles. Less exacting but fuller is yet another *Writings of Thomas Jefferson*, ed. Andrew A. Lipscomb and Albert E. Bergh, 20 vols. (Washington, D.C.: Thomas Jefferson Memorial Association, 1903–04), with most texts reprinted from earlier editions. Specialized works of use for parts of Jefferson's writings include *The Adams-Jefferson Letters: The Complete Correspondence between Thomas Jefferson and Abigail and John Adams*, ed. Lester J. Cappon, 2 vols. (Chapel Hill: University of North Carolina Press, 1959) and *Letters of the Lewis and Clark Expedition, with Related Documents*, ed. Donald Jackson, 2nd ed., 2 vols. (Urbana: University of Illinois Press, 1978).

BIBLIOGRAPHICAL GUIDES

Huddleston, Eugene L. *Thomas Jefferson: A Reference Guide*. Boston: Hall, 1982.
Index to the Thomas Jefferson Papers. Washington: Library of Congress, 1976.
Massachusetts Historical Society. *Catalogue of Manuscripts of the Massachusetts Historical Society*. Boston: G. K. Hall, 1969. For Jefferson holdings, see 4:164–271.
Shuffleton, Frank. *Thomas Jefferson: An Annotated Bibliography, 1981–1992*. New York: Garland, 1992.
——. *Thomas Jefferson: A Comprehensive, Annotated Bibliography of Writings About Him (1826–1980)*. New York: Garland, 1983.
Sowerby, E. Millicent. *A Catalogue of the Library of Thomas Jefferson*. 5 vols. Washington, D.C.: Library of Congress, 1952–59.

BIOGRAPHICAL STUDIES

Brodie, Fawn M. *Thomas Jefferson: An Intimate History*. New York: Norton, 1974.
Ellis, Joseph J. *American Sphinx: The Character of Thomas Jefferson*. New York: Random House, 1996.
Malone, Dumas. *Thomas Jefferson and His Time*, 6 vols. Boston: Little, Brown, 1948–81.
Peterson, Merrill D. *Thomas Jefferson and the New Nation: A Biography*. New York: Oxford University Press, 1970.
Randall, Willard S. *Thomas Jefferson: A Life*. New York: Henry Holt, 1993.

THE DECLARATION OF INDEPENDENCE

Becker, Carl. *The Declaration of Independence: A Study in the History of Political Ideas.* New York: Harcourt, Brace, 1922.

Boyd, Julian P. *The Declaration of Independence: The Evolution of the Text as Shown in Facsimiles of Various Drafts by Its Author.* Princeton, N.J.: Princeton University Press, 1945.

Detweiler, Philip F. "The Changing Reputation of the Declaration of Independence: The First Fifty Years." *William and Mary Quarterly* 3rd ser., 19 (1962): 557–74.

Fliegelman, Jay. *Declaring Independence: Jefferson, Natural Language, and the Culture of Performance.* Stanford, Calif.: Stanford University Press, 1993.

Ginsberg, Robert, ed. *A Casebook on the Declaration of Independence.* New York: Crowell, 1967.

NOTES ON THE STATE OF VIRGINIA

Gerbi, Antonello. *The Dispute of the New World: The History of a Polemic, 1750–1900.* Trans. Jeremy Moyle. Pittsburgh: University of Pittsburgh Press, 1973. See pp. 252–68.

Kimball, Marie. *Jefferson: War and Peace, 1776 to 1784.* New York: Coward-McCann, 1947. See pp. 259–305.

Lewis, Clayton W. "Style in Jefferson's *Notes on the State of Virginia.*" *Southern Review* 14 (1978): 668–76.

Marx, Leo. *The Machine in the Garden: Technology and the Pastoral Idea in America.* New York: Oxford University Press, 1964. See pp. 73–144.

Medlin, Dorothy. "Thomas Jefferson, André Morellet, and the French Version of *Notes on the State of Virginia.*" *William and Mary Quarterly* 35 (1978): 85–99.

Notes on the State of Virginia. Edited with an Introduction and Notes by William Peden. Chapel Hill: University of North Carolina Press, 1955.

Notes on the State of Virginia. Edited with an Introduction and Notes by Frank Shuffleton. New York: Penguin, 1999.

O'Callaghan, E. B. "The Revised Proofs of Jefferson's *Notes on the State of Virginia.*" *Historical Magazine* 13 (1878): 96–98.

Verner, Coolie. *A Further Checklist of the Separate Editions of Jefferson's Notes on the State of Virginia.* Charlottesville: Bibliographical Society of the University of Virginia, 1950.

GENERAL STUDIES

Burstein, Andrew. *The Inner Jefferson: Portrait of a Grieving Optimist.* Charlottesville: University of Virginia Press, 1995.

———. *Jefferson's Secrets: Death and Desire at Monticello.* New York: Basic Books, 2005.

Cohen, I. Bernard. *Science and the Founding Fathers: Science in the Political Thought of Jefferson, Franklin, Adams, and Madison.* New York: Norton, 1995.

Dumbauld, Edward. *Thomas Jefferson and the Law.* Norman: University of Oklahoma Press, 1978.

JEFFERSON AND SALLY HEMINGS

Gordon-Reed, Annette. *The Hemingses of Monticello: An American Family.* New York: Norton, 2008.

———. *Thomas Jefferson and Sally Hemings: An American Controversy.* Charlottesville: University of Virginia Press, 1997.

Lewis, Jan Ellen, and Peter S. Onuf, eds. *Sally Hemings and Thomas Jefferson: History, Memory, and Civic Culture.* Charlottesville: University of Virginia Press, 1999.

Index

Aborigines. *See* Indians

Adair, Douglas, 500*n*

Adair, James, 330–32

Adams, Abigail: in Brodie's criticism, 463; in Burstein's criticism, 514; death of, 361*n*; mentioned in letters, 327, 357

Adams, John: Bishop discussing, 412*n*; in Burstein's criticism, 484, 488, 493*n*, 519; complaints about lack of privacy, 493*n*; confirming Revolution's recollections, 346*n*; correspondence with Cunningham, 363*n*; death of, 427*n*; Federalist Party and, 524*n*; in Fliegelman's criticism, 476; on issue of independence, 16, 18; letters to, 211, 277–78, 329–32, 342–46, 355–57, 361–64; in McDonald's criticism, 521–22; as member of Continental Congress, 521; mentioned in letters, 245, 325–28; in Miller's criticism, 474*n*; in Paris, 222*n*; passage of Alien and Sedition Acts, 290*n*; presidential race, 285*n*; publications by, 245*n*, 329*n*; referring to mammoth cheese, 407*n*; in Tyler's criticism, 437, 439, 441; writing during Revolution, 285*n*

Adams, John Quincy: campaign for presidency, 363*n*; Federalist Party and, 413*n*; publications by, 329*n*; satire on Meriwether Lewis, 413–16; in Tyler's criticism, 441

Adams, Samuel, 285–86, 439

Administration of Justice Act, 452

Agricultural Society of Paris, 313

Albemarle, Duke of, 150

Alexander, William, 145–46

Alexander I, Czar of Russia, 335–36

Alien and Sedition Acts, 284*n*, 290*n*

Alleghaney (Allegheny) Mountains, 34–35

Alleghaney (Allegheny) River, 32

Allen, Paul, 319*n*, 336–42, 360

Ambler, Jacquelin, 217–18

American Philosophical Society: du Ponceau and, 360*n*; mentioned in letters, 272, 339, 361; Michaux and, 274*n*; Smith and, 369*n*; Thomson and, 159*n*, 217, 534

American Revolution: Adams confirming recollections of, 346*n*; Adams writing during, 285*n*; Armand's service during, 393*n*; Burke on, 443; Burstein on, 484, 517; in Burstein's criticism, 517, Clark's service during, 219*n*; Colburn on, 450; de Beauvoir on, 392; du Ponceau service during, 360*n*; fighting on British side during, 288*n*; Fliegelman on, 483; Gibson's service during, 179*n*; Hawkins' service during, 289*n*; Jay as diplomat during, 258*n*; Jay settling disputes lingering from, 290*n*; Kościuszko's service during, 321*n*; Lewis' service during, 46*n*; making gunpowder during, 44*n*; McDonald on, 523; Miller on, 468, 472; in Miller's criticism, 472; Monroe's service during, 286*n*; Onuf on, 529, 531, 533; Peale's service during, 328*n*; Price writing about, 226*n*;